T0189615

IFIP Advances in Information and Communication Technology

448

IFIP – The International Federation for Information Processing

IFIP was founded in 1960 under the auspices of UNESCO, following the First World Computer Congress held in Paris the previous year. An umbrella organization for societies working in information processing, IFIP's aim is two-fold: to support information processing within its member countries and to encourage technology transfer to developing nations. As its mission statement clearly states,

> *IFIP's mission is to be the leading, truly international, apolitical organization which encourages and assists in the development, exploitation and application of information technology for the bene t of all people.*

IFIP is a non-profitmaking organization, run almost solely by 2500 volunteers. It operates through a number of technical committees, which organize events and publications. IFIP's events range from an international congress to local seminars, but the most important are:

- The IFIP World Computer Congress, held every second year;
- Open conferences;
- Working conferences.

The flagship event is the IFIP World Computer Congress, at which both invited and contributed papers are presented. Contributed papers are rigorously refereed and the rejection rate is high.

As with the Congress, participation in the open conferences is open to all and papers may be invited or submitted. Again, submitted papers are stringently refereed.

The working conferences are structured differently. They are usually run by a working group and attendance is small and by invitation only. Their purpose is to create an atmosphere conducive to innovation and development. Refereeing is also rigorous and papers are subjected to extensive group discussion.

Publications arising from IFIP events vary. The papers presented at the IFIP World Computer Congress and at open conferences are published as conference proceedings, while the results of the working conferences are often published as collections of selected and edited papers.

Any national society whose primary activity is about information processing may apply to become a full member of IFIP, although full membership is restricted to one society per country. Full members are entitled to vote at the annual General Assembly, National societies preferring a less committed involvement may apply for associate or corresponding membership. Associate members enjoy the same benefits as full members, but without voting rights. Corresponding members are not represented in IFIP bodies. Affiliated membership is open to non-national societies, and individual and honorary membership schemes are also offered.

Ralf Denzer   Robert M. Argent
Gerald Schimak   Jiří Hřebíček (Eds.)

Environmental Software Systems

Infrastructures, Services and Applications

11th IFIP WG 5.11 International Symposium, ISESS 2015
Melbourne, VIC, Australia, March 25-27, 2015
Proceedings

 Springer

Volume Editors

Ralf Denzer
Environmental Informatics Group
Goebenstrasse 40, 66117 Saarbrücken, Germany
E-mail: ralf.denzer@enviromatics.org

Robert M. Argent
Bureau of Meteorology
GPO Box 1289, Melbourne, VIC 3001, Australia
E-mail: r.argent@bom.gov.au

Gerald Schimak
Austrian Institute of Technology GmbH
Bundesstrasse 60, 2444 Seibersdorf, Austria
E-mail: gerald.schimak@ait.ac.at

Jiří Hřebíček
Masaryk University
Kamenice 126/3, 62500 Brno, Czech Republic
E-mail: hrebicek@iba.muni.cz

ISSN 1868-4238   e-ISSN 1868-422X
ISBN 978-3-319-38668-3   ISBN 978-3-319-15994-2 (eBook)
DOI 10.1007/978-3-319-15994-2
Springer Cham Heidelberg New York Dordrecht London

Preface

20 Years ISESS Conference Series

The International Symposium on Environmental Software Systems (ISESS) is one of several overlapping forums discussing issues of environmental information systems, environmental decision support systems, environmental software systems, environmental informatics, eco-informatics or Enviromatics.

ISESS was founded by Ralf Denzer and Gerald Schimak in 1995, with support from the German Informatics Society Working Group 4.6 "Computer Science for Environmental Protection," the International Federation for Information Processing (IFIP) Working Group 5.11 "Computers and Environment," and our friend David Russell at the Pennsylvania State University (PSU) campus in Malvern, PA. The first symposium received great support from PSU and turned out to be one of many success stories.

Since then the symposium has been held in the following countries: the United States, Canada, Austria, New Zealand, Switzerland, Portugal, the Czech Republic, Italy; in several editions joint sessions were held in conjunction with the biennial meeting of iEMSs (International Environmental Modelling and Software Society). ISESS has been an IFIP event since 1995 and is organized by WG 5.11.

Since its establishment, WG 5.11 has been led by Giorgio Guariso (1991–1999), Ralf Denzer (1999–2005), and Dave Swayne (2005–2011). Since 2011 it has been in the hands of Gerald Schimak. Several individuals have served as vice-chairs and secretaries of the WG and many members of the WG have been active supporters for a long time without holding an official position.

For more than two decades, ISESS has brought together researchers dealing with environmental information challenges trying to provide solutions using forward-looking and leading-edge IT technology.

Previous ISESS Publications

During the past 20 years we have seen the publisher of IFIP change several times, and electronic publishing has become the most important medium for scientific publications. ISESS has followed this transition and therefore there is *not one place* where all ISESS proceedings can be accessed.

The first and second proceedings (ISESS 1995, ISESS 1997) were published by IFIP publisher Chapman & Hall:

- R. Denzer, D. Russell, G. Schimak (eds.), Environmental Software Systems, Chapman & Hall, 1996, ISBN 0-412-73730-2 (print).
- R. Denzer, D. A. Swayne, G. Schimak (eds.), Environmental Software Systems Vol. 2, Chapman & Hall, 1998, ISBN 0-412-81740-3 (print).

Then IFIP changed publisher and the third proceedings (ISESS 1999) were published by IFIP publisher Kluwer Academic Press:

- R. Denzer, D. A. Swayne, M. Purvis, G. Schimak (eds.), Environmental Software Systems Vol. 3 - Environmental Information and Environmental Decision Support, Kluwer Academic Publishers, 2000, ISBN 0-7923-7832-6 (print).

As print publications were becoming increasingly difficult (particularly their cost for smaller conferences), the fourth and fifth proceedings (ISESS 2001, ISESS 2003) were published by the organizers of the symposium under IFIP ISBN:

- D. A. Swayne, R. Denzer, G. Schimak (eds.), Environmental Software Systems Vol. 4 - Environmental Information and Indicators, International Federation for Information Processing, 2001, ISBN 3-901882-14-6 (print).
- G. Schimak, D. A. Swayne, N.T. Quinn, R. Denzer (eds.), Environmental Software Systems Vol. 5 - Environmental Knowledge and Information Systems, International Federation for Information Processing, 2003, ISBN 3-901882-16-2 (print).

The sixth and seventh proceedings (ISESS 2005, ISESS 2007) were published, but this time as electronic versions under IFIP ISBN:

- D. A. Swayne, T. Jakeman (eds.), Environmental Software Systems, Vol. 6 - Environmental Risk Assessment Systems, International Federation for Information Processing, 2005, ISBN 3-901882-21-9 (CDROM).
- D. A. Swayne, J. Hřebíček (eds.), Environmental Software Systems, Vol. 7 - Dimensions of Environmental Informatics, International Federation for Information Processing, 2007, ISBN 978-3-901882-22-7 (USB).

The eight proceedings (ISESS 2009) were again published electronically, but not under IFIP ISBN:

- D. A. Swayne, R. Soncini-Sessa (eds.), Environmental Software Systems, Vol. 8, 2009, University of Guelph, ISBN 978-3-901882-364 (USB).

Today, Springer is the official IFIP publisher and ISESS is published by Springer in *IFIP Advances in Information and Communication Technology (AICT)*[1]. Proceedings number nine and ten were published as follows:

- J. Hřebíček, G. Schimak, R. Denzer (eds.), Environmental Software Systems, Vol. 9 - Frameworks of eEnvrionment, IFIP AICT 359, 2011; ISBN 978-3-642-22285-6 (eBook), ISBN 978-3-642-22284-9 (hard cover), ISBN 978-3-642-26878-6 (soft cover).

---

[1] http://www.springer.com/series/6102

- J. Hřebíček, G. Schimak, M. Kubásek, A.E. Rizzoli (eds.), Environmental Software Systems, Vol. 10 - Fostering Information Sharing, IFIP AICT 413, 2013; ISBN 978-3-642-41151-9 (eBook); ISBN 978-3-642-41150-2 (hard cover)

Today Springer also has the rights of the early Kluwer and Chapman & Hall books (ISESS 1995, ISESS 1997, ISESS 1999), as Kluwer merged with Springer in 2004 and Chapman & Hall had been bought by Kluwer in 1997. Therefore all proceedings that were published by a publishing house are in one place today and can be accessed through Springer. They are available as hard cover and/or soft cover, as eBooks and (most of them) as individual articles.

The proceedings that were self- published under the copyright of IFIP are being made available at this conference in a new form. Specific ISESS sessions at IEMSS are available through the IEMSS web site[2]. This book also contains an overview article that gives a complete history of what ISESS has contributed to the research community in the past 20 years[3].

Down Under – Topics and Trends in 2015

In 2015 we welcomed ISESS to Australia for the first time. Australia has a significant history in environmental modelling and software systems, and has contributed strongly to ISESS and similar conferences (MODSIM, iEMSs, SIM-MOD) since the 1970s.

The environmental software systems community in Australia is relatively small and diverse, although well connected, with a history of cooperative research across the environmental and technological domains, and also with a clear focus on practical applications to address the unique challenges of understanding and managing Australia's environment.

Historically, the Australian science presented at ISESS has focused on the land and water resources domain, including data management, modelling system development and application, and integrated assessment.

ISESS 2015 presented a significantly broader perspective of Australia's contributions to the international body of work in environmental software systems. This includes the high-level themes of computing infrastructures, high-performance computing, extracting value from big data, and utilizing the opportunities offered by linked data. Paper topics reflect key contributions of Australia's university sector, along with state and commonwealth research institutions, and include coverage of numerical prediction of weather and natural hazards, climate dynamics, emergency response, landscape hydrology and natural resources, and fundamental informatics.

---

[2] www.iemss.org
[3] See: Ralf Denzer, Topics in Environmental Software Systems, in this book

Participants attending ISESS 2015 in Australia had a grand opportunity to strengthen and extend their research and application networks internationally, and we enjoyed welcoming participants to Melbourne.

ISESS 2015 Reviewing Standards

The ISESS conferences have always had a high standard of peer reviewing. For ISESS 2015, we published the complete reviewing data for the first time in this preface.

First of all, we decided to go back to requesting *extended abstracts of three to four pages*, a strategy which we had applied in many early conferences but not in recent years. There was a hot discussion as to whether this would negatively influence the number of submissions but it turned out that this was not the case. A total of *104 extended abstracts* were submitted for consideration. Due to some inconsistencies in communication and because many authors of previous years were used to one-page abstracts we also received one-page abstracts that we reviewed as well but that received even more scrutiny in the full-paper review than the extended abstracts of three to four pages. Of 102 extended abstracts, 64 (61.5%) were extended abstracts.

Each extended abstract was assigned for review by *three independent reviewers* in this first stage alone. In all, 21 submissions were rejected, which amounts to 20.2%. Of the remaining submissions, 29 submissions were categorized as *accept conditionally*, which meant that there were serious issues with either their focus or their quality but were borderline enough that they were given a chance to be submitted as a full paper. Where reviewing deadlines were not met, we requested additional reviews from other reviewers. Only in 13 cases (12.5 %) did we take decisions based on two reviews, but only if these results were very clear and the two reviews did not have a conflicting opinion.

For stage 2, the review of the full papers, *two independent reviewers* were assigned to each full paper, and in many cases at least one individual was a different person than the reviewers in the first stage, which means that many papers had a total of at least three reviewers. Finally, *61 papers were accepted* in the full paper review and published in this book after an editorial process, which amounts to a *total rejection rate of 41.3%*.

Acknowledgments

The editors are grateful to all authors for their valuable contribution to the conference, and to the members of the Program Committee for their time spent in reviewing more than 100 submissions.

Special thanks are given to representatives of the International Federation for Information Processing and Working Group 5.11 for their kind support of the organization of ISESS 2015. We thank all partners involved in the preparation of this conference and all sponsors for their valuable support.

We would like to thank the following institutions and partners particularly:

- The Australian Bureau of Meteorology (BOM), the conference host and organizer
- The Environmental Informatics Group (EIG)
- The Austrian Institute of Technology, its Department Safety & Security (AIT)
- The Masaryk University, its Institute of Biostatistics and Analyses
- The National Computational Infrastructure of Australia (NCI)
- The Czech Software First company and Mrs. Lucie Soukopová for their administrative support
- Miroslav Kubásek, Jiří Kalina, and Jakub Gregor for establishing and maintaining the conference website
- The Environmental Informatics Institute (EII) for their continued support

This time a very special thank you goes to IFIP, in particular Eduard Dundler, IFIP publications officer, and Erich Neuhold, IFIP TC5 chairman, for granting the rights to re-publish the 2001–2009 proceedings as second editions in an effort to make them publicly available. From now on, every article that has ever been published is either available at Springer / Springer Link (1995, 1997, 1999, 2011, 2013, 2015 and future books) or via the website www.enviromatics.org (2001, 2003, 2005, 2007, 2009). This concludes a major achievement.

January 2015

Ralf Denzer
Robert Argent
Gerald Schimak
Jiří Hřebíček

Organization

Conference Chair

Robert Argent   Bureau of Meteorology, Australia

Program Chair

Ralf Denzer   Environmental Informatics Group, Germany

Organizing Committee

Robert Argent   Bureau of Meteorology, Australia
Ralf Denzer   Environmental Informatics Group, Germany
Jiri Hrebicek   Masaryk University, Czech Republic
Gerald Schimak   Austrian Institute of Technology, Austria

Program Committee

Gab Abramowitz   University of New South Wales, Australia
Ioannis Athanasiadis   Democritus University of Thrace, Greece
Allesandro Annoni   Joint Research Center, Italy
Dan Ames   Brigham Young University, USA
Robert Argent   Bureau of Meteorology, Australia
Lars Bernard   Technical University of Dresden, Germany
Arne Berre   SINTEF, Norway
Lindsay Botten   National Computational Infrastructure,
                                 Australia
Ralf Denzer   Environmental Informatics Group, Germany
Albert van Dijk   Australian National University, Australia
Peter Fischer-Stabel   Hochschule Trier, Germany
Peter Fitch   CSIRO, Australia
Steven Frysinger   James Madison University, USA
Omar el Gayar   Dakota State University, USA
Lars Gidhagen   SMHI, Sweden
Reiner Güttler   Environmental Informatics Group, Germany
Denis Havlik   Austrian Institute of Technology, Austria
Daryl Hepting   University of Regina, Canada

Table of Contents

Decision Support Tools and Systems

Modelling and Simulation Systems

Architectures, Infrastructures, Platforms and Services

Requirements, Software Engineering and Software Tools

Analytics and Visualization

High Performance Computing and BigData

A Provenance Maturity Model

Kerry Taylor[1,2], Robert Woodcock[3], Susan Cuddy[4],
Peter Thew[1], and David Lemon[4]

[1] CSIRO Digital Productivity, Canberra, Australia
[2] Australian National University, Canberra, Australia
[3] CSIRO Mineral Resources, Canberra, Australia
[4] CSIRO Land and Water, Canberra, Australia
`firstname.lastname@csiro.au`

Abstract. The history of a piece of information is known as "provenance". From extensive interactions with hydro-and geo-scientists in Australian science agencies we found both widespread demand for provenance and widespread confusion about how to manage it and how to develop requirements for managing it.

We take inspiration from the well-known software development Capability Maturity Model to design a Maturity Model for provenance management that we call the PMM. The PMM can be used to assess the state of existing practices within an organisation or project, to benchmark practices and existing tools, to develop requirements for new provenance projects, and to track improvements in provenance management across an organisational unit.

We present the PMM and evaluate it through application in a workshop of scientists across three data-intensive science projects. We find that scientists recognise the value of a structured approach to requirements elicitation that ensures that aspects are not overlooked.

Keywords: provenance, reproducibility, lineage, pedigree, requirements.

1 Introduction

As the trend towards data-intensive cyberscience picks up pace, scientists are becoming increasingly concerned about data provenance. As consumers of data, scientists need to know: Where did this data come from? Is it good enough for me to use? Can I trust it? As producers of data and expert opinion, scientists need to ensure their results are scientifically credible, repeatable, and justified by the methods used and the reasoned interpretations made.

Knowledge of the history of a piece of information (where it came from, what it was generated for, and the workflow that generated it) is known as "provenance", although the terms "audit trail", "lineage" and "pedigree" are common synonyms. Understanding the provenance of a piece of information can be as important as the information itself. Using provenance, it should be possible to understand whether or not a piece of information is fit for the intended purpose or whether the information should be trusted.

R. Denzer et al. (Eds.): ISESS 2015, IFIP AICT 448, pp. 1–18, 2015.

While these general concerns are quite widespread, implementing software systems for long-term provenance management needs much more thought about requirements for the business context, capture, representation and storage, retrieval, and usability. From extensive interactions with hydro-and geo-scientists in Australian science agencies we found widespread confusion around how to move from high level descriptions of outcomes towards statements of requirements for selection of tools and methods for implementation. This problem is magnified in multidisciplinary science projects.

In this paper a novel tool for developing requirements for provenance is presented, the Provenance Maturity Model (PMM). The PMM has been developed together with a method for provenance requirements elicitation that is not further discussed here. It has been specifically developed for a context of multiple, disconnected stakeholders who are generally unaware of the drivers, challenges and tradeoffs of provenance management, but it can be useful in any scenario where an implementation of provenance management is required, such as hydrological modelling [15], agricultural research [3], emergency management [13] and chemistry lab notebooks [2]. The PMM can also be used to classify existing or aspirational tools and approaches to provenance to aid in tool selection after requirements are established.

Our development of the PMM was driven by our experience in the Bioregional Assessment program of the Australian Government; a program to understand the potential impacts of coal seam gas and large coal mining on water resources and water-related assets. It is a complex inter-governmental resource development decision-making process, with expectations of significant long term commercial and public interest in the decisions to be made. While there was very strong awareness of the necessity for provenance amongst the stakeholders, we struggled to discuss the breadth and depth of the impact of simple requirements statements. Elements of *maturity* have a major impact on the cost, distance from current practice, the ability to capture, and the ability to interoperate over organisational and disciplinary boundaries.

The content of the PMM was assembled by the authors' analysis of remarks and expectations of stakeholders in that and previous resource-exploitation scenarios. A survey of the research literature was also used to insert capabilities and maturity points that we may have missed. The PMM then provided a way to hold the conversations that were necessary to understand these issues where previously we had role, process and scope confusion. We needed the additional dimension of maturity to facilitate the conversation along with a context of cost-benefit and risk.

2   The PMM

Like the Capability Maturity Model (CMM) [12], the PMM contains a matrix of capabilities described at five levels of maturity. The capabilities are grouped into *Provenance Business, Data Management, Provenance Capture, Provenance Representation and Storage, Provenance Retrieval,* and *Usability.*

Table 1. PMM Capabilities(Rows)

PROVENANCE BUSI-NESS	This category relates to the adoption and commitment to provenance management. It also contains a grab bag of issues that need to be addressed for any particular provenance venture
Longevity	How long are provenance records designed to be kept?
Software maturity	What is the maturity of the software being used; for example does it have a known history of usage elsewhere or is it unknown to the organisation?
Organizational awareness: culture and behaviour	Is there a culture that understands and appreciates provenance?
Value recognition	Does the organisation care about provenance?
Governance	How formalised is the approach to provenance?
Perspective	The social extent of provenance sharing and inter-pretability
Transaction costs: Production vs. retrieval cost	How to balance the cost of detailed record keeping versus the cost of collection recording to provide an answer to a query
DATA MANAGEMENT	This category of capabilities relates not so much to provenance as to the management of the underlying data over which provenance operates. It is included here because certain features are necessary preconditions to provenance maturity
Data safety	The resilience of data (that is the subject of provenance) to failures in hardware and/or processing errors
Data versioning	Is there a scheme to identify data versions?
Data lineage	Is information kept to identify the source of data?
Identifier Management	Is the underlying data unambiguously identified?
Digital Preservation	How well preserved are the digital artefacts that are the subject of provenance?
PROVENANCE CAP-TURE	This category refers to the processes, methods and tools for initial capture, or record-keeping, of provenance
Decision making and consultation	What records are kept on decisions made by people and groups and how integrated are these records to a provenance database?
Temporal scope (Start and end points)	In the scope of a process, when do we start capturing provenance and when does it end?
Granularity of capture	The smallest unit of a process that generates a provenance record - from a complete workflow down to individual executables and commands
Temporality/Currency	When was the provenance record made with respect to the execution of the process: during the process step-by-step, at specific stages or after the fact?
Software tools used in process	What information is captured on software used within a workflow & the workflow system itself; for example version number?

Table 1. *(Continued)*

Hardware/platform	Information on the hardware environment when a workflow is executed
Provenance capture integration	How integrated is the collection of provenance records in the process execution? For example does the carrying out of the process generate provenance transparently or are the provenance records obtained by post-processing log files or independent data entry?
Provenance quality	How trustworthy is the provenance record that is kept?
Sophistication of automation	How automated is the capture of provenance record; for example manually or embedded into workflow processes
PROVENANCE REPRESENTATION & STORAGE	These capabilities discuss the static aspect of provenance information; in between creating it and using it
Provenance format	Do the provenance records adhere to a standard, and is that standard an international one or bespoke to the organisation?
Provenance language	How formalised is the content of the provenance records; for example free text or a strictly controlled language (with specific meanings)
Provenance security	Can the provenance records be validated or can they be corrupted or altered after collection; is there a way to determine if corruption has occurred?
PROVENANCE RETRIEVAL	These capabilities address the methods and support for obtaining provenance information
Provenance availability	How easy it is for people (or systems) to access the provenance records?
Provenance discovery	How easy is it to find the particular provenance record they need?
Licence to use provenance	Are the conditions of use of the provenance itself well understood?
PROVENANCE USABILITY	These capabilities refer to how provenance can be, or is, used: what is it all for?
Human readable	What attention is given to supporting the human interpretation of the provenance record?
Repeatable by automation	Can a workflow be repeated using the provenance records to identify all components and parameters that were used in the original workflow?
Reusable, that is, repeatable with improvement	Can a workflow be repeated using the provenance records but also allow deliberate substitutions; for example, an updated model or new dataset?
Transparent	Can you see what judgement decisions were made, and why?
Answerable (variation in results can be explained)	Can the provenance records identify the component that is the source of error or difference within a workflow with respect to an alternative?
Cross-disciplinary application	Is everyone talking the same language? Are they being forced inappropriately to talk the same language?

The five levels of maturity (columns) are labelled and described as follows where the original CMM title *Repeatable* has been replaced with *Tactical* to avoid conflicts with the use of that term in the study of provenance. The descriptions of each level have been modified to be more appropriate for provenance.

Initial(Chaotic). It is characteristic of provenance treatment at this level that it is (typically) undocumented and in a state of dynamic change, tending to be driven in an ad hoc, uncontrolled and reactive manner by users or events. This provides a chaotic or unstable approach to provenance management and provenance services and certainly implies that any services developed will be of very low functionality and scope.

Tactical. It is characteristic of provenance treatment at this level that many aspects of data production and management are carried out with record-keeping in mind. Some attention is being made to ensure that identified processes are repeatable in some circumstances, possibly with consistent results. Discipline is unlikely to be rigorous, but where it exists it may help to ensure that following an audit trail is possible under stress.

Defined. It is characteristic of provenance treatment at this level that there are sets of defined and documented standard processes established and routinely followed. These standard processes both require and enable standard tools to be developed and used. Such tools both assist in the implementation of the processes and offer provenance services to derive value from provenance across the organization or community.

Managed. It is characteristic of provenance treatment at this level that it has become uncontroversial: moved into the background as well-managed practices that are embedded in the fabric of business, travelling smoothly from project to project. It is consistently and effectively controlled and widely used.

Optimising. It is a characteristic of provenance management at this level that the focus is on continually improving performance of provenance management itself as a lever for continuous improvement of performance of the underlying scientific or administrative processes, through both incremental and innovative technological improvements. Provenance is a highly valued component of business delivering transparency, accountability and knowledge management.

The full PMM matrix of 33 capabilities by 5 maturity levels is included at the end of this paper.

3   Evaluation

The PMM was used for requirements elicitation for three projects of two government science agencies in August 2013, over a two-day workshop. Background material was provided, including the PMM evaluation of some existing tools, many of which were known to the participants, such as ISO-19115-LE [6] and Prov-O [7]. The workshop included a half-day of presentations on the nature of provenance and some known tools and methods; brief presentations on the selected projects' goals; an introduction on the PMM and how to use it; a hands-on application of PMM to the three projects in project groups; a subsequent requirements documentation exercise; a plenary analysis of consequent requirements for the agency as a whole; and the joint development of an architecture sketch for the agency-wide provenance management. Those who were present for the full two days excluding the PMM developers and facilitators, that is 13 people, were surveyed at the beginning and again at the end of the workshop.

The survey participants were invited to respond to 21 questions of which 18 were phrased on a 5-level balanced Likert scale and all 21 included requests for free-text comments. In some cases participants indicated responses either in between or spanning consecutive levels; in all cases these have been treated as if the lowest (i.e. least positive) level was selected.

The lowest-scoring question overall was the pre-workshop question *"Please rate your familiarity in dealing with issues or tools relating to provenance (1=not all aware, 5=extremely aware)"*, for which the minimal response was 1, the maximum 5, and the average 3.2. The highest-scoring question overall was the post-workshop *"The approach to provenance management for your project will benefit by the application of the PMM as you have used it in the workshop (1=strongly disagree, 5=strongly agree)"*. The minimum response was 3 and the maximum was 5, with average 4.8. Other high-scoring questions referred to the contribution of the PMM towards developing user requirements. The lowest-scoring post-workshop question (average 3.7) referred to the ease of determining evaluation criteria, an element of the PMM application methodology that is out of scope for this paper. We can conclude that the participants found the PMM worthwhile.

The participants were also invited to suggest needs for clarification or other improvement to the PMM version that was used in the workshop. The PMM presented here has had some wording and sequencing adjustments since the workshop to take account of those suggestions.

4   Related Work

We have evaluated some existing tools and methods with respect to the PMM in order to provide some benchmarks to assist in interpretation of the PMM, and on the other hand, to assist project designers to locate tools that might help them achieve desired maturity levels. In this context, Prov-O [7] features due to its potential contribution towards high-maturity provenance Representation and Storage, therefore also contributing to high maturity Retrieval and Usability. Because of both its underlying flexible graph representation, and the ontology inference coupled with domain-specific ontology extensions, it is possible to use it to traverse widely differing domain-oriented provenance records through semantic, executable mappings to Prov-O, such as described in [3]. This can be done even when the primary record-keeping may be entirely ontology-unaware, such as is enabled by the mapping from ISO19115 Lineage to Prov-O [14].

An alternative ISO19115-driven extension to Prov-O has been developed [9] that would be useful when an early commitment to Prov-O is made. We can envisage the particular utility of the Prov-O graph representation to support dynamic provenance assembly for federated information systems like [16], [1] and [17] that support retrieval of data products or query-answering over compositions of resources. In unpublished work, we are also exploiting the inference capability to support arbitrary provenance comparison, building on the graph matching of [8].

Recent work on provenance for an integrated ecosystem approach to management of large marine ecosystems [5] demonstrates a high level of maturity for Capture, whereby a Web application for the development of data products and charts, tables, and map visualisations also keeps track of steps taken then embeds the provenance in the final PDF report. The related Global Change Information system will demonstrate a high level of maturity for Data Management, particularly for identifier management over a heterogenous contributor community [10].

The notion of *Research Objects*[11], especially computational research objects [4], contributes to a very high level of maturity in Usability, with provenance records very closely tied to executable components for repeatability and reusability and also to the scientific practice.

5   Conclusion

We present the Provenance Maturity Model as a part of a structured approach to developing requirements for provenance management in data-intensive science. The PMM lays out many characteristics of provenance management in a matrix where preferred options may be considered and selected in the context of some evaluation criteria. We found that scientists recognise the value of a structured approach to requirements elicitation that ensures the depth and breadth of the issues are considered and that aspects are not overlooked. The value of the framework in clarifying the language in an "industry standard" approach is also appreciated.

We recommend using the PMM in a workshop environment once the scientific content of a project is well enough understood to commence. We recommend developing an evaluation criteria then proceeding to check cells in the PMM by consensus, adding additional rows if necessary. Later, system and software requirements can be developed in a conventional way, with frequent reference to the instantiated PMM. A record of tools and business processes that have previously been benchmarked by the PMM can help to fill in a solution architecture. Much later, the PMM can help to review provenance goals and to consider advancing the maturity.

In future work we would like to re-evaluate the PMM in an alternative cultural, organisational and problem context, and also to track the influence on project results through project life-cycle case studies.

Acknowledgement. The authors thank the anonymous reviewers and the many collaborators for their questions and insight, especially Neal Evans and Brian Hanisch of Geoscience Australia.

References

1. Ackland, R., Taylor, K., Lefort, L., Cameron, M.A., Rahman, J.: Semantic Service Integration for Water Resource Management. In: Gil, Y., Motta, E., Benjamins, V.R., Musen, M.A. (eds.) ISWC 2005. LNCS, vol. 3729, pp. 816–828. Springer, Heidelberg (2005)
2. Adams, N., Haller, A., Krumpholz, A., Taylor, K.: A semantic lab notebook—report on a use case modelling an experiment of a microwave-based quarantine method. In: Linked Science (LISC 2013), vol. 1116, CEUR proceedings (October 2013)
3. Compton, M., Corsar, D., Taylor, K.: Sensor data provenance: SSNO and PROV-O together at last. To appear 7th International Semantic Sensor Networks Workshop (October 2014)
4. De Roure, D.: Towards computational research objects. In: Proceedings of the 1st International Workshop on Digital Preservation of Research Methods and Artefacts, DPRMA 2013, pp. 16–19. ACM, New York (2013)
5. Di Stefano, M., Fox, P., Beaulieu, S., Maffei, A., West, P., Hare, J.: Enabling the integrated assessment of large marine ecosystems: Informatics to the forefront of science-based decision support. In: AGU Fall Meeting, number Poster IN51A-1689, San Fancsisco, American GeoPhysical Union (December 2012)
6. ISO 19115-2:2009 geographic information - metadata - part 2: Extensions for imagery and gridded data. ISO19115-2 Standard (2009)
7. Lebo, T., Sahoo, S., McGuinness, D., Belhajjame, K., Cheney, J., Corsar, D., Garijo, D., Soiland-Reyes, S., Zednik, S., Zhao, J.: PROV-O: The PROV ontology. W3C Recommendation (2013), http://www.w3.org/TR/prov-o/ (accessed April 23, 2014)
8. Liu, Q., Zhao, X., Taylor, K., Lin, X., Squire, G., Kloppers, C., Miller, R.: Towards semantic comparison of multi-granularity process traces. Knowledge-Based Systems 52, 91–106 (2013)
9. Lopez, F.J., Barrera, J.: Linked map VGI provenance schema. Deliverable D1.6.1, Planet Data Network of Excellence (March 2014)
10. Ma, X., Fox, P., Tilmes, C., Jacobs, K., Waple, A.: Capturing provenance of global change information. Nature Climate Change 4(6), 409–413 (2014)
11. Page, K., Palma, R., Hołubowicz, P., Klyne, G., Soiland-Reyes, S., Cruickshank, D., Cabero, R.G., Cuesta, E.G., Roure, D.D., Zhao, J., Gómez-Pérez, J.M.: From workflows to research objects: An architecture for preserving the semantics of science. In: 2nd International Workshop on Linked Science 2012: Tackling Big Data (LISC2012), Boston, USA, vol. 951. CEUR Proceedings (November 2012)
12. Paulk, M.C., Curtis, B., Chrissis, M.B., Weber, C.V.: Capability maturity model, version 1.1. IEEE Software 10(4), 18–27 (1993)
13. Power, R., Wise, C., Robinson, B., Squire, G.: Harmonising web feeds for emergency management. In: Piantadosi, J., Anderssen, R.S., Boland, J. (eds.) MODSIM 2013, 20th International Congress on Modelling and Simulation, pp. 2194–2200. Modelling and Simulation Society of Australia and New Zealand (December 2013)
14. Shu, Y., Taylor, K.: ISO 19115 lineage ontology (January 2013) (accessed November 2013)
15. Shu, Y., Taylor, K., Hapuarachchi, P., Peters, C.: Modelling provenance in hydrologic science: A case study on streamflow forecasting. Journal of Hydroinformatics (2012)

16. Taylor, K., Austin, T., Cameron, M.: Charging for information services in service-oriented architectures. In: Proceedings, International Workshop on Business Services Networks (BSN 2005), Workshop of IEEE International Conference on e-Technology,e-Commerce and e-Service, Kong Kong, pp. 112–119 (March 2005)
17. Woodcock, R., Simons, B., Duclaux, G., Cox, S.: AuScope's use of standards to deliver earth resource data. In: Geophysical Research Abstracts, volume 12:EGU2010-1556. European GeoPhysical Union General Assembly (2010)

Table 2. The PMM capabilities × Maturity levels

PROVENANCE BUSINESS *This category relates to the adoption and commitment to provenance management. It also contains a grab bag of issues that need to be addressed for any particular provenance venture.*

Capability	Initial (Chaotic)	Tactical	Defined	Managed	Optimising
Longevity	No provenance	Lifetime of a process instance execution	Lifetime of an identified problem or project to which knowledge is being applied	Lifetime of a consequent action plan or agreement	Deliberately unbounded without prescription in advance; i.e. evolutionary
Software maturity	Tools are not aware of provenance	Experimental developed	Extensively trialled	Several alternative implementations available, at least some are robust	Appropriate products are available and are also supported and maintained
Organisational awareness: culture and behaviour	No support for provenance	Individual or small team initiative	Major organisational support for trial or development but lacking maintenance commitment	Policy; Long term commitment supported by explicit funding stream	Legislation or Regulation
Value recognition	No support for provenance	Value of provenance is recognised in the custodian (asset)	Value of provenance is exploited opportunistically	Provenance value exploitation is intrinsic part of business model	Provenance is recognised as a knowledge base of evolving scientific method and used for continuous improvement processes

Capability	Initial (Chaotic)	Tactical	Defined	Managed	Optimising
Governance	No support for provenance	Implicit (everybody knows it, but it is not formally captured)	Explicit. Written, formal, contractual management	Provenance record management plans are comprehensive and followed	Formal accountability and governance throughout lifecycle established with & between parties
Perspective	No support for provenance	Individual: I know what I did	Team: We know what we did	Organisation: we know what our teams did	Community: we all know what everyone did
Transaction costs: Production vs. retrieval cost	No support for provenance	Low cost of production but retrieval is very expensive and slow and not always possible	Trade-off recognised and accommodated in many cases	Incremental cost of retrieval close to zero where justified	Identified cost / benefit habitually used in design decisions

DATA MANAGEMENT *This category of capabilities relates not so much to provenance as to the management of the underlying data over which provenance operates. It is included here because certain features are necessary preconditions to provenance maturity*

Capability	Initial (Chaotic)	Tactical	Defined	Managed	Optimising
Data safety	No backups	Data is manually backed up	Data backup is part of an automated backup process	Data backups are stored off-site	Data backups undergo regular restore tests

Capability	Initial (Chaotic)	Tactical	Defined	Managed	Optimising
Data versioning	Unknown versions	Old data replaced by new data. Version identification associated with new data	Old data is archived and associated with version identification.	Version control of collections	Data elements (e.g database tuples) dated and annotated with provenance
Data licensing	Unknown	Licence conditions are recorded, or a system wide standard licence applies	Licence need not be system-wide and conditions are retrievable from point of access to data	Licence need not be system-wide and conditions are retrievable from point of access to data	Flexible licencing policies can be expressed and computationally validated in the context of the intended use of the data
Identifier Management	None	Locally-scoped identifiers are assigned, possibly through a file-naming convention	Systematic, unique identifier assignment, crossing datatypes and technology platforms, supporting retrieval of identified objects	Systematic, globally unique and resolvable identifier management	International standards followed; resolvable identifiers maintained over time
Digital preservation	None	Some project materials and output data are archived	Systematic data preservation mechanisms are in place for identified strategic data	Digital preservation strategies extend to digital artefacts such as software and minuted decisions	Digital preservation strategies follow international standards and are regularly reviewed for scope, best practice, and longevity

PROVENANCE CAPTURE *This category refers to the processes, methods and tools for initial capture, or record-keeping, of provenance*

Capability	Initial (Chaotic)	Tactical	Defined	Managed	Optimising
Decision making and consultation	No records	Decision-taking meetings and individual choices in process are documented and justified	Documentation retrievable from multiple access points	Judgement choices are entirely transparent and fully integrated into provenance record and services	Reasoning services incorporated e.g. to identify decisions that follow policy (or not)
Temporal scope (Start and end points)	No provenance	Case-by-case; driven by other procedural concerns	Defined and applied at project level with end purposes in mind	System-wide principles for provenance established that determine scope	Generally lifecycle-complete, but entirely adaptable to cases without loss of verity
Granularity of capture	Undetermined	Coarse grained. Resources and methods are loosely described	High-level components captured but not all well described in terms of role or properties	Low-level components captured from the point of view of decisions made, steps taken, tools and data used	Granularity of capture is driven by understanding of future requirements
Temporality / Currency	Provenance not captured	Reconstructed on demand, after the fact	Constructed on demand from contemporary notes	Real time production but decaying record	Designed for long term storage and interpretation
Software tools used in process	Untraceable	Identified by commonly understood monikers	Versions, dates and providers rigorously identified	Originals archived with descriptions, including metadata	Fully integrated into provenance services

Capability	Initial (Chaotic)	Tactical	Defined	Managed	Optimising
Hardware / platform	Untraceable	Identified by commonly understood monikers	Versions, dates and providers rigorously identified	Originals archived with descriptions, including metadata	Fully integrated into provenance services
Provenance capture integration	No integration	Provenance is created by separate processes, usually running in parallel to workflows	Integration into tools and workflows	Standards based capture from tools and workflows	Plug and play with whatever is needed, tracking provenance
Provenance quality	Unknown	Unreliable or partial; user feedback collected and published	Measured occasionally; quality may be inferred from other attributes such as author, date	Measured routinely, quality limits and impact are understood	Effective methods to detect and improve bad provenance in place. All provenance is trustworthy; or trustworthiness is well documented
Sophistication of automation	None / manual	Policies for collection are established and followed but interpretations are localised	Habitual recording in a systematic (e.g. tablular) way in identifiable documents that are systematically archived and validated	Capture is embedded in data- and decision-processing software; some aspects demanding operator input	Integrated into the culture and toolsets

PROVENANCE REPRESENTATION & STORAGE *These capabilities discuss the static aspect of provenance information; in between creating it and using it*

Capability	Initial (Chaotic)	Tactical	Defined	Managed	Optimising
Provenance format	No provenance	Provenance may be mentioned in key papers; simple schemes like filename conventions and time stamps may be used	Formal standard for provenance format adopted and practised at key places	Flexible standard or tool-dependent formats prescribed and followed according to minimal capture granularity	Interoperable mappings over multiple formats implemented; may rely on overarching standard
Provenance language	None	Interpretation relies on natural language methods	Information is captured by link to controlled vocabulary with glossary	Semantics is captured by link to a formal ontology	Representations are interpreted for interoperability and adaptation to context of use
Provenance security	None	Original provider of provenance identifiable	Formal processes for authentication and audit trail	Provenance is signed and tamper-proof, within an organisation on selected transactions	Non-repudiation

PROVENANCE RETRIEVAL *These capabilities address the methods and support for obtaining provenance information.*

Capability	Initial (Chaotic)	Tactical	Defined	Managed	Optimising
Provenance availability	Clueless	Non-automated; requires judgement	Database or web page	Web Service	Direct availability to analysis and reporting tools; API supporting structured queries
Provenance discovery	"Phone a friend"	Retrievable from point of data product identification	Full text search over provenance records-can retrieve corresponding data through provenance search	Search by provenance structure and components: can retrieve corresponding data	Search for provenance patterns: can analyse provenance itself as subject of enquiry
Licence to use provenance	Unknown	Licence conditions are recorded or a system-wide standard licence applies	Licence need not be system-wide and special conditions are retrievable from point of access to provenance	Privacy or confidentiality conditions on access to provenance are enforced by tools	Flexible licencing policies can be expressed and validated computationally at the point of access to provenance

PROVENANCE USABILITY *These capabilities refer to how provenance can be, or is, used: what is it all for?*

Capability	Initial (Chaotic)	Tactical	Defined	Managed	Optimising
Human readable	No	Only	Predominantl with some machine-processable structure	Detailed, but detail can obscure meaning	Presentation tools take account of user perspective and purpose
Repeatable by automation	No	There is some chance that automated sub-processes are repeatable with considerable investment of effort	Partially automated to the extent that the general method can be reapplied for (typically) different results	Fully automated, repeatable results is possible in some cases	Processes are auto-matically repeatable
Reusable, that is, repeatable with im-provement	Opaque	There is some chance (decreasing over time) that sub-processes are repeatable with considerable investment of effort	Editing of parameters or selected data for rerun is supported	Processes may be arbitrarily edited or built upon or varied for improved results	Patterns in provenance are discernible and used for process im-provement
Transparent	Opaque	Only within small project teams	Formalised approach to trans-parency ensures that some decision points are noted and justified	Methods and tools are unam-biguously identified but may not be interpretable by interested parties	Open access to justified methods and tools for all nominated parties; explanatory capability

Capability	Initial (Chaotic)	Tactical	Defined	Managed	Optimising
Answerable (variation in results can be explained)	Impossible to say	Some sub-processes may be examined to explain variation but confidence is low	Variation can be attributed to plausible differences based on managed time-stamps or versions	Failure to reproduce can be diagnosed to identifiably different components	Automated; diagnosis limited only by original provenance collection granularity; user feedback quality included
Cross-disciplinary application	Unsuitable	Relies on serendipity	Provenance is available in a widely-used format that may be partly accessible to multiple discipline areas; generally relies on a lowest-common-denominator approach	Provenance is made available through multiple portals or in multiple formats to suit different discipline areas	Provenance management works for complex and intractable cross-disciplinary problems; Inter- or trans-disciplinary working is deliberately supported through management of multiple viewpoints

Challenges in Modelling of Environmental Semantics

Ioannis N. Athanasiadis

Democritus University of Thrace, Xanthi, Greece
ioannis@athanasiadis.info

Abstract. Modelling environmental semantics is a prerequisite for model and data interoperabilty and reuse, both essential for integrated modelling. This paper previews a landscape where integrated modelling activities are performed in a virtual environmental information space, and identifies challenges imposed by the nature of integrated modelling tasks and new technology drivers such as sensor networks, big data and high-performance computing. A set of requirements towards a universal framework for sharing environmental data and models is presented. The approach is demonstrated in the case study of a semantic modelling system for wildlife monitoring, management and conservation.

Keywords: Environmental semantics, Intergrated modelling, Environmental Information Space, Service orientation, Internet of the Things.

1   Introduction

Environmental modeling, almost since its infancy, was challenged with issues of integration and reuse. Today it has become natural to conduct integrated studies by putting together data and models originating from diverse sources. The process starts with the selection of *suitable* models, i.e. capable of producing the desired outputs directly, or outputs that can be easily transformed to the desired ones. Then, model input requirements needs to be matched with data, so that the models can be executed. While this simplification makes it sound as an easy task, in the contrary the reality is very challenging. This process is never a two-step action, rather an on-going, iterative process: data limitations have an impact on the models chosen, and model performance drives the needs for additional data sources. At the same time, questions to be answered change with the better understanding of the system, so that more aspects are covered: the better we understand the system behavior via simulations the more we change it. In this respect, scientists performing integrated modeling are challenged to develop skills that span from tedious data reformatting to advancing science, by creating new models. Integrated modeling is challenged with developing methodologies that manage with the inherit properties of environmental data and models.

Environmental data are spatiotemporally referenced, but (more importantly) uncertain to some degree, as they inherit the measurement instruments' failures, biases and noise [1]. At the same time, environmental data is a resource in scarcity. Already in Agenda 21, it was highlighted that "the gap in the availability, quality, coherence, standardization and accessibility of data between the developed and the developing

R. Denzer et al. (Eds.): ISESS 2015, IFIP AICT 448, pp. 19–25, 2015.

world has been increasing, seriously impairing the capacities of countries to make informed decisions concerning environment and development." [2]

Today, we experience the lack of information not only in the developing countries, where limited data records are available, but also in the developed ones, as we are flooded with data, which are not universally accessible. Environmental data are often hidden in silos, encoded with poor standards, in legacy systems, and some times are not available digitally, or human intervention is needed to access them. Issues of copyright and licensing, though changing fast, still limit open access to environmental data. Despite the abundance of data available still we need scientists to scout for data that are needed for integrated studies.

Environmental models inherit the complexity, uncertainty, scaling, and integration qualities from the physical world [3], which are observed as characteristic properties of the environmental systems. Rizzoli and Young in [4] summarized environmental systems as heterogeneous, spatiotemporal dynamic systems, with stochastic and periodic components. Denzer (2005) [5] to overcome the problems in environmental model integration insisted on model abstraction, communication and generality as three essential tests for model integration. Undoubtedly, most models today wouldn't pass those tests.

Model implementations today are poorly designed and documented, as they have been originally developed for single, or limited use. Model reuse, composition and chaining via workflows are characteristics that we have never designed for. Furthermore, one needs to consider that when an environmental model is encoded in a programming language, new limitations are introduced compared to the original modeling assumptions. Hardly ever can these assumptions be represented directly in the implementation language of choice; on the contrary, this knowledge resides with the modelers [3].

Both data and models encode domain knowledge that resides with the specialists. However this knowledge often is not accessible, and integrated modeling teams need to establish contact with original data and model producers to be trained to use them properly. Undoubtedly, we have not reached a level where data and models come with such a detailed documentation so that third-party scientists can reuse them soundly, or detailed meta-information so that machines can invoke them directly. We are still far away from the vision of a common environmental information space (Figure 1), where agencies, organizations and the public will have unhampered, universal access to environmental data and models.

2   Semantics for an Environmental Information Space

Common information spaces have been realized in other application areas (ie retail, banking, entertainment, travel, etc), so one could argue that it is a matter of time or resources to happen for environmental information. However, this is not the case due to the **subjective** nature of environmental information. In contrast to other areas, both data and models in the environmental sector are *subject to interpretation*. In the case of data collection, attributes measured, instruments used, sampling methods and quality check procedures depend on the particular goal of the specific study. Have the goals been different; one may have selected different equipment or applied different methodologies, which will have led to other results. The same holds for modeling, as theory, scale and boundaries depend on the problem definition. For such reasons, model integration and reuse in a common environmental information space needs to allow for *interpretation*. There is no universally agreed view of environmental information, which means that we need interpretations relevant for an individual, a project or a community.

Semantic modeling has been proposed as a remedy for overcoming longstanding issues of model integration. In our previous work with Villa and Rizzoli [7] we identified two approaches to semantic modeling. In the *mediation* approach, formal knowledge is the key to automatic integration of datasets, models and analytical pipelines. The next step, applied experimentally at this stage, is the *knowledge-driven* approach, where the knowledge is the key not only to integration, but also for overcoming scale and paradigm differences, and automated knowledge discovery.

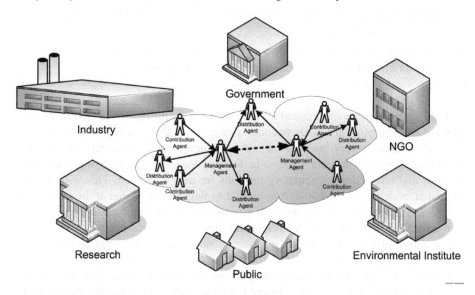

Fig. 1. A vision of a common environmental information space (Figure from [6])

Today, more than ever we are in need for developing common environmental information spaces that enable integrated modeling, following a sharing resource model (Figure 1). Each peer offers data or models, and others are able to discover and reuse them. The prime requirement of such an information space is the need for subjective interpretations: The same data or models can be interpreted differently for different studies. In the mediating approach, the challenge is for semantic annotations that allow for subjectivity. While there have been significant efforts to build domain ontologies by several projects, there was limited take up by broader communities. Apart from a few very basic nomenclatures, the rest of the domain ontologies I have used (or developed) were in one or another way biased by the problem at hand.

The second key requirement for such a common environmental information space is the *transferability* of scientific workflows. We have experienced times and again how difficult it is to perform the same study even in a nearby location: Data sources are missing, models do not converge, and corrective actions or new assumptions are needed. The major problem here is that the expert knowledge is hidden in model implementation or data archives, and our tools are not capable for manipulating our sources. Expert intervention is needed to "*adjust data*" and "*turn model knobs*". A semantically-aware common environmental information space needs to make such dependencies explicit and offer tools to match data offerings with model requirements.

Additionally, a common environmental information space for integrated modeling needs to:

a. Overcome obstacles of syntactic interoperability, by offering plug and play services for transforming data sources
b. Allow for data and model substitution, to enable model comparison in scientific workflows
c. Offer uniform services for output visualization, to allow for less engagement in producing visualizations
d. Document results provenance, ensuring the transparency of results
e. Allow for uncertainty quantification and error propagation
f. Allow for sensitivity analysis

Today, a common environmental information space is further challenged by the Internet of the Things: In the years to come we expect an abundance of sensory data to become available at very low cost, at real near time, over the Internet. This has already started to transform our view on performing local studies, engaging with communities and employing participatory methods for data collection. This will change integrated modeling methodologies, as more data will be around, but at the same time it will raise the bar for discovering such information, annotating them and evaluating their added value. A common environmental information space needs to hook up to sensor networks and allow models not only to run again as new data arrive, but to adapt as conditions change.

Another important factor that challenges our view on integrated modeling is the raise of high performance computing and the technologies for manipulating big data. Hardware acceleration and virtual computing infrastructures already allow massive simulations at a very large scale. However, still there is an entry barrier for making such computing infrastructure available. A common environmental information space needs to provide with seamless access to virtual computing infrastructures.

3   Case Study

In the following, I present a case study where we try to meet some of the challenges of integrated modelling with sensor data using semantic technologies. Based on a Greek NGO experience in large carnivores conservation in the mountain ecosystems of northern Greece, we built a generic architecture for wildlife information fusion, sharing and reuse. The ALPINE wildlife modeling system (hereafter, ALPINE for short) is a semantic modelling system for wildlife monitoring, management and conservation. ALPINE aims to demonstrate how live streaming data from animal tracking sensors can be effectively combined with geo-statistical analysis models, in order to assess habitat suitability, and to quantify the risks of wildlife interaction with man-made infrastructures. The overall system architecture (Figure 2) involves three layers of services, and is currently under development using Thinklab [7], the semantic modelling infrastructure of ARIES [8].

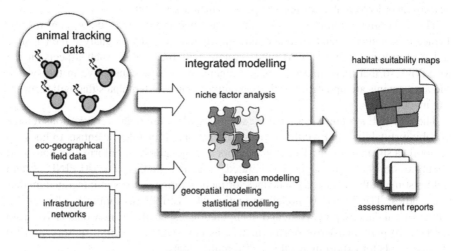

Fig. 2. The ALPINE architecture for wildlife monitoring (Figure from [9])

The first service layer deals with making available environmental data, originating either directly from sensors, or public and private archives. Animal tracking data from collars and eco-geographical field data and infrastructure networks are made available to a common environmental space. The semantic modelling system smooths out technical details for retrieving and transforming data, and also allows for interpretations tailored to the specific modelling exercise. The ALPINE system simplifies access via using open data protocols and making data discoverable through rich annotations. Open Geospatial Consortium standards have been employed to offer syntactic interoperability: Sensor Observation Service [10] for sharing sensor data, and Web Coverage Service [11] for datasets of geographical nature. Both field data, collected by ALPINE sensors (i.e. from GPS/GSM collars), and background information are annotated with problem-specific semantics, which offer interpretations for the particular problem and allows data to be matched to models.

Second, the integrated modeling layer employs statistical, geospatial and Bayesian models for ecological niche factor analysis. Models are annotated with problem-specific semantics and made available to a common environmental space. Thinklab semantic modeling engine allows for chaining models in scientific workflows, substituting models with alternatives, and feeding models with data to produce results. Specifically, three kinds of models are made available through the ALPINE system: Geospatial models allow operational interpretations of spatial sources and are typically used for creating derived information from original data, as buffering functions and density analysis. Bayesian models are employed for building probabilistic models in order to incorporate causal associations from evidence. For a more detailed discussion on Bayesian modeling for ecological risk assessments see [12]. Last, Ecological Niche Factor Analysis (ENFA) is a statistical procedure that uses only presence data, suitable to compare distributions among spaces that a population has a reasonable probability to occur using eco- geographical variables and the global space [13]. The ALPINE integrates seamlessly these three kinds of models in a platform in order to enable scientists to perform their assessments.

Third, the presentation layer generates maps and reports with the system results. Typically scientists spend adequate amount of time in order to analyse their results and post-process them. The ALPINE system will incorporate such aspects in the workflow, so that maps and reports are generated, as new data arrive in the system and assessments are updated. For this we employ reusable templates that will incorporate model results.

The ALPINE system is intended for scientists who aim to answer questions related to habitat suitability and wildlife-human interactions. It enables scientists to hook up sensor data streams coming live from sensors with geographical information and build scientific workflows to support integrated modeling studies. The ALPINE system tackles some of the semantic challenges for incorporating sensors in integrated modelling studies: The Thinklab modelling engine of ALPINE (a) minimizes human involvement in data preprocessing and manipulation, especially as new data arrive from sensors; (b) makes easier to re-run models, as new data arrive from sensors; and (c) provides tools for exporting results in different formats.

4   Epilogue

This paper aimed to preview some challenges for integrated modeling through a common information space of semantically shared environmental data and models. I believe we are close in realizing such a vision. Many of the building blocks are already in place. We have several success stories for standardizing nomenclatures, offering data as services through long-term archives, making model available as services and enabling model composition and execution in local or remote infrastructures. At the same time we are trapped with legacy software and institutional problems that do not allow such a vision to come true. Another significant part I didn't touch in this paper is the human side of the problem. In the current academic and scientific system there are very little incentives for building a sharing culture, which is a prerequisite for a common information space for integrated modeling.

Acknowledgements. Research in this study has received funding by European and national funds from NSRF 2007-2013, OP Competitiveness and Entrepreneurship, Cooperation 2011, in the context of the ALPINE project (grant 11SYN-6-411). I am grateful to Prof Ferdinando Villa for the insightful discussions that led me to the views presented here.

References

1. Rizzoli, A.E., Athanasiadis, I.N., Villa, F.: Delivering environmental knowledge: a semantic approach. In: Proc. 21st International Conference on Informatics for Environmental Protection (EnviroInfo 2007), pp. 43–50. Shaker Verlag, Warsaw (2007)
2. UN Earth Summit: Agenda 21. Department of public information, United Nations, Rio de Janeiro, Brazil (1992)
3. Athanasiadis, I.N., Villa, F.: A roadmap to domain specific programming languages for environmental modeling: key requirements and concepts. In: Proc. 2013 ACM workshop on Domain-Specific Modeling, pp. 27–32. ACM (2013)
4. Rizzoli, A., Young, W.: Delivering environmental decision support systems: Software tools and techniques. Environmental Modelling & Software 12, 237–249 (1997)
5. Denzer, R.: Generic integration of environmental decision support systems - state-of-the-art. Environmental Modelling & Software 20, 1217–1223 (2005)
6. Athanasiadis, I.N.: Towards a virtual enterprise architecture for the environmental sector. In: Protogeros, N. (ed.) Agent and web service technologies in virtual enterprises, pp. 256–266. Information Science Reference, Hershey (2007)
7. Villa, F., Athanasiadis, I.N., Rizzoli, A.E.: Modelling with knowledge: a review of emerging semantic approaches to environmental modelling. Environmental Modelling and Software 24, 577–587 (2009)
8. Villa, F., et al.: Thinklab software repository (2013)
9. Villa, F., Bagstad, K.J., Voigt, B., Johnson, G.W., Portela, R., Honzak, M., Batker, D.: A methodology for adaptable and robust ecosystem services assessment. PLoS ONE 9, e91001 (2014)
10. Athanasiadis, I.N., Villa, F., Examiliotou, G., Iliopoulos, Y., Mertzanis, Y.: Towards a semantic framework for wildlife modeling. In: Marx Gomez, J., et al. (eds.) Proc. 28th International Conference on Informatics for Environmental Protection (Enviroinfo 2014), pp. 287–292. BIS-Verlag, Oldenburg (2014)
11. OGC: Sensor Observation Service, Open Geospatial Consortium Standard (2007)
12. OGC: Web Coverage Service, Open Geospatial Consortium Standard (2012)
13. Pollino, C.A., Woodberry, O., Nicholson, A., Korb, K., Hart, B.T.: Parameterisation and evaluation of a bayesian network for use in an ecological risk assessment. Environmental Modelling & Software 22, 1140–1152 (2007)
14. Hirzel, A.H., Hausser, J., Chessel, D., Perrin, N.: Ecological-niche factor analysis: how to compute habitat-suitability maps without absence data? Ecology 83, 2027–2036 (2002)

Topics in Environmental Software Systems

Ralf Denzer

Environmental Informatics Institute (EII), Gaiberg, Germany
ralf.denzer@enviromatics.org

Abstract. Environmental software systems (ESS) are software systems supporting activities of environmental protection, environmental management, environmental policy and environmental sciences. ESS often overlap with adjacent
application fields like security, agriculture, health or climate change. The ISESS
conference series is one of several overlapping events which are devoted to environmental modelling and software systems. ISESS is probably the one international event which has the strongest focus on the software angle.

This paper gives a historic perspective of 20 years of ISESS conferences.
Starting with a historic review of the development of the field named "environmental software systems", it puts the ISESS conference into the greater perspective of similar activities. Using the original materials the paper identifies
typical themes subsumed under ESS, and highlights typical topics for the time.

The paper is the only existing complete collection of activities of the IFIP
working group 5.11 "Computers and Environment". Material of all events,
ISESS conferences as well as co-organised workshops has been collected in one
central place and will also to be kept up to date in the future.

Keywords: environmental software systems, ESS, environmental information
systems, EIS, environmental decision support systems, EDSS, ISESS, environmental informatics, enviromatics.

1   Introduction

It is probably impossible to define a clear "problem space" or "discipline/domain
boundary" for the ICT application domain named "environmental informatics" or "environmental software systems" (ESS). The more concrete one tries to capture these
boundaries the larger the problem space seems to get and the boundaries become fuzzy
and difficult to grasp. There have been discussions whether this is a "discipline" (a pure
computer scientist will say: no), an "applied discipline", a "domain" and so forth. For
the remainder of this article I shall call it "field of work" or just *"the field"* because this
sounds neutral enough.

Starting early on, there have been attempts to classify what environmental software
systems are, to provide an overview of research and application, like for instance in
the first paper [1] of the first ISESS book [2]. An early book [3] is structuring the
field according to the dividing line between technology and application [3]. Reading
some of the material today reveals interesting aspects.

R. Denzer et al. (Eds.): ISESS 2015, IFIP AICT 448, pp. 26–43, 2015.
© IFIP International Federation for Information Processing 2015

Seeing it today, some material looks naïve, but I have always been surprised how many of the hard problems which our field is dealing with today have already been identified 25 years ago, and on what impressive level, considering that informatics as a discipline was in its infancies. My own entry into the field was on September 30 and October 1, 1986, when my boss at the time, Dr. Andreas Jaeschke of KfK (today Karlsruhe Institute of Technology, KIT) organised the first recognised scientific event regarding environmental software systems, figure 1. It was my first day at work after university. The proceedings were published as a KfK report [4] and are probably the earliest proceedings published in the field.

I remember a talk in which a representative of a German federal state ministry reported about an analysis being carried out towards an integrated state-wide information system. That analysis had revealed that the state operated *several hundred information systems* relevant for environmental applications (unfortunately that statement was not published in the paper, so you just have to believe me). Needless to say that most of them were incompatible with each other – this just seems to be the way how ICT's grow in large organisations in an uncontrollable fashion – a situation which many readers today may be able to relate to.

Fig. 1. First ESS proceedings [4]

Every book or proceedings on ESS has to find a way to structure the content, which is nothing else than *trying to structure the current status of the field*. Some books try to apply the *dividing line: methodology / application* while others don't, and clearly each volume is influenced by actual research and policy trends. For instance the 2013 and 2011 proceedings [5,6] have a mixed approach (technology chapters like *future internet* or *semantics* vs. application chapters like *risk management* or *climate change*) while the 2015 book [7] applies a pure ICT structuring approach as follows:

- context articles, including keynotes and discussion papers
- information systems, information modelling and semantics
- decision support tools and systems
- modelling and simulation systems
- architectures, infrastructures, platforms and services
- requirements, software engineering and software tools
- analytics and visualization
- high performance computing and BigData

During the late 1990's there have been on-going discussions whether an *environmental information system* (EIS) is something different than an *environmental decision support system* (EDSS). A workshop report [10] of ISESS 1999 [11] is trying to answer that question. In order to avoid exclusions I have used myself the term "EIDSS" for *environmental information and decision support system*, a terrible acronym. I have personally gone back to the term *environmental software system*, because it is neutral enough and relatively clear: a software system supporting environmental applications.

Another important topic has been the *"meta thing"*. In the early days, particularly in the German scene which was heavily data centric, there was a never ending discussion about *meta-data* or *meta-information*, for instance as far back as [8]. Sometimes the "meta things" are hyphened, sometimes written together, sometimes written apart, but the never ending mystery of what "the meta things" are has not ceased to exist, although some so-called "meta-data standards" are applied in everyday life today. Still, many colleagues have come to the conclusion that the distinction is artificial because whether something is "meta" or not depends on the use, as has been stated in [9]. Actual real world meta-data standards and some service interface designs probably do not hold for long under this viewpoint.

Then it has been obvious for a long time that there is a very strong connection to *environmental modelling and simulation*, as many applications, particularly those for decision support apply models to investigate alternatives, specifically policy alternatives and planning alternatives. Looking into existing conferences and journals one must acknowledge that there are many more articles about modelling than (at least high quality) articles about ESS, and the only relevant journal, *Environmental Modelling & Software*, which has first been driven from the modelling side, still finds it a challenge to attract high quality innovative software papers.

This paper is trying to put ISESS into an international context of several related activities, and also aims at identifying typical patterns appearing over and over again in ESS. Starting with the international landscape and a complete record of ISESS events, I will make an attempt to analyse typical ISESS topics, based on a rough review of all ISESS proceedings [2,5,6,7,11,12,13,14,15,16,17].

2   The Conference Landscape

2.1   EnviroInfo

The first symposium [4] developed from 1987 on into a conference named "Symposium Informatik im Umweltschutz" which later became the "EnviroInfo" conference series. In parallel a working group named "Informatik im Umweltschutz" (computer science for environmental protection)[1] was installed as a committee of the German Informatics Society [2]. That working group can be considered as the nucleus of the field in the early days. EnviroInfo has been held in Germany and neighbouring countries since 1997. For an overview dated in 2011 see [18].

2.2   ISESS

The IFIP working group WG 5.11 "Computers and Environment" was founded in 1992, and was the first attempt to make the field, which was very much dominated by

---

[1] http://enviroinfo.eu
[2] http://www.gi.de

German speaking countries, more international. ISESS 1995 was the first event organised by the WG and it has been organised since on a biannual schedule. ISESS attempts to provide a world-wide coverage of ESS topics and has been held in North America, Europe and Australia / New Zealand (see sections 3 ff.)

2.3   MODSIM

The Modelling and Simulation Society of Australia and New Zealand (MSSANZ[3]) has been organising the MODSIM conference since the 1970's. MODSIM has a thematic relationship to our field in the sense that there are always sessions related to environmental modelling and for about 10 years there have been sessions related to environmental software which were co-organised by individuals of WG 5.11 in order to bridge the gap between the modelling and the software community. MODSIM is held in Australia and New Zealand, the last one being held in 2013 [19].

2.4   IEMSS

The International Environmental Modelling & Software Society[4] has been organising the IEMSS conference since 2002, and ISESS respectively WG5.11 have often co-organised sessions about environmental software at IEMSS. IEMSS has a strong focus on modelling, yet at the same time a considerable thematic overlap with ISESS in the field of software. IEMSS has a world-wide coverage of topics and has been held in Europe and North America. The last IEMSS conference was held in 2014 [20].

2.5   The White Spots on the Map

None of the above conferences has ever been held in South America, Africa or Asia. These parts of the world are to be covered yet.

3   The ISESS Conference Series

As illustrated above, the International Symposium on Environmental Software Systems (ISESS) is one of several overlapping forums discussing issues of *environmental information systems, environmental decision support systems, environmental software systems, environmental informatics, eco-informatics* or *enviromatics*.

ISESS was founded by Ralf Denzer and Gerald Schimak in 1995, with support from the German Informatics Society Working Group 4.6 "Computer Science for Environmental Protection", the International Federation for Information Processing (IFIP) Working Group 5.11 "Computers and Environment" and our friend David Russell at the Pennsylvania State University (PSU) campus in Malvern, PA. The first symposium received great support from PSU and turned out to be one of many success stories.

---

[3] http://www.mssanz.org.au
[4] http://www.iemss.org

Since then the symposium has been held in the following countries: the United States, Canada, Austria, New Zealand, Portugal, the Czech Republic, Italy; in several years, joint sessions were held in conjunction with the biennial meeting of iEMSs (International Environmental Modelling and Software Society). ISESS has been an IFIP event since 1995 and is organized by WG 5.11.

Since its establishment WG 5.11 has been led by Giorgio Guariso (1991-1999), Ralf Denzer (1999-2005) and Dave Swayne (2005-2011). Since 2011 it is in the hands of Gerald Schimak. Several individuals have served as vice-chairs and secretaries of the WG and many members of the WG have been active supporters for a long time without holding an official position.

For more than two decades ISESS has brought together researchers dealing with environmental information challenges trying to provide solutions using forward-looking and leading-edge IT technology.

4   A Complete History of Events

4.1   ISESS Conferences

During the past 20 years we have seen the publisher of IFIP change several times and electronic publishing has become the most important medium for scientific publications. ISESS has followed this transition and therefore there is *not a single place* where all ISESS proceedings can be accessed.

The first and second proceedings (ISESS 1995, ISESS 1997) were published by IFIP publisher Chapman & Hall (C&H):

- R. Denzer, D. Russell, G. Schimak (eds.), Environmental Software Systems [2]
- R. Denzer, D. A. Swayne, G. Schimak (eds.), Environmental Software Systems Vol. 2 [12]

Then IFIP changed publisher and the third proceedings (ISESS 1999) were published by IFIP publisher Kluwer Academic Press:
- R. Denzer, D. A. Swayne, M. Purvis, G. Schimak (eds.), Environmental Software Systems Vol. 3 - Environmental Information and Environmental Decision Support, [11]
As print publications were becoming increasingly difficult (particularly their cost for smaller conferences), the fourth and fifth proceedings (ISESS 2001, ISESS 2003) were published by the organizers of the symposium under IFIP ISBN:

- D. A. Swayne, R. Denzer, G. Schimak (eds.), Environmental Software Systems Vol. 4 - Environmental Information and Indicators, International Federation for Information Processing [13]
- G. Schimak, D. A. Swayne, N.T. Quinn, R. Denzer (eds.), Environmental Software Systems Vol. 5 - Environmental Knowledge and Information Systems [14]

The sixth and seventh proceedings (ISESS 2005, ISESS 2007) were published, but this time as electronic versions under IFIP ISBN:

- D. A. Swayne, T. Jakeman (eds.), Environmental Software Systems, Vol. 6 - Environmental Risk Assessment Systems [15]
- D. A. Swayne, J. Hřebíček (eds.), Environmental Software Systems, Vol. 7 - Dimensions of Environmental Informatics [16]

The eight proceedings (ISESS 2009) were again published electronically, but not under IFIP ISBN:

- D. A. Swayne, R. Soncini-Sessa (eds.), Environmental Software Systems, Vol. 8, [17]

Today, Springer is the official IFIP publisher and ISESS is published by Springer in IFIP Advances in Information and Communication Technology (AICT)[5]. Proceedings number nine and ten were published as follows:

- J. Hřebíček, G. Schimak, R. Denzer (eds.), Environmental Software Systems, Vol. 9 - Frameworks of eEnvrionment, IFIP AICT 359 [5]
- J. Hřebíček, G. Schimak, M. Kubásek, A.E. Rizzoli (eds.), Environmental Software Systems, Vol. 10 - Fostering Information Sharing, IFIP AICT 413 [6]

and the current conference, ISESS 2015 in Melbourne is again a Springer book in the IFIP AICT series

- R. Denzer, R. M. Argent, G. Schimak, J. Hřebíček, (eds.), Environmental Software Systems, Vol. 11 – Infrastructures, Services and Applications, IFIP AICT 448 [7]

Table 1. ISESS Conferences

Event and topic	Publisher	Pages	Papers
ISESS 2015: Environmental Software Systems Vol. 11 - **Infrastuctures, Services and Applications**, 25.3.-27.3.2015, Melbourne, Australia	Springer, IFIP AICT	611	61
ISESS 2013: Environmental Software Systems Vol. 10 - **Fostering Information Sharing**, 9.10.-11.10.2013, Neusiedl am See, Austria	Springer, IFIP AICT	696	65
ISESS 2011: Environmental Software Systems Vol. 9 - **Frameworks of eEnvironment**, 27.6.-29.6.2011, Brno Czech Republic	Springer, IFIP AICT	674	74
ISESS 2009: Environmental Software Systems Vol. 8, 6.10.-9.10.2009, Venice, Italy	IFIP Series	251	24
ISESS 2007: Environmental Software Systems Vol. 7 - **Dimensions of Environmental Informatics**, 22.-25.5.2007, Prague, CZ	IFIP Series	624	61
ISESS 2005 - Environmental Software Systems Vol. 6 - **Environmental Risk Assessment Systems**, 24.-27.5.2005, Sesimbra, PT	IFIP Series	243	26
ISESS 2003: Environmental Software Systems Vol. 5- **Environmental Knowledge and Information Systems**, 27.-30.5.2003, Semmering, AT	IFIP Series	470	43

---

[5] http://www.springer.com/series/6102

ISESS 2001: Environmental Software Systems Vol. 4 - **Environmental Information and Indicators**, 22.-25.5.2001, Banff, CA	IFIP Series	235	24
ISESS 1999: Environmental Software Systems Vol. 3 - **Environmental Information and Decision Support**, 30.8.-2.9.1999, Dunedin, NZ	Kluwer	268	28
ISESS 1997: **Environmental Software Systems Vol. 2**, 28.4.-2.5.1997, Whistler, CA	C&H	360	45
ISESS 1995: **Environmental Software Systems**, 13.-15.6.1995, Malvern, US	C&H	290	25

Today Springer also has the rights of the early Kluwer and Chapman & Hall books (ISESS 1995, ISESS 1997, ISESS 1999), as Kluwer was merged with Springer in 2004 and Chapman & Hall had been bought by Kluwer in 1997. Therefore all proceedings which were published by a publishing house are in one place today and can be accessed through Springer and Springer Link. They are available as hard cover and/or soft cover, as eBooks and (most of them) as individual articles.

4.2   ISESS Workshops and Co-organised Events

In addition to the bi-annual conference in odd-numbered years, the ISESS community has organized workshops and co-organised events in most even-numbered years. These co-organized events were either published with IEMSS, or as best paper peer-reviewed journal issues.

From the events in 1998 and 2000, the best papers were invited to be extended and improved in a peer review process, and were published as special issues of Environmental Modelling and Software (EM&S) and Advances In Environmental Research (AIER):

- Journal Environmental Modelling & Software (EM&S), Volume 16 No. 5 (2001)
- Journal Advances in Environmental Research, Vol. 5 No. 4, November 2001

Along with the first IEMSS conference in Lugano, WG 5.11 co-organised a session which is available through IEMSS:

- ISESS Session at IEMSS 2002, Tool integration in environmental decision support systems, in [21], see www.iemss.org/iemss2002/special_sessions.phtml#isess, pp. 271-389

The 2004 workshop published a special issue of EM&S, again based on the best contributions at that workshop:

- Journal Environmental Modelling & Software (EM&S), Volume 22 No. 4 (2007), pp.415-448, Special Section : Environmental Risk and Emergency Management, for an introduction see [22]

In 2006, 2008, 2010 and 2014, WG 5.11 was again co-organizer of specific sessions at IEMSS conferences.

- ISESS Special Session at IEMSS 2006, Integrated software solutions for environmental problems - architecture, frameworks and data structures, in [23], see, www.iemss.org/iemss2006/sessions/s5.html
- ISESS Special Session and Workshop at IEMSS 2008, Session S1: Data and sensor networks and environmental modelling and Workshop W1: Creating robust sensor networks architecture and infrastructure, in [24], see www.iemss.org/iemss2008/index.php?n=Main.S1
- ISESS Special Session at IEMSS 2010, Interaction Design for Environmental Information Systems, in [25], see www.iemss.org/iemss2010/Volume3.pdf
- ISESS Special Sessions at IEMSS 2014, Session A4: Smart and Mobile Devices for Environmental Applications, Session A5: Parallel Simulation of Environmental Phenomena, Session A6: Semantics, Metadata and Ontologies of Natural Systems, in [26], volume 1, see: www.iemss.org/sites/iemss2014/papers/Volume_1_iEMSs2014_pp_1-602.pdf

Table 2. ISESS workshops and co-organised events at IEMSS

Event and topic	Publisher	Pages	Papers
ISESS Sessions at IEMSS 2014, A4: **Smart and Mobile Devices for Environmental Applications**, Session A5: **Parallel Simulation of Environmental Phenomena**, Session A6: **Semantics, Metadata and Ontologies of Natural Systems**, 15.-19.6.2014, San diego, USA	IEMSS	125	17
ISESS Session at IEMSS 2010: **Interaction Design for Environmental Information Systems**, 6.7.2010, Ottawa, Canada	IEMSS	39	5
ISESS Session at IEMSS: **Data and Sensor Networks and Environmental Modelling**, 7.7.-10.7.2008, Barcelona Spain	IEMSS	96	14
ISESS Session at IEMSS 2006: **Integrated Software Solutions for Environmental Problems**, 9.-13.7.2006, Burlington, US	IEMSS	169	29
ISESS 2004 Workshop **Environmental Risk and Emergency Management**, 18.-21.5.2004, Harrisonburg, US	EM&S	33	6
ISESS Session at IEMSS 2002: **Tool Integration in Environmental Decision Support Systems**, 22.5.-25.5.2001, Lugano, Switzerland	IEMSS	119	20
ISESS 2000 Workshop: **Integration in Environmental Information Systems**, 28.5.-2.6.2000, Zell am See, AT	AIER	144	16
ISESS 1998 Workshop: **Design Principles for Environmental Information Systems**, 15.-18.6. 1998, St. Nikolai, AT	EM&S	50	8

5   ISESS 2001-2009 Second Editions and Enviromatics.org

The proceedings of 2001, 2003, 2005, 2007 and 2009 were published under IFIP copyright in different formats (print, CD, USB) and were neither available from Springer nor on-line at one central place. Following an official request in November 2014, IFIP granted me the right to re-publish these proceedings. They are now available *as second-editions*, for now in a relatively simple form, as one downloadable PDF. They will be available permanently as follows:

- R. Denzer (ed.), Environmental Software Systems Vol. 4 - Environmental Information and Indicators, Second Edition [27]
- R. Denzer (ed.), Environmental Software Systems Vol. 5 - Environmental Knowledge and Information Systems, Second Edition [28]
- R. Denzer (ed.), Environmental Software Systems, Vol. 6 - Environmental Risk Assessment Systems, Second Edition [29]
- R. Denzer (ed.), Environmental Software Systems, Vol. 7 - Dimensions of Environmental Informatics, Second Edition [30]
- R. Denzer (ed.), Environmental Software Systems, Vol. 8, Second Edition, [31]

From March 2015 on, the website www.enviromatics.org will maintain a complete repository of these volumes and will point readers to all other ISESS related publication information.

6   A Review of ISESS Topics

A rough review of topics of all ISESS books presents the reader with a large variety of topics, software tools and applications. Table 3 shows the tables of content of each ISESS conference publication.

Table 3. ISESS tables of content (omitting keynotes, workshops and tutorials)

Event	Topics
1995	Environmental information systems Modelling and simulation Environmental management Decision support Distributed environmental information Artificial intelligence applications Environmental data visualization
1997	Ecological and agricultural applications Decision support Environmental information systems and meta information Industrial applications GIS applications Modelling and simulation Object orientation
1999	Environmental information systems tools and techniques Environmental information systems implementations Environmental decision support systems

2001	Environmental indicators Environmental modelling Environmental information systems Environmental decision support systems
2003	Environmental information systems Environmental information services Environmental assessment, modelling and simulation Integration Environmental knowledge and decision support systems EC 5th framework applications
2005	Special session on successes and failures Corporate and public environment information systems Tools and techniques Wide scale monitoring Risk management State information systems Applied decision support systems Integrative tools
2007	Next generation of environmental information and risk management systems ICT tools for ecological and human risk assessment Artificial and computational intelligence for environmental modelling Open source GIS and environmental modelling systems Environmental engineering education, presentation of environmental information to nonscientists Software tools and component-based environmental modelling Integrated modelling and decision support systems for watershed and lake management Human factors in enviromatics Distributed and parallel environmental modelling paradigms
2009	Software systems for policy analysis Sensor webs and sensor networks Human factors in environmental information systems
2011	eEnvironment and cross-border services in digital agenda for Europe Environmental information systems and services – infrastructures and platforms Semantics and environment Information tools for global environmental assessment Climate services and environmental tools for urban planning and climate change applications and services
2013	Environmental applications in the scope of the future internet Smart and mobile devices used for environmental applications Information tools for global environmental assessment Environmental applications in risk and crisis management SEIS as a part of the 7th environment action programme of the EU Human interaction and human factors driving future EIS / EDSS developments Environmental management, accounting and statistics Information systems and applications
2015	Information systems, information modelling and semantics Decision support tools and systems Modelling and simulation systems Architectures, infrastructures, platforms and services Requirements, software engineering and software tools Analytics and visualization High performance computing and BigData

In the sequel I would like to point the reader to a selection of papers from each of the proceedings, which I think were typical for the developments at the time:

- 1995
  - [32]: gives an introduction into requirements of integrated information systems from an ecological point of view
  - [33]: identifies early on the problems of processing large amounts of earth observation data
  - [34]: based on the example of ecological monitoring, the paper shows how hard it can be to analyse environmental data, and that it may be difficult to grasp; the paper identifies methods and tools from artificial intelligence
  - [35]: shows the use evolving methodologies of scientific data visualization
- 1997
  - [36]: shows the needs and system design challenges for integrated decision support based on GIS, visualisation, models and data management components
  - [37]: demonstrates an early application of web technologies
  - [38]: is one of the first environmental planning applications demonstrating the integration across national borders
  - [39]: shows the need to integrate models into information systems for environmental research
- 1999
  - [40]: identifies real time processing needs for water quality management in a catchment involving many stakeholders with conflicting interests
  - [41]: is one of the early papers discussing distributed design of information systems, integrating spatial and fact information coming from different data sources over networks
  - [42]: discusses the integration of simulation models for flood management into decision support
  - [43]: is a workshop report discussing problems and solutions for water-related software systems
  - [10]: is a workshop report discussing the boundaries between environmental information systems and environmental decision support systems
- 2001
  - [44]: discusses the fundamental role of indicators in the generation of higher level information suitable for decision support
  - [45,46]: show typical system designs for environmental monitoring systems
  - [47]: identifies decision theory as baseline for decision support systems
  - [48]: presents requirements and use cases for participatory processes involving a wide stakeholder audience
- 2003
  - [49]: discusses integration efforts on the way from data to knowledge
  - [50]: shows the use of services to wrap simulation models
  - [51]: presents GPS based tracking for the optimisation of logistics processes
  - [52]: is a discussion of workflow systems for environmental administrations
  - [53]: presents the reader with a discussion of complexity issues related to human factors of ESS

- [54]: is one of the early papers describing multi governmental reporting, in this case for the European Water Framework Directive; this paper was one of several papers related to projects of the European research framework program, which became an important research driver at the time [55]
- 2005
  - [56,57]: give a good perspective on typical government information systems at state and national level
  - [58]: is one of the first papers discussing sensor web enablement
  - [59]: discusses integrated modelling toolkits and their frameworks
  - [60]: shows how the combination of analysis and visualisation methods are embraced towards interactive environmental data analytics
  - [61]: is the first publication of a series of research papers towards environmental service infrastructures - research which has dominated the ESS part of the European 6th framework research program, see also [62]
- 2007
  - the first papers on semantics and ontologies appear, both for use in the data and in the modelling sphere [63,64,65,66]
  - [67] is a large project to progress sensor web enablement and its standards
  - [68] is one example out of a class of applications devoted to risk management, a DSS integrating various tools, based on free software
  - [69,70] are two of several articles discussing the communication of information to the public
  - [71,72] are papers on evolving open source software in the area of geographical information systems
- 2009
  - [73] describes the ICT-Ensure project, which has amongst others established a literature repository around the EnviroInfo community[6]
  - [74] discusses coupling of models using OpenMI
  - [75] is one of the first papers on crisis management; ISESS here and there overlaps with the community on ICT for crisis management [7]; see also [76]
  - [77] is one of many papers to come (and yet to come) on climate change
- 2011
  - in Europe, the landscape is progressively understood as part of the Digital Agenda for Europe and the so-called Single Information Space for the Environment [78]; many papers in the 2001 proceedings [5] are in relationship to this theme
  - along this line, there is a number of articles related to platforms and standards allowing the composition of services, e.g. [79,80,81]
  - this includes infrastructures for semantics [82]
  - climate change applications are progressing more and more, see e.g. [83]

---

[6] http://www.iai.kit.edu/ictensure
[7] http://www.iscramlive.org

- 2013
  - ESS pick up developments of the Future Internet initiative, see e.g. [84]
  - mobile applications on smart mobile devices play an increasingly important role; in [85] an example is given to use crowd sourcing to cope with illegal waste dumping
  - again many papers are in relationship to pan national information infrastructures, e.g. for reporting [86]
  - [87] is giving an introduction into visual analytics methods and tools

The most obvious new theme in the 2015 edition of ISESS is High Performance Computing. A workshop is organised in collaboration with the Australian NCI (National Computing Initiative)[8].

7   Patterns in Environmental Software Systems?

It is difficult to draw more fundamental conclusions about the nature of the field without a more in-depth analysis. ESS are often defined as software systems, a) which contain heterogeneous space-time information, often geospatial multi-dimensional scientific information with some uncertainty, b) which often support complex decision making processes, c) which often use different software tools and methodologies to solve a problem, d) which often have to integrate data across boundaries of various sorts, e) where often information is re-used beyond its original intention, f) where it is necessary to bridge the gap between science and practical application.

Although there are several overview papers of the field, I have not found a real classification or taxonomy in the literature.

One approach to look at it which I would like to repeat here is one which was developed in a project to define a curriculum on environmental informatics, as part of an EU-Canadian education project [88]. While this curriculum was never implemented in terms of course modules, the structure defined by the project is probably still somewhat useful, though some terms may be outdated and it is probably not complete. The idea is to structure the information processing in terms of a level-of-complexity approach, which clearly distinguishes between situations in which information is produced, processed, integrated and re-used. Table 4 shows this proposal.

Whether there are typical patterns in ESS or not, one point is becoming very clear when going through the history of ISESS from back to front, namely that:

> The field which we call Environmental Software Systems is progressively defined as a synthesis of infrastructures, platforms, re-usable services and tools which provide end users with local-to-global transparent access to information and services; the challenge remains to supply software developers with improved means to build reliable, integrated, multi-tool systems at reasonable cost.

---

[8] http://nci.org.au

Table 4. Proposed enviromatics curriculum, taken from [89]

I: WHY ENVIROMATICS ?
1. History of Enviromatics Developments
2. Application Areas
3. Introduction into the ECCEI Course
4. Introduction into the Common Example

II: ENVIROMATICS BASE METHODS
II.A Problem Definition and System Analysis
5. Problem Definition
6. System Analysis
II.B Data Management / Information Modelling
7. Environmental Data, Data Preparation and Acquisition
8. Monitoring
9. Environmental Databases and Environmental Information Systems (EIS)
10. Information Modelling
11. Meta Information in Environmental Databases
II.C Data Analysis
12. Environmental Statistics
13. Geographical Information Systems
14. Visualization
II.D Diagnosis and Interpretation
15. Environmental Risk and Impact Assessment
16. Environmental Models
17. Environmental Indicators
18. Diagnosis and Artificial Intelligence

II.E Decision Support
19. Target Groups for Decision Support
20. IT Techniques and Systems for Decision Support
21. Scenarios
22. Presentation in DSS

III: ENVIROMATICS INTEGRATION METHODS
III.F EIS Interoperability
23. Integration Problems
24. Environmental Data Standards
25. Building and Managing Environmental Data Networks
III.G Meta Information Systems
26. Properties of Meta Information
27. Environmental Data Catalogs
28. Environmental Catalogs on the World Wide Web
29. Multilingual Information Systems
III.H Open EIS Architectures
30. Properties of Open EIS Architectures
31. Review of Architectures
32. Generic EIS Infrastructures

References

1. Page, B.: Environmental informatics – towards a new discipline in applied computer science for environmental protection and research. In: [2], pp. 3–22
2. Denzer, R., Russell, D., Schimak, G. (eds.): Environmental Software Systems. Chapman & Hall (1996) ISBN 0 412 73730 2 (print)
3. Avouris, N.M., Page, B. (eds.): Environmental informatics – methodology and applications of environmental information processing. Kluwer (1995) ISBN 0-7923-3445-0
4. Jaesche, A., Page, B.: Informatikanwendungen im Umweltbereich, KfKreport 4223 (March 1987) ISSN 0303 4003
5. Hřebíček, J., Schimak, G., Denzer, R. (eds.): Environmental Software Systems. IFIP AICT, vol. 359. Springer, Heidelberg (2011)
6. Hřebíček, J., Schimak, G., Kubásek, M., Rizzoli, A.E. (eds.): ISESS 2013. IFIP AICT, vol. 413. Springer, Heidelberg (2013)

7. Denzer, R., Argent, R.M., Schimak, G., Hřebíček, J. (eds.): Environmental Software Systems. IFIPAICT, vol. 448. Springer, Heidelberg (2015)
8. Schütz, T.: Bericht der Arbeitsgruppe Metainformation. In: Güttler, R., Geiger, W. (eds.) Workshop Integration von Umweltdaten, Schloß Dagstuhl, ch. 2, pp. 159–162. Metropolis (February 1994) ISBN 3-89518-032-7
9. Schimak, G., Bügel, U., Denzer, R., Havlik, D.: Meta-Information – A basic instrument in developing an Open Architecture and Spatial Data Infrastructure for Risk Management. In: International Symposium on Environmental Software Systems 2007 (ISESS 2007), Prague, May 22-25. IFIP Conference Series (2007)
10. Swayne, D.A., et al.: Environmental Decision Support Systems – Exactly what are they? In: [11], pp. 257–268. Kluwer Academic Publishers
11. Denzer, R., Swayne, D.A., Purvis, M., Schimak, G. (eds.): Environmental Software Systems Vol. 3 - Environmental Information and Environmental Decision Support. Kluwer Academic Publishers (2000) ISBN 0 7923 7832 6
12. Denzer, R., Swayne, D.A., Schimak, G. (eds.): Environmental Software Systems, vol. 2. Chapman & Hall (1998) ISBN 0 412 81740 3 (print)
13. Swayne, D.A., Denzer, R., Schimak, G. (eds.): Environmental Software Systems Vol. 4 - Environmental Information and Indicators, International Federation for Information Processing (2001) ISBN 3 901882 14 6 (print)
14. Schimak, G., Swayne, D.A., Quinn, N.T., Denzer, R.: Environmental Software Systems Vol. 5 - Environmental Knowledge and Information Systems, International Federation for Information Processing (2003) ISBN 3 901882 16 2 (print)
15. Swayne, D.A., Jakeman, T. (eds.): Environmental Software Systems, Vol. 6 - Environmental Risk Assessment Systems. IFIP (2005) ISBN 3-901882-21-9 (CDROM)
16. Swayne, D.A., Hřebíček, J. (eds.): Environmental Software Systems, Vol. 7 - Dimensions of Environmental Informatics. IFIP (2007) ISBN 978-3-901882-22-7 (USB)
17. Swayne, D.A., Soncini-Sessa, R. (eds.): Environmental Software Systems, vol. 8. University of Guelph (2009) ISBN 978-3-901882-364 (USB)
18. Pillmann, W.: EnviroInfo Conferences: Knowledge Exchange Platform for Information Technology in Environmental Sustainability Research, State 2011 and Outlook. In: EnviroInfo 2011: Innovations in Sharing Environmental Observations and Information, Shaker Verlag Aachen ISBN: 978-3-8440-0451-9
19. Piantadosi, J., Anderssen, R.S., Boland, J. (eds.): MODSIM 2013, 20th International Congress on Modelling and Simulation. Modelling and Simulation Society of Australia and New Zealand, pp. 2506–2512 (December 2013), ISBN: 978-0-9872143-3-1, http://www.mssanz.org.au/modsim2013/L5/ahamed.pdf
20. Ames, D.P., Quinn, N.W.T., Rizzoli, A.E. (eds.): 2014 Proceedings of the 7th International Congress on Environmental Modelling and Software, San Diego, California, USA, June 15-19 (2014) ISBN: 978-88-9035-744-2
21. Rizzoli, A.E., Jakeman, A.J. (eds.): iEMSs 2002 International Congress: Integrated Assessment and Decision Support. Proceedings of the 1st biennial meeting of the International Environmental Modelling and Software Societey, Lugano, Switzerland, vol. 3, pp. 271–389 (June 2002) ISBN 88-900787-0-7
22. Quinn, N.W.T.: Environmental Risk and Emergency Management. Journal Environmental Modelling & Software (EM&S) 22(4), 415 (2007)
23. Voinov, A., Jakeman, A., Rizzoli, A. (eds.): Proceedings of the iEMSs Third Biennial Meeting, Summit on Environmental Modelling and Software. International Environmental Modelling and Software Society, Burlington (2006) ISBN 1-4243-0852-6, 978-1-4243-0852-1

24. Sànchez-Marrè, M., Béjar, J., Comas, J., Rizzoli, A., Guariso, G. (eds.): Proceedings of the iEMSs Fourth Biennial Meeting: International Congress on Environmental Modelling and Software (iEMSs 2008). International Environmental Modelling and Software Society, Barcelona (2008) ISBN: 978-84-7653-074-0

25. Swayne, D.A., Yang, W., Voinov, A., Rizzoli, A., Filatova, T. (eds.): Modelling for Environment's Sake, Proceedings of the Fifth Biennial Conference of the International Environmental Modelling and Software Society, Ottawa, Canada, July 5-8 (2010) ISBN: 978-88-9035-741-1

26. Ames, D.P., Quinn, N.W.T., Rizzoli, A.E. (eds.): 2014 Proceedings of the 7th International Congress on Environmental Modelling and Software, San Diego, California, USA, June 15-19 (2014) ISBN: 978-88-9035-744-2

27. Denzer, R. (ed.): Environmental Software Systems vol. 4 - Environmental Information and Indicators, 2nd edn. International Federation for Information Processing (originally 2001), 2nd edn. (December 2014), doi: 10.13140/2.1.3519.6481

28. Denzer, R. (ed.): Environmental Software Systems, vol. 5 - Environmental Knowledge and Information Systems, 2nd edn. International Federation for Information Processing (originally 2003), 2nd edn. (December 2014), doi: 10.13140/2.1.3683.4887

29. Denzer, R. (ed.): Environmental Software Systems, vol. 6 - Environmental Risk Assessment Systems, 2nd edn. International Federation for Information Processing (originally 2005), 2nd edn. (December 2014), doi: 10.13140/2.1.3824.0325

30. Denzer, R. (ed.): Environmental Software Systems, vol. 7 - Dimensions of Environmental Informatics, 2nd edn. International Federation for Information Processing (originally 2007), 2nd edn. (December 2014), doi: 10.13140/2.1.3773.6001

31. Denzer, R. (ed.): Environmental Software Systems, vol. 8 (originally 2009), 2nd edn. (December 2014), doi: 10.13140/2.1.3561.8888

32. Lenz R.: Requirements of integrated information systems from an ecological point of view. In: [2], pp. 41–53

33. Zingler, M., Pintaritsch, H.: Complex metadata management in earth observation for environmental research. In: [2], pp. 90–100

34. Walley, W.J., Dzeroski, S.: Biological monitoring: a comparison between Bayesian, neural and maschine learning. In: [2], pp. 229–240

35. Mayer, H.F., Haas, W., Züger, J., Loibl, W.: Visualizing the spatial and temporary dynamics of ozone concentration data. In: [2], pp. 272–277

36. Booty, W.G., et al.: Great lakes toxic chemical decision support system. In: [12], pp. 95–101

37. Yow, T.G., et al.: Inside an environmental data archive WWW site. In: [12], pp. 168–174

38. Burgard, J., Güttler, R.: Environmental problems - a transnational solution supporting co-operation of all relevant social forces. In: [12], pp. 175–181

39. Clemen, T.: Integrating simulation models into environmental information systems – model analysis. In: [12], pp. 292–299

40. Quinn, N.: A decision support system for real time management of water quality in the San Joaquin River, California. In: [11], pp. 232–246

41. Güttler, R., Denzer, R., Houy, P.: An EIS calledWunDa. In: [11], pp. 114–121

42. Leon, L., et al.: Water quality model integration in a decision support system. In: [11], pp.187–194

43. Argent, R.: Environmental software systems in water resources: problems and approaches. In: [11], pp. 249–258

44. Braaten, R., et al.: A framework for using indicators and environmental software systems for analysis of catchment condition. In: [27], pp. 13-27, doi: 10.13140/2.1.3519.6481

45. Martin, R.W., et al.: A river biology monitoring system (RBMS) for English and Welsh rives. In: [27], pp. 152–163, doi:10.13140/2.1.3519.6481
46. Schimak, G., et al.: Environmental monitoring system UWEDAT - a flexible computerized system for monitoring of environmental issues. In: [27], pp. 164–176, doi: 10.13140/2.1.3519.6481
47. Swayne, D., et al.: Putting the decision in DSS. In: [27], pp. 207–216, doi: 10.13140/2.1.3519.6481
48. Argent, R.M., Grayson, R.B.: A modelling shell for participatory assessment and management of natural resources. In: [27], pp. 58–67, doi:10.13140/2.1.3519.6481
49. Pillmann, W.: Integrating environmental knowledge with information and communication technologies. In: [28], pp. 11–19, doi:10.13140/2.1.3683.4887
50. Smiatek, G.: Web service-based mapping tool for meteorology and chemistry transport models. In: [28], pp. 113–121, doi:10.13140/2.1.3683.4887
51. Steffens, T., Fischer-Stabel, P.: Integration of heterogeneous system components to realize an operational tracking service. In: [28], pp. 276–285, doi:10.13140/2.1.3683.4887
52. Fiala, J., Ministr, J., Racek, J.: Workflow model of environmental municipal administration in the Czech Republic. In: [28], pp. 286–294, doi:10.13140/2.1.3683.4887
53. Frysinger, S.P.: Human factors of environmental decision support systems. In: [28], pp. 318–327, doi:10.13140/2.1.3683.4887
54. Usländer, T.: Motivation for an IT framework for the implementation of the European Water Framework Directive. In: [28], pp. 391–398, doi:10.13140/2.1.3683.4887
55. Denzer, R., Colotte, P., Weets, G.: Enviromatics in the 5th European Framework program. In: [28], pp. 357–358, doi:10.13140/2.1.3683.4887
56. Hrebicek, J., Pitner, T., Racek, J.: Analysis of environmental information management in the Czech Republic. In: [29], doi:10.13140/2.1.3824.0325
57. Geiger, W., et al.: Examples of public environmental information systems and portals in Baden-Wuerttemberg. In: [29], doi:10.13140/2.1.3824.0325
58. Fleming, G., et al.: Sensor web enabling the advanced fire information system. In: [29], doi:10.13140/2.1.3824.0325
59. Argent, R.M., Fowler, K.: A new approach to integrated catchment modelling: the catchment modelling toolkit. In: [29], doi:10.13140/2.1.3824.0325
60. Andrienko, G., Adrienko, N.: Interactive aggregation methods for analysing results of environmental modelling. In: [29], doi:10.13140/2.1.3824.0325
61. Denzer, R., et al.: ORCHESTRA – development of an open architecture for risk management in Europe. In: [29], doi:10.13140/2.1.3824.0325
62. Usländer T.: Service-oriented design of environmental information systems. KIT Scientific Publishing (2010) ISSN 1863-6489, ISBN 978-3-86644-499-7
63. Gendarmi, D., et al.: Water protection information management by syntactic and semantic interoperability of heterogeneous repositories. In: [30], pp. 158–168, doi: 10.13140/2.1.3773.6001
64. Huber, D., et al.: Development and application of component-based generic farm system simulator implementing a semantically enriched integrated modelling framework. In: [30], pp. 245–258, doi:10.13140/2.1.3773.6001
65. Bügel, U., Hilbring, D., Denzer, R.: Application of semantic services in ORCHESTRA. In: [30], pp. 19–30, doi:10.13140/2.1.3773.6001
66. Dokas, I.M.: Ontology to support knowledge representation and risk analysis for the development of early warning system in solid waste management operations. In: [30], doi:10.13140/2.1.3773.6001

67. Havlik, D., et al.: SANY (Sensors Anywhere) Integrated Project. In: [30], pp. 140–146, doi:10.13140/2.1.3773.6001
68. Stewart, R.N.: SADA: a freeware decision support tool integrating GIS, sample design, spatial modelling and risk assessment. In: [30], pp. 211–221, doi:10.13140/2.1.3773.6001
69. Quinn, N.W.T.: An environmental monitoring data management system for providing stakeholder assurances toward meeting contaminant mass loading policy objectives. In: [30], pp. 312–323, doi:10.13140/2.1.3773.6001
70. Leger, K., Elshout, S., Heich, H.: Communicating air quqlity. In: [30], pp. 324–335, doi:10.13140/2.1.3773.6001
71. Neteler M. et al.: Free and open source GIS applications in environmental modelling. In: [30], pp. 417–427, doi: 10.13140/2.1.3773.6001
72. Jolma, A.: Geoinformatica: a modelling platform built on FOSS. In: [30], pp. 324–335, doi:10.13140/2.1.3773.6001
73. Geiger, W., et al.: The ICT-ENSURE European Research Area project in the field of ICT for environmental sustainability and its research programmes information system. In: [31], doi:10.13140/2.1.3561.8888
74. Booty, W.G.: Improving Lake Winnipeg integrated environmental modelling with Open-MI. In: [31], doi:10.13140/2.1.3561.8888
75. Racek, J., et al.: Process analysis and geo visualisation support of emergency management. In: [31], doi: 10.13140/2.1.3561.8888
76. van de Walle, B. (ed.): nformation Systems for Emergency Management. M.E. Sharpe Publishers (2010) ISBN 978-0-7656-2134-4
77. Wrobel M. et al.: Interactive access to climate change information. In: [31], doi: 10.13140/2.1.3561.8888
78. Hrebicek J., Pillmann W.: eEnvironment: reality and challenges for eEnvionment implementation in Europe. In: [5], pp. 1–14
79. Gadica C. et al.: Using negotiation for dynamic composition of services in multi-organisational environmental management. In: [5], pp. 177–188
80. Jolma, A., Karatzas, K.: Software architectures for distributed environmental modelling. In: [5], pp. 255–260
81. Roman, D., et al.: Open environmental platforms: top-level components and relevant standards. In: [5], pp. 217–225
82. Nesic S., Rizzoli A.E., Athanasiadis I.N.: Towards a semantically unified environmental information space. In: [5], pp. 407–418
83. Sander, S., Hoppe, H., Schlobinski, S.: Integrating climate change in the urban planning process – a case study. In: [5], pp. 631–640
84. Usländer, T., et al.: The future internet enablement of the environmental information space. In: [6], pp. 109-120
85. Kubasek, M.: Mapping of illegal dumps in the Czech Republic – using a crowd-sourcing approach. In: [6], pp. 177–187
86. Schleidt, K.: INSPIREd air quality reporting: European air quality e-reporting based on INSPIRE. In: [6], pp. 439-450
87. Komenda, M., Schwarz, D.: Visual analytics in environmental research: a survey on challenges, methods and available tools. In: [6]
88. Swayne, D.A., Denzer, R.: Teaching EIS Development – The EU Canada Curriculum on Environmental Informatics, Environmental Software Systems. In: [11], pp. 152–156
89. Denzer, R.: A Computing Program for Scientists and Engineers - What is the Core of Computing? In: Cassel., L., Reis, R. (eds.) Informatics curricula and teaching methods. IFIP Series, pp. 69–75. Kluwer Academic Publishers (2003)

The Framework for Environmental Software Systems of the European Environment Agency

Jiří Hřebíček[1], Stefan Jensen[2], and Chris Steenmans[2]

[1] European Environment Agency, Scientific Committee
Copenhagen, Denmark
hrebicek@iba.muni.cz
[2] European Environment Agency,
Copenhagen, Denmark
{Stefan.Jensen,Chris.Steenmans}@eea.europa.eu

Abstract. The European Environment Agency (EEA) is the authoritative European environment node and hub, and a key initiator within networks of knowledge co-creation, sharing and use in European Union (EU). It ensures the quality, availability and accessibility of environmental data and information needed to support strategic area: informing policy implementation and assessing systemic challenges. It actively communicates data, information and knowledge to policymakers, the public, research communities and others (non-governmental organizations, businesses) as well as to regional and international processes including those of the United Nation and its specialised agencies and promotes information governance as a driver of public empowerment and behavioural change. In the past few years the EEA's environmental information systems as well as environmental modelling with the support of environmental software systems have been supporting decision making processes within the EU Systems have undergone rapid development and grew up to support the knowledgebase of European Commission and EU Member States. Specifically, new infrastructure to support supply services (collection of data); networking (knowledge management); workflows (planning, automation, quality management); development of final products and public services (reports, web sites, public data and information services) were put in place. EEA strengthens the infrastructure for environmental data and information sharing both at the EEA and in the European Environment Information and Observation Network with cooperating countries too, taking into account the Shared Environmental Information System (SEIS) and the Infrastructure for Spatial Information in Europe (INSPIRE) developments. The paper presents the framework for the of development of EEA environmental software systems and information services accepted in Multiannual Working Plan of the EEA for 2014 – 2018 and its implication for ICT.

Keywords: EEA, environmental data, information system, environmental services, environmental monitoring, Eionet, SEIS, Copernicus and INSPIRE.

R. Denzer et al. (Eds.): ISESS 2015, IFIP AICT 448, pp. 44–55, 2015.
© IFIP International Federation for Information Processing 2015

1   Introduction

Environmental software systems in the European Union (EU) should support the current *Environment Action Programme* to 2020 (7th EAP) entitled *Living well, within the limits of our planet* entered into force in January 2014. This programme is based on a 2050 vision of EU centred on ecological limits, a circular economy and society's resilience. To move towards this vision, the 7th EAP sets out nine priority objectives, comprising three thematic objectives, four enabling objectives, one urban objective, and one global objective [1].

The 7th EAP aims at achieving existing objectives and targets in a mid-term perspective to 2020/2030, with EU policies [2, 3, 4]: the Climate and Energy Package 2020 and associated roadmaps; the EU Strategy for Adaptation to Climate Change; Europe 2020 and the Resource Efficiency Roadmap; the Biodiversity Strategy to 2020; and specific legislation for water, waste, air etc. In addition, the 7th EAP promotes new ways of thinking and innovation in order to realise the EU 2050 vision beyond existing policy targets. This gives a large framework of application Information and Communication Technologies (ICT), and it updates and developes the environmental software systems.

The overall aim of the 7th EAP is to step up the contribution of environment policy to the transition towards sustainability, understood as a resource-efficient, low-carbon economy in which natural capital is protected and enhanced, and the health and well-being of citizens is safeguarded. The 7th EAP is also the basis for EU involvement in global agendas such as Rio+20, the United Nations Framework Convention on Climate Change [5], the Montreal Protocol on Substances that Deplete the Ozone Layer [6], and the Convention on Biological Diversity [7], as well being the basis for wider European activities, which are increasingly framed in a 2050 perspective [8].

The *European Environment Agency* (EEA) [9] is one of the most important agencies of the EU with ICT support to environment protection. It is located in Copenhagen, Denmark. Its main task is to provide sound, independent environmental information. The EEA is a major information source for those involved in developing, adopting, implementing and evaluating environmental policy, and also the general public. Currently, the EEA has 33 member countries. The Regulation [10] establishing the EEA was adopted by the EU in 1990. It came into force in late 1993 and its work started in earnest in 1994. This Regulation also established the *European Environment Information and Observation Network* (Eionet) [11]. EEA's mandate is to help the EU and cooperating countries make informed decisions about improving the environment, integrating environmental considerations into economic policies and moving towards sustainability and coordinate the Eionet.

According to the above 7th EAP visions [1], EEA aims to support sustainable development and to help achieve significant and measurable improvements in information about Europe's environment, through the provision of timely, targeted, relevant and reliable information to policy making agents and the public.

The aim of the paper is an introduction of the recent independent evaluation of the EEA and discussion how EEA operates in a complex, multi-level and multi-actor governance setting at EU (e.g. Copernicus, Eurostat, INSPIRE and SEIS), national, and global levels, which also includes research institutes (e.g. Joint Research Centre), businesses, and nongovernmental organizations (NGOs). We discuss the specific role of the EEA to build the capacity of for environmental software systems in member countries, using the Eionet as its unique partner to generate two-way flows of quality-assured environmental data and information.

The EEA's understanding of the nature of environmental challenges has evolved in recent decades, requiring corresponding changes to information flows and assessments with using ICT. The continuous flow of new information and updated scientific insights into environment and climate issues improves the knowledge base for environment and climate policies [2, 3, 4]. Fulfilling its role as an interface between science and policy, the EEA will work closely with the European Commission (EC), its DG Research and Innovation (RTD), DG Communications Networks, Content and Technology (CNECT), DG Environment (ENV), DG Health and Consumers (SANCO), Eurostat (ESTAT) and Joint Research Centre (JRC), as well as others in seeking to influence activities under the EU Framework Research Programmes (Horizon 2020 and earlier). The EEA also aims to exploit the insights that result from these programmes.

Furthermore, we introduce the key goals of environmental software systems and decision making processes of the EEA in the new Multiannual Work Programme 2014-2018 (MAWP) [12] and introduce important environmental software systems and ICT used in SEIS, Copernicus and INSPIRE activities.

2   Structure of the Multiannual Work Programme 2014-2018

In order to secure the knowledge and evidence base for a framework of the Priority objective 5 of the 7th EAP [1], the MAWP [12] is structured around four strategic areas:

- **Strategic area 1 (SA1): Informing policy implementation.** There is providing feedback and input to long-established and emerging policy frameworks, objectives, and targets through reporting on progress in recognised environmental themes, including links to those sectors that are the primary sources of environmental pressures, and through reporting on the state of and trends in natural environment systems (atmosphere, oceans, territories) using the DPSIR assessment framework (Driver Forces, Pressures, State, Impacts and Responses).
- **Strategic area 2 (SA2): Assessing systemic challenges.** There is providing support to improving synergies and policy coherence across environmental, economic and social systems by applying established and experimental integrated assessment techniques and prospective analysis, with both a short-term and a long-term perspective. This work supports the long-term vision for 2050 set out in the 7th EAP.
- **Strategic area 3 (SA3): Knowledge co-creation, sharing and use.** There is providing support to the work in the above areas by building and maintaining networks of people and information systems as the basis for sharing and co-creating content, whether that be data, indicators, or assessments, in a transparent manner with other actors at national, European and global levels. Communications in the broadest sense of the word will also play a major role in ensuring that information promotes

a dialogue with a dialogue with stakeholders and reaches out to the society at large. Targeted information, communication and participation are important instruments for achieving significant and measurable improvement in Europe's environment, responding to emerging challenges and societal developments.

- **Strategic area 4 (SA4): EEA management.** EEA management, administration, and operational services make up a fourth area of work. The guiding principles of this work area are strict adherence to all the principles, rules, and regulations that apply to the EEA, as well as continuous improvement of the efficiency and effectiveness of EEA management.

These strategic areas cover complete EEA/Eionet information processes.

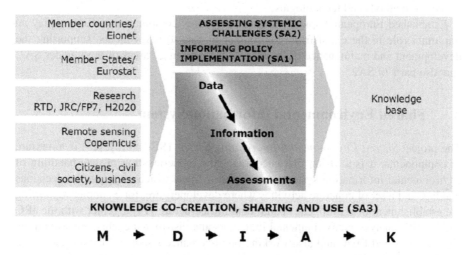

Fig. 1. Strategic areas SA1, SA2, SA 3 and EEA/Eionet core processes (Source [12])

We can see at the bottom of the Fig. 1 the overall EEA/Eionet core processes from Monitoring (in the broadest sense) through Data, Information and Assessments to Knowledge. This value-adding chain is at the heart of the work of the EEA and Eionet.

The development of the architecture of the environmental software systems of EEA has evolved in line with the principles of *Shared Environmental Information System* (SEIS) [13] and will contribute to the full implementation of the *Infrastructure for Spatial Information in Europe* (INSPIRE) [14] by 2019. The activities will support the European Open Data Portal [15], the Open Data Strategy of the EU 2020 Digital Agenda [16], and it will ensure compliance with the Åarhus Convention [17]. Highlights include the provision of:

- thematic data and expertise to support the involvement of EEA member and cooperating countries in international conventions and related activities, as described in many areas under SA1 and SA2;

- expertise, data, and assessments to ensure European contributions to global and United Nation (UN) activities, including to UN Environment Program (Global Environmental Outlook [18], UNEP-Live [19]) as well as the post Rio+20 activities [20];
- expertise and capacity-building in networking and information partnerships. This is based on Eionet and SEIS approaches, particularly towards cooperating countries and the European Neighbourhood and towards countries and regions following EU priorities. Involvement in the Global Earth Observation System of Systems (GEO/GEOSS) [21] and Copernicus [22] are included here.

Enhanced involvement of the Eionet network to decision making processes of the EEA is sought across the strategic areas in the fields of data flows, indicators, policy effectiveness analysis, integrated assessments, communications, and the use of new analytical methods and technologies.

Established European Topic Centres[1] (ETCs), key components of Eionet, play an important role in the chain from environmental data to assessments, supporting the development and maintenance of the knowledge base in all areas of work under SA1, and also parts of SA2.

3   Shared Environmental Information System

The project *Shared Environmental Information System* (SEIS) [13], [23] is a mixture of components: it is a vision that encourages the modernisation of data handling of environmental information systems; a set of principals which underpin the decisions making; and a set of concrete activities where developers are, for example, supporting the establishment of a European spatial data infrastructure [14] together with the JRC and the EC; analysing environmental indicators and distributed exchange between the EU countries and EEA; and also working on governance issues in Mediterranean and North African countries.

SEIS is based on seven principles [23]. Environmental information should be:

1. Managed as close as possible to its source.
2. Collected once, and shared with others for many purposes.
3. Readily available to easily fulfil environmental reporting obligations.
4. Easily accessible to all users.
5. Accessible to enable comparisons at the appropriate geographical scale, and citizen participation.
6. Fully available to the general public, and at the national level in the relevant national language(s).
7. Supported through common, free open software standards.

---

[1]   European Topic Centres are currently eight consortia of institutions across EEA member countries dealing with a specific environmental topic and contracted by the EEA to perform specific activities as defined in the EEA Strategy and the MAWP and the Annual Management Plan.

Under SEIS, EEA has worked with numerous EU institutes (e.g. DG ENV, JRC, ESTAT, etc.) and initiatives (Copernicus and INSPIRE) in order to reach successful implementation of its principles. These include:

- Achieving effective streamlining of legislative environmental reporting require-ments, through such actions as the thematic strategy on air pollution (CAFE) [24];
- Directive 2007/2/EC – Developing an infrastructure for spatial information in Europe (INSPIRE) [14];
- Fostering a contemporary approach to the production, exchange and use of envi-ronmental data and information through, for example, the Water Information Sys-tem for Europe (WISE) [25], European Marine Observation and Data Network (EMODnet) [26], BISE on biodiversity [27];
- Directive 2003/4/EC – Public access to environmental information (the Aarhus Convention) [17];
- The Copernicus initiative [22];
- European Environment Agency (EEA) services [9, 10];
- Group on Earth Observation (GEO) [21], which aims at building a Global Earth Observation System of Systems (GEOSS) [28];
- Other the EC funded activities for the effective distribution of open environmental software systems for environmental management.

The data input side of SEIS is predominantly based on environmental monitoring, which happens at the EU country level. The monitoring happens based on environ-mental legislation that individual countries must adhere to.

SEIS is not only about making information available for public access, it is also about making the data available for network communication via standard APIs (appli-cation programming interfaces) and open data formats [15]. Implementing and sup-porting SEIS-friendly ICT tools is one of the core activities of the EEA.

Basically, everything you see on our EEA's website [9], [11] is harvestable via ex-ternal systems and linked data spiders, so the environmental data and information may be easily re-used, integrated and re-distributed by to a wider network of users. As a practical example, organisations are now able to easily exchange their catalogues of datasets creating more complete federated dataset catalogues, also known as Open Data Catalogues. The ICT makes it almost effortless for the EEA to contribute to the EU Open Data Portal [15].

Through EU legislation and based on its's mandate, the EEA is in a position to promote free access to environmental data. Resource wise, the EEA cannot afford to keep paying for data, and there is a policy framework in EU which supports this issue. There are three things in particular: one is the Aarhus Convention [17], which ad-dresses countries outside EU and focuses on free access to environmental informa-tion, but also ensures citizens having the opportunity to, for example, go to court if certain organisations are not sharing data. Secondly, the Publish Sector Information Directive (PSI) [29] pushes public access administrators to make data available. And thirdly, the EEA has an access to information directive at the EU level that underpins the Aarhus Convention.

Another component of SEIS is remote sensing which means that data are received from satellites (e.g. Copernicus [22] and GEOSS [28]). As another source over the past five years, citizen science in Europe has grown massively, and citizens have become actively involved in the collection of environmental data. In addition, EEA and Eionet are cooperating with the research community to gather research and statistics data.

4   Copernicus

The Global Monitoring for Environment and Security, GMES, is an earth observation programme in Europe. The name has changed from GMES to Copernicus. This initiative is in partnership with the European Space Agency (ESA).

The origins of the Copernicus programme may be traced back to a series of meetings involving the EC and European space industry representatives in Baveno, Italy, in 1998. The result was the Baveno Manifesto, which called for a *"long-term commitment to the development of space-based environmental monitoring services"* in Europe [31].

Currently in the early stages of implementation, Copernicus will produce data to inform EU, national and local level environmental policymaking and to support environmental monitoring, policy evaluation, modelling, forecasting and reporting. It is intended that Copernicus will make key contributions to EU flagship initiatives, including Resource-Efficient Europe [3], which focuses on securing Europe's needs in terms of natural resources, such as food, soil, water, biomass, ecosystems, fuels and raw materials [32].

Copernicus may be considered as a building block together with other EU initiatives, such as SEIS and INSPIRE. As a member of the GEO, the EC is also collaborating with 88 participating governments in order to build a worldwide GEOSS [28]. The aim is to inform environmental decision-making in a world facing increasing environmental pressures and to realise societal benefits such as improved management of energy resources and sustainable agriculture.

4.1   Earth Observation of the Land Services of Copernicus

By definition, the land service addresses a broad range of environmental data including soil, forests, ecosystems, biodiversity, water and waste. The land monitoring component of Copernicus became operational under the GMES Initial Operation (GIO) Land services, building on precursor activities, in particular, the Geoland2 [33] 7th Framework Programme (FP7) project.

Based on user consultation, a stepwise approach was defined starting with common *"multi-purpose"* information at Global, Pan-European and local level. The Pan-European and local land services are coordinated by the EEA in cooperation with DG ENV. A global extension of the land service is coordinated by the JRC and will provide basic terrestrial parameters relating to bio-geophysical factors, radiation and water, at global scale in near real-time. These will be relevant for crop monitoring, carbon budget, biodiversity and climate change monitoring at a worldwide level.

4.2 Copernicus and INSPIRE

Many Copernicus projects contributed in different ways to the development of INSPIRE. For instance, experts from the Copernicus Marine Service (MyOcean [34] project) contributed to the relevant INSPIRE data specifications. The discussions with Atmospheric Service (MACC [35] project) and the down-stream service PASODOBLE [36] were mainly related to metadata. The interaction with Land and Emergency Services and INSPIRE took place indirectly by the introduction and promotion of INSPIRE components within these services through the GIGAS [37] FP7 project.

The role of INSPIRE in Copernicus' in situ data component was addressed by the GMES In-situ Coordination (GISC [38]) project led by EEA. Its aim was to act between data providers and to develop an initial framework for in situ data that also takes into account how demand will change over time.

4.3 Copernicus Services Challenges

Prior to the Baveno Manifesto, it was recognised that real value would not emerge from satellite observations alone; space-based monitoring would need to be combined with data collected on the ground (*in situ data*). In the same way that meteorologists combine satellite and in situ observations to make predictions about the weather, Copernicus integrates satellite and in situ observations to yield useful analysis of a wide range of environmental data.

Public and private sector partners are involved in data processing and the conversion of raw data from space into useful maps and applications-focused information, provided as Copernicus "*services*". Access to data is a real challenge for Copernicus as it relies on a number of scientific networks funded by research projects, entailing risks for long-term sustainability. Another challenge is the consistency of in situ data, which are often collected at national and local level, closely linked to the work on the INSPIRE Directive and SEIS initiative, as well as with the development of sectoral knowledge bases (for example, the water related system WISE [25]; BISE on biodiversity [27], and others on soils [33]).

5 INSPIRE

The INSPIRE Directive [14] laid down the general rules establishing the spatial data infrastructure (SDI) in the EU countries in support of EU environmental policies and policies or activities that may have an impact on the environment since 2007. This was very important for development of environmental software systems of the EEA and the EU countries. INSPIRE is to be based on the infrastructures for spatial information that are created by the EU countries. These infrastructures should ensure that [14]:

- spatial data are stored, made available and maintained at the most appropriate level;
- it is possible to combine spatial data from different sources across the EU in a consistent way and share them between several users and applications;

- it is possible for spatial data collected at one level of public authority to be shared between other public authorities;
- spatial data are made available under conditions that do not unduly restrict their extensive use;
- it is easy to discover available spatial data, to evaluate their suitability for the purpose and to know the conditions applicable to their use.

In particular, the spatial data sets and services provided by EU countries to EU institutions and bodies in order to fulfil their reporting obligations under EU legislation relating to the environment shall not be subject to any charging.

Article 17 of the INSPIRE Directive [14] defines the spatial data sharing requirements in more detail. It requires EU countries to adopt measures for the sharing of spatial data sets and services that enable its public authorities to gain access to these spatial data sets and services, and to exchange and use those spatial data sets and services for the purposes of public tasks that may have an impact on the environment. The measures should preclude any restrictions likely to create practical obstacles to the sharing that might occur at the point of use. Hence, procedures regarding, for example, property rights, licensing and charging must be fully compatible with the general aim of facilitating the sharing of spatial data sets and services between public authorities.

The state of implementation of INSPIRE [39] shows that INSPIRE is implemented across the EU with some delay, and non-uniformity, but so far it is in line with expected costs and benefits. INSPIRE starts to achieve its objectives, which according to 92 % of respondents in the 2014 public consultation are as pertinent as ever. Moreover, as indicated in [38], INSPIRE is increasingly recognised as a foundation framework for integrating on a spatial basis and making more effective and efficient a range of policies affecting the environment. The strong connection established between the flagship Copernicus programme and INSPIRE can be a very significant element in the implementation of the INSPIRE directive in coming years.

5.1   INSPIRE Enabled Interoperability of Spatial Data Sets and Services

The measures defined by INSPIRE to achieve the interoperability of spatial data sets and services are without a doubt the core of INSPIRE, and one that sets it apart from other similar SDIs in the world. The most of these measures have yet to be implemented. Evidence from the public consultation also indicates that this part of INSPIRE is technically complex, which is perceived by about 20 % of respondents as an obstacle to implementation and use INSPIRE [39].

There is little doubt that the measures put in place by INSPIRE are complex, but no alternative could be identified in order to achieve the interoperability objective. Whilst the actions related to interoperability are appropriate, further modifications might be taken into consideration in order to enable further benefits.

The INSPIRE roadmap for implementation spans until 2020, and it is therefore natural that there are still gaps in implementation, in particular for obligations for which deadlines have not yet passed. From the public consultation and the direct observations it is also evident that some aspects of the INSPIRE Directive — notably the coordination at national and cross-border levels, and the removal of obstacles to data sharing at the point of use — would increase the EU added value if better addressed.

6   Conclusion

The adoption of the EEA and Eionet model of implementing environmental software systems and environmental modelling and information systems as well as SEIS and INSPIRE principles at regional/Pan-European and international/global level may ensure coherence at all levels and also helps streamlining efforts at national level. Consequently, and decision-making processes of the EEA shall take this into account, the fast developments in environmental software systems and related ICT, their links and synergies will need to be strengthened and further explored with initiatives such as the EU Digital Agenda [16], the European Earth Observation Programme (Copernicus) [22], [31, 32], the Global Earth Observation System of Systems (GEO/GEOSS) [28], UNEP live [19], and other key initiatives related to data and information sharing [39].

The knowledge of the EEA of the development of environmental software systems is increasingly co-created, shared and used in the Eionet network (flexibility in terms of membership, roles assumed, goal orientation, type of knowledge created, shared or used, etc are important factors here). A flexible and strategic vision on the EEA role as initiator, node, hub or switch is important to continue knowledge co-creation, sharing and use between EEA, Eionet and beyond.

Strengthening the integration of EEA and Eionet activities, including capacity building, remain central to the MAWP 2014-2018. An integral part of this is a deepening of Eionet via an enhanced collaboration and integration between EU countries and EEA activities following the principles of SEIS, INSPIRE and Copernicus.

Key objectives of EEA environmental software systems therefore are:
- Ensure the quality, availability and accessibility (based on SEIS and INSPIRE principles) of data and information needed to support SA 1 and SA 2.
- Communicate actively data, information and knowledge to policymakers, the public, the academic world, to regional and international processes including those of the UN and its specialized agencies.
- Promote information governance as a driver of public empowerment and behavioural change.
- Provide support to the work in the above areas by building and maintaining networks of people and - where needed - environmental software systems as the basis for sharing and co-creating content.
- Communications will also play a major role in making sure that information is targeted and ensures a dialogue with stakeholders and the society at large. Targeted information, communication and participation remain important instruments.

EEA will further enhance and focus its outreach capacities responding to emerging challenges and societal developments. Societal trends such as the ways to access information, networking, and co-creation of knowledge are influencing the way the EEA is asked to work and communicate.

References

1. Decision No 1386/2013/EU of the European Parliament and of the Council of 20 November 2013 on a General Union Environment Action Programme to 2020. Living well, within the limits of our planet. OJL 354, 171–200 (2013)
2. EU action on climate,
   http://ec.europa.eu/clima/policies/brief/eu/index_en.htm
3. The Roadmap to a Resource Efficient Europe,
   http://ec.europa.eu/environment/resource_efficiency/about/roadmap/index_en.htm
4. EU Biodiversity Strategy to 2020 – towards implementation,
   http://ec.europa.eu/environment/nature/biodiversity/comm2006/2020.htm
5. United Nations Framework Convention on Climate Change,
   http://unfccc.int/2860.php
6. Montreal Protocol on Substances that Deplete the Ozone Layer,
   http://ozone.unep.org/new_site/en/montreal_protocol.php
7. Convention on Biological Diversity, http://www.cbd.int/convention/
8. Global Europe 2050, Publications Office of the EU, Luxembourg (2012), doi: 10.2777/79992
9. European Environment Agency, http://www.eea.europa.eu/
10. Regulation (EC) No 401/2009 of the European Parliament and of the Council of 23 April 2009 on the European Environment Agency and the European Environment Information and Observation Network (Codified version). OJL 126, 13–22 (2009)
11. Eionet, http://www.eionet.europa.eu/
12. Multiannual Work Programme 2014-2018. Expanding the knowledge base for policy implementation and long-term transitions. Publications Office of the EU, Luxembourg (2014), doi:10.2800/10814
13. Shared Environmental Information System,
    http://ec.europa.eu/environment/archives/seis/index.htm
14. INSPIRE Directive, http://inspire.ec.europa.eu/
15. EU Open Data Portal, https://open-data.europa.eu/en/data
16. Digital Agenda for Europe, http://ec.europa.eu/digital-agenda/
17. Århus Convention, http://ec.europa.eu/environment/aarhus/
18. UNEP Global Environmental Outlook, http://www.unep.org/geo/
19. UNEP live, http://www.uneplive.org/
20. Rio+20, http://www.unep.org/rio20/
21. Global Earth Observation System of Systems,
    http://www.earthobservations.org/geoss.php
22. Copernicus, http://www.copernicus.eu/
23. Shared Environmental Information System, http://www.eea.europa.eu/about-us/what/shared-environmental-information-system-1
24. Clean Air for Europe programme (CAFE),
    http://ec.europa.eu/environment/archives/cafe/
25. Water Information System for Europe, http://water.europa.eu/
26. European Marine Observation and Data Network, http://www.emodnet.eu/
27. Biodiversity Information System for Europe,
    http://biodiversity.europa.eu/info
28. GEOSS Portal, http://www.geoportal.org/

29. PSI Directive, http://www.epsiplatform.eu/psi-directive
30. Europe Space Agency, http://www.esa.int/ESA
31. Brachet, G.: From initial ideas to a European plan: GMES as an exemplar of European space strategy. Space Policy 20, 7–15 (2004), doi:10.1016/j.spacepol.2003.11.002
32. Science Communication Unit, University of the West of England, Bristol (2012). Science for Environment Policy. Future Brief: Earth Observation's Potential for the EU Environment. DG Environment, Brussels (2013),
    http://ec.europa.eu/science-environment-policy
33. Geoland2, http://www.geoland2.eu/
34. MyOcean, http://www.myocean.eu/
35. MACC, http://www.gmes-atmosphere.eu/about/project/details/
36. PASODOBLE, http://www.myair.eu/
37. GIGAS, http://www.thegigasforum.eu/project/project.html
38. GISC, http://gisc.ew.eea.europa.eu/
39. Mid-term evaluation report on INSPIRE implementation. EEA Technical report, No 17/2014, Publications Office of the EU, Luxembourg (2014)

Crowdsourcing in Crisis and Disaster Management – Challenges and Considerations

Gerald Schimak, Denis Havlik, and Jasmin Pielorz

AIT Austrian Institute of Technology GmbH, Donau-City-Straße 1, 1220 Wien
{Gerald.Schimak,Denis.Havlik,Jasmin.Pielorz}@ait.ac.at

Abstract. With the rise of social media platforms, crowdsourcing became a powerful tool for mobilizing the public. Events such as the earthquake in Haiti or the downfall of governments in Libya and Egypt indicate its potential in crisis situations. In the scope of this paper, we discuss the relevance of crowdsourcing in the area of crisis and disaster management (CDM). Starting with a general overview of the topic, we distinguish between different types of crowds and crowdsourcing and define what is meant by crowdtasking in the area of CDM. After considering technological, societal and ethical challenges for using crowdsourcing in crisis management, applications of crowdsourcing tools in ongoing projects are described and future developments outlined.

Keywords: crowdsourcing, crowdtasking, data analysis, big data, social media, crises and disaster management, volunteers, volunteered geographic information.

1   Introduction

Crowdsourcing is rapidly gaining recognition as important source of information in crisis situations. The potential of crowdsourcing in crisis management is undeniably enormous: past experiences, e.g. in Haiti and Libya [1], show that information obtained through crowdsourcing is often more detailed and just as accurate as the information gathered through hardware sensors and through official channels. Successfully managed crowdsourcing can result in nearly instantaneous situation awareness (crisis mapping). However, crowdsourcing requires adequate tools, capable moderators and professional crisis managers that are willing and able to accept the crowdsourcing as an additional tool with its own advantages and limitations. A very good overview of the challenges related to crowdsourcing in crisis situations has been given in [2] and a very critical analysis of the four use cases which are often mentioned as *best practices* is given in [3].

After accepting crowdsourcing as a powerful crisis management tool, the next logical step for crisis managers is to attempt tasking the individual crowd members and smaller groups with well-defined activities. Properly organized crowdtasking can bring multiple benefits over spontaneous crowd self-organization. For the start, the available volunteer resources can be mobilized more rapidly and deployed more efficiently to provide information where it is missing or to quickly confirm and improve unreliable or imprecise reports. Information received through crowdtasking is therefore inherently

R. Denzer et al. (Eds.): ISESS 2015, IFIP AICT 448, pp. 56–70, 2015.
© IFIP International Federation for Information Processing 2015

much more reliable and also easier to interpret than information that has been gathered by data mining from existing social networks. In addition, citizens could be individually instructed to help themselves and their neighbors, taking into account real needs, as well as individual aptitudes and capabilities.

However, it is important to understand that the "crowd" is inherently non-hierarchical, has means to self-organize and will do so with or without crisis managers. This is a challenge for the crisis managers, since their professional experience indicates that crisis management requires a hierarchic organisation and that self-organization of inexperienced civilians can be outright dangerous in crisis situations. On the other hand, the attempt to overmanage the crowd could severely limit the number of ad-hoc volunteers willing to participate in the crowdtasked activities.

On the subject of "using the crowd as a valuable crisis management resource" we therefore distinguish between: (1) information and activities of individuals and self-organized groups, which are supported by general-purpose platforms such as Facebook or Waze[1] and (2) information and activities of loosely organized volunteer groups, whose activities are, to a certain extent, coordinated by professional crisis managers and supported by a dedicated mobile crowdtasking platform.

In section 2, we present some general remarks about crowdsourcing, thereafter we present several examples of crowdsourcing and crowdtasking at work, discuss key characteristics and challenges of crowdsourcing in crisis management and finally outline the generic methodology and functional architecture for future dedicated crisis management crowdtasking tools.

2   Crowdsourcing in Crisis Management

2.1   What Is Crowdsourcing?

According to [4], the term crowdsourcing was first coined by Jeff Howe, who used it in an article published in June 2006 for the Wired magazine. Following Howe's original conception of the term, we define crowdsourcing as a "method for recruiting and organizing ad-hoc labor, using an open-call for participation" [5]. Crucial to this definition is the notion of an extremely fluid workforce, one that is devoid of managerial and contractual directives inherent to other, more traditional labor models, such as "outsourcing." *The crowd has the freedom to do what it pleases, when it pleases, and it is often up to designers to find clever ways to recruit and retain this kind of ad-hoc workforce.*

Unlike the crowd itself, the entity requesting crowdsourced work is rarely fluid or loosely defined. Indeed, the request for work usually comes from a distinct organization or individual (known as the "requester", in crowdsourcing parlance). This distinguishes crowdsourcing from other, more decentralized labor structures, such as commons-based peer production, as well as from the "smart mobs" which use the social networking for self-organization [6]. While crowdsourcing can take many forms, three dominant types

---

[1]   https://www.waze.com/events

of platforms have emerged in the past decade: (1) games with a purpose, (2) micro-task markets and (3) open innovation contests.

2.2   Social Data Mining and Crowdsourcing in Crisis Management

In the domain of crisis management, the term crowdsourcing usually refers to the gathering of information from the crowd in all phases of a crisis and results in so-called crowdsourced crisis mapping. The request for work in this type of crowdtasking usually remains at the level of general calls for action. In fact, the border towards social data mining is fuzzy because in this case data from general purpose social media (e.g. geo-tweets) is often used instead, or in addition to, the data received through dedicated platform such as Ushahidi[2].

From an organizational point of view, social data mining is the simplest form of crowdsourcing. Information relevant to a crisis will automatically appear in the social media, even if nobody explicitly asks for it. However, the general purpose social networking platforms such as Facebook or Google+ lack some features which are important for the crisis managers.

To begin with, much of the information is shared only with friends and family and therefore cannot be used by crisis managers without raising privacy issues. If, however, people share their information with the public, automatic filtering and interpreting the available information (e.g. from twitter or from a fictive "friends of Red Cross" Facebook group) is challenging. When reporting about a crisis event, people can use any language, slang and choose a hashtag or topic they find relevant, making it very difficult to understand the actual content of a post. In addition, most posts or tweets currently have no geographical location tagged to them, so that a crisis manager cannot be sure about the exact location of an incident.

In order to circumvent these difficulties, crisis managers can organize an ad-hoc platform for gathering of information from the population. This has been successfully done in the past [1], and crisis mapper[3] volunteers excel in using such information for ad-hoc mapping of the crisis development.

2.3   Crowdtasking and Micro-task Markets

In order to distinguish between this already established practice and more fine-grained crowdsourcing of both, information and more physical tasks, (e.g. "fill sacks with sand") in crisis situations, we use the word "crowdtasking" for the process, and "ad-hoc volunteers" for the participants.

Crowdtasking can be seen as a special form of a micro-task market. Both forms of crowdsourcing have in common that (1) organizers can request concrete and well-defined actions within a limited temporal and spatial scope; (2) participants are explicitly asked to

---

[2] http://www.ushahidi.com/
[3] http://crisismappers.net/

perform specific micro-tasks; and (3) participants are not obliged, or even expected, to work beyond the concrete tasks they choose to complete.

However, the crowdtasking puts much stronger emphasis on space and time. Ad-hoc volunteers are asked to visit particular location(s), report requested state parameters (e.g. "is this house damaged?") using a mobile device and possibly perform some limited physical actions (e.g. "help the inhabitants to prepare for evacuation"). Due to the inherent dynamics of the crisis, the tasks are often urgent and the probability of endangering the ad-hoc volunteers is not negligible.

In order to optimize the tasking process and minimize the risk for volunteers, tasking organizations need to know the volunteers' capabilities and whereabouts. Therefore the volunteers need to enroll prior to action. In the case of *Team Austria*, volunteers can register themselves online at any time and indicate their skills and address. However, a verification of the data by Red Cross personnel is required to reach the status of a *trusted volunteer*. In this way, triggering and tasking can be done very efficiently and with a minimal risk for volunteers.

3   Use Cases, Existing Systems or Applications

In this chapter we present several examples of crowdsourcing and crowdtasking for crisis management. The examples are ordered by complexity of the tasking process considered, starting with a passive approach of gathering relevant information from social media platforms and ending with a prototypic implementation of a dedicated crowdtasking methodology and platform, which has been developed specifically for crisis management.

3.1   Social Sensors for Security Assessments and Proactive Emergency Management

Social media statistics such as 20 million tweets related to hurricane "Sandy" or disaster-related photos shared at a rate of 10/sec on Instagram provide tangible evidence that security forces and civil protection agencies could greatly benefit from the effective blending of social media information into their processes. Due to its versatility, social media could serve in the crisis management domain as both a valuable data source for first responders and an effective communication tool to reach the public. However, despite the widespread use of social media in various domains, e.g. in marketing or finance, there is still no structured and effective way to leverage several social media in crisis management applications.

In order to tackle this challenge, the EU FP7 project SUPER (Social sensors for security assessments and proactive emergencies management)[4] aims at developing a holistic and privacy-friendly approach to exploit social media for emergencies and security incidents. In a joint effort of experts from the security and social media domain, the project addresses all phases of crisis management, i.e. before, during and

---

[4] http://super-fp7.eu/

after a crisis occurred and will integrate social media within existing security and management systems for tactical operations.

The exploitation of social media for emergencies requires efforts far beyond the adaptation, customization and effective blending of existing social media processing algorithms in the emergencies and security domains. This is because of the sensitive nature of security incidents and emergencies, their real-time nature, the fact that they are (more) susceptible to social networks compromise and manipulation, the need to combine multiple social media platforms and processing algorithms, and the dynamics of security and emergency management applications.

So far, the following key topics for research were identified by the project, providing a useful overview of the tools/methods lacking in crowdsourcing for the crisis management domain:

- Using behavioral theories in order to understand and model citizens' social media-behavior before, during and after emergencies.
- Automatic identification and verification of emergency-relevant information from social media in real-time.
- Fast extensible search across multiple social media streams.
- Community analysis across social media sources to infer the sentiments, bias and motivations of reporters and the public during emergencies.
- Behavioral analysis and sentiment identification.
- Topic Based Community Tracking.
- Leveraging Virtual Spaces for evaluating public opinion.
- Plug n' play integration and fusion of social sensors.

Resulting methods will be integrated into the SUPER concept as illustrated in **Fig. 1**, which provides an overview of how information stemming from social media will be processed and exploited. This can either happen through social sensors (i.e. algorithmic components that process social media and social networking feeds) or based on games, debates, role-playing and other applications that can solicit citizens' feedback in virtual spaces.

Apart from individual social sensors, SUPER will also offer possibilities for combining and reasoning over the outcomes of multiple processing algorithms, with a view to achieving credible results associated with the analysis of citizens' behavior, but also to become able to detect events in nearly real-time. The outcomes of the analysis of social media (based on both social sensors and virtual spaces applications) will be used to drive a number of security and emergency management applications, which will include COP generation, management of real-time operations, policy simulations and ahead planning of strategies associated with security and emergencies incidents.

SUPER will be validated in the scope of different and complementary scenarios, one dealing with emergency management during disasters (i.e. earthquakes) and another dealing with police services.

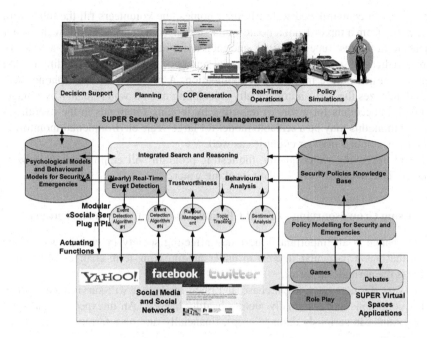

Fig. 1. SUPER Framework overview[5]

3.2 Environmental Crowdsourcing Techniques for Improved Water Quality in Rural India

A three-continent research consortium[6] is evaluating an environmental crowdsourcing technique that relies on inexpensive tests kits (53-cents) that turn purple in the presence of bacterial contamination.

With more than 10 million service points, India's rural drinking water system provides a real monitoring challenge for public health officials. Studied in eight villages during this summer (2014) and scheduled for more widespread evaluation in 2015, the technique could empower residents to check their own water quality and address the problems they find more efficiently. It would be impossible to pay somebody to go out and take all these samples, bring them back to a central lab and process them under controlled conditions.

The set-up is as following: volunteers are given the test kits, which include a test tube containing a material that changes color in the presence of E. coli, a bacterium

---

[5] http://backend.mymeedia.com/data/super-fp7/
c5627e14-ddf0-4b7b-935d-72d30164e5b4.pdf

[6] The research has been sponsored by the U.S. Institute of International Education. Partner agencies include the National Environmental Engineering Research Institute (NEERI) in India, and the London School of Hygiene and Tropical Medicine in the United Kingdom. Contacts: John Toon (jtoon@gatech.edu) Research News, Georgia Institute of Technology, 177 North Avenue, Atlanta, Georgia 30332-0181, USA.

often present in contaminated water. In their homes, the volunteers fill the tubes with water, either from a tap or from a home water storage container. They allow the water to incubate in the test tube overnight, and then use a mobile phone to text a series of numbers indicating, whether the test material remained yellow -corresponding to safe water – or turned purple indicating contamination. A programmed smartphone receives and analyzes the texts, automatically calculating overall water quality by village. The program accounts for errors in reporting by looking for trends in the overall results. We think this may be a scalable model for large-scale environmental monitoring that could be applied in other countries as well.

Beyond improving water quality, the testing program will empower rural citizens of India to take responsibility for their drinking water.

3.3   Using Crowdsourcing to Fight Climate Change Effects on Agriculture

Climate change is an important issue today affecting society in various ways. One domain that has a particular interest in understanding long-term changes of weather patterns is the agriculture sector.

Each year, farmers have to purchase and plant seeds that will survive appropriate weather conditions and eventually yield a healthy harvest. An unexpected cold spell or heavy rains can seriously damage crops, financially ruining a farmer or even leading to famines.

In order to combat this problem in developing nations, some scientists start making use of crowdsourcing techniques. As part of the Seeds for Needs initiative, for example, the CGIAR Research Program on Climate Change, Agriculture and Food Security[7] (CCAFS) has been looking at how to turn farmers into citizen observers.

According to [7] CCAFS's Jacob van Etten, the Seeds for Needs initiative can be understood as a series of projects addressing the issue to give farmers more access to crop varieties and landraces to help them adapt to climate change. As part of that initiative, the CCAFS is currently running a program in Vaishali[8], a district in India's northeastern Bihar state, to test the robustness of different wheat varieties in this region.

Variety is key here: each kind of crop has unique traits, and some particular crop types may be more suitable than others to a region. Wheat, for example, is highly sensitive to heat during flowering, writes van Etten, so planting varieties of wheat that flower earlier and later than usual can ensure that at least part of the harvest is safe.

Here is where the crowdsourcing aspect of Seeds for Needs comes in. To find out which crop varieties perform best, CCAFS is turning farmers into citizen scientists by asking them to evaluate the harvest. Van Etten describes the project thus:

"Each farmer grows a combination of three varieties drawn from a broader set of ten. The farmer then ranks them according to different characteristics such as early vigour, yield, and grain quality. The idea is to make things as easy as possible for the farmers, and then we, the researchers, use some nifty statistics methods to combine the rankings and share the results with the farmers. With this information, farmers can

---

[7] http://ccafs.cgiar.org/
[8] http://ccafs.cgiar.org/atlas-ccafs-sites#.VIgyTjGG98E

then identify the best varieties for their conditions and preferences. Farmers become citizen crop scientists, actively contributing to science with their time, effort and expertise. In India, 800 farmers are now testing wheat varieties as citizen scientists."

Van Etten laid out his plan for a project like this in [7]. While [7] focused on another region, the underlying process is the same: distribute seeds to a large number of farmers, have them report the harvest results, analyze the data, and share the information among their communities. Adding gamification elements would increase the motivation to participate, the author writes. Farmers in areas with low internet penetration could report their observations through mobile phones.

The goal is to make the crop improvement process cheaper and faster, van Etten claims. The early results in Vaishali have been positive enough for CCAFS to plan two similar programs in East Africa[9] and Central America. Information above was posted by Anton Root[10].

3.4 Resilience Enhancement by Crowdsourcing and -Tasking

Crisis and disaster management relies to a large extent on a community of volunteers with a strong commitment and almost professional experience in handling crisis situations. However, due to the increasing mobility of people, the enduring and formal membership in voluntary crisis management has lost its appeal and organizations such as the Red Cross are looking for new ways of loosely binding volunteers to their organizations.

The Austrian research project "Resilience Enhancement by Advanced Communication for Team Austria" [11] (RE-ACTA, [9]) addresses this challenge by defining and testing new processes and workflows for volunteer coordination and developing a platform that supports these workflows in close collaboration with the Austrian Red Cross as end user. The prototype will allow pre-registered volunteers from the "Team Austria" to use their mobile devices for accepting tasks and communicating their results. At the same time, crisis managers will be able to use the platform as a crowdtasking tool for selecting a specific group of volunteers according to their profile and geo-location.

The concept of crowdtasking will be developed even further in the recently started project "Driving Innovation in Crisis Management for European Resilience" [12] (DRIVER[13]). This huge pan-European project intends to establish a set of experimental facilities for testing the crisis management methods and technologies in several EU member states. Within DRIVER, the concepts of crowdsourcing and crowdtasking will be tested in various scenarios and with different volunteer profiles, with the aim

---

[9] http://www.bioversityinternational.org/
     e-library/publications/detail/seeds-for-needs-in-east-africa/
[10] http://www.crowdsourcing.org/profile/anton-root/5824
[11] http://www.kiras.at/gefoerderte-projekte/detail/projekt/
     re-acta/; or http://www.reacta.at
[12] http://driver-project.eu/
[13] http://driver-project.eu/sites/default/files/driver/files/
     content-files/articles/DRIVER%20Newsletter_1-2014.pdf

to establish the best practices for increasing the societal resilience through increased involvement of the citizens in the crisis management process. On a technical level, the crowdtasking platform is based on Ubicity platform for data-driven applications. The Ubicity platform is a result of complete rewrite of the experimental Mobile Data Acquisition Platform (MDAF, [8]) backend with the intention to turn the research prototype in a robust product which can be used in crisis management. Ubicity is capable of storing and analyzing large amounts of unstructured and semi-structured geographically and temporally referenced data from multiple domains in near real-time[14].

In order to ensure privacy of volunteer profiles, the storage of observations is separated from the volunteer data. For the production of situation reports and the monitoring, e.g. of social media, this platform has a generic interface that can be easily connected to different analysis or visualization tools. In order to support a continuous process of communication between crisis managers and volunteers, a web portal provides up-to-date information and allows volunteers to register at any time, as well as to download the mobile application. With the mobile application, volunteers can use their own smartphones to accept or reject tasks that the crisis manager sent out. **Fig. 2** illustrates the functional building blocks of the whole platform as they are implemented in the RE-ACTA approach for crowdtasking management [9].

The advantage of such a system is the increased awareness of the situation development in real-time based on spontaneous input from a large number of persons.

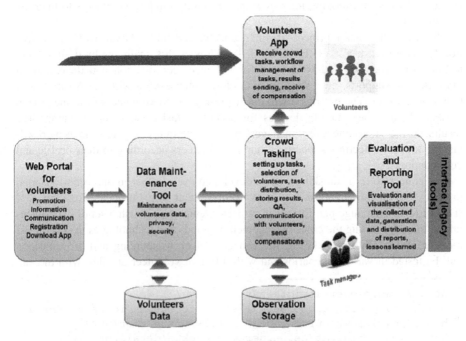

Fig. 2. Building Blocks of the RE-ACTA platform

---

[14] Ubicity details available on github´; https://github.com/ubicity-principal)

Additionally, spontaneous volunteers can easily be included into the communication process by e.g. registering on a web portal. Spontaneous volunteers are automatically assigned lower level of trust by the crowdtasking system until their profiles are verified by the Red Cross personnel. As a result, they are assigned to easier and less critical tasks and the observations they provide are trusted less than the observations provided by pre-registered volunteers.

4 Key Challenges of Crowdsourcing and Crowdtasking in Crisis Management

4.1 Information Extraction and Uncertainty

Information gathered from citizens is a-priory less reliable than the one gathered from hardware sensors. In spite of the good experiences with use of this information so far, there is no guarantee that the citizens will not post misleading information in the future. The reason for false observations could be lack of knowledge, mischief or even the wish to have some fun [10]. Social data mining brings additional issue of machine-interpreting the messages written by and for humans. As illustrated in section 3.1, this is a difficult and error-prone task. Under the assumption that the misleading information is posted by a minority of users, the quality of information can be improved using statistical methods.

These issues are far less pronounced in a crowdtasking use case, for following reasons:

- Since we have a good knowledge of the users' profile, it's easier to estimate the uncertainty of the received observations.
- Observations are well-defined and therefore easier to process by a machine.
- In case of doubt, additional users can be easily asked to confirm an observation.

4.2 Self-organization

During a crisis event, the available resources should be rapidly deployed to the most appropriate tasks. In reality, the globally optimal resource allocation is impossible because the Command Centre has neither a perfect situational awareness nor the capacity to compute the right decision strategy in real-time. The usual strategy for reaching the near-optimal solution in these circumstances is to rely on a combination of written preparedness plans, (incomplete) situation maps and "gut feeling" of the experienced crisis managers [11]. This is incompatible with the self-organization mechanisms of smart mobs and similar social-networking enabled ad-hoc organizations, where decisions are made without prior plans and hierarchical structured organization [12].

Self-organization is implicitly accepted as a way to go whenever the social data mining is used in the context of crisis management (as mentioned in section 3.1). This laisse-faire attitude drastically changes in the moment crisis managers consider the idea of steering and tasking the crowd. Our experience with the development of the crowdtasking system for the Austrian Red Cross (related to section 3.4) shows that the crisis managers consider the self-organization a liability and strive to implement a strict task assignment process which avoids the risk of self-organization. In particular, the ad-hoc volunteers should not be given a possibility to directly discuss the situation with other volunteers, invent own tasks or delegate tasks to other volunteers. This has initially led to a design of the system where tasks can be performed exactly once after accepting the assignment.

Apart from the obvious "wouldn't it be better to let them self-organize using your platform than using a platform you have no access to?" objection, we have recently discovered that some level of self-decision must be allowed by design in order to make the crowdtasking more resilient to mobile network disruptions. Since we can't rely on uninterrupted internet connection during the crisis, the ad-hoc volunteers must be pre-assigned with a basic set of tasks appropriate for the crisis situation already in the early warning phase and trusted to perform some of the pre-defined tasks as they fit if the network is interrupted. The next logical step in development would be to enable decentralized phone to phone networking and update the local situation view with the reports from nearby volunteers. In our opinion, the crisis managers will eventually have to accept and even nourish some level of self-organization in crowdtasking platform(s) under their control. Finding a right balance between "total control" and "full self-organization" is a difficult task and the end result is likely to be a platform which allows relatively high level of self-organization while still allowing the crisis managers to request tasks in a top-down manner as well as to interfere with the counterproductive self-organization efforts.

4.3   Incentives for Participation

When considering new crowdsourcing systems, perhaps the most important design question pertains to incentive structures. Since crowdsourcing systems are typically open to anyone, and do not rely on contractual relationships, people are not bound to participate. Instead, they must feel somehow compelled to participate, and so the factors that make a given system compelling might also those that make it succeed or fail. In the case of crisis management, the motivation is likely to be high during the crisis and low otherwise, so the main question we need to answer is: how to incite the participation in preparatory phase?

There are many ways to attract crowdworkers, but researchers such as Malone [13] describes three main motivation factors which can be influenced by crowdsourcing platform owners as "money, love and glory" paradigm.

Money: The dominant incentive mechanism on micro-task markets is money. Different markets have different norms for remuneration rates, but higher pay generally gets more workers to do more work more quickly [14]. In some cases, money can be the only motivator that will work. When the work is tedious and unpleasant (such as transcribing pages and pages of hand-written documents), crowdworkers are unlikely to participate unless fair monetary compensation is guaranteed. Money is not necessarily the best way to ensure quality, however. Researchers studying MTurk (Amazon's Mechanical Turk service) have found that higher rates of pay do not necessarily lead to higher quality work as mentioned in [14] and [15].

Love: Of course, money is not always required to touch people's heart. If workers simply love the task itself, they will contribute their time for free. Some people love tasks that challenge them and encourage them to help and support, especially in emergency situation or when a disaster occurs.

Glory: Finally, the possibilities to boost own social status by becoming a "hero of the crowdtasking platform" is both a strong incentive and one that is relatively easily realized. Glory incentive relies on measuring the users' performance, e.g. in terms of "points" for performed tasks and giving the visibility to "best" users, e.g. by adding a "beginner"/"experienced"/"hero" attribute to their usernames, distinctively visualizing the different user categories on a map or listing the "heroes of the day" on a special memorial page.

How can we apply these motivation factors to crisis management? A-priory, the volunteers are most likely to be motivated primarily by the factors which we can't influence, such as "moral obligation" or the wish to make the world a better place.

Relying on money as a driving force for ad-hoc volunteers is counterproductive and could be even dangerous, since most of the work in crisis management is already performed by unpaid volunteers and the available budget is tight. However, the re-compensation for charges incurred as a result of tasking (e.g. fuel costs) should be considered, if possible. Monetary compensations could play a more prominent role in preparatory phase, when tasks tend to be less exciting and the societal benefits more difficult to understand.

Helping others is a highly emotional activity. Simple ways to boost users' motivation at the "love" level are: pointing out the societal usefulness of the tasks, thanking the users for performed tasks and by visualizing the added value of the ad-hoc volunteers' work during and after the crisis. In a broader context, the "fun factor" can be seen as part of the love incentive. Presenting the tasking as a game (e.g. scavenger hunt tape of game) is therefore a good way to boost volunteers' motivation.

Finally, appealing to the "glory" factor is a good way to additionally strengthen the users' inner motivation for helping others by boosting the social status of the active volunteers. In addition, the "hero of today" score-tables can be used both to advertise the most helpful volunteers and to boost the love/fun factor by adding a touch of competition to the tasking platform.

Even more "glory" can be given to most useful ad-hoc outside of the crowdsourcing platform, e.g. by mentioning the importance of ad-hoc volunteers at post-crisis press event or inviting the most active volunteers to annual Christmas gala dinner. At this level a care must be taken not to over-compensate the ad-hoc volunteers with respect to the crisis management professionals and the institutional volunteers who do not participate in crowdtasking activities.

4.4 Ethical Considerations

Crowdsourcing is still an evolving field and many of the ethical implications it raises have yet to be resolved. Since internet has no borders, crowdsourcing could easily evolve into a digital sweatshop with the majority of the work done by "professional crowdworkers" from low income countries such as India [16]. In addition, crowdworkers are often given tedious, stupefying tasks that contribute little towards gaining new, marketable job skills. More effort should therefore be undertaken to help crowdworkers develop new, meaningful skills that can be applied to other work domains, as shown in the example "Environmental crowdsourcing techniques for improved water quality in rural India" above.

Unlike remuneration, which is unlikely to play an important role in crisis management, in crowdtasking applications the issue of liability could seriously impede the ability of crisis managers to work with the crowd. Since organizers and volunteers both play an active role in the system, it is unclear to which level they can be made responsible for the accuracy or validity of the crowdtasked information. This becomes important in case of damage or injuries caused by crowdworkers or when decisions affect the safety of crowd members. In order to minimize this type of risks, organizers should assure that tasks are always accompanied with adequate instructions and warnings. In addition, organizers should try to educate the crowdworkers to comply with relevant safety standards and to certify this knowledge, e.g. through micro-learning.

The next issue concerns privacy and misuse of data stored in user profiles or misuse of user tracking information. As a rule, the user profile data should be protected by design and the sensitive data (e.g. health-related) should never be shared with third parties, nor even be accessible to operators. Tracking of the users' positions is a special case. In our opinion, the tracking functionality should only be used with explicit users' consent, and this consent should only be requested for a well-defined area and time duration. As described in [10], the targeted geofencing could even be implemented without the need to track the users.

On a positive side, the issue of falsified profiles (e.g. minors pretending to be 18+) is unlikely to become a serious problem as long as the tasking organizations stick to the policy of validating the users profile in a face to face (offline) session. Finally, parceling of the work into tiny bits is a good way to hide the motives behind task requests from the crowdworkers. A malicious organizer could thus easily trick crowdworkers to participate in unethical activities, such as identifying and tracking of dissidents in a large crowd of people.

5   Conclusions

In this paper, we have presented several crowdsourcing use cases, which are relevant for crisis management. The use cases range from merely using whatever information becomes available on the web to actively managing and tasking the crowd. Examples from large-scale crisis incidents and ongoing research projects show that crowdsourcing techniques have a lot to offer in the field of crisis management. In crises situations any environmental, economic and health sector can be affected. However, in order to obtain real-time, accurate and trustworthy information of ongoing crisis incidents and to establish crowdsourcing as additional tool for crisis manager, significant technological and methodological advances are necessary.

Due to the massive user community of general purpose social networking platforms such as Facebook or Twitter, we see on a short time-scale two important developments with high impact in the CDM domain: (1) improved algorithms that accurately detect relevant information out of tons of data to a specific topic/theme (social media monitoring) and (2) methods for understanding emotions in the context of short messages or in posts..

On a long-term perspective, crowdtasking has the highest potential for improving the overall societal resilience. However, this is also the form of crowd use which is most difficult to implement and most sensitive to the issues mentioned in the previous section and most difficult to handle at the organizational level.

In principle, designing such a system is relatively simple, but in our opinion crowdsourcing tools are like English: it is easy to develop one, but quite difficult to do it in such a way that it optimally supports crisis managers, while at the same time attracting large numbers of users. In summary, the ideal crowdsourcing application should be designed to support crisis managers in managing issues related to user motivation, to mitigate privacy and ethical issues, as well as to support a right balance between top-down and self-organization of volunteers per design.

Acknowledgments. The research leading to this paper has been performed in the scope of DRIVER and RE-ACTA projects. The DRIVER FP7 project has received funding from the European Union's Seventh Framework Programme for research, technological development and demonstration under grant agreement no 607798. RE-ACTA was funded within the framework of the Austrian Security Research Program KIRAS[15] by the Federal Ministry for Transport, Innovation and Technology.

Paper authors would also like to acknowledge the work of following developers: Clemens Geyer, Herman Huber and Peter Kutschera who developed the initial version of the MDAF software; Jan van Oort, who started the Ubicity development by rewriting the MDAF backend from scratch; Christoph Ruggenthaler, who is currently the main Ubicity backend developer; and Maria Egly, who is responsible for the mobile application as part of the Ubicity development.

References

1. Meier, P.: Crisis Mapping in Action: How Open Source Software and Global Volunteer Networks Are Changing the World, One Map at a Time. Journal of Map & Geography Libraries: Advances in Geospatial Information, Collections & Archives (May 2012)
2. Bott, M., Gigler, B., Young, G.: The Role of Crowdsourcing for Better Governance in Fragile State Contexts. International Bank for Reconstruction and Development / The World Bank (2014)
3. Sutherlin, G.: A voice in the crowd: Broader implications for crowdsourcing translation during crisis. Journal of Information Science 39(3), 397–409 (2013), http://jis.sagepub.com/content/39/3/397
4. Morris, R.R., McDuff, D.: Crowdsourcing Techniques for Affective Computing. The Oxford Handbook of Affective Computing (Forthcoming) Edited by R. Calvo, S.K. D'Mello, J. Gratch, A. Kappas, 10.1093/oxfordhb/9780199942237.013.003 (Online Publication Date: April 2014)
5. Howe, J.: The rise of crowdsourcing. Wired Magazine 14(6), 1–4 (2006)

---

[15] http://www.kiras.at/

6. Rheingold, H.: Smart Mobs: The Next Social Revolution. Basic Books (2007), ISBN-13: 978-0738208619
7. van Etten, J.: Crowdsourcing Crop Improvement in Sub-Saharan Africa: A Proposal for a Scalable and Inclusive Approach to Food Security. IDS Bulletin 42, 102–110 (2011), doi:10.1111/j.1759-5436.2011.00240.x
8. Havlik, D., Kutschera, P., Geyer, C., Egly, M.: Geospatial Service Interfaces and Encodings for Mobile Applications in EnviroInfo 2012 Proceedings Part 1: Core Application Areas, Shaker Verlag Aachen, ISBN: 978-3-8440-1248-4
9. Sebald, C., Neubauer, G., Foitik, G., Flachberger, C., Lankmayr, G., Tellioglu, H., Havlik, D.: The RE-ACTA Approach - Resilience Enhancement by Crowdsourcing and Crowdtasking. Poster at the 11th International Conference on Information Systems for Crisis Response and Management, ISCRAM 2014, May 18-21. Penn State University, University Park (2014)
10. Havlik, D., Egly, M., Huber, H., Kutschera, P., Falgenhauer, M., Cizek, M.: Robust and trusted crowd-sourcing and crowd-tasking in the future internet. In: Hřebíček, J., Schimak, G., Kubásek, M., Rizzoli, A.E. (eds.) ISESS 2013. IFIP AICT, vol. 413, pp. 164–176. Springer, Heidelberg (2013)
11. Deri, O., Havlik, D., Rafalowski, C.: Accidental spillage from a container at large city port (Israel). In: Havlik, D., Dihé, P., Frings, S., Steinnocher, K., Aubrecht, C. (eds.) CRISMA Catalogue. CRISMA consortium (2014), https://crisma-cat.ait.ac.at/print/188 (retrieved on December 11, 2014)
12. Havlik, D., Javier, S., Granell Carlos, G., Middleton, S.E., van der Schaaf, H., Berre Arne, J., Pielorz, J.: Future Internet enablers for VGI applications in EnviroInfo 2013 Proceedings - Environmental Informatics and Renewable Energies. In: 27th International Conference on Informatics for Environmental Protection - Informatics for Environmental Protection, Sustainable Development and Risk Management - Part I and II, pp. 620–630 (2013) ISBN 978-3-8440-1676-5
13. Malone, T.: Harnessing Crowds: Mapping the Genome of Collective Intelligence. MIT Sloan Research (2009)
14. Mason, W., Watts, D.J.: Financial incentives and the "performance of crowds". In: Proceedings of the ACM SIGKDD Workshop on Human Computation - HCOMP 1909, p. 77 (1909), Presented at the ACM SIGKDD Workshop, Paris, France (2009)
15. Rogstadius, J., Kostakos, V., Kittur, A., Smus, B., Laredo, J., Vukovic, M.: An Assessment of Intrinsic and Extrinsic Motivation in Crowdsourcing Markets. In: ICWSM 2011, Presented at the Association for the Advancement of Artificial Intelligence (AAAI), Barcelona, Spain (2011)
16. Fort, K., Adda, G., Cohen, K.B.: Amazon Mechanical Turk: Gold Mine or Coal Mine? Computational Linguistics 37(2), 413–420 (2011)

Evolution of Environmental Information Models

Katharina Schleidt

Umweltbundesamt GmhH Austria
Katharina.Schleidt@umweltbundesamt.at

Abstract. Access to environmental data, based on standardized data models and services, is becoming ever more prevalent, providing stakeholders with access to a wide range of standardized environmental data from diverse sources. However, exactly this success brings new problems, with thematic extensions based on these standardized models being created by disparate thematic communities based on their specific requirements. In contrast to the traditional standards development process, which includes mechanisms for maintaining alignment of concepts across different sections of the standard, once these standards are extended by a larger and not so strictly structured community, the alignment process becomes increasingly difficult. This position paper sketches this problem, as illustrated by example of the European INSPIRE process, and serves as a basis for the conference workshop discussion that aims to capture both further facets of the problem as well as possible solutions.

Keywords: Environmental data and service modeling, extension of standardized data models, collaborative data modeling, semantic alignment approaches, processes and governance structures for collaborative data modeling.

1   Introduction

Access to environmental data is necessary for environmental research and control; often, this requires the use of data from different sources. This in turn entails a tedious process of accessing data in various formats, identifying the relevant concepts in the various data, then aligning and merging this data before the necessary analyses can be performed.

To ease this process, various initiatives have been launched around the world with the aim of providing standardized access to environmental data. While these initiatives differ in thematic focus, spatial extent or governance, they all strive to provide standardized data models and service specifications for the access to and use of environmental data.

Based on these developments, easy access to standardized and harmonized environmental data should be a simple process. Unfortunately, this initial impression is deceptive. Many of the existing standards only cover the core concepts of a domain; extensions are left to the thematic communities using these standards. As these thematic extensions grow and develop, they rapidly introduce new concepts not aligned

R. Denzer et al. (Eds.): ISESS 2015, IFIP AICT 448, pp. 71–80, 2015.

with similar concepts stemming from a different thematic area [1], we find ourselves dangerously close to the starting point.

Thus, an ongoing revision process becomes necessary, with many similar characteristics as the initial standardization process, but with additional challenges such as:

- A wider participant scope, as the adoption of the existing standardized data models leads to wider uptake;
- More complex concepts, as the scope widens through extensions;
- Less governance, as officially the problem is considered to be solved.

This paper sketches the requirements for such ongoing collaboration on a standardized data model for environmental data. It gives an overview of the types of problems already identified as well as those likely to happen in the foreseeable future. Based on these findings, it describes possible mechanisms to support this process.

2   Background

Various initiatives, stemming from various environmental sub-domains, have been launched in the last years with the goal of allowing for easy access to relevant data through the standardization of data models and service specifications. These include thematically narrow initiatives such as the Long Term Ecological Research or Biodiversity communities (see the ILTER[1], GBIF[2] and TDWG[3] sites) as well as thematically broad initiatives such as Research Data Alliance[4] or the European INSPIRE Initiative [2]. While data standards are often in place for core concepts, there is always a need to extend these in order to support new or alternative requirements.

In this paper, we use the European INSPIRE Initiative [2] as an illustrative example of both the challenges faced in such an undertaking as well as to provide examples of ways to manage these problems. However, the challenges described are the same for all initiatives attempting this task, and thus the conclusions reached have a wider validity.

2.1   The INSPIRE Directive

The INSPIRE Directive entered into force on the 15th of May 2007. It recognizes that definition and enforcement of European Community policy on the environment requires the easy availability of high quality spatial data. The Infrastructure for Spatial Information in the European Community (INSPIRE) should assist policy-making in relation to policies and activities that may have a direct or indirect impact on the environment. The 34 spatial data themes covered by INSPIRE have been structured in the three annexes to the directive, the themes are as follows:

---

[1] http://www.ilternet.edu/
[2] http://www.gbif.org/
[3] http://www.tdwg.org/
[4] https://rd-alliance.org/

ANNEX I

1. Coordinate reference systems
2. Geographical grid systems
3. Geographical names
4. Administrative units
5. Addresses
6. Cadastral parcels
7. Transport networks
8. Hydrography
9. Protected sites

ANNEX II

1. Elevation
2. Land cover
3. Orthoimagery
4. Geology

ANNEX III

1. Statistical units
2. Buildings
3. Soil
4. Land use
5. Human health and safety
6. Utility and governmental services
7. Environmental monitoring facilities
8. Production and industrial facilities
9. Agricultural and aquaculture facilities
10. Population distribution — demography
11. Area management/restriction/regulation zones and reporting units
12. Natural risk zones
13. Atmospheric conditions
14. Meteorological geographical features
15. Oceanographic geographical features
16. Sea regions
17. Bio-geographical regions
18. Habitats and biotopes
19. Species distribution
20. Energy resources
21. Mineral resources

INSPIRE is based on the European Member States (MS) spatial information infrastructures, that are made compatible with common implementing rules and are supplemented with measures at Community level. These rules and measures should ensure that the infrastructures for spatial information created by the MS are compatible and usable in across administrative levels and national boundaries.

Due the wide diversity of formats and structures in which spatial data are orga-nized and accessed in the Community, data specifications have been provided to faci-litate the use of spatial data from different sources across the MS's. Network services for sharing spatial data between the various levels of public authority in the Commu-nity make it possible to discover, transform, view and download spatial data and to invoke spatial data and e-commerce services.

3   Process and Stakeholders

Before we go into technical details, we must first consider the processes required for the creation, and subsequent extension of a harmonized data model, as well as the various stakeholders involved in this process. According to Craglia [3], INSPIRE has some characteristics that make it particularly challenging [1]:

1. The infrastructure is built on those of 27 Member States of the European Union in more than 23 languages. This requires the coexistence and collaboration of very different information systems, professional and cultural practices,
2. Given this complexity, it was necessary to adopt a consensus-building process, involv-ing hundreds of national experts, to develop the technical specifications for INSPIRE,
3. Existing standards must be tested in real distributed and multilingual settings,
4. Standards that are not mature enough, or leave too much room for different inter-pretation (because of the legally mandated implementation) have to be refined,
5. Standards which do not yet exist must be developed,
6. Inconsistency and incompatibility of data and metadata must be addressed for the 34 themes that fall within the scope of the Directive [1]

In order to counter these challenges, the following development process was defined:

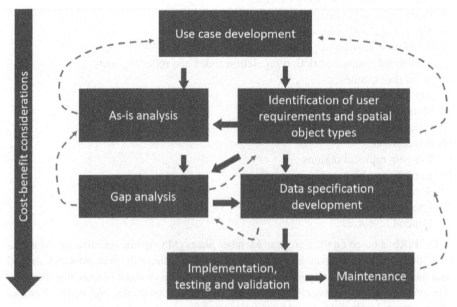

Fig. 1. Steps in the INSPIRE data specification cycle [1]

All the tasks leading to the Data specification development were undertaken by the members of the Thematic Working Group (TWG) constituted for developing the data model for a specific theme. Based on the use cases provided, and utilizing the ISO 191XX suite of standards, data models have been developed for the representation of the data themes listed above. The TWG members were supported by JRC staff in finding points for alignment between themes, as well as making the best use of existing data types stemming from both the underlying ISO standards as well as the INSPIRE base models.

Once the data specification development was advanced to the point where the TWGs were satisfied with their thematic data models, these data models together with their specification were made available to interested parties from the European Member States (MS). The MS were encouraged to test these preliminary data models both through manual scrutiny of the data specifications provided as well as by filling these data models with data stemming from their national data holdings. The feedback from this testing and validation process was in turn sent to the responsible TWGs, for a second round of data specification development (with all ensuing feedback loops illustrated above). More information on the INSPIRE data specification development process can be found in the JRC deliverable D2.6 Methodology for the development of data specifications [4]

Unfortunately, while the implementation, testing and validation step performed by the MSs did give much valuable feedback on thematic requirements, it provided little support for the task of harmonizing and aligning the data model itself. This is due to the fact that this thematic feedback usually came from dedicated thematic departments within the national environmental agencies as well as other stakeholders. Thus, while let's say the air quality department provided thorough feedback on the requirements stemming from air quality monitoring and the water management group provided feedback on requirements stemming from the water domain, there was little consideration on the fact that similar concepts from these two domains could be encoded in the same manner; this task was left to the TWG members as well as the coordinators from the JRC. Thus, despite best effort from all parties involved, inconsistencies in the INSPIRE data models were not avoidable.

Already within the harmonized INSPIRE data specifications, despite the constraints set out by the INSPIRE Generic Conceptual Model [5], equivalent concepts from individual thematic data specifications vary due to difficulties in alignment across thematic domains.

Now that the INSPIRE data and service specifications have been finalized and are being implemented on both the national as well as the European levels, further extensions are being created of these base INSPIRE data models. For example, an extension of the INSPIRE data models for European Air Quality Reporting has been finalized and is now operational[5]; the same approach is currently being followed for various other environmental reporting obligations. While these extended data models will be tailored to the requirements of a specific reporting obligation, they will undoubtedly be adding certain similar concepts such as an European station code to the base INSPIRE models. At present there is no mechanism in place to enable alignment of equivalent concepts across the various pending extensions of the core data models.

---

[5] http://www.eionet.europa.eu/aqportal

76   K. Schleidt

4   Examples

In the following section, we shall provide some examples from the INSPIRE domain. In the first example, we shall show how inconsistencies crept into the tightly governed INSPIRE data specification process. In the second example, we shall show how this problem will certainly be exacerbated now that the INSPIRE data models are available and being extended for thematic purposes, with little or no governance to assure alignment.

4.1   INSPIRE Data Specifications - Tight Governance

In theory, the INSPIRE Generic Conceptual Model (GCM) as well as the Methodology for the development of data specifications govern the data specification process. However, despite vigilance by all parties concerned, discrepancies appeared such as follows:

- In the INSPIRE data specification for Area management/restriction/regulation zones and reporting units, the name of the zone is defined as the INSPIRE base type GeographicalName.
- In the INSPIRE data specification for Environmental Monitoring Facilities, the name of the facility is defined as the ISO 19103 type CharacterString.

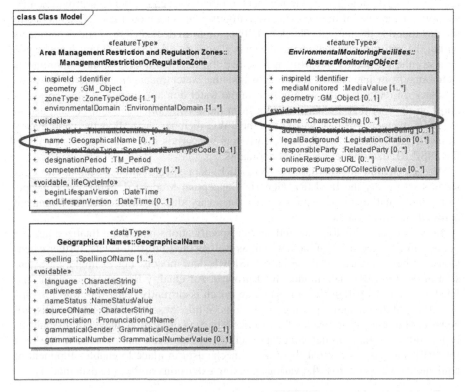

Fig. 2. Example - Name in INSPIRE

The rationale behind this difference is that within the TWG responsible for the Environmental Monitoring Facilities theme the decision was reached that the complexity of the Geographical name type was far greater than the requirements for Environmental Monitoring Facilities (see cost/benefit considerations in the INSPIRE data specification cycle shown above). However, this is sure to cause confusion in developers creating applications for multiple INSPIRE Themes.

4.2   INSPIRE Extensions - Loose Governance

Now that the INSPIRE data and service specifications have been finalized and are being implemented on both the national as well as the European levels, further extensions are being created of these base INSPIRE data models. An extension of the INSPIRE data models for European Air Quality e-Reporting has been finalized and is now operational[6]; the same approach is now being followed for various other environmental reporting obligations [6]. While these extended data models will be tailored to the requirements of a specific reporting obligation, they will undoubtedly be adding some similar concepts such as an European station code to the base INSPIRE models. At present there is no mechanism in place to enable alignment of equivalent concepts across the various pending extensions of the existing data models.

In the example below we show the AQD_Station class developed for the European Air Quality e-Reporting and derived from the INSPIRE EnvironmentalMonitoringFacility Class. Based on the requirements of the underlying air quality directive 2008/50/EC [7] and Commission Implementing Decision 2011/850/EU [8], in addition to the basic name provided by the INSPIRE EnvironmentalMonitoringFacility Class, a European Station Code must be provided. This attribute has been added to the AQD_Station definition as shown below.

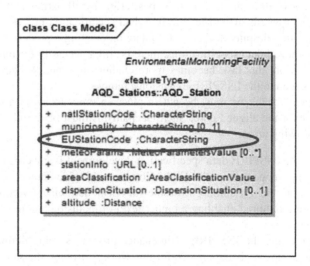

Fig. 3. Example - INSPIRE Extension

---

[6] http://www.eionet.europa.eu/aqportal

The process performed for European Air Quality e-Reporting shall now be repeated for various environmental reporting obligations, in each case the concepts ensuing from the legal requirements stemming from the relevant legislation shall be identified and the base INSPIRE data models will be extended accordingly. The likelihood that a concept such as a European Station Code will be required in other thematic domains is high; however, there is no mechanism in place to assure that this will be done in the same manner in each case, leading to subtle differences in these data specifications, and hindering reuse of mechanisms and code when working across thematic areas.

While this divergence could conceivably be managed by the European Environment Agency (EEA) when it pertains to the data specifications required in the environmental reporting domain, there is currently no mechanism in place for such coordination on extensions stemming from other areas or actors (i.e. national thematic extensions).

The INSPIRE Maintenance and Implementation Framework (MIF) is currently being set up between the European Commission and the Member States to guide further development of the INSPIRE process. An expert group called INSPIRE Maintenance and Implementation Group (MIG) with representatives of the INSPIRE national contact points has been established. Of the tasks identified under the Maintenance and Implementation Work Programme (MIWP), the problems discussed here will be addressed by MIWP-14: Theme specific issues of data specifications & exchange of implementation experiences in thematic domains [9].

5   Lessons Learned

The examples above illustrate how despite best effort by all parties involved there is an inherent creep towards diversification in a data specification process. This can be seen as evidence that despite all the work to date on creating a process for the development of harmonized data specifications, there is still a necessity for further work in this area. In addition, this task becomes more challenging once the governance becomes looser as seen in the INSPIRE extension example.

Thus, further mechanisms must be put in place in order to avoid a new level of chaos to creep over the aligned core. Such mechanisms must be defined and put into place in the following areas:

- Governance: the INSPIRE data specification development is governed by the JRC, with increasing support from the EEA. However, this does not cover extensions ensuing from drivers not coming from the European administrative domain. Thus, mechanisms are required enabling a higher level of inclusion among a wider range of stakeholders.
- Processes: currently the INSPIRE maintenance process is being defined and various working groups are being created for this work. However, the same problem as pertains to governance is also active here, with little support for Non-European extensions. In addition to inclusion of a wider base of stakeholders, mechanisms will be necessary that facilitate the access of data stemming from outside parties.

Also, as illustrated above, even with the rigid processes set up by the JRC for the base INSPIRE data specification work, discrepancies still occurred.

- Tools: Various web sites as well as a common repository for the UML data models provide support in finding agreement on necessary extensions to the INSPIRE data specifications. However, the alignment of concepts remains a manual process, depending on the meticulous perusal of the various specifications by humans. If tools were available that support the alignment between different concepts, this would make the alignment process much easier and less prone to human error.

Coming back from the more specific INSPIRE example detailed above to the general question of collaborative extension of environmental data models, it becomes clear that the challenges described in the INSPIRE process apply to other similar initiatives. Similar difficulties encountered in maintaining compatibility among extensions have been seen in the various other thematic data sharing initiatives mentioned earlier. The problems described become ever more difficult to handle the larger and more disparate the user community becomes. A great deal of effort has been put into the development of processes and supporting tools for collaborative data model development by various stakeholders in different thematic and geographic areas, but there is still a long way to go until this fully supports the requirements of the communities involved. These must also be adapted to allow for thematic extension of existing standardized data models by diverse stakeholders without this leading to a new level of diversification.

Based on examples from the INSPIRE data specification process, we have seen how easily such discrepancies arise, both with tight governance and even more so with loose governance. Only if the problems identified are properly addressed, and the necessary steps taken will it be possible to provide a truly harmonized and usable data system across thematic domains both for now as well as for future requirements.

References

1. Tóth, K., Portele, C., Illert, A., Lutz, M., de Lima, M.N.: A Conceptual Model for Developing Interoperability Specifications in Spatial Data Infra-structures. JRC Reference Report (2012), http://inspire.ec.europa.eu/documents/Data_Specifications/IES_S patial_Data_Infrastructures_(online).pdf (retrieved)
2. Directive 2007/2/EC of the European Parliament and of the Council of 14 March 2007 establishing an Infrastructure for Spatial Information in the European Community (INSPIRE), http://eur-lex.europa.eu/legal-content/EN/TXT/?uri=uriserv:OJ.L_.2007.108.01.0001.01.ENG, More available at: http://inspire.ec.europa.eu/
3. Craglia, M.: Building INSPIRE: The Spatial Data Infrastructure for Europe. ARC News, 5-7. Redlands, California (2010), http://www.esri.com/news/arcnews/spring10articles/building-inspire.html (retrieved)
4. JRC, D2.6 Methodology for the development of data specifications (2008), http://inspire.ec.europa.eu/reports/ImplementingRules/DataSpeci fications/D2.6_v3.0.pdf (retrieved)

5. INSPIRE Generic Conceptual Model,
    `http://inspire.ec.europa.eu/documents/Data_Specifications/`
    `D2.5_v3.4.pdf` (retrieved)
6. Schleidt, K.: INSPIREd air quality reporting. In: Hřebíček, J., Schimak, G., Kubásek, M., Rizzo-
    li, A.E. (eds.) ISESS 2013. IFIP AICT, vol. 413, pp. 439–450. Springer, Heidelberg (2013)
7. Directive 2008/50/EC of the European Parliament and of the Council of 21 May 2008 on am-
    bient air quality and cleaner air for Europe, `http://eur-lex.europa.eu/`
    `legal-content/en/ALL/?uri=CELEX:32008L0050` (retrieved)
8. COMMISSION IMPLEMENTING DECISION of 12 December 2011 laying down rules for
    Directives 2004/107/EC and 2008/50/EC of the European Parliament and of the Council as re-
    gards the reciprocal exchange of information and reporting on ambient air quality
    (2011/850/EU), `http://eur-lex.europa.eu/LexUriServ/LexUriServ.do?`
    `uri=OJ:L:2011:335:0086:0106:EN:PDF` (retrieved)
9. MIWP-14: Theme specific issues of data specifications & exchange of implementation ex-
    periences in thematic domains, `https://`
    `ies-svn.jrc.ec.europa.eu/issues/2136` (retrieved)

An Interactive Website for the River Eurajoki

Ari Jolma, Anne-Mari Ventelä, Marjo Tarvainen, and Teija Kirkkala

Pyhäjärvi Institute, Eura, Finland
{ari.jolma,anne-mari.ventela,marjo.tarvainen,
teija.kirkkala}@pji.fi

Abstract. The project "Our Common River Eurajoki" aims for a long-term sustainable and collaborative platform for improving and managing the river water quality. We describe a website that supports the project by linking social media to environmental monitoring and web mapping. The website development was based on five-tiered software architecture and on several systems working together. Coding was minimized by re-using existing software components. We discuss the workflows supported by the website and the role of information system standards in environmental monitoring.

Keywords: Environmental management, Web, Web services, Geospatial, Sensor observation.

1 Introduction

River Eurajoki in South West Finland has for decades been heavily impacted by human activities. For example the waste water treatment plant (WWTP) of the Eura municipality and two companies discharged raw sewage into the river for a long time due to insufficient capacity of the plant. The plant management kept the bypass secret for many years. Also, for example in May 2011 a paper mill leaked 50 kg of 2,2'-diallyl-4,4'-sulfonyldifenol (a chemical used in coating paper and on the Nordic Council of Ministers' list of chemicals that are dangerous for the environment) into its sewer and most of that probably went trough the WWTP into the river. Similar and even worse leaks have happened before. Microbiological studies made this year (2014) from the river water have often revealed concentrations of enterococci and E. coli that are over the limits for water used, e.g., for vegetable irrigation. The use of the river water was forbidden for swimming and irrigation from September 2012 to the summer of 2013 and again in spring 2014. The poor condition has led to citizen activism and much concern among municipalities and environmental authorities [1].

"Our Common River Eurajoki"[1] is a joint project carried out by the Pyhäjärvi Institute, University of Turku, and JVP-Eura (the company running the WWTP in Eura municipality). It is coordinated by the Pyhäjärvi Institute and runs from March 2013 to April 2015. The project aims for a long-term sustainable and collaborative platform

---

[1] http://www.pyhajarvi-instituutti.fi/english/image/
pdf-tiedostot/yhtejoki_leaflet_brief.pdf

R. Denzer et al. (Eds.): ISESS 2015, IFIP AICT 448, pp. 81–90, 2015.
© IFIP International Federation for Information Processing 2015

for improving and managing the river and its catchment by linking citizen activism and environmental monitoring to water quality planning and management. The goal is to increase awareness, facts, and knowledge about the environmental situation while at the same time acknowledging the existing data sources and social media. The work plan of the project comprises development of a website, real-time water quality monitoring, and a sociological study about the relationship between the river and the public. The website is planned to support and link existing activities and to provide access to existing and new data about the river. In this paper we focus on the website the project is developing. The website is online as eurajoki.info.

Using the web for collaboration rather than just as a media for publishing content is a change that has happened in the last ten years [2]. The term "Web 2.0" has been used to describe the development. According to Wikipedia, a Web 2.0 site may allow users to interact and collaborate with each other in social media dialogue as creators of user-generated content in a virtual community. Collaborative websites can be used for environmental management. Geospatial information and mapping is often a core element of the reported attempts. For example [3] discusses large-scale citizen-generated content in the web and its role in environmental monitoring and crisis management. A collaborative environmental decision support system that uses standards based web services is demonstrated in [4].

2   Materials and Methods

2.1   River Eurajoki and its Observation

Eurajoki is a 52.9 km long river in Southwestern Finland with a catchment area of 1336 km^2. It originates at Lake Säkylän Pyhäjärvi, whose ecological status is good, but there are several point sources polluting the river, and many smaller streams with possibly poorer water quality enter the main branch. Also non-point source pollution from agriculture, forestry, peat production, and rural areas may be significant at times. The average discharge of the river at its mouth is 9.6 m^3/s. Eurajoki flows into a bay in the Bothnian Sea, which is a part of the Baltic Sea.

There are 18 observation and measurement sites along the river and in the database that have been used for hydrological (water quantity and quality) measurements. Some sites have been used for continuous measurements; some have been sampled at regular or irregular intervals, some both. Observations and measurements have been done and/or commissioned by private organizations (Pyhäjärvi Institute is one of them) or companies, and by municipal or governmental authorities. Private citizens also sometimes share observations in social media. The observation/measurement workflow depends on who makes the measurement but it is often rather complex involving more than one party and many types of data cleansing and processing especially in the case of continuous measurements and averaged and derived values.

2.2   Requirements

Requirements engineering is according to [5] the process of discovering the purpose of the software by identifying the stakeholders and their needs, and documenting these for analysis, communication, and implementation.

The eurajoki.info website was initiated with several goals in mind: 1) to create a hub for existing sites and social media, 2) to aid in formulating the future water quality management work, 3) to display the existing and new water quality data, 4) to aid in collecting and displaying cultural and experiential data and stories about the river, 5) to display map datasets of the river and its catchment, and 6) to allow access to existing and new reports about the river and its environmental state. It was understood that a website is only one product for water quality data and that there is a need for improved information management in general. Especially support for collaboration and data exchange among individuals and organizations, and publication of data and results was seen important. This strengthened the interest in modern web technologies and distributed systems that are based in standard protocols.

Web mapping and presentation of water quality data were core requirements. It was seen important to be able to visualize the data and spatial information together. The measurement and observation locations, measured quantities (variables), and data itself and their attributes should be browsable. Annotating data was seen important. Public, after adequate identification, should be allowed to add stories to the map and participate in discussions. "A story" was defined as text and pictures that are attached to a point location.

New requirements appear as experience is obtained. For example the state of a web page should be attainable simply with a single URL. The reason for this is how information is often shared in social media with links.

2.3   Architecture

Five-tiered software architecture, such as the one presented by [6], was selected as the basis for the development. The tiers are visualization, presentation, business, data access, and data.

We define the visualization tier as the website as presented by the web browser. A website consists of web pages, which may be static or dynamic. Web pages are written in HTML (or one of its versions), which allows embedding of objects such as images, interactive forms, program code for interactive and dynamic content, etc.

We define the presentation tier as the data formats and the communication between the client (user) application and the servers. For a website http and HTML are naturally the most important communication standards. When it comes to geospatial and observation data, the OGC (Open Geospatial Consortium) offers at least two standards, namely WFS (Web Feature Service) and SOS (Sensor Observation Service) for publishing data [7]. SOS is a part of the SWE (Sensor Web Enablement) framework of OGC; the other parts are standards for observation and measurement data, sensor and observation processing descriptions, and sensor planning service. The OGC discussion paper 'CUAHSI WaterML' defines another family of web services, called WaterOneFlow, that was developed for communicating hydrologic data. WaterOneFlow was created by the CUAHSI (Consortium of Universities for the Advancement of Hydrologic Science, Inc.) community of US universities.

We define the business tier as the code which implements and enables the workflows that the website supports. The business tier may be implemented on the server side or on the client side. Server side code is executed on demand (when a client requests a web page), possibly taking parameters or other input from the client, and it may use any resources it has available to produce a web page or other content for the client.

The data access tier is the code which connects to the database and prepares data for the presentation or business tier, or stores data coming from those tiers to the database.

The data tier is the database and database management system, which accepts connections to the database, and typically interprets the data access and management commands. The database schema is an important element of the database.

2.4   Software

There are several web mapping and other interactive data visualization technologies for the web. Common ones include Adobe Flash, Microsoft Silverlight, Apache Flex, HTML5, and JavaScript. Each alternative has its pros and cons. We chose JavaScript because it is well supported by web browsers and operating systems, and because of the availability of good free and open source libraries that we could use.

There are several options for developing web pages using JavaScript. These include JavaScript libraries and server side APIs, especially for web mapping, which to use. Our first try was to use the Ext JS library for time series visualization. Ext JS is a large framework for rich interactive and visual web content. GeoExt project develops a library for integrating the mapping library OpenLayers with Ext JS. However, we later found out about the Flot library for time series visualization, which in our opinion supports better time series visualization. For example it can handle missing data, which is common in environmental data sets. Flot is based on jQuery, which was thus selected as the core library instead of Ext JS.

OpenLayers was chosen over other alternatives because of its good functionality, and support for standard and common geospatial data services[2].

The 52°North Sensor Web Community has developed a SOS server, for which various clients exist, including Javascript ones[3]. For WaterOneFlow there is server software but currently no JavaScript client library exists to our knowledge. Despite of these existing solutions it was decided to develop a lightweight ad hoc solution as a

---

[2]   JavaScript web mapping libraries are compared for example on page
http://tinyurl.com/o8k3b4k (URL made tiny and tested 2014-10-04)

[3]   A demonstration website which uses 52°North SOS and a JavaScript client has been developed by British Antarctic Survey (http://tinyurl.com/my2erpv). Their JavaScript client uses the Flot library, which was the inspiration for us to use Flot. CSIRO has implemented a Google Maps based client for 52°North SOS (http://tinyurl.com/nxgae7k). (URLs made tiny and tested   2014-10-04)

simple initial attempt and as a learning experience. Both the server and the client side of the ad hoc solution are described below.

On the server side we used Perl CGI programs for WFS, for story editor/server, and the ad hoc server. The overlay raster maps were developed into map tiles and set up as tile service. The WFS we used is a part of the Geoinformatica suite and built on top of GDAL and its Perl API.

PostgreSQL relational database management system (RDBMS) with PostGIS extension was used as the main data storage (image and pdf files are stored in file system). phpPgAdmin and Perl CGI programs were used for administrative data management.

3 Results and Discussion

The architecture of the developed system is shown in figure 1. The system is implemented on four subsystems: client web browser, website (eurajoki.info), dedicated services (ajolma.net), and common services (Google map tiles, OpenStreetMap map tiles, and National Land Survey of Finland map tiles). The five tiers of the conceptual architecture are divided between these subsystems. Visualization is defined mostly by the content downloaded from the website and tiled maps downloaded from services. Presentation is based on standards except for time series. Business logic is implemented partly in JavaScript that runs on the client and partly in dedicated services. Data access is based in SQL within dedicated services. Data is in ten tables in the RDBMS.

The web pages of eurajoki.info comprise several types of files. PHP is used to compose the HTML pages and to create certain pieces of JavaScript into the HTML (see below). The website architecture is flat and consists of seven web pages with uniform style. The pages are front page, management plan, water quality mapping, story map, atlas, reports, and about page. Each page has its own Facebook discussion thread. The front page has also the Facebook feed from the citizen activists' Facebook account. The management plan page is currently a stub and it will be developed more at a later stage. The water quality mapping page (figure 2.) has an OpenLayers map panel and a Flot time series panel. The story map and the atlas have a map panel for browsing and editing (story map). The overlays (historical maps and aerial photos) are tiled maps so they load fast and are easy to pan. The reports page contains PDF reports about the river environment. The about page contains information about the site, its developers, data, etc.

The JavaScript code developed for the website is divided into ten files and totals 973 lines[4].

3.1 Water Quality Mapping

The water quality mapping page (figure 2) contains panels for a map, site information, control form, and time series graph. The JavaScript code associated with the page

---

[4]   The code is available at
http://tinyurl.com/leg4yp9 (URL made tiny and tested 2014-10-04)

obtains data from services, and displays it on the panels. The measurement and observation sites are obtained as a WFS layer object. The time series data is obtained from the service as JSON (JavaScript Object Notation) and handed over to the Flot library for visualization. Both map and time series panels have interactive functionality that is mostly managed by the two libraries.

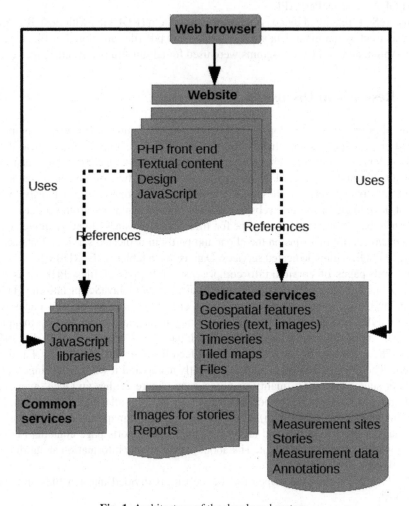

Fig. 1. Architecture of the developed system

The control panel contain standard HTML form widgets for the locations and variables (select multiple list boxes), begin and end dates (text entries with associated jQuery calendar widgets), and a button for updating the time series graph. The locations and variables lists are updated with data obtained from the time series data server (retrieved also as JSON). The locations are linked to WFS features in JavaScript through a key attribute. Thus the selection in the list widget can be synchronized with selected features on the map. The locations are also linked to variables from which

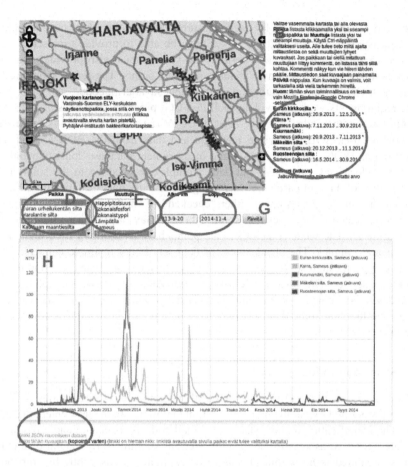

Fig. 2. A screenshot of the water quality mapping page. A is the map panel, five features/locations are selected and one that is not selected has a popup information box. B is general information to the user. C is information about the selected locations. D is the list of locations. E is the list of variables. F is the time period. G is the button to update the graph. H is the time series graph. I is links to raw data and URL of the visualization.

there is data in this location. Thus it is possible to synchronize the selected locations with the selected variables.

A solution to the state-in-a-URL problem (section 2.2), was to use PHP to create JavaScript that sets selected locations, variables and time period in initialization code. The current implementation of the solution is not complete because it does not set the selected locations in the map panel and it does not restore the possible zoom and pan of the time series graph.

3.2   Ad Hoc Observation Service

The requirements for the time series services were the following. The server must be able to list at least the locations, the measured variables for each location, and the period from which there is data for each measured variable; the server must be able to list the measured variables; and the server must be able to provide time series from requested locations, variables, and period. The service must also provide notes and comments linked to the locations, variables, and data points. The server should return the data as JSON for easy consumption by the client JavaScript code.

The requirements were met with a small Perl CGI program (409 lines of code) that supports three commands: `GetDatasets`, `GetVariables`, and `GetDataset`. The program uses SQL to retrieve metadata and data from the RDBMS and then sends it out as JSON. The observation and measurement database consists mainly of three tables: locations, variables, and data. Complexity is added to the solution by characteristics of data, in particular data being either daily data or data with arbitrary measurement time, and data being either "checked" or "not checked". The former is further complicated by the fact that some data sets may have data points that have only an arbitrary date while some other data points have an arbitrary time stamp (i.e., also hour and minute). The checkedness of data sets is not a simple concept; some datasets can go through several checks and may change more than once due to new calibration data etc. The current solution has four data tables: two for checked data (checked data is shown by default) and two for daily data and two for data with time stamps. The fact that some data sets may have data points in two tables complicates the service code.

3.3   Story Map Editor

The story map was required to have user authentication for editing stories. This requirement was filled by adding an identification dialog before the user enters the story editor. The identification dialog asks for an email address (or name) and a password. These are later used as keys to the data the user has submitted. By default data that a user has submitted is not public. It has to be explicitly set as public by somebody having appropriate rights to the database.

The story editor (its mapping part) is based on transactional WFS (WFS-T). In order to keep things simple on the client side, the stories are always served through the same WFS layer. However, for this to work, the service had to be changed to require the email and password fields and serve features according to those fields: no values: serve public data, values given: serve private data specified by those fields. This feature is not a part of WFS specification.

3.4   Overall Assessment

The result fulfills the baseline requirements. The website uses Facebook social plugins and allows public to create content, however the content has to be published by admins. The solution uses two servers on the Internet, one for the website and one for the dedicated services. The latter has a database and custom CGI programs. The solution we developed in this study did not require extensive development as the program code line counts show.

4   One or Two Standards for Geospatial Features and Observation Data?

Several middleware programs were developed for the services. Some of them are standard, some are standard but extend the standard somehow, some could be standard, and some are specific to this purpose.

According to the CUAHSI WaterML Web Services page[5] WaterOneFlow has eight functions (requests), which are very close to the ad hoc time series server we implemented in this study. The OGC SWE, due to its generic nature, is rather complex and thus it may be difficult to implement considering varying database schemas, and server and client software. Noting this, [8] defined a lightweight SOS profile for facilitating its practical application. The lightweight profile is very similar to the ad hoc profile of this study but it goes beyond ours by including a transactional part for inserting observations and sensors, which in our case can be done but only via separate tools.

The application scenario of [8] is European-wide sharing of environmental data. Our case study focuses on a single river, which is a part of a river basin. The river basin falls mostly within one administrative region, but constitutes only a fraction of it. It is worth considering what types of data services are needed and useful at each level. It could be argued that at higher level the data and information needs about lower level parts would be simpler or less dimensioned (averages, loads at system boundaries, etc.) and when the focus is on a specific system, there data needs are more detailed and also of different kind.

Our system uses two services, WFS and sensor data service, at the same time and in coordination. The coordination is to a large degree ensured by the use of a single database. Although the features (observation and measurement sites) appear in different services and thus as separate instances, they are in reality the same entities in the database. The reason for two services is also practical: WFS layers are well supported by common web mapping clients while SOS is not so well supported.

From a user point of view the technology behind a website has little importance if they do not affect the user experience. However, interoperability becomes very apparent when for example one measurement data stream cannot be added to the same graph as the others.

5   Conclusion

The website has been online since December 2013. The project ends in April 2015 but the website will be kept online after that. Currently the website has a rather steady usage with 150 or more unique visitors per month. Statistics show that water quality mapping and reports are the most popular pages on the site and only a small fraction view the stories or the tiled overlay maps. Only the project team has so far used the story editor. The discussion forum on the front pages has attracted some use but

---

[5] http://his.cuahsi.org/wofws.html

forums on other pages only little. However, this was expected since the activist Facebook forum (which is shown on the front page) is the main forum for discussions.

Future work will focus on making the provided data and information more meaningful for the public and developing the page that is dedicated to supporting the development of the water quality management plan.

Acknowledgements. The "Our Common River Eurajoki" project is funded by the Regional Development Fund of the European Union (project code A32601).

References

1. Saavalainen, H.: Eurajoki became an open sewer - City of Rauma still using it as a water supply. Helsingin Sanomat (May 25, 2014) (in Finnish)
2. O'Reilly, T.: What Is Web 2.0: Design Patterns and Business Models for the Next Generation of Software, http://www.oreilly.com/pub/a/web2/archive/what-is-web-20.html (retrieved March 11, 2014) (2005)
3. Boulos, M.N.K., Resch, B., Crowley, D.N., Breslin, J.G., Sohn, G., Burtner, R., Pike, W.A., Jezierski, E., Chuang, K.-Y.S.: Crowdsourcing, citizen sensing and sensor web technologies for public and environmental health surveillance and crisis management: trends, OGC standards and application examples. Int. J. Health Geographics 10, 6 (2011)
4. Sikder, I.U., Gangopadhyay, A., Shampur, N.V.: Interoperability in Web-Based Geospatial Applications. Int. J. Information Technology and Web Engineering (IJITWE) 3(3), 66–88 (2008), doi:10.4018/jitwe.2008070105
5. Nuseibeh, B., Easterbrook, S.: Requirements Engineering: A Roadmap. ICSE 2000 Future of Software Engineering [1]. ACM Press. (2000)
6. Tafti, A.P., Janosepah, S., Modiri, N., Noudeh, A.M., Alizadeh, H.: Development of a Framework for Applying ASYCUDA System with N-Tier Application Architecture. In: Zain, J.M., Wan Mohd, W.M.b., El-Qawasmeh, E. (eds.) ICSECS 2011, Part III. CCIS, vol. 181, pp. 533–541. Springer, Heidelberg (2011)
7. Bermudez, L., Bogden, P., Bridger, E., Cook, T., Galvarino, C., Creager, G., Forrest, D., Graybeal, J.: Web Feature Service (WFS) and Sensor Observation Service (SOS) Comparison to Publish Time Series Data. In: CTS 2009. International Symposium on Collaborative Technologies and Systems, pp. 36–43. IEEE (2009)
8. Jirka, S., Bröring, A., Kjeld, P., Maidens, J., Wytzisk, A.: A Lightweight Approach for the Sensor Observation Service to Share Environmental Data across Europe. Transactions in GIS 16(3), 293–312 (2012)

An Information Model for a Water Information Platform

Pascal Dihé, Ralf Denzer, and Sascha Schlobinski

Cismet GmbH, Altenkesseler Straße, 17, 66117 Saarbrücken, Germany
Ralf.denzer@enviromatics.org

Abstract. Sharing of open government data is amongst other reasons hindered by incompatibility of data models in different data collections. Only a few areas in the environmental domain have progressed towards commonly used data models. The purpose of this paper is to share with the community a data model which is used in a spatial information platform being built for the purpose of sharing open government data in the domain of water sciences. The objective when building the information model was not to be restricted to one and only one (meta)data standard. The information model therefore uses several standards and extension mechanisms: the ISO19000 series, the Comprehensive Knowledge Archive Network (CKAN), dynamic tag extension and dynamic content extension. The CKAN domain model can also be mapped to semantic-web-compatible standards like Dublin Core and the Data Catalogue Vocabulary of the World Wide Web Consortium.

Keywords: water information platform, water data model, spatial data infrastructure, spatial information platform.

1 Introduction and Related Work

The re-use of publicly funded governmental data has received a lot of attention recently. In the environmental domain, it is clear that improved public services need exchange of data across governments at all levels. Governments keep producing information products at all levels, and some of them are more or less readily available. Reporting obligations in the EC, for instance demanded by the Water Framework Directive (WFD)[1], are direct inputs to European datasets.

Water-related information is progressively made available on-line by a large variety of actors, including water data from operational monitoring and reporting of authorities. In Europe, the EEA plays an important role by providing water information through WISE and the water data centre[2]. Data does not only include monitored or reported data but also fundamental information like basin networks [1]. Over the past years, the Australian government has made large efforts in building water information platforms, information systems and tools [2]. Similarly, in the United States, CUASHI [3] acts as an alliance to

---

[1] http://ec.europa.eu/environment/water/
water-framework/index_en.html

[2] http://www.eea.europa.eu/themes/water/dc

R. Denzer et al. (Eds.): ISESS 2015, IFIP AICT 448, pp. 91–101, 2015.

improve water information and associated ICT. At international level the GEOSS data core also lists many water-related information resources [4].

However, *on-line* means different concepts to different people, from just presenting data to full service integration, with or without registration and authentication [5], and *re-use of data* is not happening at large scale, and platforms, particularly those developed in R&D projects often do not survive long after the project. Recent discussions in the community [6] have identified a fundamental gap between concepts, research and implementation. This gap is given by a) a distance between the modelling community / modelling environments and infrastructure developers / providers, b) a lack of tools supporting the uptake of infrastructures being built and a lack of understanding, how "re-purposing" (re-use under different context) of data can be supported.

As part of the SWITCH-ON project, a Spatial Information Platform (SIP) is being developed, which supports the reuse of information products for the water science domain. This platform is used by water scientists and aims at integrating water related data from various sources including open government data. The re-use (re-purposing) of data is a central element of the platform. The concept of this SIP has been published recently [5] and a first version is on-line[3].

The core platform is implemented with a stack of freely available open source software compiled in the CIDS product suite of CISMET GmbH. This software suite consists of a set of software components, application programming interfaces (APIs), management and development tools, services and applications, with a special focus on interactive solutions which need to integrate geo-spatial systems with databases, sensor networks, document-oriented systems, unstructured information sources and numerical models. CIDS is particularly suited for solutions which have to be built across existing heterogeneous information systems, which may be under control of different organizations. CIDS has been used in numerous projects since 1999. For recent projects see [7,8].

2   Platform Architecture

The architecture of the SIP is separated horizontally into three disparate layers: a *GUI Layer* (graphical user interface), a *Service Layer* and a *Data Layer* (figure 1). Each layer contains several components or sets of components. Interaction between components happens between components of adjacent layers. Apart from a few exceptions, GUI components, for example, do not communicate directly with the data repositories. These three layers are accompanied by a vertical *Tools Layer*.

The *Data Layer* is concerned with the storage and management of data and metadata (e.g. catalogue data). The most important component of the Data Layer is the Meta-Data Repository, a software component which is responsible for the storage and management of the meta-data compliant with the information model described in this article.

---

[3] http://www.water-switch-on.eu/sip.html

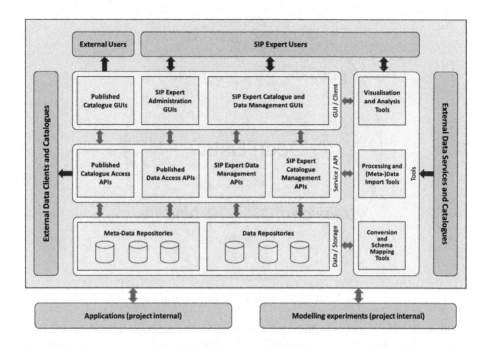

Fig. 1. SIP architecture

The *Service Layer* contains components that offer public service interfaces (APIs) which can be used by public and expert client components of the SIP. Those services also implement most of the (server-side) business logic of the SIP. They are supported by tools which provide additional functionality (e.g. data conversion) and which can be directly embedded in the respective service implementation.

The *GUI layer* of the SIP architecture contains user interface and user interaction components for expert and external users. External users include the general public which is able to use the public GUIs of the SIP without prior registration. Expert users have more access rights than external users, e.g. for the manipulation of data and meta-data.

The Tools Layer contains several supporting components that provide common or specialized functionality which are used by many different components of any other layer. Some tools are implemented as services and can be called from within other services and GUIs, while other tools represent algorithms or processes that can be embedded in services or (expert) GUIs. Some tools provide their own user interfaces.

3   Considerations about Standards and Information Models

The main purpose of the SIP information model is to support an extension of the common *publish-find-bind* pattern towards re-purposing of data (re-using data in a different context, see [6]). This extended pattern is *publish, find, bind, transform* (figure 2). As users re-use data, they not only include data in their analytics, they often also transform data into a new context or frame of reference.

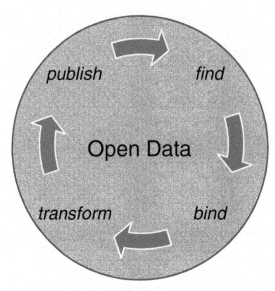

Fig. 2. Extended pattern for re-purposing of data

Although widely adopted information models for the description of data and services exist (e.g. ISO19115 [9] and ISO 19119 [10]) the decision was taken that the information model for the water information platform should not be based on one of these standards alone.

This is especially true for the requirement to consume and possibly to feed-back open data from existing catalogues. This leads to the imperative to support different (meta)data formats and standards which demand a flexible information modelling approach. Accordingly, the commitment to one (meta)data standard or profile may hinder external providers of open data that are compliant with the Standard Information Model to publish their open data to the SIP. Furthermore, support for the documentation of scientific analyses, the description of software (tools), aspects related to re-repurposing open data, inherent features for cataloguing, and other topics that have to be considered at the level of the information model, are only partially covered by existing (meta)data standards.

For instance, the commitment to one and only one (meta)data standard or profile could hinder external providers of open data to publish their open data or results of their studies to the SIP.

The design aim for the SIP was to support different (meta)data formats and standards in order to provide a flexible framework. This demands a flexible information modelling approach. Thus, instead of defining one fixed information model that is based on a selection of particular meta(data) standards or profiles, the information model for the SIP can be tailored to actual needs.

An interesting approach which goes in the same direction has been adopted by the federal German Open Data portal (GovData.de) [11]. GovData's information model is based on a meta-data structure (domain model) developed by the Open Knowledge Foundation for the Comprehensive Knowledge Archive Network (CKAN) [12].

CKAN is a de-facto standard for catalogues of Open Government Data (OGD). The CKAN domain model distinguishes between resources (e.g. data, services and tools) and their actual ("physical") representation (e.g. database, file, service endpoint, etc.). It defines a fixed set of mandatory or optional attributes to describe resources and their representations (title, description, license, contact, etc.) and allows the extension of the model by introducing arbitrary "extra attributes". GovData has made extensive use of this extension mechanism and created its own CKAN-based OGD meta-data schema [13].

Furthermore, the CKAN domain model can be mapped to semantic-web-compatible standards like Dublin Core [14] and the Data Catalogue Vocabulary (DCAT) of the W3C [15]. While at first glance CKAN seems like the ideal the candidate for the information model for the water information platform, one must consider that catalogue functionality, essentially providing access to a collection of datasets, is just one small part of the SIP. Furthermore, the SIP also has to interface with other types of catalogues like OGC Web Catalogue Service (CS-W) [16] to ensure that resources managed by the SIP can also be exposed in CS-W, among others. Nevertheless, the concepts of the CKAN domain model as well as support for meta(data) standards like Dublin Core, ISO 19115, etc., were considered in the design of the information model for the water information platform.

4   Platform Information Model

The design of the SIP information model follows a graduated approach with three different levels of increasing extensibility and flexibility: a *relational model*, *dynamic tag extensions* and *dynamic content extensions*.

The first layer is a relational information model (figure 3) which simultaneously defines the outline of the two subordinate layers. It is implemented as object relational database model of the CIDS platform and supports the core business processes of the SIP. Besides basic classes for resources, their relationships and representations, the model uses several categories from the ISO 19115 meta-data standard to define a set attributes needed to describe those classes. The relational model is also the basis for both the internal and external catalogues of the SIP. The most important classes of the relational model are

- *Resource*
  Resources are the central entity of the information model and the catalogue. They logically describe a dataset, a service, a tool, etc. Resources have a set of core attributes that have been derived from the basic ISO 19915 metadata categories. Furthermore, arbitrary additional metadata can be associated with a resource.
- *Representation*
  Among other roles, the representation defines how to actually access a particular instance of a logical resource. A resource may have different representations. For example, a dataset may be available in different spatial or temporal resolutions or different formats.

- *Relationship*
  This class is used to specify relationships (e.g. "derived from") between resources, e.g. to track and document data transformations and processing (lineage) of resources. The type of the relationship can be identified by a respective tag and arbitrary additional meta-data can be associated with a relationship.

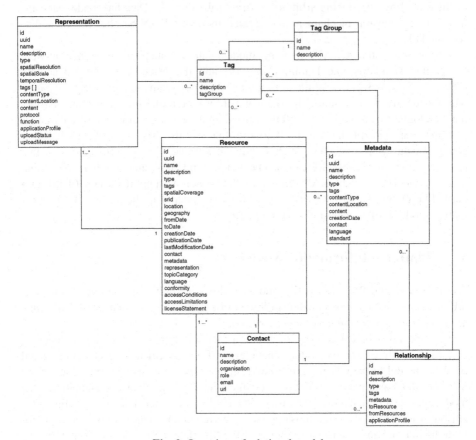

Fig. 3. Overview of relational model

- *Metadata*
  The metadata class represents additional meta-data about a resource or a relationship in a structured or semi-structured format, for example meta-data on data quality.
- *Tag* and *Taggroup*
  Tag and Taggroup represent the dynamic tag extension layer of the Standard Information Model. Taggroups define a general classification for tags and thus can be used to create lists of predefined tags (e.g. code lists).

Dynamic tag extensions provide the possibility to extend the information model for the water information platform without causing changes to the relational model itself. Accordingly, new information-needs of SIP client applications (external catalogues, tools, etc.) can quickly be fulfilled without the need to change the internal database structure of the Meta-Data Repository. Besides the possibility for extending the relational model by introducing new tag groups, tags and tag groups are mainly used to define fixed value lists like standardized topic categories, INSPIRE compliant key-words lists and so on.

Dynamic content extension is a simple mechanism for further extending the information model by either dynamically injecting arbitrary content encoded in plain text into the model or by providing references (URIs) to externally stored content.

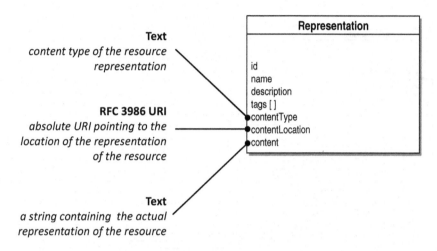

Fig. 4. Dynamic Content Extension

In the relational model, dynamic content extensions are represented by triples of attributes "contentType", "contentLocation" and "content". The "content" attribute contains the actual content encoded in plain text, for example a JSON or XML document. Although this type of content is not directly part of the relational data base model, it can be used to store structured or semi structured information that can be processed by content-aware tools or clients. The attribute "contentLocation" defines the location of the content when the content is not dynamically injected but is referenced. The type of this attribute is a URI (RFC 3986).

The "contentType" attribute refers to standardised Internet Assigned Numbers Authority (IANA) media types (image/png, text/plain,...) as well as to custom industry standard media types (application/x-netcdf, application/gml+xml,...).

While the content type is in general sufficient to identify the data stored in the content field of the representation, a URL that is stored in the contentLocation field may however not directly point to actual data. Instead, the link may lead to an online form for accessing the data (in different formats) or a service endpoint. Therefore additional information about the handling, access and processing of content must be provided.

For this purpose, dynamic tag extensions can be used to introduce new tag groups like "function" and "protocol". "Function" defines for example the function that can be performed when following the "contentLocation" link to the resource representation. Examples of such functions may include "download" which enables the user to directly download the resource representation or "order" where the link value is an URL of a web application that requires user interaction to order/request access to the resource representation.

Classes of the relational model with support for dynamic content extension, and thus containing the three aforementioned attributes, are "Representation" and "Metadata". In the case "Representation", content is generally provided by reference. Thus the "contentLocation" attribute contains a URI that points to actual resource data.

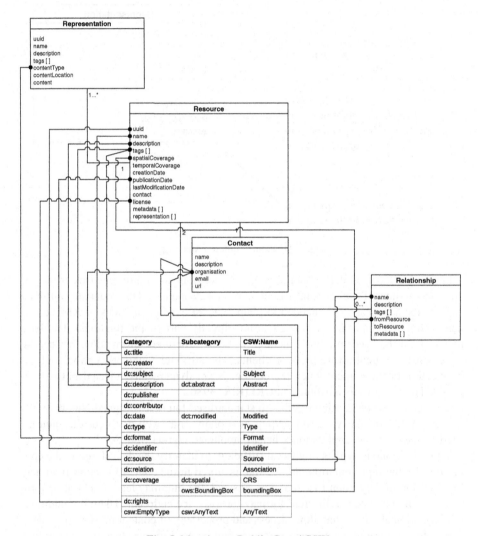

Fig. 5. Mapping to Dublin Core / CSW

5   Mapping to Related Standards

The SIP also has to interface with other types of catalogues like OGC Web Catalogue Service (CSW) or Open Knowledge Foundation for the Comprehensive Knowledge Archive Network (CKAN) catalogues. For this purpose, Published Catalogue Access APIs have been introduced which provide public and standards based access to meta-data stored in the SIP meta data repositories.

Because OGC CSW is one of the most commonly used data catalogues, the open source CSW implementation pyCSW (which is the reference implementation of CSW) has been selected as one realization of a Published Catalogue Access API. Since pyCSW retrieves its complete data from a relational database model, a mapping of the relational model of the SIP to the Dublin Core encoding of CSW Core Metadata schema could also been defined.

This mapping is shown in figure 4. The tables represent an excerpt of the Dublin Core meta-data profile as adopted by the CSW standard. The boxes represent the respective tables of the data model. The connections represent the mapping.

6   Future Work

Since provenance of re-used data and modelling experiments is important, it should be considered also in the relational model of the SIP. Up to now provenance information has not yet been considered systematically in the project. The "Relationship" class can be used to describe the relationship (lineage) between resources and Dynamic content Extensions can be used to represent the actual lineage meta-data.

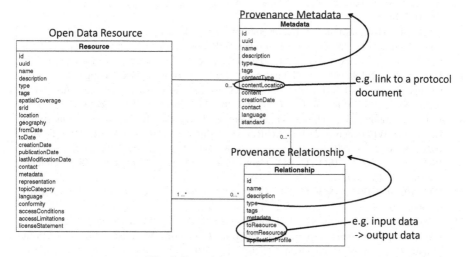

Fig. 6. Potential provenance extension

This simple relationship (fromResource / toResource) can for example be used to describe the I/O of an experiment (model run), a script for repurposing, etc. The type of the relationship can be identified by a respective tag. Interestingly, arbitrary additional meta-data can be associated with a relationship. This is where the actual lineage meta-data, e.g. a link to the protocols of an experiment, or a description could be stored. These considerations are part of future work.

Acknowledgements. The SWITCH-ON project is funded under the European Framework Program FP7 (contract number 603587).

References

1. ECRINS EEA, EEA Catchments and Rivers Network System, ECRINS v1.1, ISSN 1725-2237 (2012), http://www.eea.europa.eu/publications/eea-catchments-and-rivers-network
2. BOM. Austrian Government, Bureau of Meteorology, Improving Water Information Programme, Progress Report, Advances in water information made by the Bureau of Meteorology in 2013 (2013), http://www.bom.gov.au/water/about/publications/document/progress_report2013.pdf
3. CUASHI
4. GEOSS. Group on Earth Observation, GEO-IX, 22-23 November 2012, Report of Data Sharing Working Group, Document 13 (2013), https://www.earthobservations.org
5. Denzer, R., Schlobinski, S., Boot, G., Keppel, F., De Rooij, E.: An information platform fostering re-use of water data. In: International Congress on Environmental Modelling and Software (2014), http://www.iemss.org/sites/iemss2014/proceedings.php ISBN: 978-88-9035-744-2
6. Denzer, R.: Hydroinformatics: Interoperability, standards and governance of water information infrastructures. In: Proceedings of the WIRADA Science Symposium, pp. 120–124 (2012), http://www.csiro.au/WIRADA-Science-Sympsosium-Proceedings
7. Denzer, R., Schlobinski, S., Gidhagen, L., Hell, T.: How to Build Integrated Climate Change Enabled EDSS. In: Hřebíček, J., Schimak, G., Kubásek, M., Rizzoli, A.E., et al. (eds.) ISESS 2013. IFIP AICT, vol. 413, pp. 464–471. Springer, Heidelberg (2013)
8. Hell, T., Kohlhas, E., Schlobinski, S., Denzer, R., Güttler, R.: An information system supporting WFD reporting. In: Hřebíček, J., Schimak, G., Kubásek, M., Rizzoli, A.E. (eds.) ISESS 2013. IFIP AICT, vol. 413, pp. 403–413. Springer, Heidelberg (2013)
9. ISO 19115 (2002), ISO/TC 211 Geographic information/Geomatics. ISO reference number: 19115 (2002)
10. ISO 19119 (2007), ISO/TC 211 Geographic information/Geomatics. ISO reference number: 19119 (2007)
11. Marienfeld, F., Schieferdecker, I., Lapi, E., Tcholtchev, N.: Metadata aggregation at GovData.de - An experience report, Association for Computing Machinery. In: ACM 9th International Symposium on Open Collaboration 2013, Proceedings, Hong Kong, China, August 5-7, pp. 638-6. WikiSym + Opensym (2013)

12. CKAN, Comprehensive Knowledge Archive Network, CKAN Domain Model, `http://docs.ckan.org/en/ckan-1.8/domain-model.html`
13. OGD-METADATA, Fraunhofer FOKUS, Schema and documentation to be used by the German Open Data Portal, `https://github.com/fraunhoferfokus/ogd-metadata`
14. Dublin Core Metadata Initiative, `http://dublincore.org/`
15. Maali, F., Erickson, J., Archer, P.: Data Catalog Vocabulary (DCAT), World Wide Web Consortium (W3C), W3C Recommendation 16 January 2014, `http://www.w3.org/TR/vocab-dcat/`
16. Nebert, D., Whiteside, A., Vretanos, P. (eds.): OpenGIS® Catalog Services Specification, Version 2.0.2, OGC 07-006r1, Open GIS Consortium Inc. 218 p. (2007)

Towards Linked Data Conventions for Delivery of Environmental Data Using netCDF

Jonathan Yu[1], Nicholas J. Car[1], Adam Leadbetter[2], Bruce A. Simons[1],
and Simon J.D. Cox [1]

[1]Land and Water Flagship: CSIRO, Highett and Dutton Park Labs, Australia
[2]British Oceanographic Data Centre, Liverpool, United Kingdom
{jonathan.yu,nicholas.car,bruce.simons,simon.cox}@csiro.au,
alead@bodc.ac.uk

Abstract. netCDF is a well-known and widely used format to exchange array-oriented scientific data such as grids and time-series. We describe a new convention for encoding netCDF based on Linked Data principles called netCDF-LD. netCDF-LD allows metadata elements, given as string values in current netCDF files, to be given as Linked Data objects. netCDF-LD allows precise semantics to be used for elements and expands the type options beyond lists of controlled terms. Using Uniform Resource Identifiers (URIs) for elements allows them to refer to other Linked Data resources for their type and descriptions. This enables improved data discovery through a generic mechanism for element type identification and adds element type expandability to new Linked Data resources as they become available. By following patterns already established for extending existing formats, netCDF-LD applications can take advantage of existing software for processing Linked Data and supporting more effective data discovery and integration across systems.

Keywords: netCDF, linked data, data discovery, environmental data.

1   Introduction

Scientific data is increasingly being made available from environmental agencies, universities, research organisations and government departments via web services. There is, however, a need for better integration and discoverability across datasets from the various services. The Network Common Data Form (netCDF) is a suite of software libraries and a data format for producing array-oriented scientific data, which is commonly used to exchange environmental data organized as images, grids and time-series[1]. netCDF has been developed and maintained by Unidata, which is part of the University Corporation for Atmospheric Research (UCAR) funded by the United States National Science Foundation. The Open Geospatial Consortium (OGC) has adopted netCDF and formalized it as an implementation standard to support encoding of geospatial information to

---

[1] http://www.unidata.ucar.edu/software/netcdf

R. Denzer et al. (Eds.): ISESS 2015, IFIP AICT 448, pp. 102–112, 2015.
© IFIP International Federation for Information Processing 2015

communicate and store multi-dimensional data[2]. netCDF datasets are typically published through service interfaces using Thematic Real-time Environmental Distributed Data Services (THREDDS), which allows users to find and access the data, and use them without necessarily downloading the entire file. The THREDDS Data Server (TDS) is a web service to access catalogues, metadata and data, and allows sub-sampling of the data using OpenDAP, OGC Web Coverage Service (WCS), OGC Web Map Service (WMS), and netCDF subset service interfaces. The netCDF format is not proprietary and THREDDS and TDS have been made available online at the Unidata website and via their GitHub repository (https://github.com/Unidata/thredds). As such, this technology stack has been widely used to publish large datasets and provide the ability to efficiently query subsets of the data.

netCDF files are designed to be 'self-contained', through headers that describe the structure and content of the dataset. Standardization is based on a community 'convention' for a set of vocabulary names, with the Climate and Forecasting (CF) conventions [1] most widely known. However, these names are only text values, and often conflate various concerns. These pose a key challenge in providing automatic semantic mediation between datasets to compare equivalent parameters by its conceptual meaning. A number of controlled vocabularies and ontologies currently enable the definition, publication and access of these semantics on the web [2–6], however, there is no facility in the netCDF headers to link to and reference externally defined terms and semantics. Although, the CF community and other communities publish standard names, the publishing of these names can be a lengthy process involving review of new proposed names by the respective committee, and some names may be duplicated and have different meaning or be incomplete [7]. Figure 1 gives an example of the current practice where applications request data using multiple names that may refer to the same concept or set of vocabulary terms.

The World Wide Web Consortium (W3C) has developed principles for publishing data on the Web. Known as "Linked Data" [8], the primary feature is the use of HTTP Uniform Resource Identifiers (URIs) to link between any information resources (data or metadata), including non-hypertext formats, so that more information can be discovered. The Linked Data principles have stimulated the design of a lightweight extension to JSON [9] which is a commonly-used data format in browser applications. JSON-LD (for "Linked Data") annotates JSON data with URIs, allowing JSON data to be interpreted as Linked Data with minimal additions to the original structure. The JSON-LD pattern has now been proposed for annotation of tabular data formatted as Comma-Separated-Values or similar in the W3C activity 'CSV on the Web'[10].

Thus, extending netCDF by borrowing and adopting the *-LD pattern from JSON-LD and 'CSV on the Web' is a natural extension in order to link and reference existing controlled vocabularies and terms via the Semantic Web. In this paper, we describe initial work in defining netCDF-LD conventions, which allow netCDF to be interpreted as Linked Data with non-intrusive annotations. The netCDF-LD conventions allow the use of URIs to define the identity of a netCDF file, attribute names and attribute values. The aim is to enhance existing netCDF datasets with metadata that

---

[2] http://www.opengeospatial.org/standards/netcdf

J. Yu et al.

links to standardized vocabulary terms and to express precise semantics about the data so that it can be better discovered, integrated and used. By following patterns already established for extending existing formats, netCDF-LD applications will be able to take advantage of existing software for processing Linked Data; existing controlled vocabularies describing environmental domains published as Linked Data; and allow data, such as environmental data, to be more easily discovered, interpreted and integrated into applications, such as environmental models (see Fig. 2 for an example).

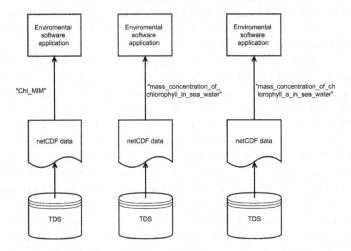

Fig. 1. Current practice of applications consuming netCDF data via TDS services

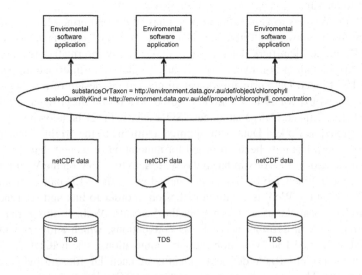

Fig. 2. Proposed data integration example consuming netCDF-LD

2   Linked Data and JSON-LD

Linked Data is a methodology for publishing data and metadata in a structured format so that links may be created and exploited between objects. The key enabling components are URIs, HTTP, the Resource Description Framework (RDF) and the SPARQL Protocol and RDF Query Language (SPARQL) [8]. RDF is the component which provides a data model for describing subject and their relationships to other objects via predicates thus forming 'triples'. RDF data is encoded in a number of serializations including RDF/XML, N-Triples, Turtle, and RDF/JSON. RDF data can be loaded into repositories called 'triple stores' and queried using the SPARQL language. Tooling has also been developed to exploit Linked Data as RDF such as Linked Data browsers and mashups, semantic search engines, and data extraction tools. To date, there are around 700 million triples across about 1,800 vocabularies discoverable in publicly available linked data services [11].

2.1   JSON-LD

JSON-LD is a W3C recommendation and is a format that adds URIs to JSON data, allowing JSON data to be interpreted as Linked Data by supporting links from JSON data to other data [12]. JSON-LD provides an interchange language for libraries utilizing JSON, such as client applications, web services, and NoSQL or unstructured databases (e.g. *CouchDB* and *MongoDB*).

```
{
    "@id": "http://foo.bar/linked_netCDF_example",
    "@type": [
        "http://www.w3.org/ns/prov#Entity",
        "http://www.w3.org/ns/dcat#Dataset"
    ],
    "http://data.ba.gov.au/def/ba#dataOwner": [
        {"@id":
"http://data.ba.gov.au/id/person/car587"}
    ],
    "http://purl.org/dc/elements/1.1/created": [
    {"@type": "http://www.w3.org/2001/XMLSchema#dateTime",
        "@value": "2014-10-15T23:23:25+11:00"}
    ],
    "http://purl.org/dc/elements/1.1/title": [
        {"@value": "Victorian Biodiversity Atlas"}
    ]
}
```

Fig. 3. A JSON-LD object with ID ("@id") of http://data.ba.gov.au/dataset/f4107720 and type ("@type") http://www.w3.org/ns/prov#Entity & http://www.w3.org/ns/dcat#Dataset, each defined at their URIs. Other properties ("created", "title", "dataOwner") defined in well-known vocabularies such as Dublin Core or in a project-specific vocabulary.

JSON-LD introduces:

- URI identifiers for JSON objects
- contexts or namespaces to disambiguate keywords in JSON documents
- a linking mechanism
- a way to associate datatypes with values such as dates and times
- a way to express one or more graphs in a single document

Tooling has been developed for reading JSON-LD data and creating an RDF graph, as well as serializing RDF data into JSON-LD, for example the *rdfLib-jsonld* plugin for Python, *JSONLD-JAVA*, and *PHP-JSON-LD*. JSON-LD contributes to the design of other microformats, such as the extension of GeoJSON with JSON-LD, called *GeoJSON-LD*.

The precedent of JSON-LD is being followed in the W3C 'CSV on the Web' [10] project, another effort to enrich a well-known format with more rigorous definitions and semantics. 'CSV on the Web' directly reuses key features of JSON-LD to allow terms to be assigned URIs and values bound to datatypes.

3   netCDF-LD

Given this uptake and prior work, we propose to apply the same approach for netCDF, to be called netCDF-LD. In this section we outline the conventions for netCDF-LD, based on the general approach from JSON-LD, and present examples of netCDF-LD encodings and the interpreted Linked Data content. The intention is that interpreted Linked Data content encoded as RDF could be used to support richer queries for data aggregation and query.

3.1   netCDF Conventions

netCDF-LD uses the "context" array concept from JSON-LD and maps it onto global variables within the NetCDF file. This allows variable names within the netCDF file to be used as shorthand for the URI of an external (Linked Data) resource, which should provide details of the variable definition. A reserved global variable, "context-id", assigns a URI to the netCDF file itself. The suffixes "_a" and "_ref" are reserved for the assignment of an RDF class and a URI to any variable level attribute within a netCDF file. The RDF datatype may be inferred from the declaration of the datatype in the netCDF file. The "_lang" variable level suffix is reserved for occasions when a human readable language is required to be assigned to an attribute or data value.

In the following sections, the reserved global attribute names and variable level suffixes are defined, and example encodings of a generic netCDF file and a Climate and Forecast (CF) metadata conventions compliant netCDF file are shown.

The "context-" Global Attributes.

The JSON-LD "@context" array is modelled in netCDF-LD as a series of global attributes with the "context-" prefix. netCDF does not allow the use of the "@" symbol as the opening character of an attribute name, and the "_" character is reserved for use by system attributes only.

Boilerplate code of three (with an optional fourth) "context-x" global attributes is recommended, and as many more as necessary may be added (see Fig. 4). Optionally, the rdf:datatype property may be declared as shown below in Fig. 5. Finally, a generic vocabulary from which all attribute URIs in the netCDF-LD file are used may be assigned as shown below in Fig. 6. Any given attribute name to be used on variables may be assigned a URI as shown below in Fig. 7.

```
:context-id = "http://foo.bar/baz";
:context-a = "http://www.w3.org/1999/02
                    /22-rdf-syntax-ns#type";
:context-ref = "http://www.w3.org/1999/02
                    /22-rdf-syntax-ns#resource";
```

Fig. 4. Boilerplate code for netCDF-LD using Common Data form Language (CDL) syntax. CDL provides a human readable text respresentation of netCDF data.

```
:context-datatype = "http://www.w3.org/1999/02
                    /22-rdf-syntax-ns#datatype";
```

Fig. 5. Declaration of the datatype in the boilerplate code section for netCDF-LD

```
:context-vocab = "http://def.seegrid.csiro.au
                /isotc211/iso19156/2011/observation#";
```

Fig. 6. Declaration of default vocabulary in the context block for netCDF-LD

```
:context-attribute_ref = "http://bar.foo/baz";
```

Fig. 7. Declaration of attribute URI reference in netCDF-LD

Assigning URIs to Variable Level Attributes

A netCDF variable may be defined by a URI in netCDF-LD by adding a "ref" attribute with a value equal to the URI.

```
variable:ref= "http://vocab.nerc.ac.uk
                /collection/P07/current/CFSN0600/";
```

The values of variable level attributes may be defined by URIs thus:

```
variable:unit = "Meters";
variable:unit_ref = " http://qudt.org/vocab
                                    /unit#Meter";
```

3.2   Example Encodings and Resulting RDF Graphs

The following example encodes the netCDF file example from http://www.unidata.ucar.edu/software/netcdf/docs/CDL.html using the netCDF-LD conventions. In the example, the dimensions and variables blocks near the start of the file define the respective dimensions and variables contained in the metadata headers. The next block provides the global attributes to describe boilerplate content for the contexts of the attributes as described in the previous section. LD attributes are specified next for the listed variables, e.g. lat, lon, time, and z, each having the appropriate URI references for its value. For example, 'lat:ref' allows the value to be bound to the URI 'http://vocab.nerc.ac.uk/collection/P07/current/CFSN0600/'. This is then used as the subject for the statements bound to the variable 'lat', so that the other attributes are related objects, e.g. its units, its type, and the data values. Figure 9 shows the RDF encoding from the netCDF-LD example where the URI values and data values are mapped.

```
netcdf foo {// Example netCDF specification in CDL
  dimensions:
      lat = 10, lon = 5, time = unlimited;
  variables:
      int    lat(lat), lon(lon), time(time);
      float  z(time,lat,lon), t(time,lat,lon);
      double p(time,lat,lon);
      int    rh(time,lat,lon);

  // Global attributes
  :context-id = "http://foo.bar/linked_netCDF_example";
  :context-units = "http://qudt.org/1.1/schema/qudt#unit";
  :context-ref = "http://www.w3.org/1999/02/22-rdf-syntax-ns
                                            #resource";
  :context-quantityKind = "http://environment.data.gov.au/def
                                       /op#ScaledQuantityKind";
  :context-dcPartOf = "http://purl.org/dc/terms/isPartOf";
  :context-a = "http://www.w3.org/1999/02/22-rdf-syntax-ns#type";
  :Conventions = "LD-1.0";

  lat:ref = "http://vocab.nerc.ac.uk/collection/P07/current
                                            /CFSN0600/";
  lat:units = "degrees_north";
  lat:units_ref = "http://qudt.org/vocab/unit#DegreeAngle";
  lat:a = "http://environment.data.gov.au/def/op#ScaledQuantityKind";
  lat:dcPartOf = "http://foo.bar/linked_netCDF_example";
  lat:datalink = "http://www.w3.org/1999/02/22-rdf-syntax-ns#value";
```

```
lon:ref = "http://vocab.nerc.ac.uk/collection/P07/current
                                          /CFSN0554/";
lon:units = "degrees_east";
lon:units_ref = "http://qudt.org/vocab/unit#DegreeAngle";
lon:a = "http://environment.data.gov.au/def/op#ScaledQuantityKind";
lon:dcPartOf = "http://foo.bar/linked_netCDF_example";
lon:datalink = "http://www.w3.org/1999/02/22-rdf-syntax-ns#value";


time:units = "seconds";
time:units_ref = "http://qudt.org/vocab/unit#SecondTime";
time:a = "http://environment.data.gov.au/def/op#ScaledQuantityKind";
time:dcPartOf = "http://foo.bar/linked_netCDF_example";


z:units = "meters";
z:units_ref = "http://qudt.org/vocab/unit#Meter";
z:a = "http://environment.data.gov.au/def/op#quantityKind";
z:dcPartOf = "http://foo.bar/linked_netCDF_example";
z:valid_range = 0., 5000.;


p:_FillValue = -9999.;


rh:_FillValue = -1;


data:
   lat   = 0, 10, 20, 30, 40, 50, 60, 70, 80, 90;
   lon   = -140, -118, -96, -84, -52; }
```

Fig. 8. Example netCDF-LD encoding

```
@prefix unit: <http://qudt.org/vocab/unit#> .
@prefix qudt: <http://qudt.org/1.1/schema/qudt#> .
@prefix op: <http://environment.data.gov.au/def/op#> .
@prefix rdf: <http://www.w3.org/1999/02/22-rdf-syntax-ns#> .
@prefix dcterms: <http://purl.org/dc/terms/> .
@prefix xsd: <http://www.w3.org/2001/XMLSchema#> .


<http://vocab.nerc.ac.uk/collection/P07/current/CFSN0600/>
   a op:ScaledQuantityKind;
   qudt:unit unit:DegreeAngle;
   dcterms:isPartOf <http://foo.bar/linked_netCDF_example>;
   rdf:value
      "{0, 10, 20, 30, 40, 50, 60, 70, 80, 90}"^^xsd:integer .


<http://vocab.nerc.ac.uk/collection/P07/current/CFSN0554/>
```

```
    qudt:unit unit:DegreeAngle;
    a op:ScaledQuantityKind;
    dcterms:isPartOf <http://foo.bar/linked_netCDF_example>;
    rdf:value "{-140, -118, -96, -84, -52}"^^xsd:integer.

_:z qudt:unit unit:Meter;
    a op:ScaledQuantityKind;
    dcterms:isPartOf <http://foo.bar/linked_netCDF_example>.

_:time qudt:unit unit:SecondTime;
    a op:ScaledQuantityKind;
    dcterms:isPartOf    <http://foo.bar/linked_netCDF_example> .
```

Fig. 9. RDF description based on example netCDF-LD metadata

4   Discussion and Related Work

The use of Linked Data within netCDF headers makes the headers less readable by humans but far more powerful for machine interpretation. Tools able to understand and process Linked Data can "follow their nose" in order to collect more information about resources as needed. When encountering a header or other term not understood directly, such as a new variable type, a Linked Data tool will be able to dereference its type URI and obtain further metadata about that variable. With current string-based controlled terms, if a variable is not understood it is unusable. The issue of reduced human readability can, we believe, be bypassed with client tooling. Commonly used netCDF tools such as Python's *ncdump* program can easily be extended to render data from a netCDF-LD file as readable to humans as the headers from a regular netCDF file.

The inverse may not be true: it may not be possible to convert existing netCDF files into Linked Data files with as rich semantics as a netCDF-LD file would offer with new tooling. Such tools would need to contain all of the metadata about string-based terms used in current netCDF files locally in order to reference it when needed – there is no equivalent to the "follow-your-nose" procedure for string values. This would be very hard to implement as instances of such a tool would need to be kept up-to-date with all possible netCDF terms metadata in order to be relevant. This precludes tools such as netCDF Markup Language (NcML) generators.[3]

netCDF-LD adapts related work on decorating netCDF variable names with URIs. Metadata linkages in netCDF were presented by [13]. In netCDF-U [14], the *:ref* and *:rel* suffixes are used to link netCDF variable declarations with URIs, but only relate specifically to concepts of uncertainty. In [15], a similar pattern is used to append variable declarations to link to ontology classes in the Observable Property ontology and concepts defined in the Water Quality vocabulary. However, these are limited to *scaledQuantityKind_id*, *unit_id*, *substanceOrTaxon_id*, *procedure_id*, and *medium_id*.

---

[3] See http://www.unidata.ucar.edu/software/thredds/current/ netcdf-java/ncml/ for a description of the NcML and links to generators.

netCDF-LD adapts these ideas for a generic mechanism for variable annotation and aligns it with current Linked Data best practice from JSON-LD. The approach used in netCDF-LD allows the whole netCDF metadata header to be translated into RDF as presented in this paper, compared with the other approaches which only map partial aspects of the netCDF metadata header.

Translating netCDF headers into RDF allows tooling to be developed to support data discovery and dataset aggregation. Figure 10 shows how the RDF descriptions from the netCDF-LD metadata headers can be harvested into a data brokering component. The data brokering component essentially would provide automated semantic mediation between netCDF datasets. This would allow applications or end users to browse or search over the available datasets based on the identifiers of the variables. An example query could be search for all datasets with 'chlorophyll concentration'.

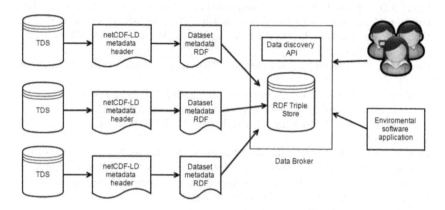

Fig. 10. Using netCDF-LD to support data discovery and dataset aggregation via a data broker

5   Conclusion and Future Work

In this paper, we have proposed initial work towards a netCDF-LD specification which applies principles from the *-LD pattern to netCDF data. The intention of netCDF-LD is to allow it to be interpreted as Linked Data with non-intrusive annotations to standard netCDF encodings. netCDF-LD conventions were presented which aim to be consistent with Linked Data design principles, allowing the use of URIs to define the identity of a netCDF file, its attribute names and the attribute values. These conventions allow existing netCDF datasets to be enhanced with structured metadata conventions for linking to standardized vocabulary terms. This allows binding to precise semantic descriptions and vocabularies which enables netCDF data exposed via THREDDS to be better discovered, integrated and used. Also by following patterns already established for extending existing formats, netCDF-LD applications can take advantage of existing semantic web tooling for handling querying and reasoning over RDF triples translated from netCDF-LD data.

How large volumes of data is to be encoded in netCDF-LD files has not been explored. The direct serialization of array data as JSON arrays, as given in **Fig. 6**, is unlikely to be attractive to netCDF with large data volumes (potentially much greater than 2GB for netCDF4) given its verbosity compared with binary data arrays. Future work will see us test various methods for data encoding while still retaining the same netCDF-LD approach to header metadata encoding. Semantic data formats such as WaterML present a number of options that may be used.

References

1. Eaton, B., Gregory, J., Drach, B., Taylor, K., Hankin, S.: NetCDF Climate and Forecast (CF) Metadata Conventions (2011)
2. Cox, S.J.D., Simons, B.A., Yu, J.: A harmonized vocabulary for water quality. In: 11th International Conference on Hydroinformatics (HIC), IWA Publishing, New York (2014)
3. Cox, S., Yu, J., Rankine, T.: SISSVoc: A Linked Data API for access to SKOS vocabularies. Semant. Web (2014)
4. Caracciolo, C., Stellato, A., Morshed, A.: The agrovoc linked dataset. Semanit. Web (2013)
5. Leadbetter, A., Lowry, R.K., Clements, O.: The NERC Vocabulary Server: Version 2.0. EGU General Assembly, pp. 29–43. Copernicus, Vienna, Austria (2012)
6. Summers, E., Isaac, A., Redding, C., Krech, D.: LCSH, SKOS and Linked Data. CoRR. abs/0805.2 (2008)
7. Peckham, S.D.: The CSDMS Standard Names: Cross-Domain Naming Conventions for Describing Process Models, Data Sets and Their Associated Variables. In: Ames, D.P., Quinn, N.W.T., Rizzol, A.E. (eds.) International Environmental Modelling and Software Society (iEMSs), San Diego, California, USA (2014)
8. Berners-Lee, T.: Linked Data - Design Issues
9. Crockford, D.: The application/json Media Type for JavaScript Object Notation (JSON) (2006)
10. Herman, I., Archer, P.: CSV on the Web Working Group Charter (2013), http://www.w3.org/2013/05/lcsv-charter
11. LODStats, http://stats.lod2.eu
12. Sporny, M., Kellogg, G., Lanthaler, M.: JSON-LD 1.0 -A JSON-based Serialization for Linked Data, http://www.w3.org/TR/2013/CR-json-ld-20130910/
13. Palmer, D.: WaterML 2.0 – Timeseries – NetCDF Discussion Paper (2012)
14. Bigagli, L., Nativi, S.: NetCDF Uncertainty Conventions (NetCDF-U) 1.0 (2011)
15. Yu, J., Simons, B.A., Car, N., Cox, S.J.D.: Enhancing water quality data service discovery and access using standard vocabularies. In: 11th International Conference on Hydroinformatics (HIC). IWA Publishing, New York (2014)

Information Technology and Solid Residue Management: A Case of Study Using Freeware and Social Networks

José Tarcísio Franco de Camargo[1], Estéfano Vizconde Veraszto[2],
Adriano Aparecido Lopes[3], and Tainá Ângela Vedovello Bimbati[3]

[1]Regional University Center of Espirito Santo do Pinhal, Sao Paulo, Brazil
jtfc@bol.com.br
[2]Federal University of São Carlos, Araras, Sao Paulo, Brazil
estefanovv@cca.ufscar.br
[3]Municipal Faculty "Professor Franco Montoro", Mogi Guaçu, Sao Paulo, Brazil
adrianoalopes2008@yahoo.com.br, tavbimbati@gmail.com

Abstract. Separation, collection, processing and disposal of waste considered recyclable are currently one of the greatest challenges of human beings in their quest for sustainability. With consumption levels in ever-higher levels, the reutilization of recyclable waste, which would likely target the garbage, becomes an obligation of society as a whole. Thus, addressing in an appropriate manner the issue of selective collection of recyclable materials can contribute to the solution of several problems associated with it – mostly under the views of environmental, social and economic ways. This way, the Project iCARE (Instrumentation for the Assisted Collection of Recyclable Waste) is based on an experiment that aims to provide computational tools that could significantly contribute to the issue of the reuse of solid recyclable waste. Specifically, the iCARE software aims to contribute to the integration between donors and collectors of recyclable materials, establishing a communication channel where ordinary people or companies may announce the availability of recyclables to collectors. These, in turn, can check through the same software the availability of certain wastes, coming to contact consumers for possible collection and subsequently forward the waste to processing companies. This software also offers a "routing module", which allows the collector to establish an optimized collection route according to certain criteria. All software developed in iCARE's framework must provide a user friendly interface, making its use very simple. iCARE is a project of free use and also a social tool, which seeks to contribute to the solution of the complex problem of disposal of recyclable waste.

Keywords: Waste disposal, recycling, computational tools, sustainability.

1 Introduction

Nowadays, there is a consensus that the sustainability of life on the planet necessarily passes by the rational use of the limited resources available. The human being realized that the unbridled consumption inevitably will lead to a depletion of the natural sources. Thus, separation, collection, processing and disposal of waste considered recyclable are,

R. Denzer et al. (Eds.): ISESS 2015, IFIP AICT 448, pp. 113–120, 2015.
© IFIP International Federation for Information Processing 2015

currently, one of the great challenges of humanity in the quest of sustainability. With high levels of consumption, the reutilization of recyclable waste, which would likely target the landfills, has become an obligation of society as a whole [1-3].

In this way, the planning and implementation of programs dedicated to the selective collection of recyclable materials can contribute to the solution of various environmental, social and economic problems. Under the economic point of view, the selective collection effectively promotes the solution of some problems relevant to society, considering that discarded materials can go back to the cycle of consumption, thus reducing the use of natural resources in the manufacture of new products.

Under the environmental point of view, the reuse and recycling of materials would probably promote direct impact on the preservation of natural resources, conserving raw materials, water and energy in production processes and, consequently, a decrease in the amount of trash sent to landfills as well as its useful life [2]. In the social aspect, the selective collection has positive impact on socioeconomic conditions of recyclable material collectors, who are the first actors in the selective collection and recycling chain.

In this context, this work presents an experiment carried out in a city in Sao Paulo State, Brazil. The work that is being carried out includes the creation of computational tools which intend to support the process of selective collection of recyclable materials. At first, a software called "iCARE bulletin board" was developed, which aims to promote the integration between "consumers" (recyclable waste producers) and "pickers" (responsible for the collection and disposal of waste). The following section presents the fundamentals of this project within the region where it is developed.

2   Science, Technology and the Environmental Issue

Having the Club of Rome as an important delegate, environmentalists from the decades of 1960 and 1970 gave emphasis that world growth was limited due to accelerated population increase, to deficiency of agricultural production (aggravating to hunger), the exhaustion of natural resources, the destruction of the environment and the increase in global industrial production. This vision, transparent in the work of Meadows [4,5] had a remarkable accession in the postwar period, with questions about the side effects of technological development on society and economy. The dangers brought by pollution and by widespread environmental degradation were key factors for a resumption of the Malthusian paradigm, whose central idea stressed that the saturation of the world growth would be in a hundred years [6,7]. From the years 1970, began a series of investments in clean technologies or alternatives in various countries in response to the demands of the environmental movement. In the decades of 1980 and 1990 the debate on environmental issues was expanded and relations with the technology got new directions. The Bariloche Group, along with other world references, was pointing out that the economic system has self-regulatory mechanisms that allow modification or reversal of patterns before the system reaches the point of catastrophe [3,8]. In the decade of 1980, sustainable development was defined and studies aimed at reducing poverty and alleviating social problems were initiated [1].

However, it was only in early 1990 that the concepts of previous years have been implemented. The concept of the role of technology on environmental issues has changed, enabling the belief that it is possible to recover degraded areas and increase the efficiency of natural resources in parallel with the increase of productivity. The technology thus is seen not as an external factor, but as an integral element of the decision-making processes. The development of S&T adapted to environmental issues then must know how to handle these challenges and dilemmas by internalizing the environmental variable in the process of innovation and seeking efficiency and quality in the development of new products, processes and/or services. (Passing not only by raising awareness about environmental issues, but also considering legal and economic aspects) [2,9,10]. In view of the foregoing, we can establish relationships with other works [11,12] to point out that both the technology and social organization can be managed and improved in order to provide a new era of economic growth, so that humanity will be able to make sustainable development possible.

Thus, environmental, scientific and technological developments are not separate challenges. Making the environmental issue the record on political agendas is an item of great importance with regard to the economy and resources [11-13].

The development of the S&T front of environmental issues can become more efficient if supported by a strong and articulate public policy. It is also necessary to create and maintain mechanisms to link research and development in the sectors of production to their demands, as well as the creation of new energy sources and new materials, in order to seek solutions to social problems [7,9,14].

It is in this sense that the work proposed here is developed. Thus, the aim of this paper is to contribute to sustainability through methods and techniques that promote technological innovation and social inclusion. These are the points that will be presented in the sequence.

2.1   A Local Context to the Issue of Waste Recycling

The steps in the process of collection and disposal of recyclable waste can be viewed in a simplified way, as follows:

1. **Separation:** this is the step where each citizen must separate, from non-reusable waste, those materials which can be recycled. This is a step based on education and awareness of people about the need to reuse materials that can go back to the cycle of consumption.
2. **Collection and Disposal:** this step has a "logistic profile", since it involves several costs for those that are collecting reusable materials. Collect which materials? Which is the minimum amount viable for collecting? How to collect and give destination? These are some of the main questions to be considered at this stage.
3. **Processing:** as well as the collection and disposal stages, this one can also be seen as a "business", where a particular company may have focused on the reuse of recyclable waste and its subsequent commercialization. This is the step of the recycle chain that is more distant from "ordinary people", considering that here the "main actor" is a businessman.

In this chain, the "picker" (or "collector") is the leading actor in the production of recycled materials, making approximately 80% of all the work, collecting an average of 600 kg of materials per day [15].

The project dealt with in this paper was born in the city of Mogi Guaçu, Sao Paulo State, Brazil. It is a medium-sized town, with an expanding industrial pole and a large number of companies in the service sector. This city has possessed, approximately fifty years ago, an economy almost entirely based on agriculture, and experienced an intense population expansion on the last forty years, when the population jumped from about 30,000 to 130,000 inhabitants. This expansion was due mainly to the migration of people from other states of the country, searching for new jobs, which actually ended up experiencing social exclusion. As a consequence, the population of recyclable materials collectors came to be composed mostly by migrants who come from other regions to work in the rural area and ended up facing unemployment. Excluded from school for avoidance or lack of access, they are also excluded from the labour market and therefore of society. To escape from hunger, these people found the possibility to work in the city from collecting discarded materials.

Regarding the problem of the garbage generated and processed in the city, according to data presented by the Secretary of Municipal Services, the rate of garbage collection in the city is around 99%. Among the total municipal waste generation, the share of production of household garbage by the population is approximately 105 tons/day, of which 32% are recyclable materials, 52% are organic and 16% are considered waste.

In this scenario, a matter that can be displayed is: how to integrate consumers, who generate such amount of potentially recyclable material (that is currently going to junk), and collectors, who while may give the appropriate disposal waste can also improve their source of income? It is in this scope that iCARE presents itself, as a technological arm that aims to generate computational tools that will contribute to the solution of socio-economic and environmental issues, among them the problem of proper collection and disposal of recyclable materials.

3   Computational Tools to Support Selective Collection

Although described in a simplified way in this paper, the complexity of the presented chain induces specialization from "actors" involved in the same. The proposal here introduced intends to contribute significantly to the integration of the actors responsible for the second step: consumers who generate recyclable waste and pickers who dispose of these materials.

Currently, with the expansion of the internet connection services, a considerable part of the population has access to the World Wide Web in their own homes, and among the most common habits of this population, is the communication through social networks. These new mechanisms of communication have promoted the exchange of messages and information in a manner so intense that its potential currently transcends social barriers. Even the lowest economic classes of the population have access to cheap portable devices which allow access to all these networks.

In this scenario, the software created under this project aims to contribute to the integration of "producers" and "pickers", establishing a communication channel where ordinary people or companies may announce the availability of recyclables to possible collectors. These, in turn, can check via software the availability of certain wastes, contact consumers for collection and subsequently forward the waste to processing companies.

In order to facilitate the collection and disposal of waste collected, this software also offers a "routing module", which allows the collector to establish an optimized collection of routes, according to certain criteria (distance and time of travel, for instance).

This software was built to provide a "friendly" interface, making its use very simple. In its current stage, the only preconditions for this software to be used are a "JAVA ready" device and an internet connection for access to data.

This software aims as well to keep a democratic and decentralized spirit. Democratic in the sense that its use and sharing is free for anyone, either to announce or to collect recyclable or reusable materials; and decentralized because any community can implement its own network, answering specifically the subject of a particular region.

4   Introducing iCare

As mentioned previously, iCARE means "Instrumentation for the Assisted Collection of Recyclable Waste". This software provides a tool for the communication between donors and collectors of recyclable materials, in this case, a Java application that is a virtual "bulletin board", through which users can make and schedule waste collections, and a database, which will store data about recyclable materials offered for disposal. Any community may set up its own database in a local server, providing data to the local citizens or companies.

To provide data, a local server must run "Apache Derby", an open source RDBMS that is based on Java technology and SQL, which will manage the database where all information will be stored. This database will serve users through a "bulletin board", written in Java, which will promote the interaction among users.

Currently, this bulletin board was built in order to provide the following functionality for its users:

- an "interface for sending messages", through which an user can offer the donation of materials that can be recycled;
- an "interface for receiving messages", through which an user can check the materials available for collection and contact the respective donors to this schedule;
- a "route generator interface", through which a collector can establish a collection of routes through certain criteria.

The interface for sending messages is presented in Figure 1.

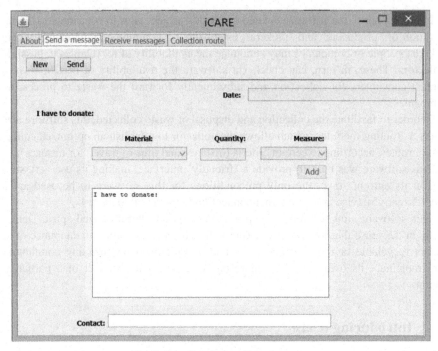

Fig. 1. Interface for sending messages

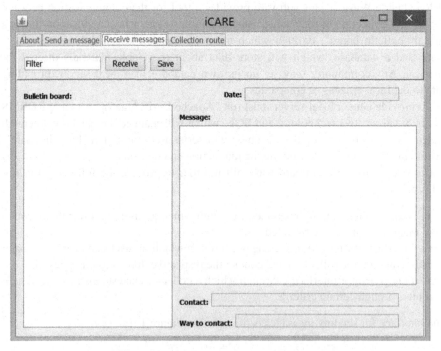

Fig. 2. The interface for receiving messages

Through this feature, the user can send to the Bulletin Board a list of recyclable materials that would be available for collection. The user can select from a list the materials that he wants to make available, indicating the available quantity. The user can insert more than one type of material for target.

The interface for receiving messages is shown in Figure 2.

The feature "Receive Message", allows collectors to receive these messages on their devices and, in this way, select the materials that interest them and contact the respective disposers to schedule a pickup.

The last feature available is the interface for creating collection routes, where is possible to schedule the gathering of recyclable materials. The problem then becomes the definition of the best way to carry out the collection and disposal of materials. The interface for creating routes allows the user to enter multiple addresses for collection and an optimized route will be calculated. This feature is based on Google Maps Java-script API. Figure 3 presents a picture of the interface for calculating routes.

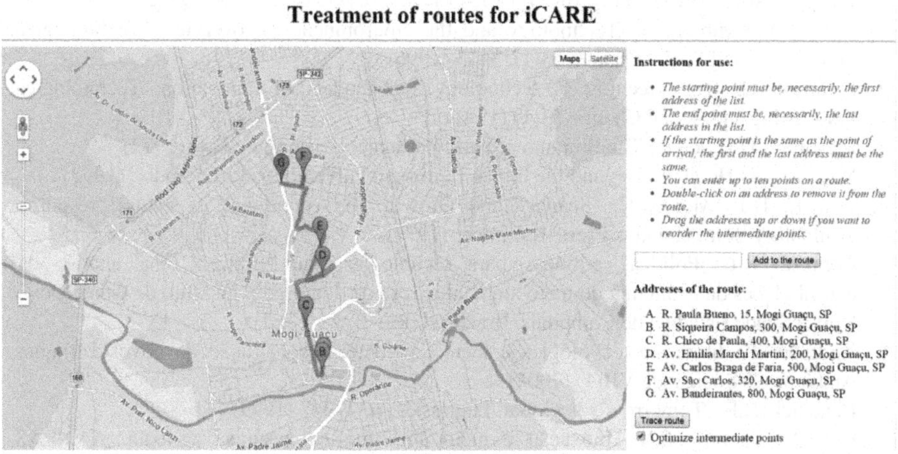

Treatment of routes for iCARE

Fig. 3. Interface for route calculation

5   Concluding Remarks

The iCARE project aims to contribute with the separation, collection and proper disposal of solid wastes, as a way to minimize the socio-economic and environmental problems arising from the inappropriate treatment of waste.

The use of this software has allowed the operation of a structure for the collection and disposal of waste, which has been organized by the Association of Collectors of Mogi Guaçu, SP, Brazil, ensuring the entry of materials to the collective work of everybody involved. The proposal of a programmed logistics makes selective collection activity itself less impressive due to the reduction of fuel consumption and emission of greenhouse gases in the collecting of materials with the planning of routes.

Considering the Brazilian national solid waste policy [16], in compliance with the law Number 12,305/2010, regarding the separate collection, recycling, reverse logistics and the strengthening of the concept of shared responsibility, the software comes to interact with companies and organizations in the area of social and environmental responsibility for the correct disposal of waste generated by its activities, with the obligations of all links in the production chain. There is also a reformulation of the concept of waste, because it happens to be seen by society as a material of value, and that the generator is responsible for their proper disposal.

The iCARE project is still in an early-stage and seeks to involve the largest possible number of people interested in the collection and disposal of recyclable waste. Other initiatives are planned for future work within the scope of the project. Among them we can mention the mapping of disposal points, which could be coupled directly to the module "Bulletin Board".

References

1. UNEP, United Nations of Environment Program. Global Environment Outlook 3, UNEP, Earthscan Pun. Ltd. London Sterling VA (2002),
   http://www.unep.org/geo/geo3/english/pdfs/chap1.pdf
2. Foray, D., Grübler, A.: Technology and the environment: an overview. Technological Forecasting and Social Change 53(1), 3–13 (1996)
3. Freeman, C.: The greening of technology and models of innovation. Technological Forecasting and Social Change 53(1) (1996)
4. Meadows, D.H., et al.: The limits to growth. Potomac, Washington D.C (1972)
5. Meadows, D.H., et al.: Beyond the limits. Earthscan Publications Ltd, London (1992)
6. Barnett, H.J., Morse, C.: Scarcity and Growth: the economics of natural resources availability. John Hopkins Press, Baltimore (1977)
7. Corazza, R.I.: Políticas públicas para tecnologias mais limpas: uma analise das contribuições da economia do meio ambiente. Tese de doutorado. Instituto de Geociências. Universidade Estadual de Campinas, Brazil (2004)
8. Andrade, T.: Inovação tecnológica e meio ambiente: a construção de novos enfoques. Ambiente & Sociedade VII(1) (2004)
9. Benedick, R.E.: Tomorrow's is global. Futures 31, 937–947 (1999)
10. Bin, A., Paulino, S.R.: Inovação e meio ambiente na pesquisa agrícola. ANNPAS. Indaiatuba/SP, Brazil (2004)
11. Herrera, A., et al.: Las Nuevas Tecnologías y el Futuro de América Latina. Siglo XXI. México (1994)
12. Worlf Commission On Environment And Development. Our Common Future. Oxford University Press. Oxford and New York. Em português: Comissão Mundial sobre meio ambiente e desenvolvimento. Nosso futuro comum. Rio de Janeiro: Ed. da Fundação Getúlio Vargas, 430 p. (1987)
13. Healy, S.A.: Science, technology and future of sustainability. Futures 27(6), 611–625 (1995)
14. Grübler, A., Gritsevskyi, A.: A Model of EndogenousTechnological Change Through Uncertain Returns on Innovation. In: Grübler, A., Nakicenovic, N., Nordhaus, W.D. (eds.) Technological Change and the Environment, 464 p. IIASA, Washington DC (2002)
15. CBO, Movimento Nacional dos Catadores De Materiais Recicláveis. Classificação Brasileira de Ocupações (2014),
    http://www.mncr.org.br/box_2/instrumentos-juridicos/
    classificacao-brasileira-de-ocupacoes-cbo
16. MMA. Brazilian Goverment. Ministério do Meio Ambiente. Plano Nacional de Resíduos Sólidos. Brasília (2012),
    http://www.mma.gov.br/port/conama/reuniao/dir1529/PNRS_consu
    ltaspublicas.pdf

Joining the Dots: Using Linked Data to Navigate between Features and Observational Data

Robert A. Atkinson[1], Peter Taylor[2], Geoffrey Squire[2], Nicholas J. Car[3],
Darren Smith[4], and Mark Menzel[4]

[1] Metalinkage, Australia
[2] Digital Productivity and Services Flagship: CSIRO, Hobart, TAS, Australia
peter.taylor@csiro.au
[3] Land and Water Flagship: CSIRO, Brisbane, QLD, Australia
[4] Information Systems and Services Division (Environmental Information Management):
Bureau of Meteorology, Melbourne, VIC, Australia

Abstract. Information about localized phenomena may be represented in multiple ways. GIS systems may be used to record the spatial extent of the phenomena. Observations about the state of one or more properties of the phenomena are available from real-time sensors, models, or from archives. The relationships between these data sources, or specific features in different data products, cannot easily be specified. Additionally, features change over time, their representations use different spatial scales and different aspects of them are of concern to different stakeholders. This greatly increases the number of potential relationships between features. Thus, for a given feature we can expect that heterogeneous information systems will exist, holding different types of data related to that feature. We propose the use of Linked Data to describe the relationships between them. We demonstrate this in practice using the Australian Hydrologic Geospatial Fabric (Geofabric) feature dataset and observational data of varying forms, including time-series and discrete measurements. We describe how different resources, and different aspects and versions of them, can be discovered and accessed. A web client is described that can navigate between related resources, including using the Geofabric's feature relationships, to navigate from one observational dataset to another related by hydrological connectivity.

Keywords: linked data, spatial data infrastructure, spatial information platform, hydrological features.

1 Introduction

An identifiable real world phenomenon within a spatial context, or a "feature", may be represented in many different information systems in different ways, for different purposes. A Geographical Information System (GIS) may be used to record the spatial extent of the phenomena, as defined or observed. Observations about the state of one or more properties of the phenomena, such as the height of a stream, may be available through real-time sensors, or from archives. Different systems may use different, but related, views of the phenomenon, characterized by different Feature Types and

R. Denzer et al. (Eds.): ISESS 2015, IFIP AICT 448, pp. 121–130, 2015.

relations between them. For example, a river may have multiple views of its channel, connectivity, banks, cross-section etc. A "Domain Model" may be developed to describe these relationships, although each data representation is often structured in terms of a simplified "Product Model" that only describes a single viewpoint. Data representations are usually tied to these simplified Product Models, and currently they are not easily discovered or navigated using the relevant Domain Model. The relationships between data products, or between specific features in different data products, cannot easily be specified using the types of specialized systems in use.

Different information sources may be linked in a customized application that is configured to know the location and type of each available source. This may be by pre-loading data into a specific data store, or by consuming it from (web-based) services, with the semantics of each dataset understood and hard-coded directly within an application. This results in systems that hide valuable relationships between datasets, for example between specific features (e.g. rivers) and observations (e.g. height, flows, water quality). These applications tend to be single-purpose and inflexible.

Linked Data [1] is an approach to standardize aspects of semantics and encoding in a Web-based environment. Linked Data does not standardize semantics or vocabularies, and the cost of standardizing access and format needs to be borne by the data provider. Links need to be embedded by data providers also, and no guidance as to the semantics of these links is directly provided by Linked Data.

"Domain models" standardize the semantics used in an individual domain, and describe the relationships that may exist between features. ISO19109 [2] describes how domain models may be formalized using UML, which supports the generation of exchange schema using GML, and more recently using OWL semantics as described in ISO/DIS 19150-2 [3] .

The Geofabric [4] is an Australian spatial data product that describes a range of hydrological features from catchments to river networks. Individual data products describe data structures within a dataset of the Geofabric, not the relationships between datasets. HY_Features [5] is a candidate conceptual model for describing hydrological features and their relationships. The Geofabric is designed to have navigable relationships consistent with the HY_Features model. The question is how to make these relationships visible and usable in practice?

This paper describes how we have used Linked Data to describe how alternate data product representations and observational data may be linked to specific features. We show further how domain models can be used to standardize and document links between different features. We demonstrate this in practice using the example of the Geofabric dataset and a river flow rating observational dataset. We describe some example use cases where this capability brings significant data integration benefits.

2   System Overview

We propose the use of Linked Data to describe the relationships between systems. Domain models standardize these relationships and provide common vocabularies for

data description. We use standard Semantic Web vocabularies, including the Vocabulary of Interlinked Datasets (VoID) [6], RDF-Datacube [7] and SKOS [8] to describe datasets and cross-references between them. Inter-feature relationship discovery is provided as a service, so it is not necessary to embed every possible relationship as a link in every dataset.

Multiple "views" of a resource are made available from a resource URI, with each view corresponding to a specific data product. The syntax for this follows the Linked Data API [9], extended to allow discovery of available views within a generalized framework for spatial data in a Linked Data context [10].

For example, persistent identifiers are created for specific catchments, e.g. 'http://environment.data.gov.au/water/id/catchment/110535'. A listing of available views for a resource is provided through a "_view=alternates" URL. E.g. http://environment.data.gov.au/water/id/catchment/110535?_view=alternates. Resolution of this URL follows the pattern [11] of using an HTTP redirect (303) to display the available named views (of which 'alternates' is one). Views provided for Geofabric features include:

- **SimpleFeatures:** provides a Web Feature Service (WFS) Simple Features view, useful for accessing with GIS or spatially aware software;
- **ahgf:cartographic:** a cartographic, image-based view of mapped streams for this feature;
- **ahgf:AHGFManmade:** WFS query that returns anthropogenic features within a feature (e.g. damns within a catchment);
- **related:** lists spatial features that are topologically related in some way to this feature. E.g. for catchments, this may contains references to upstream catchments, outflow nodes or a containing basin.
- **monitoringpoints:** lists monitoring points that are contained within this feature.

Each resource listed through these calls behaves in the same way. This provides predictable behavior for navigating between resources.

The software architecture to support these functions is provided by a number of distributed services. An overview is shown in Fig. 1. The design shows the use of Sparqlify [12] to map identifiers and context of spatial features through to a RESTful API provided by ELDA [9]. ELDA provides a means to expose APIs over SPARQL endpoints, simplifying access to RDF data. This is the mechanism for indexing the spatial features into a Linked Data representation.

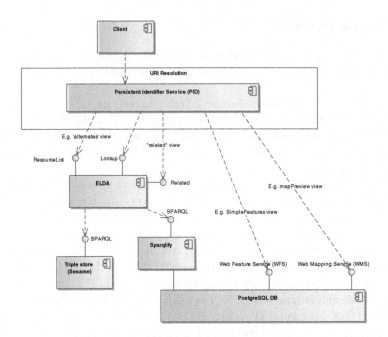

Fig. 1. Architecture Overview

3   Implementation

The Geofabric is published using a range of OGC web services, such as Web Feature Services (WFS) and Web Map Services (WMS). We use the VoID vocabulary to describe the available datasets, including descriptions of the data access endpoints. A void:Linkset describes relationships between hydrological features and monitoring points, described using WaterML2.0. This provides the data backbone allowing navigation between spatial features and monitoring points, which supports the following example use cases:

1. A user starts at a monitoring point to gain an understanding of the local hydrological conditions (e.g. local river gauge/flow conditions, channel shape etc.) and then wants to explore details of upstream conditions or the nature of the containing catchment.
2. A user interested in the national/state level, and wants to explore the hydrology of a particular catchment. This involves catchment level data, but also typically leads to more granular exploration such as river-based observations.

Using the views described in section 4, details for resources can be retrieved through requests against a resource URI. An example call flow for requesting details of a catchment is shown in Fig. 2.

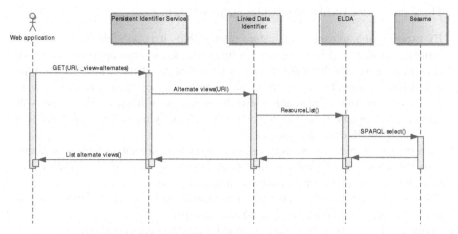

Fig. 2. Requesting alternate views of a resource URI

A screenshot of the prototype web client that makes use of the data and link rich environment is shown in Fig. 3. The workflow for the web client is as follows (numbers correspond to steps show in Fig. 3):

1. A user navigates a spatial overview showing all monitoring points within a basin. She selects a monitoring point of interest, and identifies its unique URI reference.

2. The containing catchment (http://environment.data.gov.au/water/id/catchment/110741) is found by requesting the 'related' view using the monitoring point URI. (The 'related' view itself may be "well-known" or discovered via the 'alternates' view of the monitoring point.)

3. To get a visual representation of the catchment requires finding a suitable view. For convenience, we have chosen to make default GIS views available using the special view name 'SimpleFeatures' however it is possible to interrogate the 'alternates' view to discover available views, which may be classified and annotated to support this discovery. In this case a WFS service is linked to the 'SimpleFeatures' view of the catchment. Invoking this view (e.g. for XML http://environment.data.gov.au/water/id/catchment/110535?_view=SimpleFeatures&_format=gml3) is used by the client to retrieve a GeoJSON representation and rendered in the client.

4. Additionally, the monitoring point location and containing river network views are also requested via 'SimpleFeatures' views and rendered on the same map.

5. Further context for the catchment, in terms of its hydrological relationships to other features, is requested using the 'related' view. These are shown in the table on the right of the image. In future work the prototype will support automated and user-driven navigation further into the Geofabric feature set. E.g. show up-stream catchment, outflow nodes etc.

Access to individual features facilitates access to the relevant parts of the Geofabric, rather than having a flat image-based view of all the features (e.g. through rendering an image from a WMS). This allows enhanced visualisations to be created. For example, the stream network within the catchment is dynamically rendered according to the size of the stream segment and whether it is perennial (blue) or non-perennial (green).

The approach described here provides multiple benefits:

1. By exposing the semantics of feature relationships it is possible to identify how different resources relate to a given starting point. Each client application does not need to have an inbuilt model of each feature-type in advance, how feature-types have been implemented, or where to access them. These aspects are all discoverable by introspection of available views for a feature of interest. This reduces the cost of development as well as removing the reliability on highly specialized software, such as GIS desktop packages.
2. Data transfer is reduced, as users are not required to download large spatial contexts for processing on localized areas (e.g. downloading the whole Geofabric Surface Network data product for analysis on one catchment).
3. Other specialized data products and relationships can be added in a dynamic way, without expensive changes to software and infrastructure.
4. Multiple formats can be provided, suitable for different client platforms.

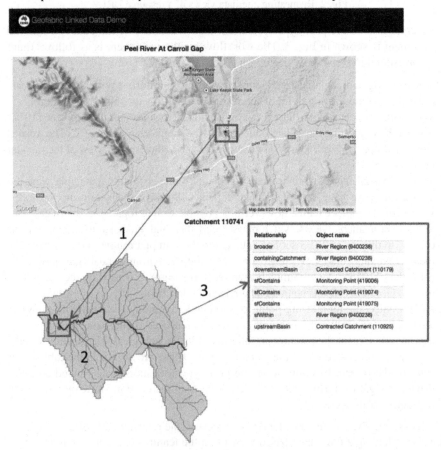

Fig. 3. Web client screenshot

4   Related Work

There is a vast body of work related to the principles of the various Internet based architectures exploited, including the World Wide Web, Semantic Web, Sensor Web, Linked Data and Spatial Data Infrastructures. This section focuses specifically on use of Linked Data for enabling hydrological and spatial data infrastructures.

Spatial Data Infrastructure (SDI) approaches [13] introduce standardized protocols and formats for delivering feature data. For example, under the INSPIRE legislation (EC 2007) EU member states will standardize the delivery of datasets via Web services, including hydrologic features [14]. INSPIRE does not, however, specify how individual features may be referenced in a Web environment, or dictate that a single representation of a feature exists.

A candidate standard formalized model for hydrological feature definitions, HY_Features, provides a domain model for feature types and their relationships [5]. HY_Features is focused on the issue of object identity rather than sharing representations.

The UK Location Strategy [15] makes distinctions between identifiers, definitions, and "spatial objects" which implement representations. It provides a pattern for implementing Linked Data using alternative representation forms, provided the "thing" in question is reliably identified.

Janowicz et al. [16] outline the key challenges in bringing semantics to SDIs. They propose a semantic enablement layer that injects semantic annotation into responses from WFS, WMS, SOS or other OGC Web Services. Our approach varies slightly in that it does not modify service responses, but augments with semantics through exposing a SPARQL (and subsequent REST) interface for indexing. The approach outlined by Jones et al. [17] and Harvey et al. [18] addresses a different challenge: serving RDF data using a WFS endpoint, thus making Linked Data available to existing GIS consumers.

Key challenges for next generation SDIs are identified by Adams and Gahegan [19]. They propose a 'model space' concept that covers the complex dimensions of large scale data integration. Our work here primarily touches on the spatio-temporal, semantic and authority dimensions. Additionally Adams and Gahegan [19, p. 127] identify the representation of spatial features and sets of features as a key challenge. Our work proposes some potential next steps in this area.

Linking raster data to the Linked Data Web is explored by Scharrenbach et al. [20]. Their approach of using semantics to describe contextual information for raster data is consistent with our work of indexing WMS calls with relevant spatial bounding boxes. This allows raster data to be included without resorting to encoding every pixel into RDF [20, p. 4].

Having observations of phenomena associated with features is important for understanding the context of an observation. WaterML2.0 part 1 [21] and the proposed part 2 [22] provide standard information models for representing hydrological observational data. Using WaterML2.0 with HY_Features is conceptually consistent, but use cases have not been widely tested or implemented. This work brings these together with Linked Data.

Much recent work has investigated representation of observational and sensor data as Linked Data [23]–[29]. Our work focuses on bridging between spatial features and monitoring points (the source of observations and sensor data); the representation of observational data as Linked Data is not tackled, rather we describe existing data sets using Linked Data.

5   Discussion

We propose linking directly from a view of a feature to relevant related information using the approach described offers advantages to the current alternatives. There are two existing options: Having all links hard-coded into each feature (document-centric Web architecture) or using a catalog of datasets and services (service oriented architecture).

We can dismiss a document-centric approach for several reasons:

- it places all the burden on knowing what data is related on the original source dataset;
- these relationships need to be expressed in a standard way that both data provider and client understand;
- all possible relationships need to be encoded in the document (which may be large and costly to produce);
- the approach does not scale to large datasets, or dynamic numerical models or sensors producing data not known in advance;

For a catalog-centric approach the best case is a data catalog coupled with a service catalog describing access points to services providing each specific dataset. This approach is fraught with challenges, especially the very high burden it places on the client to know:

- The location of a relevant dataset catalog service;
- How the catalog is organized (i.e. keywords it can be searched on);
- The catalog access protocol;
- The response format and content;
- Which services it can utilize for the task in hand, using the descriptions provided.
- How to install and configure specific software able to interpret the spatial or observational data.

Even if relevant catalogs can be found, there is still no standard way to describe exactly how features in different datasets relate, or how to invoke a service to access a view for a particular feature. The Linked Data API implementation described here utilizes URI resolution to perform all these roles seamlessly; all the client needs to do is to choose a view that it can understand.

6   Conclusion

Distributed heterogeneous data sources are a necessary reality in the case of wide-spread phenomena with multiple stakeholder perspectives, such as is the case with water resource monitoring. Using traditional dataset centric approaches to cataloguing, one quickly runs into a lack of a canonical means to describe relationships between features. We show how we can exploit domain models to standardize such relationships, then implement and utilize them for individual feature instances in a Linked Data environment. This approach avoids placing the burden on data providers to realize every possible link, or to transform existing data into a new Linked Data format. This approach results in easily discoverable data sources that can be used without significant data management overheads and specific software availability. The use of both Linked Data services and data-specific services (e.g. WFS, observational services) provide a less abrupt transition into the Linked Data world and ensures that well-established access patterns are reused.

Acknowledgements. This work is part of the water information research and development alliance between CSIRO's Water for a Healthy Country Flagship and the Bureau of Meteorology. The authors would like to thank Simon Cox for his thorough review and assistance, and the anonymous reviewers for their suggestions.

References

[1] Bizer, C., Heath, T., Berners-Lee, T.: Linked data-the story so far. Int. J. Semantic Web Inf. Syst. 5(3), 1–22 (2009)

[2] ISO TC211, 19109.3 Geographic information-Rules for application schema. Int. Organ. Stand. (2005)

[3] ISO TC211, ISO/DIS 19150-2 Geographic information – Ontology – Part 2: Rules for developing ontologies in the Web Ontology Language (OWL), p. 103 (June 2014)

[4] Bureau of Meteorology, Australian Hydrological Geospatial Fabric (Geofabric), http://data.gov.au/dataset/australian-hydrological-geospatial-fabric-geofabric (accessed: December 09, 2014)

[5] Atkinson, R., Dornblut, I., Smith, D.: An international standard conceptual model for sharing references to hydrologic features. J. Hydrol. 424-425, 24–36 (2012)

[6] W3C, VoID Vocabulary. RDF Schema vocabulary (2013), http://www.w3.org/TR/void/

[7] W3C, TheRDF Data Cube Vocabulary. RDF Schema vocabulary.http:// (2014), http://www.w3.org/TR/vocab-data-cube/

[8] Miles, A., Pérez-Agüera, J.R.: SKOS: Simple Knowledge Organisation for the Web. Cat. Classif. Q. 43(3), 69–83 (2007)

[9] Epimorphics, Elda: The linked-data API in Java (2014)

[10] Atkinson, R.: Spatial Identifier Reference Framework (SIRF)-A Case Study on How Spatial identifier data structures can be reorirnted to suit present and future technology needs. In: Proceedings of the Pole-26th International Cartogrphic Conference, Dresden, Germany, pp. 25–30 (2013)

[11] Cyganiak, R., Sauermann, L.: Cool URIs for the Semantic Web. W3C, Note (2008)

[12] AKSW/Sparqlify, GitHub, `https://github.com/AKSW/Sparqlify` (accessed: December 9, 2014)

[13] Rajabifard, A., Williamson, I.P.: Spatial data infrastructures: concept, SDI hierarchy and future directions (2001)

[14] d' Aquin, M., Noy, N.F.: Where to publish and find ontologies? A survey of ontology libraries. Web Semant. Sci. Serv. Agents World Wide Web 11, 96–111 (2012)

[15] UK Location Council, Place Matters: The Location Strategy for the United Kingdom (2008)

[16] Janowicz, K., Schade, S., Bröring, A., Keßler, C., Maué, P., Stasch, C.: Semantic Enablement for Spatial Data Infrastructures. Trans. GIS 14(2), 111–129 (2010)

[17] Jones, J., Kuhn, W., Keßler, C., Scheider, S.: Making the Web of Data Available Via Web Feature Services. In: Huerta, J., Schade, S., Granell, C. (eds.) Connecting a Digital Europe Through Location and Place, pp. 341–361. Springer International Publishing (2014)

[18] Harvey, F., Jones, J., Scheider, S.: Little Steps Towards Big Goals. Using Linked Data to Develop Next Generation Spatial Data Infrastructures (aka SDI 3.0)

[19] Adams, B., Gahegan, M.: Emerging data challenges for next-generation spatial data infrastructure

[20] Scharrenbach, T., Bischof, S., Fleischli, S., Weibel, R.: Linked Raster Data. In: Seventh International Conference on Geographic Information Science, vol. 7478 (2012)

[21] Taylor, P., Cox, S., Walker, G., Valentine, D., Sheahan, P.: WaterML2.0: development of an open standard for hydrological time-series data exchange. Journal of Hydroinformatics (2013)

[22] Taylor, P., Sheahan, P., Hamilton, S., Briar, D., Fry, M., Natschke, M., Valentine, D., Walker, G., Lowe, D., Cox, S.: An information model for exchanging hydrological rating tables. In: Proceedings of Hydroinformatics Conference 2014, New York, p. 8 (2014)

[23] Janowicz, K., Bröring, A., Stasch, C., Schade, S., Everding, T., Llaves, A.: A restful proxy and data model for linked sensor data. Int. J. Digit. Earth 6(3), 233–254 (2013)

[24] Le-Phuoc, D., Hauswirth, M.: SensorMasher: Enabling open linked data in sensor data mashup (2009)

[25] Broering, A., Foerster, T., Jirka, S., Priess, C.: Sensor bus: an intermediary layer for linking geosensors and the sensor web, New York, NY, USA, pp. 1–8 (2010)

[26] Page, K., Roure, D.D., Martinez, K., Sadler, J., Kit, O.: Linked Sensor Data: RESTfully serving RDF and GML, Washington DC, USA, vol. 522, pp. 49–63 (2009)

[27] Barnaghi, P., Meissner, S., Presser, M., Moessner, K.: Sense and Sens'ability: semantic Data Modelling for Sensor Networks (2009)

[28] Wei, W., Barnaghi, P.: Semantic annotation and reasoning for sensor data, Berlin, Heidelberg, pp. 66–76 (2009)

[29] Compton, M., Barnaghi, P., Bermudez, L., GarcíA-Castro, R., Corcho, O., Cox, S., Graybeal, J., Hauswirth, M., Henson, C., Herzog, A.: others, "The SSN ontology of the W3C semantic sensor network incubator group,". Web Semant. Sci. Serv. Agents World Wide Web 17, 25–32 (2012)

An SMS and Email Weather Warning System
for Sheep Producers

Anna Weeks[1], Malcolm McCaskill[2], Matthew Cox[3], and Subhash Sharma[3]

[1] Agriculture Division: Department of Environment and Primary Industries,
Rutherglen, VIC, Australia
[2] Agriculture Division: Department of Environment and Primary Industries,
Hamilton, VIC, Australia
[3] Agriculture Division: Department of Environment and Primary Industries,
Parkville, VIC, Australia
{anna.weeks,malcolm.mccaskill,matthew.cox,
subhash.sharma}@depi.vic.gov.au

Abstract. Sheep are vulnerable to hypothermia shortly after birth and shearing. Since the 1970's sheep weather alerts have been reported at a regional scale by the media up to 24 hours prior to a chill event. The SMS and email weather warning system was designed as an enhanced service to provide sheep producers with advanced warnings of forth-coming chill events, based on local weather forecasts, with personalized chill warnings delivered by SMS and email. A trial was conducted with 30 sheep producers who selected one or more local weather stations and a low, medium or high sensitivity threshold to control the frequency at which messages were sent. Sensitivity thresholds were calculated for each weather station from historical data. Numerical forecast data were sourced from the Bureau of Meteorology, and an email and SMS sent each morning whenever forecast chill exceeded the warning threshold within the 7-day forecast period. Participants were interviewed by telephone after a 2-month trial. The alerts were found to be clear and reasonably accurate, but produced an unexpected high number of false warnings at some sites. The SMS format was well received, and farmers were generally happy to continue the trial. False warnings were attributed to over-prediction of wind speeds at some sites relative to on-ground weather stations, most of which were in northern Victoria.

Keywords: Sheep, forecast skill, evaluation, chill index.

1 Introduction

Sheep in southern Australia are at risk of death through hypothermia shortly after shearing and in the first 3 days after birth. Since the early 1970's the Australian Bureau of Meteorology (BoM) has issued "Sheep Weather Alerts", based on an algorithm that incorporates the effects of wind speed, temperature and rainfall on heat loss from the sheep [2]. These have been broadcast through the mass media up to 24 hours prior to a chill event, but until recently were not issued in Victoria during winter, to avoid "warning fatigue". More recently, the availability of the BoM numerical forecast data has

R. Denzer et al. (Eds.): ISESS 2015, IFIP AICT 448, pp. 131–140, 2015.
© IFIP International Federation for Information Processing 2015

enabled the Department of Environment and Primary Industries (DEPI) to provide seven-day, site-specific forecasts of sheep wind-chill on its website. However, a limitation of a web service is that users are unlikely to check at times when a stress is not expected. Surprise chill events can occur in summer, such as the chill-event reported by Bird and Cayley [1] where 100,000 off-shears sheep died in south-west Victoria in December 1987. To utilize the new weather forecast dissemination capabilities, DEPI has developed and trialed a subscription service that provides advance warning of extreme chill events to sheep producers in Victoria via SMS and email notifications. This paper describes development of the system, the accuracy of forecasts, and user feedback.

2   Methodology

2.1   System Architecture

The SMS and email weather warning system ran daily as an automated service on the Victorian Resources Online server [5] (**Fig. 1**). Through a subscription web-page, subscribers selected from 56 weather stations and specified the sensitivity threshold at which warnings were sent (low, medium or high). The thresholds were based on a statistical analysis of historical weather station data, with relationships derived for each station describing the expected number of warnings per threshold.

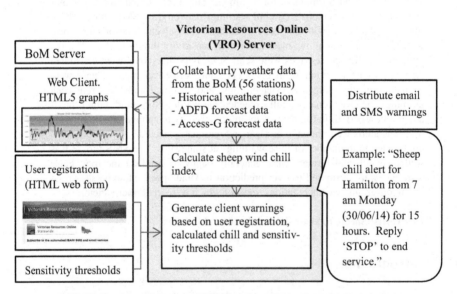

Fig. 1. System architecture of SMS and email weather warning system

Weather data (**Table 1**) were downloaded from the BoM Server via an ftp link and comprised; historical weather station data, seven days of the ~3km resolution Australian Digital Forecast Data (ADFD) and seven days of the ~40km resolution Access-G Forecast. The Access-G precipitation forecast was required because the ADFD only provided a one-day forecast. Inputs were converted to standard units of Co-ordinated Universal Time (UTC), wind speed (m/s), hourly rainfall (mm/hr) and temperature (°C). Accumulated 3-hourly rainfall was downscaled to an hourly basis and missing data in-filled by linear interpolation.

The service ran a series of scheduled tasks early each morning. Historical and seven-day forecast data were first copied from the BoM server then chill-indices calculated for each weather station. Forecasts of wind-chill were made available on the corporate website through an interactive graphical display then a sub-routine compared the forecast to the subscriber threshold. An email and/or SMS was issued based on the first occurrence and length (hours) of the first forecast event that exceeded the specified threshold.

Table 1. BoM Weather data used for sheep-wind-chill calculations

Period	Source	Time units	Element	Units	Frequency
3-weeks historical data	BoM Australian Weather Station Feed	[Year, month, day, hour] local time	Wind speed	m/s	hourly
			Rainfall since 9am	mm	hourly
			Temp	°C	hourly
Forecast day 1-7 (except for rain)	Australian Digital Forecast Grid (ADFD) ~3km grid	Co-ordinated Universal Time UTC	Wind speed	knots	hourly
			3-hr expected rainfall	mm/3hr	3-hourly
			Temp	°C	hourly
Forecast day 2-7	Access-G (IDY25001) ~40km grid	Seconds since start date UTC	Accum. rainfall over model assimilation	mm/3hr	3-hourly

2.2   Chill Modelling and Calculation of Thresholds

Sheep wind chill was calculated using the chill index of Nixon-Smith [2], which estimates the potential hourly heat loss from new-born lambs $(C_{hr}, kJ/m^2.hr)$ from air temperature $(T, °C)$, wind speed at a 0.4m height $(v_{0.4}, m/s)$ and rainfall $(R, mm/24hr)$ accumulated over the previous 24 hours:

$$C_{hr} = (11.7 + 3.1\sqrt{v_{0.4}}(40 - T) + 481 + 418(1 - e^{-0.04R}) \tag{1}$$

The BoM wind speed at 10m (v_{10}) was down-scaled to a lamb height of 0.4m using the empirical relationship developed by McCaskill *et. al* (unpublished).

$$v_{0.4} = \begin{cases} 0.104 + 0.0667v_{10} & v_{10} < 2.682 \\ -0.863 + 0.427v_{10} & v_{10} \geq 2.682 \end{cases} \tag{2}$$

Three thresholds were calculated for each weather station from historical data to give subscribers the option to control the sensitivity of the warning service. The low, medium and high thresholds were set so that approximately 10, 15 and 20 events would be triggered each year, noting that with a seven-day forecast, subscribers could potentially receive up to seven warnings for each event. The annual chill events for a given threshold value was found to be well approximated by the *upper incomplete gamma function* $(p(\alpha, x, P))$; shown in **Fig. 2** for the Rutherglen weather station.

$$p(\alpha, x, P) = \frac{P}{\Gamma(\alpha)} \int_x^\infty e^{-t} t^{\alpha-1} \, dt \ where \ \Gamma(\alpha) = \int_0^\infty e^{-t} t^{\alpha-1} dt \ and \ x = \frac{k-1000}{\theta} \quad (3)$$

Here α, θ and P are fitted constants and the threshold value (k) has a lower limit of 1000 kJ/m^2/h. The chill relationship of **eqn. 1** is presented in **Fig. 3** illustrating the wind, rainfall and temperature conditions required to trigger a warning under the low, medium or high threshold values derived for the Rutherglen weather station. Values of α, θ P and k for this and other representative weather stations are presented later in the paper (see **Table 3**).

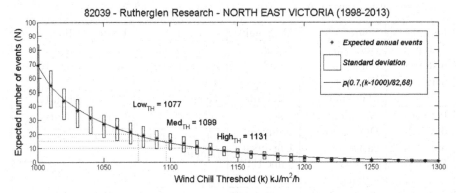

Fig. 2. The expected annual number of sheep-wind-chill events for wind-chill threshold (k), calculated from historical hourly data (1998-2013) for the Rutherglen weather station

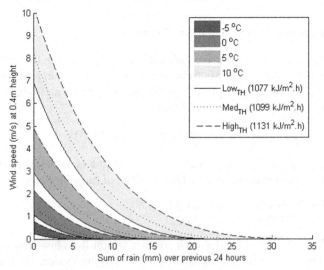

Fig. 3. Illustration of the sheep-wind-chill relationship of **eqn. 1**, showing the combination of wind speed, temperature and   rainfall required to trigger thresholds for the Rutherglen station

2.3   Forecast Skill

The forecast skill of each weather station was assessed for forecasts 1 to 7 days ahead over the 77 days between the 20th July to the 4th October 2014. Consistent with the approach used to quantify forecast skill for dichotomous forecasts by the BoM [4], skill was evaluated by means of a contingency table (**Table 2**) and calculations of bias and Equitable Threat Score (ETS).

Table 2. Contingency table to assess the types of errors being made

		Forecast		
		Yes	No	
Observed	Yes	Hits	Misses	Observed yes
	No	False alarm	Correct negative	Observed no
		forecast yes	forecast no	Total

Bias compared the frequency of forecast chill-events to observed events indicating whether the system tended to under-forecast (*Bias<0*) or over-forecast (*Bias>1*).

$$Bias = \frac{hits+false\ alarms}{hits+misses} \qquad 0 < Bias < \infty, \ Perfect\ score = 1 \qquad (4)$$

The Equitable Threat Score (ETS) compared the forecast occurrence of events to the observed, adjusting for hits associated with random chance (h_r) to reduce the effect of different climatic conditions (eg. wet or dry) .

$$ETS = \frac{hits-h_r}{hits+misses+false\ alarm-h_r} \qquad -\frac{1}{3} < ETS < 1, \ No\ skill = 0, \ Perfect = 1 \quad (5)$$

$$where\ h_r = \frac{(hits + misses)(hits + false\ alarm)}{total}$$

The predictive skill of the hourly forecast data was assessed using the Nash-Sutcliff Coefficient of Efficiency (*CoE*) which ascertains whether the forecast is a better predictor of observed data than the observed mean. The *CoE* was calculated as

$$CoE = 1 - \frac{\sum_{t=1}^{T}\left(Q_o^t - Q_f^t\right)^2}{\sum_{t=1}^{T}(Q_o^t - \overline{Q_o})^2} \qquad No\ skill \leq 0, Perfect = 1 \qquad (6)$$

where Q_o is the observed data, $\overline{Q_o}$ the mean observed data, and Q_f the forecast data The mean bias ($\overline{Q_f} - \overline{Q_o}$) between forecast and observed data was also calculated.

2.4   Trial Evaluation

Victorian Sheep producers were recruited for an initial trial of the system at the 'Best Wool/Best Lamb' Conference in Bendigo in late June 2014. The trial evaluation was conducted by an independent reviewer [3] in September and October of 2014 in which 30 subscribers were interviewed by telephone. Participants included large, medium and small-scale sheep farmers drawn from across the state. The interviews included both open and closed questions. Findings were organized to answer each of the overarching questions (i) "Were clear, accurate and timely alerts received?", (ii) "Did alerts lead to reduced lamb losses?", and (iii) "Did farmers value the alerts?"

3   Results

3.1   Trial Results

In general, the alerts were found to be clear and reasonably accurate although there were some timing issues possibly attributable to technical glitches. The SMS format was well received. Farmers were generally happy to continue the trial and would potentially be happy to pay a small amount for a commercial service.

The evaluation found that the alerts did not lead to farm responses that saved lives during lambing except for small-scale farming where sheep could be managed individually. This was primarily due to the fact that due to the risks involved in moving ewes during lambing most farmers had already taken the precaution of providing as much protection for their birthing ewes as possible.

However, almost all farmers saw significant potential value in the alerts for shearing when surprise cold can cause significant losses amongst newly shorn sheep. Participants cited greater flexibility to respond using a range of options such as moving sheep into shelter or rescheduling shearing.

The independent reviewer recommended that the trial be continued through shearing with the scope expanded to include sudden changes in weather that might be experienced during the summer months that are potentially dangerous to newly shorn sheep, generally between November and May.

3.2   Forecast Skill

The forecast skill of each weather station was assessed for forecast days one to seven, under the low, medium and high thresholds over the 77 days between the 20th July to the 4th October 2014. Key determinants of skill included calculations of bias and ETS which have been presented in **Table 3** along with other results for a subset of weather stations.

During the trial period the ETS measure of forecast skill varied with weather station, forecast day and the threshold, ranging from a perfect score of 1.0 at Horsham to 0.2 at Wangaratta (**Table 3**) for the day-one forecast. Stations with a lower ETS generally predicted actual chill events well however their score was reduced by the frequent occurrence of 'false alarms'; represented by a bias>1 in **Table 3**. Across the 56 weather stations there was a significant (P < 0.05) decline in forecast skill from day one to day seven (Fig. 4a). In contrast, there was less differentiation in the forecast skill between the low, medium and high thresholds (Fig. 4b).

Table 3. Forecast skill (bias and ETS) for selected weather stations for the 77 day trial between 20th Jul and 4th Oct 2014. Includes parameters (α, θ and P) to estimate the number of events, low, medium and high thresholds. For the medium threshold (Med_{TH}); the number of warnings sent (N_W), the number of observed events (N). For forecast-day one; the forecast events (N_F), the hits (1|1), misses (1|0), false alarms (0|1) and false negatives (0|0).

Station	ID	α	θ	P	Threshold			Med_{TH}		N_F	Forecast day = 1, Med_{TH}				Bias	ETS
					Low	Med	High	N_W	N		1|1	1|0	0|1	0|0		
Horsham	79100	0.979	55.1	107.3	1095	1113	1137	15	3	3	3	0	0	74	1.0	1.0
Latrobe V.	85280	1.182	76.3	83.5	1133	1158	1193	9	3	3	3	0	0	74	1.0	1.0
Kilmore Gap	88162	1.292	70.2	192.9	1198	1223	1258	5	1	1	1	0	0	76	1.0	1.0
Geelong	87184	0.950	74.0	43.2	1059	1081	1113	21	6	7	6	0	1	70	1.2	0.8
Melbourne	86282	0.954	48.9	72.1	1062	1077	1098	23	11	9	9	2	0	66	0.8	0.8
Westmere	89112	0.867	77.0	96.9	1111	1134	1166	11	4	5	4	0	1	72	1.3	0.8
Stawell	79105	1.084	73.0	51.8	1080	1103	1136	9	2	3	2	0	1	74	1.5	0.7
Hamilton	90173	0.918	80.3	120.7	1137	1162	1197	10	3	5	3	0	2	72	1.7	0.6
Nhill	78015	0.949	62.1	60.6	1068	1087	1113	16	4	4	3	1	1	72	1.0	0.6
Mildura	76031	0.777	70.1	23.4	1010	1026	1050	31	10	16	10	0	6	61	1.6	0.6
Ballarat	89002	0.992	74.8	147.4	1152	1177	1212	11	3	6	3	0	3	71	2.0	0.5
Bendigo	81123	0.753	86.7	64.7	1079	1102	1135	16	5	4	3	2	1	71	0.8	0.5
Shepparton	81125	0.765	87.3	59.3	1075	1098	1131	18	4	5	3	1	2	71	1.3	0.5
Rutherglen	82039	0.733	82.2	68.8	1077	1099	1131	29	4	10	4	0	6	67	2.5	0.4
Omeo	83090	0.903	74.0	130.6	1133	1156	1188	25	4	9	3	1	6	67	2.3	0.3
Kyabram	80091	0.965	70.0	23.9	1012	1033	1063	38	5	14	4	1	10	62	2.8	0.2
Wangaratta	82138	0.734	87.8	74.8	1089	1113	1147	18	2	4	1	1	3	72	2.0	0.2

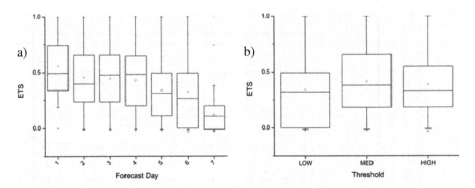

Fig. 4. The ETS range over 56 stations where box-plot represents [99,75,50,25,1] percentile, (*=mean) for (a) forecast day one to day seven, (b) low, med and high threshold

The Coefficient of Efficiency (CoE) was used to evaluate the forecast skill of the hourly sheep-chill-index and underlying temperature, rainfall and wind-speed forecast data. Overall the sheep-chill-index forecast skill was 'good' with over 75% of stations achieving a *CoE*>0.6 for forecast days one to four (**Fig. 5**). This could be attributed to forecast skill of temperature which far exceeded that of rainfall and wind-speed. The accumulated rainfall saw a sharp decline in CoE between days one and two which coincided with the transition between the 3km grid ADFD forecast to the 40 km grid Access-G rainfall forecast. The Wind-speed forecast showed less skill with only 25% of stations achieving a *CoE*>0.6 by day four.

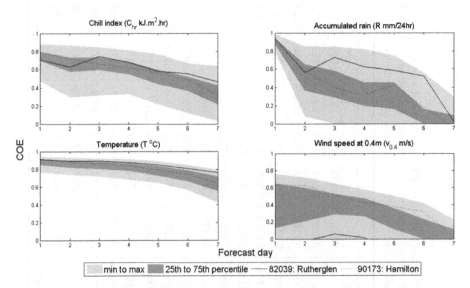

Fig. 5. Range of CoE over 56 stations for chill-index, accumulated rain, wind speed and temperature showing decline in predictive skill over seven days. Example response given for Hamilton and Rutherglen stations.

Forecast bias across the 56 stations showed little change with increasing forecast length (**Fig. 6**), apart from a greater divergence in bias at longer forecast lengths. In general the forecast wind-speed exceeded the observed with over 75% of stations showing a positive mean-bias. This followed through to the calculation of chill-index where the mean forecast chill-index exceeded the observed by more than 10 kJ.m^2.hr for over 75% of stations. For example at Rutherglen, wind speed was overestimated by 1.1 m/s from the one-day forecast and chill by 22 kJ/m^2.hr. Overall there was a strong correlation between over-prediction of mean wind-speed and the number of false alarms triggered.

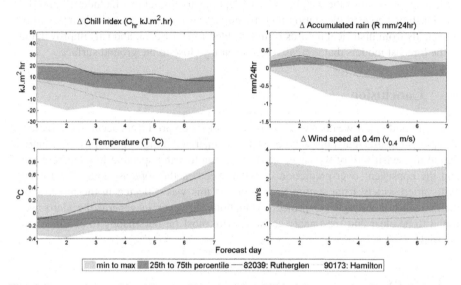

Fig. 6. Range of mean-bias (Δ) over 56 stations for chill-index, accumulated rain, wind speed and temperature.   Example mean-bias given for Hamilton   and Rutherglen stations.

4   Discussion

The forecast skill varied widely from station to station and this was reflected in the mixed comments received through the project evaluation. In general, although there was a decline in performance over successive forecast days, weather stations that had a high forecast skill on day-1 maintained that performance over the seven day forecast. Of the 56 weather stations, 33% performed well with a day-1 forecast skill as measured by the ETS of > 0.6. A further 46% of stations performed moderately-well with a day-1 ETS of between 0.2 and 0.6. Chill events were generally well forecast for these stations but the forecast score was brought down by a high number of false alarms.   Significantly, many of the stations that triggered multiple false alarms were located across the Northern region of Victoria (eg. Rutherglen, Wangaratta), where severe frosts often bring hourly temperatures to below zero. Subscribers to these stations commented on the fact that occasionally alerts were "*clearly just for frost*" rather than the "*holy trinity of wind rain and cold*" [3]. It was found that at low temperatures the wind-chill algorithm is highly sensitive to small changes in wind-speed (**Fig. 3**) and that the cold temperatures combined with an over-prediction of wind-speed across these locations was enough to trigger a series of false-alarms. Enforcing a precipitation requirement was found to effectively reduce false-alarms for these stations as simply increasing the threshold made little improvement to the ETS.

The difference between the forecast wind and that observed at the weather station highlights not only the difficulty of accurately predicting wind speed but also one of the fundamental assumptions made by this system that the 3 km gridded ADFD data and the 40 km gridded Access-G rainfall provide an adequate representation of the climate at the point of the weather station. Options to correct this include (i) empirical relationships between the station and the numerical forecast, (ii) calculating warning thresholds from historical records of the gridded forecast data, and (iii) improvements to the forecast models that increase their accuracy close to the ground surface.

5   Conclusion

The SMS and email weather warning service for sheep producers accurately predicted sheep-wind-chill events, but at some stations generated a high number of false alarms due to the sensitivity of the sheep chill algorithm to wind-speed at low temperatures, and the consistent over-prediction of wind speed in the forecast data. The forecast skill varied widely from station to station and this was reflected in the mixed comments received through the project evaluation. However in general the alerts were found to be clear and reasonably accurate with most farmers happy to continue with the trial.

References

1. Bird, R., Cayley, J.: Bad weather, shelter and stock losses. Agricultural Science: The Journal of the Institute of Agricultural Science 4(4), 18–19 (1991)
2. Nixon-Smith, W.F.: The forecasting of chill risk ratings for new born lambs and off-shears sheep by the use of a cooling factor derived from synoptic data. Working paper No. 150, Bureau of Meteorology, Melbourne (1972)
3. Revium. Department of Environment and Primary Industries Systems for Enhanced Farm Services Program. Spatial Discovery &Visualisation – SDV1: IBAW Trial Participants Survey. Report 1-39 (2014)
4. Stanski, H.R., Wilson, L.J., Burrows, W.R.: Survey of common verification methods in meteorology. World Weather Watch Tech. Rept. No.8, WMO/TD No.358, WMO, Geneva, 114 p. (1989)
5. VRO Victorian Resources Online, Internet Based Agricultural Warnings (2014), http://vro.depi.vic.gov.au/dpi/vro/vrosite.nsf/pages/ibaw

The Emergency Response Intelligence Capability Tool

Robert Power, Bella Robinson, Catherine Wise, David Ratcliffe,
Geoffrey Squire, and Michael Compton

CSIRO, Canberra, ACT, Australia
{robert.power,bella.robinson,catherine.wise,david.ratcliffe,
geoffrey.squire,michael.compton}@csiro.au

Abstract. The Emergency Response Intelligence Capability (ERIC) tool, http://eric.csiro.au, automatically gathers data about emergency events from authoritative web sources, harmonises the information content and presents it on an interactive map. All data is recorded in a database which allows the changing status of emergency events to be identified and provides an archive for historical review.

ERIC was developed for the Australian Government Department of Human Services Emergency Management team who is responsible for intelligence gathering and situation reporting during emergency events. Event information is combined with demographic data to profile the affected community. Identifying relevant community attributes, such as languages spoken or socioeconomic information, allows the department to tailor its response appropriately to better support the impacted community.

An overview of ERIC is presented, including its use by the department and the difficulties overcome in establishing and maintaining a nationally consistent harmonised model of emergency event information. Preliminary results of republishing the emergency event information using the Australian Profile of the Common Alerting Protocol, an XML standard to facilitate the construction and exchange of emergency alert and warning messages, are also presented.

Keywords: Disaster Management, Situation Awareness, Situation Reporting, System Architectures, Web Feeds.

1 Introduction

The Emergency Management team within the Australian Government Department of Human Services (the department) is responsible for the coordination of the department's response to emergencies, with a focus on delivery of departmental services and disaster assistance on behalf of the Australian Government to the affected community. The Australian disaster season is from early October through to late March and often involves bushfires, floods and cyclones with many events often occurring at the same time across State and Territory borders.

ERIC allows the Emergency Management team to easily monitor events occurring around the country and provides fast and intuitive access to a wide collection of information. The aim was to provide software support to help the Emergency Management

R. Denzer et al. (Eds.): ISESS 2015, IFIP AICT 448, pp. 141–150, 2015.
© IFIP International Federation for Information Processing 2015

team perform their tasks more efficiently and effectively, allowing them to better utilise their time in the analysis of information.

During large scale emergency events, the Emergency Management team creates a Situation Report as a Microsoft Word document. The information recorded includes specific event details (the event type, its location, impact to the community) and the tasks undertaken by the department (the number of staff mobilised, the impact on business as usual activities, statistics about the number of phone calls received and claims made by members of the community for Commonwealth Disaster Assistance). This information is tracked and reported on during the course of the emergency events and may continue well after the initial emergency response. The Situation Report is used by senior managers in the department to make informed decisions.

Dynamic data is sourced from public 'live' web feeds that provide content to the existing State and Territory emergency services web sites. See for example the Rural Fire Service websites for New South Wales[1] and Queensland[2]. A web feed is a web accessible resource that is updated frequently as new information becomes available from the content provider. This information is produced in many formats, for example RSS, GeoRSS, ATOM, JSON, GeoJSON, KML, HTML, XML, GML, XLS and plain text.

ERIC integrates information from numerous other sources such as statistical data from the ABS including population demographics; 'departmental demographics' such as the number of people receiving different payment types; the 'live' web feeds noted above; a repository of historical data collected via these 'live' web feeds; and an arc-hive of previous situation reports. The integrated information can be focused to a specific region under investigation where an emergency is underway and collated semi-automatically to generate a pre-populated Situation Report as a web form that is then completed by the user. This may include content from a previous Situation Report with updates to the current situation automatically highlighted.

The example screen shot of Fig. 1 shows the status of the New South Wales (NSW) State Mine Fire. It highlights how overlaying information from two different agencies (the NSW Rural Fire Service and Geoscience Australia) provides more in-sight into events. This figure demonstrates some of the important features of ERIC: the recorded information remains available for review and the map provides an easy and intuitive interface for users to navigate the information available from different sources.

A public version of ERIC is available at http://eric.csiro.au/. This version does not include any of the department's data (for privacy reasons), and the situation report function is not available. Some web feeds are also excluded for copyright reasons. Notably, the state of Victoria does not allow republication of their emergency web site content.

---

[1] http://www.rfs.nsw.gov.au/dsp_content.cfm?cat_id=683
[2] https://ruralfire.qld.gov.au/map.html

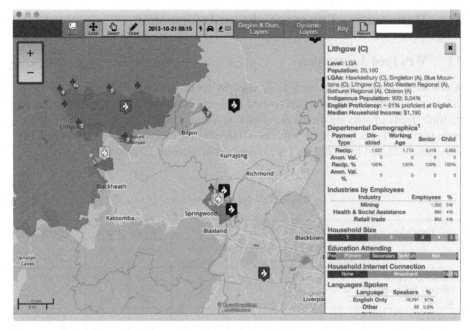

Fig. 1. State Mine Fire, near Lithgow NSW on 21 October, 2013

2   Related Work

There are existing web feed aggregators that provide some of the ERIC features to combine content from the 'live' web feeds[3], however they do not support the diverse range of formats currently managed by ERIC. Similarly, some of the ERIC mapping and geospatial features are provided by Geospatial Information Infrastructures and Web 2.0 'mashups'[4], however, they require the data to be available in specific formats and do not support the identified Situation Report features.

The central task of the Emergency Management team is to maintain situational awareness throughout the response and recovery phases of disaster events. The Situation Report embodies this knowledge. A number of Situation Awareness models exist to help characterise this process. For example, Endsley [1] defines three levels: perception (sensing the environment), comprehension (combining sensory data to discover information) and projection (using the information to predict possible futures). ERIC helps with the first two levels, perception and comprehension, by assembling information from various sources into a single coherent picture. Predicting possible consequences remains the task of the user, although this could be an area of future work.

---

[3] See http://www.rss-readers.org/list-of-rs-feed-reader/
[4] For example, see GeoCommons: http://geocommons.com/

3   Harmonising Emergency Event Information

3.1   Web Feed Aggregation

A summary of the different web feeds used by ERIC is shown in Table 1 indicating the content, word count and formats used for each. Note that some agencies maintain multiple feeds of varying types. As shown in Table 1, ERIC tracks nine RSS feeds, eight GeoRSS feeds, two KML sources, 10 GeoJSON sources, and 13 GML files. The providers indicated by a 'dagger'[†] are discussed in more detail below.

Table 1. Web Feed Summary

Provider	Content				Word count		Format
	Traffic details	Fires	Weather warnings	Other incidents	Mean	Std Dev	
Australian Capital Territory Emergency Services[†]	✓	✓		✓	1,694	1,548	GeoRSS
Bureau of Meteorology			✓				13 GML, 8 RSS, text, XML
Geoscience Australia		✓					GeoRSS
Queensland Traffic	✓						GeoJSON
Queensland Community Safety	✓			✓			GeoJSON
NSW Roads	✓						6 GeoJSON
NSW Rural Fire[†]		✓			5,186	4,993	GeoRSS
Rural Fire Queensland[†]		✓	✓		4,053	2,906	GeoRSS, XLS
South Australian Country Fire[†]		✓			852	773	KML
Tasmanian Fire[†]	✓	✓		✓	9,833	10,979	GeoRSS, KML
Victorian Country Fire[†]	✓	✓		✓	3,024	2,765	2 GeoRSS, RSS
Victorian Environment		✓		✓			2 GeoJSON
Victorian Roads	✓						JSON
West Australian Fire[†]		✓	✓		17,948	10,822	GeoRSS

3.2   Common Web Feed Model

The dynamic 'live' web feed data is polled regularly with the results stored in a database. These web sources are heterogeneous in many ways and a common model has been defined which is the basis of the database schema. The variety of data formats and information content used by the various agencies around Australia can be seen in Table 1. In general however, the web feed content is similar for each: a web feed has a URL endpoint which provides regular information updates. These updates consist of one or more posts describing the individual events. Each post contains: an identifier that uniquely identifies the event described; a timestamp for the individual post; the description of the event; the event category; a link to further information from the source; and the location as either a point or region. This model is shown in Fig. 2, from [2].

The process of harmonising the various web feeds into the common structure of Fig. 2 is one of the tasks performed by the ERIC web server: each web feed is regularly checked for updates (currently every 10 minutes, which is configurable) with new information recorded in a database. Note that only new information is recorded in the database – new content consists of a collection of posts where some posts contain updated information while others remain unchanged. Identifying differences between subsequent posts about the same event is part of the user alerting process.

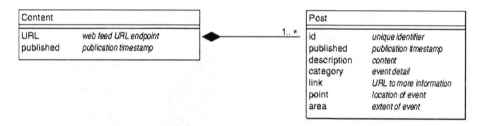

Fig. 2. Common Web Feed Model

3.3   Harmonising Examples

Further examination of the web feed contents is focused on the seven web feeds indicated by the 'dagger'[†] in Table 1. These fire feeds were targeted since they provide coverage for the whole country, are representative of the diverse formats used and include geospatial content. The target feeds are mostly rural fire services from around the country, except for the Australian Capital Territory Emergency Services and West Australian Fire which includes posts about other event types as well. There were 21 different categories of events derived from the content of these feeds recorded for the period 1 October 2012 – 1 May 2014, ranging from hazard reduction, permitted burns, car incidents, false alarms, electrical fires and so on. Of these, the information of interest is the fire 'alert level': the fire warnings to the community.

In general, the progression of alert levels for fires are 'Advice': an indication that a fire has started and there is no immediate danger; 'Watch and Act': a heightened level of threat where preparatory action by the community is required; and 'Fire Emergency': the highest alert level where there is immediate threat to the community.

The different agencies report this information in different ways. Of the seven target web feeds† in Table 1, four produce fire warnings in the three alert level categories noted above. One has an indication in the event title that can be used to derive the alert level. The remaining two do not directly state the alert level, but instead provide detailed descriptions of the type of fire, such as 'grass fire'. In these two cases, the alert levels are mapped as an Advice for all reported fires.

Fig. 3 shows the distribution of fire events showing the different reporting styles of the agencies: across the Eastern Seaboard, and into Tasmania, the agencies report very frequently. By comparison, Western Australia has far fewer reports, and the Northern Territory has none. Reports are widespread in Victoria, and Tasmania, but in the other eastern states they cluster along the coast with the population.

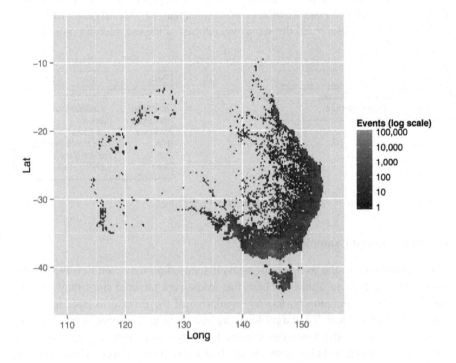

Fig. 3. Map of reports

The agencies describe events with a sequence of key-value pairs, for example the 'Type' and 'Status'. Of the seven sources investigated, all but one show a strong indication of a few standard ways of reporting fires. This was measured by counting the number of fields; approximated by the number of colons (:) in the description of the posts and illustrated in Fig. 4. West Australian Fire was the exception, with a highly prosaic format and long reports, as shown by the mean description length in Table 1. As such, they have been excluded from Fig. 4 because they do not use the key-value pairs and their data obscures the other results.

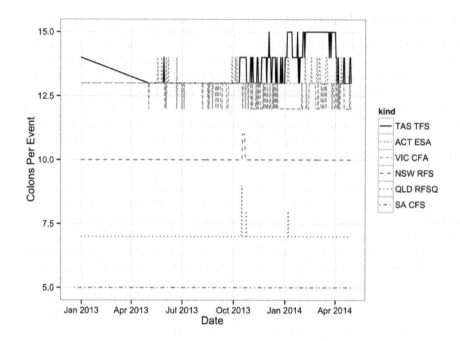

Fig. 4. Colon ':' count per event per day

We can compare Fig. 3 and Fig. 4 to tease out some of the diversity of reporting present in these feeds. In Queensland, the reports are concentrated towards the south and the east, however the reporting format is very static. In fact, it is quite brief, and despite the large number of reports many of them are almost indistinguishable. This is even more extreme in South Australia. Here the reports concentrate heavily around Adelaide and the Eyre Peninsula, and are very rigidly formatted. This is in part due to the Victorian Country Fire's choice of using KML as the reporting format, which is highly structured.

In contrast are Victoria and Tasmania. Both have a spread of reports covering the majority of the state, and both have a fluctuating reporting format, although unlike Western Australia the format is still structured. This structure is not because of the format, since Queensland and Western Australia also use GeoRSS.

Different agencies have informally extended the file formats with structured text formats, such as the use of colon-seperated fields and values. In some cases, such as Queensland, this new format is strictly adhered to; however other agencies are not so strict, changing their customisations as they feel the need. The GeoRSS format is particularly amenable to this extension, with the main 'post' tag allowed to contain arbitrary XML, although most commonly HTML or plain text is used.

4   Discussion and Future Work

4.1   Architectural Improvements

All ERIC data is managed as a data warehouse. While this is necessary for the web feed content to provide an historical archive, some of the other data layers could be provided using services provided by the data custodians. These services are currently not universally available, but it is expected they will be established over time.

Another benefit of a service based approach is the ability of users to include spatial data layers of their choosing. This is best achieved using a standards based approach to service integration, such as adopting relevant Open Geospatial Consortium service standards, such as the Web Feature Service and the Web Mapping Service.

Such integration currently requires a skill set beyond the average user. In order to empower users to integrate their own data, a new generation of supporting tools are needed. We have investigated the use of a web-based user interface to allow non-programmers to easily upload newly available data.

Using the web-based upload/update tool, users may upload their data in a number of file formats (currently ESRI Shapefiles and CSV, with nested data formats like XML/JSON to follow, for example: KML, RSS and RDF). The tool then presents the schema of the uploaded files against an ontology (a conceptual schema), terms from which are then used to describe the semantics of the uploaded data. The user's description of their data in ontology terms describes a 'mapping', which is automatically interpreted and executed by the tool to extract data from the uploaded file, transform it to the relevant data structure and load it into the system, completely automating the manual Extract/Transform/Load process.

This process was aimed at allowing the user to update the data warehouse with new versions of data without the need of a system administrator. This tool could be adapted to semantically integrate new data sources from service end points. Instead of simply providing a new dataset as a visual layer in ERIC, the content could optionally be merged with existing data layers.

4.2   Common Alerting Protocol

The Common Alerting Protocol (CAP)[5] is an international XML standard to facilitate the construction and exchange of emergency alert and warning messages. The Australian Government has created an Australian Profile of the standard[6] and are

---

[5] http://docs.oasis-open.org/emergency/cap/v1.2/CAP-v1.2.html
[6] http://www.em.gov.au/CapAuStd

encouraging all Australian emergency agencies to adopt it. This is a significant undertaking with only one agency listed in Table 1 doing so to date[7].

Since ERIC harmonises web feed data from various emergency related agencies, initial work has been carried out to evaluate the difficulty for ERIC to produce CAP compliant messages. The most challenging task to date has been determining the mapping between each agency's category of events to the standard CAP event categories. For example some agencies describe an incident as a 'scrub fire' to which there is no direct CAP mapping. The options in this case are: fire, bushfire, forest fire, grass fire, structure fire and industrial fire.

Data integration would be simplified if the agencies published information using CAP. This is an area of further work requiring liaison with key agencies to demonstrate how this can be done using the CAP messages produced by ERIC.

4.3   Social Media Integration

The tasks achievable using ERIC can be extended by including crowd sourced social media. Some progress has been made in ERIC by linking to the CSIRO Emergency Situational Awareness (ESA) platform [3] which continuously retrieves and analyses new Twitter posts originating from Australia and New Zealand. It is able to detect high frequency words and alerts the user to these using a tag cloud. ESA also uses machine learning methods to classify Tweets containing earthquake and fire related keywords, to see if they relate to current or new emergency events. ESA provides a search interface allowing the user to search for Tweets matching specific criteria.

ERIC includes a hyperlink in an event's popup to the ESA search interface for every fire event. The search terms are preset so that ESA will search for Tweets from the region surrounding the selected event that have been classified as positive fire related Tweets. Tweets from official agencies and the general public often contain extra information that is not available via the official web feeds. This extra information may include pictures or videos of the event and detailed impact information.

In future we plan to explore a more comprehensive integration of web feed and social media content. Instead of simply linking ERIC and ESA, we would like to present the social media data within the ERIC tool. An identified issue to be resolved is the trustworthiness of this information source [4,5]. This is especially important for emergency managers who are mainly concerned with verifiable information.

5   Conclusions

CSIRO has developed the ERIC web based tool that demonstrates the usefulness of data integration for emergency managers. ERIC improves the situational awareness of the Emergency Management team in the Australian Government Department of Human Services by integrating information from authoritative public real time web feeds with demographics data to provide a national picture that is available for historical

---

[7] http://www.rfs.nsw.gov.au/feeds/majorIncidentsCAP.xml

review. ERIC also identifies when the current situation changes and informs the user, reducing the need for the operator to do so.

ERIC was developed to support the intelligence gathering and situation reporting activities performed by the department's Emergency Management team. This has been successful, reducing the time taken to produce a Situation Report from approximately two hours to about 20 minutes. This is one of the main activities of the team during emergency events and their aftermath. It is critical that this information be reported in a timely manner. There have been other benefits also: the workflow of creating a Situation Report has been revised and improved; a standard Situation Report template defined and a method of naming events established.

A public version of ERIC is available at http://eric.csiro.au/ demonstrating the utility of data integration for the purposes of emergency management. All departmental information has been removed from the public version for privacy reasons and the situation reporting features disabled. While ERIC was developed for the department's Emergency Management team, we are actively promoting it for use by other agencies, the not for profit sector and the general public.

Acknowledgements. ERIC was funded under the Human Services Delivery Research Alliance between the CSIRO and the Australian Government Department of Human Services. The ESA project was originally financially supported through the National Security Science and Technology Branch within the Department of the Prime Minister and Cabinet.

References

1. Endsley, M.R.: Toward a theory of situation awareness in dynamic systems: Situation awareness. Human Factors 37(1), 32–64 (1995)
2. Power, R., Wise, C., Robinson, B., Squire, G.: Harmonising Web Feeds for Emergency Management. In: Piantadosi, J., Anderssen, R.S., Boland, J. (eds.) MODSIM2013 20th International Congress on Modelling and Simulation. Modelling and Simulation Society of Australia and New Zealand, pp. 2194–2200 (December 2013),
http://www.mssanz.org.au/modsim2013/K5/power.pdf
ISBN: 978-0-9872143-3-1
3. Power, R., Robinson, B., Colton, J., Cameron, M.: Emergency Situation Awareness: Twitter Case Studies. In: Hanachi, C., Bénaben, F., Charoy, F. (eds.) ISCRAM-med 2014. Lecture Notes in Business Information Processing, vol. 196, pp. 218–231. Springer, Heidelberg (2014)
4. Hiltz, S.R., Kushma, J., Plotnick, L.: Use of Social Media by US Public Sector Emergency Managers: Barriers and Wish Lists. In: 11th International Conference on Information Systems for Crisis Response and Management (ISCRAM), Pennsylvania, USA (May 2014)
5. Thomson, R., Ito, N., Suda, H., Lin, F., Liu, Y., Hayasaka, R., Isochi, R., Wang, Z.: Trusting Tweets: The Fukushima Disaster and Information Source Credibility on Twitter. In: The 9th International Conference on Information Systems for Crisis Response and Management (ISCRAM), Vancouver, Canada (April 2012)

Civic Issues Reporting and Involvement of Volunteers as a Phenomenon in the Czech Republic

Miroslav Kubásek

Institute of Biostatistics and Analyses, Masaryk University, Brno, Czech Republic
kubasek@iba.muni.cz

Abstract. Today's smartphones can unlock the full potential of crowdsourcing and take eParticipation to a new level. Users are allowed to transparently contribute to complex and novel problem solving. Engagement of citizens is still challenging but the proliferation of smartphones with geolocation have made it easier than before. In this paper we will introduce the ZmapujTo project - a reporting platform in the form of a mobile application and responsive web page intended for citizens to report civic issues. We will also describe used technology stack and system architecture. In addition, we will introduce "Uklid'me Česko" (Clean up the Czech Republic) which is a maiden event taking place in the Czech Republic. We explain how ZmapujTo is applied in this event and the ICT tools that are offered to volunteers and organizers for communication and management of the event.

Keywords: Crowdsourcing, smartphones, illegal landfills, geolocation, web portal, GIS, mapping, human sensors.

1 Introduction

Illegal waste dumping is a serious environmental concern in many countries[1,2]. These illegal dumps decrease the quality of human life in surrounding areas. Illegal dumping of garbage, discarded appliances, old barrels, used tyres, furniture, yard debris, oil, antifreeze and pesticides can threaten human health, wildlife and the environment.

Engaging citizens is challenging but due to the proliferation of personal smartphones with geolocation it is easier to develop a reporting system that can be used by every citizen. Timely elimination of illegal dump sites can limit the extent and severity of the damage (soil and water contamination, hazard of fire etc.).

Solving these issues was the main reason for creating the ZmapujTo. Project was started in mid 2011 as an e-Participation project and became the most popular environmental project in the Czech Republic. ZmapujTo is based on community phenomenon and thus leverages the power of crowd. It enables each one of us to be heard [3,4,5].

R. Denzer et al. (Eds.): ISESS 2015, IFIP AICT 448, pp. 151–159, 2015.
© IFIP International Federation for Information Processing 2015

2   The ZmapujTo Web Portal

In this chapter we shortly explain the framework of the Web portal ZmapujTo and introduce the technology of interactive mapping which enables detailed viewing of reported issues. We use several advanced GIS technologies to improve the visualization of reported illegal dumps (Fig. 1).

The first technology is the Google Street View[1], which enables users to get a very detailed overview of the situation around the reported illegal dump. The Google Street View is a feature of Google Maps that provides 360° panoramic street-level views and allows users to view parts of selected cities and their surrounding metropolitan areas at ground level. The Google Street View displays photos that were previously taken by a camera mounted on an automobile. Due to the fact that illegal dumps are mostly located near roads, we found the Google Street View as a useful tool to add a situation overview about the reported illegal dump.

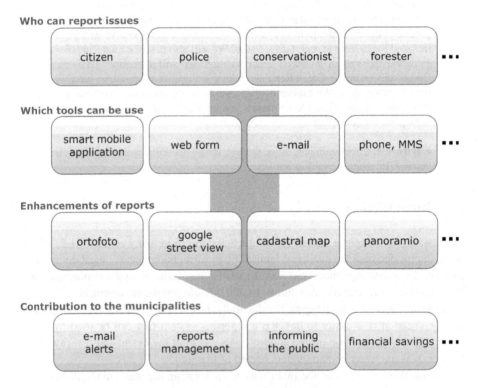

Fig. 1. Framework of the project ZmapujTo

---

[1] http://maps.google.com/intl/cs_cz/help/maps/streetview/

Next we integrate the cadastral maps of the Czech Republic[2] to the web portal
ZmapujTo. This technology can simply identify the owner of the illegal dump site and
project a specific plot of this. The municipal authority can thus directly contact this
owner.

The map of illegal dump sites also provides a set of layers which can be explored
by the users. The user can select from the menu of the portal the ortofoto layer, hybrid
layer and a terrain layer.

We gained experience using the initial version of ZmapujTo portal since 2011 and
we have collected a list of opinions, proposals and criticisms. For example a lot of
municipalities wanted to extend the types of reports (we had only one possibility to
report illegal dumps, so they proposed to extend reports e.g. about overloaded bins).
Some authorities closely cooperated with their city police department to help monitoring illegal dumps in their cities. They were interested to integrate a reporting system
directly into the police information and communication systems etc.

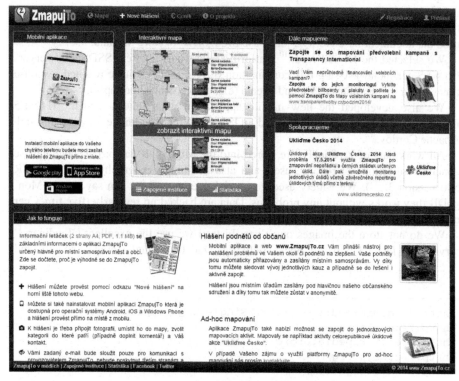

Fig. 2. Welcome page of ZmapujTo

Based on user feedback we launched a new version of the ZmapujTo portal in
Spring of 2014 (Fig.2). The main properties of this new version are: an extension
of report types, an extensive list of mobile platforms which will allow running the

---

[2] http://nahlizenidokn.cuzk.cz/

ZmapujTo mobile application, and an improved web page to employ a responsive design paradigm and enable the use of tablets and phones to browse and manage reported issues.

3   System Architecture

The general system architecture (Fig. 3) is proposed to utilize existing technical solutions and services as much as possible. We have tried to design the system so that it can be deployed on a distributed environment if it will be necessary, e.g. in case of large traffic.

We analyzed the state-of-the-art information and communication technologies (ICT) and decided to use a single page application approach of SPA[3] technology in order to improve the web portal response time. We selected the AngularJS[4] JavaScript[5] framework. We also applied the JavaScript language in cooperation with NodeJS[6] (JavaScript event-driven runtime) and Express[7] (the web application framework for nodeJS on the server side). We decided to leave traditional relation databases and used the document base NoSQL[8] database MongoDB[9] to store the data.

We selected the DigitalOcean[10] platform for hosting (it offers SSD cloud servers from \$5 per month). Using this combination of ICT tools we have reached response times under 70 ms on user frontend events (e.g. map zoom, filter apply).

We also developed the new mobile application with Sencha Touch[11] HTML5 framework and ported it to Android, iOS and Windows Phone devices through Apache Cordova[12].

All work data of ZmapujTo are stored into the MongoDB database. This database contains collections of reports, users and also additional geographical data (ArcČR 500 version 3.1[13]). We widely used geospatial queries and we can say that in MongoDB they works without any problems. Data are backed up regularly (five times per day) on geographically remote location.

We do not store the images ourselves. Instead we use the excellent Cloudinary[14] service for fast CDN-based image delivery. Due to limited storage capacity and

---

[3] http://en.wikipedia.org/wiki/Single-page_application
[4] http://angularjs.org/
[5] http://en.wikipedia.org/wiki/JavaScript
[6] http://nodejs.org/
[7] http://expressjs.com/
[8] http://en.wikipedia.org/wiki/NoSQL
[9] https://www.mongodb.org/
[10] https://www.digitalocean.com/
[11] http://www.sencha.com/products/touch
[12] http://cordova.apache.org/
[13] http://www.arcdata.cz/produkty-a-sluzby/geograficka-data/arccr-500/
[14] http://cloudinary.com/

bandwidth of Cloudinary we store here only processed images (resized to 500x500 px). Original images we uploaded into Amazon S3[15] online file storage to keep them for possible future use.

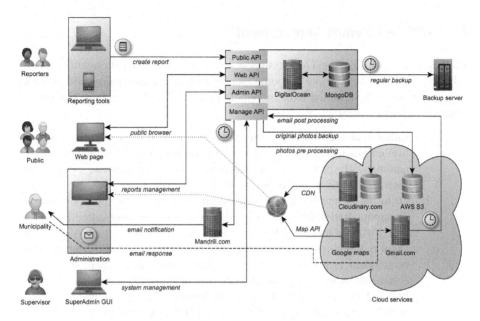

Fig. 3. System architecture

We created RESTful server with several APIs, where we combine the best of No-deJS and PHP worlds. We use NodeJS mostly for critical, the most widely used parts (e.g. filtering of reports in map, on-line providing of the data).

In our system we have proposed four APIs. The first "Public API" is intended to be a backend server for mobile applications. Its main objective is to receive photos and reports from mobile applications and from on-line form. The second API "Web API" is intended to serving data for web application (based on AngularJS framework). "Admin API" with authentication is intended to municipalities, which are able to manage reports in their regions. Last "Manage API" is used by supervisor and enable to manage and processing of new reports, processing of photos, management of e-mail notifications etc.

For email notifications of municipalities we utilized the Mandrill[16] which has a easy to use really good API. For processing of emails from municipalities we simply utilized Gmail[17] service. We use email prefixing (append a plus "+" sign and any combination of words or numbers after your email address) to enable automatically unique identification of related report.

---

[15] Amazon Simple Storage Service http://aws.amazon.com/s3/

[16] https://mandrill.com/

[17] https://mail.google.com

The system in this configuration works very well for last 10 months. In this time period we did not notice loss of services used. System responses are despite the growing interest in ZmapujTo still very fast and sufficient.

4   Efficient Report Management

The key issue of the ZmapujTo reporting system is the communication with municipal authorities. In the ZmapujTo portal, the responsible municipality will receive information about the reported issue by e-mail. Municipal authorities have two possibilities to solve this event:

1. Either to answer directly to this email with response. Mostly it is information on whether they are aware of this issue or not. These responses are automatically processed and the content of these response e-mails are inserted directly to the record list of specific events;
2. Or to log-in into ZmapujTo web portal and process the report directly in its administration interface (Fig. 4). The aim of this application is to provide a simple tool, which will give to the authorities actual information about reported issues in their district. The administrator of the municipality assigned to a specific issue can change its, change location or leave comments as well. The administrator can also use the statistics of the district and a set of widgets (Fig. 5), which can be placed into the municipality web site and thus inform the visitors that the municipality is involved in the project, and how many issues have been reported and solved

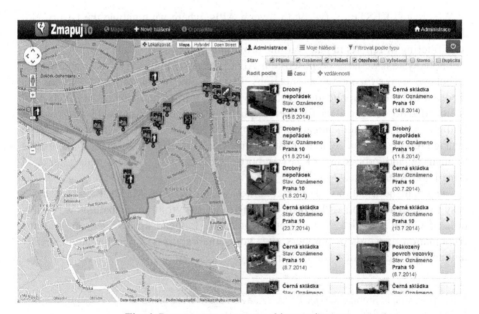

Fig. 4. Reports management and interactive map

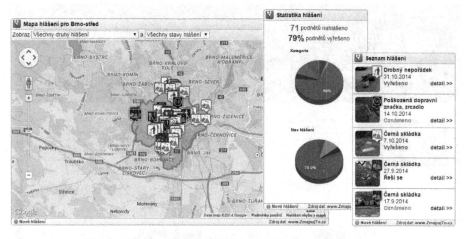

Fig. 5. Widgets which can by placed into municipality webpage

Currently, 470 municipalities and institutions from the entire Czech Republic are involved into ZmapujTo.

5   Voluntary Event

In 2014 for the first time, an event called "Uklid'me Česko" (Clean up the Czech Republic) took place in the Czech Republic (Fig. 6). It was inspired by past events from abroad (e.g. "Let's do it!"[18]), and hopes to address the continued lack of success in cleaning the dumps. The main goals were to warn and inform the public about the problems of illegal dumps and subsequently clean them up with the help of volunteers.

The cleaning was scheduled for 17th May 2014. This cleaning event collaborated closely with the ZmapujTo project and used its platform for mapping and registration of illegal dumps. The event was driven by volunteers, municipalities and non-governmental organizations.

"Uklid'me Česko" participants were divided into groups, with having at least one organizer per group. The organizer was responsible for arranging group meetings in order to discuss various issues regarding the event.

One volunteer in the group used an interactive map (Fig. 7) on the web portal to register. Dark-colored points are drawn on the map to show all the registration points. Each of these points contains information about the number of registered participants (organizers and volunteers separately) in a particular location. Therefore one can check whether there is any organized group already present in his place of interest or whether it is necessary to establish a new one. Those interested persons can register to one particular point at any part of a city or a village.

---

[18] http://www.letsdoitworld.org/

Fig. 6. Web page of the cleaning event

Thanks to the registration in this information system, organizers gain access (password required) to their account created directly on the web portal. Each organizer can manage a number of volunteers, choose a meeting point and an cleaning area (illegal dumps from ZmapujTo project are seamlessly integrated, so the organizer can select specific illegal dumps, which going to be cleaned up). This organizer's account also mediates communication with associated volunteers and with other organizers, for example from their neighborhoods.

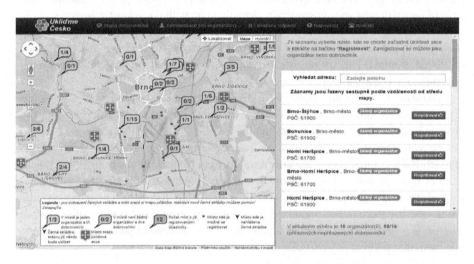

Fig. 7. Interactive map of volunteers integrated with illegal dumps from ZmapujTo

6   Conclusion

The ZmapujTo project fulfills its aim to inform the public of the Czech Republic about the dangers related to illegal dump sites, motivates the public to report them, and offers municipalities and other organizations a tool for administration of these reports.

We followed various feedbacks collected from users and developed a new version of the web portal with state-of-the-art information technologies. An extension of the report types and automatic communication with all municipal authorities in the Czech Republic are the main benefits of the new version. The user-friendliness has been improved by using up-to-date and more efficient technologies. We utilize existing technical solutions and services as much as possible. We chose young technology as a NoSQL MongoDB database, Node.js, Express web framework and AngularJS for creating Single Page Application. Despite the initial fears, we can tell now, that during the operation of the system we didn't encountered a single failure or a major problem.

During the event "Clean up the Czech Republic" which took place on Saturday 17th May 2014 the participants collected 350 tons of garbage, the volunteers participated in 280 places over the whole country. Based on feedback from the organizers and volunteers who used the ZmapujTo mobile application and the interactive map of volunteers we can state that the our systems fulfills our expectations.

References

1. Europol, Europol warns of increase in illegal waste dumping,
   `https://www.europol.europa.eu/content/simplenews/`
   `europol-warns-increase-illegal-waste-dumping-1057` (last accessed: March 15, 2014)
2. HCCREMS, Hunter & Central Coast Regional Environmental Management Strategy Illegal Dumping (2013), `http://www.hccrems.com.au/Programs/Environmental-Compliance/Sub-projects/Illegal-Dumping.aspx` (last accessed March 15, 2014)
3. Kubásek, M., Hřebíček, J.: Crowdsource Approach for Mapping of Illegal Dumps in the Czech Republic. International Journal of Spatial Data Infrastructures Research 8, 144–157 (2013)
4. Kubásek, M.: Mapping of Illegal Dumps in the Czech Republic – Using a Crowd-Sourcing Approach. In: Hřebíček, J., Schimak, G., Kubásek, M., Rizzoli, A.E. (eds.) ISESS 2013. IFIP AICT, vol. 413, pp. 177–187. Springer, Heidelberg (2013)
5. Kubásek, M., Hřebíček, J.: Involving Citizens into Mapping of Illegal Landfills and other civic issues in the Czech Republic. In: Ames, D.P., Quinn, N.W.T., Rizzoli, A.E. (eds.) Proceedings of the 7th International Congress on Environmental Modelling and Software, pp. 978–988. iEMSS, San Diego (2014) ISBN 978-88-903574-4-2

Mobile Field Data Collection for Post Bushfire Analysis and African Farmers

Bradley Lane, Nicholas J. Car, Justin Leonard, Felix Lipkin, and Anders Siggins

Land and Water Flagship: CSIRO, Highett and Clayton, VIC and Brisbane, QLD, Australia
bradley.lane@csiro.au

Abstract. In recent years CSIRO has been trialling field data collection using mobile devices such as phones and tablets. Two recent tools that have been developed by CSIRO are the CSIRO Surveyor (Post Bushfire House Surveyor) and DroidFarmer. Challenges tackled include mapping field documents to mobile data through QR (Quick Response) codes, rapid input of survey data, accurate capture of GPS locations and offline operation. Throughout this paper we detail the design choices made for these systems. We give details of how well field data collection was performed and discuss our planned future developments in this space.

Keywords: DroidFarmer, CSIRO Surveyor, AusAID, Bushfire, Africa, Farmer, GIS, Questionnaire, Android, MongoDB, SQL Server.

1   Introduction

CSIRO Surveyor and Droid Farmer applications (apps) were designed to fulfil a need to easily and efficiently collect field data. Each tool faced different challenges due to differing design requirements. The key issues for Droid Farmer were linking field documents to app-collected data, getting accurate GPS readings and enabling offline data recording (i.e. local phone storage) for areas with poor network coverage. CSIRO Surveyor had to handle issues of efficiency in GIS and survey data entry, map caching for offline use and the possibility of communications infrastructure breakdown.

Throughout this paper we explain how we attempted to resolve these issues through mobile application system design and software architectures.

2   CSIRO Surveyor

CSIRO Surveyor was initially developed for the New South Wales Rural Fire Service (RFS) to enable detailed data capture in areas recently affected by bushfire. After a bushfire front passes an area and it is deemed safe, trained survey teams with tablets carrying the Surveyor application are sent into the field. The app delivers two primary functions: firstly, the detailed marking of houses, trees, water tanks and other types of objects using a Graphical Information System (GIS) user interface (see Fig. 2) and secondly, a novel Survey Questionnaire Response System (SQRS, see Fig. 3). Along

R. Denzer et al. (Eds.): ISESS 2015, IFIP AICT 448, pp. 160–168, 2015.

with the main app a cut-down version was developed for Rapid Impact Assessment, which provided a means to easily visually track bushfire-affected houses via a central desktop GIS dashboard.

The data collected was used for public reporting of statistics and then post bushfire analysis. Analysis of the affected areas gives information on how to reduce the impact of bushfires in the future.

2.1   Basic System Design

The basic system design for CSIRO Surveyor is displayed in Fig 1.

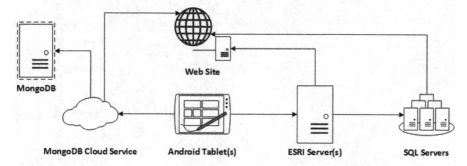

Fig. 1. The main technologies used were ESRI GIS Servers, SQL Databases (for ESRI data and Questionnaires), Android Devices, ASP.NET Web Sites and MongoDB Cloud Services

[4] discusses a similar Android data collection system and points to the importance of ease of input, consideration of the availability of internet connectivity and data visualisation. We address these considerations below.

GPS Touch Input

The GIS interface (see Fig. 2) was developed using Android and ESRI [1] APIs. Maps are loaded before travelling to a site. Once on location, the user marks houses, trees, water tanks and other entities of interest regarding bushfires by first touching the entity type on the right and then marking its location on the screen. After marking the entity locations the questionnaire activity starts.

There were three different methods of marking entity locations on the screen depending on the type of entity. To record a polygon entity such as a house the user marked each point and then pressed the starting point again to complete the shape. For a single point entity the user just marked the desired location once. Finally for multi-point entities like trees the user marked each position with a screen tap for each point and then completed the entry process by tapping the final point a second time.

Questionnaires

The tablet-optimized Survey Quick Response System (SQRS) was developed using the standard Android API. Questionnaires were structured in a hierarchical fashion using a separate web tool and then uploaded to a central MongoDB cloud-base store [2] on creation; editors were also able to update the cloud store questionnaires. Tablets then communicated with the cloud store allowing them to automatically update their local copies of the questionnaires. Questions could be 'removed' by disabling/hiding them. No questions were deleted from the cloud store to prevent older responses being orphaned (no question left to link to an answer).

Fig. 2. The above image shows the GIS input interface

Questionnaire Construction

Questionnaires were built by creating questions with appropriate responses and adding them to a hierarchy which ensured only necessary information was collected when certain question's answer invalidated other questions. Questions responses could be either multiple choice or numeric, with individual responses being linked to any number of further questions in the hierarchy.

Multiple choice responses were the simplest to implement as new questions could be easily linked to individual responses. Linking numeric responses to new questions was achieved using value ranges, for example, when a user enters value in range of 0 to 20 we could ask questions x, y and z.

Questionnaire Input

Due to the hierarchical structure of the questionnaires users could complete input actions very quickly. For multiple choice questions, a single tap on a response immediately moved one to the next appropriate question. For numeric answers, the user had to enter a value before tapping a button to continue.

When a mistake was made, the user could press a 'Back' button to backtrack through the questions. The questions followed a specific track, with questions being asked until the end of a branch with hierarchy recursion used to find the next relevant question. A summary of questions and responses is given on the right side of the SQRS interface in Fig. 3.

Some questions required the user to enter information regarding a specific face or side of a building. To make this process easier for the user we dynamically labeled them for the user as A, B, C and D (see Fig. 3) then referred to these specific labels in the questionnaires.

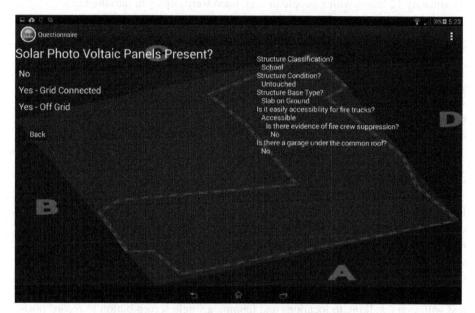

Fig. 3. The above image shows the SQRS input interface

2.2   Consideration of Infrastructure Breakdown

To cater for mobile phone network infrastructure breakdown, the CSIRO Surveyor and RIA tools incorporated offline capabilities. This was implemented using a SQLite database to cache data that had not been sent to the cloud store. When the user of a tablet caching data later moved into network connectivity, the cached data could then be transmitted. Since data could be cached, phone network infrastructure state does not affect the effectiveness of the app. Results could not be displayed on the desktop GIS dashboard until successful data upload.

2.3   Data Integrity and Cross Checking

For comparison and data integrity purposes, two copies of the questionnaire results were transmitted; one to the ESRI Database and one to MongoDB. This was very helpful in both ensuring that results were successfully transmitted to both systems and that the results matched. Data was transmitted with a globally unique identifier (GUID) and a time stamp for quick matching.

2.4   Usage Statistics

Between October 20th and 30th 2013, 4,715 questionnaires were submitted from one bushfire. These included 24 different types of questionnaires plus separate storage of other types of data such as photos. To collect the data from all affected houses approximately 12 teams with 2 people in each team were deployed into the field.

2.5   Planned Improvements

The current system is designed for use with bushfires but could easily be modified to support other disasters. To accomplish this, we intend to make certain sections of the system more generic. For example, the interface for selecting the type of entity to record (see Fig. 2) is partially hard coded. By making the screen layout and entities configurable, the application could easily support different disaster types.

3   DroidFarmer

DroidFarmer is an Android mobile phone application built to collect crop and spatial data for farm surveys in Africa. The app was designed using standard Android tools and built for compatibility with early Android devices. It was also designed to be very simple to operate in order to cater for users not familiar with Smartphones. It used offline storage with online sync to handle poor cellular/wireless internet availability in farm areas. GPS readings were taken for spatial objects such as trees and field areas and with users walking to locations and tapping a single screen button to record position. After transmission to a central server, recordings were displayed as map points and polygons on a web map interface.

This app is essentially a 'mapping app' as described by [5] however, unlike the proposition in that paper that such apps require potentially costly and time-consuming post-collection data analysis, such steps are not required where app users are the beneficiaries of the field data collection (e.g. farmers using the app to measure their field areas and results can be related on screen). Where scientists are the beneficiaries of aggregated field data, normal results processing is required.

The data collected had numerous uses. One example was the collection of soil moisture data from field instruments to assist farmers in choosing appropriate crops. Another example was the recording of field size and position, which enabled farmers to order goods and services without being overcharged.

3.1   Basic System Design

The basic system design for DroidFarmer is shown in Fig 4.

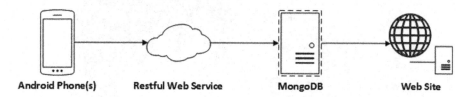

Android Phone(s)   **Restful Web Service**   **MongoDB**   **Web Site**

Fig. 4. Main technologies used were Android Devices, MongoDB RESTful Web Services and a Web Site

Document Linking

One novel aspect of DroidFarmer was its linking of paper field records, readings from field equipment and phone gathered data through interpreting Quick Response (QR) codes and its function reuse.

Fig. 5. The DroidFarmer logo and a QR Code

QR codes were printed on paper survey sheets and affixed to field instruments via stickers. This was designed to prevent data confusion and loss when data was recorded in multiple forms. The approach worked well with many thousands of complete bundles of field data being recorded and incomplete bundles instantly identifiable after data upload. This rapid understanding of data gathering completeness saved much time in deciding which fields to resurvey. Extensive input validation of phone input data and QR recording sequences was implemented which reduced data entry errors compared with paper-based recording. Several data gathering workflows were implemented that utilized the same GPS recording, QR code handling and form entry functions which are able to be used still further. The code scanning was done using a 3rd party tool called "Barcode Scanner" developed by ZXing Project [3]. Data visualisation was done via a website (see Fig. 6), where recorded data was marked on a map with pins; additional data and images could then be accessed by clicking on a pin.

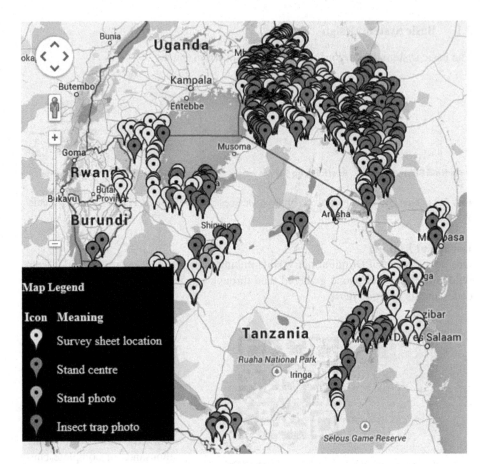

Fig. 6. A screenshot of a large number of DroidFarmer-reported survey locations in East Africa. Four different types of icons are shown for four different data types: the locations of survey sheet completions (in the field), the centres of stands of crops, photos of stands of crops and photos of insect traps.

Improving the Accuracy of GPS Readings

To aim for the best accuracy, we deployed multiple strategies based on observations from testing. Two key things we observed in testing were that GPS tracking took time to initiate and that accuracy improved the longer a user stayed in one spot.

To take advantage of this we started tracking locations as soon as the user entered the activity. Once started we continually polled for new readings with each new reading being added to a short stack. When a user requested a location be marked we would first look at the top reading, if it met our accuracy requirements it was used, if not we would check the stack for one that does, if none was found we took the average position.

Because the user needed to spend time entering data before taking a reading (not a coincidence), the device was normally in a good position to take the first reading.

In either case the process was fast because the stack was continually updated the moment the activity was started.

Our goal was to have readings accurate to 10m or less. Using the above mentioned approaches we were generally able to achieve this target.

3.2   Dealing with a Low Tech Community

The overall level of smart phone technology was low in Africa. Due to this we needed to design the software to run on the lowest possible version of Android while taking into consideration our design needs.

3.3   Data Validation and Statistics

Most spatial data could be easily validated visually (GIS view) from the website upon the users return. At the time of writing there were several thousand submitted recordings across the various categories.

4   Controlling the User Experience

Use of the CSIRO Surveyor app was a controlled user experience as it was manually loaded onto tablets which were then handed to individuals and small groups after receiving training. DroidFarmer on the other hand was delivered to phones using the Google Play online app store meaning access to it was available to all. Scientists familiar with Smartphones wanting to capture data could do so easily, but farmers not familiar needed to be guided through the process.

5   Platform Specific vs. Platform Independent

After considering various platform-specific vs platform-independent designs, we decided to go for a hybrid model. We utilised RESTful technologies whenever possible; but for devices we chose to be dependent on Android. This decision was made after careful consideration of the level of control we needed over device hardware.

6   Conclusions

Both DroidFarmer and CSIRO Surveyor were received well by their intended audience. Users appreciated the effort that was taken to meet their specific needs which we were able to achieve while retaining a large amount of application code reuse. DroidFarmer enabled, and continues to enable, farmers and researchers to collect data in Africa and have it instantly available for study world-wide. CSIRO Surveyor is continuing to enable the rapid collection of post disaster survey data. These systems met their intended design use and are continuing to be developed and enhanced for future use.

References

1. Environmental Systems Research Institute, Inc. ArcGIS Runtime SDK for Android. Software Application. ESRI, Redlands, CA, USA (2013),
2. https://developers.arcgis.com/android/ (accessed October 30, 2014)
3. ObjectLabs, Corporation. MongoDB-as-a-Service. MongoLab, San Francisco, CA 94110, United States (2014), https://mongolab.com/ (accessed October 30, 2014)
4. GitHub, Inc., ZXing Project (Barcode Scanner) (2014),
5. https://github.com/zxing/zxing/ (accessed October 30, 2014)
6. van der Schaaf, H., Rood, E., Watson, K.: A mobile application for reporting disease incidents. In: Hřebíček, J., Schimak, G., Kubásek, M., Rizzoli, A.E. (eds.) ISESS 2013. IFIP AICT, vol. 413, pp. 188–195. Springer, Heidelberg (2013)
7. Plewe, D.A.: A visual interface for deal making. In: O'Grady, M.J., Vahdat-Nejad, H., Wolf, K.-H., Dragone, M., Ye, J., Röcker, C., O'Hare, G. (eds.) AmI Workshops 2013. CCIS, vol. 413, pp. 205–212. Springer, Heidelberg (2013)

Provenance in Systems for Situation Awareness in Environmental Monitoring

Markus Stocker, Mauno Rönkkö, and Mikko Kolehmainen

Department of Environmental Science, University of Eastern Finland, Kuopio, Finland
{markus.stocker,mauno.ronkko,mikko.kolehmainen}@uef.fi

Abstract. As environmental monitoring systems increasingly automate the collection and processing of environmental sensor network data, the technical components of such systems can automatically obtain and maintain higher levels of situation awareness—awareness of the monitored part of reality. In order to increase confidence in the correctness of situation awareness maintained by such systems it is important to explicitly model provenance. We present an alignment of the PROV ontology with ontologies used in a software framework for situation awareness in environmental monitoring, called Wavellite. The extended vocabulary enables the explicit representation of provenance in Wavellite applications. We demonstrate the implementation for a concrete scenario.

Keywords: Situation awareness, situation theory, provenance, environmental monitoring, Wavellite.

1   Introduction

Endsley defined situation awareness as the "perception of the elements in the environment within a volume of time and space, the comprehension of their meaning, and the projection of their status in the near future" [1]. Over decades, situation awareness has been receiving considerable attention in various communities, e.g. human factors and ergonomics [2, 3, 4, 5]. Whether situation awareness is purely an "individual psychological phenomenon" [6] or is distributed between human and technical agents continues to be debated [2, 5, 6, 7]. However, applications of situation awareness theory and systems have been largely limited to military and security domains [2, 8].

Recently, Stocker et al. [9, 10, 11] have adopted Situation Theory [12, 13] and technologies [14] for situation awareness in environmental monitoring. Today, environmental monitoring systems often rely on environmental sensor networks [15] to implement the measurement [16] of properties of physical phenomena over time and space. Data resulting from measurement is collected, processed, and analyzed in order to obtain information about the monitored environment. Environmental monitoring systems are arguably not just technical systems. In fact, on one hand the monitored entities are often organisms or entire ecosystems. On the other hand, people are part of environmental monitoring systems, in roles such as technicians, scientists, or citizens. Thus, environmental monitoring systems may perhaps be described as (enviro-)sociotechnical systems [17].

R. Denzer et al. (Eds.): ISESS 2015, IFIP AICT 448, pp. 169–177, 2015.

Situations are structured parts of reality [13]. The concept of situation is interesting in environmental monitoring for at least three reasons. First, the monitored entity is a part of reality. For instance, in urban air pollution monitoring the particular volume of urban ambient air is the monitored entity and is a part of reality. Second, the entity is structured. In our example, the structure of the particular volume of urban ambient air is defined by the relations among the objects that are constituents of the entity, such as particulates and gases. It is properties of such objects that are typically measured. Third, environmental monitoring is concerned with gaining information about the monitored part of reality, i.e. information about situations.

In environmental monitoring, situation awareness is, traditionally, in the mind of people, typically experts. Here, Endsley's model is particularly suitable. However, as the technical components of environmental monitoring systems become increasingly more "intelligent," distributed situation awareness models [5] are of interest as well. Indeed, as the technical components increasingly implement data collection and processing, as well as knowledge extraction and representation, the technical parts can arguably hold higher levels of situation awareness—shared with people, such as scientists.

With increasing automation of data collection, data processing, knowledge extraction, and knowledge representation, it becomes important to automatically model (data) provenance. Provenance enables tracing the processes involved in producing data and knowledge. It can increase confidence in the correctness of situation awareness obtained and maintained by environmental monitoring systems, in particular that of their technical parts. Our aim in this paper is to extend an alignment of ontologies [18] used in a software framework for situation awareness in environmental monitoring, called Wavellite, with the PROV Ontology (PROV-O) [19]. As our main contribution, we present the alignment and discuss its application for a concrete example.

2   Materials and Methods

Wavellite[1] [9, 10, 20] is designed to support the implementation of data collection, data processing, knowledge extraction, and knowledge representation. Collection is, often, for data resulting in measurement implemented by environmental sensor networks. Such data are sensor observations, which are aligned with the term Observation of the Semantic Sensor Network (SSN) ontology [21]. Processing is for dataset observations, which are aligned with the term Observation of the RDF Data Cube Vocabulary (QB) [22]. Knowledge is for situations and is, specifically, situational knowledge. Situational knowledge is extracted from dataset observations and is represented as Situation, a term of the Situation Theory Ontology (STO) [14].

An alignment of these three ontologies, plus OWL-Time [23] and GeoSPARQL [24] for the representation of time and space, respectively, has been proposed in [18]. This alignment forms the Wavellite Core Ontology (WCO) which we extended with Wavellite terms (e.g. SensorObservation) to form the Wavellite Entity Ontology (WEO). Here we modify WCO to include PROV-O, and propose an alignment between PROV-O and

---

[1] http://uef.fi/envi/projects/wavellite

WEO. As a result, PROV-O joins the WCO family of upper ontologies used in Wavellite to represent data, knowledge, metadata, and now provenance. We used Protégé[2] to create the alignment. Note that such alignment is independent of concrete software implementations, such as Wavellite.

PROV-O is a specification for provenance designed for the representation of the origins of digital objects in form of descriptions "of the entities and activities involved in producing and delivering or otherwise influencing a given object" [25]. In PROV-O, provenance is, generally, of entities, which can be physical, digital, or conceptual. Entities can be derived from other entities and they are generated by activities. Activities are the processes through which entities come into existence. Associated with activities are agents, e.g., persons or, of most interest here, software.

In addition to the ontology alignment, we also extend Wavellite such that the software framework supports the representation of provenance in concrete applications. Thus, provenance records can be persisted and retrieved in a similar manner as sensor observations, dataset observations, and situations are persisted and retrieved in Wavellite.

3   Results

In this section, we briefly describe the main elements of the alignment. Sensor observation, dataset observation, and situation are digital objects and, thus, PROV-O entities. Aligning sensor observations with PROV-O is extensively addressed in [26]. The authors propose an alignment that aims at reconciling different aspects of modelling sensor observations in the SSN ontology (constrained by its alignment to the DOLCE Ultralite ontology [27]), OGC Observations and Measurements [28], and PROV-O. As a consequence, the resulting alignment relies on the introduction of several additional classes.

We follow [26] by adopting a lightweight subset of the alignment axioms. Specifically, SSN `Observation` is a sub class of PROV-O `Entity`; SSN `Stimulus` is a sub class of PROV-O `Activity`; and SSN `Sensor` is a sub class of PROV-O `Agent`. Sensor observations are generated by stimuli, are attributed to sensors, and stimuli are associated with sensors. Thus, the SSN object property `observedBy`, used to relate observations and sensors, is a sub property of PROV-O `wasAttributedTo`. In Wavellite, sensor observations are not derived from entities.

Wavellite implements *operators* that translate sensor observations into dataset observations [20]. Translation is an *operation*. Operators are software and thus PROV-O agents. Operations are PROV-O activities. Operations are associated with operators. Dataset observations may be derived from sensor observations, are attributed to operators, and are generated by operations. Wavellite also implements operators that process a source set of dataset observations into a target set of dataset observations. Thus, dataset observations may also be derived from dataset observations. Such operators are associates for the *processing* operation, which uses and generates dataset observations. For instance, the `Aggregate` operator with function `mean` and time period `hour` is a PROV-O agent and associate for the *aggregation* activity that uses

---

[2] http://protege.stanford.edu

source sets of dataset observations within one hour window and generates a singleton target set with hourly mean dataset observations. Finally, QB `DataSet` is a PROV-O `Entity` and datasets can thus be derived from datasets.

STO objects, notably situations, elementary infons, relations, individuals, attributes, and values are PROV-O entities. Any of these objects may be derived from dataset observations. In this case, extraction (or acquisition) operations (PROV-O activities) that are associated with extractors, the operators (PROV-O agents), use dataset observations, and generate STO objects. For instance, a classification operation may be associated with a machine learning operator and classify (use) dataset observations to generate (information about) an individual involved in a situations. However, any STO object may also be derived from STO objects. For instance, given information for storms and the location of drivers, a system may infer information for situations in which drivers are at higher risk due to storms [29].

In Wavellite, PROV-O enables the explicit representation of metadata describing the origin of sensor observations, dataset observations, and situations. This is particularly interesting at the derivation layer of the Wavellite architecture, where applications can implement arbitrary complex chains of dataset processing. By modelling datasets and dataset observations as PROV-O entities, we can explicitly model the derivation of datasets and dataset observations from other datasets and dataset observations, respectively, as well as the responsible processes (activities) and involved software (agents). However, provenance is interesting also at the situation layer of the Wavellite architecture, where applications implement the representation of situational knowledge acquired (extracted) from dataset observations. Here provenance enables Wavellite to relate situational knowledge to the dataset observations from which it is derived and with the agents, e.g. data-driven or physically-based models, and activities involved in knowledge acquisition.

4   Discussion

This section discusses a concrete example. The scenario builds on related work [10, 30] and can be summarized as follows. The pavement of a road section is measured for vibration by a sensor network consisting of accelerometers installed into the ground at one side of the road. Occasionally, vehicles travel the road section and modify the vibration pattern measured by sensors. Using a trained artificial neural network, such patterns can be classified in order to detect and characterize vehicles, for instance as 'light' or 'heavy'.

Figure 1 is an example sensor observation in this scenario. As expected, the example relies on the SSN ontology to model (meta-)data about the observation, and on OWL-Time for temporal data. Figure 2 displays the provenance information for the example sensor observation in Figure 1. The sensor observation `ex:44b` is modelled as a PROV-O `Entity` that was generated by the `ex:vibration` PROV-O `Activity` (SSN `Stimulus`) and was attributed to the `ex:sd1` PROV-O `Agent` (SSN `SensingDevice`). The graphs in figures 1 and 2 can be joined via node `ex:44b`.

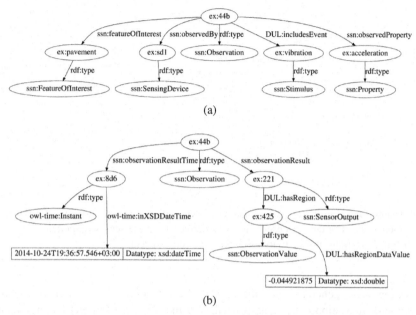

(a)

(b)

Fig. 1. Sensor observation ex:44b that resulted in measurement of road pavement vibration by accelerometer sensing device ex:sd1 on October 24, 2014 at 19:36:57.546 with observation value -0.044921875. For the sake of readability, the graph is split into two sub graphs. Figure (a) shows the feature, sensor, stimulus, and property related to the observation. Figure (b) shows the temporal location and measurement value. The two sub graphs can be joined via node ex:44b.

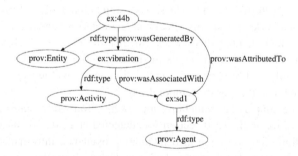

Fig. 2. Provenance information for the example sensor observation (Figure 1). Modelled are in particular the involved PROV-O entity, activity, agent and relations among them.

Sensor observations are translated to dataset observations. Figure 3 shows the result of such translation for our example sensor observation. Dataset observation ex:3bc relates to dataset ex:d1 as well as to time and the acceleration value via two component properties. The graph includes provenance information. It states that the dataset

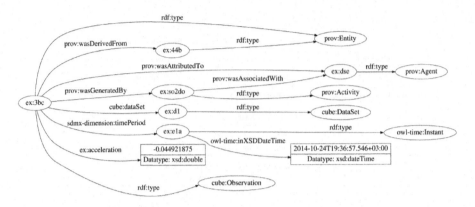

Fig. 3. Dataset observation ex:3bc of dataset ex:d1 with component properties for time and acceleration value. The dataset observation was derived from the sensor observation ex:44b and generated in a translation activity associated to a certain agent.

observation was generated by the ex:so2do (sensor observation to dataset observation) translation activity associated with the ex:dse (dataset engine) agent. The graph also states that the dataset observation ex:3bc was derived from the sensor observation ex:44b.

In the discussed scenario, for a specified time window length and at regular time intervals, dataset observations in time domain are processed to vibration patterns in frequency domain [10]. Vibration patterns are dataset observations with component property for time and one component property for each represented frequency component. Vibration patterns are then classified using trained Multi-Layer Perceptron artificial neural networks in order to detect and characterize vehicles travelling on the road section. Characterization determines whether the observed vehicle is light or heavy. Detected vehicles are individuals in situations. We can model such situations as supporting an infon with vehicle-at-relation and two objects, one for the individual vehicle and the other for the temporal location.

Figure 4 is an example. The situation supports an infon which states that a vehicle (ex:640) travelling on the road section was detected at 20:05:36 and was characterized as being light. The example also includes provenance information for the vehicle individual. It states that the individual was derived from the ex:aa3 PROV-O Entity (which an expanded graph would additionally type as dataset observation) and that it was generated in the ex:classification PROV-O Activity associated with the ex:se (situation engine) PROV-O Agent.

The discussed example demonstrates how the provenance of information for objects observed in real world situations by an environmental monitoring system can be traced through a complex data processing chain down to the original sensor observations. Provenance also tracks the activities and agents involved in transforming entities.

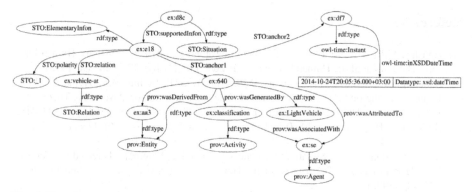

Fig. 4. Situation supporting a `vehicle-at`-relation infon involving two objects, an individual light vehicle and a temporal location. The graph also includes provenance information for the vehicle individual.

Systems can query the RDF data according to whether the interest is for situational knowledge or for the provenance of such knowledge.

5   Conclusion

We presented an alignment of a suite of ontologies useful to situation-aware environmental monitoring systems with PROV-O, the W3C provenance ontology. Related work on the alignment of the SSN ontology and PROV-O proved useful here. We have presented a basic alignment of PROV-O with entities beyond sensor observations, required in situation-aware environmental monitoring systems, namely dataset observations and situations.

The discussed example for situations involving vehicles travelling a road section demonstrates how systems can annotate, during processing, sensor observations, datasets and their observations, and situations with provenance information. Provenance can thus support making transparent the often complex data processing and knowledge extraction chains implemented in situation-aware environmental monitoring systems.

There exist several directions for future work. On one hand, our alignment consists of only few key axioms. More work can be done to study how to improve the alignment. On the other hand, the ideas and implementation presented here can be developed for a concrete system and application. The data and provenance information resulting in such a system can be used to more concretely study the potential of provenance information in a situation-aware environmental monitoring system.

Acknowledgements. This research is funded by the Academy of Finland project "FResCo: High-quality Measurement Infrastructure for Future Resilient Control Systems" (Grant number 264060).

References

1. Endsley, M.R.: Toward a theory of situation awareness in dynamic systems. Human Factors: The Journal of the Human Factors and Ergonomics Society 37(1), 32–64 (1995)
2. Salmon, P.M., Stanton, N.A., Jenkins, D.P., Walker, G.H., Young, M.S., Aujla, A.: What Really Is Going on? Review, Critique and Extension of Situation Awareness Theory. In: Harris, D. (ed.) HCII 2007 and EPCE 2007. LNCS (LNAI), vol. 4562, pp. 407–416. Springer, Heidelberg (2007), http://dx.doi.org/10.1007/978-3-540-73331-7_45
3. Smith, K., Hancock, P.: Situation Awareness Is Adaptive, Externally Directed Consciousness. Human Factors: The Journal of the Human Factors and Ergonomics Society 37(1), 137–148 (1995)
4. Bedny, G., Meister, D.: Theory of Activity and Situation Awareness. International Journal of Cognitive Ergonomics 3(1), 63–72 (1999), http://dx.doi.org/10.1207/s15327566ijce0301_5
5. Stanton, N.A., Stewart, R., Harris, D., Houghton, R.J., Baber, C., McMaster, R., Salmon, P., Hoyle, G., Walker, G., Young, M.S., Linsell, M., Dymott, R., Green, D.: Distributed situation awareness in dynamic systems: theoretical development and application of an ergonomics methodology. Ergonomics 49(12-13), 1288–1311 (2006), http://dx.doi.org/10.1080/00140130600612762, pMID: 17008257
6. Stanton, N.A., Salmon, P.M., Walker, G.H., Jenkins, D.P.: Is situation awareness all in the mind? Theoretical Issues in Ergonomics Science 11(1-2), 29–40 (2010), http://dx.doi.org/10.1080/14639220903009938
7. Endsley, M.R.: Automation and Situation Awareness. In: Parasuraman, R., Mouloua, M. (eds.) Automation and human performance: Theory and applications, pp. 163–181. Lawrence Erlbaum Associates, Inc., Mahwah (1996)
8. Salfinger, A., Retschitzegger, W., Schwinger, W.: Maintaining Situation Awareness Over Time – A Survey on the Evolution Support of Situation Awareness Systems. In: Conference on Technologies and Applications of Artificial Intelligence (TAAI 2013), pp. 274–281. IEEE Computer Society (2013)
9. Stocker, M., Baranizadeh, E., Portin, H., Komppula, M., Rönkkö, M., Hamed, A., Virtanen, A., Lehtinen, K., Laaksonen, A., Kolehmainen, M.: Representing situational knowledge acquired from sensor data for atmospheric phenomena. Environmental Modelling & Software 58(0), 27–47 (2014), http://www.sciencedirect.com/science/article/pii/S1364815214001108
10. Stocker, M., Rönkkö, M., Kolehmainen, M.: Situational knowledge representation for traffic observed by a pavement vibration sensor network. IEEE Transactions on Intelligent Transportation Systems 15(4), 1441–1450 (2014)
11. Stocker, M., Nikander, J., Huitu, H., Jalli, M., Rönkkö, M., Kolehmainen, M.: Disease pressure situation modelling in agriculture. Computers and Electronics in Agriculture (Submitted, 2014)
12. Barwise, J., Perry, J.: Situations and Attitudes. The Journal of Philosophy 78(11), 668–691 (1981), http://www.jstor.org/stable/2026578
13. Devlin, K.: Logic and Information. Cambridge University Press (1991)
14. Kokar, M.M., Matheus, C.J., Baclawski, K.: Ontology-based situation awareness. Inf. Fusion 10(1), 83–98 (2009)
15. Hart, J.K., Martinez, K.: Environmental Sensor Networks: A revolution in the earth system science? Earth-Science Reviews 78(3-4), 177–191 (2006)

16. Finkelstein, L.: Theory and Philosophy of Measurement. In: Sydenham, P.H. (ed.) Handbook of Measurement Science. Theoretical Fundamentals, vol. 1, pp. 1–30. John Wiley & Sons (1982)

17. Walker, G.H., Stanton, N.A., Salmon, P.M., Jenkins, D.P.: A review of sociotechnical systems theory: a classic concept for new command and control paradigms. Theoretical Issues in Ergonomics Science 9(6), 479–499 (2008), http://dx.doi.org/10.1080/14639220701635470

18. Stocker, M., Rönkkö, M., Kolehmainen, M.: Towards an Ontology for Situation Assessment in Environmental Monitoring. In: Ames, D.P., Quinn, N.W., Rizzoli, A.E. (eds.) Proceedings of the 7th International Congress on Environmental Modelling and Software, vol. 3, pp. 1281–1288. International Environmental Modelling & Software Society, San Diego (2014), http://www.iemss.org/society/index.php/iemss-2014-proceedings

19. Lebo, T., Sahoo, S., McGuinness, D.: PROV-O: The PROV Ontology. W3C Recommendation, W3C (April 2013), http://www.w3.org/TR/prov-o/

20. Stocker, M., Rönkkö, M., Kolehmainen, M.: A software framework for situation awareness in environmental monitoring. Knowledge-Based Systems (Submitted, 2014)

21. Compton, M., Barnaghi, P., Bermudez, L., García-Castro, R., Corcho, O., Cox, S., Graybeal, J., Hauswirth, M., Henson, C., Herzog, A., Huang, V., Janowicz, K., Kelsey, W.D., Phuoc, D.L., Lefort, L., Leggieri, M., Neuhaus, H., Nikolov, A., Page, K., Passant, A., Sheth, A., Taylor, K.: The SSN ontology of the W3C semantic sensor network incubator group. Web Semantics: Science, Services and Agents on the World Wide Web 17(0), 25–32 (2012)

22. Cyganiak, R., Reynolds, D., Tennison, J.: The RDF Data Cube Vocabulary. Recommendation, W3C (January 2014), http://www.w3.org/TR/2014/REC-vocab-data-cube-20140116/

23. Hobbs, J.R., Pan, F.: Time Ontology in OWL. Working draft, W3C (September 2006), http://www.w3.org/TR/owl-time/

24. Perry, M., Herring, J.: OGC GeoSPARQL - A Geographic Query Language for RDF Data. Tech. Rep. OGC 11-052r4, Open Geospatial Consortium (September 2012)

25. Gil, Y., Miles, S.: PROV Model Primer. W3C Working Group Note, W3C (April 2013), http://www.w3.org/TR/2013/NOTE-prov-primer-20130430/

26. Compton, M., Corsar, D., Taylor, K.: Sensor Data Provenance: SSNO and PROV-O Together At Last. In: Proceedings of the 7th International Workshop on Semantic Sensor Networks 2014 (SSN2014), 13th International Semantic Web Conference, Riva del Garda, Trentino Italy (October 2014)

27. Masolo, C., Borgo, S., Gangemi, A., Guarino, N., Oltramari, A., Oltramari, R., Schneider, L., Istc-cnr, L.P., Horrocks, I.: WonderWeb Deliverable D17. The WonderWeb Library of Foundational Ontologies and the DOLCE ontology (2002)

28. Geographic information – Observations and measurements (2011), http://www.iso.org/iso/catalogue_detail.htm?csnumber=32574

29. Stocker, M., Kauhanen, O., Hiirsalmi, M., Saarela, J., Rossi, P., Rönkkö, M., Hytönen, H., Kotovirta, V., Kolehmainen, M.: A Software System for the Discovery of Situations Involving Drivers in Storms. In: Denzer, R., Argent, R., Schimak, G., Hřebíček, J. (eds.) ISESS 2015. IFIP AICT, vol. 448, pp. 229–237. Springer, Heidelberg (2015)

30. Stocker, M., Rönkkö, M., Kolehmainen, M.: Making Sense of Sensor Data Using Ontology: A Discussion for Road Vehicle Classification. In: Seppelt, R., Voinov, A., Lange, S., Bankamp, D. (eds.) 2012 International Congress on Environmental Modelling and Software, pp. 2387–2394. iEMSs, Leipzig (2012)

Decision Making and Strategic Planning for Disaster Preparedness with a Multi-Criteria-Analysis Decision Support System

Sascha Schlobinski[1], Giulio Zuccaro[3], Martin Scholl[1], Daniel Meiers[1], Ralf Denzer[1,2], Sergio Guarino[3], Wolf Engelbach[4], Kuldar Taveter[5], and Steven Frysinger[1,2]

[1] Cismet GmbH, Saarbrücken, Germany
{sascha.schlobinski,martin.scholl,
daniel.meiers,steven.frysinger}@cismet.de
[2] Environmental Informatics Group, Saarbrücken, Germany
ralf.denzer@enviromatics.org
[3] CENTRO STUDI PLINIUS, Napoli, Italy
{zuccaro,guarino}@unina.it
[4] Fraunhofer IAO, Stuttgart, Germany
wolf.engelbach@iao.fraunhofer.de
[5] Tallinn University of Technology, Tallinn, Estonia
kuldar.taveter@ttu.ee

Abstract. In the context of the CRISMA FP7 project we have developed a seamless decision support concept to connect simulated crisis scenarios and aggregated performance indicators of impact scenarios with state of the art Multi-Criteria Decision Analysis (MCDA) methods. To prove the practicality of the approach we have developed a decision support tool realising the important aspects of the method. The tool is a highly interactive and user-friendly decision support system (DSS) that effectively helps the decision maker and strategic planner to perform multi-criteria ranking of scenarios. The tool is based on state-of-the-art web technologies.

Keywords: impact scenario simulation, indicator, criteria, decision support system, multi-criteria-analysis, disaster preparedness, strategic planning.

1 Introduction

Decision making and strategic planning for disaster preparedness can be extensively supported by simulations of crisis scenarios. Such scenarios can provide insight into the overall course, cause and effect of many aspects of a future crisis. A powerful high level way to look at a crisis is by relating hazards, the exposure of elements at risk and their vulnerabilities, resulting in probabilities of damage or other effects. A simulation following this concept will produce the so-called impact scenarios that show the potential damage of a crisis, e.g. the effect of an earthquake on buildings and population [1]. Impact scenarios are particularly suited to supporting strategic decision making as they focus on the causal connection between a specific threat and

R. Denzer et al. (Eds.): ISESS 2015, IFIP AICT 448, pp. 178–186, 2015.
© IFIP International Federation for Information Processing 2015

the potential effects on the objects of concern. The construction of impact scenarios requires the integration of a potentially large number of complex data sets either based on static data (such as census data) or simulation results (such as risk maps). These data usually come from various sources and thus are inherently heterogeneous with respect to format, resolution and semantics.

One way to considerably reduce the complexity of impact scenarios while preserving their key properties is to aggregate scenario data into so called (key) performance indicators [2]. This kind of approach to complex data has a long history in economics and business management e.g. [3] and such indicators are the de-facto standard in measuring the performance of emergency services (e.g. [4]). While performance indicators pertaining to impact scenarios allow comparison of individual indicator values decision makers (DM) still face multiple, often-conflicting decision objectives involving more than one criterion. As a result, the selection of a specific scenario (e.g. intervention) with the "best" performance is very difficult. For example, a particular mitigation action will come with a cost but will reduce the potential impact of a disaster. So the objective of minimal cost for mitigation measures in combination with the objective of minimizing disaster impact leads to a trade-off decision problem (np-hard [5]) where optimization approaches (for example) are hardly applicable in real world solutions. However, established methods of Multi-Criteria Decision Analysis (MCDA) e.g. [6] offer solutions to the problem.

This paper describes a seamless decision support concept developed within the CRISMA FP7 project [7] to connect simulated crisis scenarios and aggregated performance indicators of impact scenarios with state of the art Multi-Criteria Decision Analysis (MCDA) methods [8].

2   Concept Overview

The overall idea is to: (a) Let the Decision Maker (DM) produce and use scenarios in support of the decision; (b) provide aggregated but representative information about scenarios (indicators); (c) support the DM in defining an explicit decision strategy (criteria, priorities, Andness and Orness (see section 3)); and (d) assist in comparing and ranking impact scenarios according to the decision strategy.

The overall concept consists of seven elements - four data and three functional - to support the DM: (1) an impact scenario consisting of information required to take a decision, e.g. representing the possible consequences of a flood for people living in the flooded area; (2) an indicator function to map an impact scenario to indicators; (3) a set of representative scenario indicators consisting of aggregated scenario information, e.g. the number of homeless, or the building damage or cost; (4) a criteria function mapping each element of the indicator set to satisfaction; (5) a level of satisfaction in a normalised scale (0-1 or 0%-100%); (6) a ranking function mapping normalized indicator sets to values; and (7) corresponding scalar values (ranks/score). The DM can use the four data elements as a basis for the decision and define an individual decision strategy mapping indicators to criteria with the help of criteria functions. In addition they are supported in assigning priorities to indicators as well as defining the

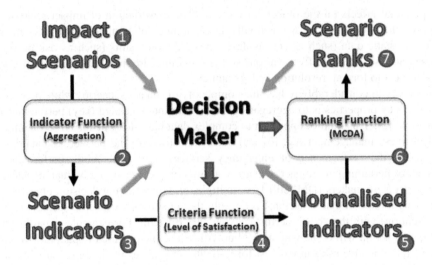

Fig. 1. Decision Support Concept Overview

level of "Andness" and "Orness" of the ranking function [9] through the parameterization of a MCDA method [6]. More concretely the DM is supported in:

- Using indicators derived from impact scenario data (usually aggregated) to quickly assess and compare impact scenarios
- Defining a decision strategy by:
  - Mapping performance indicators to decision criteria (defining the level of satisfaction for each indicator)
  - Defining priorities by assigning weights to indicators
  - Defining the level of Andness and Orness to be considered when computing the rank of an impact scenario
- Dealing with a multi-criteria decision problem by obtaining a ranking of scenarios with respect to the defined decision strategy.

3   Ordered Weighted Averages as a Means for Decision Support

Decision problems considering more than one criterion on the basis of impact scenarios require appropriate methods to assess the performance of specific scenarios. In our concept we have selected the Ordered Weighted Averages method (OWA) [6,10,11] that allows one to specify a particular decision strategy that defines the properties of a good solution. The OWA method allows us to:

- Implement several decision makers' perspectives (multiple points of view);
- Make the decision strategy explicit;
- Obtain a score/rank for each scenario;
- Let the DM choose between different strategies (e.g. optimistic, neutral, pessimistic);
- Compare results obtained under different strategies.

The OWA method is based on multi-criteria aggregation operators proposed by Yager [6]. OWA is characterized by a vector of ordered weights in addition to the importance weights assigned to each criterion. Using OWA, normalized indicator values are multiplied with a corresponding level of importance. The vector of weighted levels of satisfaction for all indicators is re-ordered according to their values and weighted according to their position in the vector. The vector of ordered weights determines an instance of an OWA operator. E.g. the vector of ordered weights (1, 0, ..., 0) will give full weight to the criterion with the highest level of satisfaction independent of all other criteria (maximum level of Orness). As a consequence, alternatives with a single outstanding property will be ranked highest. This is called a risk-taking or optimistic decision strategy. In contrast, the vector of ordered weights (0, ..., 0, 1) will give full weight to the criterion with the lowest level of satisfaction. As a consequence alternatives with the best "poor" criterion will rank highest (maximum level of Andness). This is called a pessimistic decision strategy. Obviously, between these two extremes there is a large number of intermediate strategies. Another easily interpreted strategy is the neutral strategy that does not emphasize any position in the re-ordered criterion values (simple weighted average). The vector of ordered weights can be calculated to fit to a specific decision strategy [10] but of course they can be defined manually by the DM as will be shown in the next section.

4   The Implementation

The concept described above has been implemented including a HTML5 [12] (Angular JS [13]) based User Interface (UI). The software is part of the CRISMA Integrated Crisis Management System Framework [14]. It is available under an open source license as a github project [15]. For illustration, the figures visible in the screenshots refer to three fictional alternative mitigation strategies for an earthquake in L'Aquila (Italy), since that is one of case studies addressed in the CRISMA project[1].

4.1   Scenario Analysis and Comparison View

The Scenario Analysis and Comparison View consists of several widgets and visually represents indicator and criteria data to compare different simulated scenarios side by side. The indicators vector is mainly based on quantities (e.g. number of victims who died) calculated from a scenario. To be effectively used in a decision support context indicators need to be qualified. Here qualification basically means assigning a level of satisfaction to the indicator data. The "normalised" indicators can be better used as decision criteria. As indicators and criteria data have the same format (vector of scalar values) both can be displayed in the same fashion.

---

[1] For reasons of security sensitivity the data used in this paper consist of test data sets that do not reflect reality in any way.

4.1.1   Indicator Table Widget

Fig.2 shows the normalised indicators of three example scenarios in a tabular form.

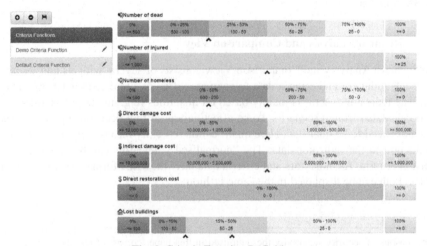

Criteria	L'Aquila (M=7 +BR)	L'Aquila (M=7)	L'Aquila (M=7) (edited)
Casualties			
Number of dead	80 Percent	90 Percent	54 Percent
Number of homeless	9 Percent	38 Percent	83 Percent
Number of injured	68 Percent	67 Percent	79 Percent
Economic cost			
Direct damage cost	76 Percent	86 Percent	53 Percent
Indirect damage cost	67 Percent	70 Percent	65 Percent
Direct restoration cost	47 Percent	5 Percent	65 Percent
Damaged buildings			
Lost buildings	73 Percent	7 Percent	1 Percent
Unsafe buildings	8 Percent	97 Percent	8 Percent
Damaged infrastructure			
Number of damaged road segments	30 Percent	45 Percent	96 Percent
Evacuation cost			
Total evacuationcost	28 Percent	45 Percent	84 Percent

Fig. 2. Criteria Table

4.1.2   Criteria Function Definition Widget

The Criteria Function Definition Widget depicted in Fig. 3 allows the definition of functions converting indicator values to criteria.

Fig. 3. Criteria Function Definition

The view presented in Fig.4 allows users to correlate individual indicator and criteria values.

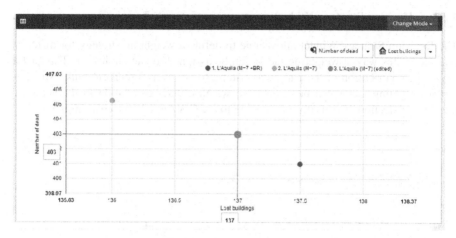

Fig. 4. Indicator Scatter Plot

Fig. 5 shows the data as spider charts in order to support the quick assessment of the overall performance of the selected scenarios. In addition a "reference scenario" (in the example L'Aquila (M=7) visualised in orange) can be selected.

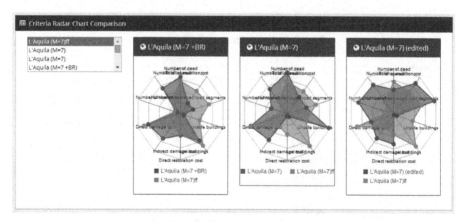

Fig. 5. Criteria Radar Chart

4.2   Multi Criteria Analysis and Decision Support View

While the Scenario Analysis and Comparison View (see section 4.1) allows a comparison of indicators and criteria for different scenarios, the Multi Criteria Analysis and Decision Support View allows a ranking of different scenarios with respect to a specific decision strategy.

In this it adds supplemental decision support functionalities. The view is composed of two different widgets: The Decision Strategy Widget and the Decision Ranking Widget.

4.2.1   Decision Strategy Widget

The Decision Strategy Widget allows one to define a weighting strategy for different criteria. In this way, a weighting factor can be assigned to each indicator. This factor scales the contribution of the particular criteria to the overall scenario rank. An additional weighting factor can be selected to weigh criteria in relation to the achieved level of satisfaction. This is done according to the OWA method (see section 3).

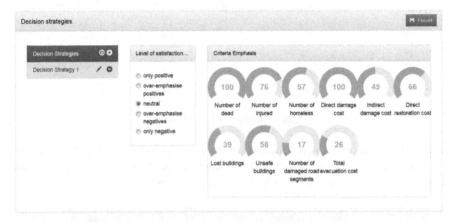

Fig. 6. Decision Strategy Definition

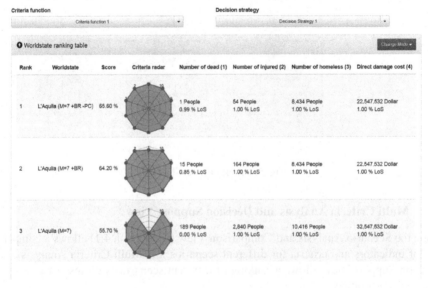

Fig. 7. Scenario Ranking

4.2.2   Decision Ranking Widget

The Decision Ranking Widget allows the selection of a previously defined decision strategy and criteria function. It applies the selection to the available scenarios and produces a ranking.

5   Conclusion and Outlook

We have presented a seamless decision support concept to intended connect simulated crisis scenarios and aggregated performance indicators of impact scenarios with state-of-the-art Multi-Criteria Decision Analysis (MCDA) methods. To prove the practicality of the approach we have developed a decision support tool realising the important aspects of the method. The tool effectively supports the decision maker and strategic planner in applying a multi-criteria decision strategy to the ranking of scenarios. The tool is based on state-of the art web technologies and is freely available under an open source license. Currently, the presented approach and DSS are evaluated in a number of different disaster management preparedness case studies in the context of the project.

Future work includes the integration of uncertainty indicators that will allow decision makers to take the inherent uncertainty of scenario data into account. Also, as we do not necessarily know in advance what is important for successful crisis management (what are the relevant indicators). Crisis managers may need to explore what *has led* to particular indicator values rather than what *are* the values of particular indicators. We plan to work out a method and the corresponding software enabling to compare the dynamics of scenario evolvement in alternative scenarios.

Acknowledgements. The research leading to this paper has been performed within the CRISMA project, which is co-funded under the European Community's Seventh Framework Programme FP7/2007 - 2013 (grant agreement no. 284552).

References

1. Zuccaro, G., Cacace, F.: Seismic Casualty Evaluation: The Italian Model, an Application to the L'Aquila 2009 Event, Human Casualties in Earthquakes Advances in Natural and Technological Hazards Research, vol. 29, pp. 171–184 (December 8, 2010)
2. Engelbach, W., Frings, S., Molarius, R., Aubrecht, C., Meriste, M., Perrels, A.: Indicators to compare simulated crisis management strategies. In: 5th International Disaster and Risk Conference IDRC Davos (2014)
3. Business Measures-Modes and Key Performance Indicators,
   http://publib.boulder.ibm.com/infocenter/dmndhelp/v6rxmx/ind
   ex.jsp?topic=/com.ibm.btools.help.modeler.bmeasures.doc/doc/
   concepts/measures/kpis.html
4. Zygowicz, W.: Key Performance Indicators in EMS,
   http://www.usfa.fema.gov/pdf/efop/efo44984.pdf
5. Garey, M.R., Johnson, D.S.: Computers and Intractability; A Guide to the Theory of NP-Completeness. W. H. Freeman & Co., New York ©1990ISBN:0716710455

6. Yager, R.R.: On ordered weighted averaging aggregation operators in multi-criteria decision making. IEEE Transactions on Systems, Man and Cybernetics 18(1), 183–190 (1988)
7. Heikkilä, A.-M., Molarius, R., Rosqvist, T., Perrels, A.: Minimising the outcome of disasters by simulating the effects of different actions. In: The Second Nordic International Conference on Climate Change Adaptation, pp. 29–31 (August 2012)
8. Steuer, R.E.: Multiple Criteria Optimization: Theory, Computation and Application. John Wiley, New York (1986)
9. Dujmović, J.: Properties of Local Andness/Orness. In: Castillo, O., Melin, P., Ross, O.M., Cruz, R.S., Pedrycz, W., Kacprzyk, J. (eds.) Theoretical Advances and Applications of Fuzzy Logic and Soft Computing. AISC, vol. 42, pp. 54–63. Springer, Heidelberg (2007)
10. Yager, R.R.: Quantifier guided aggregation using OWA operators. International Journal of Intelligent Systems, 11–49 (1996)
11. Zuccaro, G., Filomena, P.: Multi-criteria analysis in vulnerability assessment. Second Egyptian Conference on Earthquake Engineering, Aswan, Egypt (1997)
12. http://www.w3.org/TR/html5/
13. https://angularjs.org/
14. Dihé, P., Denzer, R., Polese, M., Heikkilä, A., Havlik, D., Sautter, J., Hell, T., Schlobinski, S., Zuccaro, G., Engelbach, W.: An architecture for integrated crisis management simulation. In: 20th International Congress on Modelling and Simulation (MODSIM 2013), Adelaide, South Australia, December 1-6 (2013)
15. https://github.com/crismaproject

A Cotton Irrigator's Decision Support System and Benchmarking Tool Using National, Regional and Local Data

Jamie Vleeshouwer[1], Nicholas J. Car[1], and John Hornbuckle[2]

[1]Land and Water Flagship: CSIRO, Brisbane, QLD Australia
Jamie.Vleeshouwer@csiro.au
[2]Agriculture Flagship: CSIRO, Griffith, NSW Australia

Abstract. We are developing a smart phone application that provides irrigation water management advice using satellite imagery, weather stations and field-scale farmer provided data.

To provide tailored advice we use high resolution satellite imagery with national coverage provided by Google Earth Engine services to estimate field-specific crop growth information – crop coefficients – and we are among the first systems to do so. These coefficients combined with regional scale weather station data for major cotton growing regions and farmer-supplied data means we can run daily water balance calculations for every individual cotton field in Australia and provide irrigation decision support advice.

We are using automated data processing to ensure the latest satellite and weather data is used for advice without manual effort.

We will also deliver benchmarking data to farmers based on their previous seasons as well as peers' farms in order to compare absolute (calculated) and relative (benchmarked) advice.

Keywords: irrigation, satellite data, weather station, mobile phone app, evapotranspiration.

1 Background

IrriSAT is a weather based irrigation scheduling service which is used to inform farmers how much water their crop has used and how much how much irrigation they need to apply. Information is produced daily, and can work with different crop types, across large spatial scales. The system is being developed by the Commonwealth and Industrial Research Organisation (CSIRO) for the Cotton Research and Development Corporation (CRDC).

The system uses satellite images to determine the Normalized Difference Vegetation Index (NDVI) for each field, from which the plant canopy size can be determined and a specific crop coefficient (Kc) can be estimated (Hornbuckle et al, 2009). By combining Kc with daily reference Evapotranspiration (ET0) observations from a nearby weather station, the crop water usage can be determined and advice can be provided regarding the amount of irrigation to be applied.

R. Denzer et al. (Eds.): ISESS 2015, IFIP AICT 448, pp. 187–195, 2015.

Successful trials of the service have previously been undertaken with grape and citrus irrigators, leading to further trials with cotton in the Gwydir, Border Rivers and Lower Namoi valley areas from 2009 - 2012. In the final season of these trials, 72 irrigators were using the service, whereby the preferred interface for interacting with the service was via SMS messages. (Car et al 2012). The SMS interface allowed an irrigator to enter codes which represented their identity and their fields, along with how much irrigation had been applied to the field (from observed rainfall, or applied by an irrigation system). This information was then used to calculate the daily water balance for their field and provide a response via SMS with the water deficit to aid with managing irrigation schedules.

Whilst the SMS interface provided an efficient way for irrigators to register their data with the IrriSAT service, it was also subject to data entry errors such as codes / water quantities often being mistyped (either by miskeying, or the mobile phone's autocorrect features modifying the inputs). Recent investments will allow the technology overcome these issues and to be further developed for the next generation of services which include: automated near-real time forecasting; regional crop water use productivity benchmarking, and in season yield production. To better deliver these services to irrigator's, smart phone and tablet applications will be developed, along with the required automated data feeds in standardized exchange formats to drive the next generation IrriSAT applications.

2   The IrriSAT Concept

Rule-based irrigation advice is generated using data from sources shown in Fig. 1 according to the equation (1). The water balance for a crop is determined by representing the field as a closed-system summing the daily calculated water balance of the field which is determined by equation (2).

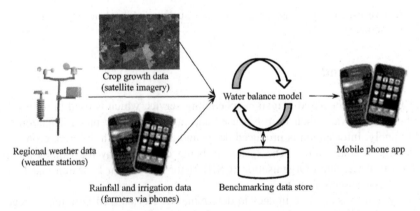

Fig. 1. A basic information flow diagram of the IrriSAT system

The water balance is calculated by subtracting crop evapotranspiration, calculated by reference evapotranspiration multiplied by a crop coefficient (for cotton), from water inputs (irrigation and rainfall). Whilst irrigation and rainfall simply can be obtained observations with appropriate shaping (reduction) functions to cater for runoff, the crop evapotranspiration (ETc) is determined by a variant of the Penman-Montieth equation according to (Allen et al, 1998). The modification is for 'tall crops' which models cotton better than the standard for 'short crops (grass).

$$WB_d = \sum_i^d WB_i \tag{1}$$

$$d \ (day \ in \ season) \in [1 - n]$$

$$WBd = total \ season \ waterbalance \ to \ day \ d$$

$$WB_i = Sh_I I_i + Sh_R R_i - (ET_0 K_c) \tag{2}$$

$$WB_i = daily \ waterbalance$$
$$Sh_I = shaping \ function \ for \ rainfall$$
$$Sh_R = shaping \ function \ for \ rainfall$$
$$ET_0 = reference \ evapotranspiration$$
$$K_c = crop \ coefficient$$

WB_d is translated from millimeters depth into irrigation pump run times by knowing the application rate of the field's irrigation system. This allows a user to program a system to run in order to return WB_d to zero (or other desired level) without further calculation.

In addition to this water balance rule-based decision support advice, the next generation of IrriSAT will deliver case-based, benchmarked decision support advice to irrigators via the methods described in Section 3.4.

3   Establishing the Next Generation IrriSAT

In recent years smartphones and tablets have become very popular, and we now aiming to make IrriSAT services more easily accessible through Android and iOS applications. A key factor to making these services functional are the data feeds which are required as inputs to the decision support system (DSS). These data feeds need to be: made available on demand for near real time decision support; be encoded in standardized data exchange formats; and be easily accessible over the internet via web services. Alternate forms of decision support advice are able to generated by non-rule-based artificial intelligence systems such as Case-Based reasoning. The next generation IrriSAT system will test one such form.

3.1   Remotely Sensed Imagery

Within previous trials of the IrriSAT service, Landsat 5 imagery was used which provided a spatial resolution of 30m which was sufficient for capturing the spatial variability of the crop water use across an irrigator's field. An email would be sent to the IrriSAT administrator when new Landsat imagery was made available. The tasks the administrator would then undertake would be:

1. Downloaded the latest imagery
2. Manually screen away the clouds based upon inspection within ERDAS IMAGINE
3. Execute an ERDAS script to produce a CSV file containing field Kc values
4. Upload the CSV to the IrriSAT database for further processing

This process was often time-consuming for the administrator, and had to be repeated approximately every 8 days as new imagery became available. However recent advancements in accessing remotely sensed data warehouses and executing scientific algorithms aim to make tasks like these mentioned more efficient. Two services currently in development include: The Australian Geoscience Data Cube (AGDC); and Google Earth Engine (GEE). Both of these services utilize supercomputing to allow users to run custom algorithms upon remotely sensed imagery via API's. Here, we have undertaken a scoping study to assess whether GEE is capable of being used for processing the modeling required for the backend IrriSAT services.

The GEE platform allows users to run algorithms on satellite imagery and earth observation data for scientific analyses and visualisation (Gorelick, 2013). It contains a petabyte-scale archive of global imagery which spans the past 40 years and uses a distributed computational model using a just-in-time approach, meaning that processing is run in real-time, however won't occur until it is required as an output or as an input to another process. This is achieved by exchanging a description of the processing activities and their sequences with GEE servers through a restful web services. Algorithms can be written using the GEE Application Programming Interface (API) which is available in both Python and Javascript programming languages.

For this study we used a combination of Landsat 8 OLI and Landsat 7 ETM+ imagery since the Landsat 5 program is no longer operational. Similarly to Landsat 5, both Landsat 8/7 exhibits a 30m spatial resolution, takes 16 days to observe Earth, and is made available in 8-day cycles. Given that Landsat 8 is offset by 8 days to Landsat 7 our approach was to combine Landsat 8/7. Whilst differences exist between the OLI and ETM+ sensors, it has been shown that the two sensors are broadly compatible across the Australian landscape with differences of approximately 5% for NDVI (Flood, 2014).

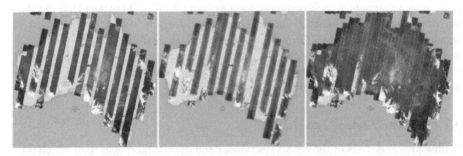

Fig. 2. Landsat 8 (left), Landsat 7 (centre) and combined Landsat 8/7 (right) TOA reflectance for 16 October 2014

The approach of combining the two datasets typically provides near full coverage for Australia every 8 days (Fig. 2), which would provide the most up to date crop water usage information to irrigators in near real time.

It is well known that the influence of cloud cover can cause remotely sensed NDVI to be underestimated (Liaw, et al 1995). In order to address this problem we are using the SimpleCloudScore algorithm which is provided within the GEE Algorithms API (Fig. 3). This algorithm works by determining a cloud-likelihood score in the range [0,100] using a combination of brightness, temperature, and NDSI from the TOA reflectance imagery.

Fig. 3. Illustration of Landsat 8 TOA reflectance for 16 irrigation fields with visible cloud cover (left). The GEE SimpleCloudScore algorithm used to generate a mask for removing cloud cover from Landsat imagery (right). Detected clouds are shown in magenta.

The SimpleCloudScore algorithm is not a robust cloud detector, and is intended mainly to compare multiple looks at the same point for relative cloud likelihood, however we have found it to give adequate performance at detecting clouds when a cloud-likelihood score threshold of 17 is set. At present, an implementation of the Fmask v3.2 automated cloud detection algorithm (Z. Zhu and C.E. Woodcock, 2012) is being incorporated into the GEE API. The Fmask algorithm is an object-based cloud detection algorithm which is able to detect clouds, cloud shadows and snow with an average overall accuracy of 96.41%. When the algorithm is made available it would be useful to trial it out as cloud shadows can also lead to NDVI misinterpretations.

By combining a cloud mask with the Landsat NDVI datasets available within GEE we are then able to determine the pixels which represent a valid values.

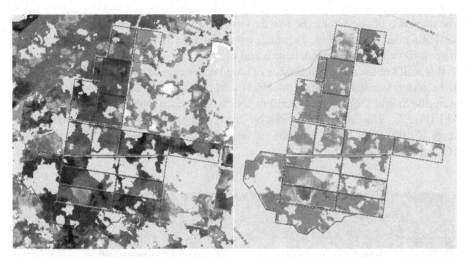

Fig. 4. Landsat 8 NDVI for the same day as is Fig. 3. The cloud mask is used the remove pixels which are determined to be invalid data (left). This image is then used to determine the crop coefficient (Kc) for cotton using a linear scaling (right).

Examining one of these fields over the 2013-2014 cotton growing season (Fig. 5) illustrates how the crop coefficient initially starts with values of ~0.1 (bare soil) and increases to ~1.0 (grown cotton), with harvesting taking place usually at the end of the first quarter of each year.

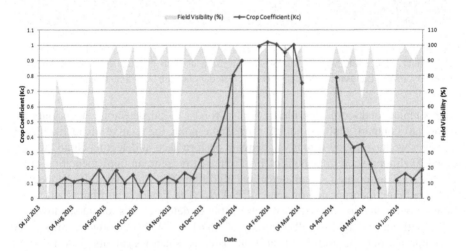

Fig. 5. Crop coefficient for an irrigators field over the 2013-2014 cotton growing season

3.2   On-ground Weather Observations

In order to provide regionalized evapotranspiration observations to irrigators, CSIRO maintains a network of Automatic Weather Stations (AWS). These services are currently tightly-coupled to the current IrriSAT system, however we will be working to expose this data via web services. This allows users or devices to be able to query and retrieve observations over the web which will play an important role for consuming data within a mobile app. To improve the accessibility of this data we are currently implementing the Sensor Observation Service (SOS) which provides a way to query real-time sensor data in a standardized data exchange. Utilising this standardized exchange format will allow us to easily expand upon our current coverage of weather stations, allowing us to query and consume SOS observations from other organisations such as the Bureau of Meteorology and also enables this technology to also work internationally.

3.3   Irrigation and Rainfall

The mobile app will provide a way for irrigators to enter how much irrigation they have applied to each field, and also how much rainfall has fallen as it occurs. This information needs to be supplied by the user since most irrigation pumps are not telemeted, and rainfall from a nearby weather station is not local enough to accurately determine how much rainfall was observed on their fields. The new application user interface will provide a richer user experience, and more accurate methods of data entry over the previous SMS message approach. The application being developed will be similar in functionality to the Smartirrigation Cotton app (Vellidis et al, 2014) which has been developed for use in the United States (Fig. 6)

Fig. 6. Smartirrigation Cotton application developed for iOS

3.4   Benchmarking-Based Irrigation Decision Support

Unlike the previous generation of IrriSAT system, this next generation will deliver advice to irrigators based initially on the water balance (rule-based) system and then, after a season of operation for baselining, advice from a benchmarking, case-based reasoning system will also be delivered.

Time-delimited periods of irrigation practice (weekly or monthly) will be treated as cases in a Case-Based Reasoning (CBR), as described by Aamodt & Plaza (1994). The input conditions to these cases (the weather and crop data) will be used with a measure of utility of the case results (the irrigation decision(s) made within the time-frame) according to standard CBR methodology. The utility measure will be gathered from yield data at the end of the first season's operation.

From the start of the second season's operation (2015/2016) onwards, the CBR system will compare a current irrigator's situation (the 'current case' in CBR terminology) with past, similar situations (the 'case base') and provide advice in parallel with the rule-based advice. How this advice will be presented to the irrigators is future work.

4   Conclusion

Through the GEE case study, we have found the API to be adequate for undertaking the desired processing tasks required for determining paddock scale crop coefficients required by IrriSAT. The work from this case study is currently further being integrated into the next generation IrriSAT DSS which will be capable of: providing more regular Kc estimates than previously by using both Landsat 8 and Landsat 7 imagery; and will also provide a completely automated data processing pipeline. Adopting the GEE platform will allow us to access and run algorithms on the full Earth Engine data archive, all using Google's parallel processing platform in real time, enabling the next generation IrriSAT to easily scale across all of Australia.

Exposing the weather observations via SOS allows our applications and any other applications, to easily query and retrieve information over the web. We have currently migrated all historic weather station data into 52 north's SOS implementation. Further work involves developing automated data ingestion routines to ensure the datasets are kept up to date for near-real time accessibility.

Once the application is developed, irrigation information will be able to be collected from a limited selection of farmers throughout the first cotton growing season. This will enable us to develop the benchmarking products required to compare water usage against other cotton irrigators in nearby regions and also against previous growing seasons.

Our use of new and sophisticated datasets and web services at the national and regional (weather station) levels will enable us to avoid much of the data preparation complexity of previous generation DSS. The DSS core application will be capable of requesting information from the external data services to run a water balance calculation; whilst all of the raw data management and preparation steps generating the required products have already been undertaken by the data providers.

References

1. Aamodt, A., Plaza, E.: Case-based reasoning: Foundational issues, methodological variations, and system approaches. AICom - Artificial Intelligence Communications 7(1), 39–59 (1994)
2. Allen, R.G., Pereira, L.S., Raes, D., Smith, M.: Crop Evapotranspiration - Guidelines for Computing Crop Water Requirements. FAO Irrigation and Drainage Paper 56 (1998)
3. Car, N.J., Christen, E.W., Hornbuckle, J.W., Moore, G.A.: Using a mobile phone Short Messaging Service (SMS) for irrigation schedulingin Australia – Farmers' participation and utility evaluation. Computers and Electronics in Agriculture 84, 132–143 (2012)
4. Flood, N.: Continuity of Reflectance Data between Landsat-7 ETM+ and Landsat-8 OLI, for Both Top-of-Atmosphere and Surface Reflectance: A Study in the Australian Landscape, remote sensing (2014)
5. Gorelick, N.: Google Earth Engine,Geophysical Research Abstracts, vol. 15, EGU2013-11997, 2013 EGU General Assembly (2013)
6. Hornbuckle, J.W., Car, N.J., Christen, E.W., Stein, T.M., Williamson, B.: IrriSatSMS – Irrigation Water Management by Satellite and SMS – A Utilisation Framework. CRC for Irrigation Futures Technical Report No. 01/09and CSIRO Land and Water Science Report No. 04/09. CSIRO Land and Water,Griffith, NSW, Australia (2009)
7. Liaw, Y.P., Cook, D.R., Sisterson, D.L., Gao, W.: Comparison of Satellite-Derived and Observer-Based Determinations of Cloud Cover Amount at the Southern Great Plains Cloud and Radiation Testbed Site. Fifth Atmospheric Radiation Measurement San Diego, California (March 1995)
8. Vellidis, G., Liakos, V., Perry, C., Tucker, M., Collins, G., Snider, J., Andreis, J., Migliaccio, K., Fraisse, C., Morgan, K., Rowland, D., Barnes, E.: A smartphone app for scheduling irrigation on cotton. In: Boyd, S., Huffman, M., Robertson, B. (eds.) Proceedings of the 2014 Beltwide Cotton Conference, New Orleans, LA, National Cotton Council, Memphis, TN (2014) (paper 15551)
9. Zhu, Z., Woodcock, C.E.: Object-based cloud and cloud shadow detection in Landsat imagery. Remote Sensing of Environment 118, 83–94 (2012)

Water Pollution Reduction: Reverse Combinatorial Auctions Modelling Supporting Decision-Making Processes

Petr Šauer, Petr Fiala, and Antonín Dvořák

University of Economics, Prague, Czech Republic
{sauer,pfiala,advorak}@vse.cz

Abstract. This paper presents a model that contributes to finding cost-effective solutions when making decisions about building wastewater treatment plants in the planning process defined in the Framework Directive 2000/60/EC of the European Parliament and of the European Council. The model is useful especially when construction and operation of joint wastewater treatment plants is possible for several (neighbouring) municipalities, where a huge number of theoretical coalitions is possible. The paper presents the model principles for one pollutant and for multiple pollutants, describes the CRAB software used for computing the optimal solutions and presents selected applications. It concludes that the computations can contribute directly to decision-making concerning environmental protection projects and also serve for calculating background models for economic laboratory experiments in the area.

Keywords: environmental protection, environmental management, decision-making, CRAB software, water pollution, combinatorial auctions.

1   Introduction

There are still situations in the area of surface water quality that require solutions in the Czech Republic and other advanced countries, in spite of a noticeable improvement since the 1980s, as municipalities with more than 2000 equivalent inhabitants have had to ensure sewerage and wastewater treatment by the end of 2010 pursuant to the implemented Framework Directive 2000/60/EC of the European Parliament and of the Council [1]. It is important to respond to the need for timely adaptation to climate change in progress, secure drinking water sources, increasing demands for recreational water quality as a consequence of improving living standards, enhancements in nature protection, and creation of conditions for further scientific and technical development in water quality improvement.

Planning for river basins consists of a series of decisions leading to the implementation of appropriate water protection projects. A new planning process concerning waters is defined in the Directive 2000/60/EC, establishing a framework for Community action in the field of water policy. This Framework Directive has been progressively transposed into the Czech legal system by a series of legislative standards. This fact has brought about a significant change to the whole system since 2004, and new

R. Denzer et al. (Eds.): ISESS 2015, IFIP AICT 448, pp. 196–206, 2015.
© IFIP International Federation for Information Processing 2015

national documents in the area of water management planning have had to be developed. Planning concerning waters has become a systematic policy area managed by the national government. Updates of the plans are made every 6 years.

Our modelling support relates to so-called *sub-catchment plans*. They define goals in protection of water as an environmental component (i.e., environmental goals) to be achieved in water bodies by 2015 or in the next two six-year planning periods. New functional forms of coordination of involved parties are being sought, i.e., not only those responsible for developing the plans but also other stakeholders, including professional and non-governmental organizations.

Increasing emphasis is placed on the economic efficiency of proposed and implemented measures, not only due to the current economic situation. This is particularly true in cases where a subsidy from public sources is offered to relevant projects (at the national or EU level). There is a wealth of literature dealing with finding cost-efficient solutions in wastewater treatment.

One of the ways of ensuring cost-effective solving of surface water quality problems is to find technical projects/designs shared by multiple polluters (so-called "coalition designs"). A new strategy is being promoted: reducing the risks caused by increasingly smaller sources. The specific feature of this strategy is that it allows implementation of so-called coalition projects, i.e., joint projects implemented by multiple polluters. A typical example is the construction and operation of joint wastewater treatment plants for several (neighbouring) municipalities.

Auctions are important market mechanisms for the allocation of goods and services. Reverse combinatorial auctions serve as a theoretical framework for the approach presented in the paper. Combinatorial auctions [4] are those auctions in which bidders can place bids on combinations of items, so-called bundles. The advantage of combinatorial auctions is that the bidder can express his preferences more fully. It is possible to formulate single-sided combinatorial auctions, forward auctions and reverse auctions. In forward auctions, a single seller sells resources to multiple buyers. In reverse auctions, a single buyer attempts to source resources from multiple suppliers.

The paper intends to demonstrate the possibilities of model support to this decision-making process in two areas: (i) model support to finding a cost-effective solution to a given task of reducing pollution by a specified key pollutant. A typical example is the task of reducing phosphorus emissions to a certain level to reduce eutrophication in surface waters; (ii) and model support to decision-making, which includes multiple criteria. The CRAB software [2], which makes it possible to compute results for quite complex situations, is described, followed with a presentation of selected applications.

2   Decision-Making Diagram

The simplified decision-making diagram for the planning process in the field of sewerage and wastewater treatment as described above is presented in Figure 1. The main decision-making stages are identified in it.

Based on the documents elaborated within the first analysis of the problem, it is decided if the solved problem is complex and requires optimization with using a combinatorial auction model. If yes, input data are collected and verified and it is decided

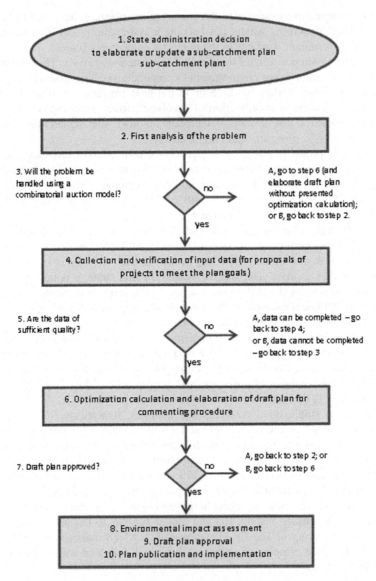

Fig. 1. Diagram of the planner's (entire) workflow

whether they are of sufficient quality for the modeling. If yes, the optimal solution is calculated and is commented within the draft plan by experts and stakeholders. In the case the plan is approved, the stages of Environmental impact assessment procedure, the plan final approval and its publication follow.

The calculation model supporting the decision-making process is shown in steps 3-7 in particular. For a more detailed description of the whole process, see the Methodology for economic and environmental optimization of reducing pollution in watercourses approved by the Czech government [3].

3   Models for Calculating a Cost-Effective Solution with Environmental Criteria

3.1   Model with One Environmental Criterion

We propose to use a model for reverse combinatorial auctions searching for a cost-effective combination of projects to reduce pollution. We assume that one environmental indicator is reduced to the desired level for all the projects. Therefore, it is possible to focus on the cost side of the problem.

We present a reverse combinatorial auction [4] of projects with one authority and several polluters. Let us suppose that m potential polluters $S_1, S_2, ..., S_m$ offer a set R of r projects, $j = 1, 2, ..., r$, to one buyer A.

A bid made by the polluter S_h, $h = 1, 2, ..., m$, is defined as

$$b_h = \{C, c_h(C)\},$$

where
$C \subseteq R$ is a combination of pollution sites, and
$c_h(C)$ is the price offered by the polluter S_h for the combination C.

The objective is to minimise the buyer's costs given the bids made by polluters. Constraints establish that the procurement provides at least a set of all items.

Bivalent variables are introduced for the model formulation:
$y_h(C)$ is a bivalent variable specifying whether the combination C is bought from the polluter S_h ($y_h(C) = 1$).

The reverse combinatorial auction can be formulated as follows

$$\sum_{h=1}^{m} \sum_{C \subseteq R} c_h(C) y_h(C) \rightarrow \quad \min$$

subject to

$$\sum_{h=1}^{m} \sum_{C \subseteq R} y_h(C) \geq 1, \quad \forall j \in R, \tag{1}$$

$$y_h(C) \in \{0,1\}, \quad \forall C \subseteq R, \quad \forall h, h = 1, 2, ..., m.$$

The objective function expresses the costs. The constraints ensure that the selection of projects includes all the pollution sites.

See section 5 for an illustration of this approach.

3.2   Model with Multiple Environmental Criteria

The basic model (1) can be extended for situations with multiple environmental criteria. We assume k environmental indicators, $i = 1, 2, ..., k$. A bid made by the polluter S_h is extended by $e_{ih}(C)$ is the reduction in the environmental indicator i offered by the polluter S_h for the combination C.

The reduction in the environmental indicator i in the whole region is given by the limits E_i, $i = 1, 2, ..., k$. Then the environmental aspect of the problem can be modelled by a set of constraints

$$e_{ih}(C)y_h(C) \geq E_i, i = 1, 2, ..., k. \tag{2}$$

In situations without limits, the problem can be extended in a multi-objective version of the problem (1) with a set of added objective functions

$$\sum_{h=1}^{m} e_{ih}(C)y_h(C) \rightarrow \max, i = 1, 2, ..., k. \tag{3}$$

The multi-objective programming problem can be solved by corresponding approaches.

See section 5 for an illustrative example of this approach.

4   CRAB – CombinatoRial Auction Body Software System

A need for an input problem generator arose during our research into combinatorial auctions. The CATS [5], software developed by Stanford University can be used for combinatorial auction problems, but it does not meet the specific needs of our problem. To satisfy our needs, we have developed our own software tool: CRAB [2]. This tool has several advantages comparing CATS, namely:

- fast problem generation,
- combinations are generated in a more predictable way,
- combinations are generated only in given subset of all items,
- CSV is used as the primary data format,
- fine-grained control over problem generated,
- built-in linear problem solver,
- multiple output formats.

This tool is implemented in Ruby. We choose Ruby for performance reasons, mainly for its dynamic, agile nature with enables us to quickly experiment with different approaches.

4.1   Overview

A combinatorial auction problem is given by the number of buyers and the number of all feasible combinations of goods – bundles. Prices of bundles – bids – and a budget are also needed for each buyer. The number of goods is read in the vector form where the number of vector components (comma separated) is equal to the number of bundles. Each vector component corresponds to the number of goods in the bundle.

All the combinations of goods in each bundle (except the empty set) are generated in the first phase. This step is done for every bundle. In this way, all the bundles are generated. The list of these bundles is saved in a file (*.csv) – one bundle per row – and one column is prepared for each buyer. The first row contains a column label and the second row is given to the buyer's budget.

The user of the CRAB software can load the CSV file into a text editor or a spreadsheet and fill in the bids (i.e., the price offered by the buyer for a particular bundle) and budgets for each buyer. If the user uses CRAB only for tests, he/she can use automatically generated prices and budgets. In both cases, the final file has to be saved in the CSV format again.

In the second phase, the file is transformed into a binary programming problem. The bundles correspond to variables and the bids correspond to prices of the objective function that is being maximized. The problem consists of automatic constraints for each good (each good can be sold only once) and each buyer (a buyer cannot exceed his budget). The user is free to change the automatically generated constraints and remove or add (for example non-typical) constraints. All the data have to be saved in the CSV format again.

Finally, the problem can be passed to the built-in binary programming solver to find out the optimal solution for the given combinatorial auction. If so, the problem is transformed into a form with minimizing the objective function with non-negative prices and all the constraints in the "less or equal" form. Afterwards, the transformed model is passed to the Balas algorithm [6]. The CRAB architecture gives a possibility to extend the system, especially about the implemented models and algorithms.

4.2   Practical Use

CRAB can operate in two modes: (i) an interactive mode, and (ii) a command line mode. CRAB can be run in an interactive mode, which means that the user is prompted for data interactively. Contrary to interactive mode, the CRAB can operate in a command line mode, which means that all input data as well as all options have to be supplied on the command line.

The CRAB can generate combinatorial problems. The principal command is:

```
ruby crab.rb --output <outfile> generate --buyers <nb> --
bundles <bundlespec>
```

where <nb> is the number of buyers (non-negative integer value) and <bundlespec> is a vector specifying the number of items in each bundle. The number of bundles is determined by the dimension of the vector. The vector should be entered as a comma-separated sequence of positive integer values with no spaces in between. CRAB can also generate random prices for each bundle as well as a budget for each buyer.

The generated file is an ordinary CSV (Comma Separated Values) file and thus editable by almost every spreadsheet application. The first row contains only column labels and no data. The second row contains a budget for each buyer. The rest of the rows specifies bids of bundles given by each buyer.

The first two columns contain only labels and no data. The first column denotes the bundle, the second one denotes the particular goods combination within the bundle.

A bundle is denoted by the ID of the first and last goods item in the bundle; the combination is denoted by a minus-separated list of goods IDs. The following columns contain the bids made by the buyers.

4.3   Transforming Combinatorial Auction to Binary Programming Problem

Once the combinatorial auction is generated, it can be transformed to the form of a binary programming problem and passed to the binary programming solver afterwards. The principal command for the combinatorial auction transformation is:

```
./ruby crab.rb --output <output file> transform --bids
<input file>
```

where `<input file>` is the CSV file specifying the combinatorial auction. The form of the input file must be the same as the output of the generate command. Optionally, the user can use the --format option to specify the output format. CRAB currently supports two output formats: (i) CSV (which is the default) and (ii) XA. The first one is the one used by the built-in solver; the latter can be passed directly to the XA integer solver [7].

The following command will transform the file bids.csv into a binary programming problem, saving the output to a file named problem.csv using the CSV format.

```
./ruby crab.rb --output problem.cvs transform --bids
bids.csv
```

The following command will create a binary programming problem specification file as used by the XA solver:

```
./ruby crab.rb --output problem.lp transform --format xa
--bids bids.csv
```

4.4   Solving

CRAB contains a built-in binary programming solver based on Balas's method [6]. The form of the input file must be the same as the output of the transform command using the CSV format. The CRAB tool also provides a few options to control the Balas algorithm. The first option controls the overall strategy to walk through the state space. Two strategies are available: depth-first (specified by the --depth-first option) and breadth-first (which is the default, specified by the --breadth-first option).

The second option deals with branching logic. If --one-first is specified, then the one-filled branch is tried first, if --zero-first is specified, the zero-filled branch is taken first. The one-first strategy is the default. Based on a few experiments, breadth-first combined with one-first gives the best results (measured by the number of iterations required to solve a particular problem).

The output of the built-in solver is as follows:

```
Iteration 1000: 47 solutions in queue (delta 46)
   z_f = 25930.0, z = 32702, z_max = 26433.0]
Iteration 2000: 123 solutions in queue (delta 76)
   z_f = 25930.0, z = 32702, z_max = 26807.0]
Iteration 3000: 269 solutions in queue (delta 146)
   z_f = 25991.0, z = 32702, z_max = 26812.0]
Iteration 4000: 321 solutions in queue (delta 52)
   z_f = 27285.0, z = 32702, z_max = 28251.0]
Iterations done: 4214
Solution: Vector[1, 1, 1, 1, 1, 1, 0, 0, 0, 0, 0, 0, 0, 0,
0, 0, 0, 0, 0, 0, 0, 0, 0, 0, 0, 0, 0, 0, 0, 0, 0, 0, 0, 0,
0, 0, 0, 0, 0, 0, 0, 0, 0, 0, 0, 0, 0, 0, 0, 0, 0, 0, 0, 0,
0, 0, 0, 0, 0, 0, 0, 0, 0], z = 5203
```

As the solver is solving the problem, it prints some statistical information: the total number of partial solutions in the queue, the delta from the last output and the values of a few other internal variables. After the solver finishes the computation, it prints out the number of iterations made, the solution and the value of the objective function.

5   Case Studies Results

5.1   Case with Single Environmental Criterion

The Rozkoš recreational lake in Eastern Bohemia serves as a practical example of application where a single environmental criterion was introduced. Phosphorus pollution reduction has become an issue, since it has a significant impact on the water quality for recreational purposes. It was taken as the most important (single) environmental criterion in the case. The experts evaluated investment costs for:

- all of the 20 individual projects (i.e., a situation where each of the municipalities would build its own wastewater treatment plant); they were coded as A1, A2, A3, A4, B1, B2, B3, B4, C1, C2, C3, C4, D1, D2, D3, D4, E1, E2, E3, E4;
- all of the 14 "promising" coalition projects, i.e., costs of such coalition projects that cannot be excluded from the analysis beforehand for technical, economic, environmental, morphological, political or other reasons; they were coded as A1+A2, A3+A4, A3+A4+B1+B3, B2+B3, B2+B3+B4+C2, B4+C1+C2, C3+C4, C3+C4+D2, C3+C4+D1+D3, D1+D2+D3, D1+E1, D4+E2, D4+E2+E3.

The CRAB software was used. The calculated optimal solution is as follows:

- 7 individual projects: B1, C1, C3, C4, E1, E3, E4
- 3 two-member coalitions: A1 +A2, A3 + A4, D4+ E2
- 1 three-member coalition: D1 + D2 + D3
- 1 four-member coalition: B2 + B3 + B4 + C2

Total costs of coalition solutions = CZK 720,600 thousand

Total costs of individual solutions = CZK 1,212,400 thousand

Cost saving if the coalition solutions are applied = CZK 491,800 thousand; i.e., about 40%.

See the simplified case in section 5.2 for the design of the mathematical model of this exercise.

5.2   Case with Multiple Criteria

An ideal case, close to a practical situation, has been created and called the Powder Brook case. It is an illustrative application to a case of a small river basin with 4 municipalities polluting a brook with one tributary. In spite of some necessary simplifications, the authors have striven for maximum approximation to the real situation in one of the tributaries to the Elbe river basin in Bohemia (Czech Republic).

Environmental criteria entering the analysis in this case were adopted from pollution production monitored pursuant to Government Regulation No. 61/2003 Coll. [8], and ČSN 75 6401 [9], which specifies the daily production of BOD_5 at 0.06 kg/EI, P_{total} at 0.0025 kg/EI, N_{total} at 0.015 kg/EI, and $N-NH_4+$ at 0.011 kg/EI. These environmental parameters were adopted and modelled as a set of constraints (2) as described in section 3.2.

The mathematical model of the exercise for the analysis is as follows:

$$N = 6500\ y_A + 16{,}250\ y_B + 29{,}000\ y_C + 32{,}750\ y_D + 27{,}750\ y_{AB} + 41{,}750\ y_{BC} + 59{,}000\ y_{BD} + 65{,}000\ y_{CD} + 50{,}000\ y_{ABC} + 69{,}000\ y_{BCD} + 73{,}000\ y_{ABCD} \rightarrow \quad min$$

The optimum solution to this exercise:

$$y_A = 0,\ y_B = 0,\ y_C = 0,\ y_D = 0, y_{AB} = 0,\ y_{BC} = 0,\ y_{BD} = 0,\ y_{CD} = 0,\ y_{ABC} = 0,\ y_{BCD} = 0,\ y_{ABCD} = 1.$$

One coalition project – ABCD – should be implemented.

The total costs N = CZK 73,000 thousand = saving of CZK 11,500 thousand compared to individual projects (common practice; CZK 84,500 thousand).

The case was very simple (only 4 subjects-municipalities where the presented software is not actually needed) for two reasons: (i) it serves as an understandable illustration of the methodology mentioned above developed by the authors of this paper [3]; and (ii) the results served as a background model for economic laboratory experiments, which are mentioned in the discussion. The authors of this paper are currently working on quite sophisticated applications.

6   Discussion and Conclusion

The calculations using the CRAB software produce very usefully information for support of decision-making of a public authority (government) when finding the cheapest solutions to water pollution reduction in situations where coalition (common) projects exist and experts are able to assess all the important information. The result is a cost-effective solution, which, in complex situations, would be very difficult to find by traditional computational methods.

In reality, especially in situations where the polluters are offered some financial support from public funds (subsidies), there is an information asymmetry between the authority and the polluters. It means that the polluters do not tell the truth about their abatement costs and try to apply for as much as possible from the funds. In such situations, the calculation using the CRAB software can help to calculate the optimal solution for testing the polluters' behavior in the form of economic laboratory experiments. The experiments then test how close or far from the optimal solution the negotiated outcomes are. For more details about these experiments, see [10] and [11]. In other words, the laboratory experiments can help test alternative institutional settings in the field, including settings where multiple criteria are introduced. See [12] and [13] for a costs-effectiveness analysis of public spending on environmental protection when multiple criteria are applied in the Czech conditions. Computing optimal solutions would also be helpful when testing alternative settings with public participation in decision-making. See [14] and [15] for a discussion of public participation in decision-making, and [16] for a typical Czech research in this area.

Acknowledgement. The paper was developed with the support of the Czech Science Foundation, grant no.13-07036S "Modelling of Negotiations in Environmental Policy under Information Asymmetry".

References

1.   Directive 2000/60/EC of the European Parliament and of the Council of 23 October 2000 establishing a framework for Community action in the field of water policy (2000)
2.   Fiala, P., Kalčevová, J., Vraný, J.: CRAB – CombinatoRial Auction Body Software System. Journal of Software Engineering and Applications 3, 718–722 (2010)
3.   Šauer, P., Dvořák, A., Fiala, P., Prášek, J.: Methodology for economic and environmental optimisation of reducing pollution in watercourses, University of Economics & Ministry of Agriculture, certificate no. 79469/2013-MZe, Prague (2013)
4.   Cramton, P., Shoham, Y., Steinberg, R. (eds.): Combinatorial Auctions. MIT Press, Cambridge (2006)
5.   Leyton-Brown, K., Pearson, M., Shoham, Y.: Towards a Universal Test Suite for Combinatorial Auction Algorithms. In: The Proceedings of ACM Conference on Electronic Commerce (EC 2000) (2000)
6.   Balas, E.: An Additive Algorithm for Solving Linear Programs with Zero-one Variables. Operations Research 13, 517–546 (1965)
7.   XA: Linear Optimizer System (2003), http://www.sunsetsoft.com/ (approached December 28, 2009)
8.   Government Order of 29 January 2003 No 61/2003 Coll., on the indicators and values of permissible pollution of surface water and wastewater, mandatory elements of the permits for discharge of wastewater into surface water and into sewerage systems, and on sensitive areas (Czech Technological Norm; in Czech) (2003)
9.   ČSN 75 6401 Sewage treatment plants for more than 500 of population equivalents.

10. Fiala, P., Šauer, P.: Application of Combinatorial Auctions on Allocation of Public Finan-
    cial Support in the Area of Environmental Protection: Economic Laboratory Experiment.
    Politická ekonomie 59(3), 379–392 (2011) (in Czech)
11. Šauer, P., Fiala, P., Dvořák, A.: Environmental negotiation under information asymmetry:
    a laboratory experiment for coalitions of four parties. Actual Problems of Econom-
    ics 154(4), 544–550 (2014)
12. Soukopová, J., Struk, M.: Methodology for the efficiency evaluation of the municipal
    environmental protection expenditure. In: Hřebíček, J., Schimak, G., Denzer, R. (eds.) En-
    vironmental Software Systems. IFIP AICT, vol. 359, pp. 327–340. Springer, Heidelberg
    (2011)
13. Soukopova, J., Bakos, E.: Assessing the efficiency of municipal expenditures regarding
    environmental protection. In: Aravossis, K., Brebbia, C.A. (eds.) Environmental Econom-
    ics and Investment Assessment III. Book Series: WIT Transactions on Ecology and the
    Environment, vol. 131, pp. 107–119 (2010)
14. Koontz, T.M., Johnson, E.M.: One size does not fit all: Matching breadth of stakeholder
    participation to watershed group accomplishments, Policy Sciences 37(2), 185–204 (2004)
15. Priscoli, J.D.: What is public participation in water resources management and why is it
    important? Water International 29(2), 221–227 (2004)
16. Slavikova, L., Jilkova, J.: Implementing the Public Participation Principle into Water
    Management in the Czech Republic: A Critical Analysis. Regional Studies 45(4), 545–557
    (2011)

Scenario Planning Case Studies
Using Open Government Data

Robert Power, Bella Robinson, Lachlan Rudd, and Andrew Reeson

CSIRO. GPO Box 664 Canberra, ACT, 2601, Australia
{robert.power,bella.robinson,lachlan.rudd,
andrew.reeson}@csiro.au

Abstract. The opportunity for improved decision making has been enhanced in recent years through the public availability of a wide variety of information. In Australia, government data is routinely made available and maintained in the http://data.gov.au repository. This is a single point of reference for data that can be reused for purposes beyond that originally considered by the data custodians. Similarly a wealth of citizen information is available from the Australian Bureau of Statistics. Combining this data allows informed decisions to be made through planning scenarios.

We present two case studies that demonstrate the utility of data integration and web mapping. As a simple proof of concept the user can explore different scenarios in each case study by indicating the relative weightings to be used for the decision making process. Both case studies are demonstrated as a publicly available interactive map-based website.

Keywords: urban planning, environmental planning, decision support, government data, public transport.

1 Introduction

This paper addresses the issue of characterising the demand for community services, and presents a framework for evaluating existing service locations in terms of their accessibility by public transport and ability to meet demand. To demonstrate the approach, we fit simplistic models to show the types of policy enhancing results that are possible. The main objective is to encourage government to push more data into open access; then more complex models could be fit to the actual datasets. The simplistic models we use show the results that are possible and highlight the power of the mapping tool for policy makers to interpret large amounts of data.

This approach can be applied to a range of services. Here we demonstrate its applicability using two case studies drawing on publicly available datasets. The first focuses on government shopfronts (used in Australia for the delivery of welfare and other government services), and the second looks at environmental services in the form of urban parks.

The framework allows users (modelers, decision-makers or other interested parties) to explore and evaluate scenarios using an interactive map-based website. This exploration

R. Denzer et al. (Eds.): ISESS 2015, IFIP AICT 448, pp. 207–216, 2015.

allows the user to define appropriate parameters to the decision making model. The model results are then computed in a database to produce the final results which are made available on the map-based website.

The demand for services varies across the community. This demand can be categorised based on the expected community need. Different categorisations define scenarios to help assess services which form the basis of the decision making model. An example of a service is a school, shopping centre, swimming pool, playground, government service centre or shopfront. The community need for these services varies. Some services will be needed by the general public, but will be used more by some than others; for example a shopping centre or swimming pool. Other services will predominantly be used by specific community subgroups; for example schools are used by families with school aged children.

The aim of our investigation is to explore how publicly available datasets can be used to help assess services using a methodical, repeatable, transparent and evidence based process that makes use of an interactive map-based website to allow modelers to better explore the data and its interrelationships. The focus is on services provided at specific locations, and we consider that demand is determined by demographics, accessibility by public transport (since not all have access to private cars), and the availability of alternatives.

2   Related Work

Demand for services varies spatially, with population density, demographics and transport as key determinants of accessibility. Location-allocation models are used to optimise the locations of service centres. A specific review in the health sector, found that greater availability of geographic data (e.g. GIS) and enhanced computing power has greatly expanded the range of data applications [1]. More recent applications include using mathematical optimisation techniques to identify optimal locations for defibrillators in urban areas [2,3].

A decision support system was developed using a mixed integer programming model to determine the efficient location of government service delivery offices by identifying which offices could be closed with the least impact on customers [4]. Such models can be used to explore a number of different scenarios, and provides decision-makers with an objective method of making, and justifying, service delivery decisions. A review of the use of geo-information technologies to support collaborative and participatory decision-making found that this can help to engage a greater range of stakeholders and elicit more local knowledge [5].

The simplest approach to accessibility considers Euclidean distance from locations, while more detailed models include roads and other transport features [6]. Accessibility by private car can be estimated from traffic flow models, but public transport has proved more complex due to the vagaries of routes and timetables [1]. Spatial optimisation has been applied in environmental management, including conservation [7] and natural resource management [8].

3   Methodology

The following process describes the steps taken to develop the interactive map-based website for use by a domain matter expert: the modeler. This process requires expertise in data management and website administration. While these skills are available in the Information Technology (IT) section of most organisations, they are also becoming a common skill set within reach of researchers. We believe the skills required to accomplish the tasks outlined below are increasingly within the capability of modelers themselves, especially as supporting software tools become available in the field of semantic web and linked data.

3.1   Problem Definition

The first step is to clearly define the problem to be solved. While this may seem obvious, it is sometimes assumed to be self-evident and therefore overlooked. By taking the time to define the problem to be solved using clear and unambiguous language, all participants in the task will share a common understanding of the goal to be achieved.

3.2   Obtain the Data

Central to the methodology is the need to understand the community for whom services are being provided (usually using census information) and the preferred means of accessing the services (in our case public transport). A summary of these two critical datasets are described in Section 4 below.

The other necessary dataset for the decision making process is the locations of the services being evaluated. This is expected to be available to the subject matter expert: the modeler. There may be other datasets necessary and again, it is the responsibility of the modeler to provide these and describe how they are to be used.

In some cases the required data will not be available and so proxies must be identified. This occurs when the necessary level of detail is not available and so approximations are required or where the specific data is not available, but known correlations can be found. An example is presented in the first case study where the home locations of customers for a government shopfront are not known, but are approximated using the Department of Social Security (DSS) payment recipients by postcode data from data.gov.au.

3.3   Load the Data

In order to load the data into a database, the data needs to be in a machine readable format. This process may require the data to be 'cleaned' (free of errors or inaccuracies), restructured (only relevant data extracted) and pre-processed (transformed to be suitable for the database loading tools) before it can be loaded. In some cases the data may need to be modified to make it compatible with other datasets. For example, the identifiers used to reference common artifacts (such as postcodes, suburbs, street names and so on) may need to be modified to match other datasets. This is often necessary when combining data managed by different custodians.

3.4   Define the Decision Making Model Function

There are three elements to the definition of the decision making model, outlined below. Note that this is intentionally a simplistic approach that is quick to implement with publicly available datasets as a proxy for actual usage data. As actual data is released, more powerful models can be used.

1. Categorise the community to reflect different service demands.

   For the example case studies below, we categorised the community into demand groups (e.g. levels of high, medium and low demand). The number of categories and how their membership is defined is dependent on the problem under investigation and at the discretion of the modeler. It is likely to include demographics (e.g. families with young children and families living in high density housing, are likely to have a higher demand for urban parks) and the availability of alternatives (e.g. households with broadband internet are more likely to access government services online, and so will have reduced demand for shopfronts).

2. Combine the different measures of service accessibility.

   The service accessibility includes public transport travel time but can also include other measures (e.g. walking or driving distance).

3. Include parameters to account for relative competing service demands.

   The contribution of each variable parameter to the overall result will change based on modeler supplied weights. This is how outcomes are prioritised. For example, decision-makers may assign a higher weighting to certain disadvantaged groups, or long travel times.

3.5   Update the Website

Geographic data can be explored visually in order to gain deeper insight into the available data. As well as making the input datasets available, the parameterised decision making model function is included as a derived data layer. This is how the modeler explores different scenarios – by providing different model parameters and viewing the results.

4   Gathering Data

4.1   The Australian Statistical Geography Standards (ASGS)

The Australian Bureau of Statistics (ABS) divides the country into a structure of hierarchical non-overlapping regions called the Australian Statistical Geography Standard (ASGS). These regions are used to present aggregate statistical information, such as population density, economic indicators, and so on. The main regions are termed Statistical Areas defined in four levels: SA1 (Statistical Area Level 1), SA2, SA3 and SA4. A collection of SA1 regions are grouped to form an SA2; the SA2s are grouped to form an SA3 and so on. There are 54,805 SA1s; 2,214 SA2s; 351 SA3s; 106 SA4s. SA1 data has been used in the case studies described below. These are the smallest regions for which the ABS releases census data and they vary in size to have a population of 200 to 800 people with an average of about 400 people.

4.2   Public Transport Travel Times

One of the measures of accessibility to a service is the travel distance to its location. A different accessibility measure is the travel time using public transport. Websites exist for people to plan travel on road networks, see for example Google Travel Planner[1]. Similarly, public transport journey planners are available for all Australian capital cities and some regional areas. It would not be feasible to manually use these journey planner websites to calculate the travel time to the nearest service.

Software was used to perform this task. Public Application Programming Interfaces (APIs) are available that provide a software interface to public transport journey planners, such as Google's Directions API[2] and the SilverRail[3] Journey Planner. However, these APIs have strict licensing conditions and/or only allow a small number of requests before a fee is required. For example, Google's Directions API only allows 2,500 requests per day and the results must be displayed on a public Google Map. An alternate open source solution was found along with timetable information, based on OpenTripPlanner and OpenStreetMap. By installing this software locally, we could make as many requests as necessary.

Software was written to systematically use OpenTripPlanner to generate travel plans for the 34,172 SA1s (62%) that were within the regions of Australia for which we had public transport data. For each SA1, travel plans were generated from the SA1 centroid to all service locations that were within a specific radius of the SA1. OpenTripPlanner can generate several alternate itineraries for each SA1 service location combination. Only the journey with the shortest duration was recorded in the database. Further details are provided in the case studies below.

5   Government Office Locations Case Study

5.1   Description

Government services have traditionally been provided to citizens through face-to-face interactions at shopfronts or through telephone services provided by call centre staff. More recently, there has been a push to transition customers to self-management through digital services with the aim of reducing service delivery costs while maintaining customer satisfaction. Over time, face-to-face government services can be combined between departments and call centres consolidated providing efficiencies.

---

[1] http://maps.google.com.au/intl/en/landing/transit/
[2] https://developers.google.com/maps/documentation/directions/
[3] http://www.silverrailtech.com/journeyplanner

5.2   Process

For this investigation we worked with the Australian Government Department of Human Services (the department) to evaluate alternative options for service delivery to meet anticipated customer needs balanced against the department's resources. There are 304 existing government shopfront locations, referred to as customer service centres, or simply offices, available from data.gov.au. Another public dataset used was Detailed Payment Demographic Data which included payment recipient numbers by postcode for the March 2014 quarter[4]. There were 27 payment categories such as age pension, carer allowance, disability support, unemployment benefit and so on. This data was de-aggregated from postcodes to SA1 regions using ABS socioeconomic indicators by matching the expected customer profile to the different benefit types. For example, areas of high socio-economic need are allocated more customers for specific benefit types, such as unemployment payments, compared to areas of lower socio-economic need [9].

In summary, the aim of the investigation was to evaluate the accessibility of existing offices in terms of public transport for the department's customers and to model the potential for customers to transition to self management through digital services.

The ability of citizens in the different geographic areas to transition to self management through digital services can be approximated by the broadband availability and usage in their local area. The idea being that digital services are best provided to areas that are currently well serviced and utilised by the community. This information was available from two sources: the ABS census data (which includes an indication of the Internet availability for dwellings for each SA1 region) and the Australian Government Department of Communications MyBroadband website[5].

The demand for services was modeled by categorising the customers into three groups; high, medium and low, using the payment demographic data. Those customers with high need likely require regular and possibly intensive meetings with front line customer service staff. Those with low need are expected to understand their obligations and (mostly) meet these requirements using self service interactions, preferably online. Customers categorised as medium fall between these two and will have some irregular face-to-face or phone contact with the government while also fulfilling some aspects of their interactions through self service mechanisms.

A demand (d) measure for each SA1 region is calculated by combining the customer category numbers (customers categorised as being high (h), medium (m) or low (l) need) with the services expected to support them. This is a weighted combination using parameters (w_h for high weightings, w_m medium and w_l for low) as follows:

$$d = w_h \cdot h \cdot t_i + w_m \cdot m + w_l \cdot l \cdot b_s$$

Here t_i is the travel interval in a range of 1-10 and b_s is the broadband scale. In both cases, 1 is good (short travel time or good broadband) and 10 is bad. The demand

---

[4] http://data.gov.au/dataset/dss-payment-demographic-data
[5] https://www.mybroadband.communications.gov.au/

measures for the SA1 regions close to an office are then summed, normalised and scaled and the results ranked to allow comparisons between offices.

The rankings were used to divide the centres into deciles loosely based on customer need. If the need was low, policy makers could consider downsizing the centre and shifting more services online. Demand for a centre's services was defined as the sum of the SA1 rankings in the centre's catchment. This sum accounts for the volume of customers weighted by their service requirements (high, medium or low) and their access to public transport or broadband.

Once demand was calculated and centres were arranged into deciles, policy makers could look at the distribution of customers at any given service centre. Univariate statistics like the mean, median, skew and kurtosis were generated to help evaluate large groups of service centres within a decile and a histogram of customer need scores was generated for each individual centre.

Using the univariate statistics, policy makers are able to identify centres with concentrations of one particular customer type, or centres with skewed distributions indicating a wider mix of customer demand. The histograms of key centres can then be analysed prior to considering changes to the services offered by a centre. This allows the impact of change on the full spectrum of customer types to be considered.

The data is available to explore on the http://rapt.csiro.au/rprc website.

6   Urban Parks Accessibility and Demand Case Study

6.1   Description

The next case study examined the expected use of parks in the Brisbane metropolitan area. Urban parks offer a range of environmental services, which are likely to become increasingly important as housing density increases. The 2,042 park locations and descriptions of their facilities were obtained. The park facilities indicate, among other information, the presence of playgrounds, sporting areas (fitness exercise equipment, netball courts, soccer fields), recreation areas (bike paths, skating areas, bushwalking) and picnic facilities (barbeques and seating).

The aim of this investigation was to measure park accessibility and demand by using public transport. Some parks will be more attractive than others based on the facilities they provide. This equates to an 'attractiveness' measure, defined by the number of facilities provided, ranging from 0 (no facilities), 1 (one of playgrounds, sporting areas, recreation areas and picnic facilities) up to 4 (includes all facilities).

6.2   Process

Two stages of data preparation were required: calculate the walking and public transport travel times to the various parks from the SA1 regions and identify members of the community most likely to want to use the different parks.

Parks with playgrounds were expected to be used by families with small children, recreation parks used by teenagers, parks with picnic areas by people who live in dwellings without a yard and so on. To reduce the calculations required, thresholds were placed on the distance people will travel to a park based on the attractiveness measure: people are expected to only walk up to two kilometers to a '0' park (attractiveness measure of 0, i.e. a park with no facilities) and optionally use public transport to travel to the other parks. For a '1' park, the maximum distance travelled is set to 3 kms, 5 kms to a '2', 7 kms to a '3' and 10 kms to a '4'. We are assuming that people will be willing to travel further on public transport to parks with more facilities (ie those with a higher attractiveness score). The travel planner software was configured to calculate public transport travel plans for each SA1 – park combination that meets these park attractiveness and distance constraints.

The model used is an arbitrary proxy to demonstrate the types of inferences that can be drawn from this type of data. More powerful models could be constructed using the local council's actual usage statistics. Our model's advantage is in using publicly available data and easy to implement methods for early stage exploratory analysis and to demonstrate what can be learned if more data is pushed into open access. Additionally the linking of public transport information and the readily interpreted map-based display of model outputs is of high utility to policy makers.

The data is available to explore on the http://rapt.csiro.au/parks website.

7   Discussion and Future Work

There have been a few lessons learned in undertaking these case studies. While there is an abundance of open government data published in Australia, the same data is available from different agencies, in different formats, with different structures and includes different content. The data.gov.au site is a central repository of authoritative government data, however state governments maintain the same data on their own data repositories or agency specific websites with content that is more up to date and more extensive. For example, the Brisbane park data was obtained from the Brisbane City Council website[6] not data.gov.au.

Finding data relevant for a particular investigation has become easier and governments are more willing to describe and share their data. However, improvements in data related outcomes can still readily be achieved if governments are able to interlink their releases with existing public and private datasets. Interactive map-based websites are becoming ubiquitous and user expectations of the features available from them are increasing. This is in our view an opportunity and was the motivation for our case studies: combining readily available open government data for new purposes and making it available in a publicly accessible and interactive website. However to achieve these aims we have had to exploit specialist skills in data management, software engineering, web application development and statistics.

While the short term aim was to demonstrate the benefits of combining these skills to deliver the solutions presented, this process is not sustainable. Instead, tools need to be developed to allow users to readily incorporate web accessible datasets of their own choosing. This integration needs to be more than simply making datasets appear as a new 'layer' on the website. It needs to be combined in the context of the datasets already present. This can be achieved by utilising emerging standards and supporting tools in the field of the semantic web. This is an ongoing area of our research.

---

[6] http://data.brisbane.qld.gov.au/index.php/datasets/

Another area of further work is to move away from a data warehouse solution and utilise a services oriented architecture. This requires the data custodians to introduce suitable services which adopt appropriate standards. While these services are not currently universally available, it is expected they will be established over time.

Other future work includes automating the process of exploring and evaluating the scenario generation process, mechanisms to combine private data using authentication controls and to extend the public transport analysis. For example, to preference trains over buses, use different thresholds for the maximum number of transfers, varying the maximum walking times for different customer cohorts and including more timetable options, such as weekends and different times of the day.

8   Conclusions

We have presented a methodology for characterising the demand for community services, with a focus on evaluating existing service locations in terms of their accessibility by public transport and ability to meet demand. The methodology has been demonstrated by two case studies using publicly available datasets. It provides a methodical, repeatable, transparent and evidence based process for users to perform scenario planning. The scenarios are explored by users providing parameters to the decision making model with the results available as an interactive map-based website.

The aim of the first case study was to demonstrate what could be done without actual access to the required data. We weren't subject matter experts, did not have access to the detailed customer data, and did not try to build the most accurate model. Our objective was to demonstrate what could be achieved if government were to open access to more data. We showed possible results and how they could be used by decision makers to enhance policy outcomes.

If the data was to become open, our model for demand would change drastically (mixed integer programming, approximate Bayesian computation, hierarchical regression models with spatial correlations). We could tailor the model to the data itself. In this paper we are using a balance between simplicity and general applicability to make a case for releasing more data. The second case study examined the expected use of parks in the Brisbane metropolitan area based on park facilities, demand and accessibility by using public transport.

These examples show that the decision making process is available to non-expects such as members of the general public who have an interest in exploring such issues in their community. In order to fully realise this aim, the user needs to be able to integrate their own data and define their own decision model function. The availability of relevant public datasets goes some way to achieve this aim. The next stage is to develop advanced tools based on semantic technologies and linked data to allow users to integrate content, visually explore data and to model relationships. The result would be a general purpose web accessible 'spatial spreadsheet', combining features found in web mapping, databases, Geographical Information Systems and spreadsheet tools.

Acknowledgements. This work was funded under the Human Services Delivery Research Alliance between the CSIRO and the Australian Government Department of Human Services. Thanks go to David Lovell (CSIRO) who provided helpful advice during the project.

References

1. Tanser, F., Gething, P., Atkinson, P.: Location-allocation Planning. In: A Companion to Health and Medical Geography, pp. 540–566. Wiley-Blackwell (2009)
2. Tsai, Y.S., Ko, P.C.I., Huang, C.Y., Wen, T.H.: Optimizing locations for the installation of automated external defibrillators (AEDs) in urban public streets through the use of spatial and temporal weighting schemes. Applied Geography 35, 394–404 (2012)
3. Chan, T.C.Y., Li, H., Lebovic, G., Tang, S.K., Chan, J.Y.T., Cheng, H.C.K., Morrison, L.J., Brooks, S.C.: Identifying locations for public access defibrillators using mathematical optimization. Circulation 127, 1801 (2013)
4. Narasimhan, R., Talluri, S., Sarkis, J., Ross, A.: Efficient service location design in government services: A decision support system framework. Journal of Operations Management 23, 163–178 (2005)
5. McCall, M.K., Dunn, C.E.: Geo-information tools for participatory spatial planning: Fulfilling the criteria for 'good' governance? Geoforum 43, 81–94 (2012)
6. Noor, A.M., Amin, A.A., Gething, P.W., Atkinson, P.M., Hay, S.I., Snow, R.W.: Modelling distances travelled to government health services in Kenya. Tropical Medicine & International Health 11, 188–196 (2006)
7. Moilanen, A., Wilson, K.A., Possingham, H.P.: Spatial conservation prioritization: quantitative methods and computational tools. Oxford University Press, United Kingdom (2009)
8. Bryan, B.A., Crossman, N.D., King, D., Meyer, W.S.: Landscape futures analysis: Assessing the impacts of environmental targets under alternative spatial policy options and future scenarios. Environmental Modelling & Software 26, 83–91 (2011)
9. Power, R., Robinson, B., Rudd, L.: Planning the Future Face to Face Service Delivery Footprint. CSIRO Australia (2014)

Training Support for Crisis Managers with Elements of Serious Gaming

Denis Havlik, Oren Deri, Kalev Rannat, Manuel Warum, Chaim Rafalowski,
Kuldar Taveter, Peter Kutschera, and Merik Meriste

Austrian Institute of Technology, Vienna, Austria
Denis.havlik@ait.ac.at

Abstract. This paper presents a methodology and a prototypic software implementation of a simple system supporting resource management training for crisis managers. The application that is presented supports the execution and assessment of a desktop training for decision makers on a tactical and strategic level. It introduces elements of turn-based strategic "serious gaming", with a possibility to roll back in time and re-try new decision paths, while keeping the graphical user interface as simple as possible. Consequently, the development efforts concentrated on: (1) formulating and executing crisis management decisions; (2) assuring responses of all simulated entities adhere to natural laws of the real world; and (3) analyzing progress and final results of the training exercise. The paper presents the lessons learned and discusses the transferability and extensibility of the proposed solution beyond the initial scenario involving accidental release of toxic gas in an urban area in Israel.

Keywords: crisis management, training, resource management.

1 Introduction

Organizing realistic trainings which force crisis managers and other training participants to understand that "there is no ideal solution to a complex crisis" is difficult [1]. Trainers, trainees and other stakeholders often oversee the obvious mistakes in both, planning of the (field) trainings and assessing the training results. Typical omissions include: the unlimited availability of resources, unrealistically fast arrival of resources at the scene, instantaneous and unfailable performing of some tasks such as a triage, as well as the superhuman endurances of the responders and patients alike.

The CRISMA project team developed a methodology and a set of software tools which can be used to make trainings quite realistic, by keeping most of the training organization unchanged and, where needed, taking into account the peculiarities of the local crisis management organization.

Below we start with a presentation of one concrete use case targeted in the "Accidental pollution" application of the CRISMA project. Thereafter, in section 3, we introduce the technical implementation of the application and section 4 presents the lessons learned in application development and testing, and close with the discussion on transferability and extensibility of the proposed solution.

R. Denzer et al. (Eds.): ISESS 2015, IFIP AICT 448, pp. 217–225, 2015.

2   Decision Support Concept and the Resource Management Training Scenario

The CRISMA project is a European Union funded project focusing on simulation of multi-sectorial large scale crisis scenarios with multi-dimensional effects on the society. According to the CRISMA architecture [2,3] the aspects of the *World* we are interested in must be modelled as a set of representative *World State* data (*WSs*) which develops in discrete steps (*World Transitions*), depending on the inherent characteristics of the problem at hand as well as on the users' decisions (*Decision Chain*).

Depending on the selected use case, new WSs may be generated at regular time intervals, following the users decisions (e.g. "evacuate"), or to capture the results of a specific model execution (e.g. "ambulance has arrived to the scene"). In most CRISMA applications, the user can test the effects of alternative decisions. This results in distinct *Scenarios, i.e.* sets of WSs corresponding to unique *Decision Chains.*

WSs and whole Scenarios can be compared and assessed using a set of *Indicators* relevant to a problem at hand. In addition to indicators, CRISMA also supports *Criteria* – a normalized form of the Indicators which take into account the desired values of the Indicators (e.g. "evacuating the critical patients in less than 30 min is *good*"). This simplifies the task of analyzing the results and ranking the different Scenarios. However, the Criteria are both subjective and extremely sensitive to small changes in the problem definition. Consequently, the criteria must be defined separately for each training or planning session, e.g. as a part of the training setup.

The CRISMA decision support concept can thus be summarized as: *help the users to assess the results of their decisions, but do not suggest a course of action nor impose any particular solutions.*

2.1   Resource Management Training Scenario

The CRISMA concepts and the software framework have been tested in five pilot applications covering various aspects of the crisis management planning and training [4]. Two of these applications target the long-term infrastructure and organizational planning, one concentrates on the development of operational plans, and the final two address the planning, execution and assessment of the resource management trainings. Here and now we only concentrate on the resource management training application.

During an emergency, commanders in emergency organizations have to decide which resources (ambulances, fireman, police officers, etc.) to deploy, where to send them, and what their tasks should be. In our trainings, the commanders (trainees) are confronted with initial crisis situation and have to express their decisions as they would do during a real accident. Thereafter, the decisions are entered into the system by a steward, the application calculates a new situation, and the result is presented to the trainees. At every step, the trainee can issue additional commands or even step backwards and revise previous decisions (**Fig. 1**).

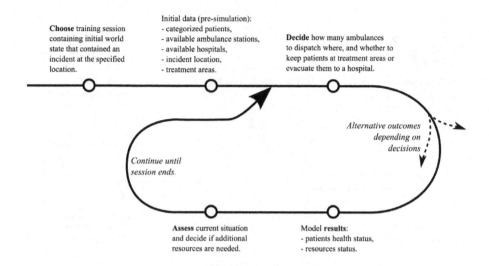

Fig. 1. Resource management training workflow

A concrete accident scenario addressed in the resource management training pilot deals with an accidental spilling of chemicals (i.e. bromine) from a container in a major port. The resulting plume poses a threat to a large number of inhabitants in the neighboring city and the severity of the impact depends on the commander's decisions. The main purpose of the application is to assure the impact of the decisions taken by the trainees is realistic, in a sense that the impact is guided by the natural laws and peculiarities of the training setup. For example:

- Resources have to be actively deployed and their arrival to the scene is delayed based on their distance from the scene, type of the road, and weather conditions.
- The condition of the patient will deteriorate based of one's previous medical history, exposure to the contamination and the help received (e.g. decontamination).
- The condition of resources also changes as result of the interaction between the resource and the environment and/or patient. At some point, resources may become exhausted and cannot perform additional actions.

3   Concept and Implementation

A CRISMA resource management training application is realized by using six generic "Building Blocks" (BBs) of the CRISMA framework (**Fig. 2**).

- *Integrated Crisis Management Middleware (ICMM)* is the core CRISMA middleware service. It acts as a catalogue of the WSs and Scenarios and also supports the work with Indicators and Criteria. *Objects of Interest World State Repository (OOI-WS Repository)* and the *Agents Platform* assure that resources of interest for the application are represented in a common form and that their state changes over time, similarly to a way it would be in 'real life'. Main OOIs and activities modeled in the pilot are illustrated in the **Fig. 3**.

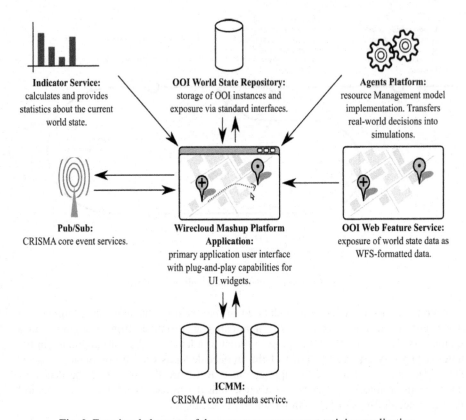

Fig. 2. Functional elements of the resource management training application

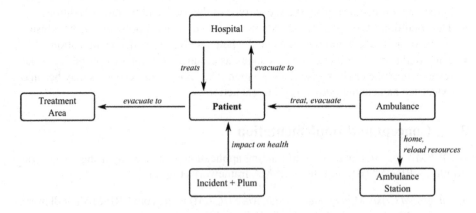

Fig. 3. Main Objects of Interest and activities

- *Indicator Service* calculates the relevant indicators whenever a new World State has been generated by the user or by the agents' platform. Indicators (e.g. "number of dead", "utilization of resources" or "time required for evacuation of critical patients") are used to analyze the progress and final outcome of the training.

- *Pub/Sub service* provides support for event-driven application designs. In this application, all changes to the WS are advertised using the Pub/Sub service. Software elements such as the agents' platform or the indicator service are subscribed to these events and automatically activated as needed.
- Finally, the *Wirecloud Mashup Platform* provides a flexible platform for implementing the application GUI elements and building mashup applications.

The following sections provide more information on three central system components: OOI-WS repository, Agents platform and the Mashup application.

3.1   Objects of Interest -World State Repository

OOI-WSR is a service which enables archiving, querying and manipulation the Objects of Interest world state data. It provides a central information exchange and data storage point for all other BBs which consume and manipulate world state data.

The repository data is organized in simulation sessions. Each repository session corresponds to a distinct training and consists of multiple world state snapshots. Each of the snapshots represents the state of the world at specific points (in time) and contains the states of all OOIs relevant for the training.

The starting properties of all OOIs in the initial world state (e.g. initial positions and states of citizens and ambulances) are postulated by a trainer. Subsequent world state snapshots are generated by the agents' platform BB and reflect both the inherent model logic and the trainees' decisions.

The OOI-WSR provides an easy http based access to data and enables data manipulations for authorized services. It exposes the stored data in a variety of industry standard such as REST/JSON and OGC WFS/GML in order to support out-of-the-box integration with other web technologies. The repository assures that each OOI is an instance of a specific OOI type representing some real-world resource (e.g. "ambulance"). In order to facilitate data analysis, typed OOIs also prevent the trainers from instantiating the "impossible" resources as a part of the training setup.

3.2   OOI Models and Serious Gaming

The general logic and architecture of CRISMA favor the development of strategic turn-based "serious gaming" applications. This type of applications emphasizes making strategic and/or tactical decisions by the players, rather than elaborate graphics or real time reaction skills. A central concept in serious gaming is that of an "agent", which is understood as a proactive and social entity capable of reasoning [1,5,6,7,8].

In our training application, each of the OOI types defined in the OOI-WSR has to be associated with an active representation (agent) of the same OOI. The properties and behavioral models of the software agents corresponding to various OOI types are specified as requirements for the agent-based simulation, using the method put forward in [5,6].

The agent-based simulation runs as an autonomous client-server application, using OOI-WSR for obtaining the initial World State (WS0) and recording the consecutive intermediate World States (WS1 ... WSn) back to OOI-WSR. The consecutive WSs reflect the evolution of the World and the emerging states for each agent as a result of interactions between different types of agents (for example, Ambulances⟵→Patients) and the impact of the environment (e.g. weather conditions, chemical plume, etc.) on these agents. Our agent-based simulation environment supports behavioral models of the following two types:

1. Behavioral models for each agent type, such as Ambulance and Patient;
2. Scenarios, specifying "what is played" for different games.

Agent types are designed to be as generic as possible, and the sub-typing (e.g. different ambulances) can be achieved through parameterization at the level of the OOI repository. The agents can also communicate with external models via HTTP or some other fixed protocol. This feature simplifies the calculation/estimation of the agent/environment interactions and also makes agent-based simulation models easily expandable, and allows us to solve rather complicated tasks by means of external services.

However, in many cases different games need game-specific agent types because each agent type must support the scenario(s) foreseen for the game by having all the properties and behavioral models that support realization of the game`s scenarios. In addition, the agent types should also be designed to support the calculation of Key Performance Indicators (KPIs) required by the application owner for decision(s) making for a concrete application. Finally, at the level of scenario, each application of the serious game of resource management requires its specific overall agent-based simulation model developed jointly with the application owner.

3.3   User Interfaces

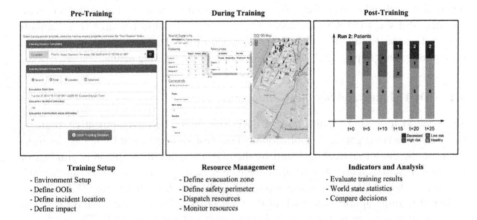

| Pre-Training | During Training | Post-Training |

Training Setup	Resource Management	Indicators and Analysis
- Environment Setup	- Define evacuation zone	- Evaluate training results
- Define OOIs	- Define safety perimeter	- World state statistics
- Define incident location	- Dispatch resources	- Compare decisions
- Define impact	- Monitor resources	

Fig. 4. Main User Interface Views

At the level of graphical interfaces, the application implements three of the "views" foreseen by the CRISMA architecture (**Fig. 4**). The views have been realized as web mashup applications running on a Wirecloud Platform. As a consequence, the whole application is built by "wiring" the simpler GUI widgets which are implemented in

JavaScript and HTML5. The application runs in any modern web browser as well as many mobile devices, and the further development and improvements can be easily achieved by replacing or adding new widgets and re-wiring the mashup.

The *Pre-training View* focuses on the initial creation of a training exercise and allows the user to specify details about the incident from a pre-defined set of templates. This includes the ability to modify each OOI's state and availability. Templates are set up by an expert and already contain a sample configuration of a training exercise but can further be tuned in the pre-training stage. This view is designed to be used by the trainer rather than the trainee.

The *Training View* allows the trainee to play out decisions such as allocation of resources for the training exercise created during the pre-training step. This is achieved by a turn-based approach where the trainee issues any number of orders and then receives the information on a new situation at discreet time intervals. At any point in time, the trainee can issue new orders if deemed necessary, or go back in time and try alternative approaches.

Finally, the *Post-training Analysis View* presents the user with indicators that allow measuring and comparing individual outcomes generated during the training exercise. These comparisons render one or more outcomes as a time series to assess how different decisions played a part in the overall progression. Currently, these statistics cover an aggregated view of the health categorization of patients (healthy, injured, severely injured, and dead), how this status compares to the initial health (improved/deteriorated), as well as the resource utilization over time, but additional indicators can be easily implemented using the Indicator Service.

The fact that results are measurable, and can be correlated with decisions is of major importance for the trainees, as it enables evaluation of the decision processes and not just of the results. In this way, the Analysis View can help the trainees to understand the influence of own decisions on the results.

4   Transferability and the Path Ahead

At a time of writing the article (October 2014), the first version of the training application has been developed and tested by the end-users, and the work on the second application version is underway. Second version of the application is due in March 2015.

The v1 application version already incorporated all the functional elements (**Fig. 2**), OOIs (**Fig. 3**) and GUI elements (**Fig. 4**) which have been introduced in the previous section, but the implementation is still incomplete. In particular, the v2 application will feature: (1) improved patients "life model"; (2) improved interaction between the OOIs (patients, resources) as well as the interaction between OOIs and the environment (e.g. temperature, light conditions, weather, road blocks); and (3) possibility to determine zones with different concentrations and simulate the plume movement during the incident.

Tests of the v1 application with end-users from Magen David Adom (MDA) have confirmed the usability of the application concept and provided a valuable feedback concerning the shortcomings of the design of the graphical interface. For example, the way in which the commands are given to resources in the v1 application differs from the way such commands are given in the command center and the v2 application will be amended accordingly. Nevertheless, all testers agreed that the fully-developed application could enhance the learning experience of the crisis managers' and contribute towards improved preparedness at the MDA. Moreover, the technical development team is confident that the current application design can be easily extended and transferred to new domains and use cases.

Wirecloud offers a solid platform for prototyping and the individual widgets can be easily embedded in other projects at a later time; ICMM simplifies housekeeping and working with indicators and criteria; the Indicator Service simplifies the task of calculating indicators; and the combination of OOI-repository and the Pub/Sub event broker assures that application parts can be developed in parallel without undue overhead.

At the end of the day, the application flexibility remains essentially limited by the functionality of available agent models and by the cost of implementing the missing model features. While no "silver bullet" solution to this issue exists, following features at least mitigate the issue:

• new sub-types of agent models can be introduced in the application by defining a new subtype of OOIs with specific parameters (e.g. max speed, max transport capacity, types of patients which can be treated, etc. for ambulances) within OOI-WSR; and
• as agents can communicate with arbitrary external models, existing models can be easily re-used as is or with small changes where appropriate.

One of the interesting opportunities for future development is in supporting the trainer to choose realistic environmental conditions, e.g. by taking into account past situations and/or forecasting new ones.

Another interesting possibility is extending of the software to support the task of defining and testing of the operational plans. Related work is already underway and the results will be presented in a separate paper later on.

Acknowledgements. The research leading to this paper has been performed within the CRISMA project, which is co-funded under the European Community's Seventh Framework Program FP7/2007 - 2013 (grant agreement no. 284552).

All of the software mentioned in the paper, with the exception of the agents' platform (property of TTU) is licensed under Open Source licenses and can be re-used and extended in other projects.

— Pub/Sub and WireCloud have been developed in the scope of the EC Future Internet Public Private Partnership initiative,
— Remaining software has been developed by CRISMA partners AIT Austrian Institute of Technology, Cismet, and NICE, but may be based on or include third party open source products. Full information on all software used and developed within the project is available at the CRISMA catalogue [9].

References

1. Hawe, G.I., Coates, G., Wilson, D.T., Crouch, R.S.: Agent-based simulation for large-scale emergency response: A survey of usage and implementation. ACM Computing Surveys (CSUR) 45(1), 8 (2012)
2. Dihe, P., Denzer, R., Polese, M., Heikkilä, A.-M., Havlik, D., Sautter, J., Hell, Th., Schlobinski, S.: An architecture for integrated crisis management simulation. In: 20th International Congress on Modelling and Simulation, Adelaide, Australia (December 2013)
3. Dihe, P., et al.: CRISMA framework architecture v2. Project report (2014), http://www.crismaproject.eu/deliverables/CRISMA_D322_public.pdf
4. CRISMA consortium (2013), http://www.crismaproject.eu/usecases.htm
5. Sterling, L., Taveter, K.: The Art of Agent-Oriented Modeling. MIT Press, Cambridge (2009)
6. Miller, T., Lu, B., Sterling, L., Beydoun, G., Taveter, K.: Requirements Elicitation and Specification Using the Agent Paradigm: The Case Study of an Aircraft Turnaround Simulator. IEEE Transactions on Software Engineering 40(10), 1007–1024 (2014)
7. Dignum, F.: Agents for games and simulations. Autonomous Agents and Multi-Agent Systems 24(2), 217–220 (2012)
8. Gentile, M., La Guardia, D., Dal Grande, V., Ottaviano, S., Allegra, M.: An Agent Based Approach to designing Serious Game: the PNPV case study. International Journal of Serious Games 2(1) (2014)
9. Havlik, D., Dihé, P., Frings, S., Steinnocher, K., Aubrecht, C. (eds.): Catalogue of CRISMA applications, framework building block specifications and software implementations. CRISMA consortium (2015), https://crisma-cat.ait.ac.at/content/crisma-catalogue-book

A Software System for the Discovery of Situations Involving Drivers in Storms

Markus Stocker[1], Okko Kauhanen[1], Mikko Hiirsalmi[2], Janne Saarela[3], Pekka Rossi[4], Mauno Rönkkö[1], Harri Hytönen[5], Ville Kotovirta[2], and Mikko Kolehmainen[1]

[1]Department of Environmental Science, University of Eastern Finland, Kuopio, Finland
{markus.stocker,okko.kauhanen,mauno.ronkko,
mikko.kolehmainen}@uef.fi
[2]VTT Technical Research Center of Finland, Espoo, Finland
{mikko.hiirsalmi,ville.kotovirta}@vtt.fi
[3]Profium Oy, Helsinki, Finland
janne.saarela@profium.com
[4]Finnish Meteorological Institute, Helsinki, Finland
pekka.rossi@fmi.fi
[5]Vaisala Oyj, Vantaa, Finland
harri.hytonen@vaisala.com

Abstract. We present an environmental software system that obtains, integrates, and reasons over situational knowledge about natural phenomena and human activity. We focus on storms and driver directions. Radar data for rainfall intensity and Google Directions are used to extract situational knowledge about storms and driver locations along directions, respectively. Situational knowledge about the environment and about human activity is integrated in order to infer situations in which drivers are potentially at higher risk. Awareness of such situations is of obvious interest. We present a prototype user interface that supports adding scheduled driver directions and the visualization of situations in space-time, in particular also those in which drivers are potentially at higher risk. We think that the system supports the claim that the concept of situation is useful for the modelling of information about the environment, including human activity, obtained in environmental monitoring systems. Furthermore, the presented work shows that situational knowledge, represented by heterogeneous systems that share the concept of situation, is relatively straightforward to integrate.

Keywords: Environmental knowledge systems, situation theory, ontology, knowledge representation, MMEA, Wavellite.

1   Introduction

Computational models [1], in particular empirical and physically-based models, can be used on data to obtain information. In some environmental software systems, data is obtained in environmental monitoring and information is about the environment. Data is, specifically, the result of measurement, defined as "the process of empirical,

R. Denzer et al. (Eds.): ISESS 2015, IFIP AICT 448, pp. 226–234, 2015.

objective, assignment of numbers to properties of objects or events of the real world in such a way as to describe them" [2]. To automatically sample physical properties at high spatiotemporal resolution, measurement is often implemented by environmental sensor networks.

An environment monitored in space-time can be abstracted as structured parts of reality, in other words situations [3]. The Situation Theory, developed in the 1980s by Barwise and Perry [4] and Devlin [3], proposes a mathematical ontology for information about situations. A situation is said to support infons, whereby and infon is a tuple consisting of a relation, a set of objects, and the polarity to state whether or not the objects stand in the relation. Environmental phenomena, including humans in activity, are objects. Such objects have attributes and stand in relation to each other.

Models can be used on measurement data to obtain information about situations. The term *situation* can serve as the most abstract concept in a framework that models information about structured parts of reality monitored in space-time. We present the application of such a framework, called Wavellite, to the modelling of situations with storms and driver locations as the objects. The resulting system reasons over situational knowledge to detect those in which storms and drivers overlap in space-time. Such situations are of interest because people may be at higher risk of accident.

The contribution of this work is two-fold. First, together with our related work [5, 6], we underscore the suitability of the notion of situation for the modelling, i.e. explicit representation, of situational knowledge obtained using models from processed data collected and managed by environmental monitoring systems, possibly building on environmental sensor networks. Second, we present the integration of situations with information about the environment (storms) and situations with information about human activity (driver locations). The application suggests that the notion of situation is suitable not only to model situational knowledge about the natural environment but also situational knowledge about human activity occurring in the built environment. The application arguably supports the claim that to share the concept of situation among heterogeneous environmental monitoring systems facilitates situational knowledge processing, including integration and reasoning.

2   Materials and Methods

The presented system builds on the Measurement Monitoring and Environmental Assessment (MMEA) Platform,[1] the Profium Sense[2] semantic technology-based software platform, and Wavellite.[3] The MMEA Platform is a software infrastructure for the collection, storage, processing, and distribution of (processed) observation and forecast data resulting in environmental monitoring. The platform implements an Enterprise Service Bus (ESB) based architecture and was developed within the Finnish MMEA CLEEN/SHOK research program.

In this work, the MMEA Platform handles the collection and processing of data and initiates situational knowledge extraction. The platform also powers the user interface.

---

[1] http://mmea.fi/

[2] http://www.profium.com/en/profium-sense

[3] http://www.uef.fi/en/envi/projects/wavellite

Profium Sense serves as RDF database for the persistence and retrieval of situational knowledge. Wavellite is a software framework for situation awareness in environmental monitoring. It supports the collection and processing of data, specifically data of environmental sensor networks, and the representation of situational knowledge acquired from data using models, in particular empirical (data-driven) and physically-based environmental models. In this work, Wavellite builds on top of the MMEA Platform, reuses platform functionality and extends it with situational knowledge extraction and representation.

We use radar data for the reflectivity of rainfall intensity in Finland. Radar data is obtained by the Finnish Meteorological Institute (FMI) and is made available by FMI as GeoTIFF encoded images via its Open Data INSPIRE-compliant interface.[4] FMI also provided a MATLAB script that implements an algorithm for the extraction of storm polygon data from radar data. Because the MMEA Platform uses Octave,[5] we implemented the MATLAB program logic as Octave script. Given a scheduled driver direction (consisting of departure time, origin, and destination) we use Google Directions[6] to obtain (alternative) routes, driving distance and estimated driving time.

The MMEA Platform continuously (configurable time interval) retrieves radar data and processes it to extract polygon coordinate data. Polygon data is Well-Known Text (WKT) encoded and wrapped in MMEA observation messages, which are published to the ESB for further processing. We implemented a Wavellite derivation reader, i.e. the component of the Wavellite architecture that reads Wavellite dataset observations, as ESB listener for MMEA observations messages containing storm polygon data. Upon incoming message, the derivation reader converts the MMEA observation message to a Wavellite dataset observation with two component properties, one for time and one for the WKT polygon data. Wavellite dataset observations are then processed by a Wavellite situation engine, i.e. the component of the Wavellite architecture that represents situations with knowledge extracted from dataset observations. For storms, situations s_{sa} support the infon

$$\ll storm - at, \dot{s}, \dot{t}, \dot{l}, 1 \gg$$

where $\dot{s}$, $\dot{t}$, and $\dot{l}$ are parameters for a storm, a temporal location, and a spatial location, respectively. Given a dataset observation with component properties for spatiotemporal locations it is thus straightforward to map dataset observations to situations by anchoring a new individual (representing the storm) to $\dot{s}$ and the temporal and spatial locations of the dataset observation to $\dot{t}$ and $\dot{l}$, respectively. The infon states that at time anchored to $\dot{t}$ the storm with identifier anchored to $\dot{s}$ covers the spatial region delineated by the polygon anchored to $\dot{l}$.

Upon user registration of a scheduled driver direction – consisting of origin, A, destination, B, and departure time – a component of the MMEA platform uses Google Directions to obtain a route, r, between A and B. Given r, the component computes route segments and driver location for each segment. The component uses locations for which there exist situations s_{sa} to segment the route. It is thus temporal locations

---

[4] https://en.ilmatieteenlaitos.fi/open-data
[5] https://www.gnu.org/software/octave/
[6] https://developers.google.com/maps/documentation/directions/

at which radar images are obtained, or at which storm situations are projected, that determine time steps. For driver locations, situations s_{da} support the infon

$$\ll driver - at, \dot{d}, \dot{t}, \dot{l}, 1 \gg$$

where $\dot{d}$ is a parameter for a driver and $\dot{t}$, $\dot{l}$ are parameters for temporal and spatial locations, respectively. The infon states that at time $\dot{t}$ the driver $\dot{d}$ is located at $\dot{l}$. Users can register driver directions using the prototype Web user interface.

A reasoning component of the MMEA Platform uses situations s_{sa} and s_{da} to discover situations s_{hr} that support the infon

$$\ll higher - risk, \dot{d}, \dot{t}, \dot{l}, 1 \gg$$

which states that the driver $\dot{d}$ is in a higher risk situation at temporal and spatial locations $\dot{t}$ and $\dot{l}$, respectively. The parameter $\dot{l}$ for spatial location is optional in this infon, as it can be obtained from the situation with driver-at-relation infon with same objects anchored to parameters $\dot{d}$ and $\dot{t}$. Situations s_{hr} are of interest to drivers.

The discovery of such situations is implemented as SPARQL [7] queries that leverage on Profium Sense support for quantitative spatial reasoning and qualitative spatial relations in SPARQL queries. Specifically, the query is for situations with storm-at-relation infon and situations with driver-at-relation infon with same temporal locations and driver spatial location *inside* storm spatial location.

Of particular interest in this system is situation *projection*. The projection of situations s_{da} is trivial, as it amounts to the registration of a point of departure at some future temporal location. The projection of situations s_{sa} is, however, more complex. Indeed, the task amounts to forecasting the future spatial location of storms. As a proof of concept, we have implemented Octave program logic to support forecasting storms. The method uses temporal clustering [8] and recursively searches for matching storms in consecutive radar images to form storm tracks over time. At each time step, a storm has no predecessors if it just formed; one predecessor if it has a defined path from the previous time step; more than one predecessor if several storms have merged together since the previous time step; or it disappeared. A storm can progress in one direction or multiple directions, if it has split into different storms [9]. For each storm track, the method then fits a suitable model to observed storm centroids and projects the storm using the model. The weighted linear regression model assigns smaller weights to older observations in order to make projection more sensitive to newer observations. The direction vector of the storm centroid is used to displace all storm polygon vertices.

The Web graphical user interface is a JavaScript client that makes use of Open-Layers,[7] jQuery,[8] Google Direction Service,[9] and a Web service for communication with the MMEA Platform (retrieval of situations and addition of directions). In

---

[7] http://openlayers.org/
[8] http://jquery.com/
[9] https://developers.google.com/maps/documentation/javascript/directions

Wavellite, situations are individuals, instances of the class Situation. The class is defined in the Situation Theory Ontology (STO) [10] and reflects Situation Theory semantics. Thus, Wavellite builds on Semantic Web technologies, in particular the Resource Description Framework (RDF) [11] and the Web Ontology Language (OWL 2) [12]. Wavellite interacts with Profium Sense to store and retrieve RDF.

3   Discussion

The system operates in near real-time and populates the RDF database with situational knowledge, which can be visualized. Figures 1 and 2 provide examples.

Upon user registration of an origin (e.g. Kuopio) and a destination (e.g. Tampere) for a scheduled driver direction starting at temporal location t_l, the system segments the route and computes situations s_{da}. Given situations s_{da} and s_{sa}, we can create visualizations such as the map shown in Figure 1 where the driver location (circle) is shown along the direction between Kuopio and Tampere and the spatial location of the storm is shown as polygon. The system reasons over such situational knowledge to discover higher-risk situations in which the driver location and storm location overlap in space-time. Figure 2 visualizes several higher-risk situations. Drivers may want to be aware of such situations.

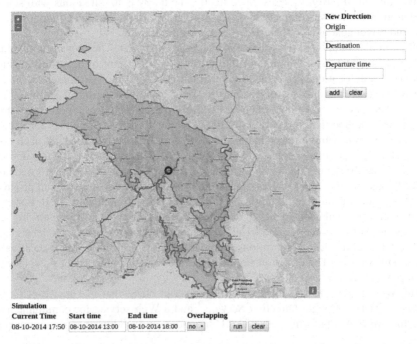

Fig. 1. Overview of the Web graphical user interface. Situations are shown animated on a map according to simulation parameters (start and end time). On the right hand side, new directions can be added. Visible are situations at 17:50, including a large storm and the location of a driver (circle) on a direction from Turku to Kuopio. The direction is highlighted.

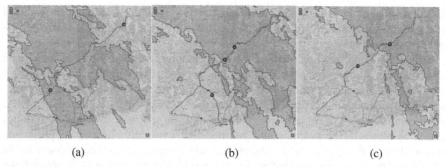

(a)   (b)   (c)

Fig. 2. Examples for situational knowledge visualization for storm and driver locations at several points in time on October 10, 2014, between 13:00 and 18:00. At 14:15, Figure (a), a driver travelling from Turku to Kuopio is within the storm. A second driver travelling from Kuopio to Tampere is not. The storm has left Turku and is over Helsinki. At 15:55, Figure (b), a third driver travels from Tampere to Helsinki and is not affected by the storm. The storm is approaching Kuopio. At 17:00, Figure (c), the driver travelling to Helsinki had arrived. The driver travelling from Kuopio to Tampere exited the storm. The storm is now over Kuopio.

Figure 2 shows situations at three time steps on October 10, 2014: at 14:15, Figure 2(a); at 15:55, Figure 2(b); and at 17:00, Figure 2(c). The relatively large storm is moving south-west to north-east from Turku to Kuopio. At the same time, several drivers are located along directions, Turku-Kuopio, Kuopio-Tampere, and Tampere-Helsinki. At various times, drivers overlap the storm. Only the driver directed from Tampere to Helsinki is never in a higher-risk situation.

The presented software system is a proof of concept. The aim was to demonstrate the integration of situational knowledge obtained from heterogeneous data sources using a set of technologies, including the MMEA Platform, in an environmental monitoring context. However, with further development the system could mature so that it can be deployed for active use.

Drivers are perhaps the obvious potential interest group for such a system. Directions scheduled in a calendar could be automatically 'safety checked' hours prior to departure. The system could inform drivers accordingly. For end consumers, such as drivers, mobile applications may be of particular interest. The presented Web graphical user interface is a lightweight JavaScript application. It communicates via HTTP requests with map, direction, and situation services, which implement the bulk of the program logic. Thus, developing a graphical user interface for mobile platforms should be fairly trivial.

The current system can also be extended to integrate more situational knowledge, and thus improve situation awareness [13]. For instance, during winter road conditions are critical. In addition to snow storms, of particular interest is situational knowledge for road sections that may be covered with ice, of poor visibility, or congested. Such information is likely to result from data processed by different systems. However, because of the shared ontology, the integration of situational knowledge would be as straightforward as in the case presented here.

Google Directions suggests alternative directions. This feature can be exploited when higher-risk situations are discovered. For such situations, the system can notify drivers and suggest (1) alternative directions with same departure time, (2) same direction with earlier or later departure time, or (3) to postpone travelling altogether if no direction can be scheduled for which the driver will not find herself involved in a higher-risk situation.

Critical for future work, in particular work that aims at a mature system deployable for active use, is the evaluation of situation projection. This can be achieved through analysis of how well forecasts agree with observations, which requires the construction of a dataset that appropriately aligns storms in space-time. Of particular interest is the comparison of storm polygon centroids and storm spatial extent. Uncertainties related to storm development could be modelled explicitly. Instead of projecting storms along a line, or path, a system that takes uncertainties into account could project storms along regions that widen the further the projection is in space-time. Rather than to search for higher-risk situations along a line, the system could thus search for such situations in the region in which a storm will likely be. Naturally, such a search is computationally more demanding. Further issues need to be addressed in work that aims at a system deployed for active use, including liability in case of system failure. Such concerns are however beyond the scope of this paper.

Route planning is an old problem and algorithms have been developed that are constraint aware. For instance, authors have proposed estimating the cost of travelling through particular grid cells, whereby factors such as weather conditions can influence the cost value [14]. In [15], the authors present a personalized mobile traffic information system capable of handling weather information, including rainfall.

There exist online services for road trip planning that include weather information. For instance, AccuWeather[10] supports this feature. Together with the direction, the service shows (forecast) weather at various locations along the direction. The Weather Channel[11] offers a similar feature. Aside the obvious difference between weather and storms as well as the nature of the data involved, the main novelty here is arguably in technologies that support the explicit representation of situational knowledge with machine readable and interpretable semantics specified in ontologies that can be shared among heterogeneous environmental monitoring systems.

4   Conclusion

We presented an environmental software system that obtains, integrates, and reasons over situational knowledge about storms and driver directions. As such, the system demonstrates the integration of situational knowledge about natural phenomena and situational knowledge about human activity. All knowledge is represented explicitly. As a consequence, the system can manipulate situational knowledge. Spatio-temporal situation reasoning is an example for such manipulation. As we demonstrated, inferring situations in which drivers are at higher risk can be achieved by means of a simple SPARQL query. The work underscores the suitability of the concept of situation, as defined in Situation Theory, for the modelling of situational knowledge obtained using computational models from processed data collected and managed by environmental monitoring systems.

---

[10] http://www.accuweather.com/en/driving-directions-weather
[11] http://www.weather.com/travel/trip-planner

A thorough discussion of the advantages and disadvantages of the presented system could be valuable. However, such an evaluation requires at least one comparable system that uses a different set of technologies. We currently do not have such a comparable system. Aside from the discussed advantages, a disadvantage of the presented system may be the potentially large number of generated RDF statements. However, such concerns need to be addressed primarily by the RDF database.

Naturally, the described system could be extended to include situations of various other types that are of interest to driver Situation Awareness [13, 16]. For instance, situations involving road sections possibly covered with ice may be of interest. It is trivial to see how such additional situational knowledge can be integrated in the present system. Other directions for future work include the development of mobile applications and the integration with driver assistance systems.

Acknowledgements. We thank the Finnish Funding Agency for Technology and Innovation (TEKES) and the Academy of Finland for funding this research. This work has been carried out in TEKES funded CLEEN SHOK programme "Measurement, Monitoring and environmental Assessment" (MMEA, decision number 427/10) and in the Pathway project funded by the Academy of Finland.

References

1. Mulligan, M., Wainwright, J.: Environmental Modelling: Finding Simplicity in Complexity. In: Modelling and Model Building, pp. 7–73. John Wiley & Sons, Ltd (2004)
2. Finkelstein, L.: Theory and Philosophy of Measurement. In: Sydenham, P.H. (ed.) Handbook of Measurement Science. Theoretical Fundamentals, vol. 1, pp. 1–30. John Wiley & Sons (1982)
3. Devlin, K.: Logic and Information. Cambridge University Press (1991)
4. Barwise, J., Perry, J.: Situations and Attitudes. The Journal of Philosophy 78(11), 668–691 (1981), http://www.jstor.org/stable/2026578
5. Stocker, M., Baranizadeh, E., Portin, H., Komppula, M., Rönkkö, M., Hamed, A., Virtanen, A., Lehtinen, K., Laaksonen, A., Kolehmainen, M.: Representing situational knowledge acquired from sensor data for atmospheric phenomena. Environmental Modelling & Software 58, 27–47 (2014), http://www.sciencedirect.com/science/article/pii/S1364815214001108
6. Stocker, M., Rönkkö, M., Kolehmainen, M.: Situational knowledge representation for traffic observed by a pavement vibration sensor network. IEEE Transactions on Intelligent Transportation Systems 15(4), 1441–1450 (2014)
7. Prud'hommeaux, E., Seaborne, A.: SPARQL Query Language for RDF. Recommendation, W3C (January 2008), http://www.w3.org/TR/2008/REC-rdf-sparql-query-20080115/
8. Ester, M., Kriegel, H.P., Sander, J., Xu, X.: A Density-Based Algorithm for Discovering Clusters in Large Spatial Databases with Noise. In: Proceedings of 2nd International Conference on Knowledge Discovery and Data Mining (KDD-96), pp. 226–231. AAAI Press, Menlo Park (1996)

9. Dixon, M., Wiener, G.: TITAN: Thunderstorm Identification, Tracking, Analysis, and Nowcasting–A Radar-based Methodology. Journal of Atmospheric and Oceanic Technology 10(6), 785–797 (1993)

10. Kokar, M.M., Matheus, C.J., Baclawski, K.: Ontology-based situation awareness. Inf. Fusion 10(1), 83–98 (2009)

11. Manola, F., Miller, E., McBride, B.: RDF Primer. W3C Recommendation, W3C (February 2004)

12. W3C OWL Working Group: OWL 2 Web Ontology Language Document Overview (Second Edition). Recommendation, W3C (December 2012),
http://www.w3.org/TR/2012/REC-owl2-overview-20121211/

13. Endsley, M.R.: Toward a theory of situation awareness in dynamic systems. Human Factors: The Journal of the Human Factors and Ergonomics Society 37(1), 32–64 (1995)

14. Szczerba, R., Galkowski, P., Glicktein, I., Ternullo, N.: Robust algorithm for real-time route planning. IEEE Transactions on Aerospace and Electronic Systems 36(3), 869–878 (2000)

15. Balke, W.T., Kiessling, W., Unbehend, C.: A situation-aware mobile traffic information system. In: Proceedings of the 36th Annual Hawaii International Conference on System Sciences (January 2003)

16. Stanton, N.A., Stewart, R., Harris, D., Houghton, R.J., Baber, C., McMaster, R., Salmon, P., Hoyle, G., Walker, G., Young, M.S., Linsell, M., Dymott, R., Green, D.: Distributed situation awareness in dynamic systems: theoretical development and application of an ergonomics methodology. Ergonomics 49(12-13), 1288–1311 (2006),
http://dx.doi.org/10.1080/00140130600612762 pMID: 17008257

An Application Framework for the Rapid Deployment of Ocean Models in Support of Emergency Services: Application to the MH370 Search

Uwe Rosebrock, Peter R. Oke, and Gary Carroll

CSIRO Oceans and Atmosphere Flagship, Hobart, TAS, Australia
{uwe.rosebrock,peter.oke,gary.carroll}@csiro.au

Abstract. Ocean models are beneficial to many different applications, including industry, public-good, and defence. Many applications use high-resolution models to produce detailed maps of the ocean circulation. High-resolution models are historically time-consuming to configure – often taking weeks to months to properly prepare. A system for automatically configuring and executing a model to predict the past, present, or future state of the ocean – named TRIKE – has been developed. TRIKE includes a sophisticated user interface allowing a user to easily set a model in minutes, control data management and execute the model run on a supercomputer almost instantly. TRIKE makes it feasible to configure and execute high-resolution regional models anywhere in the world at a moments notice. TRIKE was used to support the recent search for MH370 that is thought to have crashed somewhere in the South Indian Ocean.

Keywords: integrated environmental modeling, software control framework, connectivity, large data management, model management.

1   Introduction

Ocean models are routinely applied to predict the past, present, and future state of the ocean to better understand ocean dynamics and to support a range of industrial, public-good and defense applications. Since the advent of the Global Ocean Data Assimilation Experiment (GODAE; www.godae.org), a global initiative to develop operational ocean forecasting capabilities, several global and basin-scale ocean forecast systems have been developed with resolution of up to 10 km [5]. This is beneficial to many applications, but delivers forecasts at insufficient resolution for many situations that require resolution of up to 1 km. For these applications requiring high-resolution, it is common to configure and run regional models, where the domain extends only a few hundred kilometres or less. Historically, regional ocean models are time-consuming to configure, requiring an expert modeller to configure a grid – carefully setting the spatial extent of the model domain and the model resolution. The expert continues the process by acquiring the data to support the running of the ocean model. This generally involves the gathering of the data from multiple sources to set the bathymetry, coastline, initial conditions as well as forcing fields. The modeller then reformats the various datasets to meet the requirements of the specific ocean

R. Denzer et al. (Eds.): ISESS 2015, IFIP AICT 448, pp. 235–241, 2015.

model and configures the ocean model dynamics for the chosen region – carefully considering the dominant physical processes and requirements to properly represent the important characteristics of the regional circulation. The modeller selects a suite of model parameters, numerical schemes, and boundary conditions that are appropriate for the chosen application. In the past, this process would take several weeks for an experienced modeller, and several months for a less-experienced modeller, making real-time applications inconceivable. Moreover, the idea of a non-expert user (e.g. a marine biogeochemist) was merely a pipe dream.

However, the development of a system called TRIKE (or 'wheels for modellers'), by the CSIRO has made the configuration and execution of a regional ocean model simple. With a sophisticated user interface, a user can quickly and easily set up a model domain, select the desired input data sources, and execute the model. TRIKE allows a user to run a model simulation for any historical period, or for a forecast – predicting the ocean circulation for several days into the future. This paper documents the salient features of TRIKE, and describes a recent application that supported the Australian Maritime Safety Authority in the search for the ill-fated flight MH370.

2   Trike

The TRIKE user interface (Fig. 1) allows a user to use a graphical interface to set the model domain, the model resolution, the input data sources, and other key specifications of the model run (e.g., what time-period to simulate, and when to execute the

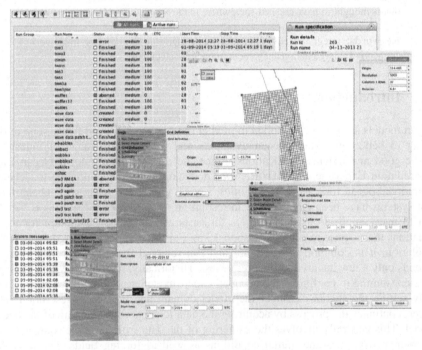

Fig. 1. The TRIKE user interface and wizard

model). The back-end of TRIKE then configures a state-of-the-art ocean model [4] for a specific area. Ocean models solve mathematical equations on a computer to simulate the time-evolution of the ocean circulation; representing impacts of surface forcing (e.g. wind) and tides [2]. A large amount of data is needed for every application. TRIKE automates this process of configuring the model and massively reduces the setup time required to less than a minute (historically weeks to months). TRIKE consists of several software components, including an extensive data management and interrogation component. The software components manage the user interactions and apply extensive heuristics to create the scientific modelling domain.

2.1 Defining the Model Domains

TRIKE provides a simple-to-use application that uses the notion of a "run wizard" to select model characteristics such as the model type and the temporal and geographical extent. The original aim in developing TRIKE was to provide a facility to allow the running of complex models with minimal human effort. This was extended to also allow users with minimal understanding of the actual modelling process access to initiate, configure and execute model runs independently. The result is a "desktop-client" leading a user through the process of setting up a model run with simple steps. (Depending on the permissions of users more sophisticated options are made available.) The complexity of the various parameter ranges from output directives to creating sophisticated interpolations of a domains bathymetry. In addition TRIKE provides the facility of high level scheduling and repetitions (e.g. run process every 12 hours). The scheduling extends from simple run-later to creating dependencies between runs (e.g. process x starts after process y has finished).

2.2 Data Preparation

The nature of numerical models dictates very comprehensive input data requirements. TRIKE is capable of maintaining an extensive database of forcing data and automates the process of data preparation for a particular model; configuring a model process and selects, extracts, prepares and assembles the appropriate input data. To be able to utilise different data sources and to meet the requirements of an ocean model, a matching from provided to the required data is necessary. As an example of a data provider; the Australian Bureau of Meteorology performs many weather forecasts each day. Internationally, many weather centers perform equivalent forecasts to the Bureau, generating equivalent data, but disseminating data in different formats (e.g., with different variable names, units etc). TRIKE matches the data sources it manages to what is required by a model by using metadata vocabularies and runs processes to convert data so the receiving model can ingest the data correctly. The regional data used can be available through online services or stored locally. The ingestion of data can also be localised or provided through online services. The provisioning of the data is a very important aspect of the model preparation process, particularly for data sets updated on a regular basis, the TRIKE sub-system is capable of monitoring and responding to changes in the data availability.

2.3   Running a Model

Once the modeling process has been prepared it can then be run on a remote high-performance computer, on a local compute server, or the workspace can be made available as an archive to be run on user infrastructure outside TRIKE. The progress of the computational process can be monitored through the application's user interface as the modelling process is executed (see Fig. 1). The execution may utilise high per-formance computing job queues or simply execute a process remotely. Either is mon-itored and can be aborted. Deployment into cloud-based compute-resources has also been implemented as a prototype.

TRIKE consists of several components that function independently of each other and communicate with each other via dedicated protocols. Fig. 2 shows an overview of the management component Run Coordination System (RCS), the Data Management Framework (DMF) and the interface to the individual modelling components. Fig. 3 shows a generalised workflow of creating a modeling process. Once the process has successfully finished, post-processing can consist of further analysis and/or packaging. After a process is complete, results are transferred to a server for further analysis. Scientific users of TRIKE can receive bundled model run workspaces that allow the user to fine-tune the model configuration and rerun the process.

Originally TRIKE was developed for the Royal Australian Navy (RAN), under the Bluelink partnership [6]. Today the RAN uses a dedicated customised system routinely for tactical briefings prior to operations. TRIKE also has enormous potential benefits for public applications including search and rescue at sea, modelling of effluent dispersal following oil spills, environmental prediction of ocean currents to inform industry of risks during operations (e.g. oil and gas exploration), and storm surge prediction during tropical cyclones.

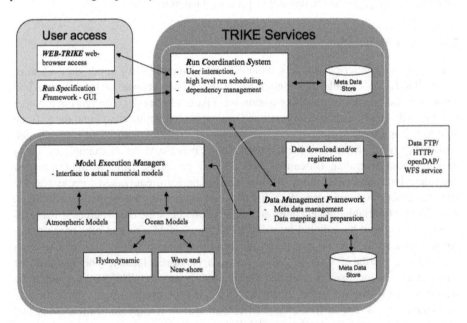

Fig. 2. An overview of the TRIKE framework

As a research tool it can provide easy access to determine for example biological connectivity, path of invasive species [1], marine debris in general [3], abandoned fishing equipment [7] or support more general coastal inundation modelling. TRIKE currently supports several ocean models and wave models as well as a regional atmospheric model. It has the capacity for further integration of models or any other data driven processes as well as creating dependencies between modelling process (nesting of one model within the data space of another, parameter estimation).

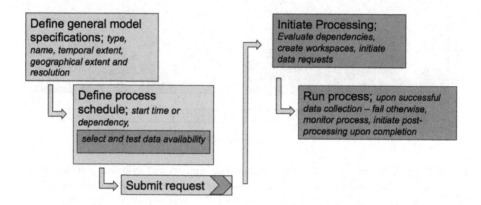

Fig. 3. The general workflow to initiate a TRIKE process, the background colours correspond to the location and correspondence of components in Figure 2

2.4   Current and Future Work

A web-based user interface has been developed under the MARVL (http://www.marvl.org.au) project to simplify maintenance and expand the user uptake. It forms the basis for several other projects within CSIRO such as eReefs (http://www.ereefs.org.au). Further developments under the 'Australian Wave Energy Atlas' are underway to incorporate the advances provided by accessing the local graphical processing unit (GPU) from within a web-browser to present and edit complex geometries defining the modelling domain. The intention for future development is to also move some of the processes, like interpolations currently performed on the server, into the GPU to improve the user experience.

3   Application to MH370

Malaysian Airlines Flight 370 disappeared on 7 March 2014 at 17:20 UTC. A multinational search effort subsequently began, initially focusing on the Gulf of Thailand and the South China Sea, before shifting to the South Indian Ocean. Using a range of different techniques, several possible "splash-points" were identified – but all with relatively high-levels of uncertainty. Many groups around the world began trying to predict the possible fate of surface debris that may have resulted from the crash.

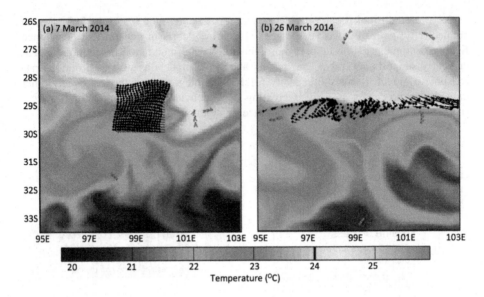

Fig. 4. Examples of the modelled ocean temperature (colour) and modelled particles (black cells) tracking the possible trajectories of surface debris from a possible crash site of the MH370 plane for 7 March 2014 and 26 march 2014. The pink arrowheads show the location and velocity of surface drifters.

Many different estimates of surface velocities were used to support the search, including near-real-time maps of sea-level and surface velocities from satellite altimetry (e.g. oceancurrent.imos.org.au), estimates of the past, present, and future ocean circulation from operational ocean forecasts and regional ocean forecasts generated by TRIKE. An example of the type of analysis performed using 2-km resolution TRIKE forecasts (limited by computation resources) are shown in Fig. 4, showing the locations of a cluster of hypothetical particles (intended to represent debris from a possible crash site) at the time that MH370 is thought to have crashed, and locations of the particles 19 days later. In this example, there was a front separating relatively warm water (yellow-orange in Fig. 4) and colder water (green-blue in Fig. 4). For this simulation, the model predicts that if the plane crashed into the ocean along this front, then any resulting surface debris would likely spread along the front. Information like this was disseminated to decision-makers who were coordinating the search effort for MH370.

The data produced by TRIKE that formed the basis of the analysis outlined as well as the imagery shown in Fig. 4, can easily be incorporated as a post-processing step of a modeling process managed in TRIKE.

4   Conclusion

As environmental computational modelling is becoming a more and more standard tool used in science and environmental services, it appears crucial that a supporting infrastructure is also developed. TRIKE has demonstrated to be capable of supporting numerous numerical models as well as the versatility to meet a broad set of demands. The current state of TRIKE is the result of many years of development. The Royal Australian Navy has made use of a derived version of TRIKE called ROAM (Relocatable Ocean and Atmosphere Modelling framework) for some time. The lessons learnt from that deployment and the re-investment into the concept have saved innumerous hours of science time and promises to lower the hurdle of access to numerical modeling further through the current developments.

Although the search of the MH370 plane did not result in a positive detection of the remains of the aircraft, the applications allowed the developers of TRIKE to showcase its versatility. It will undoubtedly be used for future applications such as support for search and rescue, oil spill response and as a research tool.

References

1. Brinkman, D.: Could ocean currents be responsible for the west to east spread of aquatic invasive species in Maritime Canadian waters? Marine Pollution Bulletin 85, 235–243 (2014)
2. England, M.H., Oke, P.: Ocean modeling and prediction. In: Leslie, L., Peng, P., Shao, Y. (eds.) Environmental modelling and prediction, pp. 125–171. Springer (2001)
3. Hardesty, B.D., Wilcox, C.: Understanding the types, sources and at-sea distribution of marine debris in Australian Waters. Final report to the Department of Sustainability, Environment, Water, Health, Population and Communities (2011)
4. Herzfeld, M.: Improving stability of regional numerical ocean models. Ocean Dynamics 59(1), 21–46 (2009)
5. Hurlburt, H.E., Brassington, G.B., Drillet, Y., Kamachi, M., Benkiran, M., Bourdalle-Badie, R., Chassignet, E.P., Jacobbs, G.A., Le Galloudec, O., Lellouche, J.-M., Metzger, E.J., Oke, P.R., Pugh, T.F., Schiller, A., Smedstad, O.M., Tranchant, B., Tsujino, H., Usui, N., Walcraft, A.J.: High-resolution Global and Basin-Scale Ocean Analyses and Forecasts. Oceanography 22(3), 80–97 (2009)
6. Schiller, A., Meyers, G., Smith, N.: Taming Australia's last frontier. Bull. Am. Met Soc., 436–440 (April 2009)
7. Wilcox, C., Hardesty, B.D., Sharples, R., Griffin, D.A., Lawson, T.J., Gunn, R.: Ghostnet impacts on globally threatened turtles, a spatial risk analysis for northern Australia. Conservation Letters 1(2012), 1–8 (2012)

Exposure Modeling of Traffic and Wood Combustion Emissions in Northern Sweden

Application of the Airviro Air Quality Management System

Lars Gidhagen[*], Cecilia Bennet, David Segersson, and Gunnar Omstedt

Swedish Meteorological and Hydrological Institute, Norrköping, Sweden
{lars.gidhagen,cecilia.bennet,david.segersson,
gunnar.omstedt}@smhi.se

Abstract. Traffic and residential wood combustion (rwc) constitute the two dominating local sources to fine particulate matter PM2.5 concentration levels in Sweden. In order to meet the authorities' requirements of air quality assessments, a national modelling system SIMAIR has been developed. The system is based on the commercial Airviro air quality management software, a three tier client/server/web system which includes modules for measurement data collection, emission databases and dispersion models with very high performance in terms of data access and model execution. The technical characteristics of Airviro databases and models have facilitated web based national air quality systems, of which some examples are given.

The present Airviro/SIMAIR application had the objective to assess the impact of rwc in three urbanized areas in northern Sweden. The Airviro Scenario module was used to determine exposure and health impact of the rwc contribution. The estimated mortality due to PM2.5 concentrations from residential wood combustion is about 4 persons/year, which corresponds to approximately 0.4% of the total number of deaths (excluding accidents). Cities which have well established district heating facilities have a lower rwc use and a very different exposure to locally generated PM2.5. Umeå, one of the three areas in the study, is such a city. A similar assessment with impact only from traffic emissions shows an increase of 4.4 deaths for the Umeå population, while the impact of wood combustion in the city contributes with 2.5 deaths per year. The advantages of using the Airviro software in combination with annually updated databases for input data on the national scale, are summarized. The approach facilitates for municipal end users and non-meteorological professionals like epidemiologists to perform by themselves advanced dispersion simulations and health impact assessments.

Keywords: Airviro, dispersion modelling, residential wood combustion, PM2.5 health.

1 Introduction

Fine particles with diameter <2.5µm (PM2.5) suspended in ambient air constitute a leading risk factor contributing to premature death [1,2]. In Sweden the most

R. Denzer et al. (Eds.): ISESS 2015, IFIP AICT 448, pp. 242–251, 2015.

important local source is road traffic emitting particles generated both by combustion and by road wear and brake abrasion. Another important source is residential wood combustion (rwc) and people living in smaller cities with rwc are exposed to elevated PM2.5 levels. According to a recent health review [3] these rwc particles may have a similar effect on health as traffic combustion particles. Strong impact of wood combustion is common not only in northern Sweden but also considered to be a large and well spread source of PM2.5 in Europe [4].

To facilitate the supervision of local air pollution hot spots and allow urban planning where air pollution levels can be held below European and Swedish standards, the Swedish EPA, the Swedish National Road Administration and the Swedish Energy Agency jointly commissioned the development of the web tool SIMAIR [5,6]. SIMAIR is a coupled model system covering all Swedish regions and urbanized areas, where local authorities can assess the current status of air quality. The SIMAIR system is based on a commercial air quality management software used in many locations around the world, the Airviro system [7]. SIMAIR has most of the environmental and activity data required in dispersion modeling preloaded, e.g. the entire Swedish road network. For Sweden this gives possibilities of annual overviews of spatial and temporal variations in PM10, PM2.5, NO2, CO and benzene levels. The system has previously been used to simulate national exposure of particulate matter for a specific year (2004) [8]. The exposure was then related to self-reported health problems [9]. The Airviro software has also been used as a platform for an integrated climate change enabled Environmental Decision Support System (EDSS) [10]. Recent development of the Airviro system includes a module, Airviro Scenario, where the exposure on the entire population can be assessed with respect to health outcomes and economical costs for different air quality scenarios. In much this module bears a strong resemblance with U.S. EPAs BenMap system [11]. The present study describes how the Airviro software, including Airviro Scenario, has been used together with SIMAIR input data to assess the health impact of air pollution from residential wood burning and road traffic. We also discuss potential users to this health impact assessment tool.

2   Software

The Airviro system has been developed during more than 30 years, originally for powerful (at the time) work stations and then migrated to Linux servers, i.e. it did not raise from personal computer platforms. Its highly optimized databases assure a rapid access of time series, both point and field data, which has made it ideal for large regional and national systems. The principal and fully integrated functionalities of the Airviro system are

- data collection, storage, validation and presentation
- emission database for point, area, line and grid sources
- dispersion models

Through requirements from users in Europe, Asia and Latin America there is now a great flexibility for users to select among e.g. some 20 data collection protocols and an extensive list of dispersion models including Airviro models for different scales and purposes as well as open-source models like AERMOD, CALPUFF and AUSTAL2000.

A strength of the Airviro system is the capacity to process very large emission inventories with a mix of individual sources and gridded emissions. Also, the integration with the time-series database allows the use of live data, such as continuous stack measurements, traffic flow measurements or ship movements to be described in near real-time. A specialized type emission source has been developed to represent ship emission sources, in which the movements of the ships are described based on the positions of the individual ships found in AIS (Automatic Identification System) data for the sea area of interest. By adding information on ship engine data from available sources, Airviro allows the emissions from ships to be described with high temporal and spatial resolution. The emission database for residential wood combustion presented in this paper is another example of an advanced emission model for a very large number of individual sources.

Current versions Airviro 3.2x is a three tier client / server / web system. It runs on Linux platforms but Red Hat, Fedora and CentOS Linux are the preferred operating systems. The clients normally run on PCs using Java JRE (run time plugin) compatible web browsers such as Internet Explorer and Firefox. The web server side is using lean CGI scripts and heavy programs written primarily in C. The pages at the client side use html and java script and are built on the server. Some small applets written in Java are also used on the client side primarily for caching, maps and user interfaces that are too complex to be written using html and JavaScript. All models are written using FORTRAN.

The Airviro databases are based on the FairCom CTREE™ server version 4.3 or on proprietary solutions. Communication of data into and out of the Airviro databases is performed through ASCII or EXCEL interfaces, or through Web services using HTTP or HTTPS protocols. An OGC compliant service layer to access, interrogate, execute models and upload/download gridded time series in Airviro was developed as part of the EU FP7 project SUDPLAN [10].

The great flexibility of the Airviro system gives advantages to large applications. National monitoring databases in Singapore, UK, Estonia and Chile are operated by Airviro. In a current upgrade of the Singapore system data collection is extended to high resolution precipitation sensors and other climate instruments. Other countries like Estonia, Chile and Sweden also uses the data collection together with emission inventories and dispersion models on a national scale. Airviro has recently been implemented in Turkey to collect and quantify emissions from ship traffic in the Bosphorus straight and adjacent seas. Smaller systems are serving local authorities and industries in some 20 countries.

The flexibility and generality of the system has the drawback that it makes it complex to configure and new users often require support for setting up the system and fill it with useful information serving the purpose of air quality management (which is not only doing diagnostic work of how things are today, but also to be able to identify air pollution control actions and project their effects on future air quality as part of a planning procedure). While this is manageable for large and specialized institutions, it is for users in individual cities or industries a threshold that is sometimes difficult to overcome. This is why the SIMAIR system, to be described in the next section, has been developed. SIMAIR is basically a simplified Airviro interface where less experienced users can access the preloaded information required to execute dispersion models for whatever location within Sweden.

3   Method

Figure 1 gives an overview of the Air Quality Management system and the work flow required for an health impact assessment based on a given emission scenario.

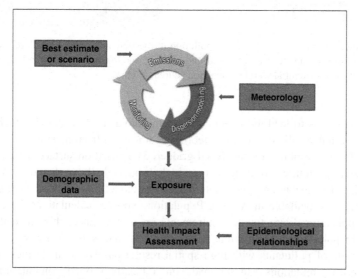

Fig. 1. Overview of data flows in the Airviro Air Quality Management System which involve four major modules: Emission Database, Dispersion models, Time series database/presentation/analyzing tool and the Scenario module with exposure assessments.

Starting point is the formulation of an emission scenario. Health effects can be based on absolute emissions, but it is also common to quantify the health benefits by comparing a scenario with reduced emissions to a reference (business-as-usual) scenario, i.e. health benefits achieved by a certain change in emissions. The results to be presented below will separately quantify the different health effects of the two largest local PM2.5 sources in Swedish cities (Figure 2).

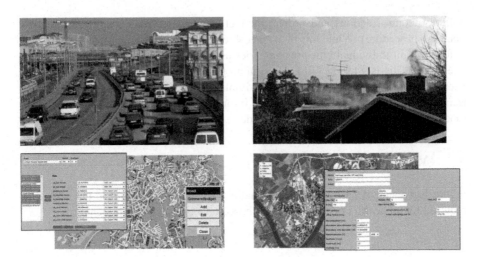

Fig. 2. The two major sources to PM2.5 pollution in Sweden and how the GUIs of the Airviro Emission Database can be used by local end-users to modify/update information of mobile sources (left) and residential wood combustion sources (right).

The next step is to feed the system with meteorological information, which can be taken – if available - directly from meteorological towers, from meteorological model output or from a combination (analyzed gridded data based on surface data, meteorological models, satellite and radar data routinely produced all over Sweden). With this it is possible to execute an appropriate dispersion model among those Gaussian and Eularian models available in Airviro. Population exposure calculations for entire cities are applications with tough requirements on performance, this since the rapid decrease in pollutant concentrations close to roads makes it necessary to describe the dispersion of pollutants with high spatial resolution. To facilitate these calculations, Airviro simulations can be made on a locally refined computational grid (Fig. 3).

Fig. 3. Example of refined computational grid – named quad grid - along a main highway. The original grid of 800x800 m is refined to 50x50 m along all roads where traffic emission intensity is above a specified threshold. For this example the number of grid cells are only 4.13% of that of a regular grid with 50x50 m resolution.

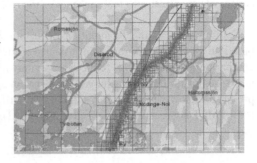

Since all models produce hourly time series of pollution concentrations, it is possible to evaluate model output through a comparison with monitor data. Such quality assurance comparisons should always be performed when measured concentrations are at hand. It is common to find rather severe errors in the emission description, calling for a new round in the emission-dispersion-monitoring cycle of Fig. 1.

When confidence in simulated concentrations has been achieved, the Airviro Scenario module can be used to combine the dispersion model results with demographic data to assess the health effect on the population. For Sweden this means the use of high resolution population data with 100x100m grid, separated into age intervals of 5 years. The Scenario module can handle health outcomes of long-term exposure, either mortality or the incidence of different diagnosis like cardiovascular or respiratory diseases. Concentration-response relationships should be taken from epidemiological studies published internationally. The present study has assessed the relative risk of mortality (the risk of dying in exposed population compared to the risk of dying in non-exposed population) due to PM2.5 particles and the concentration-response relationship was set to 1.17 per 10 µg/m3 [12].

The calculations were performed for three different locations in northern Sweden close to the city Umeå (63.8N, 20.3E): the villages Vännäs (population 6062), Sävar (population 2976) and the city Umeå (population 90230). Air quality parameters of particles - PM2.5 and sot, polyaromatic hydrocarbons, elementary carbon and black carbon - were measured in four different places and used for validation.

The emissions were estimated from chimney sweeps registers, including detailed data for about 3700 wood boilers and about 16900 stoves. Heating habits and wood consumption were estimated from interviews in 176 houses using a standardized form.

4   Results and Discussion

Figure 4 shows measured and modelled local daily mean concentrations of PM2.5 ($\mu g/m^3$) from residential wood combustion in Sävar. The local contribution of the measurement is estimated as the difference between the measured local concentrations and the background concentration. In average the local contribution in Sävar is small, about 2 $\mu g/m^3$. The daily variations are large, some days the local contribution can be higher than 10 $\mu g/m^3$. These variations are typical for residential wood combustion in Sweden. As shown in the figure the model can reproduce these variations and the long term average rather well.

The results of the health impact assessment are summarised in Table 1. The calculated maximum concentrations due to wood combustion vary between 2 and 4 µg/m3 while the traffic in the regional capital Umeå contributes up to 6 µg/m3.

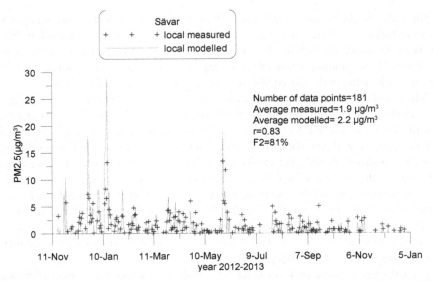

Fig. 4. Comparison of measured (blue cross) and modelled (red line) local daily mean PM2.5 concentrations ($\mu g/m^3$) at Sävar. r is the correlation coefficient and F2 denotes fraction of calculated concentrations that are within a factor of two of the measured concentrations.

The calculated population averaged concentrations due to wood combustion vary between 0.2-0.9 $\mu g/m3$ and are higher in the villages Vännäs and Sävar than in the city Umeå. This is due to the fact that extensive district heating system is used in Umeå but not in the two villages. The fraction of households using wood for residential heating is therefore much lower in Umeå where most wood stoves are used primarily for comfort and well-being and not as the main source of heating the house. This is also seen in the exposure histogram Figure 5.

Table 1. Summary of results from the calculations of annual mean concentrations, exposure and health impact

Location	source type	PM2.5($\mu g/m^3$)yearly mean		Health Impact Assessment	
		Max	Population average	Population (number of people	Mortality (number of people/year)
Umeå	local wood comb.	2.38	0.165	90230	2.50
Umeå	local traffic	6.20	0.295	90230	4.40
Vännäs	local wood comb.	2.47	0.913	6062	0.93
Vännäsby	local wood comb.	3.85	0.887	2976	0.44

The estimated mortality due to PM2.5 concentrations from residential wood combustion for the summed population in the three locations of about 100 000 people is about 4 persons/year, which corresponds to approximately 0.4% of the total number of deaths (excluding accidents). Scaling up this estimate to the whole population of

Sweden, the estimated mortality due to PM2.5 from wood combustion is about 374 persons per year. This number can be compared with earlier estimates of about 100-340 persons per year by Forsberg et al. [13] and about 216-282 persons per year by Brandt et al. [14] for Denmark. Scaling up the Danish estimate to the Swedish population, by the ratio between the Swedish and the Danish population i.e. 9.6/5.6, it means that the estimated mortality is about 370-483 persons per year. The estimated mortality due to PM2.5 from local wood combustion in this project is thus close to earlier estimates in Sweden and Denmark.

For the Umeå population the traffic impact is higher (4.4 deaths per year) than the impact of wood combustion (2.5 deaths per year). Traffic impact was not assessed in the smaller cities, but it is obvious from Table 1 and Fig. 5 that wood combustion is there the dominating source contributing to PM2.5 exposure.

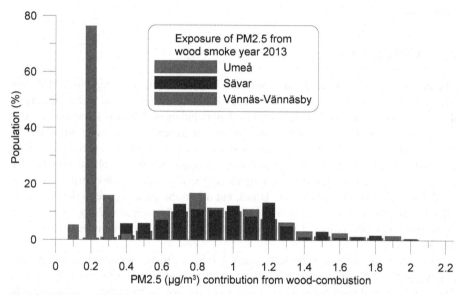

Fig. 5. Calculated number of persons (%) that are exposed to locally generated PM2.5 from residential wood combustion in different concentrations intervals

The Airviro application presented, in which the impact of the two largest contributors to PM2.5 - traffic and residential wood combustion - have been assessed in urbanized areas with different characteristics, can easily be repeated for whatever city in Sweden. This because input data and model tools are available and updated each year, in order to allow the municipal authorities assess compliance to EU directive and Swedish environmental objectives. The concept behind the national modelling system SIMAIR can be summarized as making available on the web the Airviro software plus all input data:

- Use of Airviro software with all input provided for a first preliminary assessment in whatever Swedish location, i.e. long range transported contributions, urban contributions, local emissions and local meteorological information, all pre-stored as hourly data in a national database inside Airviro.

- The municipal user just has to execute the local model to get a first preliminary result of total pollution concentrations, separated in different contributions. By reviewing and adjusting the local data that he or she are best suited to deliver, i.e. local traffic intensities, share of heavy duty vehicles etc., improved impact assessments are made for traffic environments. Similar improvements in wood combustion areas can be made with access to local chimney-sweeper data and interviews/questionnaires on wood consumption.

As for health impact studies this can also be done by external users, however experiences show that a health impact assessment require some training and understanding of epidemiological concentration-response relationships. Potential users of the health impact module are found at the regional health authorities rather than at individual municipalities.

5   Conclusions

The Airviro modeling system with the health impact calculation Scenario module has been used to assess the number of premature deaths from residential wood burning in the northern part of Sweden. In a summed population of 100 000 inhabitants, local wood combustion is estimated to cause about 4 premature deaths per year, which is about 0.4% if the total number of deaths in this area. The fraction of the population exposed to large pollution contributions due to residential wood combustion is smaller in the city of Umeå compared to the neighboring villages, this since district heating is available to almost all residences in Umeå, but not in the same degree in the other two villages. However, for the Umeå population the traffic impact is higher with 4.4 deaths per year, as compared to wood combustion which there contributes with 2.5 deaths per year.

The advantages of using the web based Airviro software in combination with annually up-dated databases for input data on the national scale have been described. The approach facilitates for municipal end users and non-meteorological professionals like epidemiologists to perform by themselves advanced dispersion simulations and health impact assessments.

References

1. Lim, S.S., et al.: A comparative risk assessment of burden of disease and injury attributable to 67 risk factors and risk factor clusters in 21 regions, 1990—2010: a systematic analysis for the Global Burden of Disease Study. The Lancet, 380, 9859, 2224-2260 (2012)
2. Health Effects Institute, Ambient air pollution among top global health risks in 2010 (2013), http://www.healtheffects.org/International/GBD-Press-Release.pdf
3. WHO, Review of evidence on health aspects of air pollution – REVIHAAP Project, Technical report, 280 p. (2013)

4. Genberg, et al.: Light-absorbing carbon in Europe – measurement and modelling, with a focus on residential wood combustion emissions. Atmos. Chem. Phys. 13, 8719–8738 (2013), doi:10.5194/acp-13-8719-2013
5. Gidhagen, L., Johansson, H., Omstedt, G.: SIMAIR – Evaluation tool for meeting the EU directive on air pollution limits. Atmospheric Environment 43, 1029–1036 (2009)
6. Omstedt, G., Andersson, S., Gidhagen, L., Robertson, L.: New model tools for meeting the targets of the EU Air Quality Directive: description, validation and evaluation of local air quality improvement due to reduction of studded tyre use on Swedish roads. Int. J. Environment and Pollution 47(1/2/3/4), 79–96 (2011)
7. http://www.smhi.se/airviro
8. Gidhagen, L., Omstedt, G., Pershagen, G., Willers, S., Bellander, T.: High resolution modeling of residential outdoor particulate levels in Sweden. J. Expos. Sci. & Environ. Epidem., 1–9 (2013), doi:10.1038/jes.2012.122
9. Willers, S., Eriksson, C., Gidhagen, L., Nilsson, M.E., Pershagen, G., Bellander, T.: Fine and coarse particulate air pollution in relation to respiratory health in Sweden. Eur. Resp. J. 42, 924–934 (2013), doi:10.1183/09031936.00088212
10. Denzer, R., Schlobinski, S., Gidhagen, L., Hell, T.: How to Build Integrated Climate Change Enabled EDSS. In: Hřebíček, J., Schimak, G., Kubásek, M., Rizzoli, A.E. (eds.) ISESS 2013. IFIP AICT, vol. 413, pp. 464–471. Springer, Heidelberg (2013)
11. U.S. EPA.Environmental Benefits Mapping and Analysis Program (BenMAP), http://www.epa.gov/airquality/benmap/index.html
12. Jerrett, M., et al.: Spatial Analysis of Air Pollution and Mortality in Los Angeles. Epidemiology 16(6), 727–736 (2005)
13. Forsberg, B., Hansson, H.C., Johansson, C., Areskoug, H., Persson, K., Järvholm, B.: Comparative health assessment of local and regional particulate air pollutants in Scandinavia. Ambio 34, 11–19 (2005)
14. Brandt, J., Silver, J.D., Christensen, J.H., Andersen, M.S., Bonlokke, J.H., Sigsgaard, T., Geels, C., Gross, A., Hansen, A.B., Hansen, K.M., Hedegaard, G.B., Kaas, E., Frohn, L.M.: Contribution from ten major emission sectors in Europe and Denmark to the health-cost externalities of air pollution using the EVA model system – an integrated modelling approach. Atmos. Chem. Phys. 13, 7725–7746 (2013)

Medium-Term Analysis of Agroecosystem Sustainability under Different Land Use Practices by Means of Dynamic Crop Simulation

Sergey Medvedev[1], Alex Topaj[1], Vladimir Badenko[2], and Vitalij Terleev[2]

[1] Agrophysical Research Institute, St.Petersburg, Russia
glorguin@yandex.ru, alex.topaj@gmail.com
[2] St.Petersburg State Polytechnical University, St.Petersburg, Russia
vbadenko@gmail.com, vitaly_terleev@mail.ru

Abstract. The role of dynamic crop models as an intellectual core of computer decision support systems in agricultural management increases significantly in recent time. However, the scope of model applications is often limited by short time scale i.e. crop simulation/forecasting is performed within a particular vegetation season. The use of dynamic models in long-term planning is still much less developed. This contribution presents the author's efforts in development and improvement of the integrated system of crop simulation «APEX-AGROTOOL» for its use as a tool of model-oriented analysis of land use environmental sustainability. Attention is paid to the modification of the existing software in order to provide an ability to simulate agro-landscape dynamics taking into account crop rotation effects.

Keywords: crop rotation, sustainable agriculture, generic crop simulator, computer experiment, multivariate analysis, simulation software.

1 Introduction

Maintaining or even increasing the fertility of agricultural landscapes during their active agricultural use is one of the most important scientific problems in theoretical agricultural science. The importance of this issue has recently increased due to significant changes in land use. For example, the new energy-oriented agriculture needs scientific support in many aspects: choice of the proper cultures, choice of crop rotation scheme, choice of crop allocation in different spatial scales etc. The main problem is to bridge the gap between economic requests and scientific methodological support of sustainable land use. In recent years agricultural science reinforced the efforts to achieve agrolandscape environmental sustainability instead of maximum productivity [1]. The paper presents efforts for development and improvement of the integrated system of crop simulation «APEX-AGROTOOL» for analysis and investigation of alternative medium-term planning strategies in land use, taking into account the crop rotation influence on environmental sustainability and saving resources.

R. Denzer et al. (Eds.): ISESS 2015, IFIP AICT 448, pp. 252–261, 2015.

2   Material and Methods

The use of dynamic imitation models is well-known and wide-distributed modern tool in agroecology and crop production for analyzing, forecasting and decision support. Numerous benefits of this approach in comparison with statistical and regression models are:

- improved accuracy and approximation of the calculations by taking more factors into account;
- obtaining multiple results based on the wider range of variations of input data;
- results produced as distributions of indicators on probability samples of external conditions can be readily used in risk analysis;
- almost unlimited number of monitored indicators of the agroecosystem model (productivity, environment, fertility, etc.);
- reduced uncertainty of model calculations, etc.

All these advantages of dynamic models are the basis of their wide application to real-time forecasting and crop management in the short time scale (within a particular growing season) [2]. However, their use for long-term planning is still much less developed. Until recently, it was mainly caused by technical limitations such as computational efficiency or memory size. At present, however, due to the progress in hardware engineering as well as in information technologies, the most significant restrictions have been overcome. Thus the subject-oriented requirements have become the principal feature for the applicability of imitation models in mid-term forecasting in agriculture [3].

An appropriate solution requires adaptation of both the models and the computer simulation environment for fulfilling the relevant task requirements. First of all, it refers to the need for a full description of the changes during the long-term crop rotation [4]. The latter involves the following specific requirements to imitation model:

- Universal character of the simulation algorithm. It includes structural identity of the models for different cultures/cultivars, soil-climate conditions and technologies.
- Comprehensive sequence analysis. The model should fully take into account the influence of culture predecessors in all significant aspects such as decomposition of crop residues and changes in the agrochemical and the physical properties of the soil, symbiotic nitrogen fixation legumes, etc. [5,6].
- «Wintering» imitation. The model should be able to simulate abiotic processes in the agroecosystem (soil frost penetration and thawing, snowfall and snow melting etc.) during off-seasons period.
- Environmental orientation. The model should be able to estimate yield as well as the dynamics of various parameters of the sustainability, such as soil fertility indexes (humus content, carbon sequestration), energy-matter balance of the agro-landscape (emission of greenhouse gases, biogen transfer to water body), etc.

In addition, special software for planning and performing the computer experiments with the model must be developed to provide the following:

- Multivariate analysis of the studied crop model. It means multiple running of the model with different input data sets defined during preprocessing. Moreover, crop rotation research needs strong sequence of scenario execution.
- GIS interface or integration with GIS software for visualization of simulated results (economical as well as ecological variables) on a farm scale.
- Built-in tools of model information support for model-based forecasting (weather and field test databases, stochastic weather generator, etc.)

Only the existence of a comprehensive ecologically oriented crop model and a special software providing cyclical scheme of model computation (taking into account crop rotation) will solve the problem of analyzing long-term trends of indicators of soil fertility and other parameters of the environmental sustainability of agricultural landscapes. The above mentioned requirements to a «model-centric» computer system of analysis and decision making support in sustainable agriculture seem to be rigorous. Nevertheless, the prototypes of such a system have been developed. For example, DSSAT (leading solution for crop modeling in the USA) includes special application for crop rotation analysis that assess economic risks and environmental impacts taking into account irrigation, fertilizer management, climate variability and changes, soil carbon sequestration, and precision management [7].

Examples of successful DSSAT applications for crop rotation analysis and optimization of combination of crop residue and N application rate for sustainable production are also known [8,9]. One of the most known European solutions for model-based analysis incorporating mid-term planning in farm scale is LandCare-DSS developed in the Leibniz Center of Agrolandscape Research [10]. LandCare-DSS features includes an original cartographical interface, close connection with a built-in module of economic analysis and the usage of different type of crop simulators depending on the spatial resolution of the investigated problem: from simplified regression model YieldStat at regional level to dynamic crop model MONICA at farm or field level.

Integrated simulation environment «APEX-AGROTOOL» is, probably, the most advanced Russian product providing information support, planning and running of multivariate computer experiments in crop modeling. The system was developed in Agrophysical Research Institute (Saint-Petersburg) and consists of two main parts: dynamic crop model AGROTOOL [11] and the system of model multivariate analysis APEX [12]. The principal modifications which have been made in software for «APEX-AGROTOOL» system to satisfy the above mentioned requirements of long term environmental analysis of agroecosystem dynamics are presented further.

3   Changes in the AGROTOOL Software

The simulation algorithm of AGROTOOL can be written in the form of recurrent discrete expression:

$$\mathbf{x}(k+1) = \mathbf{f}(\mathbf{x}(k), \mathbf{a}, \mathbf{w}(k), \mathbf{u}(k)), \quad \mathbf{x}(0) = \mathbf{x_0}, k = 0,1...T \tag{1}$$

where $\mathbf{x}$ - vector of dynamic state variables; $\mathbf{a}$ - vector of constant parameters; $\mathbf{u}$ - vector controlled external impacts (agricultural technician); $\mathbf{w}$ - vector uncontrollable external impacts; k - the time step for the model (time step is equal to one day), $\mathbf{f}$ - the evolution operator (a logical essence of the simulation algorithm).

Thus, AGROTOOL model recursively computes the vector of values of the modelling characteristics of the agroecosystem in the next step of the calculation on the base of the vector from the previous step. The main technical feature of the current version of AGROTOOL software is that all the data necessary for the calculation are stored in the model operational database, which is a multi-sheet Microsoft Excel document. Moreover, the same Microsoft Excel document also stores a detailed simulation results in the form of the state vector model at each step for calculating $\mathbf{y}(k)=\mathbf{y}(\mathbf{x}(k))$. Another important feature of AGROTOOL is the universal character of the simulation algorithm, i.e. it is so-called *generic crop simulator*.

A special modification has been developed for sequential modeling of crop rotation using AGROTOOL. Now it uses data from the operational database, stored there during the previous stage of calculation (for the predecessor crop) to be used as initial state for the calculation of the next crop. A formal procedure to perform recalculation is following: $\mathbf{x_0}^{i+1}=g(\mathbf{y}^i(T))$. In turn, the results of this calculation can be used to generate the initial state of the calculation of the crop of the successor of the second order, and thus closes the next "round" of crop rotation.

To carry out model calculations within the crop rotation in the current version of AGROTOOL software, it is necessary to know the dry biomass residue (separately for aboveground and root parts), nodule nitrogen (if the predecessor culture is legume), the total mineral nitrogen content and the humus in the soil. These values are fixed at the end of the season for the predecessor crop and "frozen", i.e. do not change until the time of sowing of the next succeeding crops. In the future, it is planned to develop an algorithm to study the behavior of these characteristics for non-vegetation period (wintering), including a simplified description of the transformations of these variables.

4   Changes in the APEX Software

The APEX software can be considered as a versatile repository of external crop model descriptors. Its interface permits users to register its own crop model or model version. Also APEX provides a universal environment for the polyvariant model analysis. It means designing and preparation of a multivariate computer case study, performing the model runs in batch mode and applying advanced procedures of statistical treatments for results obtained. Each set of input data forms a single scenario calculation. The scenario is a cortege of references to specific gradation of selected factors (information domain) specific to the subject area. These factors are following "soil", "culture", "area", "initial state", "technology" and "weather." During the registration of the model the software allows the user to specify the structure of variables and parameters for the specific model and to generate a list of tables and their fields, as well as an array of metadata. A more detailed description of the structure and principles of operation of the APEX software can be found in [12].

Rigid specification of the predefined factors enabled to perform "semantically rich" analysis of the results obtained using specialized software tools for preparation of input data (e.g. weather generator), although these features limit flexibility of the system. In particular, it allows implementation of the calculation of the crop rotations within the APEX software.

For automated calculation of crop rotations in APEX it is necessary to develop the following additional functionality:

- To implement a mechanism for the explicit specification of the sequence for the execution of scenarios in a framework of the   project of computer experiment and to specify "boundary" scenarios, defining the beginning of the crop rotation block for a particular agricultural field.
- To create a flexible interface for specification the method for the "continuity" of the results of the previous scenario during the formation of the initial state for the next scenario (taking into account the "predecessor crop") in the procedure of the metadata specification describing the connected model.

The fundamental idea underlying the formation of an ordered list of scenarios in a structured polyvariant project calculation of crop rotation can be demonstrated by analogy with SQL-queries in a relational database (Fig.1). A simple project, realized by all possible combinations of all gradations of predefined factors (a full factorial experiment) in the framework of this analogy, can be represented by a QUERY1 (Fig. 1 – red), where the WHERE clause explicitly chooses the set of gradations for each of the predefined factors. The result of such query will be the Cartesian product of "all vs. all", generating $N * M * K * P * Q * R$ scenarios in a project.

Obviously, not all combinations of the factor gradations are meaningful. So it is clear that in a given year on the specific field only one crop involved in the crop rotation can grow. Thus, it is necessary to restrict the number of possible combinations and to form an incomplete factorial experiment scheme – QUERY2 (Fig.1 – green). Here, the second block of the AND clause is a set of additional links between the factor gradations. They are defined by the user in the specific APEX interface designed for the so-called "factor coupling".

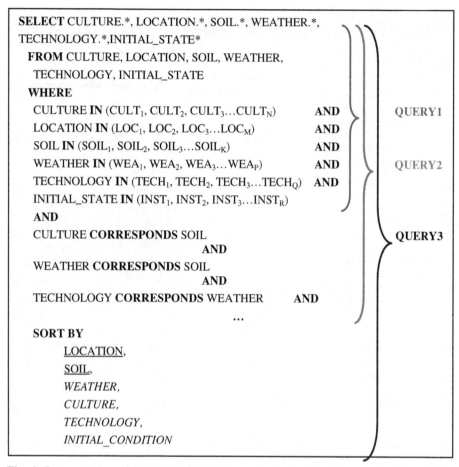

Fig. 1. Demonstration of the fundamental idea approach (syntax does not coincide with the standard SQL)

A significant feature of the crop rotation project is the clear sequence of the execution of scenarios as results of the previous calculation can be used to generate the initial state at the next startup model in strict accordance with the scheme of crop changing. This is achieved by including a mechanism of the explicit specification of the order within factor gradations and between factors. The latter can be demonstrated by the introduction of sorting like QUERY3 (Fig.1 – blue).

The sequence of these factors in the SORT BY clause completely defines the scenario ordering within the project. The wizard dialog for creation of a new project for a simple "three-field - three-year" crop rotation scheme is shown in Fig. 2.

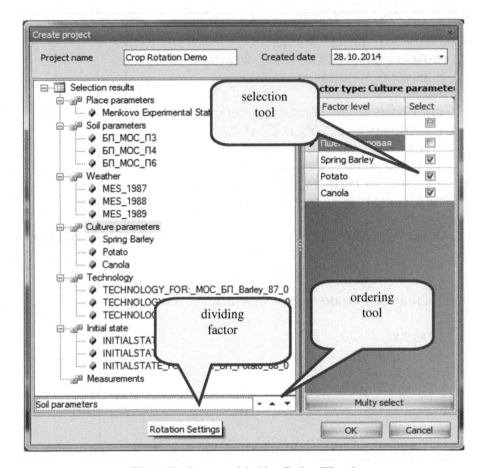

Fig. 2. The first step of the New Project Wizard

Fig.2 shows which factor used as a "separator" in the determination of the crop rotation (in this case, this factor is "soil"). As a result, a user can transparently specify the correct scenario order and define the boundaries of the "result continuity" blocks within simulated crop rotation. APEX performs the transfer of the results from the previously calculated variant to initial state of next variant inside every block following by the separating scenario. Thus, a set of scenarios, which make up the project, and a series-parallel scheme of their execution are fully defined. A typical interface with the project created in APEX is shown on Fig. 3.

The method for transferring the results of the previous calculations into the certain fields of the gradation of the INITIAL_STATE factor for the next variant is described via a special APEX interface that is part of the input metadata about the connected models. Currently APEX supports two following modes: a) the selected INITIAL_STATE field can be directly equated to the value of selected calculation result and b) it can be declaratively assigned to a constant value. The latter method is used in conjunction as "environment APEX + model AGROTOOL».

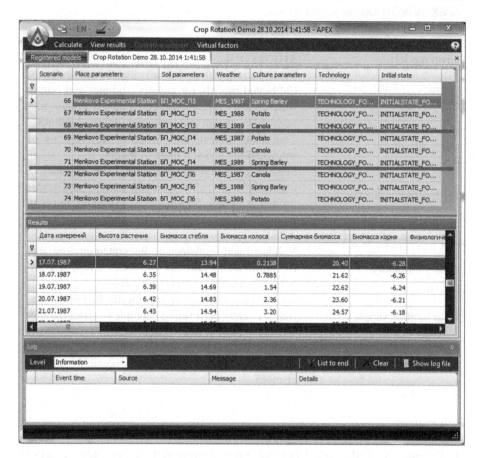

Fig. 3. Project visualization in APEX (red line – the boundaries of the crop rotation logic blocks)

5   Results

The degree of conformity of the achieved functionality of APEX and AGROTOOL with the above mentioned requirements of mid-term planning in land use is briefly summarized in Table 1. The abilities of the developed integrated environment cover the needs completely and thus, the «APEX-AGROTOOL» system can be used as a tool of model-oriented analysis of land use environmental sustainability [13].

Table 1. Correspondence between mid-term planning requirements and abilities of «APEX+AGROTOOL» integrated software

Requirement	Current state
Crop model:	**AGROTOOL:**
Generic simulator	Versatile algorithm for all maintained cultures. Calibrated models for cereals (summer and winter wheat, winter rye, barley, oats), maize, potato, root vegetables, annual and perennial forages, legumes.
«Wintering»	Continuous calculation. Modified descriptions of snow melting and soil thermal regime.
Predecessor influence	Separated calculation of litter and root residues in the module of carbon-nitrogen transfer and transformation in soil. Sub-model of symbiotic nitrogen fixation and nodule nitrogen dynamics.
Simulation infrastructure:	**APEX:**
Multiple running	Validated and implemented integrated environment for multivariate analysis and automation of computer experiments with crop models.
Crop rotation support	Special plug-in for planning not full factorial experiments and performing complex serial-parallel schemes of scenario computation.
Forecasting	Built-in stochastic generator of daily weather variables taking into account possible climate changes.

References

1. Costanzo, A., Bàrberi, P.: Functional agrobiodiversity and agroecosystem services in sustainable wheat production. A review. Agronomy for Sustainable Development. 34(2), 327–348 (2014)
2. Tonitto, C., Li, C., Seidel, R., Drinkwater, L.: Application of the DNDC model to the Rodale Institute Farming Systems Trial: Challenges for the validation of drainage and nitrate leaching in agroecosystem models. Nutrient Cycling in Agroecosystems 87(3), 483–494 (2010)
3. Belcher, K.W., Boehm, M.M., Fulton, M.E.: Agroecosystem sustainability: A system simulation model approach. Agricultural Systems 79(2), 225–241 (2004)
4. Dury, J., Schaller, N., Garcia, F., Reynaud, A., Bergez, J.E.: Models to support cropping plan and crop rotation decisions. A review. Agronomy for Sustainable Development. 32(2), 567–580 (2012)
5. Alva, A.K., Marcos, J., Stockle, C., Reddy, V.R., Timlin, D.: A crop simulation model for predicting yield and fate of nitrogen in irrigated potato rotation cropping system. Journal of Crop Improvement 24(2), 142–152 (2010)
6. Davari, M.R., Sharma, S.N., Mirzakhani, M.: Effect of cropping systems and crop residue incorporation on production and properties of soil in an organic agroecosystem. Biological Agriculture and Horticulture 28(3), 206–222 (2012)

7. Jones, J., Hoogenboom, G., Porter, C., Boote, K., Batchelor, W., Hunt, L., Ritchie, J.: The DSSAT cropping system model. European Journal of Agronomy 18(3-4), 235–265 (2003)
8. Sarkar, R., Kar, S.: Sequence Analysis of DSSAT to Select Optimum Strategy of Crop Residue and Nitrogen for Sustainable Rice-Wheat Rotation. Agronomy Journal 100(1), 87–97 (2008)
9. Salmerón, M., Cavero, J., Isla, R., Porter, C.H., Jones, J.W., Boote, K.J.: DSSAT nitrogen cycle simulation of cover crop-maize rotations under irrigated mediterranean conditions. Agronomy Journal 106(4), 1283–1296 (2014)
10. Wenkel, K.O., Berg, M., Mirschel, W., Wieland, R., Nendel, C., Köstner, B.: LandCaRe DSS –An interactive decision support system for climate change impact assessment and the analysis of potential agricultural land use adaptation strategies. J. Environ. Manag. 127, 168–183 (2013)
11. Poluektov, R.A., Fintushal, S.M., Oparina, I.V., Shatskikh, D.V., Terleev, V.V., Zakharova, E.T.: Agrotool – a system for crop simulation. Arch. Acker- Pfl. Boden. 48, 609–635 (2002)
12. Medvedev, S., Topaj, A.: Crop simulation model registrator and polyvariant analysis. IFIP Advances in Information and Communication Technology 359, 295–301 (2011)
13. Badenko, V., Terleev, V., Topaj, A.: ARGOTOOL software as an intellectual core of decision support systems in computer aided agriculture. Applied Mechanics and Materials, 635-637, 1688–1691 (2014)

SPARK – A Bushfire Spread Prediction Tool

Claire Miller[1], James Hilton[1], Andrew Sullivan[2], and Mahesh Prakash[1]

[1] CSIRO Digital Productivity Flagship, Melbourne, Australia
{claire.miller,james.hilton,mahesh.prakash}@csiro.au
[2] CSIRO Land and Water Flagship, Canberra, Australia
andrew.sullivan@csiro.au

Abstract. Bushfires are complex processes, making it difficult to accurately predict their rate of spread. We present an integrated software system for bushfire spread prediction, SPARK, which was developed with the functionality to model some of these complexities. SPARK uses a level set method governed by a user-defined algebraic spread rate to model fire propagation. The model is run within a modular workflow-based software environment. Implementation of SPARK is demonstrated for two cases: a small-scale experimental fire and a complex bushfire scenario. In the second case, the complexity of environmental non-homogeneity is explored through the inclusion of local variation in fuel and wind. Simulations over multiple runs with this fuel and wind variation are aggregated to produce a probability map of fire spread over a given time period. The model output has potential to be used operationally for real-time fire spread modeling, or by decision makers predicting risk from bushfire events.

Keywords: level set, bushfire, wildfire, modeling, simulation.

1 Introduction

Although a natural occurrence in the Australian landscape, bushfires have the ability to be devastating, particularly when they come into contact with urban environments. Improving knowledge of how these fires spread is critical for effective management and timely issuing of warnings. Unfortunately, it is difficult to predict the rate of spread of a fire as there are many elements influencing fire behavior occurring over a range of length and time scales. Fully physical computational fluid dynamics models attempt to incorporate a large number of these elements, but are computationally intensive and are not practical in an operational environment. Instead, operational models usually propagate the perimeter of the fire using spread rates based on empirical expressions. These empirical models can give an approximation of expected fire area in a significantly shorter computational time than physical models.

Two operational tools currently in use in Australia are *Phoenix Rapidfire* [1] and *Australis* [2], both developed over the last ten years. SPARK has been developed with the goal of easy adaptability. It allows user defined spread models, as opposed to the hard-coded spread models found in current operational tools. This functionality enables many aspects of simulated fire spread to be tested and investigated. One such

R. Denzer et al. (Eds.): ISESS 2015, IFIP AICT 448, pp. 262–271, 2015.

aspect is the non-homogeneity of a bushfire's local environment, which we explore in this paper.

This paper aims to familiarize readers with SPARK's architecture and development path, and to demonstrate its analysis capability for a simple fire scenario. We explore the functionality of SPARK in dealing with non-homogeneity, which highlights the requirement for correct consideration of local environmental conditions.

2   SPARK Overview

SPARK uses a level set method for the representation of the fire perimeter, which propagates over a domain according to a one-dimensional algebraic rate of spread. The model sits within a workflow environment, allowing a broad range of flexibility in the analysis and the input and output of data types. Core elements of the model are explained in further detail below, along with details on the data aspects of the tool.

2.1   Level Set Method

The level set method is used to model the propagation of the fire perimeter. Use of this method is still fairly novel for fire simulation, particularly for large-scale wildland fires. The level set method was first implemented as an interface propagation solution by [3] and has since been found useful over multiple application areas (eg. [4] and [5]). In contrast to traditional simulation methods which define front locations and propagate these locations forward in time, the level set method defines a surface over the domain according to a distance function. In this implementation the value of the distance function, Φ, is equal to the closest distance to the fire perimeter. The function is defined as positive where the fire is yet to burn and negative in burnt areas. This allows for simple identification of the front location at $\Phi = 0$. Evolution of the surface in time is determined for each grid cell using some rate of spread value, S, in a direction normal to the fire front, according to

$$\frac{\partial \Phi}{\partial t} + S|\nabla \Phi| = 0. \tag{1}$$

For a more detailed explanation of the model, see [6].

2.2   One Dimensional Spread Rates

The value of S in Equation (1) is calculated for each cell according to a one dimensional rate of spread model. This spread rate model is a function of the environmental conditions at that grid point. The level set method in SPARK uses OpenCL [7], allowing the spread rate model governing the value of S to be directly passed to the OpenCL compiler as a text string written in the C programming language. This allows the flexibility of incorporating a range of aspects and functional forms of fire spread model. An example input is shown in the lower right panel of Fig. 1.

2.3   Workflow System

The SPARK solver sits within a modular workflow environment, developed by CSIRO, called Workspace [8]. The Workspace GUI with an example workflow is shown in Fig. 1, where operations are represented by colored triangles and connections between operations are represented by the black lines. The directions of flow of information between the operations are shown as arrowheads superimposed onto the connecting lines. Workspace allows users to build computational solutions using a catalogue of these operations, shown in the panel on the left in Fig. 1. Each operation has its own function, for example fire propagation by the level set method is performed within the SPARK 'Bushfire solver' operation, circled in red. Operations are dragged from the catalogue to the main canvas, where all the operations currently in use can be seen. Input and output container types are predefined and passed between the operations to create a workflow. These connections can only be made if connected container types are compatible. Users can interchange operations by simply passing the new operation's output to replace the old one.

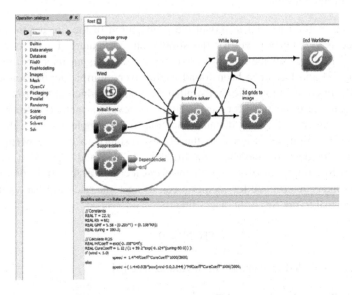

Fig. 1. An example workflow. The panel on the far left shows a catalogue of available operations. Operations and connections are shown in the upper right panel. An example operation circled in green has its outputs displayed. The lower right panel displays the C code for the rate of spread model used in the bushfire solver operation, which is circled in red.

New user-defined operations can easily be added to analyze or visualize data. The Workspace is based on the Qt framework, and all operations are written in C++. Data is held in memory to allow efficient sharing and passing between operations. Workspace allows the data to be read and written at any stage of workflow operation. This allows users to visualize progressive fire spread output from SPARK. New operations and data types are compiled as shared libraries (.dll, .so or .dylib) which act as plugins to Workspace. For example, the SPARK model and analysis operations are all contained within a single plugin. This plugin architecture allows transparent access between different data types and operations within the framework. C++ stub code for new operations and data types can be generated using code generation wizards and compiled using the included CMake build system and scripts for cross platform compilation.

As well as the Workspace GUI shown in Fig. 1, workflow execution is supported from the command line through batch execution or exposed through an API. Close integration with Qt allows complex user interfaces to be designed and transparently connected with an underlying workflow, allowing custom applications to be easily developed. Parallel APIs, such as OpenMP and OpenCL, are fully supported. Operations for running scripts in both ECMAScript and Python within Workspace are also available for non C++ developers. Furthermore, a number of existing open-source software systems have been natively compiled with the Workspace framework. These modules include; OpenCV for image analysis, which can be used to convert fire imagery to SPARK inputs, NetCDF for large data file support, which is useful for SPARK's environmental inputs and spread information outputs, and GDAL for geospatial analysis and conversion, which can convert to meter grids from latitudes and longitudes for compatibility with fire spread rate equations.

2.4   Integration with the Amicus Decision Support Tool

SPARK has been built with the capability to be integrated with the decision support tool Amicus [9] through Workspace. Amicus is a knowledge base and tool informing users on expected fire behavior metrics given a set of fuel, weather, and topographic conditions. It has been built around a number of well-established fire spread models developed for Australian vegetation. The rate of spread model functions in Amicus exist as separate operations within Workspace and can be used and tested within Amicus before being implemented dynamically within SPARK.

2.5   Data Inputs

Fires can occur over a vast range of vegetation and fuel types. By using gridded inputs for fuel properties it is possible for a variety of fuel types to occur within the same simulation, bounded only by grid size. This can include areas of un-burnable fuel, such as roads and water bodies. The development of SPARK within a workflow environment allows users to easily incorporate these environmental inputs. Fuel grids can be pre-populated and read directly into the workflow, or manipulated from other inputs, such as satellite imagery, within the workflow.

Weather conditions, in particular significant changes in weather conditions, contribute significantly to fire consequence. Atmospheric condition inputs, which often include air temperature, relative humidity, wind speed, and wind direction, are generated as time series. The time series inputs for the model are implemented as a Workspace data type with arbitrary temporal spacing between the samples.

2.6   Data Sources

In order to run SPARK, data is required for the atmospheric conditions, fuel conditions, topography, and initial fire location. This can be sourced from a range of databases discussed below, depending on the scenario. A current aim is to integrate web services into the model, such that data can be directly used by the system.

Historical data for atmospheric conditions are available from the Australian Bureau of Meteorology at half hourly intervals for a number of stations nationally. This data can be used to set parameters such as the wind, temperature, and moisture levels for simulating large historical fire events. Issues arise when the stations available are not close, in both location and environment, to the ignition location. In the future, we hope to gain access to data recorded during fire events, or gridded hindcast data, which may provide a more accurate record of the conditions. For small experimental fires, such as the case demonstrated in Section 3, atmospheric data is commonly recorded at a high frequency in locations close to the fire.

Fuel inputs are slightly more difficult to obtain. They can be manually created using basic satellite imagery, such as from Google maps. A related, but more sophisticated, method is to create classifications using satellite band imagery from LandSat. A third option is to use land use grids which can be converted to fuel types, however these tend to lack the critical details of unburnable areas such as roads and water bodies. Which of these inputs are most useful depends on the scale of the area of interest and the fuel information that is required for the rate of spread formula used.

The last input is initial fire location information. Fire ignition locations and progression maps are available online for some historical fires and hence are simple to implement. For more recent fires, fire agencies will often use airborne thermal imagery to determine current fire extent. This imagery is geo-tagged and can be converted to a fire front map. For example, some images may be false colored with the fire appearing as red in the image with the surrounding area blue. It is straightforward to split the image by color and threshold according to the value of the red channel. Additionally, this entire process can be performed within the workflow.

2.7   Data Output

The output from SPARK consists of gridded forms of both the value of the level set function at a user specified frequency and the time of ignition over the domain. This allows users to easily investigate both long term and time specific consequence of the fire.

3   A Simple Fire Scenario

A series of small scale, 35 m square, experimental burns were conducted in Ballarat, Victoria, Australia in January, 2014 [10]. Weather data was recorded during the fires, for both the wind speed and bearing, at a frequency of 10 Hz. The fire used in this example burnt for 28 seconds, with wind speeds averaging around 4 ms^{-1}. Quadcopter footage was taken of each fire, which was then stabilized and rectified to provide clear observations of the spread.

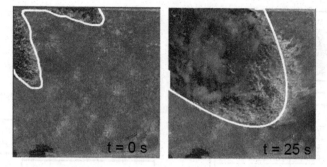

Fig. 2. A simple fire example. Simulated fire fronts (solid white line) are overlaid on fire imagery for the ignition configuration, left, and then at 25 seconds, right.

For this example, simulated spread was governed by a generic rate of spread model with an added curvature dependent component. The grid size was 0.1 m. A qualitative comparison of simulated spread to actual fire imagery indicates a good match for both fire shape and rate of spread, as shown in Fig. 2. This is largely influenced by the ability to incorporate curvature. Without the inclusion of a shape-related variable in the spread model, simulated fires on flat ground tend to maintain their initial shape.

4   A Study of Non-homogeneity

A major challenge in simulating bushfire spread is dealing with the complexities of the environments in which they occur. This can include complex topographies, often large varieties of fuel types, and local variations in weather and fuel. Operational fire spread models developed for large scale fires assume fires will attain a quasi-steady rate of spread for conditions averaged over considerable time and distance, invariably smoothing out local scale environmental variations. SPARK was used to investigate the effect of this local variation on fire spread. The use of a gridded input system allows the methods for the inclusion of variation explained below to be simply implemented. The application of these mechanisms is demonstrated in Section 5.

4.1   The Inclusion of Variation

At most scales, our environment is far from homogeneous. The software architecture has the functionality to easily incorporate spatial and temporal variation into both the fuel and wind inputs.

In order to include fuel variation, a grid was populated prior to the running of the model. Fuel values for each cell were chosen randomly, and independently of surrounding cells, from a predefined distribution. The distribution used could be different for different fuel varieties according to a fuel input grid. The random selection process enabled reproducibility by setting a seed value for the random number generator. Fig. 3 is a diagram showing the fuel population process.

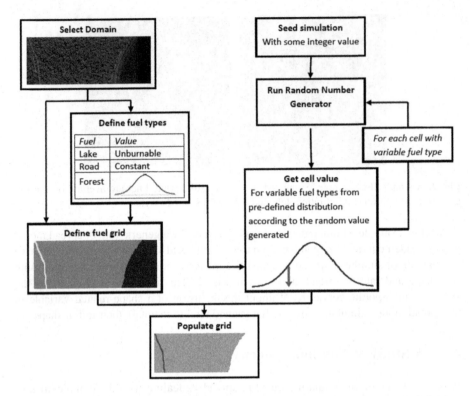

Fig. 3. The process by which fuel grids are populated. The left column focuses on the definition of multiple fuel types, the right column focuses on the incorporation of variation into the grid.

Variation was also included in wind, for both speed and direction, in a similar manner. For the wind however, the value of each parameter was randomly chosen from its predefined distribution for each grid cell spread calculation at each time step. For this preliminary investigation, the variation in both fuel and wind was assumed to be normally distributed.

The workflow system allowed the implementation of variation to be straightforwardly incorporated in the execution of the model. The seed value was given to a random number generation operation which gave a new random value every time one was requested. The random operation in this case was used for both the population of the fuel layer and the wind strength and direction.

4.2 Probability of Arrival Maps

The addition of variation into the model in this manner adds an element of randomness into the arrival time of the fire at a given location. As such, the same simulation run with a different randomly selected set of environmental values, based on the same distributions, could potentially produce a different set of arrival times. This leads to the concept of an ensemble of simulations run with different seed values for the random selection process. Producing intuitive visualizations of these results is challenging. The method we use in this paper is maps indicating the probability of arrival of the fire. These maps show, for each grid cell, the proportion of simulations in which the front passed through that cell in a given time frame. As such, they can give an indication of the probability of the fire reaching a location at a given time.

5   Complex Fire Scenario with Variation

The Deans Gap fire burned within the City of Shoalhaven, New South Wales, Australia, for over a week in January, 2013 [11]. It was a highly complex fire in terms of weather, fuel, and topography. Consequently, it provides an interesting scenario in which to demonstrate how the addition of variation can provide an increased understanding of expected spread. Our scenario focused on the first 24 hours, January 7th to 8th. Fire location data was obtained from the NSW Rural Fire Service.

For these simulations the Dry Eucalypt Fire Model [12] rate of spread for Australian forest vegetation was used. This rate of spread model was chosen as it is the most suitable for the vegetation in the fire area. The domain was an 850 by 740 grid with a cell size of just less than 30 m. Total simulated fire time was 31 hours. Wind was a triangulation of data from the surrounding weather stations of Nowra, Ulladulla, Jervis Bay, and Goulburn. The variation in the wind had standard deviation 1 km/h and 10 degrees for speed and direction respectively. Fuel height was variable with mean 50 cm and standard deviation 30 cm. The surface fuel hazard score used in the model was 2, and near-surface fuel hazard 3.5. Maximum slope over which the fire was considered able to run was 40 degrees.

Simulation results for several times are shown in Fig. 4a. Results indicate a slow spread over the first 12 hours, which is the period over the evening and night. The fire picks up during the morning of the next day as the temperature starts to heat up. There is a further increase in spread rate in the afternoon, which is the hottest and driest time of day, as would be expected.

The concept of a probability of arrival map was applied to the Deans Gap scenario using 100 simulations run from different seeds, Fig. 4b. This map highlights that the addition of variation over a 24 hour period, from a known ignition location, has a significant impact on spread. Within the 10 minute interval possible front locations stretch almost four and a half kilometers. These results show how unpredictable the fire can be, and in which areas this variation is greatest. This has implications both educationally and operationally. It shows that the influence of common local environmental events can have an impact on the final spread, which the straight empirical models do not capture. Operationally, it provides an enhanced knowledge set to assist decision making.

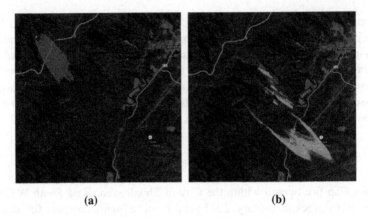

(a)   **(b)**

Fig. 4. Simulation results for Deans Gap; (a) A single simulation with the ignition point (yellow, top left) at 17:30 on January 7, and the simulation results for each subsequent 6 hourly interval finishing at 17:30 on January 8. Each new 6 hour interval is represented by a change in color, (b) Probability of arrival map for the time frame 17:20 to 17:30 on January 8. Red indicates a high proportion, and blue low, of simulations predicting the same arrival time in each cell.

6   Summary

We have provided a general introduction to SPARK, our bushfire prediction tool. The model uses a level set method for fast and simple spread propagation, combined with well-established empirical spread rates. The simple fire example demonstrated the use of a generic fire spread rate that incorporated curvature.

SPARK has been developed with the goal of providing the functionality to easily incorporate, and hence investigate, additional complexities in the model. The use of a visual workflow tool such as Workspace has made this relatively straightforward to do. This is expected to be useful for researchers to determine the roles and importance of these complexities. The complexity considered here was the addition of variation into the environmental components. Applying this to a complex bushfire scenario has indicated that this variation over an extended period of time can introduce a large amount of uncertainty into the results. Highlighting this effect, and the areas in which it is most significant, could potentially provide a more well-informed information set to fire management.

SPARK is currently being used to further investigate the effect of this variation. Future work will also be to consider the inclusion of wind and spotting models.

References

1. Tolhurst, K., Shields, B., Chong, D.: Phoenix: development and application of a bushfire risk management tool. The Australian Journal of Emergency Management 23, 47–54 (2008)

2. Johnston, P., Kelso, J., Milne, G.J.: Efficient simulation of wildfire spread on an irregular grid. International Journal of Wildland Fire 17, 614–627 (2008)
3. Osher, S., Sethian, J.: Fronts Propagating with Curvature-Dependent Speed: Algorithms Based on Hamilton-Jacobi Formulations. Journal of Computational Physics 79(1), 12–49 (1988)
4. Sethian, J.A., Strain, J.: Crystal growth and dendritic solidification. Journal of Computational Physics 98(2), 231–253 (1992)
5. Sussman, M., Smereka, P., Osher, S.: A level set approach for computing solutions to incompressible two-phase flow. Journal of Computational Physics 114, 146–159 (1994)
6. Hilton, J., Miller, C., Sullivan, A., Rucinski, C.: Incorporation of variation into wildfire spread models using a level set approach. Submitted to Environmental Modelling and Software (under review)
7. OpenCL (2014), https://www.khronos.org/opencl/ (accessed December 9, 2014)
8. Workspace (2014), http://research.csiro.au/workspace/ (accessed October 31, 2014)
9. Sullivan, A.L., Gould, J.S., Cruz, M.G., Rucinski, C., Prakash, M.: Amicus: a national fire behaviour knowledge base for enhanced information management and better decision making. In: Piantadosi, J., Anderssen, R.S. (eds.) MODSIM 2013, 20th International Congress on Modelling and Simulation, pp. 2068–2074 (2013)
10. Cruz, M.G., Gould, J., Kidnie, S., Nichols, D., Anderson, W.R., Bessel, R., Hurley, R., Koul, V.: Grass curing and fire behavior. Submitted to International Journal of Wildland Fire (under review)
11. Mackie, B., McLennan, J., Wright, L.: Community Understanding and Awareness of Bushfire Safety: January 2013 Bushfires. Research for the New South Wales Rural Fire Service. Bushfire CRC. La Trobe University (2013)
12. Cheney, N.P., Gould, J.S., McCaw, W.L., Anderson, W.R.: Predicting fire behaviour in dry eucalypt forest in southern Australia. Forest Ecology and Management 280, 120–131 (2012)

Construction of a Bio-economic Model
to Estimate the Feasibility and Cost of Achieving Water
Quality Targets in the Burnett-Mary Region, Queensland

Craig Beverly[1], Anna Roberts[2], Geoff Park[2], Fred Bennett[3], and Graeme Doole[4]

[1] Agriculture Research: Department of Environment and Primary Industries,
Rutherglen, Australia
[2] Natural Decisions, Pty Ltd, VIC, Australia
[3] Burnett Mary Regional Group Ltd, Bundaberg, QLD, Australia
[4] Centre for Environmental Economics and Policy,
University of Western Australia, WA
craig.beverly@depi.vic.gov.au

Abstract. The aim of this study was to develop a bio-economic model to estimate the feasibility and net profit (or net costs)s of achieving set water quality
targets (sediment, nitrogen and phosphorus load reductions) in the Burnett Mary
region of northern Queensland, Australia to with the aim of protecting the
southern portion of the Great Barrier Reef (GBR). Two sets of targets were evaluated – Reef Plan Targets (RPTs) which are the currently formally agreed targets, and more ambitious Ecologically Relevant Targets (ERTs) which current
science suggests might be needed to better protect the values of the GBR. This
paper describes the construct of a bio-economic optimisation framework which
has been used to underpin a Water Quality Improvement Plan (WQIP) for the
Burnett Mary region. The bioeconomic model incorporates the available
science developed from paddock and catchment scale biophysical model results
and farm economic analysis. The model enabled transparent assessment and
optimisation of net profits and costs associated with four categories of best
management practices (cutting edge unproven technologies called 'A' practice,
current best-management practices called 'B', common industry or 'C' practices, and below industry standards or 'D' practice) in the grazing and sugar cane
industries. The bioeconomic model was able to solve for RPTs or ERTs assigned to either the entire region or within each of five discrete river basins.
Key outcomes from the study were that RPTs could be achieved at an annual
cost of $3M/year on a whole of region basis. In contrast ERTs could be
achieved on a whole of region basis at as net cost of $16M/year. ERTs were not
able to be feasibly met on a basin by basin basis. This is the first time such a
comprehensive and integrated bio-economic model has been constructed for a
region within GBR using environmental software that linked available biophysical and economic modelling.

Keywords: decision support system, DSS, bio-economic optimisation framework, water quality.

R. Denzer et al. (Eds.): ISESS 2015, IFIP AICT 448, pp. 272–281, 2015.
© IFIP International Federation for Information Processing 2015

1   Introduction

The Burnett-Mary region in Queensland, Australia includes the southern-most portion of the World Heritage listed Great Barrier Reef (GBR) Marine Park and the Ramsar listed Great Sandy Strait. The region hosts biodiversity values that are globally important. The health of the coastal and inshore marine areas are influenced by the quality and quantity of runoff from five river basins. Increased loads of nitrogen, phosphorus, sediments and pesticides from adjacent catchments have led to chronic changes in environmental conditions for GBR species and ecosystems. To help protect the values of coastal and marine receiving waters, the Burnett Mary Regional Group (BMRG) with funding from the Australian Government commissioned the development of a Water Quality Improvement Plan (WQIP). The focus of the WQIP is to improve water quality through the implementation of agricultural management practices based on the 'ABCD' water quality risk framework for the sugarcane and grazing industries ([1], [2]). 'A' practice represents cutting edge unproven technologies, 'B' represents current best-management practices, 'C' is common current industry practice and 'D' is below industry practice expectations. A bio-economic model was developed to assist the Burnett Mary region transparently evaluate the feasibility and costs of various management options to achieve two sets of pollutant load reduction targets, namely Reef Plan Targets (RPTs), the currently formally agreed targets, and more ambitious Ecologically Relevant Targets (ERTs) which might be needed to better protect the values of the GBR. This paper describes the construct and underpinning data used to develop the bio-economic model that explicitly considers the feasibility and net profits/costs of achieving water quality objectives.

2   The Burnett Mary Region

The Burnett Mary region in Queensland, Australia covers 56,000 square kilometres (5.6 million ha) of land and encompasses five major river basins (Baffle, Burnett, Burrum, Kolan and Mary). The Baffle, Kolan and the Burnett catchments flow to the GBR Reef Marine Park whilst the Burrum and Mary flow to the Great Sandy Strait Marine Park. The major primary industries are grazing, sugarcane, horticulture, forestry and mining.

3   Methodology

The development of the Burnett Mary WQIP involved integrating the outputs from a number of separate supporting projects and biophysical modelling activities across various scales. The approach has built on the outcomes from previous WQIPs, findings of the Scientific Consensus Statement and priorities from Reef Plan 2013 ([4]; [10]; [14]; [15]) and new supporting studies. The key components of this approach have been:

- Use of assumptions and outputs from available science from paddock and catchment scale modelling conducted in Queensland;

- Coordination and engagement with technical experts and local stakeholders to integrate local knowledge and previous research;
- Financial economic analysis of practices for grazing and sugar cane industries;
- Development and application of a bio-economic modelling framework to assess costs in attaining targets.

3.1 Data Sources

Land use data was based on the 2009 land use map derived from the Queensland Land Use Mapping project (QLUMP, [8]). The QLUMP data was used to represent all land uses with the exception of sugar cane. For sugarcane areas, Australian Bureau of Statistics (ABS) data was utilized because the ABS data was widely accepted by stakeholders as better representing the current area of land under sugarcane. Soil data layers were provided by the Queensland Department of Natural Resources and Mines. Stream and gully mapping was provided by the Burnett Mary Regional Group whereas gully and streambank effectiveness assumptions were provided by [16].

3.2 Landscape Modelling Software

The Burnett-Mary bio-economic model utilised predictions of catchment streamflow, baseflow and loads (nutrient, sediment and pesticide) derived using Source Catchments [9] and management impacts estimated using paddock scale models. Baseline data was based on a combination of point scale modelling and calibrated catchment scale model outputs. The key components of the linked modelling approach are described below.

3.2.1 Catchment Model

The landscape model Source Catchments was used to estimate constituent generation loads and attenuation coefficients for each of the 597 sub-catchment within the Burnett-Mary region. Each sub-catchment was defined based on topography, river basins, land use and the location of existing water quality and flow monitoring stations. Source Catchments modelling from the Paddock to Reef program provides a prediction of end of catchment loads for key pollutants of interest (nitrogen, phosphorus, sediment and pesticides). The variables modelled include: Total Suspended Solids (TSS), Dissolved Inorganic Nitrogen (DIN), PSII Herbicides (PSII), Particulate Nitrogen (PN), Particulate Phosphorus (PP), Dissolved Inorganic Phosphorus (DIP). The 2008-09 baseline results from the Source Catchments modelling were analysed to provide a summary of the relative contribution from the five river basins as a proportion of total load and anthropogenic load [18].

3.2.2 Paddock-Scale Model

Farming system models were used to inform sediment and nutrient loads in Source Catchments and to estimate the constituent load reductions associated with various management practices. The APSIM [12] and Howleaky [11] models were used to simulate sugar cane systems, whereas GRASP was used to model grazing systems.

Output from the farming system models were used to assign constitutive load reductions for each practice class by soil type by management combination representing the various abatement options.

3.3   Farm Level Financial Cane and Grazing Economics

Achievement of meaningful water quality targets require practice changes in agriculture. Although infrastructure and all agricultural industries contribute to constituent loads, this study was confined to the sugar cane and grazing industries because of their importance in contributing to water quality issues and the fact that estimates of the contributions of impacts from practice changes could be quantified from modelling assumptions. Financial economic analysis was undertaken for both these industries as part of the WQIP.

The farm level financial economic analysis for sugar cane was conducted for three representative farm sizes (small 75 ha, medium 125 ha, large 250 ha) and two soil types (well drained and less well drained). The analysis included consideration of non-profit related barriers and transaction costs [17].

Similarly the financial economic analysis for grazing in the Burnett Mary region was conducted for three representative farm sizes (small 288 ha, medium 880 ha, large 4134 ha) and across three land productivity class (high, medium and low; [19]). Both profit and non-profit related financial barriers were also taken into account in the analysis, as outlined in [13].

3.4   Optimisation Model

The bioeconomic model components were solved using nonlinear programming with the CONOPT solver in the General Algebraic Modelling System (GAMS) [5]. The model seeks to maximise total net benefits for grazing and sugar cane enterprises as required to meet specified water quality targets at both the regional scale as well as by individual basin. The cost-effectiveness approach adopted in this study, where emissions goals are sought at least cost, is common ([3]; [6]; [7]) because it avoids the difficulty and cost of assessing the benefits associated with improved water quality.

There are a sub-catchments in each catchment labeled sc = [1,2..,a]. The total land area is allocated to b land use combinations labeled lu=[1,2,...,b]. These land use combinations contain permutations of sugarcane and grazing BMP options totaling 36 sugarcane management options (18 on good soil and 18 on poor soil) and 90 grazing management permutations (30 options on each of the high, medium and low productivity classes).   Three decision variables describe the management options.   First, the area allocated to each land use in each sub-catchment denoted by $A_{sc,lu}$. Second, the intensity with which gully erosion is managed in each sub-catchment denoted by G_{sc}. Third, the intensity with which streambank erosion is managed in each sub-catchment denoted by S_{sc}. The intensity of gully, streambank and permanent waterway management is the percentage of the gully system or associated length that is fenced and revegetated. Subscripts eg refers to the length of gullies and es the length of streambanks. Total profit in each catchment is computed:

π^n = landuse profit x landuse area – cost gully management – cost streambank management

$$= \sum_{sc^n=1}^{a^n} \sum_{lu^n=1}^{b^n} \pi^n{}_{sc^n,lu^n} A^n{}_{sc^n,lu^n} - \sum_{sc^n=1}^{a^n} \sum_{eg^n=1}^{d^n} cg^n{}_{sc^n,eg^n} G^n{}_{sc^n,eg^n} - \sum_{sc^n=1}^{a^n} \sum_{es^n=1}^{f^n} cs^n{}_{sc^n,es^n} S^n{}_{sc^n,es^n} \quad (1)$$

Contaminant loads (TC) are calculated as follows where C refers to either DIN, DON, Particulate N, TN, FRP, DOP, Particulate P, TP, TSS and pesticides (hexazinone, ametryn, atrazine, diuron and tebuthiuron); PP and Gload, Sload refers to exports from gully and streambank respectively:

$$TC^n = \sum_{sc^n=1}^{a^n} \sum_{lu^n=1}^{b^n} C^n{}_{sc^n,lu^n} A^n{}_{sc^n,lu^n} + \sum_{sc^n=1}^{a^n} C^n{}_{GLoad} G^n{}_{sc} + \sum_{sc^n=1}^{a^n} C^n{}_{SLoad} S^n{}_{sc} \quad (2)$$

The optimisation model seeks to maximize profit in each sub-catchment (grazing and sugar cane enterprises only) subject to target emission constraints. The model considered only transition states under the assumption that initial land use areas currently in A and B class practices would not be allowed to be reduced. As such, transitions can only move to an improved state (Figure 1). No land use change (land retirement) was also permitted – solutions could only be derived from practice change. Constraints including (1) farm distributions, (2) soil type, (3) productivity classes, (4) land practice class (A, B, C and D) and (5) land use transitions. Stream bank and gully remediation was also considered with associated opportunity costs.

3.5   Software Environment

Source catchment prediction data sets were provided in an Access database. Key data was then exported from the database and manipulated using a Fortran program into a format consistent with the GAM model input data construct. The output results from the GAMS model was post-processed using software developed in Fortran. Outputs included summary text files and raster based gridded data for importing into GIS. Model sensitivity analysis was undertaken using a Fortran wrapper program that systematically modified GAMS input data, initiated the GAMS solver and collated simulation results.

The uniqueness of the developed models is the capacity to

- Consider individual or combinations of constituent abatement targets;
- Consider meeting abatement targets at both the basin or regional scale;
- Evaluate the impact of different levels of funding;
- Estimate the area under A, B, C and D practice and the area transitioned into each of these conditions required to meet abatement targets;
- Estimate the length of streambank and gully remediation.

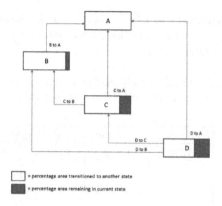

Fig. 1. Schematic of the optimisation model constituent pools

4   Application

Numerous targets were evaluated and reported to local stakeholders initially. Two sets of targets were selected as a focus for the WQIP, the Reef Plan Targets (RPTs) and Ecologically Relevant Targets (ERTs). Each target was evaluated at both the regional and individual basin scale and costs to achieve targets were assumed t be over a 20 year period

The RPTs were a 20% overall reduction in anthropogenic suspended sediment load; a 20% (based on RPT 2013 target) and 50% (based on RPT 2009) reduction in anthropogenic loads of particulate nitrogen (PN) and particulate phosphorus (PP); 50% (based on Reef Plan 2013) reduction in anthropogenic loads of dissolved inorganic nitrogen (DIN); 50% (based on 'interpreted' Reef Plan 2009) reduction in anthropogenic loads of dissolved inorganic phosphorus (DIP) and 50% (Reef Plan 2009) and 60% (Reef Plan 2013) reductions of loads of PSII herbicides (i.e. the 2009 target and the 2013 target respectively).

The ERTs considered in this study are (based on reductions in anthropogenic load from the 2008-09 baseline): 20% overall reduction in suspended sediment load; a 50% reduction in particulate nitrogen (PN) and particulate phosphorus (PP); 80% reduction in dissolved inorganic nitrogen (DIN); 50% reduction in anthropogenic loads of dissolved inorganic phosphorus (DIP) and 60% reduction of loads of PSII herbicides. It should be noted that a 50% reduction in DIP proved to be infeasible and this constituent was limited to a 20% reduction in the tested scenarios.

5   Results

5.1   Costs and Land Use Implications of Achieving Targets

The annual cost of attaining scenario targets for each river basin are summarised in Table 1, with the associated spatial distribution shown in Figure 2. Figure 3 show the spatial patterning of reductions in DIP to meet scenario targets, whereas Figure 4 show the contrasting sediment reduction achievable under limited funding of $2M/year and $8M/year respectively.

Table 1. Net profit or cost associated with meeting targets in the Burnett Mary region in individual basins or whole of regional scale. Red text indicates a net cost and black text indicates a net profit.

Scenario	Annual Cost/Profit ($M/year)				
	Baffle	Kolan	Burnett	Burrum	Mary
1. Meet RPTs by individual basins	-1.4	0.6	-4.8	0.5	-2.8
2. Whole catchment RPTs	-3.0				
3. Meet all ERTs by individual basins	-4.3	0.2	-7.8	0.2	infeasible
4. Whole catchment ERTs	-16.4				

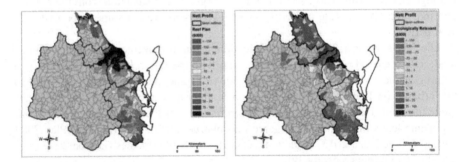

Fig. 2. Net profit associated with the RPTs (left) and the ERTs (right)

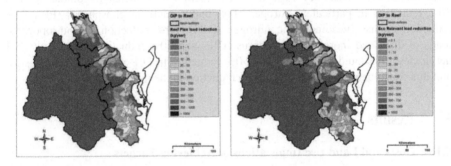

Fig. 3. Reduction in DIP associated with the RPTs (left) and the ERTs (right)

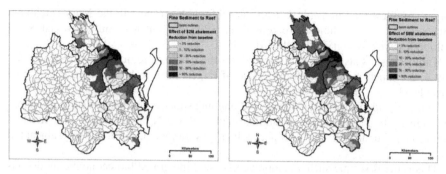

Fig. 4. Reduction in TSS for associated with a $2M (left) and $8M (right) funding program

5.2 Land Use Management Changes

The bioeconomic model predicts that for both RPTs and ERTs in cane all land is required to move to at least B practice to meet whole of basin targets. For RPTs 81% of cane is required in B practice and 19% in A practice. For the ERTs the majority of land (over 46,000 ha or 81% cane) is predicted to be required to be in A practice. The transition in grazing land management is even more challenging, with an additional 131,349 ha required in A practice for RPTs and 243,815 ha to achieve ERTs. For RPTs 19% of grazing is required in A practice, 51% in B practice, 22% in C practice and 7% in D practice. In contrast for ERTs, 22% of grazing is required in A practice, 49% in B practice, 21% in C practice and 7% in D practice.

In the context of available funds (Figure 4), the proportional cane area in practices A, B and C are predicted to be 6%, 92% and 2% for $2M and 14%, 84% and 2% for $8M respectively. A similar transition is predicted for the proportion of grazing areas in practices A, B, C and D which are predicted to be 19%, 52%, 22% and 7% for $2M and 22%, 51%, 21% and 6% for $8M respectively.

6 Discussion and Conclusion

The results for Scenario 1 (meeting the RPTs in each basin, see Table 1) indicate that targets are predicted to be achieved at a modest net profit in the Kolan and Burrum basins. This occurs because of their lesser size compared with the Burnett and Mary and the increased area of sugarcane as a proportion of land use. Net costs are predicted in the Baffle, Burnett and Mary basins because the predictions require practice changes in grazing to achieve the targets, which always incurs a net loss.

If RPTs only have to be met on a whole of region basis, then huge savings can be made (see Scenario 2 Table 1 compared to Scenario 1). The net cost is estimated to be approximately $3.0 million/year compared with a net loss of approximately $7.9 million/year from Scenario 1.

The difference between the RPTs and the ERTs are in the ambitiousness of the PN and PP targets – only 20% needs to be met under RPTs compared with 50% for ERTs. Meeting ERTs poses significant feasibility issues because particulate losses come mostly from grazing land uses, streambank and gully erosion, all of which incur large losses. As illustrated in Table 1, ERTs are infeasible to meet in the Mary catchment (Scenario 3). At a whole of region scale, ERTs pose at least an additional $13.4 million loss/year on agriculture than for RPTs.

Table 1 results also further illustrates that the whole of region targets (Scenarios 2 and 4) are much more cost effective than if targets have to be met on an individual basin level.

This study identified that (1) large and ongoing support will be needed for the grazing industry to achieve sediment and particulate P and N targets and (2) the most limiting constituent was DIP. Importantly ERTs cannot be met without substantial costs.

This is the first time such a comprehensive and integrated bio-economic model has been constructed for the study region using environmental software that links available biophysical and economic modelling. The developed framework has a demonstrated capacity to test the effectiveness of alternative land management options, the optimal likely impact from available funding (Figure 4) and the environmental impacts of traditional incentive schemes (such as water way and gully remediation).

Importantly this study has informed the development of the Burnett Mary WQIP. Integration of available science and local knowledge through development of a bio-economic model shows how net profits/costs of reaching relevant targets n can inform a more realistic implementation plan than previously possible . This is the first time such a comprehensive and integrated bio-economic model has been constructed for a region within GBR using environmental software that linked available biophysical and economic modelling.

Acknowledgements. The authors acknowledge the contributions from Dr Jon Brodie for defining the Ecological Reef Targets, Dr Mark Silburn for paddock scale effectiveness estimates and Dr Robert Ellis and Dr Banti Fentie for the provision of Source Catchments and farm scale modelling results without which the bio-economic model could not have been developed.

References

1. Anonymous. Paddock to Reef Water Quality Risk Assessment Framework for Sugar Cane. Draft November 2013 (2013a)
2. Anonymous. Reef Plan Water Quality Risk Framework for Grazing. Draft October 2013 (2013b)
3. Beverly, C., Roberts, A., Stott, K., Vigiak, O., Doole, G.: Optimising economic and environmental outcomes: water quality challenges in Corner Inlet Victoria. In: Proceedings of MODSIM 2013, Adelaide (2013), http://www.mssanz.org.au/modsim2013
4. Brodie, J., Waterhouse, J., Schaffelke, B., Kroon, F., Thorburn, P., Rolfe, J., McKenzie, L.: 2013 Scientific Consensus Statement Land use impacts on Great Barrier Reef water quality and ecosystem condition (2013)
5. Brooke, A., Kendrick, D., Meeraus, A., Raman, R.: GAMS—A user's Guide.GAMS Development Corporation, Washington, DC (2008)
6. Doole, G.J.: Cost-effective policies for improving water quality by reducing nitrate emissions from diverse dairy farms: An abatement–cost perspective. Agricultural Water Management 104, 10–20 (2012)

7. Doole, G.J., Pannell, D.J.: Empirical evaluation of nonpoint pollution policies under agent heterogeneity: regulating intensive dairy production in the Waikato region of New Zealand. Australian Journal of Agricultural and Resource Economics 56, 82–101 (2012)
8. DSITIA, Land use summary 1999-2009: Burnett Mary NRM Region, Queensland Department of Science, Information Technology, Innovation and the Arts, Brisbane (2012)
9. eWater Cooperative Research Centre. Source Catchments User Guide, eWater Cooperative Research Centre, Canberra (2010), ISBN 978-1-921543-29-6
10. Kroon, F., Turner, R., Smith, R., Warne, M., Hunter, H., Bartley, R., Carroll, C.: 2013 Scientific Consensus Statement. In: Sources of sediment, nutrient, pesticides and other pollutants in the Great Barrier Reef, ch. 4 (2013)
11. McClymont, D., Freebairn, D.: Howleaky? Exploring water balance and water quality implications of alternative land uses. A computer program. © Dept Natural Resources and Mines, Queensland, Australia (2007)
12. McCown, R.L., Hammer, G.L., Hargreaves, J.N.G., Holzworth, D., Huth, N.I.: APSIM - An agricultural production system simulation model for operational research. Mathematics and Computers in Simulation 39, 225–231 (1995)
13. Pannell, D., Roberts, A., Park, G.: Economic analysis of grazing systems for water quality improvement in the Burnett Mary catchment. Report to the Burnett-Mary Regional Group (Natural Decisions Pty. Ltd, February 2014) (2014)
14. Schaffelke, B., Anthony, K., Blake, J., Brodie, J., Collier, C., Devline, M., Warne, M.: 2013 Scientific Consensus Statement. In: Marine and coastal ecosystem impacts, ch. 1, p. 50 (2013)
15. Secretariat Reef Water Quality Plan Protection. Reef Water Quality Protection Plan (2013)
16. Thorburn, P., Wilkinson, S.: Conceptual frameworks for estimating the water quality benefits of improved agricultural management practices in large catchments 180. Agriculture Ecosystems and Environment, 192–209 (2013)
17. Van Grieken, M.E., Pannell, D., Roberts, A.: Economic Analysis of Farming Systems for Water Quality Improvement in the Burnett Mary Catchment. A report prepared for the Burnett Mary Regional Group in cooperation with Natural Decisions. CSIRO Water for a Healthy Country Flagship. Brisbane (January 2014)
18. Waterhouse, J., Maynard, J., Brodie, J., Lewis, S., Petus, C., da silva, E., Mellors, J.: Assessment of the relative risk of degraded water quality to ecosystems of the Burnett Mary Region, Great Barrier Reef DRAFT REPORT A Report for Burnett Mary Regional Group (2014)
19. Whish, G.: GRASP modelling of grazing systems in Great Barrier Reef catchments. Technical Report to Paddock to Reef Integrated Monitoring, Modelling and reporting program funded through the Australian Government's Caring for Our Country Reef Rescue. Department of Agriculture, Fisheries and Forestry, Queensland, Australia (2012)

Integrating Hydrodynamic and Hydraulic Modeling for Evaluating Future Flood Mitigation in Urban Environments

Mahesh Prakash[1,*], James Hilton[1], and Lalitha Ramachandran[2]

[1] CSIRO Digital Productivity Flagship, Melbourne, Australia
[2] The City of Port Phillip, VIC, Australia
Mahesh.Prakash@csiro.au

Abstract. We present an integrated flood modelling tool that is able to evaluate different mitigation solutions for areas that are prone to floods from storm surge and heavy rainfall. Our model integrates catchment and coastal flood modelling (spatio-temporally dynamic), including sea level rise, to provide a holistic inundation model for future flooding. Additionally, the model aims to enable simulation of a combination of flood mitigation and adaptation options. To date, the practice has been to model either drainage augmentation solutions alone, or (for coastal inundation) single coastal adaptation solutions. This tool aims to deliver the capacity to model a range of both coastal and drainage adaptation solutions to understand what combination of solutions might be effective. The model is demonstrated for example cases in the City of Port Phillip, Melbourne. Three mitigation strategies involving the use of a hypothetical off-shore reef and the combination of a single valve systems and retention/detention measures are evaluated for the region around Elwood canal for current and future scenarios.

Keywords: modular mitigation analysis, drainage augmentation, local councils, evidence based cost-benefit analysis, land-use planning.

1 Introduction

Australia has a very long coastline stretching almost 36,000 km in the mainland. A significant percentage of the population resides along this coastline especially along the eastern seaboard. Among these urban environments there are several locations that are low lying and are prone to flooding including storm surge, heavy rainfall and catchment. The Elwood Canal region in the City of Port Phillip (CoPP) in Melbourne, Victoria is particularly at risk of flooding which has been indicated through flood mapping studies carried out internally by engineers in the council as well as through AECOM [1]. However the coastal flood inundation studies have been carried out using essentially static bath tub type models which do not provide details of flooding such as duration and areas that are prone to water logging (lack of sufficient drainage). This can be particularly important to decide future infrastructure needs including the effect of sea level rise (SLR). Additionally mitigation and adaptation

---

* Corresponding author.

R. Denzer et al. (Eds.): ISESS 2015, IFIP AICT 448, pp. 282–292, 2015.

options have not been investigated using a simulation and modelling approach in the past following on from a flood modelling exercise. An integrated flood modelling tool that is able to evaluate different mitigation solutions has therefore been developed by CSIRO for the CoPP so that the council:

1. Continues to have new (as becomes available) catchment and coastal data modelled into an integrated hydrodynamic model in order to understand what climate risks might present design and maintenance challenges to a range of municipal assets and land use planning processes. Specifically, we want to have a clear perspective on the future behaviour (shape, extent and duration) of flooding, and what changes how and when.
2. Is able to model a range of adaptation solutions and land use planning changes to test their effectiveness in mitigating flooding, in order to understand what future infrastructure and land-use needs might be.

These then give councils a basis for understanding where and when critical infrastructure and land-use changes may need to be made, as well as the required investment plan for new adaptive infrastructure. The tool is currently being investigated by the Association of Bayside Municipalities (ABM), Victoria for Port Phillip bay-wide deployment.

2   Key Components of the Tool

The mitigation modeling tool being developed consists of the following key components:

1. **Hydrodynamic Module** - A 2D shallow water based model will be used to simulate the flow hydrodynamics for the scenarios. The solver is able to concurrently simulate flood inundation due to sea level rise, storm surge, tides and rainfall allowing scenarios with multiple flood interactions possible. This is especially important for coastal councils where there is a significant likelihood of combined coastal and catchment flooding.
2. **Topography Clean-Up Module (Terrain/Bathymetry)** - The solver is integrated with a LiDAR pre-processing capability that allows input of raw/processed LiDAR data at varying resolutions to be used as input into the hydrodynamic model. The model allows specification of variable drag maps resulting from regions with varying vegetation composition and other resistance (infrastructure) overlays.
3. **Hydraulic Module** - Drainage is handled either as an infiltration sink or by using an explicit 1D network model connection into the 2D solver for complex urban drainage infrastructure.
4. **Mitigation Module** - Mitigation solutions are integrated into the hydrodynamic/hydraulic model either as modules (eg: drainage augmentation, retention/detention systems) or as structures that can be designed in AutoCAD or similar and imported into the model.
5. **Analysis and Visualisation Module** - An integrated visualisation tool allows the results of the hydrodynamic solver to be produced in a visual 3D Google Earth-like environment. The flood inundation can be visualised as depth/velocity/force maps to provide a before and after quantitative assessment of the assessed mitigation scenario(s).

A detailed description of the computational models and the mitigation models is provided in the sections below.

3   Computational Models

The tidal and pluvial hydrodynamics were modelled using a shallow water model developed by CSIRO. The method has been specially adapted for modelling wide-spread areas of urban inundation. The model is well suited to both heavy rainfall events and tidal inundation. Recent applications include the impact of heavy rainfall events leading to the flash floods in Toowoomba in 2012 and the effects of possible SLR in the Kakadu region. The shallow water equations represent the depth averaged height and unit discharge of water above a fixed datum. The equations are discretised onto a fixed grid representing the land surface and computationally processed to pre-dict the water dynamics. The underlying method is based on the finite-volume methods presented by Kurganov and Petrova [2]. The method requires a combined topological and bathymetric height map above a given vertical datum as well as an initial distribution of water. In addition the method allows the input of a given boun-dary condition, which may represent a storm surge or tsunami, as well as a spatially distributed source map, which may represent a rainfall or other water source. The effect of base friction is imposed using a Manning drag model.

The underground drains were incorporated into the hydrodynamic model using a 1D pipe network model (see Fig. 1). The solution to the 1D pipe network is derived as a steady state output at every hydrodynamic model time step. This integrated solution provides an accurate estimate of the dynamic flooding across a large urban region. The models have been extensively tested and validated against benchmark test cases presented by Neelz and Pender [3].

Fig. 1. Flow in drainage network for the City of Port Phillip 3 hours after a 1 in a 10 year ARI rainfall

4   Mitigation Models

A highlight of the software tool is the ability to incorporate different types of mitigation options as applications which then can be deployed to specific parts of the region
of interest. The mitigation models can be classified into three broad categories:

- Drainage augmentation: These can be either a simple measure such as increasing
  the size of the drainage pipe, deploying back valves into existing drainage pipes or
  enhancing drainage capacity by incorporating pumps at specified locations in the
  urban drainage system.
- Retention/detention systems: Retention/detention systems are typically useful for
  low to medium level flooding where a water storage system is also utilized for managed release of water to provide for additional capacity during a predicted flood
  event (such as a flash flood). Retention/detention systems can either be at a household level (tanks), street level (underground large storage tanks) and/or large
  parks/open spaces used as dug-out storage/release facilities.
- Sea walls/off-shore reefs/protective barriers: These are large engineering or natural
  (such as mangroves) protective barriers that are specifically designed to protect a
  region in a council for its economic, heritage and/or environmental value typically
  against storm surge or similar events.

The software tool is able to incorporate all three forms of mitigation models. The
drainage augmentation and retention/detention systems are built in the tool in such a
way that they can be modularly incorporated into any mitigation analysis either by a
point and click mechanism or by assigning the mitigation model(s) to a particular
chosen location in the council. The protective barriers are incorporated typically via
an AutoCAD or similarly designed input. This is because protective barriers are specifically designed for a region of interest and cannot be modularized.

5   Data Inputs

The data requirements for the tool are summarized below:

- Terrestrial and bathymetric LiDAR data
- Land-use classification data to derive a variable drag map for the region of interest
- Historical storm surge data
- Tidal data
- Sea level rise scenario(s)
- Rainfall data
- Drainage network information   (ArcGIS compatible)
- Mitigation solutions
  - Modular (retention/detention, back valves, pumps)
  - Designed (AutoCAD or similar for custom sea walls and protective barriers and
    off shore reefs)
- Historic flood data for validation
- Previously performed flood study information for calibration

6   Modelling Process Flow Chart

The mitigation modeling process involves several components that have a specific purpose, these are described below, Fig. 2 provides a graphical flowchart summary describing the steps involved in the integrated mitigation modeling process:

1. Adoption of existing flood study data as input into an integrated flood mitigation model.

   Purpose: Effective use of existing data and to reduce rework. Existing data will also be used for validation purposes.

2. Statistical extreme event analysis

   Purpose: To understand and estimate the occurrence likelihood of extreme events such as storm surges and rainfalls for current day and for the future. This is important since there could be large variations in climatic conditions in a study region of interest. Rigorous statistical analysis provides a better basis for estimating flood frequency and amplitude. Using this approach will provide an envelope that can then be used as input into a hydrodynamic/hydraulic model for scenario simulations.

3. Statistical joint probability analysis

   Purpose: To understand and estimate the occurrence likelihood of joint flood events such as coastal and catchment flooding for current day and for the future. Very few of the previous flood studies investigated the joint likelihood of flooding. Joint probability analysis is an emerging and robust approach for a holistic analysis of encompassing all possible avenues for flooding.

4. Integration of hydrodynamic modelling with a comprehensive drainage network (hydraulic) model

   Purpose: To accurately predict flooding in an urban environment. A key outcome from the case study (described below) conducted for the City of Port Phillip study (2014) was that drainage networks contribute to flood inundation especially when there is a storm surge event and/or sea level rise due to the drainage pipes working as a reverse carrier of water from the sea further inland. This will be especially important for low-lying inland locations.

5. Incorporation of outputs from the statistical modelling into the hydrodynamic/hydraulic model.

   Purpose: For simulation scenario analysis that uses an occurrence likelihood approach including joint (coastal and catchment) flood events. This provides a robust statistically based envelope for flood inundation predictions that is relevant for coastal councils.

6. Analysis of future flooding to investigate the effect of sea level rise.

   Purpose: This is important since any future infrastructure (overland or underground) will need to be justified from a cost/benefit perspective.

7. Integration of suggested mitigation and adaptation strategies.

Purpose: This relates to quantitatively assessing the effect of suggested mitigation and adaptation strategies for specific "hot spot" locations. This approach provides a quantitative method of assessing the effectiveness of flood mitigation and adaptation strategies especially for future flooding.

8. Provide further guidance on flood mitigation following on from the integrated analysis in step 7 above.

Purpose: This is a feedback loop that allows the planners/engineers to test various suggested strategies and potentially enhance their effectiveness.

The modelling components are linked and packaged (see Fig. 3) utilizing the CSIRO Workspace: A scientific workflow platform [4]. Workspace has the following advantages that are advantageous for the development of the mitigation modelling tool including:

1. Ability to modularly include different mitigation options
2. Ability to seamlessly connect computational models such as the 2D hydrodynamic model with the 1D network model for drainage
3. In-built capability to manage distributed computing such that a set of simulation scenarios can be assigned to different GPUs/CPUs and results drawn back into a unified analysis/visualization environment
4. In-built visualization facility

7   Case Studies

7.1   Simulation Scenarios

Table 1 summarises the simulation scenarios investigated for the integrated flood impact study. These scenarios were derived following on from a preliminary joint probability analysis as described in section 6 above. A maximum storm surge height of 1.3 m was chosen on the basis of the gauge measurements at St Kilda marina by Melbourne Water [5]. It is acknowledged that the maximum storm surge height recorded in St Kilda marina is higher than the one recorded at Williamstown (1.15 m) in the work of McInnes et al. [6]. The higher value is used for the purposes of evaluating a severe but very likely future scenario. The rainfall input condition was finalised following on from discussions with Melbourne Water for a typical storm event in CoPP. The same scenarios were repeated for evaluating the effect of mitigation described in section 4.

Table 1. Simulation scenarios

No	Max. Stm ht. (m)	Rain (ARI)	Rain (hrs)	SLR (m)	Max ht (AHD)
1	1.30	100	3	0.0	1.30
2	1.30	100	3	0.4	1.70
3	1.30	100	3	0.8	2.10
4	1.30	100	3	1.1	2.40

7.2   Designed Mitigation – Off-Shore Reef

The first case study is used to demonstrate the application of the tool to evaluate the effectiveness of a hypothetical off-shore reef designed to attenuate the effect of a storm surge wave impacting the Elwood region in the City of Port Phillip. The off-shore reef was introduced into the model by importing a design concept proposed by Prof. Rob Roggema (Urban Design, Swinburne University, Melbourne). The off-shore reef is 3 m tall, 150-200 m in width and approximately 2 km offshore. Fig. 4 shows the case without the seawall (left) and with the seawall (right), where the initial water level is shown in blue to highlight the difference between the maps. Fig. 5 shows the change in maximum flood extent without and with the off-shore reef for a high storm surge for current day conditions.

7.3   Modular Mitigation – Back Calves and Retention/Detention

In the second example two mitigation models (as shown in Fig. 6) have been investigated namely:

1. Non return valves included along the stretch of Elwood canal and main drains at St Kilda and end of Langridge Street and
2. Retention detention consisting of water tanks installed on all lots in the Elwood region, along roads identified as being prone to flooding and a cricket oval in north-west of Elsternwick Park.

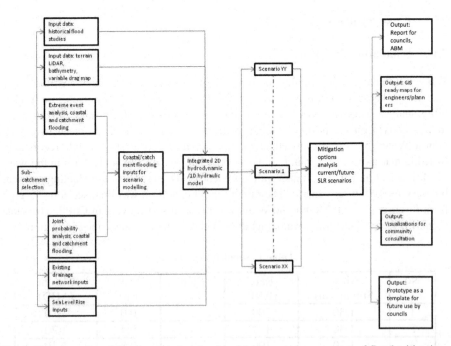

Fig. 2. Flowchart describing the steps involved in the integrated assessment of flood mitigation and adaptation strategies

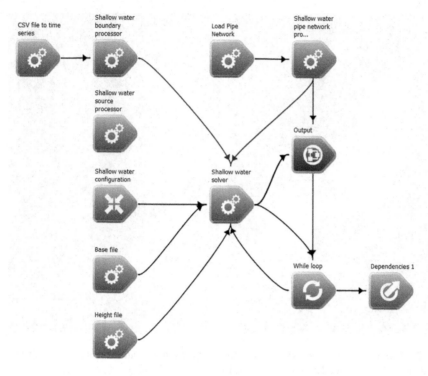

Fig. 3. Modelling components for the integrated mitigation modeling tool packaged using CSIRO Workspace: A scientific workflow platform

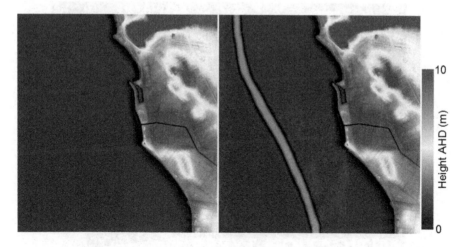

Fig. 4. The original topography and bathymetry (left) and modified with the addition of a 3 m off-shore reef (right). Initial water level shown in blue.

Fig. 5. Maximum flood extent with water coloured by depth without (left) and with (right) the off-shore reef for current day storm surge conditions

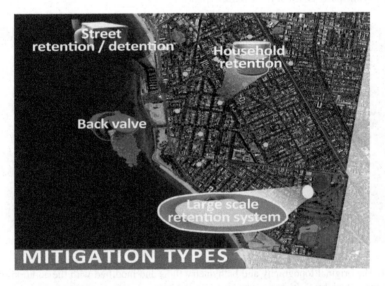

Fig. 6. Modular mitigation types and location around Elwood Canal

The flood extent averaged over time for a 0.4 m sea level rise (SLR) scenario with and without mitigation is compared in Figure 7. This demonstrates that the mitigation options selected is able to reduce the flooding to essentially nuisance levels (retention times of only around 2 hrs with flood height of 0.5 m or lower) in most regions around Elwood canal at a 0.4 m SLR.

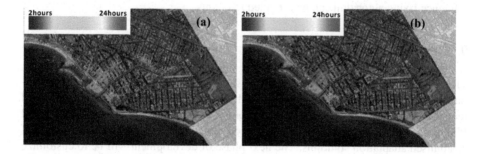

Fig. 7. Flood extent at 0.4 m SLR (a) no mitigation (b) with mitigation. Water is coloured by retention time with blue indicating 2 hrs and red 24 hrs.

8   Advantages and Limitations

a. Data inputs and methodology will necessarily change over time due to the nature of input data including LiDAR and climatic inputs. This model enables the capacity to feed in more updated datasets and methodology as they become available – this in turn provides a smarter and more cost-effective way to develop integrated flood simulations and test solutions.   At present, no tool/model does this easily.

b. Usefulness of an integrated future flood modelling tool to land use and infrastructure managers – the capacity to gain a clear perspective about future integrated (coastal and catchment) flood behaviour provides enormous potential to understand the actual extent and risks associated with inundation over time. Current practice continues to model coastal and catchment flooding separately and creates a disjoint in providing this necessary perspective.

c. The capacity to simulate a range of coastal and drainage adaptation solutions into an integrated future flood model enables a range of testing and analysis of adaptation and drainage augmentation to measure what combination of solutions works, for what types of flooding, and for how long. This type of assessment capacity also provides a sound evidence base for consequent infrastructure design and an evidence-based cost benefit analyses of local and regional solutions.

d. Such a model also enables the capacity to assess and determine areas that will not be able to provide effective adaptation solutions – this then enables an evidence-base for the consideration of different land uses or drastic changes to current land use.

e. The tool currently does not have the capacity to process point cloud LiDAR data and requires a "clean and processed" LiDAR input. CSIRO is aware of this limitation and work is underway to address this issue.

d. Visualisation of the results currently requires the LiDAR obtained terrain/bathymetry to match up with textural information. This is always not straightforward due to the inherent inconsistency associated with frames of reference for these layers. This issue is being investigated so that a Workspace based frame reference fixing algorithm can be provided to clients.

9   Conclusions

The flood modelling tool is an integrated system for stakeholders to investigate potential mitigation options in response to flood scenarios. The tool provides end-to-end modelling, analysis and visualization capability, as demonstrated by the City of Port Phillip case study. The model has also been developed to test the effectiveness of customised adaptation solutions. The next phase of development will be to customize the tool for use by land-use and infrastructure managers, especially in Local Government through a Port Phillip bay-wide approach.

Acknowledgements. The authors would like to acknowledge financial support provided by the City of Port Phillip and the CSIRO Digital Productivity and Services Flagship for conducting research towards developing the integrated flood mitigation analysis tool. The authors would also like to acknowledge the in-kind expertise and review provided by a range of key stakeholders including Melbourne Water, the Association of Bayside Municipalities, AECOM, and SGS Consulting to consider data and methodological inputs and likely adaptation solutions to be tested. Finally the authors would like to thank Fletcher Woolard from CSIRO for assistance in producing the visualisations related to this project.

References

1. AECOM, City of Port Phillip – Case Study for the Elwood Canal, Port Phillip Bay Coastal Adaptation Pathways Project (September 19, 2012).
2. Kurganov, A., Petrova, G.: A Second-Order Well-Balanced Positivity Preserving Central-Upwind Scheme for the Saint-Venant System, Commn. Math. Sci. 5, 133–160 (2007)
3. Neelz, S., Pender, G.: Benchmarking the latest generation of 2D hydraulic modeling packages, Report SC12000, Environmental Agency UK
4. Workspace, A.: scientific workflow platform, http://dx.doi.org/10.4225/08/544E4FF7B67B0 (accessed November 6, 2014)
5. Hoang, T.: Frequency analysis of tide levels for St Kilda marina (Site No: 229670) (Melbourne Water, 2011)
6. McInnes, K.L., O'Grady, J., Macadam, I.: The effect of climate change on extreme sea levels in Port Phillip Bay, Dept. of Sustainability and Environment, VIC report (2009)

Modelling of Air Flow Analysis for Residential Homes Using Particle Image Velocimetry

Rajiv Pratap[1], Ramesh Rayudu[1], and Manfred Plagmann[2]

[1] School of Engineering and Computer Science
[2] BRANZ
Wellington, New Zealand
Ramesh.Rayudu@vuw.ac.nz

Abstract. The purpose of this paper is to simulate the designed physical Particle Image Velocimetry (PIV) system, as a simulation platform to physically build and implement a system for residential building and housing research. The focus is on the angle filter; the filter used to process the images of a laser progressively scanning through a space by adjusting its angle.

An indicator of heat escape and ventilation in buildings is the airflow itself. Conventional airflow measurement techniques are typically intrusive, interfering with the data or the environment. For small flows such as that in residential housing, the error introduced can sometimes be large relative to the measured data. In contrast, PIV is a relatively a non-intrusive measurement tool that measures flows. However, there are a few problems with standard PIV techniques, for implementation in an attic space.

The proposed solution is to use dust particles, already present in the air, as tracers for the PIV system. In conclusion, our PIV system with a non-diverging laser beam produces a velocity field of similar quality to a velocity field of a standard PIV system.

Keywords: Particle Image Velocimetry, PIV, air flow measurement, building ventilation analysis, Angle filtering.

1 Introduction

NZ homes are well known to be cold, damp and poorly ventilated. There have been several papers reporting on the quality of these conditions [1,2], as well as how to mitigate these problems. In some cases it can be relatively easy to identify causes and find solutions to them, such as by adding insulation [3]. Other times it can be more difficult, such as finding gaps where heat is escaping, or identifying poor ventilation. These problems require less conventional methods to solve.

One indicator of both heat escape and ventilation is the airflow itself. Conventional airflow measurement techniques are typically intrusive, interfering with the data or the environment. For small flows such as that in housing, the error introduced can sometimes be large relative to the data measured. In contrast, Particle Image Velocimetry (PIV) is a relatively non-intrusive measurement tool that measures such flow.

R. Denzer et al. (Eds.): ISESS 2015, IFIP AICT 448, pp. 293–302, 2015.

PIV systems have been researched and implemented for decades, especially useful in wind tunnel experiments and other complex flow scenarios [4]. The typical setup for a PIV system uses a camera, tracer particles, a laser to illuminate the tracers and a data processing unit, typically a computer, to compute a vector field of the space [6]. The use of tracer particles in combination with a laser, through a diverging lens, gives a clear representation of the flow through a space, providing high contrast to the background which makes it easier to visualise and process the space.

There are a few problems with this standard setup, for implementation in an attic space. Firstly, the use of tracer particles involves adding potential pollutants to the housing space. These could get stuck in cracks and other gaps where air escapes, disrupting or changing the airflow, which would defeat the purpose of such a system. Another problem is that the reflected light intensity of particles decreases dependant on distance from the lens. This is because the mirror modifies the laser's beam to be diverging, and so the beam's power density decreases as a result of distance. When the incoming light intensity decreases, so does the reflected intensity of the particles. This limits the dimensions which the system can be used, and to compensate for it the laser's power may need to be adjusted for various scenarios.

The proposed solution uses dust particles, already present in the air, as tracers for the PIV system. Research has previously been done in use of small particle tracers for PIV [5], outlining specifications for suitable tracer particles. The scattering intensity of dust particles prevents its use as a tracer particle in standard PIV systems. However, through experimental observation it was found that the space containing dust particles could be illuminated using a non-diverging, high power laser beam. The level of illumination produced was comparable to the images used in existing PIV systems, suggesting this modified system could perform equivalently.

The purpose of this paper is to simulate the modified PIV system, as a confirmation to build and apply the system for building and housing research. The simulation provides insight to algorithm design for a new system, allowing for rapid adjustment and testing. Once simulated, the final algorithm in the simulation was implemented in a physical system, and tested in a building. This paper focuses on the simulation side of the project, in particular the angle filter used to process the images of a laser progressively scanning through a space.

2   Modelling of PIV System

The simulated PIV system was implemented in Mathematica. The PIV simulation takes in images and generates a vector field overlaid on top of the two images used for correlation, blended together.

The PIV simulation utilises a multi-frame single pulse PIV technique [6], with some additional features. The method uses two images taken a small time frame apart, divide each image into cells, and cross correlate each cell with the corresponding cell in the second image. By observing various shifts in both vertical and horizontal direction, the shift that results in the highest correlation corresponds to the estimated displacement in that time for the particles in that cell.

The convolution is calculated using the Fast-Fourier Transform (FFT), by utilizing the Convolution Theorem of Fourier Transforms. By using this property the convolution can be found significantly faster than by directly calculating the convolution. The Convolution Theorem property can be observed in the equation below.

$$F[\ a * b\ ] = F[a]\ .\ F[b] \tag{1}$$

$$a * b = F^{-1}[\ F[a]\ .\ F[b]\ ] \tag{2}$$

To prevent aliasing, the data was zero padded. This allows the correlation at the edges of the cells to be calculated without distortion from the opposite side of the cell. The details of the developed algorithm are discussed in the following sections.

2.1   Correlation Adjustment

2.1.1   Background Correlation

Background correlation as described in [7] was removed by subtracting the mean from each image. Background correlation is caused by images' direct correlation, resulting in a high correlation at '0' displacement. This is prevalent in a PIV system, as it involves repeated photographing of and at a relatively stationary point. The background would remain constant, and using small tracer particles of dust would result in a majority of the image consisting of the background. The majority of the image would have a net velocity of 0, and so the algorithm would indicate a '0' vector field. By removing the constant background correlation, the exclusive velocity vector field of the particles can be observed.

The difference in clarity of the correlation is significant, and can be seen in Fig. 1. Here, the cross correlation values can be graphically observed, both with and without the mean. Notice the sharper peak after the mean is removed, allowing for an easier decision of net velocity vector.

2.1.2   Correlation Peak Averaging

Cross correlation calculates the correlation at each integer displacement by considering the peak displacement and thereby choosing the most likely integer displacement. One drawback with this method is that velocities are locked into integer values, and so the error introduced can be ±0.5 pixels. A second drawback is the decision method cannot consider several velocities as it only takes the single peak. Both the drawbacks can be solved by peak averaging, as described in [8]. Fig. 1 depicts the case where the true velocity lies between two integer pixel displacements. Cross-Correlation PIV [8] method looks at the estimated region of peak, and determines the 'centre of gravity' by using a weighted average at that location to improve the accuracy. The modified algorithm used in the simulation takes a weighted average of all local maxima within 80-100% of the largest correlation. For this simulation, taking above the 80th percentile of peaks empirically provides a good balance between accurate vector estimation and speed.

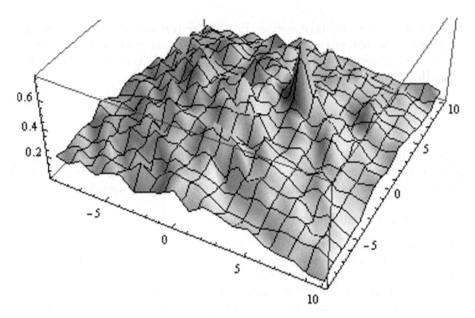

Fig. 1. (a) Mean Adjustment: before

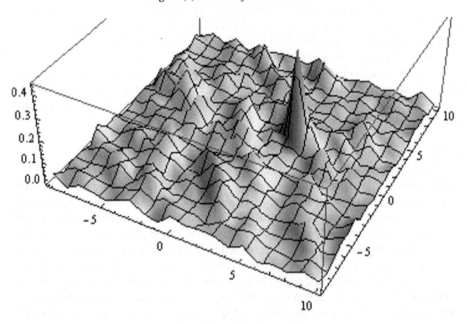

Fig. 1. (b) Mean Adjustment: after

2.2   Angle Filtering Systems

The final feature that is unique to this simulation is the filter for the laser's scanning angle. The laser may not be able to sweep the entire field in a single time frame, so utilisation of these filters allows the system to obtain partial information and can be combined to provide an accurate full field.

2.2.1   Physical Setup

There are two physical configurations (methods) for the considered angular filter: 1. Successive images per step (pre-processing) and 2. Scan the field and correlate (post processing).

Method 1 iterates through a range of angles, and for each iteration, takes two successive images. These images are directly compared against each other, and the resultant vector fields combined. Method 2 iterates through a range of angles twice; each time taking a single image. Iterating twice produces two images per angle, with a longer time step between each image.

The limiting factor for these systems is the time gap between correlations, which determines the maximum measurable velocity. To compare each system, the time gap was set constant and the space to scan was divided up into 20 segments. It was found that the time to scan the field using Method 1 required 20 times that of Method 2, and the time between each angle was 40 times that of Method 2. This suggests that for measuring a velocity field, Method 1 takes longer to scan however puts less strain on equipment. It should also be noted that Method 2 has a significant memory cost, as the system must hold the image in memory until another image appears for comparison. For 20 segments, this would require 20 images to be stored in memory at any time. The extension of this project will have access to a high speed scanner, and hence Method 2 was chosen.

Applying maximum dust speed calculations to the model, with an estimate of the laser being 1 pixel in diameter and a 1200x1000 pixel image, the time taken to scan the entire field using Method 2 is about 0.5 seconds ignoring the camera delay. A large delay is introduced from the high resolution required due to the small diameter of the laser. However, by utilising the exposure of the camera and the indirect illumination from the beam, the effective resolution and hence the time can be vastly improved. This will introduce an error due to blurring, and will require calibration and filtering to reduce the error to an acceptable level.

2.2.2   Vector Merging Algorithm.

It is possible that the laser may not cover the field fast enough to include it within one frame, and even if it does, the exposure may increase noise beyond an acceptable threshold. This scenario would instead require multiple frame comparisons, and a method to merge the resultant fields. The method of merging can be done by adding using a rectangular window; however by using more complex functions a higher accuracy can be achieved per vector coordinate, via a weighted average.

The proposed method uses a triangle function. For a particular measured angle, the following algorithm is used:

For each Vector Position,

```
If[θ_laser - angleStepSize < θ_V < θ_laser + angleStepS-
ize ]
Vector V += 1-Abs[ (θ_laser - θ_V) ] / angleStepSize *
VectorV_0
```

where

θ_laser is the angular position of the laser.

angleStepSize is the space between laser positions, determined by 'resolution'.

θ_V is the polar coordinate angle of the vector's position in the vector field.

Vector_V is the current state of the output vector at a position, and initialised as {0,0}.

Vector_V0 is the original state of the vector, produced using the correlation algorithm with the unfiltered images.

This results in the following function per vector point:

$$a = (\theta 1 - \theta\_a)/(\theta 1 - \theta 2).a2 + (\theta\_a - \theta 2)/(\theta 1 - \theta 2).a1 \qquad (3)$$

where

θ1 and **θ2** are the two closest possible angular positions of the laser

θ_a is the polar coordinate angle of the vector's position

a1 is the vector at the position generated from images at laser angle θ1

a2 is the vector at the position generated from images at laser angle θ2

The above is a basic weighing function which weighs the vectors according to the closeness to the laser in each laser's iteration. The sum across the full range of angles results in a full field with unit scaling on all vectors.

For regular repeating angles, the algorithm can be pre-processed, which allows the merging function to be implemented by simply multiplying a 'kernel' to each field, effectively applying a scalar weighting to each vector. By estimating the angle to match that of the kernel, the processing speed can be vastly improved.

The use of this algorithm allows a continuous sum that emphasises vectors that contain accurate information, by being closer to the beam. It should be noted that although a simple triangle function was used, any other window function that sums to unity would also work.

3   Simulation and Testing

3.1   Methodology

Initially the original, non-angle filtered PIV system was tested using a simulation of randomly moving pixels, with a net velocity applied to the pixels. The purpose of this simulation was to confirm that the system was processing and displaying the right velocities. Once confirmed, the original system was used as a benchmark for comparison with the new system.

A particle-based fluid dynamics simulation was developed to test the PIV system for complex flow. Here, a typical attic space was modelled in Mathematica. This attic space allowed for particles to flow in from the sides of the attic, and force applied to eject them from the top. This simulation was based on algorithms described in a fluid modelling thesis [9]. A screen-shot of the simulation can be seen in Figure 2, and the applied angle filtering algorithm in Figure 3.

The fluid simulation has several features, including particle collision, diffusion, advection, velocity damping, boundary conditions, and force. It also simulates the laser by displaying the particles at a particular depth, as well as within a range of a polar coordinate angle with a Gaussian decaying boundary. A sample of this can be seen in Figure 3. This display method assumes the light scattering of the laser on the particles is Mie scattering. Physical dust particles have a highly irregular shape and hence irregular scattering. However, for this system the dust particles move and rotate relatively slow compared to the camera and scanner, even after considering their volatility. Hence it can be assumed that scattering will not fluctuate significantly within the time frame.

The fluid simulation was run with 100 particles, simulating an attic space of dimensions 4mx5mx2m. The PIV system was then applied to these images, in various sample steps. The original and angle filtered systems were measured over the same time interval. The original system was tested over 50 steps at 0.01 seconds while the angle filtered system was measured over 1000 steps, angular resolution 1/20 of a frame, at 0.01 seconds. This provided a 0.5 sec total interval.

The test used to measure the quality of the system was correlation distance. To measure consistency, the correlation distance was measured between the original and the angle filtered system.

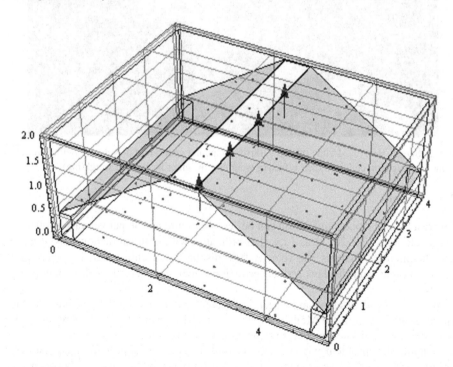

Fig. 2. Screen-shot of a 3d view of the fluid simulation. Arrows indicate a force field, replicating the force due to negative pressure.

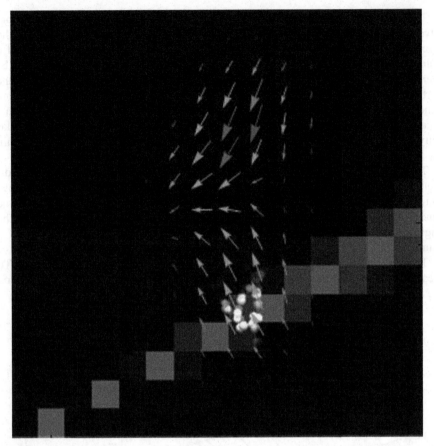

Fig. 3. Screen-shot of 2d view (rotated), during scan and generation of velocity field. Overlaid is the interrogation cells and their effective weighing (brighter is stronger weighting).

3.2   Results

The results of the pixel simulation can be seen in Figure 4. The net velocity applied to the pixels were {30, 20, 1} as {x,y,z} coordinates, with uniform randomness of up to ±5. On empirical analysis, the velocity field displays an accurate velocity where pixels are present, and displays a small error for velocities where the cell contains few pixels.

A second set of results can be seen in Figure 4. Here, a system describing an attic space, as displayed in the Methodology, is analysed for particle flow where air feeds from the sides and force applied to remove them from the top.

A noticeable problem with the system is that velocities appear to change slowly across sharp borders. An example of this can be observed in Figure 5 between the boundary of visible and non-visible particles. Only the beam of particles (visible as white dots) show a visible displacement per frame, and so it is expected that non-zero velocities only exist at the location of the particles. However, in the Figure the non-zero velocities extend to no particle space in a cell. This can be explained as an effect of linear spatial smoothing, in an attempt to generate smoother flow. The presence of this smoothing is questionable, so the effect may need to be removed or improved using a different function, depending on the desired effect.

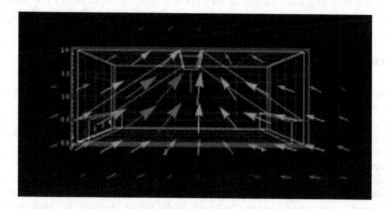

Fig. 4. Vector field describing fluid flow in an attic space

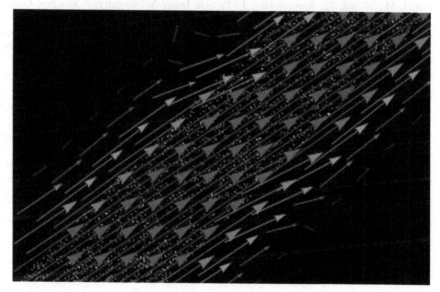

Fig. 5. Vector field of velocities due to pixel drift

4   Conclusion

In conclusion, a PIV system utilising a non-diverging laser beam produces a velocity field of similar quality to a velocity field of a standard PIV systems. By using appropriate filters the accuracy of this new system is comparable to that of standard ones, while maintaining constant beam power across a distance. The downside to this filtering produces errors at boundaries, and so is a consideration for implementation of such systems.

The simulation suggests the use of dust particle tracers works for PIV systems, and provides evidence for proceeding to implement a PIV system with this methodology.

References

1. Lloyd, C.R., Callau, M.F., Bishop, T., Smith, I.J.: The efficacy of an energy efficient upgrade program in New Zealand. Energy and Buildings 40(7), 1228–1239 (2008)
2. Isaacs, N., et al.: Energy Use in New Zealand Households: Final Report on the Household Energy End-use Project (HEEP). BRANZ Study Report 221, BRANZ Ltd, Judgeford, New Zealand (2010)
3. Howden-Chapman, P., Crane, J., Matheson, A., Viggers, H., Cunningham, M., Blakely, T., O'Dea, D., Cunningham, C., Woodward, A., Saville-Smith, K., Baker, M., Waipara, N.: Retrofitting houses with insulation to reduce health inequalities: Aims and methods of a clustered, randomised community-based trial. Social Science & Medicine 61(12), 2600–2610 (2005)
4. Raffel, M., Willert, C., Kompenhans, J.: Particle Image Velocimetry, A Practical Guide. Springer. New York (1998)
5. Cao, X., Liu, J., Jiang, N., Chen, Q.: Particle image velocimetry measurement of indoor airflow field: A review of the technologies and applications. Energy and Buildings 69, 367–380 (2014)
6. Adrian, R.J.: Particle-imaging techniques for experimental fluid mechanics. Annual review of fluid mechanics 23(1), 261–304 (1991)
7. Westerweel, J.: Fundamentals of digital particle image velocimetry. Measurement Science and Technology 8(12), 13–79 (1997)
8. Bastiaans, R.J.: Cross-correlation PIV; theory, implementation and accuracy. Eindhoven University of Technology, Faculty of Mechanical Engineering (2000)
9. Roy, T.M.: Physically-Based Fluid Modeling using Smoothed Particle Hydrodynamics (1995), http://www.plunk.org/~trina/thesis/html/thesis_toc.html (accessed February 20, 2014)

Open Data Sources for the Development of Mobile Applications and Forecast of Microbial Contamination in Bathing Waters

Gianluca Correndo and Zoheir A. Sabeur

University of Southampton IT Innovation Centre, Electronics and Computer Science, Faculty of Physical Sciences and Engineering, Southampton, United Kingdom
{gc,zas}@it-innovation.soton.ac.uk

Abstract. This paper describes a service oriented architecture for mobile and web applications and the enablement of participatory observations of the environment. The architecture hosts generic microbial risk forecast models in bathing zones, which are trained by heterogeneous input data. Open observation data sources, specializing in water quality indicators and environmental processes are used for the construction of such applications. Nevertheless, the encountered integration of the open data sources was challenging due to the various incompatibilities found in data samples. These included gaps in the data with diverse temporal and spatial coverage as well as conflicting collection policies.

Keywords: service oriented architecture, bathing water quality directives, open data, mobile and web applications.

1   Introduction

The state of bathing water quality in European Member States and beyond is important for a number of industries. These span from fisheries, aquaculture to retail business and tourism industries. With the Water Framework Directive and the later simplified Bathing Waters Directive in place, the EU set up the mandatory standards for the quality of Bathing Water throughout the European Union[1]. As a result, the respective delegated organizations by each Member State Environmental Department have the statutory mandate to monitor bathing zones and regularly report on the state of water quality at all designated bathing zones of each Member States to the European Commission (EC). Hence with the affordability of ad-hoc sensing using mobile devices and accessibility to open data from UK and international sources, it has become a reality to build new and low-cost web and mobile applications. The applications will aid bathing water quality managers, with the support of volunteers, achieve regular reporting on water quality to the EC.

   In this study, data-driven models for microbial risks predictions in bathing zones have been put in context of a service oriented architecture. The software service infrastructure provides mobile clients specializing in microbial risk alerts, which are

R. Denzer et al. (Eds.): ISESS 2015, IFIP AICT 448, pp. 303–310, 2015.
© IFIP International Federation for Information Processing 2015

generated by forecast models. The service infrastructure is also enabled for crowd sourcing and the collection of environmental parameters. The risk models have been trained and tested using open data sources prior to their operations.

2   Open Data Collection and Processing

In order to train and test the microbial risk models in bathing zones, it is important to access to open data about environmental observations and measurements such as precipitations (rainfall), river flows, hours of sunshine and so on.

2.1   Open Data for Bathing Water Quality Forecast

The relevance of environmental parameters which explain microbial contamination in bathing waters, is important to construct reliable causal models of microbial risks forecast. Access to open data in order to rapidly develop such models is paramount. The Environmental Agency (EA) of England and Wales has been collecting bathing water quality data since 1988 [2]. The EA is the official organization for England and Wales, which is delegated by the UK Department of the Environment, Fisheries and Rural Affairs (DEFRA) to collect water quality data and report back to the EC. The EA provides both an API to access to the dataset, a Linked Data interface to link to data observations; and dump files with all collected data samples. The data is also associated with UK Open Government Licensing. It includes 530 sampling locations, which cover all the bathing zones of England and Wales. The EA water quality samplings span from 1988 up until 2013. The samplings are taken within the bathing season period, starting from the end of April until the month of October each year.

2.2   Explanatory Processes and Parameters

Various environmental processes may contribute to microbial contamination in bathing zones. However, their level of influence is very complex to predict from first-principles as it will greatly depend on understanding water transport processes and land-sea morphologies near the coast [3]. In this case, models can be efficiently constructed using observation data time series to predict the causal effects of microbial contamination in bathing zones [4]. The data time series may include measurements on precipitation, river runoffs, water salinity, sea surface temperature, wind-induced currents and so on. All these measurements relate to water transport processes and water contamination processes near the bathing zones. They can be retrieved from many open sources currently. For example, the following open data was collected in this study:

- Precipitation (related to preceded 24hrs, 48hrs, 72hrs rainfalls)
- Sea surface temperature
- Wind fields(offshore and onshore)
- Hours of sunshine(also related to cloud cover)

Precipitation

This parameter can be accessed from the American National Center for Environmental Prediction (NCEP) and the National Center for Atmospheric Research (NCAR) [5]. Additionally *atmospheric pressure*, *temperature* and *cloud cover* can be retrieved. The dataset, named DOE Reanalysis 2, is recorded under a 2.5x2.5 degrees grid resolution for daily averages

Sea Surface Temperature

The American National Climatic Data Center provides historical daily measurements of sea surface temperature, sea surface temperatures anomalies, sea ice concentration, and estimated error standard deviations worldwide [6]. The dataset, named Optimum Interpolation Sea Surface Temperature (OISST), reports the measurements on ¼ degree grid and has been collected by two satellites: The American Advanced Very High Resolution Radiometer (AVHRR) and the Japanese Advanced Microwave Scanning Radiometer-EOS (AMSR-E).

Wind Fields

The DOE Reanalysis 2 source also provides daily means for wind fields components worldwide [5].

Hours of Sunshine

The UK Meteorological Office provides hours of sunshine estimates from the Spinning Enhanced Visible and Infrared Imager (SEVIRI), which is mounted on the Meteosat Second Generation (MSG) satellite. The estimates are based on the fraction of cloud cover per day [7]. The dataset spatial coverage include the whole of Europe for the period [2009, 2012]. The geographical grid is composed of 204 x 367 (longitude/latitude cells).

2.3   Open Data Access

The above mentioned open data sources are heterogeneous. The geographical coverage ranges from the national boundaries to the globe. The gridded datasets use different spatial resolutions under various coordinate systems (i.e. Latitude/Longitude or Easting/Northing). The temporal coverage is also diverse, ranging from decades to just few years. This inevitably challenges the long term analysis of the integrated open data. Such heterogeneity in open data is due to the fact that they have been collected by different organizations over time with somehow conflicting data sampling and collection policies. Hence the need for the explicit semantic descriptions of the datasets in order to support their discovery and integration will be essential. Alternatively, this can be delegated to users for discovering and inspecting such datasets and manually implementing them under data wrappers.

It is also worth mentioning that there are other datasets on relevant environmental observation for water quality than those introduced earlier. However, their licensing would not allow their direct usage for integration in this study. Redundancy is therefore an aspect to take into account when searching for open and useful data for integration (see for example, Microsoft FetchClimate[1]).

3   Open Data-Driven Models

Microbial risk forecast modelling is often validated at specific marine coastal regions. In this study, the work is on the generic deployment of the risk models into an open service oriented architecture that supports mobile and web applications. The models are efficiently trained using a common data pre-processing and modelling approach which is based on standard multi-linear regressions [4].

For every monitored bathing zone (group of beaches), a number of time series of the environmental parameters were retrieved. The data series were then harmonized and cleansed, prior to training the regressions. The strength of correlations between all selected explanatory parameters and the targeted variable Log10 (Total coliform) was analyzed. In order to find a set of regression variables for a particular beach, a backward stepwise regression is applied. The analyzed data covered several bathing zones and their respective beaches for the period 2009-2010. This was achieved using all collected open data sets with overlapping temporal coverage. For each sampling point contained in the studied region, all the relevant data (explanatory and target data) have been collected, combined and temporally harmonized to daily observations and measurements. Once the data have been quality pre-processed, a linear regression model was deployed. The linear regression based model was then simplified using a stepwise backward procedure which eliminates the statistically less relevant variables. Fig. 1 below illustrates an exemplar analysis of the open data tested for the construction of the models prior to their training, then deployment.

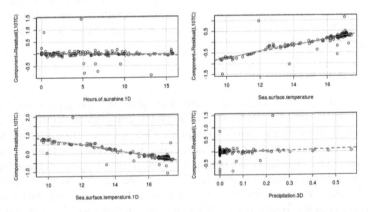

Fig. 1. Data Analysis for model deployment at Bournemouth Pier Beach (South of England)

---

[1] http://research.microsoft.com/en-us/projects/fetchclimate/

4   Mobile Application Framework

In recent years, several service oriented architectures based and web-accessible systems have been developed for environmental risk management. The users, mostly specialists, could access to web sensor observations and invoke data processing services for various environmental risk forecasts with great efficiency [8] and [9]. But with the recent advancement in mobile phone communication it is now possible for more user communities to participate in environmental monitoring at local scales. They will need however the support of new open platforms to connect their mobile applications for the ingestion of local environmental observation and measurements. In this paper, a mobile application framework for crowd sourcing environmental observations in bathing zones is considered.

The mobile application framework enables the dissemination of microbial risk alerts in of bathing zones. It is driven by open environmental data sources and made useful for the specific operational needs of environmental regulators, local authorities, industries and volunteers. The framework provides an entry point for providing information about relevant environmental parameters that may affect bathing water quality. On-site users can contribute as volunteers to collect first hand observations for local authorities (e.g. cloud coverage, presence of bird nesting near the coast, number of bathers etc.). The various type of users are described in Table 1 below.

Table 1. User typologies

User typology	Functionality
Bather	Get: daily notifications of bathing water quality
Casual data provider (Volunteer)	Provide: qualitative information (i.e. presence/absence of bathers), estimates (e.g. bathers density), mobile phone's readings (e.g. temperature, light intensity), and multimedia (e.g. pictures for estimating cloud coverage).
Environmental Officer	Provide: sensor readings (e.g. daily river flows) Get: weekly forecasts of water quality for planning samplings
Local authority Officer	Provide: Bathing location's profile (e.g. presence of waste water treatment plants in the catchment area) Get: weekly forecasts of water quality for planning bathing water quality notifications
Industrial	Get: weekly forecasts of water quality for planning operational activities

The functionalities for the target users entail a one way communication from the server to clients and also a back-channel from some users. Smartphones and tablets can be deployed with different types of sensors, some of which can measure relevant environmental properties to water quality foreacsts.

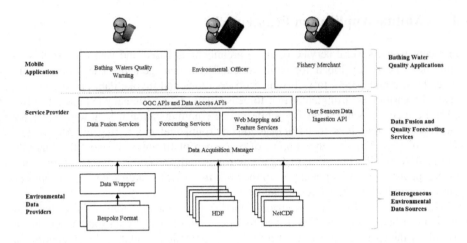

Fig. 2. Bathing water quality mobile application framework architecture

The above architecture (Fig. 2) supports a range of applications that are fed with environmental data. A Data Acquisition Manager is included to semantically enrich the ingested open data with relevant formats. Semantic enrichment will disambiguate the data dimensions such as time resolution and extent, geographical granularity and coverage, properties measured etc. For this particular study, a number of environmental data formats were identified. These include: NetCDF and HDF. Other third party data formats need software wrappers in order to be integrated in the framework. The framework maintains a semantic index of the datasets, which is managed along with the represented physical dimensions, temporal and geographical extents and resolutions. This additional metadata is used to harmonise the differences in data representations and allowing the use of ingested data for the forecasting models. The Data Fusion Services exploit the semantic description to perform the data preprocessing functionalities. These are needed in the rapid construction of the forecasting models. Specifically, it entails resampling, interpolation of missing values, temporal series composition and so forth. The Forecasting Services employ the data-driven models, while selecting the relevant parameters to be used for a given beach of interest at a bathing zone. Then risks of microbial contamination are predicted and pushed to the mobile application via an OGC compliant API. This is specifically done by mapping layers that depict the risk values via a browser accessible real-time communication API (**WebRTC**[2] protocol is considered).

WebRTC is an open project that is supported by many Internet technology providers (Google, Mozilla and Opera among others). It provides real-time communication (RTC henceforth) capabilities to web browsers. Mobile applications (depicted in the top part of Fig. 2.) access those APIs via javascript.. The project is undergoing also a phase of standardization within the World Wide Web Consortium community. Hence, it benefits from a wide adoption base with the most used browsers around (Internet Explorer supported via third party plugin).

---

[2] http://www.w3.org/TR/webrtc/

WebRTC includes the possibility to create an RTCDataChannel, which is a bi-directional data channel between peers that is not based on HTTP protocol. HTTP protocols would be extremely inefficient and slow for high data traffic mobile applications. However, Clients use HTTPS protocol only to initiate a session, while the rest of the communication switches to alternative protocols.

Once a data communication channel is established, the peers can exchange data using proprietary applicative protocols. These are implemented over a real-time carrier. RTC API is employed to communicate with the User Sensor Data Ingestion API and the submission of sensor observation and measurements. The crowd sourced observation is therefore stored using Data Access API. It will subsequently be enhanced with richer meta-information for usage by the risk models. The client layer is composed of a number of Android applications that will access the framework APIs and fetch model prediction and historic observation data. In particular, the mobile application layer supports data intensive applications which render map based visualizations and data plots. It will also sustain data backchannels to the server for the submission of user based observations with streams of sensor measurements.

Most current Android handsets have a range of sensors that fall broadly into one of these following categories:

- Motion sensors: Include accelerometers, gravity, gyroscopes and rotational vector sensors along 3D spatial axes.
- Environmental sensors: Include sensors that measure ambient temperature, pressure, illumination and humidity.
- Position sensors: Include the device physical position with orientation sensors and magnetometers.
- Camera: Include a CCD image sensor (or a CMOS sensor), ranging from 2 to 8 megapixels in resolution.

Sensor readings are usually supplied to the javascript engine. For those sensors that are not yet accessible via javascript API, Android allows to register Java methods as javascript functions. The readings are made available within the mobile application for the visualization and further processing. They are also made available in the server via **WebRTC** along with user's identification and application parameters.

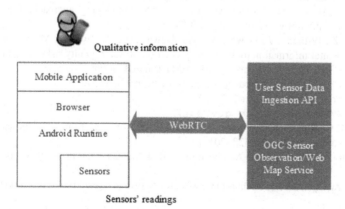

Fig. 3. Mobile Data Provisioning Interface

Users can provide the framework with qualitative observations which may be relevant to the microbial risk forecast application. Number of bathers in a beach of interest, or the presence of birds' nests along the coastline, or cloud cover levels for example are useful qualitative local observations. Cloud cover particularly can be submitted by simply providing digital pictures of the sky at the beach location of interest. The picture can be then processed to estimate the cloud cover levels (in %).

The choice of adopting Android as a target platform is attractive enough in this study. This is due to of its open source development tools and high rate of penetration in the market. This is clearly useful for maximizing crowd sourcing qualitative observation and measurement but also reducing the cost of building further mobile environmental applications and services..

5   Conclusion

This paper describes a service oriented architecture with a common approach for the deployment of generic models and mobile applications. The applications specialize in microbial risks forecast in bathing waters. The models are generically built on standard multi-linear regressions which are trained by heterogeneous open environmental data. Nevertheless, meta-information enhancements were needed to make use of the open data. The development of the mobile application using Android open platforms was also discussed. The application enables crowd sourcing qualitative observations and measurement at bathing zones. Further, it will assist environmental managers and authorities perform their statutory bathing water quality reports to the EC more effectively and at low cost.

References

[1] Directive 2006/7/EC of the European Parliament and of the Council of 15 February 2006 concerning the management of bathing water quality and repealing Directive 76/160/EEC, Official Journal of the European Union. L64/67 (April 3, 2006)
[2] http://www.geostore.com/environment-agency/WebStore
[3] Lin, B., Syed, M., Falconer, R.A.: Predicting faecal indicator levels in estuarine receiving waters – An integrated hydrodynamic and ANN modelling approach. Environmental Modelling and Software 23(6), 729–740 (2008)
[4] Sabeur, Z., Williams, J., Dewey, N., Kozakiewicz, A., Piwowarska, M.: Development of environmental information tools for the prediction of water quality risks in bathing waters. ICREW Final Technical Report. p. 128. BMT Limited (2006)
[5] http://www.esrl.noaa.gov/psd/data/gridded/
    data.ncep.reanalysis2.html
[6] http://www.ncdc.noaa.gov/sst/
[7] Good, E.: Estimating daily sunshine duration over the UK from geostationary satellite data. Weather 65(12), 324–328 (2010)
[8] Orchestra. An Open Service Architecture for Risk Management. ISBN: 978-3-00-024284-7 (2008)
[9] SANY. An Open Service Architecture for Sensor Networks (2009), ISBN: 978-3-00-028571-4

Ecohydrology Models without Borders?

Using Geospatial Web Services in EcohydroLib Workflows in the United States and Australia

Brian Miles[1] and Lawrence E. Band[1,2]

[1] Institute for the Environment, University of North Carolina, Chapel Hill, USA
[2] Department of Geography, University of North Carolina, Chapel Hill, USA
brian_miles@unc.edu

Abstract. Ecohydrology models require diverse geospatial input datasets (e.g. terrain, soils, vegetation species and leaf area index), the acquisition and preparation of which are labor intensive, yielding workflows that are difficult to reproduce. EcohydroLib is a software framework for managing spatial data acquisition and preparation workflows for ecohydrology modeling, while automatically capturing metadata and provenance information. The goal of EcohydroLib is to enable water scientists to spend less time acquiring and manipulating geospatial data and more time using ecohydrology models to test hypotheses, while making it easier for models to be shared and scientific results to be reproduced. This increased reproducibility, ease of sharing, and researcher productivity can enable both model inter comparison of interest within a country, and site inter comparison of interest across national borders. Currently, EcohydroLib allows modelers to work with geospatial data stored locally as well as high spatial resolution U.S. national spatial data available via web services, for example 30-meter digital elevation model and land cover data, and 1:12,000 scale soils data. While researchers working in watersheds outside the U.S. can use EcohydroLib, they must manually download data for their study areas before these data can be imported into EcohydroLib workflows. Though national agencies in the U.S. and Australia offer some datasets via web services, with a few exceptions these are either lower resolution datasets or data made available via Open Geospatial Consortium (OGC) Web Map Service (WMS) interfaces of use primarily for cartography, rather than via OGC Web Coverage Service (WCS) or Web Feature Service (WFS) interfaces needed for integration with numerical models. In this paper we explore: (1) availability of high-resolution national geospatial data web services in the United States and Australia; and (2) integration of Australian web services with EcohydroLib.

Keywords: hydroinformatics, workflows, ecohydrology modeling, RHESSys.

1   Introduction

Researchers working in the interdisciplinary field of ecohydrology are concerned with the cycling of energy, carbon, water, and nutrients through coupled climate-soil-vegetation systems (Rodríguez-Iturbe 2000), and with the interaction between water

R. Denzer et al. (Eds.): ISESS 2015, IFIP AICT 448, pp. 311–320, 2015.

cycling and the ecological community. Ecohydrology models require diverse geospatial datasets (e.g. terrain, soils, vegetation species and leaf area index), the acquisition and preparation of which are labor intensive, yielding workflows that are difficult to reproduce. When applied to sites with complex terrain, for example mountainous forested ecosystems or urbanized ecosystems, high spatial resolution data (<= 30-m) are needed to accurately simulate hydrologic processes (Band 1993, Band et al. 2005).

Environmental modeling can incorporate information from diverse sources and relies heavily on cyberinfrastructure (CI; e.g. hardware, software, sensors, networks, and the human and social capital necessary to make use of these) to assist in the collection, analysis, and visualization of observed and model output data. The increasing use of cyberinfrastructure to carry out complex modeling, data analysis, and visualization tasks has led to the adoption of workflow systems of increasing complexity (Deelman et al. 2009). Workflow construction tools (e.g. Cyberintegrator, Kepler, VisTrails) enable scientists to create workflows by combining a series of services needed to complete a set of tasks (e.g. data preparation, analyses and modeling, visualization; Goble et al. 2010). Over the past decade, workflow systems have been gaining use across the sciences (e.g. high-energy physics, biological science as well as climate science). More recently, domain and information scientists have turned their attention to improving cyberinfrastructure for geoscience workflows in general (cf. U.S. National Science Foundation EarthCube; http://www.earthcube.org/) and water science in particular. In an analysis of Australia's Water Information Research and Development Alliance (WIRADA), Plale (2012) identifies the benefits of adopting workflow systems to carry out tasks common to water sciences, and considers how amenable these tasks are to representation in scientific workflow systems. The tasks include: (1) data discovery; (2) data cleaning and formatting; (3) data ingest; (4) data assimilation and forecast model execution; and (5) data analysis. The challenge for workflow systems in geosciences is to enable easy: (1) workflow creation, including debugging; (2) validation of workflows; (3) running of workflows across workflow systems; (4) results visualization; (5) results publishing; (6) sharing and reuse of workflows among scientists in a community and across disciplines to allow results to be reproduced (Duffy et al. 2012; Guo et al. 2012).

EcohydroLib (https://github.com/selimnairb/EcohydroLib) is a software framework for managing spatial data acquisition and preparation workflows for ecohydrology modeling, and provides library code and workflow commands for acquiring, manipulating, and managing geospatial data needed to run a variety of ecohydrology models (e.g. RHESSys, SWAT, VIC). Workflow steps common across models can be performed using EcohydroLib commands, for example identifying a study area, or acquiring terrain or soils data via web services (Fig. 1).

Modelers can then use model-specific workflow commands built on top of EcohydroLib to transform input data into formats appropriate for direct use by a particular model. In this way, EcohydroLib increases the amount of code devoted to data acquisition that can be shared across models, reducing duplication of programming effort, and facilitating model and site inter comparison. EcohydroLib workflows are composed of loosely coupled commands for performing geospatial data acquisition and preparation; data acquired by these commands are stored in a directory on

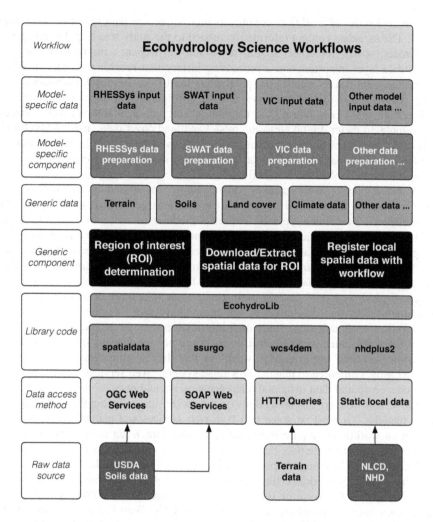

Fig. 1. Illustration of layered architecture of EcohydroLib. Read from the bottom, raw data sources are accessed using web services (yellow), or as static data stored on local files systems (yellow), using library code (green) in EcohydroLib. Generic data acquisition tools (black) are built on top of EcohydroLib library code. These tools yield data in generic formats not specific to any model (grey). Model-specific tools (magenta) use these generic data to produce model-specific input data parameterizations (grey, above magenta). The model specific data make possible ecohydrology modeling science workflows (cyan) whose goal is to answer particular science and management questions.

local disk specific to each project (i.e. the project directory). These workflows are orchestrated via a metadata store in the project directory. Workflow commands are built using task-oriented APIs defined in the package *ecohydrolib*. These commands provide tools for downloading and manipulating geospatial data needed to run ecohydrology models, information such as: digital elevation model (DEM), soils, land cover. The metadata store, essentially a key-value store (e.g. a dictionary), is used to orchestrate a series of workflow commands used to prepare data for an ecohydrology model. The metadata contain information related to the study area (e.g. bounding box coordinates, spatial reference, spatial resolution), provenance information for each spatial data layer imported, and a processing history that records the order in which commands were run as well as the parameters used to invoke each command. Currently, EcohydroLib allows modelers to work with geospatial data stored locally as well as high spatial resolution U.S. national spatial data available via web services, for example 30-meter digital elevation model and land cover data, and 1:12,000 scale soils data. While researchers working in watersheds outside the U.S. can use EcohydroLib, they must manually download data for their study areas before these data can be imported into EcohydroLib workflows.

Compared to systems for manually downloading geospatial data, web services can make it easier to acquire and integrate such data into geoscience workflows. Manual-download workflows typically require a modeler to use a web browser-based GIS tool to define the region of interest and choose a data product to download before being able to download data, perhaps after a delay of minutes to hours while the data are fetched from offline storage or otherwise processed. Once downloaded, these data may consist of several image tiles that need to be joined together before being usable in an ecohydrology model. Instead, web services can offer more-or-less instant access to seamless geospatial data covering the entire study area. Further, when accessed via workflow tools that store study area information (e.g. geographic bounding box, spatial reference) such as EcohydroLib, users are not required to specify spatial information each time within a given workflow that they acquire datasets via web services. Lastly, compared to manual-download systems, web services make it possible to acquire geospatial data in spatial reference systems and resolutions specific to each workflow, with conversions being done on the server side, reducing the work required of the modeler. It must be noted that both web services and manual-download data acquisition workflows require the modeler to take care when combining geospatial datasets to ensure that the data being combined are of commensurate spatial scales or resolutions as well as being temporally and semantically compatible.

To be of use in numerical ecohydrology models, web services must provide data as Open Geospatial Consortium (OGC) Web Coverage Service (WCS) end points (http://www.opengeospatial.org/standards/wcs) or OGC Web Feature Service (WFS; http://www.opengeospatial.org/standards/wms), rather than as OGC Web Map Service (WMS; http://www.opengeospatial.org/standards/wms), which are of use primarily for cartography applications. While national agencies in the U.S. and Australia are offering some datasets via web services, these are either lower resolution datasets or are offered as WMS end points. In this paper we explore: (1) availability of high-resolution national geospatial data web services in the United States and Australia; and (2) integration of Australian web services with EcohydroLib.

2   Availability of National Spatial Data Web Services in Australia and the United States

Geospatial datasets needed to parameterize process-based ecohydrology models include: digital elevation model (DEM); land cover; soil surface texture; and vegetation leaf area index. Some of these data are available via web services interfaces as national coverages

for both Australia and the United States (Table 1). In Australia, all data listed are provided by Geoscience Australia (GA). Currently, Australia has national-scale 1-second
(~30-m) spatial resolution DEM data available via a WCS interface, though these data
date from the 2000 Shuttle Radar Topography Mission. There is a relatively coarse
250-m land cover data dataset for Australia, however at present the GA only offers a
WMS web service for these data, not WCS. Soils data (e.g. Australian Soil Resource
Information System; ASRIS) do not appear to be available via web services at this time,
though a web browser-based download tool is provided by CSIRO (the Commonwealth
Scientific and Industrial Research Organisation) and the Department of Agriculture,
Fisheries and Forestry (http://www.asris.csiro.au/).

Table 1. U.S. and Australia national geospatial data of use in ecohydrology modeling available via
web services interfaces. AU = Australia, US = United States, GA = Geoscience Australia, USGS
= U.S. Geological Survey, NLCD = National Land Cover Database, ORNL DAAC = Oak Ridge
National Laboratory Distributed Active Archive Center for Biogeochemical Dynamics, NASA =
National Aeronautics and Space Administration, GMU = George Mason University, USDA = U.S.
Department of Agriculture. More info on GA web services: http://www.ga.gov.au/data-pubs/web-
services/ga-web-services USGS web services: http://viewer.nationalmap.gov/example/services/
serviceList.html ORNL web services: http://webmap.ornl.gov/wcsdown/index.jsp GeoBrain
WCS4DEM web service: http://geobrain.laits.gmu.edu/wcs4dem.htm SSURGO web services:
http://sdmdataaccess.nrcs.usda.gov

Country	Dataset	Spatial resolution	Web service type	Hosting organization	Notes
AU	Land cover	N/A	WMS	GA	
AU	DEM	9-second (~250-m)	WCS, WMS	GA	
AU	DEM (SRTM)	1-second (~30-m)	WCS, WMS	GA	
AU	LiDAR	20-cm	WCS	GA	Murray Darling basin only
AU	DEM (LiDAR)	1-m	WCS	GA	Murray Darling basin only
US	NLCD (1992-2011)	N/A	WMS	USGS	
US	NLCD (2011)	30-m	WCS	USGS	
US	NLCD (1992-2011)	30-m	WCS	ORNL DAAC / NASA	

Table 1. (*continued*)

US	DEM (SRTM, NED)	30-m	WCS	GeoBrain GMU / NASA
US	Soil Survey Geographic Database (SSURGO)	~1:12,000	WFS, SOAP	USDA

In the U.S., DEM data are available via WCS4DEM, a WCS service provided by the GeoBrain project at George Mason University and funded by NASA (Table 1); both high-resolution U.S. national data (National Elevation Dataset, NED; SRTM) as well as global DEM data (e.g. GLSDEM, GTOPO) coverages are available via WCS4DEM. High spatial resolution (30-m) land cover data for the continental U.S. are available over a number of years (1992, 2001, 2006, and 2011) as part of the National Land Cover Database (NLCD), which is available for download via WCS interfaces from the NASA Distributed Active Archive (DAAC) for Biogeochemical Dynamics center at Oak Ridge National Laboratory (ORNL) for years 1992, 2001, and 2006, as well as through the U.S. Geological Survey for 2011 (Table 1). Finally, U.S. soils data are available via WFS and Simple Object Access Protocol (SOAP) web services interfaces provided by the U.S. Department of Agriculture (USDA).

Unfortunately, at present there are no national-scale high spatial resolution vegetation leaf area index (LAI) data products available for either the U.S. or Australia via WCS interfaces. However, it is possible to derive 30-m peak LAI data from Landsat satellite data as well as LAI phenology (e.g. green-up, senescence) from MODIS satellite data, which are available globally. ORNL DAAC offers seasonal and yearly Landsat mosaics for 2008 and 2009 via WCS (http://webmap.ornl.gov/wcsdown/dataset.jsp?ds_id=111112) from the USGS Web-enabled Landsat Data (WELD) project (http://weld.cr.usgs.gov/). These data could serve as a data source for a prototype WCS-enabled peak LAI service.

3   Integrating EcohydroLib with U.S. and Australian National Spatial Data Web Services

When EcohydroLib 1.0 was released in July 2013, it provided the ability to acquire the following geospatial datasets from remote web services: U.S. and global DEM data from WCS4DEM, NLCD 2006 data from ORNL DAAC, and U.S. surface soil texture data from USDA SSURGO. Here we describe an additional module recently developed for EcohydroLib 1.20 to provide access to national-scale 1-second (~30-m) spatial resolution SRTM-based DEM data provided by Geoscience Australia. Geoscience Australia (GA) provides 1-second spatial resolution DEM data for all of mainland Australia and Tasmania based on the 2000 Shuttle Radar Topography Mission data. These data are offered in three forms: unsmoothed data (DEM); smoothed data

(DEM-S; with noise removed); and a hydrologically enforced version of the smoothed data (DEM-H; which includes hydrologic flowpaths derived from both SRTM data and mapped streams). The hydrologically enforced data are deemed to be suitable for watershed delineation (Geoscience Australia 2011). EcohydroLib provides access to all three datasets using the *GetGADEMForBoundingBox* command (for a full description EcohydroLib, including installation instructions and tutorials, see: https://github.com/selimnairb/RHESSysWorkflows). The EcohydroLib workflow steps required to acquire GA DEM data are summarized in Fig. 2.

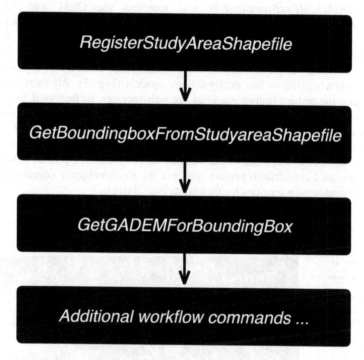

Fig. 2. Initial EcohydroLib workflow steps including acquisition of DEM data from Geoscience Australia WCS web service interface

The first workflow step, *RegisterStudyAreaShapefile*, defines the spatial extent of the study area using a single polygon encoded in an ESRI shapefile file format. This shapefile, accessed locally via a disk mounted on the computer where EcohydroLib is running, is copied into the project directory specified to *RegisterStudyAreaShapefile*; as it is copied, the shapefile is reprojected into the WGS84 geographic coordinate system (EPSG:4326). This reprojected shapefile can be visualized using a GIS such as QGIS.

Once the study area is defined, the bounding box of the study area must be derived from the study area polygon using the *GetBoundingboxFromStudyareaShapefile* command, which stores the bounding box in the *metadata.txt* file stored in the project directory. The bounding box (a.k.a. minimum bounding rectangle) is defined by two coordinate pairs that represent the upper right (e.g. northeast) and lower left (e.g. southwest) corners of a rectangle that circumscribes the study area polygon. With the bounding box defined, it is possible to obtain GIS data for the study area via web services; by default *GetBoundingBoxFromStudyareaShapefile* will slightly buffer the bounding box rectangle to help ensure that any data downloaded provide sufficient coverage of the study area watershed.

The *GetGADEMForBoundingBox* command is used to download the 1-second DEM data from web services provided by Geoscience Australia. The type of DEM to be downloaded (e.g. DEM, DEM-S, or DEM-H) can be specified using the –d (a.k.a. –demType) option. A sample DEM for an example study area is shown in Fig. 3. By default, *GetGADEMForBoundingBox* will reproject the DEM into the UTM (WGS84) zone appropriate for the centroid of the study area; the native resolution of the DEM will be maintained. Both the spatial reference and resolution of the DEM can be specified as optional arguments to *GetGADEMForBoundingBox*. With the DEM data in hand, subsequent EcohydroLib commands can be run to acquire and manipulate data needed to run ecohydrology models (Fig. 2). All subsequent data imported into the project (either acquired via web services, or imported from locally stored data) will be resampled to the spatial reference system and resolution of the DEM; the user can choose any re-sampling method supported by GDAL, or can disable raster re-sampling on import. When working in Australia, land cover, soils, and other necessary geospatial data would need to be downloaded by hand before being imported into an EcohydroLib project (e.g. via the *RegisterRaster* command), given the lack of suitable web services for these data (see above).

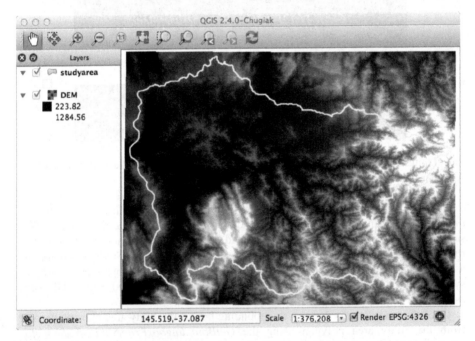

Fig. 3. QGIS visualization of Geoscience Australia DEM acquired for bounding box of study area defined by watershed shapefile

4   Discussion and Conclusion

In this paper we have described common high spatial resolution (<=30-m) geospatial data needed for parameterizing ecohydrology models, and listed known OGC web services-based interfaces for these data for the United States and Australia. We have also described a new module for EcohydroLib that provides access to high spatial resolution (~30-m) national-scale Australian DEM data accessible via OGC WCS interfaces provided by Geoscience Australia. While this new module does not address all data gaps for EcohydroLib users working in Australia, it is a useful first step toward providing easy access to geospatial data needed for parameterizing ecohydrology models for Australian catchments. Once other necessary geospatial datasets are available via suitable OGC web services interfaces (e.g. high resolution land cover raster data via WCS, and soils raster or vector data via WCS or WFS), these can be similarly integrated into EcohydroLib, providing similar ease of access currently afforded to users working in U.S. watersheds. In the mean time, EcohydroLib can still be of benefit when applied to Australia due to its ability to improve metadata and provenance information capture, even for datasets downloaded manually. Further, it is our hope that this work will show the benefits to the water science community when providers of national geospatial data make these data available via OGC WCS and WFS web services interfaces required for integration with numerical models, rather than cartography-oriented WMS services. Such web services, when integrated with tools like EcohydroLib, hold the potential to enable transformative water science by improving scientific reproducibility and researcher productivity while making model and site inter comparisons easier to achieve.

References

1. Band, L.: Effect of land surface representation on forest water and carbon budgets. Journal of Hydrology 150(2-4), 749–772 (1993), doi:10.1016/0022-1694(93)90134-u
2. Band, L.E., Cadenasso, M.L., Grimmond, C.S., Grove, J.M., Pickett, S.T.A.: Heterogeneity in urban Ecosystems: Patterns and Processes. In: Lovett, G.M., Turner, M.G., Jones, C.G., Weathers, K.C. (eds.) Ecosystem Function in Heterogeneous Landscapes, New York, pp. 257–278 (2005), http://dx.doi.org/10.1007/0-387-24091-8_13
3. Deelman, E., et al.: Workflows and e-Science: An overview of workflow system features and capabilities. Future Generation Computer Systems 25(5), 528–540 (2009)
4. Duffy, C., et al.: Designing a Road Map for Geoscience Workflows. Eos 93(24), 225–226 (2012), http://www.agu.org/pubs/crossref/2012/2012EO240002.shtml
5. Geoscience Australia, Metadata for SRTM-derived 1 Second Digital Elevation Models Version 1.0 (2011), http://www.ga.gov.au/metadata-gateway/metadata/record/gcat_72759
6. Goble, C.A., et al.: myExperiment: a repository and social network for the sharing of bioinformatics workflows. Nucleic Acids Research 38(Web Server), W677–W682 (2010)
7. Guo, D., et al.: Scientific workflow challenges. In: WIRADA Science Symposium Proceedings, Melbourne, Australia, August 1-5, pp. 54–60 (2012)

8. Plale, B.: The challenges and opportunities of workflow systems in environmental research. In: WIRADA Science Symposium Proceedings, Melbourne, Australia, August 1-5, pp. 48–53 (2012)
9. Rodríguez-Iturbe, I.: Ecohydrology: a hydrologic perspective of climate-soil-vegetation dynamics. Water Resources Research 36(1), 3–9 (2000)

A Distributed Computing Workflow for Modelling Environmental Flows in Complex Terrain

Stuart R. Mead[1,2,*], Mahesh Prakash[2], Christina Magill[1],
Matt Bolger[2], and Jean-Claude Thouret[3]

[1] Risk Frontiers, Faculty of Science, Macquarie University, Sydney, Australia
[2] CSIRO Digital Productivity Flagship, Melbourne, Australia
[3] Laboratoire Magmas et Volcans UMR6524 CNRS, IRD and OPGC, University Blaise Pascal,
Clermont-Ferrand, France
Stuart.Mead@mq.edu.au

Abstract. Numerical modelling of extreme environmental flows such as flash floods, avalanches and mudflows can be used to understand fundamental processes, predict outcomes and assess the loss potential of future events. These extreme flows can produce complicated and dynamic free surfaces as a result of interactions with the terrain and built environment. In order to resolve these features that may affect flows, high resolution, accurate terrain models are required. However, terrain models can be difficult and costly to acquire, and often lack detail of important flow steering structures such as bridges or debris. To overcome these issues we have developed a photogrammetry workflow for reconstructing high spatial resolution three dimensional terrain models. The workflow utilises parallel and distributed computing to provide inexpensive terrain models that can then be used in numerical simulations of environmental flows. A section of Quebrada San Lazaro within the city of Arequipa, Peru is used as a case study to demonstrate the construction and usage of the terrain models and applicability of the workflow for a flash flood scenario.

Keywords: Structure-from-Motion, photogrammetry, numerical modelling, rapid mass flow, natural hazards.

1   Introduction

Extreme environmental flows and mass movements such as floods, landslides, avalanches and debris flows pose significant risk to exposed populations and can cause substantial damage to buildings, infrastructure and the environment. Due to safety concerns and difficulty in predicting the occurrence of these events, field measurements are rare and, when available, are generally limited to depth and point velocity measurements (e.g. [1]). As a consequence, computational flow models are commonly employed in an attempt to predict the outcomes of specific events, understand fundamental processes and to provide a greater understanding and delineation of the hazard.

---

[*] Corresponding author.

R. Denzer et al. (Eds.): ISESS 2015, IFIP AICT 448, pp. 321–332, 2015.

Two-dimensional (2D) depth-averaged numerical models such as the shallow-water (SW) method for fluids or Savage-Hutter method for granular mass movements are widely used to simulate environmental flows. These depth-averaged approaches are suitable for predicting large scale flow features and inundation; however the shallow-ness assumption can be limiting within complex environments (such as urban areas) where there are large and sudden changes in the terrain gradient. Complex and varying topography causes the flow to have three dimensional features and varying vertical velocity profiles which cannot be captured by depth-averaged approaches. For these circumstances, three dimensional (3D) particle based flow modelling methods, such as smoothed particle hydrodynamics (SPH), may be more suitable as they have the ability to predict and track the motion of objects or debris within the flow, model complex flooding scenarios including interaction with buildings, and predict forces on structures [2]. Use of SPH and other 3D methods has traditionally been limited due to their high computational requirements. However, advances in processing power and parallel computing solutions such as OpenMP and Message Passing Interface (MPI) have created opportunities to simulate larger areas at higher resolutions.

In both depth-averaged 2D and fully 3D flow modelling approaches, topographic information (in the form of terrain models) is required as a primary input and mod-elled outcomes are highly sensitive to the accuracy of this topographic data [3]. For example, Legleiter, Kyriakidis, McDonald and Nelson [4] examined the effects of uncertain topographic data on a typical 2D depth-integrated (i.e. Shallow Water) me-thod, finding that the method was sensitive to morphological features such as point bars. Small-scale bed features were also found to affect results, albeit at a reduced level as flow depth increased. The applicability and accuracy of simulation predic-tions is therefore reliant on accurate reproduction of small scale flow-steering features and topographic obstacles in the terrain model.

While advances in computational power and remote sensing methods have general-ly increased the dimensionality and resolution of terrain models [5], quality and accu-racy has not necessarily increased at the same pace. Measurements of the terrain are commonly acquired from satellite or aerial platforms using techniques such as Li-DAR, stereo photogrammetry or radar interferometry. This information is then used to create gridded digital terrain models (DTM), a representation of the topography at a single point in time. Frequent data acquisition is critical to ensuring currency of the DTM, as sediment transport processes and human interaction continually modify the terrain and create small scale features that may affect the behavior of flows. The fre-quency of data acquisition is, however, limited by high computational requirements, costly equipment and lengthy data processing times [5], resulting in an inaccurate representation of the current shape and features of the terrain. In addition, terrain models can be limited by the acquisition platform. High altitude aerial platform me-thods are not suitable when the area of interest has large amounts of cloud cover, which is often the case before and after weather based flow events. Tall trees, build-ings and bridges may also cause occlusion, leading to inadequate representations of key terrain features.

For high resolution modelling, accurate reproduction of small-scale terrain features and the 3D terrain structure is particularly important, although grid based terrain models are limited in their ability to reproduce these 3D features. Reasons for this have been described by Kreylos, Oskin, Cowgill, Gold, Elliott and Kellogg [6] and include:

- Constraints of a rectangular grid system limits the gradient of the slope, and therefore flow direction, to eight cardinal directions.
- Re-projection of steep topographic features, such as dips, overhangs or bridges, onto a horizontal plane degrades the level of detail captured, implicitly reducing the resolution.
- Gridding can have a directional dependence, and features such as channels that do not align with the primary grid direction can be degraded.

Three dimensional terrain representations, such as triangulated irregular networks (TIN) or point based methods [6] present a feasible alternative to reduce the limitations of grid-based terrain models as well as more accurately reproducing terrain features.

Here, we demonstrate a workflow to acquire and process detailed 3D terrain models for use in 3D flow modelling and visualisation. The process utilises and integrates several core technologies to provide a fast, reliable and inexpensive method for terrain generation and numerical modelling that eliminates or reduces many of the common limitations of traditional terrain models. Open source libraries and data structures are used to enhance the flexibility of the process and allow users to extend this methodology. The workflow utilises parallel and distributed computing to allow for rapid turnaround time from terrain acquisition to output of numerical simulation results. The key components of the workflow are (1) acquisition of ground images and low altitude aerial images from a light remote control quadcopter, (2) image feature detection, matching and 3D scene reproduction using Structure-from-Motion (SfM) photogrammetry, (3) point cloud processing, including reprojection and meshing; and (4) numerical modelling using SPH. The low cost and high speed of this method allows for faster acquisition of terrain models, increasing their currency, while the point based approach enables features to be more accurately represented. The application of this workflow is demonstrated as a case study by simulating flash flood scenarios in complex terrain for the city of Arequipa, Peru.

2   Methods

2.1   Workflow Outline and Software Integration

The four stages of the terrain generation and modelling process are shown in figure 1. The first stage, image acquisition, involves capturing images of the terrain from multiple angles, taken either aerially and from ground level. The main objective of this stage is to collect as many images of the area of interest as possible. The Structure-from-Motion (SfM) stage uses these images to generate a point cloud representation of the area using photogrammetry and computer vision methods including feature identification and matching, camera pose estimation and point cloud reconstruction using multi-view stereo (MVS). The dense point cloud produced by the SfM stage is then processed using algorithms to filter out erroneous points, reduce the size of the point cloud and reconstruct a manifold, watertight surface mesh representing the terrain. In the final numerical modelling stage, the terrain mesh model is converted into an input for simulation and subsequent visualisation.

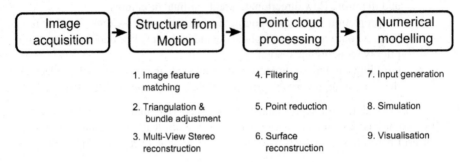

Fig. 1. Terrain generation and modelling workflow outline

The modelling and terrain generation process, shown in figure 1, is sequential with each step relying on inputs from the previous. Aside from the requirements for inputs, each component of the process is independent from each other. This makes the process well suited for implementation into a workflow tool, where each software component can be developed and modified independently. This is particularly important for image feature detection (step 1 in figure 1), surface reconstruction (step 6) and numerical modelling (steps 7-9), as these are all active areas of research where a range of approaches (e.g. fully 3d or 2d depth-averaged numerical models) could be employed and may be more appropriate depending on user requirements.

We chose to implement this process (referred to hereafter as the modelling workflow) into Workspace, a cross-platform workflow framework with a plug-in architecture [7]. The plug-in architecture exposes data types and operations, enabling the development of new workflows and operations. Other advantages of Workspace for this application are:

- 3D visualisation capabilities allows for integrated model checking, without the need for additional software packages,
- the distributed/parallel execution engine, which allows components of the workflow to be processed on multiple CPU's, both locally and distributed through TCP and cluster based systems, and,
- the engine is built upon permissive free software licenses, allowing for extensions and applications to be developed without third party licensing requirements.

Currently image feature matching, point cloud processing (steps 4-6), input generation (step 7) and visualisation (step 9) are implemented within Workspace. The triangulation, bundle adjustment and multi-view stereo processes are run separately, but are executed within the workspace from a command line operation. The SPH simulations (step 8) are run externally using the terrain model generated within the workflow.

2.2 Structure-from-Motion (SfM)

Structure-from-Motion (SfM) is a photogrammetry method that reconstructs sparse 3D points and camera viewpoints from image collections of a scene. Dense 3D point clouds can be reconstructed by coupling with MVS methods, which construct dense 3D point clouds from overlapping images and camera viewpoints [8]. The accuracy of SfM-MVS approaches is said to be nearly on par with laser scanners [9].

To obtain camera viewpoints, the SfM process is as follows: (1) within each image, find and compute descriptors for unique features such as building corners (keypoints); (2) find matching keypoints in images taken from different angles; (3) obtain an estimate of camera parameters and location through triangulation of the image matches; and, (4) optimise the matrix of camera parameters and locations (bundle adjustment). For a detailed description of the SfM process, see [10].

In the workflow, our approach differs slightly from the commonly used methods presented by Snavely, Seitz and Szeliski [10] in that we utilise the open source library OpenCV (www.opencv.org) to compute and match features. OpenCV is a BSD-licensed computer vision and machine learning software library with a feature detection and matching framework that allows for a variety of different keypoint extraction and descriptor methods. Currently implemented matching methods are SIFT [11], SURF [12] and BRISK [13]. These provide a range of keypoint descriptors that can be utilised depending on requirements for speed, robustness or commercial purposes (SIFT and SURF are patented methods, freely available for non-commercial use only).

Following the triangulation and bundle adjustment stage of the workflow, the camera pose and sparse point cloud are used to create a dense reconstruction of the scene using MVS. The MVS method used here implements view-clustering to group images in order to reduce memory requirements and reconstruction speed. For details on the view-clustering MVS method used here refer to [14].

2.3 Point Cloud Processing and Surface Generation

Following dense reconstruction, the point cloud is converted into a structure that can be used in the Point Cloud Library (PCL), a large scale open project for point cloud processing [15]. The PCL libraries contains algorithms for filtering, feature and object detection, processing and smoothing, model fitting and surface reconstruction. Currently, the following PCL operations are implemented in Workspace: (1) normal and curvature estimation using OpenMP; (2) statistical processing and filtering; (3) moving least squares smoothing and upsampling (useful for DTM generation); and, (4) iterative closest point registration. These operations, and others within the libraries can be used interchangeably in the workflow to filter, smooth and transform the point clouds depending on output requirements. As a result, the workflow can be easily modified or extended to have uses beyond the creation of surfaces for numerical modelling.

For simulation of environmental flows, a watertight reconstruction of the surface is required, with minimal artificial perturbations or mesh artefacts such as non-manifold geometry. The main challenge with creating surfaces from the SfM-MVS process is handling non-uniform point density, noise and misaligned points; while being scalable to large point clouds. There are several surface reconstruction methods currently available and research in this area is active. In this workflow, the Smoothed Signed Distance Colored (SSD-C) surface reconstruction method of Calakli and Taubin [16] is used. This method was chosen for its speed and durability, however additional methods may be easily substituted if required.

2.4   Numerical Modelling

The reconstructed surface created from the previous steps has a number of potential applications, including visualisation and as an input for numerical modelling. Here, we demonstrate an application for high-resolution numerical modelling within a complicated urban environment using 3D smoothed particle hydrodynamics (SPH). SPH is a versatile, meshless, Lagrangian particle method that has been used to model environmental phenomena such as tsunami, dam breaks, landslide initiation, lava flows and mudflows [2]. SPH is particularly advantageous for modelling complicated flows within complex environments due to the natural handling of complex topography and free surface flows, and the ability to include additional physics such as non-Newtonian rheology and entrainment of dynamic objects.

In the workflow, the reconstructed surface is converted into a data structure that can be read by the SPH software, which is run externally to the workflow due to the long computational time (in the order of weeks to months) required for high resolution simulations. Once completed, the data can be analysed and visualised within Workspace using separate data analysis workflows.

3   Case Study: Arequipa, Peru

To demonstrate the applicability of this method, we present a case study of the workflow for Arequipa City, Peru. Arequipa's central business district is located approximately 17 km south-west of El Misti, a steep potentially active volcano. The city is exposed to flash floods and lahars (volcanic debris flows) due to climatic conditions and the city's proximity to El Misti. Areas along the main quebradas (ravines) of San Lazaro and Huarangal are at risk from flash floods and lahars during the rainy season or after eruptions [17]. For example, flash floods in February 2011 destroyed 20 houses and caused damage to another 400, mostly along the quebradas and steep slopes. Much of this damage was attributed to heavy rainfall or breakout floods caused by infill obstacles such as makeshift crossings [17]. High resolution terrain models are required to represent the small scale of these features, while the rapidly changing environment requires frequent updating to accurately represent the topography for hazard simulations. This area was therefore chosen as a case study to demonstrate the value of the modelling workflow.

3.1   Image Collection

An approximately 200 m long and 200 m wide area of Quebrada San Lazaro was studied and is shown in figure 2a, looking upstream from a road bridge. The area in question contained the bridge and an upstream bend in the channel, which are thought to create overbank flow and strong 3D flow features that are ideal to test the use of SPH. In total, 2000 images of the area were acquired in September 2013; 600 images were taken from the ground and 1400 aerially. The aerial images were obtained from a DJI Phantom, a small ($35 \times 35 \times 19$ cm), lightweight (take off mass < 1 kg) quadcopter with an attached camera.

The objective of the image collection stage was to acquire as many images as possible from multiple angles to ensure all features were reproduced correctly and that there was minimal occlusion. A quadcopter is ideal in these circumstances, as its light weight and maneuverability means that it can be flown in close proximity to buildings to acquire images from multiple angles. In other areas (e.g. larger regions will less changes to terrain) a higher, more stable, but less maneuverable, aerial platform such as a helium balloon may be more suitable.

3.2   Feature Matching, SfM and MVS

Image features for the case study were detected and matched using SIFT feature descriptors. In an unordered image set, such as the one used in this case study, each image can potentially match each other image, meaning that image matching has $O(n^2)$ complexity. To reduce the time taken to match images, we parallelised this portion of the workflow, enabling matches to be determined on local and external CPU cores using the Workspace parallel execution engine. A speedup of 600% was achieved using parallel processing on 12 CPU cores (at 2.93 GHz), the speedup of the parallel implementation in this case is limited by the file I/O. Following image matching, the triangulation, bundle adjustment and multi-view stereo processes are run separately using VisualSFM [18], which utilises the CMVS-PMVS method of Furukawa and Ponce [14].

3.3   Mesh Generation

The SfM-MVS process created a dense point cloud containing ~8.5 million nodes. An image of the point cloud taken from a similar view angle to figure 2a is shown in figure 2b, where the point cloud model appears to correspond well with the real topography. The density of the raw point cloud varied due to occlusion and the number of images taken of a particular area. The maximum point cloud density was approximately 250 points in a 0.25 m^2 area. However, for this application point densities of this magnitude are much higher than required and the point cloud was reduced by 10% to have a maximum of 1 point within a 1 cm radius (7.6 million points over the entire case study area). The filtered point cloud was then reconstructed into a watertight, manifold mesh using SSD reconstruction, shown in figure 3. For this example, the entire point cloud processing workflow took 10 minutes; however the amount of required memory (~10Gb) may limit the scalability of SSD reconstruction to much larger areas.

Fig. 2. (a) Case study area in Quebrada San Lazaro and, (b) dense point cloud reconstruction from the SfM-MVS

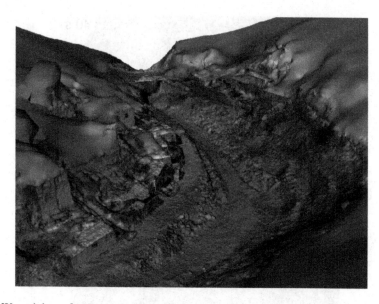

Fig. 3. Watertight surface reconstruction of the case study area using SSD (looking downstream towards bridge)

3.4   SPH Simulation

Multiple SPH simulations examining the effect of flash flood flow rates on inundation, flow structures and velocities were run, using the terrain model generated from the previous steps. Computational time for the simulations increases by the cube of particle spacing and can therefore be reduced significantly through increasing particle spacing and simplification of the terrain. Terrain resolution and particle spacing was chosen here to be the largest resolution size of the smallest features that might affect the flow. Input flow rates of 25, 50 and 150 m^3s^{-1} were considered, with a particle spacing of 12.5 cm. In the highest flow rate scenario, this required 2.8 million fluid particles to be simulated, which took 2 weeks of runtime to simulate 150 seconds of inundation on a 12 core, 2.93 GHz processor.

Figure 4 displays the velocities and inundation patterns 40 seconds after the flash flood was initiated for each flow rate. The fluid is shaded by velocity, with red being 10 ms^{-1} and blue being 0 ms^{-1}. The inundated area and velocities increase with flow rate, which is expected given the larger volume of water in the flow. The shape and magnitude of some flow structures are also different for the three flow rates. The effect of small features in the terrain is largely invisible in the highest flow rate scenario, with the flow mainly being guided by the bend in the channel. The effects of smaller features on the flow are noticeable for the 50 and 25 m^3s^{-1} scenarios. For example, the small access road into the channel (circled in figure 4) causes hydraulic jumps to form in the lower flow rate scenarios, but the high flow rate scenario is largely unaffected by this feature. This demonstrates the necessity of detailed 3D representations of terrain and modelling, particularly when considering smaller, high frequency flooding scenarios.

330   S.R. Mead et al.

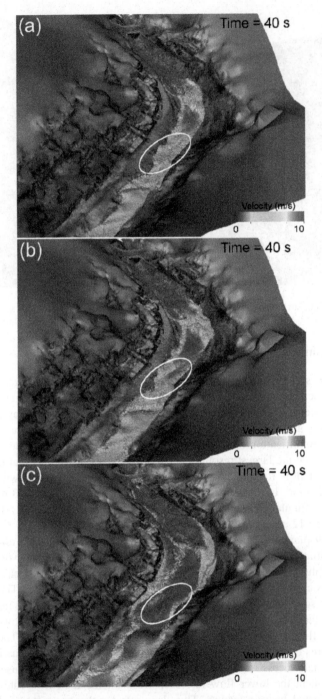

Fig. 4. SPH simulations of a flash flood in Quebrada San Lazaro with flow rates of (a) 150, (b) 50 and, (c) 25 m³s⁻¹. White circle highlights small road seen to affect flow structures in lower flow rate simulations.

4   Conclusion

The workflow presented here describes a process for generating 3D terrain models by utilising advances in structure-from-motion, multi-view stereo, point cloud processing and surface generation. The process is inexpensive, rapid, captures fine scale features and accurately represents 3D structures within complex environments. The parallel processing of image matching ensures the workflow is scalable to a large number of images. By reducing the cost and acquisition time, terrain models can be generated at a higher frequency, better capturing transient small-scale features such as flow blockages and obstacles that can affect flow behaviour. Data processing is achieved through the use of a modular workflow engine, which allows for new methods to be implemented as research into particular areas progresses. The flexibility of the workflow engine, in addition to the usage of open source libraries and data structures provides opportunities beyond the use case demonstrated here, as the process and data generated may be used in various visualisation, terrain analysis and risk assessment fields of study.

The use and an application of this workflow was demonstrated using the case study area of Arequipa, Peru, where the resulting terrain model was used to predict the impacts of flash flood events using smoothed particle hydrodynamics. In addition to the presented numerical modelling application, the resulting terrain models can be used in a variety of applications such as visualisation, building classification and vulnerability estimation.

References

1. Manville, V., Cronin, S.J.: Breakout Lahar from New Zealand's Crater Lake. Eos, Transactions American Geophysical Union 88, 441–442 (2007)
2. Cleary, P.W., Prakash, M.: Discrete–element modelling and smoothed particle hydrodynamics: potential in the environmental sciences. Philosophical Transactions of the Royal Society of London. Series A: Mathematical, Physical and Engineering Sciences 362, 2003–2030 (2004)
3. Williams, R.D., Brasington, J., Hicks, M., Measures, R., Rennie, C.D., Vericat, D.: Hydraulic validation of two-dimensional simulations of braided river flow with spatially continuous aDcp data. Water Resources Research 49, 5183–5205 (2013)
4. Legleiter, C.J., Kyriakidis, P.C., McDonald, R.R., Nelson, J.M.: Effects of uncertain topographic input data on two-dimensional flow modeling in a gravel-bed river. Water Resources Research 47, W03518, 3518 (2011)
5. Javernick, L., Brasington, J., Caruso, B.: Modeling the topography of shallow braided rivers using Structure-from-Motion photogrammetry. Geomorphology 213, 166–182 (2014)
6. Kreylos, O., Oskin, M., Cowgill, E., Gold, P., Elliott, A., Kellogg, L.: Point-based computing on scanned terrain with LidarViewer. Geosphere 9, 546–556 (2013)
7. Workspace (2014), http://research.csiro.au/workspace
8. Furukawa, Y., Curless, B., Seitz, S.M., Szeliski, R.: Towards Internet-scale multi-view stereo. In: 2010 IEEE Conference on Computer Vision and Pattern Recognition (CVPR), pp. 1434–1441 (2010)

9. Seitz, S.M., Curless, B., Diebel, J., Scharstein, D., Szeliski, R.: A Comparison and Evaluation of Multi-View Stereo Reconstruction Algorithms. In: 2006 IEEE Computer Society Conference on Computer Vision and Pattern Recognition (CVPR), pp. 519–528 (2006)
10. Snavely, N., Seitz, S.M., Szeliski, R.: Photo tourism: exploring photo collections in 3D. ACM Trans. Graph. 25, 835–846 (2006)
11. Lowe, D.G.: Object recognition from local scale-invariant features. In: The Proceedings of the Seventh IEEE International Conference on Computer Vision, vol. 1152, pp. 1150–1157 (1999)
12. Bay, H., Tuytelaars, T., Van Gool, L.: SURF: Speeded Up Robust Features. In: Leonardis, A., Bischof, H., Pinz, A. (eds.) ECCV 2006, Part I. LNCS, vol. 3951, pp. 404–417. Springer, Heidelberg (2006)
13. Leutenegger, S., Chli, M., Siegwart, R.Y.: BRISK: Binary Robust invariant scalable keypoints. In: 2011 IEEE International Conference on Computer Vision (ICCV), pp. 2548–2555 (2011)
14. Furukawa, Y., Ponce, J.: Accurate, Dense, and Robust Multiview Stereopsis. IEEE Transactions on Pattern Analysis and Machine Intelligence 32, 1362–1376 (2010)
15. Rusu, R.B., Cousins, S.: 3D is here: Point Cloud Library (PCL). In: 2011 IEEE International Conference on Robotics and Automation (ICRA), pp. 1–4 (2011)
16. Calakli, F., Taubin, G.: SSD-C: Smooth Signed Distance Colored Surface Reconstruction. In: Dill, J., Earnshaw, R., Kasik, D., Vince, J., Wong, P.C. (eds.) Expanding the Frontiers of Visual Analytics and Visualization, pp. 323–338. Springer, London (2012)
17. Thouret, J.-C., Enjolras, G., Martelli, K., Santoni, O., Luque, J., Nagata, M., Arguedas, A., Macedo, L.: Combining criteria for delineating lahar-and flash-flood-prone hazard and risk zones for the city of Arequipa, Peru. Natural Hazards and Earth System Sciences 13, 339–360 (2013)
18. Wu, C.: Towards Linear-Time Incremental Structure from Motion. In: 2013 International Conference on 3D Vision (3DV), pp. 127–134 (2013)

An Integrated Workflow Architecture for Natural Hazards, Analytics and Decision Support

James Hilton, Claire Miller, Matt Bolger, Lachlan Hetherton, and Mahesh Prakash

CSIRO Digital Productivity Flagship
james.hilton@csiro.au

Abstract. We present a modular workflow platform for the simulation and analysis of natural hazards. The system is based on the CSIRO Workspace architecture, allowing transparent data interoperability between input, simulation and analysis components. The system is currently in use for flooding and inundation modelling, as well as research into bushfire propagation. The modularity of the architecture allows tools from multiple development groups to be easily combined into complex workflows for any given scenario. Examples of platform usage are demonstrated for saline intrusion into an environmentally sensitive area and image analysis inputs into a fire propagation model.

Keywords: simulation, workflow, natural hazard.

1 Introduction

Computational simulations of natural hazards such as floods and fires can now be performed with high accuracy at speeds greatly exceeding real-time. Analytics from such models can give valuable prediction information to decision makers in the event of a crisis, aiding decision support, or allow detailed risk assessments to be performed on vulnerable regions. Such natural hazard models have specific architectural needs, such as the ability to handle large data sets, run complex computational methods and perform detailed ensemble analysis over the results of these models.

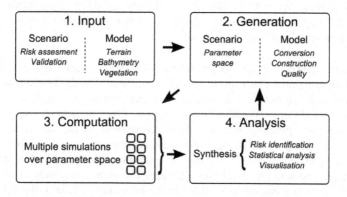

Fig. 1. Stages in modelling a natural hazard event

R. Denzer et al. (Eds.): ISESS 2015, IFIP AICT 448, pp. 333–342, 2015.
© IFIP International Federation for Information Processing 2015

A typical workflow in a natural hazard modelling process is shown in Fig. 1. This can be subdivided into a series of stages, which are:

1. Determination of the requirements for the given scenario, such as prediction of risk or impact assessment. The requirements for the scenario decide the input data requirements for the model, as well as the parameter space over which the model will be run. This input data may need to be gathered from local or remote data repositories and may be a static or real-time data source. For natural hazards this data may include items such as digital elevation models, wind predictions or measurements, precipitation levels, bathymetry measurements or land usage maps.

2. Generation of formatted data suitable for the model. The data is quality checked, cleaned, processed and converted into a format required for the model. For geophysical data this stage may involve processing such as filling missing values in data sets or geodetic re-projection into a common datum or format. The required parameters or sample space for the model are also generated during this stage. Examples of such parameter spaces include ranges of probable tidal extents for inundation scenarios, or the degree of variation in fuel load in bushfire scenarios.

3. Simulation of the given scenario over the parameter space using the cleaned, formatted data sets. One instance of an underlying computational solver is usually run for each element in the parameter space. These instances may be run sequentially or in parallel on local or remote compute nodes. Each instance requires the ability to read and write large data sets to storage which may be local or remote relative to the instance.

4. Synthesis and analysis of the multiple raw data items produced by the computation. This can be an automated or manual processes depending on the scenario, such as risk identification from spatial maps, statistical ensemble analysis or visualization of the results. In some applications, such as real-time scenarios with rapidly changing input conditions, the results from the final stage can be used to inform the choice of parameter space for subsequent simulations of the scenario.

The requirement for an end-to-end solution for these stages has led to the development of an integrated platform for modelling natural hazards. The aim of this platform is to provide all of this functionality in a user-friendly and rapidly configurable environment for different types of natural hazard. Once a particular scenario is defined, and the corresponding workflow has been constructed, the workflow can be run on multiple operating systems and hardware types, ranging from desktop systems to GPU based supercomputers. If required, interaction with the workflow can be exposed through a custom graphical user interface. The architecture behind this modular framework for natural hazards is outlined in the following section, followed by examples of two current use cases.

2   Software Architecture

A schematic diagram of the architecture behind the framework is shown in Fig. 2. The natural hazard solvers sit within the CSIRO Workspace environment, which is based on the Qt framework. There are currently two operational natural hazard solvers: SWIFT, which is a hydrodynamic modelling tool for inundation and flooding and SPARK, which is a fire perimeter propagation tool.

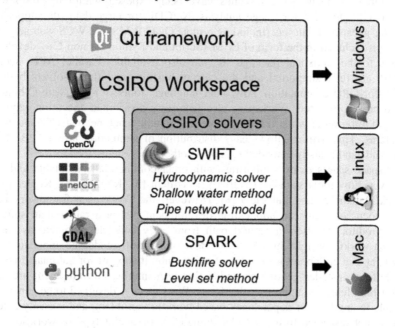

Fig. 2. Architecture of the CSIRO Workspace and natural hazard solvers

CSIRO Workspace is a cross-platform, extensible workflow and application development framework which handles three main elements; data objects, operations, and user interface elements or widgets [1]. As well as natural hazards, Workspace has been applied to a number of other scientific areas including quantitative imaging, additive manufacturing and industrial process modelling.

In Workspace, workflow stages are encapsulated into individual Workspace operations with multiple input and output data objects connected together into a dependency graph. Data is passed in-memory between operations, allowing efficient, transparent communication of data through the system. This data can be inspected and interacted with at any stage, including during execution, with various data-type specific widgets. The plugin architecture exposes data types, operations and widgets to the framework through shared libraries. Workspace plugins are shared libraries (.dll, .so or .dylib) which act as containers, exposing components to the framework. The Workspace editor includes code generation wizards to create stub code for new components and utilizes CMake for cross platform compilation. Development of complex user interfaces is supported with easy drag and drop designing within Qt Designer allowing any input or output throughout a workflow to be visualized or controlled from a simplified, abstracted user interface. Workspace provides a large library of useful data types, operations and widgets out-of-the-box, such as image manipulation, visualization, mesh processing, database support and plot generation. Workspace itself is written predominantly in C++ for performance and scalability and leverages the full power of the Qt toolkit providing a library of underlying capabilities for developers to leverage such as threading, file IO (XML, JSON etc.), networking, image processing, and 3D visualization using OpenGL.

A number of open-source modules have been exposed within the framework. These include OpenCV for image analysis, NetCDF for large data file support and GDAL for geospatial datasets (including remote OGC WMS and WCS web-services). Scripting is included in the form of ECMAScript and Python for non-C++ developers and calls to the statistical package 'R' are also available. Parallel APIs, such as OpenMP, are fully supported and the current bushfire and flood solvers both use OpenCL for GPU computation. Any other language, toolset or API with C bindings can also be incorporated. Workspace also features a distributed execution capability allowing it to farm out work to local CPU cores, remote machines via TCP and cluster job systems. This feature allows easy distribution of simulation jobs to PBS-based clusters and can be easily extended to support other job systems.

Workspace shares many similarities with other commercially available and open source workflow tools such as Taverna [2], Trident [3], KNIME [4], Kepler [5, 6], Simulink/Matlab [7] and LabView [8]. However, the Workspace framework has a stronger focus on being an application development platform rather than simply a workflow editor. It offers a natural path from early code development as part of a research workflow right through to the development of standalone applications for deployment to a collaborator or external client. Inbuilt support for automated testing, cross-platform installer generation and native user-interface development are some distinguishing features supporting this focus. Workspace is designed to be generically applicable to any kind of dependency-based workflow problem, and is easily extendable. It is not restricted to a particular domain, or particular type of workflow, and developers can easily extend its functionality by writing plug-ins. Some workflow engines (such as KNIME and Kepler) are similar in this way, while others have more domain specific focus (such as LabView for measurement and control systems and Simulink for simulation and model-based design). The system also transfers data in-memory between operations as opposed to using local storage or a database as the intermediary between operations, as implemented in workflow engines that focus on web-service connectivity such as Taverna and Trident. In-memory operation is very suited to the computationally intensive needs of natural hazard modelling, in contrast to local storage which can severely impede performance. Workspace is also the only workflow tool which can execute in continuous mode. In this mode, any modification to an operation input triggers an immediate downstream update of the workflow, including all relevant visual outputs. This event-driven approach enables users to immediately visualize factors such as changes to their input conditions or post processing steps.

Workspace is built on free software license tools, such as the Qt framework. This allows researchers and developers to freely build and distribute applications based on their workflows, or integrate them into existing software packages. Workflow-based application development like this is not well supported in open source available alternatives while commercial packages such as Simulink/Matlab and LabView require paid licenses. Furthermore, although packages such as Simulink/Matlab also provide user interface customization features, Workspace's tight integration with the Qt framework enables developers to quickly and easily develop user interfaces for their workflows. A number of specialized Qt widgets have been developed specifically for natural hazard operations, such as interactive time-series inputs and two-dimensional layer views. These can be directly built into a user interface using the Qt Designer tool and linked with an underlying workflow. Furthermore, a design goal of Workspace was for computational fluid dynamics applications, and it therefore offers far greater interactive 2D and 3D scientific visualization capabilities than alternative workflow engines.

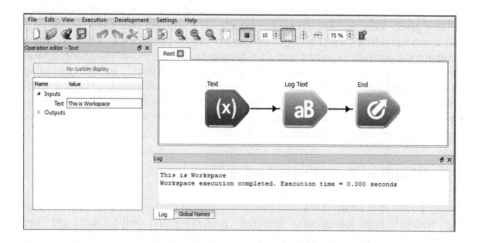

Fig. 3. A simple example of a workflow in the Workspace GUI

An example workflow is shown in Fig. 3 within the Workspace editor GUI. Individual workflow elements, or operations, are represented as colored triangular blocks which are logically joined in the GUI by dragging output data from an operation to the input of another operation. The joins, and the direction of data flow, are shown as black connection arrows in the GUI. In this simple example some text data is created ('Text' block) and passed into an operation to output the text to a log ('Log Text' block). A final block acts as an operation representing the end of the workflow ('End' block). This example passes string data, but new data types can easily be defined and added. For the natural hazard solvers both two-dimensional gridded data sets and one-dimensional time series data sets were added as new data types within Workspace. The workflow is saved as xml, and once a Workspace workflow has been developed it can be easily shared between collaborators. Workspace supports execution both from the GUI shown in Fig. 3, execution in batch mode from the command-line, or an API for stand-alone Qt-based applications.

The computational solver elements are implemented as individual operations. Each solver operation requires a set of configuration parameters specific to the particular operation. These parameters consist of items such as the total time for the solver to be run, how often to output simulation data and global physical variables for the solver. The solver inputs also include two dimensional input data sets for the starting conditions as well as two dimensional layers such as topography and land usage. The solver executes for a specified period before pausing and returning control back to Workspace. Once control is returned, Workspace operations outside the solver have access to internal data from the solver and can be used to analyze, output, display or collate the data. Once these steps are complete, control is returned to the solver which resumes, runs again for the specified period, then returns control back to Workspace. This loop is carried out until the solver reaches the specified total simulation time, at which point Workspace ends execution.

The solver operations incorporate an additional feature, called processor modules, which are exposed as a subclass of Workspace operations. These processors are subsolvers with full access to the solver data and are used to provide specific capabilities for any given scenario. The processor modules are separate operations which plug into a corresponding solver. Multiple processors can be connected to a solver, which transparently controls execution and data management within each processor. Examples of these processors for the hydrodynamic solver, SWIFT, include providing rainfall conditions, applying tidal boundary conditions, infiltration effects, evapotranspiration and coupling with a one-dimensional pipe network model. These processors can be developed separately from the solver, which was a key requirement in the design of the solvers as open platforms for collaboration.

3   Workflow for Saline Intrusion

The hydrodynamic model SWIFT is based on a finite-volume shallow water formulation, which is both conservative, positivity preserving and well-balanced [9]. The project in this example was designed to examine the effects of saline intrusion from potential sea level rise on environmentally and culturally sensitive areas of Kakadu National Park in the Northern Territory, Australia. Multiple tidal cycles were required to ensure adequate saline mixing with the freshwater from the catchments, so the simulations were run for a period of 30 days. The simulation domain was an area of approximately 150 km × 120 km, encompassing the major catchments of the park, at a resolution of 60 m.

The Workspace GUI in Fig. 4 has been arranged with input operations on the left-hand side, the solver at the center and a 3D output of Kadadu national park on the right hand side. The inputs for this model consisted of a digital elevation model (DEM) for the bathymetry and topography as well as the initial salinity state. These were supplied as files in a standard ESRI ASCII format. The 3D output was configured for this example to show the textured digital elevation model with a water layer colored by saline concentration. The processor modules are shown as the set of upper red boxes. These included a processor module to apply the tides to the northern boundary, a module for rainfall based on a time series from measured data, a module for evapotranspiration and a module for advective-diffusive saline transport and mixing.

The actual simulations for the project were run in batch mode using PBS on the CSIRO Accelerator Cluster, rather than through the interactive GUI shown in Fig. 4.

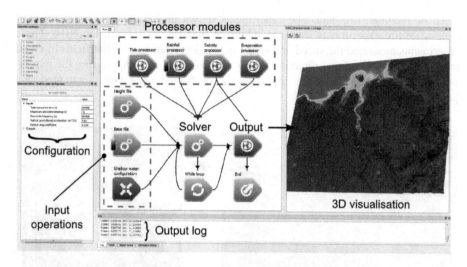

Fig. 4. Example workflow configuration for environmental impact assessment of saline intrusion in Kakadu National Park, Australia

The simulations took 42 hours to complete on a Tesla K20 GPU, with an average simulation time-step of 0.7 s. Data from the simulation was written to disk in a binary format and an analysis step was performed on this data using a second workflow to provide various time-averaged metrics such as the maximum, minimum and median water levels and salinity concentrations over the 30 day simulation. These metrics are currently being used for an impact assessment of sea level rise on freshwater species and cultural sites in the region for the NERP Northern Australia Hub.

4   Workflow for Bushfires

The scenario in this second example is a comparison between a controlled experimental fire in a plot of cured grass and a level-set based bushfire computational model, SPARK [10]. The level set method is a computational model for the propagation of an interface [11], and can be applied to numerous systems such as crystal growth, droplet dynamics and bubbles. SPARK uses the level set method to track the interface between regions in a fire that are burnt and un-burnt. The level set method has several advantages over other computational methods for interface propagation; it is raster based and therefore highly suited to GPU acceleration, it naturally handles the merging of interfaces and the interface can be given an arbitrary outward speed at any point.

The outward speed of the interface in SPARK is equal to the rate of spread of the fire. The functional form of rates of spread in real fires are known to depend on several factors relating to fire propagation including the wind speed, wind direction, fuel and moisture levels and slope of the ground. Many empirical expressions have been given for various fuel types [12, 13], but the functional form for rates of spread in two dimensions is currently an active area of research. SPARK is currently being used as a research tool for investigating new two-dimensional rate of spread empirical models based on recorded fire data. The experiments shown in this example are number of large-scale fire experiments were carried out in Ballarat, Victoria in Jan 2014. These experiments measured the speed and shape of fire propagation over flat fields of cured grass. The wind speed and direction during the fire were recorded during the experiment, and the progression of the fire perimeter was filmed using camera mounted on a quad-copter.

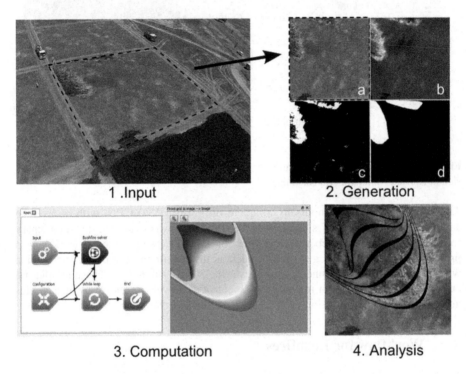

Fig. 5. Stages for comparison of experimental data to simulation results

Comparison of the simulation outputs with the recorded experimental data, shown in Fig. 5.1, required a sequence of image processing transformations. These steps are shown in Fig. 5.2, including (a) rectification of the original image onto a Cartesian grid, (b) identification of the burning areas, (c) thresholding and (d) reconstruction of the interface between burnt and un-burnt areas. Each of these steps were carried out using OpenCV operations which have been natively incorporated into Workspace. Once the data had been rectified, it could be used as the initial condition in the simulations. Fig. 5.3 shows an example configuration of SPARK in operation, where the panel on the left hand side shows the individual operations comprising the workflow, and the image on the right hand side a preview of the results. The color scale in the image represents the arrival time of the fire, with blue equal to zero and red equal to the current simulation time. In the final stage, the results of the model can be used to forward predict the behavior of the fire perimeter, shown in Fig. 5.4. The perimeter locations predicted by the model at 5 second intervals up to 25 seconds from the start of the fire are shown as black bands in the image. These are superimposed over the recorded fire perimeter at 25 seconds from ignition time.

Each of the stages in this example consists of a number of self-contained processes which operated on similar data types. Using our architecture, all stages can be directly processed from start to end within the same framework. These were logically chained together in the workflow environment for each image processing step. An operation could then be used to convert the output image directly into the initial conditions required for the bushfire computational solver after the image processing steps were complete. Finally, data from the solver was visualized for prediction of the fire perimeter. As well as a research tool, SPARK is currently being built into an operational predictive model using published empirical expressions for fire rates of spread over grassland and Eucalypt forest.

5   Conclusion

The combination of computational solvers and the CSIRO Workspace framework gives a flexible, modular platform for modelling natural hazards. All of the steps in a typical natural hazard simulation, from reading and cleaning input data, simulation, analysis and visualization, have been implemented as individual operations on common data types. These operation can be either be contained within a single end-to-end workflow or, dependent on requirements, split into sub-workflows for pre-processing, execution and post processing. The Workspace framework has a number of advantages over existing workflow engines. These include in-memory data transfer between operations, which is advantageous for the complex, real-time applications and computationally intensive simulations found in natural hazard modelling. The framework also allows workflows to be run in an interactive continuous mode. In fast natural hazard models, such as SPARK, this interactivity enables conditions to be changed on-the fly. Alternatively, workflows for detailed simulations, such as the SWIFT application in this paper, can be executed in a batch mode on high performance computing nodes.

The architecture has been demonstrated in this paper for two very different applications, environmental impact analysis from saline intrusion and image processing of real fire events as input into a fire model. These applications represent only a small subset of the potential applications for the framework. Environmental modelling workflows can be rapidly tailored for any natural hazard application, such as operational usage from data streams or detailed simulations for environmental modeling. These workflows can, if required, be packaged and run behind a Qt user interface and freely distributed by virtue of the permissive software licenses on which Workspace is built. Future work includes adding further solver components to the system, including models for dust advection, granular dynamics and mudflows. However, the open nature of the architecture allows other users and research groups to add any new computational models to the system. Alternatively, processing units can be constructed and freely added to run sub-models on any of the existing natural hazard models.

We have demonstrated the potential of this system within this paper, and expect many applications for this system in the future within the environmental modelling space.

References

1. Workspace (2014), `http://research.csiro.au/workspace/`
2. TavernaWorkflow Management System (2014), http://www.taverna.org.uk/
3. Project Trident: A scientific workflow workbench (2014), `http://tridentworkflow.codeplex.com/`
4. KNIME (2014), `http://www.knime.org/`
5. The Kepler project (2014), https://kepler-project.org/
6. Altintas, I., Berkley, C., Jaeger, E., Jones, M., Ludascher, B., Mock, S.: Kepler: an extensible system for design and execution of scientific workflows. In: Proceedings of the 16th International Conference on Scientific and Statistical Database Management, pp. 423–424 (2004)
7. Simulink simulation and model-based design (2014), `http://www.mathworks.com/products/simulink/`
8. LabVIEW System Design Software (2014), http://www.ni.com/labview/
9. Kurganov, A., Petrova, G.: A Second-Order Well-Balanced Positivity Preserving Central-Upwind Scheme for the Saint-Venant System. Commun. Math. Sci. 5, 133–160 (2007)
10. Hilton, J.E., Miller, C., Sullivan, A., Rucinski, C.: Incorporation of variation into wildfire spread models using a level set approach. Environmental Modelling and Software (under review)
11. Sethian, J.A.: Evolution, implementation, and application of level set and fast marching methods for advancing fronts. Journal of Computational Physics 169, 503–555 (2001)
12. Gould, J.S., McCaw, W.L., Cheney, N.P., Ellis, P.F., Knight, I.K., Sullivan, A.L.: Project Vesta – Fire in Dry Eucalypt Forest: Fuel Structure, Dynamics and Fire Behaviour, CSIRO Ensis and Department of Environment and Conservation: Canberra, ACT (2007)
13. Cheney, N.P., Gould, J.S., Catchpole, W.R.: Prediction of fire spread in grasslands. International Journal of Wildland Fire 8, 1–13 (1998)

Quality Control of Environmental Measurement Data with Quality Flagging

Mauno Rönkkö[1], Okko Kauhanen[1], Markus Stocker[1], Harri Hytönen[2],
Ville Kotovirta[3], Esko Juuso[4], and Mikko Kolehmainen[1]

[1] Department of Environmental Science,
University of Eastern Finland, Kuopio, Finland
{mauno.ronkko,okko.kauhanen,
markus.stocker,mikko.kolehmainen}@uef.fi
[2] Vaisala Oyj, Vantaa, Finland
harri.hytonen@vaisala.com
[3] VTT Technical Research Centre of Finland, Espoo, Finland
ville.kotovirta@vtt.fi
[4] Faculty of Technology, Control Engineering,
University of Oulu, Oulu, Finland
esko.juuso@oulu.fi

Abstract. We discuss quality control of environmental measurement data. Typically, environmental data is used to compute some specific indicators based on models, historical data, and the most recent measurement data. For such a computation to produce reliable results, the data must be of sufficient quality. The reality is, however, that environmental measurement data has a huge variation in quality. Therefore, we study the use of quality flagging as a means to perform both real-time and off-line quality control of environmental measurement data. We propose the adoption of the quality flagging scheme introduced by the Nordic meteorological institutes. As the main contribution, we present both a uniform interpretation for the quality flag values and a scalable Enterprise Service Bus based architecture for implementing the quality flagging. We exemplify the use of the quality flagging and the architecture with a case study for monitoring of built environment.

Keywords: quality control, quality flagging, enterprise service bus, environmental data, built environment.

1   Introduction

Environmental measurement and monitoring has been a growing trend for the past decade [1]. It is needed for instance for assessing the negative impact of human activities to the environment [2,3]. Environmental measurements, however, are prone to external variation and even disruptions. Therefore, raw measurement data must always be somehow preprocessed before it can be used in computations as an input. There exist standards for the representation of environmental data. For instance, the Open Geospatial Consortium provides standards for the representation and access of

R. Denzer et al. (Eds.): ISESS 2015, IFIP AICT 448, pp. 343–350, 2015.

the spatial data. However, the standards do not address the issue of data quality comprehensively. For instance, UncertML [4] was proposed as an extension to OGC, to address uncertainty representation. With UncertML, one can attach probabilistic uncertainties to environmental data sets. Still, standards do not provide sufficient support, for instance for real-time quality control of environmental data, as discussed in Section 2.

Quality flagging is a means to provide quality information on the level of individual measurement data points both in real-time and off-line. Most importantly, quality flagging is also a reversible activity, as it preserves all original measurement values. As discussed in Section 2, we focus on one specific quality flagging scheme. It is the scheme presented by Vejen et al. [5] that is recommended and used by the Nordic meteorological institutes. Since the quality flagging scheme by Vejen et al. is tailored for weather measurement data, we propose as part of the main contribution a uniform interpretation for the quality flag values to be used for the flagging of any kind of environmental measurement data. It should be noted that the quality flagging scheme by Vejen et al. is not what World Meteorological Organization (WMO) refers to when speaking of a Quality Management Framework. In particular, WMO strives after an ISO certification, whereas the quality flagging scheme is a technical implementation of a real-time and off-line computational quality procedure.

As the other part of the main contribution, in Section 3, we present an Enterprise Service Bus (ESB) [6] based architecture to perform quality flagging in a scalable and measurement device independent manner. In Section 4, we illustrate the use of the ESB based architecture to perform quality flagging of data for built environment, including room temperature and water consumption measurements. As the research work is still ongoing, we present here our complete plans. We conclude in Section 5.

2   Quality Control of Environmental Measurement Data

When considering quality control of environmental measurement data, there is practically one well-known proposed standard, UncertML [4]. With UncertML, one can attach probabilistic uncertainties to environmental data sets to support statistical preprocessing. For instance, Williams et al. [7] used UncertML to attach uncertainty information to raw weather data as provided by Weather Underground[1]. By using UncertML and INTAMAP [8], they were able to estimate the bias and residual variance, to adjust, merge, and interpolate temperature data from independent data sources. As a result, they were able to produce an interpolated temperature map for the whole UK based on the Weather Underground data with statistical corrections.

Although UncertML does provide means to improve the quality of environmental data, it operates on the level of measurement data sets. Such level of data quality, however, is not sufficient for all applications. A complementary approach is to perform quality control on the level of individual measurement data points. For this purpose quality flagging is used.

---

[1] http://www.wunderground.com

Table 1. Quality flag values and their original interpretation [5] along with the proposed generic interpretation

Flag	Original interpretation	Generic interpretation
0	No check performed	Value not checked
1	Observation is ok	Approved value
2	Suspected small difference	Suspicious value
3	Suspected big difference	Anomalous value
4	Calculated value	Corrected value
5	Interpolated value	Imputed value
6	(Not defined originally)	Erroneous value
7	(Not defined originally)	Frozen value
8	Missing value	Missing value
9	Deleted value	Deleted value

The Nordic meteorological institutes have developed a fully functioning quality flagging scheme as discussed by Vejen et al. [5]. It provides both real-time and off-line quality flagging. Vejen et al. [5] distinguish between four quality control levels. QC0 is a real-time quality control performed by the measurement devices or stations. QC1 is a real-time quality control performed by the data acquisition system prior to storing the data. QC2 is an off-line quality control performed by the data management system based on the stored data. Lastly, HQC is the final off-line quality control check performed by a human operator. Each of these levels use the same quality flag values as indicated in Table 1. Thus, the quality flag is a number with four digits: $C=E_{QC0}+10{\times}E_{QC1}+100{\times}E_{QC2}+1000{\times}E_{HQC}$, where each E_{QC0}, E_{QC1}, E_{QC2} and E_{HQC} are quality flag values for the corresponding quality control levels.

Because the quality flagging scheme by Vejen et al. is designed for weather measurements, it does not apply to generic environmental measurement data. In particular, the original interpretation can be non-informative or misleading in a generic case. Also, the original flag values do not support observations of a malfunctioning measurement device that produces constant, "frozen", or clearly erroneous measurement values. Therefore, we propose a generic interpretation for the quality flag values, as indicated in Table 1. The proposed interpretation is downwards compatible with the original interpretation, so that it could also be used for weather measurements. In particular, in the generic interpretation "suspicious value" and "anomalous value" are used instead of "small difference" and "big difference". Also, "imputation" is used instead of "interpolation", as interpolation may not be applicable in a generic case. Similarly, the generic interpretation replaces "calculated value" with "corrected value" to emphasize the difference between value correction and missing value imputation. Lastly, the generic interpretation uses the two originally unused flag values for diagnostics, to indicate a clear measurement error or a "frozen" measurement value.

It should be noted that quality flagging is a complementary approach with respect to use of UncertML. In particular, quality flagging operates on the level of individual measurement points, whereas UncertML operates on the level of data sets. Thus, both can be applied to the same data set at the same time to provide detailed information about the data quality. What makes the quality flagging an attractive approach is that it supports quality restrictions during the data queries. For instance, one can query only such data, where the final quality check has been performed. Similarly, one can query data, where there are no QC0 or QC1 failures or corrections. Implementing such queries requires no extra work, as they can be constructed based on the quality flag values. Such a query style is supported, for instance, by all SQL databases. Furthermore, queries about failures, suspicions, and corrections provide valuable information to be used with UncertML. In particular, information about bad quality can be used to select and fine tune appropriate statistical and probabilistic model for UncertML, to match the observed data quality.

Quality flagging provides also valuable information to systems diagnostics and maintenance. The frequency and trend of quality failures function as indicators for device failures or model inadequacies. Thus, the bigger the measurement network is, the more useful and valuable quality flagging becomes. This is something that is not currently addressed by methods such as UncertML that focus on interoperability at the level of datasets.

3   The Enterprise Service Bus Based Architecture

As depicted in Fig. 1, the role of the ESB is to pass measurement data as messages between services. More specifically, we use here WSO2 ESB[2]. The ESB is extended and configured so that it has a dedicated port and a mediator for each sensor. Thus, a sensor performs QC0 on the measurement data after each measurement and sends the data in its native format, such as JSON or XML, to the dedicated ESB port. The ESB then redirects the received measurement data to a dedicated mediator that performs QC1 and passes the checked measurement data back to the ESB. The ESB then redirects the checked measurement data to a data storage. The ESB is configured to trigger QC2 on stored data on regular intervals. The actual QC2 is then performed by a computational service, for which we use Octave[3]. For this purpose, a predetermined subset of the stored data is retrieved for the computational service. After QC2, the checked data is stored back to the data storage. Lastly, HQC is performed by a human operator on the data that is already checked by QC2. HQC is initiated by the human operator through a dedicated client application. The client application accesses the stored data requested by the operator through the ESB. Similarly, after HQC, the client application stores the checked data back to the data storage through the ESB.

The advantage of the ESB architecture is that it can be reconfigured by an administrator while the system is running. Therefore, it is possible to add new sensors and algorithms, as well as expand and refactor a data storage while the system is in use. The reception ports of the ESB can also be configured to receive measurement data as messages virtually in any format. For instance, the WSO2 ESB supports by default messages that are passed in HTTP and SOAP format. It should be noted that the ESB

---

[2] http://wso2.com/products/enterprise-service-bus/
[3] https://www.gnu.org/software/octave/

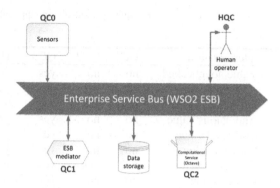

Fig. 1. An Enterprise Service Bus based architecture for quality flagging

architecture is scalable by using multiple ESB instances to improve performance by passing the messages in between them. Several concurrent instances of the ESB architecture can also be used to make the overall system more robust and fault-tolerant.

The ESB architecture also supports the use of OGC SWE Standards. The ESB architecture can be extended with ports configured, for instance, to receive and pass OGC O&M compliant data. Similarly, the architecture can be extended to support the OGC SOS standard for sensor data management.

4   Case Study

As our case study, we consider the monitoring of residential buildings. The buildings sector is the largest user of energy and CO_2 emitter in the EU, estimated at approximately 40% of the total consumption. In particular, we study a specific home monitoring system called AsTEKa [9,10]. For simplicity, we consider here only two variables: room temperature and water consumption. The sensors for these two variables are both physically and technologically different. As the research work is still ongoing, we present here our complete plans. We have already implemented the ESB architecture and we have studied various statistical methods to be used in the quality flagging. We have also implemented example mediators for quality control, but we have not yet implemented in full the quality flagging scheme that we discus next.

We decided not to consider all quality flag values for all quality control checks. Instead, only the most critical quality checks are considered, as indicated in Table 2. In particular, QC0 was not used, as AsTEKa uses low-cost sensors that do not support real-time computations. Instead, QC1 is extended to consider also the checks usually performed by QC0.

Room Temperature. Fig. 2 depicts the whole chain of quality control for room temperature data. QC1 decides coarsely if the data points are approved, suspicious, erroneous, or missing. As QC1 runs once a minute, quality controlled data points are available one minute after the measurement. Hence, such approved data points can be

Table 2. Quality flag values used in AsTEKa quality control; an applicable flag value is indicated by "yes"

Flag	Interpretation	QC1	QC2	QC3	HQC
0	Value not checked	no	no	yes	yes
1	Approved value	no	yes	yes	yes
2	Suspicious value	no	yes	yes	yes
3	Anomalous value	no	no	yes	yes
4	Corrected value	no	no	yes	yes
5	Imputed value	no	no	yes	yes
6	Erroneous value	no	yes	yes	no
7	Frozen value	no	no	yes	no
8	Missing value	no	yes	yes	no
9	Deleted value	no	no	yes	yes

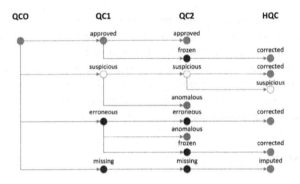

Fig. 2. Quality control of room temperature data

used for near real-time control of heating and cooling. By avoiding using suspicious and erroneous data points we can also avoid unnecessary heating and cooling.

Since QC2 runs every 2 hours, data after QC2 can be used for alerting occupants and maintenance personnel of anomalies and potential malfunctions. When considering heating and cooling, a 2 hours window is sufficient to prevent systemic failures that could cause damage to devices or structures. Thus, data after QC2 is particularly suited for diagnostic purposes and detecting occupant behavior or system settings causing to waste energy.

As HQC aims at resolving frozen, erroneous, or missing data, it is useful for analyzing structural changes in the residential building. Because structures weaken over time and the performance of heating or cooling devices also deteriorates over time, one can expect an increasing trend in use of energy over time. This trend can be computed by comparing quality controlled room temperature values with use of heating and cooling energy. As such a change is not abrupt, it is sufficient to perform HQC once a month. The frequency and number of performed corrections by HQC acts also as an indicator for the condition of the home monitoring system as a whole.

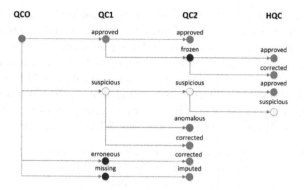

Fig. 3. Quality control of water consumption data

Water Consumption. Fig. 3 depicts the whole chain of quality control for water consumption data. QC1 decides coarsely if the data points are approved, suspicious, erroneous, or missing. As QC1 runs once a minute, only the erroneous and missing data points are of interest. In such a case, maintenance personnel could be notified and the measurement devices could be repaired quickly.

Since QC2 runs every 2 hours, data after QC2 can be used for alerting occupants and maintenance personnel of anomalies and potential malfunctions. In particular, the data after QC2 can be used to spot leaks and malfunction of valves and appliances that use water. When considering water consumption, a 2 hours window is generally sufficient to prevent systemic failures that could cause damage to appliances or structures. Thus, data after QC2 is particularly suited for diagnostic purposes and detecting occupant behavior or system malfunctions causing to waste water or causing structural damage. The frequency and number of performed corrections by QC2 indicates also the condition of the home monitoring system as a whole.

As HQC aims at resolving remaining frozen data, it is useful for analyzing the condition of appliances as well as occupant behavior that leads to wasting water. As such conditions do not evolve fast over time, it is sufficient to perform HQC once a month.

5   Conclusion

We studied the use of quality flagging as a means to perform quality control of environmental measurement data. We proposed the adoption of the quality flagging scheme introduced by the Nordic meteorological institutes to be used with any kind of environmental measurement data. We presented both a uniform, generalized interpretation for the quality flag values and a scalable Enterprise Service Bus based architecture for implementing the quality flagging. We exemplified the use of the quality flagging a case study for the monitoring of built environment. Our research is ongoing. We presented our design and approach to quality control by quality flagging. We have implemented the core ESB based architecture and we are currently implementing the quality flagging algorithms.

As for future work, we plan on studying occupant profile-based imputation of missing or erroneous values. Such profiling based models could also be used earlier in quality control, for instance, by having QC1 flagging suspicious values with respect to profile based reference values. We also plan on including different kinds of measurement variables, such as CO_2 and humidity. This would enable monitoring indoor air quality and automated notifications on degraded air quality. We are also simultaneously investigating the use of quality flagging in a sensor network monitoring water quality of lakes in Finland together with the Finnish Environment Institute.

Acknowledgements. We wish to thank the anonymous reviewers for valuable comments. This research is funded by the Tekes project "MMEA: Measurement, Monitoring, and Environmental Assessment" (Decision number 427/10).

References

1. Messer, H., Zinevich, A., Alpert, P.: Environmental Monitoring by Wireless Communication Networks. Science 312, 713 (2006)
2. Cyranoski, D., Brumfiel, G.: Fukushima impact is still hazy. Nature 477, 139–140 (2011)
3. Gilbert, N.: Drug waste harms fish. Nature 476, 265 (2011)
4. Williams, M., Cornford, D., Bastin, L., Pebesma, E.: Uncertainty markup language (UncertML),OpenGIS Discussion Paper 08-122r2, Open Geospatial Consortium Inc. (2009)
5. Vejen, F. (ed), Jacobsson, C., Fredriksson, U., Moe, M., Andresen, L., Hellsten, E., Rissanen, P., Palsdottir, T., Arason, T.: Quality Control of Meteorological Observations. Automatic Methods Used in the Nordic Countries.Climate Report 8/2002, Norwegian Meteorological Institute (2002)
6. Chappell, D.A.: Enterprise Service Bus: Theory in Practice. O'Reilly (2004)
7. Williams, M., Cornford, D., Bastin, L., Jones, R., Parker, S.: Automatic processing, quality assurance and serving of real-time weather data. Computers & Geosciences 37, 351–362 (2011)
8. Williams, M., Cornford, D., Ingram, B., Bastin, L., Beaumont, T., Pebesma, E., Dubois, G.: Supporting interoperable interpolation: the INTAMAP approach. In: Proceedings of the International Symposium on Environmental Software Systems, Prague (2007)
9. Skön, J.-P., Kauhanen, O., Kolehmainen, M.: Energy Consumption and Air Quality Monitoring System. In: Proc. of the 7th International Conference on Intelligent Sensors, Sensor Networks and Information Processing, pp. 163–167 (2011)
10. Skön, J.-P., Johansson, M., Kauhanen, O., Raatikainen, M., Leiviskä, K., Kolehmainen, M.: Wireless Building Monitoring and Control System. World Academy of Science, Engineering and Technology 65, 706–711 (2012)

Towards a Search Driven System Architecture for Environmental Information Portals

Thorsten Schlachter[1], Clemens Düpmeier[1], Oliver Kusche[1],
Christian Schmitt[1], and Wolfgang Schillinger[2]

[1] Karlsruhe Institute of Technology (KIT), Karlsruhe, Germany
{thorsten.schlachter,clemens.duepmeier,
oliver.kusche,christian.schmitt}@kit.edu
[2] Baden-Wuerttemberg State Institute for Environment, Measurements,
and Nature Conservation, Karlsruhe, Germany
wolfgang.schillinger@lubw.bwl.de

Abstract. In order to merge data from different information systems in web portals, querying of this data has to be simple and with good performance. If no direct, high-performance query services are available, data access can be provided (and often accelerated) using external search indexes, which is well-proven for unstructured data by means of classical full text search engines. This article describes how structured data can be provided through search engines, too, and how this data then can be re-used by other applications, e.g., mobile apps or business applications, incidentally reducing their complexity and the number of required interfaces. Users of environmental portals and applications can benefit from an integrated view on unstructured as well as on structured data.

Keywords: environmental information portal, architecture.

1 Motivation

Environmental portals offer a quick and comprehensive overview on available environmental information and data, which are often distributed over a variety of individual databases, systems, and business applications [1]. The information are of manifold types and ranges, i.e., structured measurement data, meta data, individual structured or semi-structured (environmental) objects, or reports on the state of the environment without an explicitly modelled information structure.

In web portals such a mix of structured, semi-structured[1] and unstructured data is typically made accessible via hierarchical navigation paths and/or a full text search.

For example, a search for 'nature reserves' in the environmental portal of the federal state of Baden-Württemberg in its present form links to about 3,000 relevant

---

[1] As semi-structured data can be transformed into a structured form [2], and both are treated analogously in the portal application, in the following only structured (as opposed to unstructured) data will be mentioned.

R. Denzer et al. (Eds.): ISESS 2015, IFIP AICT 448, pp. 351–360, 2015.

documents and also provides a direct entry into the map view of a business application. However, neither information on individual nature reserves nor a localized entry point into the map view are displayed – although all necessary data is present in databases as well as in a web-based business application, it is not available for the portal via services and interfaces.

From a user's perspective, the portal application should already provide an overview of all relevant nature reserves (in a desired area). Access to a complex business application should only be necessary for very specific tasks or advanced search requests. However, for this purpose all objects, e.g. nature reserves, must be made directly available for the portal application, which basically also applies for all other kinds of environmental information. This means that a vast number of information and environmental objects has to be made searchable in the portal. For the user, this search should be easy to use and as fast as possible.

1.1   Querying an Exploding Number of Data

With the aim to present fine-grained environmental information, the number of objects increases dramatically. Some traditional navigation approaches are therefore no longer appropriate, and the design of search interfaces becomes more important.

While full text search interfaces are usually instrumented to provide easy access to unstructured textual data, access to structured data is often implemented by querying the available data via complex search forms, data selectors, or map-based access mechanisms backed up by dedicated application logic mapped to underlying (relational) databases.

An advanced search approach based on simple full text search paradigms has to be implemented which integrates the classical (single-slot full text) search functionality with a search for structured data, and includes specialized approaches for displaying structured data such as map presentations (for the querying and representation of spatial data) or graphical and tabular presentations of measurement data.

Furthermore, search by voice input should be supported on mobile devices, which is easy as search terms are ultimately converted into textual queries anyway.

2   User Expectations and Objectives

A new search driven approach will change user behavior and raise expectations with respect to how information is accessed using mobile devices. For many users, accessing data via complex navigation paths is no longer acceptable. Especially on mobile devices, a context-based, e.g. location-based, representation of suitable information with a minimum number of user interactions is expected. Any further navigation is often done in an exploratory manner, based on the information already displayed. Every subsequent interaction can trigger a change in the search, i.e., the displayed information has to be updated if necessary. This generates great demands both on the flexibility of query interfaces and on their performance. Noticeable latencies in updating the display are unreasonable for reasons of ergonomics.

As many systems and services do not meet these requirements in practice (yet), it is desirable to prepare structured data in an optimized way for flexible and high-performance querying - an approach proven for unstructured data by means of full text search indexing. At this point, search indices maintaining the structure of data and providing advanced access functionalities come into play.

The principle of search driven websites and portals certainly also applies for structured data. Background services are used to maintain data in their original systems, e.g., relational databases, while keeping a structured search index up to date in parallel. The portal uses the query interface of the search engine for primary data access via search and takes care of data presentation.

Within a search driven portal, the primary information access is driven by search. All navigation items (including menus) as well as the contents are displayed as a result of one or several search queries. In this regard, search driven websites and portals can be characterized as being highly dynamic environments.

2.1   The Search Engine as Glue for Distributed Information

The described use of search engines can also contribute to solve further problems of the classical, service-oriented portal approach: as the landscape of environmental information systems is highly heterogeneous, the same applies for the nature of services and interfaces used. It is desired to significantly reduce the number of required interfaces within the portal software – however, for the synchronization of data with the search engine, they have to be implemented elsewhere. In turn, other applications, e.g. mobile apps, can also make use of the search engine and benefit from the availability of data by means of a single query interface.

By adding them to a structured search index, even such data can be made available for real time access that aren't available via an (accessible) service, or that are hidden behind a complex navigation or query form. Yet, even in the case of available data services, the performance they offer may often not be sufficient in order for them to be the basis for a search implementation with satisfactory response time. For example, in the context of environmental data, response times in the range of several seconds have been observed from some systems.

While importing or indexing data, these can be filtered or enriched by additional attributes, e.g., place names can be converted into explicit geographical coordinates using gazetteer services, which then can be used to implement a proximity search or bounding box queries. By integrating machine learning algorithms, even a more complex semantic enrichment of data is possible.

In summary, by using a search driven architecture for environmental information portals, the following objectives will be pursued:

- Use of data from their original source and concentration in a powerful search engine
- Comprehensive view of all available, relevant information, accessed via simple single-slot full text search queries
- Provision of additional aids for an exploratory search experience
- Both the discovery of object classes and of individual objects has to be possible

- All data is supposed to contain references to their original systems, as only the most important information is displayed in the portal or mobile application
- Reduction of the number and complexity of data interfaces (for portals and applications)
- Use of the search index by a variety of applications
- No or little extra load on original systems through additional search requests
- Querying large numbers of objects has to be as performant as a "simple" full text search
- The current state of the environment (measurements) has to be presented
- Context information (mobile devices, settings for personalization) has to be included into search

3   A Basic Architecture for Search Driven Environmental Information Portals

The presented architecture for a search driven environmental information portal is based on a JEE (Java Platform, Enterprise Edition) portal server (Liferay Portal [3]) as both a web frontend and an integration platform for underlying data services, but it also applies for a variety of other applications. The portal software provides a rich set of standard functionalities needed for an environmental portal, e.g., user authentication and authorization, support for corporate web design with responsive layouts [4], content and asset management, etc. In particular, however, its modular extensibility is important. New content and data presentation functionality can be easily added to a JEE portal using concepts like portlets and web widgets. The application logic of these extensions uses two search engines for primary data access.

3.1   Use of Specialized Search Engines

Since different search engines exist which each have their strengths in specific areas, several search engines are used in the portal. Unstructured data is indexed by a traditional full text search engine (Google Search Appliance [5]) using web crawlers and special connectors. Structured data items are stored and indexed as JSON objects in a separate structured index server based on NoSQL technology (Elasticsearch [6]). This second search engine can be easily accessed and managed through a REST interface.

The necessary tools for importing structured data into the Elasticsearch server as well as for ongoing/periodic synchronization of data are running outside the portal software and should be part of a workflow which also includes quality management for the data.

When data are not available by means of services or when access is limited, these data can be made available using generic cloud services, e.g., data from geo-referenced files can be uploaded to the Google Maps Engine, and subsequently can be used via data services or as map layers.

External search engines may complement the portal search by delivering special data, e.g., statistical data or descriptions [7] of administrative services [8]. The use of standardized interfaces like OpenSearch [9] can simplify the integration of external search engines.

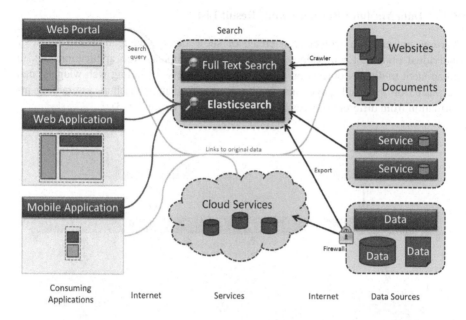

Fig. 1. Main components of a search driven architecture for web portals and (mobile) applications including two search engines and cloud services to complement original data services

3.2   Creating the Search Experience

In addition to editorial content and navigation structures, the search engine is forming the core of the portal application for data access. Queries entered in the search slot will be preprocessed and semantically enriched, e.g., by use of gazetteer services for the identification of geographic coordinates and other location context, or by identifying a time context, and then forwarded to the search engines.

In particular, the enriched queries can drive a more precise search - not only on the basis of mere string comparisons, but allowing location-aware queries finding nearby objects by radius search. Using the enhanced query terms, the search engine returns weighted results according to (configurable) relevance criteria.

The presentation of search results can be performed by various components within the portal software. Currently this is realized via web widgets, i.e., encapsulated Javascript components, each implementing a certain type of data visualization. As soon as supported by relevant web browsers, these can be replaced by standardized "Web Components" [10]. Web widgets are independent from their container application, and therefore can easily be re-used in other applications, e.g., in hybrid mobile apps [11].

For data access they use REST APIs, and for the seamless integration with the portal software every web widget is managed within a wrapper portlet. The individual widgets are kept as generic as possible, i.e., they can be configured using Mustache templates [12] for display, thus being adapted to the respective search results. For the re-use of generic components, it may be helpful to generate additional general attributes such as "title", "abstract" and "link".

3.3   Data Mashup: Beyond Simple Result Lists

Various presentation widgets can create or show menus, navigation structures, or individual objects. Each widget again can be a (complex) web application, e.g., a component to display objects on a map. Several portlets (including web widgets) can be placed on the result page, and thus form an information mashup, assembling information from different sources to a single integrated view (Fig. 3).

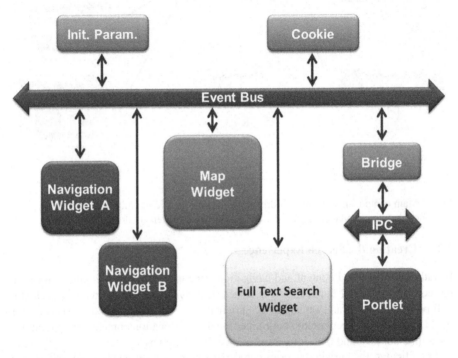

Fig. 2. Event bus connecting a set of components (widgets and portlets) on the result page. Other communication systems can be connected using bridge interfaces, e.g., the Liferay Inter-Portlet Communication (IPC).

In order to interconnect components (widgets) and to offer a rich user interface, these have to be able to communicate. An event bus implements the loose coupling of individual components (Fig. 2). Each component can do both listen to events and send own events to the bus, and is solely responsible for the events to which it responds or not. In order to achieve a coherent interaction of components, only the set of event types has to be defined for the portal application.

Additional mechanisms are integrated in the event concept, e.g., for gathering personalization information from cookies, browser storage, or a web server, or to query sensor data (GPS or coarse-grained location) on a mobile device. URL parameters or search slot queries may be sent as events as well. If required, further adapters can be connected to the event bus for handling of external or system events, e.g., the portal software.

In addition to external data from various environmental information systems, data from the portal software itself can be made available via the (structured) search engine. For large datasets or complex requests, the load on the portal software and the underlying database can be reduced significantly by intelligent preprocessing and querying in the search engine. The next major release of the Liferay portal software (Liferay 7) will provide this option by default by means of an embedded Elasticsearch engine.

4   Case Study "State Environmental Portals" and Environmental App

The described search engine-based approach has been used to perform a prototype re-implementation of the state environmental portal (LUPO) [1] (Fig. 3). In addition to the weak structured and unstructured content (about 2,000,000 documents from more than 2,000 sites), many structured data, e.g., various types of protected areas, and locations of energy systems such as windmills, biogas plants, solar panels, and hydropower plants have been stored in the Elasticsearch index. Where possible, geographical coordinates were acquired or produced for all objects. This index forms the core of a significantly expanded functionality of the portal which now integrates the display of location based search results on maps and provides a location-based search.

Each query, whether manually entered to the search slot or clicked on using the tag cloud, first generates an empty result page. After preprocessing and semantic enrichment of keywords, both search engines and additional backend systems are queried in parallel and asynchronously. While the results for the full text search engine are shown in a classic hit list, the structured hits can trigger a variety of representations. For example, the discovery of objects of certain classes can force the display of corresponding map layers within the map component. Classes and individual objects can be shown for information and further navigation. Clicking on an object class can force the display of matching instances and switches the corresponding map layers on or off. The results already contain quantitative information, e.g., how many objects of a certain class were found for the current query. Clicking on a particular object can, for example, trigger the centering of the map to this object.

Coming back to the example of the "motivation" section, a search for "nature reserves" and a place name now displays the closest reserve objects in the left column. The corresponding heading with the concept name "nature reserve" serves for further navigation and allows switching on and off the respective map layer. Clicking on a particular object (a single nature reserve) centers the map to the appropriate place. Another click on that area in the map then displays additional details and links to business applications.

Current measured values are displayed either from the search engine or from separate cloud services to match the context.

Many components of the state environmental portals (data, services, search engines, and user interface) are also used in the mobile application "Meine Umwelt" ("My Environment") [13]. It is a hybrid app whose core consists of a HTML5 application used in apps for Android, iOS and Windows Phone. The HTML5 application is organized into web widgets as well and utilizes the same services and search engines. This saves resources for both the development and the maintenance of components.

Fig. 3. Result page of a state environmental portal. Object classes and individual objects as well as measurement values are presented by multiple widgets on the left. They may trigger events toggling the display of map layers, centering of the map, or refining of search queries. Full text search results are presented below the map widget.

5   Conclusion

The procedure described can be summarized as follows: Modern web applications, and in particular mobile solutions, dynamically load data. In portal-like applications, a great variety of different data interfaces and data sources is used. In order to simplify the application and to reduce the load on the primary backend systems, data can therefore be administered in a separate search index:

- Let the engine do the hard work (preprocessing, indexing, querying)
- Existing data can be enriched
- Use structured data types to obtain individual ways to query and to present object classes
- Use generic formats and mechanisms, e.g., templates for presentation, so a variety of applications can be covered "out of the box"

What distinguishes the search driven approach in comparison to previous/alternative concepts?

- Reduction of interface diversity in the consuming applications
- Easy integration of data sets. However, it requires an operating concept for the update of the index
- (Quick!) retrieval of object classes and individual objects
- Fine-grained local search on a single object-level (as opposed to entire map layers)
- Combination of structured/semi-structured and unstructured data in the search
- Reduction of redundantly managed metadata
- Reusability of web widgets, e.g., for mobile and web applications
- Reusability of services and search indexes
- More interactivity for the user
- Prevention of a bottleneck on the server side (portal)
- Less load on the portal server by offloading and indexing content

The concept of search-driven portals and websites will stand or fall related to the relevance of their search index. Automatic updates of the search index, which have been only briefly mentioned in this paper, must not be underestimated. Basically, the operation of a search engine for information integration in principle means an added expense and also raises questions about data consistency, redundancy avoidance and operating cost.

However, the advantages of the search-driven approach clearly outweigh these concerns for the existing applications. The objectives are therefore fully met by the prototype. User feedback has been very positive and expectations are even being surpassed in many ways.

6   Outlook

Putting unstructured, semi-structured, and structured information into search engines can be considered as a first step towards a unified information access platform (UIA) [14], even if central aspects of UIA like advanced data processing or data analysis remain outside yet. However, the basic technologies create a huge potential for the generation of added value.

Most planned extensions do not affect the search-driven architecture as such, but rather the applications it supports. Especially with regard to user-experience and ergonomics, quite a number of improvements can be achieved. Due to the loose coupling of components and the use of an event-bus in the portal application, the integration of additional navigation aids and further functionality is very easy.

An improved linking of data in the search index is probably the most promising approach. Currently, many object classes in the index are data islands that are not or hardly connected to other classes. The use of shared concepts, such as in the thematic and spatial classification of data, promises a great potential, even for the generation of completely new applications. Corresponding relation or graph-oriented concepts based on Elasticsearch already exist and are waiting to be used.

References

1. Schlachter, T., et al.: LUPO - Weiterentwicklung der Landesumweltportale. In: Weissenbach, K., et al. (eds.) Umweltinformationssystem Baden-Württemberg F+E-Vorhaben MAF-UIS Moderne anwendungsorientierte Forschung und Entwicklung für Umweltinformationssysteme, Phase II 2012/14; KIT Scientific Reports 7665, pp. 65–74 (2014) ISBN 978-3731502180
2. Abiteboul, S., Buneman, P., Suciu, D.: Data on the Web: From Relations to Semistructured Data and XML. Morgan Kaufmann (1999) ISBN 978-1558606227
3. Liferay Portal: http://www.liferay.com (visited September 5, 2014)
4. Zillgens, C.: Responsive Webdesign: Reaktionsfähige Websites gestalten und umsetzen. Carl Hanser Verlag (2012) ISBN 978-3446430150
5. Google Search Appliance: http://www.google.de/enterprise/search/ (visited September 5, 2014)
6. Elasticsearch, http://www.elasticsearch.org (visited September 5, 2014)
7. Statistisches Landesamt Baden-Württemberg, http://www.statistik-bw.de (visited November 5, 2014)
8. Service-BW: http://service-bw.de/zfinder-bw-web/processes.do (visited November 5, 2014)
9. OpenSearch, http://www.opensearch.org/Home (visited December 15, 2014)
10. Web Components, http://www.w3.org/TR/components-intro/ (visited September 5, 2014)
11. Multi-channel app development, http://en.wikipedia.org/wiki/Multi-channel_app_development (visited September 5, 2014)
12. Mustache, http://mustache.github.io (visited September 5, 2014)
13. Schlachter, T., Düpmeier, C., Weidemann, R., Schillinger, W., Bayer, N.: My environment - a dashboard for environmental information on mobile devices. In: International Symposium on Environmental Software Systems, ISESS 2013 (2013)
14. Probstein, S.: Five Advantages of Unified Information Access (UIA), CIO (2010), http://www.cio.com/article/2416284/ (visited December 15, 2014)

National Environmental Data Facilities and Services of the Czech Republic and Their Use in Environmental Economics

Jana Soukopová[1], Jiří Hřebíček[2], and Jiří Valta[3]

[1] Faculty of Economics and Administration, Masaryk University
Lipová 507/41a, 602 00 Brno, Czech Republic
soukopova@econ.muni.cz
[2] Institute of Biostatistics and Analyses, Masaryk University,
Kamenice 126/3, 625 00 Brno, Czech Republic
hrebicek@iba.muni.cz
[3] Czech Environmental Information Agency, Vršovická 1442/65
100 10 Prague 10, Czech Republic
jiri.valta@cenia.cz

Abstract. National environmental data facilities and services are part of the environmental information systems of the Ministry of the Environment of the Czech Republic that have been under development since 1990. In 2010 the development of the National Information System for Collecting and Evaluating Information on Environmental Pollution project started, co-financed by the European Regional Development Fund. This project consists of an integrated system of reporting (ISPOP), an environmental help desk (EnviHELP), and the national INSPIRE geoportal, which were developed between 2010 and 2013 and were discussed at ISESS 2013. This paper introduces the current development of several national environmental and financial data facilities and services based on eGovernment implementation in the Czech Republic and the open environmental and financial data approach of the Czech Ministry of the Environment and the Czech Ministry of Finance. It also introduces the web information system that enabled us to find the relationship between environmental economics and municipal waste management in the Czech Republic.

Keywords: environmental data, information system, environmental services, eGovernment, open government data, environmental economics.

1 Introduction

The development of eGovernment is part of the current strategy for the modernisation of public administration in the Czech Republic which was approved in July 2007: "Efficient Public Administration and Friendly Public Services – Strategy on Realisation of Smart Administration in the Period 2007-2015" (further "Smart Administration Strategy"). The overall purpose of this policy instrument is for the Public Administration (PA) to achieve effectiveness comparable to that of the European Union (EU) and its

R. Denzer et al. (Eds.): ISESS 2015, IFIP AICT 448, pp. 361–370, 2015.

Member States. The "Strategic Framework of the Development of eGovernment 2014+" further develops the Smart Administration Strategy and outlines steps and measures to be taken to enhance electronic governance, to improve and upgrade its architecture, to secure its financing, and to transform it into a standard information and communication technology (ICT) tool used by all PAs in their everyday communication with their clients – the public, representatives of the business sector, and other subjects [1]. The construction of environmental data facilities and infrastructure focuses primarily on the transparent disclosure of data created during these processes. In 2013, the Ministry of the Interior (MoI) of the Czech Republic adopted the "Strategic Framework for the Development of eGovernment 2014+", which regards eGovernment as an interactive process involving PA authorities, i.e., national, regional, and municipal governments, as well as citizens, entrepreneurs, and other stakeholders. The activities of the MoI in eGovernment are connected with the information agendas of the Ministry of the Environment (MoE) and their registration in the Register of Rights and Obligations of the Basic Public Administration Registers of eGovernment [2] which have been in place since 1 July 2012. These agendas are a cornerstone of the eGovernment of the Czech Republic. Their basic objective is to help citizens, companies, and other entities that come into contact with PA by minimizing the number of their personal visits to government offices through the use of ICT tools with on-line access from anywhere, at any time. At the same time, the agendas require that the PA must perform a safe, efficient, and transparent exchange of accurate and up-to-date environmental data [3].

The strategic approach to the development of national environmental data facilities and services focuses on a high level of eEnvironment services [4] and on building support for MoE information services. The approach enables a broader effectiveness of MoE policy instruments for environmental protection. The basis for such changes is the management of the organizational framework and strategy of ICT resources, support, and services. The Environmental Information Systems (EISs) of the MoE manage the processing, retrieval, and presentation of environmental data and information, in support of the Aarhus Convention [5], [7].

In the Czech Republic there are currently about 40 different EISs in operation, including a geographic information system in compliance with INSPIRE standards [6] and several thousand environmental databases [3]. Most of these information resources are directly available to the general public, regardless of the applicability of their content.

The notification of the scope to national environmental data and services (agendas) in eGovernment of the Czech Republic has now finished [2]. This notification ensured the legitimacy of access to environmental data through the information system of the Basic Public Administration Registers of eGovernment. The information flow within the EISs of the MoE has been formalized with the necessary degree of ICT infrastructure. These EISs are reflected in the new concept of the Information Strategy of MoE [7], whose attestation took place in November 2012 [8].The PA currently publishes environmental and related data mostly through prepared EIS applications. However, these applications only suit a certain type of user. Users wishing to use the environmental data in a different manner than that intended by the PA are excluded. Data that users might want that is not published by the PA include: tenders and budgets; payments made by individual towns, cities, regions, and national institutions; and the composition of municipal representation and the individual votes of its members [9].

Various third-party developers can create many applications that display, analyse, and link the data in ways that may be interesting to the public. For example, applications can be created that show: trends in the numbers and amounts of tenders in individual regions; trends in municipal budgets in individual regions; tender-winning companies that are led by municipal representatives; and the ten biggest suppliers for each regional city.

Most of the necessary data for environmental economic modelling is produced from taxpayers' money [9] and collected by the PA information systems. The related data is even often available on the PA websites, such as those of the MoI, MoE, the Ministry of Finance (MoF), the Ministry of Regional Development (MoRD), and the Czech Statistical Office (CZSO). However, due to the way this data is published, the creation of smart custom applications is challenging for the future development of eGovernment in the Czech Republic, both financially and in terms of time [1].

In section 2 of the paper, we present our experience with the standard means of collecting environmental data through the Integrated System of Reporting (ISPOP) [10], which enables open public access to nationwide data for several EISs. It provides environmental data in a form that allows access to anyone at any time and freely allows the data to be combined. In section 3 of the paper we discuss our experience with the open data infrastructure of the MoF, which enables public access to financial data through its MONITOR web information system [25] and with the ROZPOČETOBCE [11, 12] system, which enables the comparison of financial data for every municipality in the Czech Republic in a time series. Further discussion in section 3 is devoted to our experience in creating software applications [27] for the environmental economic modelling that the public really needs.

2   National Environmental Data Facilities and Services of Public Administration

2.1   Collection of Environmental and Financial Data

Environmental legislation of the Czech Republic is in compliance with the European Union (EU) and requires organizations, companies, enterprises, etc. (i.e. environmental reporters) to provide the PA with information on the environmental impact of their activities. Their environmental reports and the duty of notification are defined by the relevant Czech environmental legislation, which obliges environmental reporters to keep prescribed records and report them to the PA of environmental protection.

The duty of environmental reporters is to deliver relevant environmental data, information, and messages to the PA authorities and institutions concerned. Legal provisions exist to control the reporting obligation. Environmental reports include primary environmental data such as air, water, and soil pollution, the generation and treatment of waste, electrical and electronic waste, etc. Most of these reports are processed by the Czech Environmental Information Agency (CENIA) [8] through the Integrated System of Reporting (ISPOP) [10] of the MoE, which was developed in collaboration with Telefonica O2 CR between 2008 and 2013. ISPOP was constructed to ensure flexibility in terms of its expansion to other environmental reporting agendas and to ensure compliance with updated environmental legislative obligations [8]. The hardware architecture of ISPOP consists of the IBM server eCenter BladeCenter, HS 22, and IBM disc array storage System Storage DS3400. Communication infrastructure is based on Cisco network elements. The software architecture consists of several modules: VMware virtualization; Novell SUSE Linux operating system; Jboss and Tomcat application servers; Oracle 11g database and ISPOP application layer (own J2EE application); CMS Magnolia (presentation); Adobe LiveCycle ES2 (operation with PDF form); Novell eDirectory (identification); and Novell Access Gateway (SSO).

The basic idea of ISPOP is a form solution in the information technology of Adobe LiveCycle ES. Electronic smart forms are available in PDF format and are part of the XML layer for computer processing [13]. The forms also include a PDF layer for an electronic signature, by means of which it is possible to authorize a document. Filling in the forms and browsing through them is possible with Adobe Reader.

Standardized PDF forms enable: obtaining and storing structured content (XML according to the valid XSD template); editing forms in Adobe Reader; online checking and sending reports to ISPOP; online submission to ISPOP Data Storage; content encoding forms into 2D bar codes.

The main technical requirement for using ISPOP is the ability to connect to the Internet, at least for the amount of time necessary for receiving/being assigned to the environmental report. A user needs an internet browser with the additional free software of Adobe Reader to work with ISPOP web applications.

ISPOP built the universal input data gateway of several EISs, providing incoming data files in a specified standardized format and the control and distribution of target processing systems. ISPOP enables the management of reports submitted using the environmental record form and the archiving and evaluation of their content (in cooperation with other related systems of eGovernment).

The Central System of State Accounting Information (CSÚIS) [28] of the MoF is designed to gather the accounting records of selected entities (accounting units, e.g. all municipalities in the Czech Republic) for the operational management of the MoF. It collects only the prescribed obligatory forms with financial data, which responsible persons submit in the automatically encrypted XML files using the Simple Object Access Protocol (SOAP) interface (the preferred option) or manually using the CSÚIS web application or the application of the batch statements. It is a similar collection method to that of the collection of environmental data through ISPOP.

2.2   Public Access to Environmental and Financial Data

The web information system EnviHELP [14] provides support for a particular operating state of ISPOP, e.g. administration for incumbents fulfilling reporting obligations under Act No. 25/2008 Coll., as well as business communities and the general public in providing environmental information in relation to Act No. 123/1998 Coll., on public access to environmental information and the Aarhus convention.

Many EISs have been developed in the Czech Republic in the past decade, but only some collect environmental data through ISPOP with standardized interactive PDF forms.

Data standards [13] for reporting through ISPOP are published every year by the MoE, where for any legislative obligation there is a data standard (in XSD format) and a detailed description (in PDF format). These data standards describe the data structures, the data formats and the automated checks of the content of the submitted information. Forms are available in the accounts of registered environmental reporters after login into the ISPOP system. Here is a brief description of two EISs using prescribed data standards:

- *Integrated Pollution Register* (IRZ), [16], in compliance with the *Pollutant Release and Transfer Register* (PRTR), is an environmental database or inventory of potentially hazardous chemical substances and/or pollutants released to the air, water, or soil and transferred off-site for treatment or disposal according to the OECD Council Recommendation [17]. IRZ is a publicly accessible database of plants for which the amount of pollution produced beyond the legal limits has been reported. The system records 93 different pollutants of every plant monitored in all types of releases and transfers, according to the established threshold, which is reported as the amount of a substance in kilograms per calendar year.
- *Information system of waste management* (ISOH) [18] is a publicly accessible database containing data on the waste generation and treatment by generators and data on facilities for treatment, recovery, and disposal of waste. The system records annual reports of more than 70,000 different generators in all 6,500 municipalities and more 3,000 facilities. The annual ISOH database contains more than 50,000 records of municipal waste generation and 10,000 records about their treatment. The nationwide database VISOH [19], which contains the aggregated data of ISOH, is accessible to the general public. The nationwide database ALLISOH [20], which contains all of the data of ISOH, is accessible for the staff of the State administration in environment protection.

MONITOR [25] is a specialized web information portal of the MoF that allows open public access to budget and accounting information from all levels of the PA. MONITOR also provides the financial statements of all PA units. The presented information comes from the Integrated Information System of the Treasury (IISSP) [25] of the MoF and CSUIS, and they are updated quarterly.

The primary version of MONITOR was released in May 2013. It replaced the previous MoF web information portals ARIS [23] (database of municipalities' accounting from 2000 to 2009) and ÚFIS [24] (database of municipalities' accounting from 2010 to 2012). In December 2013 the analytical part of portal was made available, which allows dynamic data analysis using advanced tools for financial reporting.

Unfortunately, other transparently published data by the PA in the eGovernment services are not in a proprietary format (only scanned to PDF or manually created tables). They are not published with standardized open formats that would allow the general public to: share the data freely and combine the data freely.

3   Case Study: Environmental Economic Model and Information System of Municipal Waste Management

We developed environmental economic models and information systems [21, 22] for all types of waste treatment facilities: mechanical biological treatment plants, incineration plants with energy recovery and landfills, composting and biogas plants, and sorting plants. We wanted to use a time series to investigate municipal waste management and financial data. We used municipal waste management data from ISOH with the collaboration of the CENIA agency and the MoE for the time series 2008-2013.

We also needed a time series of municipal financial data. We tried to use the publicly accessible data from the web portals ARIS, ÚFIS, and MONITOR of the MoF. However, they do not provide simple tools for downloading publicly accessible data like the systems VISOH for the public or ALLISOH for the PA.

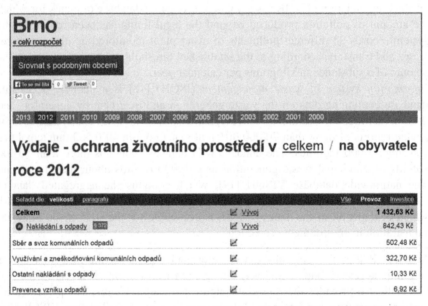

Fig. 1. Public expenditure on waste management per capita in Czech crowns [Kč] in the city of Brno in 2012

It is very difficult to find an appropriate time series of financial data of a given municipality. Therefore, we analysed the database structures of ARIS and UFIS. One student developed the web information system ROZPOČETOBCE [11, 12] in 2012 and updated it in 2013. ROZPOČETOBCE enables the presentation of publicly accessible financial data (public income and expenditure) of every municipality in the Czech Republic in the period from 2000 to 2013 from many different viewpoints. Every citizen and user of this smart web system can analyse complete public incomes and expenditures of a municipality in the Czech Republic. We chose the city of Brno as an example; see Figs. 2 and 3 where per capita expenditures in municipal waste management are presented. The expenditure of municipal waste management in the municipalities covers the costs associated with the collection, pick-up, transportation, use, disposal, other treatment, and prevention of municipal waste (Fig. 2).

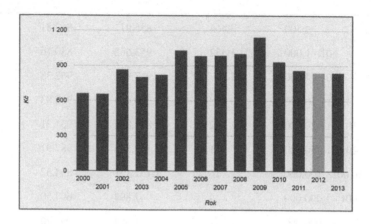

Fig. 2. Graph of per capita public expenditure on waste management in Czech crowns [Kč] in the city of Brno 2000-2013

In environmental economic models and information systems [21, 22], we also used publicly accessible data from the Information System on Public Procurement and RISY [26] of the MoRD, where we had to develop a special parser to download the required municipal data.

We continued, on the basis of the ROZPOČETOBCE system, to create a new information system [27] for the automatic visualization of public incomes and expenditures in waste management of all municipalities, districts, and regions with the use of a time series of publicly accessible data from the VISOH and ALLISOH of the MoE, ARIS, ÚFIS and MONITOR of the MoF, and RISY of the MoRD web information systems. The new complete database system has more than 15 million records.

One of the outputs of the new system [27] covers the expenditure and revenue of municipalities on waste management, the generation of waste in municipalities, and the cost of landfill waste, including their aggregation with respect to the number of municipal inhabitants. For data analysis in the system [27], we used a mathematical-statistical theory of sets and a cluster analysis of each municipality. We sorted municipalities into groups (sets) according to population. For the nine resulting groups of municipalities we compared the data on the average per capita expenditure, the maximum and minimum value of per capita expenditure, and the standard deviation of expenditure and per capita data for the entire file with the set of all municipalities in the Czech Republic; see Table 1.

Table 1. Total per capita expenditure on waste management for municipalities in the Czech Republic in 2012

Population	Number of municipalities	Total of inhabitants	Expenditure per capita in Czech crowns [Kč]	
			Average	Standard deviation
≤ 500	3,464	835,971	862.81	487.13
501 - 1,000	1,352	953,662	830.16	465.81
1,001 - 4,000	1,047	1,917,991	962.38	807.25
4,001 - 10,000	198	1,210,408	968.83	493.9
10,001 - 20,000	62	871,834	964.31	419.7
20,001 - 50,000	41	1,167,522	987.91	423.16
50,001 - 100,000	16	1,137,171	854.52	173.68
100,001 - 1,000,000	4	947,894	693.50	209.61
> 1,000,000	1	1,241,664	1,097.70	0

The information from Table 1 would be appropriate to add to the analytical tools of the MONITOR system so that a municipality could compare its own expenses with that of other municipalities (e.g., according to their position in the district or region, by size category, etc.) and thus uncover potential methods for reducing costs and increasing efficiency in waste management.

4   Conclusion

All of the PA information systems in the Czech Republic that are accessible through the web interface have similar shortcomings. Legislation in the Czech Republic has presented no centralized way to constitute and fully fulfil public data access following Directive 2003/98/EC, known as the "PSI Directive", as announced in the Smart Administration Strategy. Each Ministry created its own information system or database system, which have been in closed forms. The exception is the MoE strategy [7], which had its own format and application of EIS dependent on standardized data. The applicability of other PA information systems is difficult. For the user, this means prevented or restricted work with the data of the PA. Current social, technological, and economic changes create challenges and new expectations for national environmental data facilities and services based on ISPOP. Given that these challenges are largely intertwined, any vision for the future of public data services needs to take a multi-disciplinary approach. One solution may be embracing open government data, based on the principles of collaboration, transparency, and participation within an appropriate governance framework. Such an open government model of national data facilities and services builds on open data, open services and open decisions.

Acknowledgement. This research was supported by the Czech Science Foundation (GACR) under the project "Unfair competition and other economic factors influencing the efficiency of the provision of public services".

References

1. Action 42 in Czech Republic, http://www.egovap-evaluation.eu/indicator.php?id_country=5&action_n=42
2. Základní registry veřejnésprávy (Basic public administration registers), http://www.mvcr.cz/clanek/zakladni-registry-zakladni-registry-verejne-spravy.aspx
3. Hřebíček, J., Kubásek, M.: Environmental information systems (in Czech). AkademickénakladatelstvíCERM, Brno (2011), http://www.iba.muni.cz/res/file/ucebnice/hrebicek-environmentalni-informacni-systemy.pdf
4. Hřebíček, J., Pillmann, W.: eEnvironment: Reality and challenges for eEnvironment implementation in europe. In: Hřebíček, J., Schimak, G., Denzer, R. (eds.) Environmental Software Systems. IFIP AICT, vol. 359, pp. 1–14. Springer, Heidelberg (2011)
5. Århus Convention, http://ec.europa.eu/environment/aarhus/
6. INSPIRE standards, http://geostandards.geonovum.nl/index.php/1.3.3_INSPIRE
7. Information strategy of the Ministry of Environment (in Czech), http://www.mzp.cz/cz/informacni_strategie
8. Prášek, J., Valta, J., Hřebíček, J.: National INSPIRE Geoportal of the Czech Republic. In: Hřebíček, J., Schimak, G., Kubásek, M., Rizzoli, A.E. (eds.) ISESS 2013. IFIP AICT, vol. 413, pp. 425–438. Springer, Heidelberg (2013), doi:10.1007/978-3-642-41151-9_40.
9. Soukopová, J., Malý, I., Hřebíček, J., Struk, M.: Decision Support of Waste Management Expenditures Efficiency Assessment. In: Hřebíček, J., Schimak, G., Kubásek, M., Rizzoli, A.E. (eds.) ISESS 2013. IFIP AICT, vol. 413, pp. 651–660. Springer, Heidelberg (2013), doi:10.1007/978-3-642-41151-9_61.
10. ISPOP - Integrated System of Reporting, http://www.ispop.cz
11. Řezáč, K.: Web portal for the evaluation of public municipal budgets (in Czech). Master thesis, Masaryk University, Brno (2012)
12. Rozpočetobce, http://www.rozpocetobce.cz/
13. Data standards, https://www.ispop.cz/magnoliaPublic/cenia-project/uvod/datove_standardy_aktualne.html
14. EnviHELP - Environmental help desk, http://helpdesk.cenia.cz
15. INSPIRE geoportal, http://inspire-geoportal.ec.europa.eu/
16. Integrated register pollution, http://www.irz.cz/
17. Recommendation of the Council on Implementing Pollutant Release and Transfer Registers (PRTRs), http://acts.oecd.org/Instruments/ShowInstrumentView.aspx?InstrumentID=44&Lang=en&Book=False
18. ISOH - Waste Management Information System, http://www1.cenia.cz/www/odpady/isoh
19. VISOH - Public Waste Management Information System of the Ministry of the Environment, http://isoh.cenia.cz/groupisoh
20. ALLISOH, http://isoh.cenia.cz/allisoh/login.php?mes=sesexpired

21. Soukopová, J., Hřebíček, J.: Model of cost and price relationships for municipal waste management of the Czech Republic. Acta Univ. Agric. et Silvic. Mendel. Brun. 59, 371–378 (2011)
22. Hřebíček, J., Kalina, J., Soukopová, J.: Integrated economic model of waste management: Case study for South Moravia region. Acta Univ. Agric. et silvic. Mendel. Brun. 61, 917–922 (2013)
23. ARIS-Automatized budget information system, http://wwwinfo.mfcr.cz/aris/
24. UFIS - Monitoring of municipal finances, http://wwwinfo.mfcr.cz/ufis/
25. MONITOR, http://monitor.statnipokladna.cz/en/2014/
26. RIS - Regional Information Service, http://www.risy.cz/en/
27. Kuttner, M.: Web portal for the evaluation of the cost of waste management for municipalities, districts and regions. Master thesis. Masaryk University, Brno (2014) (in Czech).
28. CSÚIS - Central system accounting information of state,
http://www.statnipokladna.cz/cs/csuis/zakladni-popis
29. IISSP - Integrated information system of Treasury,
http://www.statnipokladna.cz/cs/
o-statni-pokladne/integrovany-informacni-system-statni-pok

A Best of Both Worlds Approach to Complex, Efficient, Time Series Data Delivery

Benjamin Leighton[1], Simon J.D. Cox[1], Nicholas J. Car[1], Matthew P. Stenson[1], Jamie Vleeshouwer[1], and Jonathan Hodge[2]

[1] Land & Water Flagship: CSIRO, Melbourne, VIC and Brisbane, QLD, Australia
Ben.Leighton@csiro.au
[2] Oceans and Atmosphere Flagship: CSIRO, Brisbane, QLD, Australia

Abstract. Point time series are a key data-type for the description of real or modelled environmental phenomena. Delivering this data in useful ways can be challenging when the data volume is large, when computational work (such as aggregation, subsetting, or re-sampling) needs to be performed, or when complex metadata is needed to place data in context for understanding. Some aspects of these problems are especially relevant to the environmental domain: large sensor networks measuring continuous environmental phenomena sampling frequently over long periods of time generate very large datasets, and rich metadata is often required to understand the context of observations. Nevertheless, timeseries data, and most of these challenges, are prevalent beyond the environmental domain, for example in financial and industrial domains.

A review of recent technologies illustrates an emerging trend toward high performance, lightweight, databases specialized for time series data. These databases tend to have non-existent or minimalistic formal metadata capacities. In contrast, the environmental domain boasts standards such as the Sensor Observation Service (SOS) that have mature and comprehensive metadata models but existing implementations have had problems with slow performance.

In this paper we describe our hybrid approach to achieve efficient delivery of large time series datasets with complex metadata. We use three subsystems within a single system-of-systems: a proxy (Python), an efficient time series database (InfluxDB) and a SOS implementation (52 North SOS). Together these present a regular SOS interface. The proxy processes standard SOS queries and issues them to the either 52 North SOS or to InfluxDB for processing. Responses are returned directly from 52 North SOS or indirectly from InfluxDB via Python proxy where they are processed into WaterML. This enables the scalability and performance advantages of the time series database to be married with the sophisticated metadata handling of SOS. Testing indicates that a recent version of 52 North SOS configured with a Postgres/PostGIS database performs well but an implementation incorporating InfluxDB and 52 North SOS in a hybrid architecture performs approximately 12 times faster.

Keywords: time, series, timeseries, SOS, OGC, sensor, database.

R. Denzer et al. (Eds.): ISESS 2015, IFIP AICT 448, pp. 371–379, 2015.
© IFIP International Federation for Information Processing 2015

1   Time Series Data, Lots is Hard to Manage

Time series data is frequently used to represent environmental properties and processes and is fundamental in environmental science. Hey and Trefethen[1], describe and predict a scientific data deluge. Managing a deluge of time series data so that it can be discovered, understood, accessed and used effectively, is an ongoing challenge.

A simple time series of numerical values requires context to be useful. For example observational time series often include a unit of measure, and some description of an observed feature. Metadata provides a richer description and context and allows more complex queries to filter or group data. Furthermore standards for metadata mean data can be more readily exchanged because compatible systems and data sets can be identified and interfaced.

Very large amounts of data can be collected by sensors or generated computationally. Metadata can further increase the size and complexity of a dataset. Better analysis and use can be made of large time series data that are richly described. Such descriptions are more computationally expensive to process, require more storage, and consume more network bandwidth.

To address these challenges we review and compare some technologies for storing, delivering and managing time series data. We introduce a hybrid approach that merges a lightweight time series database with a standardized metadata-rich service for delivering sensor observations. This approach provides good performance for a both large dataset with rich metadata. In testing this approach performs faster than a standalone combined data and metadata service.

2   Sensor Observation Service for Management

Standards and models for interacting with and describing observations help address the problem of management, and effective use, of time series data.

The open geospatial consortium sensor observation service (SOS)[2] describes a standard way of managing and querying observation data. Services compliant to this standard are capable of returning stored observations and contextual information about related real world features, sensors, and observational procedures. SOS compliant services can provide observation records that conform to the Open Geospatial Consortium's (OGC) Observations and Measurements standard (O&M)[3]. O&M provides a flexible observations model including information about an observed feature, property, and the procedure associated with making an observation. SOS implementations also provide for complex descriptions of sensors, for example, using SensorML[4].

SensorCloud[5] is an architecture and associated application that performs functions similar to those of described by the SOS standard. SensorCloud specifies a service for delivering sensor data and metadata through REST like URL requests. SensorCloud encodes observations and related data using a JSON format. Sensor metadata is closely modelled on the StarFL[6] format. SensorCloud services can provide information on networks of sensors, sensor platforms, sensors, phenomena reported by sensors, sensor calibrations and can deliver observations produced by a sensor. The SensorCloud services also provide create and insert operations for networks, sensor, platform, and observations data.

Both SensorCloud and OGC SOS standards describe ways of structuring and delivering time series data and related metadata in the scientific domain.

3   Other Databases

Beyond the scientific domain there are many databases and services for the storage and use of time series data. There is a continuum between specialised time series databases and more general purpose databases. Numerous specialized time series databases exist and many are in active development. Development of time series databases is driven by a broad need to access observations but not always in a scientific context. For example OpenTSDB[7], while somewhat general purpose, is typically used to monitor various I.T system metrics. Similarly Cube[8] is generic but was developed for use cases related to monitoring customer data, website, and system performance.

Time Series databases readily integrate with other systems and often provide web service based interfaces. REST interfaces and JSON provide rapid integration with JavaScript frameworks and thus ease integration with web based visualisation tools. KariosDB[9] is a rewrite of, and intended to be an improvement on, OpenTSDB. It provides a REST interface alongside other interfaces including a GUI and a telnet interface. Cube is built on MongoDB[10] and provides a REST like interface. InfluxDB[11] provides a REST interface.

More general purpose databases are also used for time series storage. MongoDB provides the back end database for SensorCloud as well as Cube. PostgreSQL[12] is one of the possible back-ends for 52 North SOS[13]. Cassandra[14] can be readily adapted to store time series data. Cois[15] describes a hybrid approach using Redis[16] and PostgreSQL for an environmental database prioritizing real time event detection. InfluxDB can use a variety of embedded backend databases.

Databases may be optimized for write versus read operations, can be highly normalised and efficient, or may enable rapid prototyping and querying of unstructured or loosely structured data.

4   Standards Support and Interoperability

SensorCloud and OGC SOS-compliant systems provide rich metadata models. In contrast most other time series databases provide minimal metadata and none provided any time series-specific standards conformance.

Non-relational databases, like MongoDB, provide storage of structured documents thus support arbitrary metadata schemas. Relational databases like PostgreSQL support table structures that may accommodate arbitrary metadata schemas. Neither MongoDB nor PostgreSQL provide a built in metadata model for time series data.

Specialised time series database typically provide limited and inflexible metadata capabilities that do not conform to recognised standards. OpenTSDB provides some very basic support through unique identifiers[17]. KariosDB annotates values with tags and a name[18]. Cube is much more flexible and supports arbitrary structured JSON data at each data point. In InfluxDB, a value is effectively a row consisting of multiple columns and thus simple metadata structures can be accommodated.

5   Performance Considerations for Rich Metadata Systems

Standards for interoperability and metadata are particularly important in the scientific domain. Standards provide a basis for a scientific infrastructure where data can be discovered, compared, reused, and through which experiments can be replicated [19][20]. Thus time series databases and services that conform to comprehensive metadata and encoding standard have an advantage over more general database systems and time series specific databases. Performance is always an important consideration: the ability to rapidly query, analyze and retrieve time series data is a requirement for a number of time series use cases. For example, exploratory interactive visualization of time series data is possible if data points can be quickly retrieved, processed and displayed. Similarly fast responses ensure that access to time series data is not a bottleneck in analysis, or when used as an input to a model.

An ongoing concern with the SOS standard is the performance of implementations. The well-known 52 North SOS implementation provides conformance to the SOS 2.0 standard and includes a number of extension methods and formats. Recent releases have addressed performance issues however older 52 North SOS implementations have suffered from numerous performance issues. Results[21] from performance tests for various older versions of 52 North SOS indicate that under a load of 10 concurrent requests every 5 seconds, SOS performs quite slowly. For example a GetObservation request, the average response time for a request for a yearly data set having approximately 500,000 records was 191 seconds. Similar performance issues with scaling SOS to millions of records for thousands of sensors have been discussed in the SOS community[22].

Performance has been greatly improved in 52 North SOS version 4.1[13] however with dataset sizes likely to increase more than linearly, revolutionary performance change will be needed in the longer term. Large performance gains may be possible through alternative approaches to data storage, that behind a SOS interface, leverage dedicated time series databases.

6   An Alternative Architecture

A good candidate for comparison with 52 North SOS's large data capacity is Influx DB. InfluxDB is a "Timeseries, events and metrics" database[23]. InfluxDB is easy to deploy and is packaged with an embedded backend database. Unlike 52 North SOS, InfluxDB lacks any native metadata model and provides no standards-compliant interface.

We developed a hybrid data/metadata architecture, combining InfluxDB with 52 North SOS. We tested an implementation of this architecture to determine whether it provide better performance than a standalone 52 North SOS instance.

Similar Hybrid architectures have been previously proposed. Cox[24][Fig 1.] describes scenarios in which SOS services consume data from other OGC standard Web Feature Services and Web Coverage Services. Bröring et. al. [25] describe patterns for bridging sensors and sensor delivery services in hybrid like architectures. In particular Bröring describes using Twitter as a middleware layer to store sensor metadata.

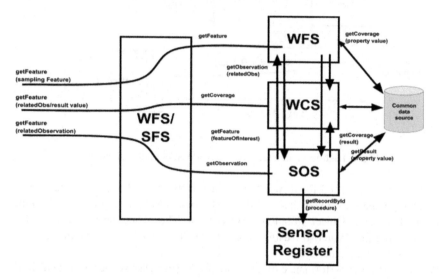

Fig. 1. Hybrid OGC architectures (adapted from Cox[24])

A prototype SOS service has also been developed that, through a heterogeneous systems architecture, provided a partially SOS-compliant service using a Web Feature Service (WFS) back-end[26].

Our hybrid architecture aims to meet multiple use cases. It provides a rich SOS implementation for standards compliant interoperability to enable sophisticated queries. For a subset of queries it provides SOS-compliant responses faster than 52 North SOS configured with a Postgres/PostGIS backend database. The system should enable exploration of data across the temporal domain with a minimum of delay to facilitate use cases such as real time interactive visualisation.

Figure 2 presents a high-level view of the hybrid architecture: SOS requests and responses are handled via a hybrid internet proxy. The hybrid proxy forwards certain requests to InfluxDB while others not able to be handled by InfluxDB are redirected to 52 North SOS.

A test implementation of the hybrid proxy is capable of processing and forwarding only a small subset of SOS queries to InfluxDB: SOS 2.0 requests provided as key value pairs (as URL arguments) where the response format is specified as WaterML2. This subset includes the main data delivery request GetObservation when WaterML2 format is used. The hybrid proxy can process queries that vary by real world feature or property of interest for a feature and can handle a temporal filter that specify results between varying start and end times.

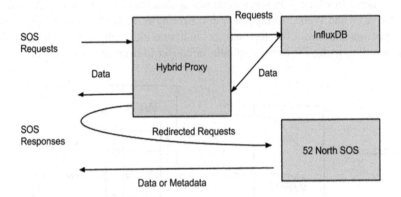

Fig. 2. High-level architecture of a hybrid SOS implementation

SOS queries identified for forwarding to InfluxDB are analysed and used to construct an equivalent InfluxDB query. InfluxDB provides simple responses back to the proxy in JavaScript Object Notation (JSON) form. The hybrid proxy translates the JSON response into WaterML (using lookup tables for variables like unit of measure) and returns it to the requester.

We compared the performance of a realistic 52 North SOS instance as a standalone service to a test implementation the hybrid proxy architecture incorporating the same 52 North SOS instance alongside InfluxDB.

The 52 North SOS version tested was 4.1 and the particular instance contained approximately 14 million weather station records stored in a backend a Postgres/PostGIS. Two configurations were tested: one in which a query was sent to a standalone 52 North SOS instance and another in which the query was sent to a hybrid proxy configuration combining 52 North SOS and InfluxDB. In the hybrid proxy configuration the 52 North SOS dataset was replicated into a parallel InfluxDB instance (version 0.7.3).

In both configurations the test used a SOS-compliant query specified as a URL with key value arguments. The test query varied between the standalone SOS instance and hybrid proxy implementation by the system specifying URL part only with key value pair arguments and format remaining the same. The test machines varied in specification and no attempt was made to compensate for hardware differences or network latencies. However our estimates are that the server 52 North SOS virtual machine was significantly more powerful than the Hybrid test virtual machine and the InfluxDB virtual machine. Therefore we expect that performance results are biased in favor of the standalone 52 North SOS instance.

The test query in both configurations retrieved approximately 52,230 hourly average air temperature records for a weather station between 19-11-2010 at midnight and 13-11-2013 at 13:00.

In both test configurations the request was sent using the cURL application. The cURL "w" parameter and a template file were used to generate response timing information. Server processing time was considered to be the time between time_pretransfer and time_starttransfer. This approach minimised noise related to network overheads and time taken to transport response data. Responses are listed in Table 1 below.

Table 1. Response times for 52 North standalone and 52 North Influx DB hybrid

Run	Hybrid	52 North SOS
First	0.45s	8.485s
Run 1	0.377s	4.891s
Run 2	0.31s	4.594s
Run 3	0.336s	4.282s
Run Average (excluding first result)	0.368s	4.589s

The first response was considered an outlier and was significantly slower than subsequent queries for both systems. It was assumed this was because parts of the databases are cached into memory after the first response. In our test the hybrid approach using InfluxDB generated responses 12 times faster on average than 52 North SOS. Our results are indicative of a significant performance benefit through the hybrid approach nevertheless further study could provide more certainty and help remove confounding factors such as differing machine and network performance.

In addition to high performance a hybrid approach offers other advantages. It maintains rich metadata capabilities. The hybrid proxy forwards SOS queries that can't be handled by InfluxDB to 52 North SOS. In our example InfluxDB replicates time series data stored in SOS but doesn't replicate any metadata. For example, InfluxDB cannot provide a response to a SOS DescribeSensor request because it doesn't store any information about the sensors used to produce a time series. The hybrid proxy can identify queries that can't be handled by InfluxDB and redirect these to the 52 North SOS instance. Thus the hybrid proxy handles a subset of queries quickly via InfluxDB but can also respond to the broader set of possible SOS requests by redirecting these to 52 North SOS. This approach improves performance while maintaining a rich metadata model. Additionally, a more general approach should be possible interfacing to other data stores. These kinds of systems could leverage existing data services and adapt those to return SOS responses. This improves the reuse of data and reduces the need to duplicate data across multiple systems. In turn this "future proofs" SOS installations against reimplementation if and when data loads require new back-end database implementations.

7   Conclusion

Time series data is prolific. There are many systems to help manage, store and deliver time series data. In the scientific domain some systems also provide metadata capabilities that provide more context for understanding and analysing data. Beyond the scientific domain, many other time series databases and services are being developed. These typically have poor metadata capabilities but may be more scalable and provide faster performance. Near real time visualisation and other use cases requiring rapid retrieval and exploration of data would benefit from a system that is standards based, provides rich metadata and performs fast. The 52 North SOS implementation provides a standards based service for management and storage of time series data along with extensive metadata capabilities. Newer versions of 52 North SOS have improved performance. To investigate whether further performance gains were possible we developed a hybrid architecture that combined 52 North SOS with InfluxDB, a light-weight dedicated time series database. We compared the performance of a standalone 52 North SOS instance and a prototype implementation of the hybrid architecture that coupled the 52 North SOS instance with InfluxDB. Under our tests performance was approximately 12 times faster in the hybrid system. There are performance benefits using a hybrid architecture compared to a standalone 52 North SOS instance other advantages maybe that loose coupling between components readily allows integration of new technologies and reuse of data in existing deployments.

References

1. Hey, A.J.G., Trefethen, A.E.: The data deluge: An e-science perspective. Wiley Sons (2003)
2. Portal.opengeospatial.org: OGC Sensor Observation Service Interface Standard (2014), https://portal.opengeospatial.org/files/?artifact_id=47599
3. Cox, S.: Geographic information: observations and measurements. Doc. OGC (2010)
4. Portal.opengeospatial.org: OGCSensorML: Model and XML Encoding Standard (2014), https://portal.opengeospatial.org/files/?artifact_id=55939
5. Peters, C.: SensorCloudRESTful API, https://wiki.csiro.au/display/sensorcloud/SensorCloud+RESTful+API
6. Malewski, C., Simonis, I., Terhorst, A., Bröring, A.: StarFL–a modularised metadata language for sensor descriptions. Int. J. Digit. Earth 7, 450–469 (2014)
7. Opentsdb.net: OpenTSDB - A Distributed, Scalable Monitoring System (2014), http://opentsdb.net/
8. Square.github.io: Cube (2014), http://square.github.io/cube/
9. Code.google.com: kairosdb - Fast scalable time series database - Google Project Hosting (2014), https://code.google.com/p/kairosdb/

10. Mongodb.org: MongoDB (2014), `http://www.mongodb.org/`
11. Influxdb.com: InfluxDB - Open Source Time Series, Metrics, and Analytics Database (2014), `http://influxdb.com/`
12. Postgresql.org: PostgreSQL: The world's most advanced open source database (2014), `http://www.postgresql.org/`
13. Hollmann, C.: 52 North SOS 4.1 (2014), `http://blog.52north.org/2014/09/02/52north-sos-4-1/`
14. The Apache Cassandra Project, `http://cassandra.apache.org/`
15. Aaron Cois, C.: Large-Scale Data Collection and Real-Time Analytics Using Redis - O'Reilly Radar (2014), `http://radar.oreilly.com/2013/03/large-scale-data-collection-and-real-time-analytics-using-redis.html`
16. Redis, `http://redis.io/`
17. Metadata — OpenTSDB 2.0 documentation, `http://opentsdb.net/docs/build/html/user_guide/metadata.html`
18. PushingData - kairosdb - Pushing data into KairosDB - Fast scalable time series database - Google Project Hosting, `https://code.google.com/p/kairosdb/wiki/PushingData`
19. Haak, L.L., Baker, D., Ginther, D.K., Gordon, G.J., Probus, M.A., Kannankutty, N., Weinberg, B.A.: Standards and infrastructure for innovation data exchange. Sci. 338, 196 (2012)
20. Hendler, J.: Science and the semantic web. Science 299(80), 520 (2003)
21. Tan, F.: SOS 2.0 Performance Test (2013), `https://www.seegrid.csiro.au/wiki/SISS4BoM/SOS2PerformanceTest`
22. Fwd: ODIP-3 Prototype SOS - Google Groups, `https://groups.google.com/forum/#!searchin/ioostech_dev/geoff/ioostech_dev/ThkMPTsrEdA/Sv9_iGib1DAJ`
23. InfluxDB Documentation, `http://influxdb.com/docs/v0.8/introduction/overview.html`
24. Cox, S.: No Title (2007), `https://www.seegrid.csiro.au/wiki/pub/AppSchemas/RecentPresentations/IN43C-07_Cox_Info_Viewpoints_Service_Architectures.ppt`
25. Broring, A., Foerster, T., Jirka, S.: Interaction patterns for bridging the gap between sensor networks and the Sensor Web. In: 2010 8th IEEE International Conference on Pervasive Computing and Communications Workshops (PERCOM Workshops), pp. 732–737. IEEE (2010)
26. Golodoniuc, P.: ThinSOS<SISS4BoM<SEEGrid (2013), `https://www.seegrid.csiro.au/wiki/SISS4BoM/ThinSOS`

Implementing a Glossary and Vocabulary Service in an Interdisciplinary Environmental Assessment for Decision Makers

Simon N. Gallant[1], Rebecca K. Schmidt[1], and Nicholas J. Car[2]

[1] CSIRO Land and Water Flagship, Canberra, ACT, Australia
[2] CSIRO Land and Water Flagship, Brisbane, QLD, Australia
{simon.gallant,becky.schmidt,nicholas.car}@csiro.au

Abstract. When delivering scientific information for decision makers, it is important to define and use appropriate terminology to ensure scientific credibility and good communication. A glossary with terms from authoritative sources for specific domains can increase the usefulness and reusability of information for decision makers as the information can be more easily used without adaptation or translation. Linked Data principles and semantic web-based vocabulary tools provide mechanisms for delivering formalised glossaries via vocabulary services for use in integrated products, both documents and information platforms.

Issues to consider when implementing a glossary and vocabulary service are covered: persuading stakeholders to accept standard external terms and gain agreement on unique terminology; requirements for gathering, controlling and maintaining terminology in a glossary to ensure transparency and persistence; formalising a glossary as a standards-based vocabulary; and efficiently implementing this glossary via automation.

Keywords: glossaries, web services, interoperable information systems.

1   Introduction

This paper explores the implementation of a glossary service in the Bioregional Assessment Programme (the Programme) [1,2]. The Programme provides information on the ecology, hydrology, geology and hydrogeology of specified bioregions with explicit assessment of the potential direct, indirect and cumulative impacts of coal seam gas and coal mining development on water resources. This scientific information will be available for all interested parties, including Australian and state government regulators, industry, community and the general public, when considering coal seam gas and coal mining developments.

The Programme is delivering over 150 products, mostly scientific reports, over the course of three years. A key requirement for these products is a high standard of scientific and editorial quality including the consistent use of terminology. For plain-English words, this is straightforward as existing literature can be used. For more technical language, standards must be agreed upon and recorded, including both negative and positive instruction ('Use *bore* not *well* in the context of groundwater.

R. Denzer et al. (Eds.): ISESS 2015, IFIP AICT 448, pp. 380–387, 2015.

Use *well* not *bore* in the context of oil or gas.'). Through interacting with experts in many fields, a Programme-specific language list has been developed, which guides the writing, integration and quality assurance of content for all Programme staff.

The limitation of this list is its simplicity. When an author knows precisely what they wish to say, but not exactly which word to use, this list provides authority. What the list cannot do is help multiple authors agree on what they mean, nor inform readers as to that meaning. For the Programme to publish its products in a way that is truly useful to and accessible by the public, the way words and concepts are used needs to be discoverable by readers. For this, a controlled, authoritative glossary service is proposed.

This paper provides a short background on the Programme, Linked Data, ontologies and controlled vocabularies in order to establish the context of the work. The processes by which terminology, both individual words and entire sets of words from particular authorities, is agreed and governed are described, as is the architecture for automatically building product-specific glossaries. Finally, the costs and benefits of such a service are discussed, as well as the implications for multiple-use services such as this, with particular reference to the difficulties of (i) conflicting requirements, (ii) multiple-context reporting and (iii) doing something rather than nothing.

2   Background

2.1   The Bioregional Assessment Programme

A bioregional assessment is a scientific analysis of the ecology, hydrology, geology and hydrogeology of a particular geographic location, with explicit assessment of the potential direct, indirect and cumulative impacts of coal seam gas and large coal mining development on water resources [1,2]. The Programme undertakes these assessments for a range of stakeholders including the Independent Expert Scientific Committee on Coal Seam Gas and Large Coal Mining Development (IESC), Australian and state government regulators, industry, community and the general public. The outputs are a suite of scientific products for each of the geographic locations currently being studied, delivered both as documents and via an information platform.

The Programme team spans both scientific disciplines and research agencies with four main collaborators: the Australian Government Department of the Environment; the Bureau of Meteorology; the Commonwealth Scientific and Industrial Research Organisation (CSIRO); and Geoscience Australia.

2.2   Linked Data, Ontologies and Controlled Vocabularies

In this Programme, multiple agencies contribute and multiple fields of research are involved so information from a diverse range of sources must be integrated. Semantic web [3] technologies such as standardised vocabularies[1] and Linked Data [4], are

---

[1] See the W3C's listing of Semantic Web technologies including vocabularies at
http://www.w3.org/standards/semanticweb/

designed with heterogeneous data integration in mind and are thus of great utility to this Programme. Terms from a range of authorities in a range of formats can be integrated for a single purpose, then placed within semantic web vocabularies. The delivery of them as Linked Data assists this greatly. By using Linked Data, terms become properties of objects that are identified using Uniform Resource Identifiers (URIs)[2] meaning they can be linked to and information about them 'dereferenced' (looked up) by following their URI. This allows the term owners (the authorities or acting on behalf of the authorities regarding their definition) to deliver them at a single point of truth and in both human- and machine-readable formats, enabling unambiguous references (links) to individual terms within text (documents, webpages). If standardised concept ontologies, such as the Simple Knowledge Organization System (SKOS) [5], are used for vocabularies, multiple properties for terms may be recorded, not simply textual definitions. SKOS allows the mapping of terms between vocabularies using a range of relationships such as *broad*, *close* and *exact*. This allows for nuanced relationships between the constructed glossary and other known, trusted vocabularies.

Software tools, such as the Spatial Information Services Stack Vocabulary Service (SISSVoc, [6]), deliver controlled vocabularies with formalised relationships between terms defined using SKOS as Linked Data. Other vocabulary delivery tools do exist, such as the Australian National Data Service (ANDS) Controlled Vocabulary Service [7], but controlled vocabularies are more commonly delivered in informal ways without standardised information models (ontologies) and without formal data formats. For example, the Australian Government's Interactive Functions Thesaurus (AGIFT) http://agift.naa.gov.au/ delivers its controlled vocabulary via regular webpages.

3   Glossary and Vocabulary Services

3.1   Persuasion and Approvals

Editorial quality is required to be of a very high standard for products of the Programme. Part of ensuring high editorial quality is ensuring that language is consistent both within and between products. This required consistency in language spans the choice of terminology to the way that concepts are used. The Programme's interdisciplinary nature has made this particularly challenging as experts from different disciplines have different ways of expressing similar concepts and different uses for the same terms. Two approaches have therefore been taken: (i) to use an external authority for definitions wherever possible, and (ii) to discuss, collate and socialise a language list which is governed by Programme management.

External authorities are valuable as they provide a point of truth, once contributors agree that it is appropriate. For instance, Programme members have agreed to use the *Australian Oxford dictionary* [8] avoiding many arguments over terminology (such as

---

[2] A 'URI' is similar to the more commonly known 'URL'. See
http://en.wikipedia.org/wiki/URI for more details.

whether to use 'modeling' or 'modelling'). In the experience of the Programme, the following is necessary to gain agreement to use an external authority:

1. the majority of Programme staff have access to that authority
2. that authority includes a sufficiently volume of terms to make it worthwhile using
3. the majority of Programme scientific leaders already agree with the majority of terms.

Similar projects have devised related language lists, for example for the Sustainable Yields projects [9] and the Great Artesian Basin Water Resource Assessment [10]. In addition, the BA methodology [2], Australian Government's *Style manual* [11] and the *Australian Oxford dictionary* [8] were accepted as authorities. This provided the Programme with a sufficiently comprehensive language list to begin with, which was endorsed by Programme management as part of the development of the products, thus developing a first-pass list of approved terms.

As the Programme progressed it became clear that it was important to move beyond simply specifying a list of approved terms, but rather to give definitions. This is best practice when writing, particularly in interdisciplinary projects where readers and co-authors from different disciplines might have different meanings for the same word. This confusion needs to be avoided within the single context of a product and the broader context of the whole Programme. Some middle ground between two disciplines must be determined, or one discipline must use a different word. This problem cannot be solved by the imposition of a rule based upon personal preferences – it can only be solved by having conversations with the scientists involved and coming to agreement. For efficiency, the discussion ideally would start with determining external authorities that each discipline accepts so that glossaries from them could be adopted, then it would move to the task of defining individual terms that are not already defined in any external authority. External authorities that will be considered by the Programme include: the METOTERM database [12], the Australian Water Information Dictionary [13], and the Water Quality vocabulary developed for the Bioregional Assessment Framework [14].

A method of discourse based in participatory research methods was used to facilitate this agreement. The involvement in the decision-making processes of parties those decisions will affect has been encouraged since the 1950s and it has been long argued (for example, [15]) that increasing this involvement will improve outcomes. The persuasion work done is best described as a Partnership [15]: groups of scientists are given the power to negotiate, trade-off and come to agreement both with each other and with the editing and managerial teams, but the editing and management teams retain the power to formalise these decisions. Once decisions are formalised, they are presumed to be fixed.

3.2   Governance

What are the requirements for the process to gather, version control and maintain terminology in a glossary in order to ensure transparency and long-term persistence? The governance of terminology in the Programme is managed from the time an undefined term is identified right through until that term is published in the glossary.

At the first step, identification, the term is entered in the glossary as 'proposed, awaiting editing'. The definition of the term is then raised with those concerned (editors, authors, managers, subject matter experts), and a member of the glossary team facilitates the discussion. The glossary team member revises the definition in the glossary, changing its status to 'edited, awaiting approval'. Edited terms are then submitted to Programme management for acceptance at which point they gain a status of 'approved'.

The glossary will hold a large number of terms in various stages at any given time. Various status-based subsets of these terms will be shown through the use of different views. Only 'approved' terms will be available in the Public view, only 'edited, awaiting approval' terms will be visible in the ForApproval view, and all terms will be visible in the Management view. All views are able to show multiple definitions for a term, but this functionality is intended to be used infrequently. It is expected, that the Public view would only ever show the most recent definition.

The Public view can be used as an authoritative list of approved terminology, fulfilling the function of enforcing consistency. An agreed list of terms is a necessary part of publishing products with a high standard of scientific and editorial quality with transparency. Using the glossary as a way of tracking the changes and approvals of the way terms are used makes it possible to ensure that the products of the Programme are consistent in their terminology, with a transparent process for defining, approving and possibly redefining terms.

This process to submit and accept terms is informed by the Geographic Information standard ISO19135 [16] and future efforts will be made to harmonise the term stage naming with existing semantic web ontologies that handle resource lifecycles.

The management and governance of the glossary is important due to its multiple requirements: (i) the glossary is the complete list of terms for which rules on usage and spelling have been made and (ii) the glossary is an audited and controlled list of important terms and their definitions. While those terms that fall under (ii) can be included in (i), the reverse is not practicable. Therefore, there is conflict in the use, governance and maintenance responsibilities and requirements for the glossary as a whole. To resolve this issue, it is helpful to simplify the idea of 'the glossary': the glossary is a structured way of storing terms, some of which may have agreed definitions. The necessary additional maturity and complexity that comes from having multiple lists of terms can therefore be solved by using filter criteria for different views. An Authors view can then be presented, showing the complete list of approved words, without definitions even when they exist (addressing (i)), and the Public and ForApproval views show only those important, defined terms (addressing (ii)).

3.3   Formalising the Glossary as a Standards-Based Vocabulary

Once glossary terms have been identified and even before definitions are agreed upon, a URI for each term is generated. These are intuitive when designed well and take the following form for the Programme's terms:

```
http://{ProgrammsDataWebsiteAddress}/glossary/term/{term-label}
```

With a URI and the text of the term (known as a *prefLabel* in SKOS) now known, the bare-minimum requirements of SKOS have been achieved. Once the term's definition is settled, that is added as a *definition* and SKOS relationships such as *broader*, *narrower* or *exact* can be determined. This information can easily be managed in the same media – a spreadsheet or database – as used to store the term's status and other information required by governance.

Once SKOS data are stored, a computer script can be used to automatically load the terms and their properties into a vocabulary service such as SISSVoc for delivery on the web.

3.4   Automated Implementation

The Public view of the glossary can also be used to generate product-specific glossaries in multiple formats.

The products are written using standard document preparation software which is easily available to all Programme contributors. For the traditional delivery of documents, a print-style glossary is required: a list of terms at the end of a product, with a definition for each. Where defined terms exist in the product, they should be linked to their individual location in the glossary through text indicating the reference. For the web-based delivery, the Public view of the entire glossary should be accessible through a link on any page and, where defined terms exist in these products, they should be hyperlinked to their individual location in the online glossary.

The production of both of these forms can be automated using computer scripts, which manipulate documents and can read information from web services. Post-processing of document files can identify defined terms used, inject referencing links and auto-assemble the print-style glossary. Similar processing can take place for marked-up files for web-based products.

4   Discussion and Conclusion

The primary cost involved in setting up a glossary service such as the one described here is time: a great deal of it is required in both system development and administration, as well as the discourse that is necessary to gain agreement on terms.

The benefits of having a glossary, however, should not be understated. The glossary is a binding context for Programme products. When a reader encounters a term they find ambiguous they are able to find its definition and can be sure that it will still be defined in the same way every time it is used. Thus, the clarity of written communication in Programme products is greatly increased and the trust that a reader places in Programme products is improved.

It is important to note that the Programme is large enough for such an activity to be worth undertaking. Relative to the total time for which the Programme will run (3 years) and the number of people involved (more than 160), the time and people required to develop and maintain the glossary system is reasonable. The same would not be true for a small project with few staff. However, the system and processes are relatively easily transferable to other projects, thus expanding the benefits without much additional cost.

The Programme is reliant on credible, authoritative external sources of definitions: if external authorities for glossary terms are *not* available or are *not* accepted by the disciplinary scientists, the cost in developing and maintaining a glossary (by writing hundreds of definitions) may not offset the benefits.

Using one glossary service to fulfil many functions adds to the maturity of the Programme. In addition to improving communication and increasing trust, the problem of conflicting requirements is solved in part: instead of having a language list for authors and editors, a printed glossary for readers and a series of meeting minutes indicating managerial approval of terms – all of which must be aligned – the Programme is able to include all the necessary information in a single store and then provide the filtered information as subsets of the whole.

The difficulties of multiple-context reporting have not been fully addressed by the Programme. While the goal of having both complete, cover-to-cover reports *and* 'chunks' of online context is admirable, the shift of context both for authors and readers is difficult. It is believed that by providing a centralised service that ensures consistent definitions for terms, some of this context shift can be avoided.

Beginning development despite fluctuating and conflicting requirements has been valuable, and parts of the system can be implemented while others mature. The need to develop the glossary system incrementally has prompted the involvement of some Programme staff earlier than would have been anticipated, which should increase buy-in from many Programme staff. This is the most important outcome of the glossary development for if it is not valued it will not be used, and a glossary that is not used is not a glossary at all.

Acknowledgements. This work was funded by the Bioregional Assessment Programme, a scientific collaboration between the Australian Government Department of the Environment, Bureau of Meteorology, the Commonwealth Scientific and Industrial Research Organisation (CSIRO), and Geoscience Australia. For more information visit http://bioregionalassessments.gov.au.

References

1. Department of the Environment: Overview of the Bioregional Assessment Programme (viewed March 26, 2014), http://www.environment.gov.au/coal-seam-gas-mining/pubs/overview-bioregional-assessment-programme.pdf
2. Barrett, D.J., Couch, C.A., Metcalfe, D.J., Lytton, L., Adhikary, D.P., Schmidt, R.K.: Methodology for bioregional assessments of the impacts of coal seam gas and coal mining development on water resources. A report prepared for the Independent Expert Scientific Committee on Coal Seam Gas and Large Coal Mining Development through the Dept. of the Environment. Dept. of the Environment, Australia (2013), http://www.environment.gov.au/coal-seam-gas-mining/pubs/methodology-bioregional-assessments.pdf

3. Berners-Lee, T., Hendler, J., Lassila, O.: The Semantic Web. Scientific American Magazine (2013), `http://www.sciam.com/article.cfm?id=the-semantic-web&print=true`
4. Heath, T.: Bizer. C.: Linked Data: Evolving the Web into a Global Data Space. Synthesis Lectures on the Semantic Web: Theory Technology, Morgan & Claypool (2011)
5. Miles, A., Bechhofer, S.: Skos simple knowledge organization system - reference (2014), `http://www.w3.org/TR/skos-reference/`
6. Cox, S., Mills, K., Tan, F.: Vocabulary services to support scientific data interoperability. In: European Geosciences Union General Assembly 2013, Vienna, Austria. Göttingen, Germany, April 7-12, p. 1. Copernicus Publications (2013), `http://meetingorganizer.copernicus.org/EGU2013/EGU2013-1143.pdf`
7. Australian National Data Service: ANDS Controlled Vocabulary Service (2014), `http://ands.org.au/services/controlled-vocabulary.html`
8. Australian Oxford Dictionary, 2nd edn. Oxford University Press. (viewed March 26, 2014), `http://www.oxfordreference.com/view/10.1093/acref/9780195517965.001.0001/acref-9780195517965`
9. CSIRO (2014) Sustainable Yields Projects (viewed October 29, 2014), `http://www.csiro.au/Organisation-Structure/Flagships/Water-for-a-Healthy-Country-Flagship/Sustainable-Yields-Projects.aspx`
10. Ahmad, M., Schmidt, R.K., Marston, F., Cuddy, S., Mahoney, J.: Editing conventions for authors and editors. A document in the CSIRO Great Artesian Basin Water Resource Assessment reporting tools series. CSIRO, Canberra (2012), `https://publications.csiro.au/rpr/pub?list=SEA&pid=csiro:EP1210495`
11. Australian Government: Style manual for authors, editors and printers, 6th edn. John Wiley & Sons, Australia (2010)
12. World Meteorological Organization:METEOTERM database, `http://wmo.multicorpora.net/MultiTransWeb/Web.mvc` (viewed October 29, 2014)
13. Bureau of Meteorology: Australian Water Information Dictionary, `http://www.google.com/url?q=http%3A%2F%2Fwww.bom.gov.au%2Fwater%2Fawid%2F&sa=D&sntz=1&usg=AFQjCNHtnJRpK23FADXkaB-uuWBjTSE_Ww` (viewed October 29, 2014)
14. Simons, B.A., Yu, J., Cox, S.J.D.: Water Quality vocabularies for the Bioregional Assessment Framework. Water for a Healthy Country Flagship Report series. CSIRO, Canberra (2013) ISSN: 1835-095X
15. Arnstein, S.R.: A Ladder of Citizen Participation. Journal of the American Institute of Planners 35(3), 216–224 (1969)
16. International Organization for Standardization: ISO 19135:2005 Geographic information - Procedures for item registration (2005), `http://www.iso.org/iso/catalogue_detail.htm?csnumber=32553`

Requirement Engineering for Emergency Simulations

Alena Oulehlová, Jiří Barta, Hana Malachová, and Jiří F. Urbánek

University of Defence, Department of Emergency Management,
Kounicova 65, 662 10 Brno, Czech Republic
{jiri.barta,alena.oulehlova,hana.malachova,jiri.urbanek}@unob.cz

Abstract. Paper deals with requirement engineering that is used in the first phase of project SIMEX (*Research and development* of *simulation tools for training cooperation of actors in* emergency *management* by *subjects of critical infrastructure.* Project SIMEX focuses on the development of simulation tools and instruments for common interoperability training of crisis staff managers, security advice bodies and liaison safety employees in the energy sector with the integrated rescue system in dealing with emergencies and their consequences. This paper also deals with the analysis of different national systems providing publicly available information and evaluates the usability and benefits of implementation of information generated into simulation tool.

Keywords: critical energy infrastructure, emergency management, information systems, security, simulation tool.

1   Introduction

Timeliness, completeness, objectivity, reliability, and accuracy are essential units to measure the effectiveness and efficiency of decision-making process in emergency or crisis situations. Monitoring and information tools play key role - in obtaining such information. Natural and anthropogenic hazard information represents statistics and other quantitative or qualitative data that are used by authorities. These authoritative bodies include, but not limited to, the emergency management authorities, individuals, households, non-governmental organizations, companies and scientific or research institutions. The same figure may render different information for different entities at the same time.

The basic information scheme about sources of danger and their transmission is similar to other information systems. This information scheme typically contains description of the transmission protocol through which the information is being transported, and the format of the information itself. One typical information format is a composition of three components: the sender, the recipient, and the information payload.

Prediction, origin and course of specific natural hazards are recorded with monitoring tools of individual environmental components managed by public authorities. Information systems in the Czech Republic that focus primarily on natural disasters caused by atmospheric changes with strongest effects are the longest and most thoroughly monitored.

R. Denzer et al. (Eds.): ISESS 2015, IFIP AICT 448, pp. 388–396, 2015.

One of the tasks carried out by the state under normal conditions and particularly in crisis situations is ensuring the functioning and protection of key system components and services. This task has been implemented by the state since its formation. However, with the growth of intensity and occurrence of anthropogenic and natural threats and impacts on society, pressure increases for the state to improve the quality of its protection and resilience, and to reduce vulnerability. Individual systems and services, due to their importance to the society, have begun to be referred to as critical infrastructure.

One of the earliest establishment of national critical infrastructure protection occurred in the United States of America. Stemming from the country's comprehensive legal definition of the subjects of critical infrastructure, USA has now been one of the leading countries in critical infrastructure protection. Germany and the Great Britain later followed suit as they begun to deal with similar issues. The discussion on the critical infrastructure protection at European level was launched at the beginning of the 21st century after incidents of several crisis situations (floods, terrorist attacks, etc.). Current documents of European critical infrastructure protection (1) were created on principles of proportionality, subsidiarity, complementarity, confidentiality and cooperation among stakeholders. Based on application of principle of subsidiarity, the critical infrastructure in the European Union is divided into National Critical Infrastructure and European Critical Infrastructure.

2   Critical Energy Infrastructure in the Czech Republic

Czech Republic adopted required European standards (1) into the Act No. 240/2000 Coll., on Crisis Management (2) and related Act (3). Ministry of Interior of the Czech Republic - General Directorate of Fire Rescue Service was appointed as the responsible body, which then delegates tasks and responsibilities to various ministries and other central administrative authorities. In order to define various elements of critical infrastructure, there are cross functional and cross sectorial criteria in the nine areas of critical infrastructure (energy, water, food and agriculture, health, transport, communication and information systems, financial market and currency, emergency services and public administration). Cross functional and sectorial criteria identifying critical infrastructure elements are defined in the Government legislation document (3). Subjects of critical infrastructure have responsibility for protecting critical infrastructure elements by law (2). Each subject has to process crisis preparedness plans, where potential functional threats towards critical infrastructure element are identified and measures for its protection are set.

National critical energy infrastructure is divided into the following sectors and subsectors:

A. Electricity
    A.1 Production of Electricity
    A.2 Transmission System
    A.3 Distribution System

B. Natural Gas
  B.1 Transmission System
  B.2 Distribution System
  B.3 Gas Storage
C. Oil and Petroleum Products
  C.1 Transmission System
  C.2 Distribution System
  C.3 Storage of Oil and Fuel
  C.4 Production of Fuel
D. District Heating
  D.1 Heat generation
  D.2 Heat Distribution

There are 228 subjects of critical energy infrastructure in the electricity sector at the national level: 58 subjects in the production of electricity subsector, 133 subjects in the transmission system subsector, and 37 subjects in the distribution system subsector.

3   Simulation Tools for Training Cooperation by Subjects of Critical Infrastructure

Although ensuring proper function of energy infrastructure is crucial for the European Union, there are other sectors that play significant role in the system of critical infrastructure protection (3). This project, entitled "Research and development of simulation tools for training cooperation of actors in emergency management by subjects of critical infrastructure (SIMEX)", focuses on the roles and responsibilities of the subjects in the critical energy infrastructure.

SIMEX project was selected from a competition held by the Technology Agency of the Czech Republic to support applied research and experimental development called "ALFA". It is classified in the sub-program of energy resources and environmental protection and preservation. The project started in September 2014. To meet the project objectives, it is necessary to identify the needs of individual stakeholders on mutual communication, quality and level of information exchange, potential threats and the state of hardware and software among stakeholders.

Without an in-depth initial requirements analysis of individual stakeholders it is not possible to create simulation software for common training of the Integrated Rescue System subjects of critical infrastructure that can improve coordination, cooperation, operability and interoperability of intervening units. The secondary objective of the project is to investigate the impacts of failure of critical energy infrastructure on environment, mitigation and prevention strategies for negative consequences from natural disasters, and the impact of protection and preservation of the environment.

3.1   Primary and Secondary Stakeholders

Requirement engineering is employed in order to achieve the project objectives (5, 6). At the currently ongoing first stage of requirement engineering, the project has identified primary and secondary stakeholders for energy critical infrastructure. Table 1 shows an overview of stakeholders who influence mitigation, solution and elimination of consequences of extraordinary event and crisis situation caused by failure of critical energy infrastructure. Identification of stakeholders was conducted in accordance to the recommendations of ISO CSR the Stakeholder Engagement Manual (7), and The Stakeholder Engagement Manual Volume II (8), focusing on emergency management in subjects of critical energy infrastructure.

Table 1. Summary of identified stakeholders in emergency management in subjects of critical energy infrastructure

Primary stakeholders	Secondary stakeholders
Security Liaison employee	Ministry of Defence – Army of the
Staff	Czech Republic (ensuring of selected
Parties (suppliers of spare parts, components, technologies, contracted subjects providing help in a crisis situation).	objects) State institution (e.g. the Government, National Security Council, The Czech Environmental Inspectorate,
Emergency services of Integrated Rescue System	Energy Regulatory Office, Administration of State Material Reserves,
Other emergency services of Integrated Rescue System	District Security Council, Czech hydrometeorological Institute)
Ministry of Interior, Ministry of Interior – the General Directorate of Fire Rescue Service of the Czech Republic	Media Civil associations (NGO - Non-Governmental Organization)
Ministry of Interior of the Czech Republic – Policy of the Czech Republic (ensuring of selected objects)	Banks
Ministry of Industry and Trade	
Influenced Customers	
Influenced Suppliers	
Owners and Subject Investors	
External processor of crisis preparedness plan	

Identifying contracting party at the primary stakeholders is meant to be generic because specific names of legal entities and individuals are stated in the emergency preparedness plan of each given subject. The subject is contracted with them for specific range of services and assistance that will be performed in case of extraordinary events and crisis situations.

3.2   Requirements Engineering: A Communication With Stakeholders

Based on the definition of stakeholders, we began to communicate with them. In the first step there we addressed the state authorities (Ministry of the Interior of the Czech Republic, Ministry of the Interior - General Directorate of Fire Rescue Service of the Czech Republic, and the Ministry of Industry and Trade). Fundamental requirements for protection of subject of critical infrastructure, realization and practices of liaison exercises related to failure of some element of critical infrastructure, were found by interviewing responsible people. Public administration authorities pointed out several requirements that the simulation software for the joint training of the Integrated Rescue System and subjects of critical infrastructure should provide.

Requirements for the simulation software in terms of further research could be divided into the following groups:

- Requirements for core functions of the system;
- Interface requirements - interface with other systems, user interface, software, hardware and communication interfaces;
- Non-functional requirements - product requirements, external resources, etc.;
- Other requirements - including legislative requirements, software multilingualism, etc.

In the second phase there is established communication with the liaison safety staff in particular subjects. There are structured and controlled interviews with the liaison security staff. Questions for structured and controlled interviews are divided a number of particular areas: emergency management and crisis preparedness plans, preparation and realization of training simulating failure of element of critical energy infrastructure, and impacts of the critical energy infrastructure on environment. In case of unsuccessful communication with the liaison security staff, we have prepared a checklist that represents basis qualitative method of risk management.

3.3   Simulation Software for Training

For a successful creation of the simulation software for liaison training to work in real time with real geo-data and models of effects of extraordinary event effects or crisis situation, it is necessary to create good quality scenarios of extraordinary event and crisis situations process. Creating of such scenarios will require wide spectrum of requirements from different interfaces, non-functional and other requirements. The first step for creating the scenario is hazard (threats) identification concerning element of critical energy infrastructure. Qualitative, semi-quantitative or quantitative methods of risk analysis will be used to verify the correctness of created registry of danger for element of critical infrastructure in the emergency preparedness plan.

To determine technological threats and their impact, we will use risk analysis methods What-if, Fault Tree Analysis (FTA), Event Tree Analysis (ETA), Failure Mode and Effects Analysis (FMEA), a Hazard and Operability Study (HAZOP), Human Reliability Analysis (HRA), Chemical Exposure Index. For the sector of critical energy infrastructure, a special method RAMCAP Plus was developed. All Hazards Risk and Resilience Prioritizing Critical Infrastructures use RAMCAP Plus approach (9).

This method is based on the general procedure of risk management (10). RAMCAP Plus, in addition, evaluates the environmental threats and mutual dependencies of regional threats. Evaluation of impact of environmental threats is based on semi-quantitative evaluation using historical data on frequency of natural threats. In relation to technological risk analysis and modelling of leakage, scatter, discharge, evaporation, explosion, and fire, many software tools were developed to facilitate the application of the above mentioned methods. These applicable methods include e.g. HAZOP Manager Version 7.0, Fault Tree +, EPRI HRA Calculator®, Security Risk Scorecard, Property Security Risk Survey, SFÉRA- ENERGY and other.

4   Proposed Solution of Simulator

To ensure the main function of proposed simulator for solution of extraordinary events of critical infrastructure subject (11), it will be necessary to take up real information about the occurrence of extraordinary event and its spread via interfaces that are available and used not only by the Integrated Rescue System. This information has at its disposal the sector of critical infrastructure and Emergency Services. Table 2 summarizes main information systems providing information about the dangers of natural extraordinary events, environmental impacts, and secondary sources of danger in case of spreading of extraordinary event or crisis situations on the environment.

From executed analysis of information and data provided by various information and monitoring systems in the area of environmental security imply that on the interface level the simulator will use data from CZRAD, EUMETSAT, Air Quality Information System (AQIS) and the Water Information System.

Radar Network CZRAD is used for detection of precipitation clouds (storms up to 250 km). It can be used to estimate the instantaneous precipitation intensity to about 150 km away from the radar (13). Real-time view of radar images of rainfall, in combination with images of lightning discharges and ward measurements, information on weather in a place where an element of critical energy infrastructure will be made available.

EUMETSAT (European Organisation for the Exploitation of Meteorological Satellites) provides data on weather, climate, and environment. It has a system of meteorological satellites that observe the atmosphere, ocean and land surface (14). It also provides the latest data to the Czech Hydrometeorological Institute that uses it for rigorous prediction of weather forecast and issuing warnings.

Table 2. Summary of significant information systems in the area of environmental safety and their operators[1]

Operator	Name of information system
Czech Hydrometeorological Institute	AMIS
Czech Hydrometeorological Institute	AWOS AVIMET
Czech Hydrometeorological Institute	CZRAD
Czech Hydrometeorological Institute	EUMETSAT
Czech Hydrometeorological Institute	Information system of the air quality (ISKO)
Ministry of the Environment of the Czech Republic	Integrated Pollution Register
Ministry of the Environment of the Czech Republic	Unified Information System for the Environment (JISŽP)
Ministry of the Environment of the Czech Republic	Information system SEA
Ministry of the Environment of the Czech Republic	Information system EIA
Ministry of the Environment of the Czech Republic	Integrated system of reporting compliance
Ministry of Agriculture of the Czech Republic	Information system Voda

Air Quality Information System (AQIS) monitors, evaluate, publish and archive data on air quality for territory of the Czech Republic through automatic air pollution monitoring stations. Local fluctuation of air pollution caused by accidents, extraordinary event and crisis situations (especially smog situations) are due to stations immediately recorded.

Water Information System "Voda" provides information about condition and flows on rivers, water levels in reservoirs, rainfall and water quality, water planning, register state of surface- and groundwater. Information in Voda Portal is provided by a wide range of authorities of Ministry of Agriculture and Ministry of Environment.

Apart from the above mentioned information systems, we recommend to incorporate interface with the Integrated Warning Service System of the Czech Hydro meteorological system. The Integrated Warning Service System issues alert for 32 dangerous phenomena, divided into 8 groups (temperature, wind, snow, frost, storm, rain, floods and fires). Alerts on storms, rains and floods are issued in cooperation with Prediction and Warning Service. Alerts on risk of flooding are already linked to the aforementioned Water Information System.

[1] Adapted in accordance with Act No. 174/2014 Coll., on significant information systems and their underlying criteria (12).

Publicly available information services provide detailed data on climate, soil, and hydrological drought that belong among the key data for the energy sector. Another optional system from the interface is Informational System POVIS (Flood Information System) that is developed for flood protection and flood authorities. The

System contains digital flood plans and books. The flood issue is added by Hydroecological Information System VÚV THM (HEIS VÚV).

National information systems are connected to external systems abroad, especially with neighbouring states for risk of flooding, or systems of European Union (MeteoAlarm, Floods Portal EFAs,) and system of international organizations, where Czech Republic is a member.

Some elements of European Critical Infrastructures are connected to the system of Critical Infrastructure Warning Information Network (CIWIN) (14). Warning Network was established by the European Commission in order to secure the exchange of best practices and provides a platform for the exchange of rapid alerts about threats and vulnerabilities.

5   Conclusion

SIMEX project is currently at the initial stage at the first phase of requirement engineering. The aim is to find out all necessary functions that the simulation tool should obtain for cooperative training of emergency management actors at subjects of critical infrastructure. We initially have identified primary and secondary stakeholders. Communication was later started with the primary stakeholders through a guided interview and checklist. At present, the results are being evaluated. For the exact definition of requirements and elimination of uncertainties in the area of user feedback, a workshop will be organized. This will be where this project puts the most pressure on the next phase.

In definition of simulation interface, there were defined broad spectrum of information and monitoring systems for technological and natural risks that could be used for creation and processing of real simulation scenarios that will subsequently be validated by training of subjects. This fact will significantly contribute to the increase reliability, portability and interoperability in real life scenario with a view to reducing environmental impacts, loss of human lives and damage to property.

References

1. European Commission. Acton the identification and designation of European critical infrastructures and the assessment of the need to improve their protection. Council Directive, 2008/114/EC
2. Czech Republic. Act No. 240/2000 Coll., on Crisis Management and on amendments of certain acts (Crisis Act)
3. Czech Republic. Act No. 432/2010 Coll., on Criteria for determining the elements of critical infrastructure

4. European Commission. Critical Infrastructure Protection - Energy Infrastructure,
   http://ec.europa.eu/energy/infrastructure/critical_en.htm
5. Software Engineering Institute. A Framework for Software Product Line Practice, Version
   5.0. Carnegie Mellon University,
   http://www.sei.cmu.edu/productlines/frame_report/req_eng.htm
6. Sutcliffe, A.G.: Requirements Engineering. In: Soegaard, M., Dam, R.F. (eds.) The Encyclo-
   pedia of Human-Computer Interaction, 2nd edn. The Interaction Design Foundation, Aarhus,
   http://www.interaction-design.org/
   encyclopedia/%20requirements_engineering.html
7. The Stakeholder Engagement Manual VolumeI: The guide to practitioners' perspectives on
   stakeholder engagement, p. 88. Stakeholder Research Associates Canada Inc. (2005),
   http://www.accountability.org/images/content/2/0/207.pdf
   ISBN 0-9738383-0-2
8. The Stakeholder Engagement Manual Volume II: The practitioner's handbook on stakeholder engagement, p. 168. Beacon Press,
   http://www.accountability.org/images/content/2/0/208.pdf
   ISBN 1901693220
9. ASME Innovative technologies institute, LLC. All-hazard risk and resilience: Prioritizing
   Critical Infrastructures Using the RAMCAP Plus Approach, 155. ASME. New York
   (2009) ISBN 978-0-7918-0287-8.
10. Bozek, F., Ješonková, L., Dvorak, J., Bozek, A.: General Procedure of Risk Management.
    Economics and Management 3, 15–24 (2012) ISSN1802-3975
11. Rehak, D., Senovsky, P.: Preference Risk Assessment of Electric Power Critical Infra-
    structure. Chemical Engineering Transactions 36, 469–474 (2014) ISSN 1974-9791, doi:
    10.3303/CET1436079
12. Czech Republic. Act No. 174/2014 Coll., on significant information systemsandtheir un-
    derlyingcriteria
13. Czech Hydrometeorological Institute. Radar net CZRAD,
    http://www.chmi.cz/%20files/portal/docs/meteo/rad/info_czrad/
14. EUMETSAT. Monitoring weather and climate from space,
    http://www.eumetsat.int/website/home/%20AboutUs/WhatWeDo/
    index.html
15. Ministry of Economy and Energy. Critical Infrastructure Warning Information Network –
    CIWIN,
    http://www.mi.government.bg/en/themes/
    critical-infrastructure-warning-informatio%20-network-ciwin-
    333-300.html

Requirements Engineering for Semantic Sensors in Crisis and Disaster Management

Bojan Božić[1], Mert Gençtürk[2], Refiz Duro[1], Yildiray Kabak[2], and Gerald Schimak[1]

[1] Austrian Institute of Technology, Vienna, Austria
[2] Software Research, Development and Consultancy, Ankara, Turkey
bojan.bozic@ait.ac.at

Abstract. This paper describes the requirements engineering methodology used for the definition of semantic sensors in a Crisis and Disaster Management framework. The goal of the framework is effective management of emergencies which depends on timely information availability, reliability and intelligibility. To achieve this, different Command and Control (C2) Systems and Sensor Systems have to cooperate and interoperate. Unless standards and well-defined specifications are used, however, the interoperability of these systems can be very complex. To address this challenge, in the C2-SENSE project, a "profiling" approach will be used to achieve seamless interoperability by addressing all the layers of the communication stack in the security field. The main objective is to develop a profile based Emergency Interoperability framework by the use of existing standards and semantically enriched Web services to expose the functionalities of C2 Systems, Sensor Systems and other Emergency and Crisis Management systems. We introduce the concepts of Semantic Sensors, describe the characteristics of Sensor Systems in Emergency Management, and the methodology of requirements engineering for such a framework.

Keywords: requirements, crisis and disaster management, semantic sensors.

1 Introduction

Emergencies and disasters caused by nature and humanity do not recognize country borders and create international problems (see e.g. [1] and [2], and references therein). These include flooding, forest fires, and industrial accidents, to name a few. The Emergency and Disaster Management hence needs cross border solutions, in order to facilitate communication, resource management and offer solutions to emergencies. This is one of the main motivations for the C2-SENSE[1] Framework, where the knowledge, capabilities and experience from a consortium of several European partners[2] is implemented.

Due to such a partnership, a specific approach in the framework development is needed, explored and implemented. Therefore, the partners decided to use a dedicated requirements engineering methodology, which is explained in Sec. 4.

---

[1] http://c2-sense.eu
[2] The list of the C2-SENSE consortium partners is given at
http://c2-sense.eu/index.php/partners

R. Denzer et al. (Eds.): ISESS 2015, IFIP AICT 448, pp. 397–406, 2015.
© IFIP International Federation for Information Processing 2015

The development of an Emergency and Disaster Management tool, such as C2-SENSE, which will apply the current achievements in semantic sensor technologies, is a complex process requiring specific development methods. In our method for the C2-SENSE framework, there exist three different levels of requirements. The first level is the Emergency Domain Inventory, which uses existing standards, real life use cases of sensors, devices, C2 systems and Emergency Management architectures for different scenarios in the security field. The second level is the common Emergency Domain Ontology, which gathers the knowledge of all stakeholders in a unique and flexible data model. The final level is the Emergency Interoperability Profiles which are developed by using the concepts in this ontology and also by taking into account both functional and operational requirements, as well as different countries' cultural, linguistic and legal issues. This is especially important since such profiles include diverse users such as local authority representatives, activists from non-governmental organizations, and police departments.

Standardization activities that aim to evolve the C2-SENSE Emergency Interoperability Framework into a standard specification for interoperability between Sensor Systems and C2 Systems are also part of the requirements engineering process. The framework developed in the C2-SENSE project will assess its outcomes in a realistic pilot that will cover the Puglia region in Italy to ensure that the developed technologies are generic and applicable in a real life setting.

In the following sections, we describe the requirements engineering process in more detail. In Sec. 2, the importance of semantic sensors is discussed. The available and relevant semantic sensor technologies for the C2-SENSE project are presented in Sec. 3. The method used in the requirements engineering process is shown in Sec. 4, while the lessons learned and conclusions are in Sections 5 and 6.

2   Semantic Sensors and Interoperability

To achieve interoperability, sensors and humans need a common ground of communication and understanding, which is expressed in the ontologies.

2.1   Current State of Data and Semantics

Sensor technology is constantly evolving at a high pace; hence we face a constant increase in the amount of new available data. Such a situation asks for an integration of plethora of sensor types that provide diverse capabilities, such as range, modality and maneuverability. Networks with multiple sensors are becoming common ([3], [4]) and can detect and identify objects of interest from great distances and under demanding conditions [5].

There is, however, a lack of proper integration of sensor data leaving us with large amounts of data, but with a low amount of knowledge about this data. For example, an air quality sensor can give us a measurement of the C02 level in the air (a datum), but will probably not provide us with the sensor calibration status or its geospatial location (additional descriptive data). To change this limitation in the field of e.g. the

Emergency Management, the sensor data should be annotated with metadata. Technologies such as Semantic Web and Sensor Web Enablement (SWE, [6], [7]) are very suitable for this task. Metadata annotation will help us in order to provide contextual as well as situational awareness information. The basis for this is the concept of spatial, temporal, and thematic metadata for sensors, which is being standardized by the Open Geospatial Consortium (OGC, [8]) and the World Wide Web Consortium (W3C, [9]). Activities related to the extension of the existing standards with Semantic Web technologies have been initiated in both organizations in order to improve the description of and access to sensor data.

2.2   Sensor Interoperability

One of these standardization activities is the development of the OGC Sensor Observation Service (SOS, [10]). This is a Web service specification defined by the OGC's Sensor Web Enablement group in order to standardize the way sensors and sensor data are discovered and accessed on the Web. Besides the main objectives, the standard is providing interoperability between repositories of non-homogeneous sensor data and applications that consume these data. As aforementioned, a lack of knowledge of what kind of environment these data represent is a serious obstacle for data handling applications and value extraction. To solve this, the data need to become smarter, which means that there should exist a more meaningful representation of sensor data. The Semantic Sensor Web initiative models the domain of sensors and sensor observations in a suite of ontologies. Semantic annotations are then added to sensor data by using the ontology models to reason over sensor observations and extend the SOS implementation with semantic knowledge. Such semantically enriched data can be queried by semantically enabled SemSOS [11], i.e. the knowledge of the environment, as well as raw sensor data, can be extracted.

3   Sensor Systems in Emergency Management

An important element in the architecture of a (semantic) sensor network in Emergency Management is related to communication, since the Sensor Systems are based on several protocol messages at different levels. This implies that besides the sensors and hardware, the used communication protocols and standards on different levels are of high relevancy.

For the communication between Sensor Web Services we use Simple Object Access Protocol (SOAP, [12]), which is transported through HTTP, TCP, and IP packets. These are in return sent as Ethernet or WiFi messages. Other kinds of sensors and standards used in the development of C2-SENSE tools are:

- Seamless Communication for Crisis Management (SECRICOM, [13]), which addresses the physical level interoperability for a pervasive and trusted communication infrastructure.

- TErrestrial Trunked Radio (TETRA, [14]), Worldwide Interoperability for Micro-wave Access (WiMAX, [15]), GSM and WiFi.
- Asset and Resource Management Standards such as Emergency Data Exchange Language - Resource Messaging (EDXL-RM, [16]), Global Justice XML Data Model (GJXDM, [17]), Joint Consultation, Command and Control Information Exchange Data Model (JC3IEDM, [18]), and Hospital AVailability Exchange Language (EDXL-HAVE, [19])
- Notification Management Standards such as OASIS Common Alerting Protocol (EDXL-CAP, [20]), OGC Sensor Web Enablement Information Standards, OMG Alert Management Service (ALMAS, [21]), News Markup Language, or Events Markup Language (EML, [22]).
- Situational Awareness Standards such as EDXL-Situation Reporting (SitRep, [23]), Tracking of Emergency Patients (TEP, [24]), and Emergency Geospatial Data Distribution Standards such as OGC Web Services (OWS, [25]), OGC Keyhole Markup Language (KLM, [26]), OGC Geography Markup Language (GML, [27]) or compact GML.

4   Requirements Engineering Methodology

Well-designed and efficient coordination of ideas and implementations is required when involving several project partners. The requirements engineering methodology implemented in the C2-SENSE framework aims at providing this in a simple and sufficiently flexible way.

4.1   Requirements Engineering Process

The requirements engineering process used in the C2-SENSE project is shown in Fig. 1. Firstly, a state-of-the-art analysis of relevant projects, tools and technologies is prepared. The analysis is used as a primary basis for the second step, i.e. the extraction of C2-SENSE requirements. Further, the requirements in general can be subdivided into system requirements and pilot application requirements. Thus, there is an interchange between these two tasks. Pilot requirements and general requirements tasks cooperate in order to provide a common understanding of the project goals, as well as to synchronize the inputs of users and technical partners who are responsible for the implementation of software components.

Concrete input for requirements engineering is provided by use case diagrams developed by each project partner. The diagrams define the functionality of the respective components, and templates for technical and user requirements, and for the requirements platform database.

The requirements platform database can be accessed via a Web platform interface and is used to categorize different kinds of requirements. It is also used to manage the requirements and their changes during the life-cycle of the framework. Finally, the requirements are used in the architecture and design tasks for defining the architecture of the C2-SENSE system.

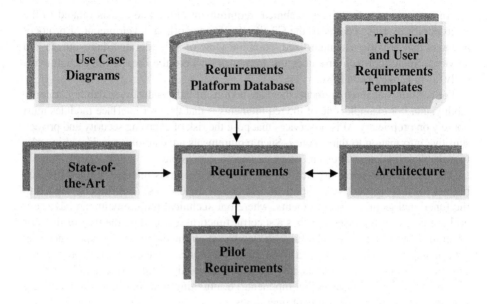

Fig. 1. Requirements Engineering Process

In the next section, a more detailed explanation of the engineering process steps is provided.

4.2   Disaster Management Requirements

The following general disaster management requirements are supported by the C2-SENSE platform:

- *Collaborative Decision Making:*
  Collaborative Decision Making supports different users, different command and control systems, and different doctrines and procedures.
- *Tasking:*
  First responders and other units and resources need to be organized, i.e., tasked with assignments.
- *Monitoring and Reporting:*
  Monitoring and Reporting provide position reports and reports on casualties and obstacles.
- *Re-tasking:*
  Re-tasking may be required during a mission to allocate a unit which is available in a given period of time.

4.3   Technical Requirements and Use Cases

C2-SENSE requirements are divided into technical and user requirements. Technical requirements are further subdivided into functional and non-functional requirements.

An example of a functional technical requirement is the one that is related to the interoperability tasks central to the C2-SENSE framework: a development of protocol adapters that provide a standardized, common view of all integrated data sources and services. Such approach produces the framework where the data is linked automatically, as in Linked Data [28].

For non-functional requirements there are notions of independency, scalability, accountability, etc. For example, one of the requirements is that the user interface modules must not rely on proprietary APIs or services that pose the risk of exposing security and privacy sensitive information to third parties. Such requirements are carefully considered in order to make their implementation and usage as smooth as possible.

The user requirements are developed based on use cases that are defined by each partner for their respective component. Moreover, the use cases are directly related to the functional technical requirements, where one technical requirement can have several use cases. A use case describes a specific function required by the user or the user program/system. These are carefully chosen based on the domain user experience (i.e. a fireman, an NGO activist, or a local authority representative), the Emergency and Disaster literature and standards, and the technical requirements. An example of a use case is the "plug and measure" component, i.e. plugging in a sensor that immediately becomes eligible for measurement operations.

When considering responsibilities, each partner is given the possibility to provide the technical and user requirements that fit to that partner's domain and expertise. At the end, the sum of all requirements corresponds to the architecture of the whole system, which means that functional requirements are bound to the system components.

4.4   Templates

In order to collect technical requirements and use cases from all project partners, templates based on [29] and [30] were provided. They were designed as forms and were also used to prepare partner input for the requirements database. The goal of this is to make the cooperation and planning simpler, to identify the possible issues at an early stage, and to ease the transition to the architecture and the implementation.

The technical requirements template consists of a general, but concise description of the C2-SENSE component, a list of use cases implied by the component, a general function description of the component, and a description of the characteristics of the intended component's users, including educational level, experience and/or technical expertise.

The use case template is more extensive. The project partners provide the following information in the template: a description of what the specific use case does and in which context the use case is applied; the scope of the use case (i.e. which system component in the framework is considered); a list of actors involved in the use case, where the actor refers to a person, a role or a system that triggers the use case in order to reach the defined goal; a description of the goal that the actor pursues upon use case execution; a trigger event and the frequency of the use case realization (e.g. once daily, weekly, etc.). Additionally, UML use case and sequence diagrams are provided to explain the use cases in more detail.

4.5   Requirements Platform

The requirements platform is an ancillary way of increasing the efficiency of the requirements engineering process. It is developed to provide a simple method for technical and user requirements input. Moreover, it is meant for the long-term management of requirement changes, as well as for input of new requirements discovered in later phases of the project.

In short, the platform is a web page[3], on which each project partner has a possibility to log and submit the changes to the existing requirements, or to provide new requirements (see Fig. 2). The web platform is structured in a way that the distinctions and relations between the technical and user requirements are very clear. This should increase the efficiency and understanding among the project partners.

Fig. 2. Screenshot of the Requirements Database platform of the C2-SENSE framework

5   Discussion

Our experience with the proposed methodology for requirements elicitation is two-fold. At first we started by defining a template in a text document and provided it to project partners based on their responsibilities. The problem, however, was to motivate every partner to participate to the collection of requirements and to show them the importance of having a complete set of framework requirements. The breakthrough idea was to initiate a web platform for requirements collection and visualize how requirements are related to each other and how the lack of information on a use case can lead to problems in the implementation phase. After understanding the linkage and the possible impacts, in addition to have an easy to use and intuitive plat-

---

[3] Requirements Database of the FP7 project is located at
http://service.ait.ac.at/c2-sense/

form for collection and management, the process of requirement engineering has improved significantly.

The feedback from all our partners was positive after the change in methodology and we managed to collect user requirements, technical requirements, and use cases in a quick and professional way. It is often very tough to decide when a list of requirements is complete; therefore pitfalls can arise when requirements management is overstressed. On the one hand one does not want to miss important requirements and have an incomplete specification, but on the other hand, putting too much effort in completing the specification phase is not only cumbersome and repetitive for the project team, but also does not lead to a lot of new insights.

Therefore, we recommend a requirement elicitation which supports a dynamic, iterative process and management of new requirements and update of already existing ones throughout the whole project phase.

6   Conclusions

This paper describes the work in the area of requirements engineering specifically applied to semantic sensors in the Emergency Management field. Our contribution is primarily in the proposed method for collection, management, and evolution of requirements, and the development of specific categories for Emergency Management sensor system requirements.

We apply templates that cover the necessary information for technical and user requirements. This is thus more important since there are several international partners involved in the project. A template keeps the ideas concise and simple, which on the other hand increases the understanding in the communication process among partners. We also introduce a web platform, which covers the whole requirements engineering process and which can be reused for similar projects. Our experience with the platform shows that it is effective and efficient, and that it provides a simple way to manage requirements for all the partners involved.

Well-designed and implemented requirements engineering is one of the keys for the success of a project such as C2-SENSE. It is a founding ground for the remaining steps in a process of a system development, and as such is of high importance. It must, however, be simple and flexible enough to allow changes at later stages in the project, and to aid the exchange of ideas among partners. Our proposed method provides the mentioned, is implemented in the C2-SENSE project, and can thus be used in similar projects.

Acknowledgements. The research leading to these results has received funding from the European Community's Seventh Framework Programme (FP7/2007-2013) under grant agreement nr. 607729.

References

[1] Seidel, J., Imbery, F., Dostal, P.: Analysis of Historical River Floods – A Contribution Towards Modern Flood Risk Management. INTECH Open Access Publisher (2012)

[2] Ulbrich, U., Brücher, T., Fink, A.H., Leckebusch, G.C., Krüger, A., Pinto, J.G.: The central European oods of August 2002: Part 1 Rainfall periods and ood development. Weather, 371–377 (2003)

[3] Hart, J.K., Martinez, K.: Environmental Sensor Networks: A revoltion in the Earth system science? Earth-Science Reviews, 177–191 (2006)

[4] Martinez, K., Hart, K., Ong, R., Brennan, S., Mielke, A., Torney, D., Maccabe, A., Maroti, M., Simon, G., Ledeczi, A., et al.: Sensor Network Applications. IEEE Computer (2004)

[5] Werner-Allen, G., Lorincz, K., Welsh, M., Marcillo, O., Johnson, J., Ruiz, M., Lees, J.: Deploying a Wireless Sensor Network on an Active Volcano. IEEE Internet Computing, 18–22 (March 2006)

[6] Jirka, S., Broring, A., Stasch, C.: Applying OGC Sensor WebEnablement to Risk Monitoring and Disaster Management. In: GSDI 11 World Conference,Rotterdam, Netherlands (2009)

[7] Open Geospatial Consortium Sensor Web Enablement (OGC SWE), http://www.opengeospatial.org/ogc/markets-technologies/swe

[8] Open Geospatial Consortim (OGC), http://www.opengeospatial.org

[9] World Wide Web Consortium (W3C), http://www.w3.org/

[10] Open Geospatial Consortium Sensor Observation Service (OGC SOS), http://www.opengeospatial.org/standards/sos

[11] Henson, C.A., Pschorr, J.K., Sheth, A.P., Thirunarayan, K.: Sem-SOS: Semantic sensor observation service. In: IEEE Proceedings of 2009 International Symposiumon Collaborative Technologies and Systems (2009)

[12] Simple Object Access Protocol (SOAP), http://www.w3.org/TR/soap12-part1/

[13] Seamless Communication for Crisis Management Project (SECRICOM), http://www.secricom.eu/

[14] Terrestrial Trunked Radio (TETRA), http://www.tandcca.com/

[15] Worldwide Interoperability for Microwave Access (WiMAX), http://www.wimaxforum.org

[16] Emergency Data Exchange Language Resource Messaging (EDXL-RM), http://docs.oasis-open.org/emergency/edxl-rm/v1.0/errata/EDXL-RM-v1.0-OS-errata-os.pdf

[17] Global Justice XML Data Model (GJXDM), http://tinyurl.com/ndw5gyx

[18] The Joint Consultation, Command and Control Information Exchange Data Model (JC3IEDM), http://tinyurl.com/nr6vgjw

[19] Emergency Data Exchange Language Hospital Availability Exchange (EDXLHAVE), http://docs.oasis-open.org/emergency/edxl-have/v1.0/errata/edxl-havev1.0-os-errata-os.html

[20] Common Alerting Protocol (CAP), http://docs.oasisopen.org/emergency/cap/v1.2/CAP-v1.2-os.html

[21] Alert Management Service (ALMAS), http://www.omg.org/spec/ALMAS/1.0/

[22] Event Markup Language (EML), http://tinyurl.com/nmzz2w7

[23] Emergency Data Exchange Language Situation Reporting (EDXL-SitRep),
`http://docs.oasis-open.org/emergency/edxl-sitrep/v1.0/`
`edxl-sitrep-v1.0.pdf`
[24] Emergency Data Exchange Language Tracking of Emergency Patients (EDXLTEP),
`http://docs.oasis-open.org/emergency/edxl-tep/v1.0/`
`edxl-tep-v1.0.pdf`
[25] Open Geospatial Consortium Web Services (OWS),
`http://www.opengeospatial.org/standards/owc`
[26] Open Geospatial Consortium Keyhole Markup Language (OGC KML),
`http://www.opengeospatial.org/standards/kml`
[27] Open Geospatial Consortium Geography Markup Language (OGC GML),
`http://www.opengeospatial.org/standards/gml`
[28] Bizer, C., Heath, T., Berners-Lee, T.: Linked Data - The story so far. In: Int. J. Semantic
Web Inf. Syst., pp. 1–22 (2009)
[29] Cockburn, A.: Writing Effective Use Cases. Addison-Wesley, (2001)
[30] Coleman, D.: A Use Case Template: draft for discussion. Fusion Newsletter (April 1998)

Context Ontology Modelling for Improving Situation Awareness and Crowd Evacuation from Confined Spaces

Gianluca Correndo, Banafshe Arbab-Zavar, Zlatko Zlatev, and Zoheir A. Sabeur

University of Southampton IT Innovation Centre, Electronics and Computer Science,
Faculty of Physical Sciences and Engineering, Southampton, United Kingdom
{gc,zdz,baz,zas}@it-innovation.soton.ac.uk

Abstract. Crowd evacuation management at large venues such as airports, sta-
diums, cruise ships or metro stations requires the deployment and access to a
Common Operational Picture (COP) of the venue, with real-time intelligent
contextual interpretation of crowd behaviour. Large CCTV and sensor network
feeds all provide important but heterogeneous observations about crowd safety
at the venue of interest. Hence, these observations must be critically analyzed
and interpreted for supporting security managers of crowd safety at venues.
Specifically, the large volume of the generated observations needs to be interpreted in context of the venue operational grounds, crowd-gathering event times
and the knowledge on crowd expected behaviour. In this paper, a new context
ontology modelling approach is introduced. It is based on knowledge about venue background information, expected crowd behaviours and their manifested
features of observations. The aim is to improve situation awareness about
crowd safety in crisis management and decision-support.

Keywords: crisis management, decision-support, sensor data, semantics, context ontology modelling, crowd behavior.

1 Introduction

Advanced situation awareness, safety of crowd and their evacuation from large mass
gathering venues during incidents is of paramount importance in crisis management.
The crowd must be evacuated rapidly towards safer zones. However, the real-time
monitoring of crowd during incidents is an enduring responsibility taken by security
managers. Nowadays security personnel is able to observe venue spaces in real-time
through using ICT based devices and use automated systems for their decision-
support. The ICT devices and systems may include a large network of deployed
CCTV cameras, multiple arrays of sensors and a Common Operational Picture (COP)
of the venue of interest. Nevertheless, security managers can be overwhelmed by
sheer volumes and complexity of observation data while making their decisions on
crowd spatial evacuation in real-time. Further, they could potentially encounter risks
of failure in their decisions since they may not be able to capture and interpret incident related situations critically on time.

R. Denzer et al. (Eds.): ISESS 2015, IFIP AICT 448, pp. 407–416, 2015.

The eVACUATE1 project specializes in crowd behaviour detection using multiple video observations under the visible, thermal and hyper-spectral light bands, which is also enhanced by high level crowd psychology and typology knowledge reasoning, modelling and fusion. This shall add value to existing crowd evacuation strategies with much improved situation awareness and decision-support. Four crowd evacuation pilot experiments are considered in the project. These include the following: 1-Evacuation of a Soccer Stadium - Real Sociedad de Futbol S.A.D (Spain); 2-Mustering and evacuation of passenger cruise ship -STX-FR (France); 3-Airport Terminal evacuation - Athens International Airport(Greece); and 4- Metro Tube evacuation – Metro Bilbao S.A (Spain).

Crowd behaviour modelling is an established discipline in numerical phenomena simulation. Also, with more affordable and easy to deploy ICT devices to monitor crowd, it has become possible to analyze human behaviour with more degrees of spatial granularities and context to advance knowledge reasoning and crowd behaviour modelling. "Normative behaviour models" are based on established cognitive psychology theories, or "Script" (Schema) theories [1]. These postulate that human behaviour can mostly be described as a set of patterns, so called "scripts". These are basically comparable to the way a written script is set with its provision of a program for actions. For example, the stringent requirements on following safety procedures on board aircrafts or cruise ships is a typical attempt to set up appropriate temporary schema to be used during emergency [2]. Therefore, it is highly desirable to investigate on the scripts which can be generated by crowd during a real evacuation event from a given venue. This will provide a good basis for understanding how crowd evacuation evolves in space and time and also learn from it for further improvement on future evacuation plans. It is worth noting that understanding usual (and unusual) behaviour in context of crowd types and gathering venues is essential to proceed with this study.

Automated usual (and unusual) behaviour detection aims at supporting security managers and decision-makers during normal crowd monitoring activities as well as during evacuation. In this paper, an ontological framework based on causality assumption on crowd behaviour is developed. This is in contrast to the traditional rigid approaches based on the creation of ad-hoc rules which describe crowd behaviour. Moreover, the proposed approach introduces context knowledge as a source of important information, to improve the crowd behaviour classification process and modelling.

2   Context Knowledge and Human Behaviour Detection

Research interest on domain knowledge usage for improving the performance of traditional machine learning based human behaviour detection classifiers from vision observation has been growing over the last few years. Concepts of ambient intelligence which are embedded in cognitive vision systems have also been explored. The use of context about crowd typology in accord with mass-gathering venue

---

1   http://www.evacuate.eu/

characteristics, including operational spaces and times are being researched for advancing the performance of crowd behaviour detection algorithms using vision in the eVACUATE project.

2.1 Contextual Knowledge in Cognitive Vision

In [3] it is presented an approach, named *key-frame*, for modelling human sequences within cognitive vision systems that allow the description and synthesis of human actions within spaces. The approach focuses on actions performed by individuals, segmenting them into key frames which are characterised by body posture configurations. At higher level of abstraction, human behaviour(s) are described in a lattice of symbolic templates, named situation graph trees. The graph trees describe the relationships between agents and the surrounding environment. Various types of semantic representations have been proposed within the framework of human sequence evaluation. Depending on the addressed domain of safety and security surveillance, they can support the classification of critical situations accordingly. Within the surveillance domain, an ontology has been proposed [4], based on the key-frame approach. The core of this ontology is introduced with the following listed concepts: 1) **Event** (or situation): Characterized by a status, which encodes metric-temporal knowledge; 2) **Contextualized Event**: Describes higher level interactions among entities; and 3) **Behaviour Interpretation**: Specifies surveillance oriented behaviors of interest, i.e. "abandoned object". One of the main issues in applying such approach for monitoring crowd in EVACUATE's confined spaces is that it will be almost impossible to maintain the identity of the monitored entities and rendering the tracking of agent's activities through frames. Moreover, there is no design pattern that will support the creation of general behaviour(s). This approach seem to be too rigidly linked to the native domain of crowd surveillance and cannot be proposed as a reusable knowledge for modelling.

2.2 Context in Ambient Intelligence

Ambient intelligence concept ontologies are used to provide high level descriptions of situations in order to support context awareness in smart applications for decision-support. The term "context" is understood to be: *"Any information that can be used to characterise the state of an entity"* [5]. The aim of ambient intelligence is also for recognising what users do so that they can be assisted in spaces around which they move. This aim somehow steps on the definition provided on "human behaviour" [6]. Context here plays a key role for understanding not only the activities performed by agents within a spatial environment, but also how these activities can be interpreted within a broad framework of relationships between other agents, entities and unfolding events. These concepts have been modelled using ontologies such as: COBRA-ONT [7] and SOCAM [8]. Nevertheless, such ontologies provide concepts only for user-oriented entities such as *Location*, *Person*, or *Activity*. They are solely focussed in personalised ambient intelligence but with less interest on the specificities of human behaviour detection.

3   Context Information in Crowd Evacuation Management

Context in ambient intelligence is understood to capture the amount of information that could characterize a situation of an entity at a given space of interest. It is partly given and/or acquired, while it remains user interactive and application centric. In eVACUATE, context information and sensor observations are kept separate. Nevertheless, Context is used in the interpretation of the sensor observation. With this in mind, context is defined as the amount of *a priori* knowledge information about expected crowd behaviour(s) at given venues of interest. This prior knowledge is assumed to give trade-offs on better interpreting and detecting crowd behaviour from video sensing. During the monitoring of crowd in real-time, it is important to model the expected interactions of crowd(s) at various spatial scales. These include macro-, meso- and micro-scales. They could represent overall people, finite number of people as a group and single individuals within the crowd respectively. These types of interactions can be modelled by representing them as causal connections across *a prior* known behaviour modes, contextual information and observed (detectable) features.

3.1   New Crowd Behaviour Contextual Modelling

Ontological models are used to describe crowd *Usual* (expected) behaviour(s) in context of venues. These models describe how behaviour manifests itself and how it compares with its detectable features through sensor observations. When discrepancies between the expected and detected behaviour occur, then the behaviour is classed as *Unusual*. Equally, when discrepancies do not occur, the behaviour is classed as *Usual*. The distinction between *Usual* and *Unusual* behaviour in this study is mainly dependent on the following: *1) Context; 2) The Model which describes the situation; and 3) The set of observations which are collected from a venue.* Similarly, subdivisions of *Context*, *Model*, and *Observations* are found in logical problem definitions such as *diagnosis* and *diagnostic* in model-based reasoning [9]. For instance, Diagnosis is described with a set of assumptions that are joint with a logical model system (i.e. Crowd at a given Venue) and context to explain observations. For example, when monitoring a flow of spectators at different parts of a venue, like a football stadium during a match, usual behaviour is specifically characterised in accord with the place that is monitored (e.g. *Entrance Gate*; *Ticket Counters, Bar, Club Fan Shop, Stands* etc.). Usual behaviour is also characterized in accord with the various stages of the unfolding event (e.g. *Pre-Match*; *Match in progress*; *Post-match*).

- *Pre-Match*: The spectators are expected to enter the stadium through the *Entrance Gates*. From there they proceed to the *Stands*.
- *Match in progress*: The expected behaviour at the stands is for spectators to be partly stationary on their benches (i.e. with oscillatory or occasional movements of small groups for toilet breaks and trips to the bar). Hence, any substantive movement of individual or groups of spectators towards opposite fans can be considered as unusual.

- *Post-Match*: Groups of individuals are expected to leave the stadium and head towards the car parking spaces.

The above mentioned example of venue and crowd type clearly shows that the various stages of the football match event together with the various monitored areas around the stadium are by far the most important knowledge for defining the expected (Usual) behaviour of spectators(crowd or fans). Specifically, crowd physical motions related parameters such as the predominant crowd velocities (speed and direction) and densities (counted number of people per unit area) become important to measure. In this case, rules that model expected crowd behaviour at a football match can be simply defined as follows:

$$BehavioralMode(usual) \land Venue(stadium) \land Time(pre\text{-}match) \land Place(gate) \vdash$$
$$Expected(flow(X, gate, benches) \land velocity(X,V) \land V \leq 5m/s) \tag{1}$$

The above logical formula (1) involves the flow velocity V (including speed and direction) of detected groups X which are represented as predicates. It also includes the context information of Venue, Type, and Place. The *BehaviouralMode* term in (2) does not belong to the context; its value (i.e. "usual") is the assumption made by the system when processing observations. Formula (1) represents the expected usual crowd motion conditions (i.e. usual behaviour). However, the spectrum of behaviour(s) can be formulated at various spatial scales of detected groups in the crowd. These concern the generic terms X and their respective estimated velocities. The system can use such formulas by adopting available contextual information and assuming usual behavior(s). Forward logical chaining can be then applied to get a set of expected values of observations. The expected values will be then matched against actual observed features that need to be detected computer vision based machine learning algorithms. (Equally, the system can use the concept of formula (1) for backward chaining observations and context to infer values of predicated behavior.

4   Ontology Design Pattern for Context Definition

In order to correctly interpret crowd sensor observations, a set of ontological behavioural templates needed to be developed against measured sensor properties (or features). The latter are extracted from crowd behaviour detection algorithms trained on vision sensor observation data sources (e.g. video feed). OGC standards on "Sensor Observations and Measurements" [10] were adopted to develop the behavioural templates of eVACUATE. OGC ontologies such as SSN ontology [11] were specifically used to semantically enhance the concept of "Observation" in this research study.

4.1   Context for Defining Crowd Behaviour

Some crowd behaviour(s) are context agnostic (e.g. Crowd stampede). These do not need further contextual information to fully define them. However, most crowd behaviour(s) are context dependent. Their interpretation depend on a number of contextual factors which are described (with examples) below:

- *Time*
  The flow of spectators at a stadium change with the expected match schedules (pre-match, during the match, after match). Or, passengers motions at an underground station platform vary depending on the train time table (before, during, after train arrives)
- *Space*
  Passengers in an airport tend to queue at check-in desks; or at ticket kiosks of an underground station. Also, spectators at a stadium are usually orderly seated at stands.
- *Venue*
  Passengers evacuating from a cruise ship are expected to behave differently from spectators evacuating a stadium.
- *Other*
  Crowd(s) behaviour expectations from instructions (i.e. Audio guided evacuation at a given venue).

The behaviour templates associate the above behaviour-like modes in this study. These have key detectable features which can be observed through sensing hods, including video cameras

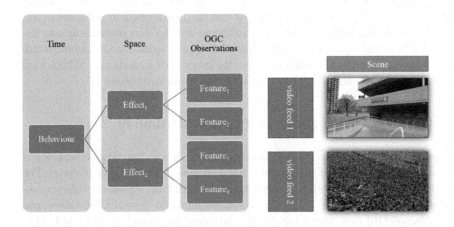

Fig. 1. Behaviour Template

At the heart of the context behaviour ontology describing behaviour templates lies the concept of causality which is used to match the interpretation of the collected sensor observations. The crowd contextual behaviour ontology distinguishes three main components (see Fig. 1): 1-*Behaviours*; 2-*Effects*; and 3-*Features*.

Sensor observations are modeled as the detected manifestations of the effects of unfolding behaviour(s). Crowd *Behaviour*(s) are described in templates of expected human interactions in a given venue. They are defined with a set of expected *Effect*(s) in space and time. *Effect*(s) are spatially tangible (or intangible) result, in terms their manifested detectable features. They are also conceptualized as spatially related to scheduled activities of crowd(s) at the venue. The manifested *Feature*(s) of such *Effect*(s) are sensory observed at the venue with specific measurable values.

OGC O&M standards on "Observation & Measurements" [10] define observation as:

"An Observation is an action whose result is an estimate of the value of some property of the feature-of-interest, at a specific point in time, obtained using a specified procedure".

Although our approach is inspired from OGC O&M standards, the crowd behaviour modelling template was developed distinctly in terms of its description of observations and features. In it, the Effect(s) are postulated as a collection of detectable Feature(s). Also, Feature(s) are constrained by a set of specific observations with detectable properties. For example, sensor readings of property, which concern crowd activities in a venue, may include crowd physical motion (Velocity: Speed and direction); and density (Number of individuals per unit spatial area) at various spatial resolutions and levels. The main distinction from OGC O&M standards in the construction of the behaviour template here, mainly concerns the restriction of the possible (and range of) values of observations of given Feature(s). This is greatly supported by the assumption that crowd(s) are expected to behave in a particular way within a given and venue and times. This new distinction enables good reasoning on observed and detectable Usual (or Unusual) crowd behaviour.

The inclusion of effects with no direct tangible features are required in order to model psychological states that involve single (or group of) individuals in the crowd(s). These are not directly detectable via sensing but undoubtedly influence the value and range of detectable features. In eVACUATE, the modelling of crowd behaviour(s), the spatial environment in which they unfold and their evolution in time, allows the abstraction of behaviour templates and instantiate them generically for different of venues and crowd(s). For example, in the expected behaviour at a stadium, which was introduced in Section 3, can be generalized using an abstract behaviour template (See Table 1) so that it can be used for different venues. (For a Stadium, the gathering places are the stands, the transition places are the gates and the internal corridors, while the exit can be the car park outside the stadium.)

4.2   Modelled Crowd(s) Features

The ontological modelling of detectable features is a process which is primarily driven by the type of information that can be collected from the deployed sensor networks at the venue. At this stage of the project, the primary source of information are

Table 1. Event Behaviour Template

		Time		
		pre	**During**	**post**
	Gathering Place	People settling in	People stably at place	People leaving from the gathering place
Space	**Transition Place**	People moving towards gathering place	Mostly empty	People moving towards the exit
	Exit	People moving towards inside the venue	Mostly empty	People moving towards the outside of the venue

CCTV cameras which are already installed at the venue. The included features in the modelling so far, include the ones which are available by the feature extraction algorithms in eVACUATE. These particularly focus on venues with the description of crowd(s) at various scales and levels. These are highlighted below:

1. *Micro-scale*: An individual is identified with measurable time-dependent position and velocity
2. *Meso-scale*: Although group of individuals are identified with measurable time-dependent positions and velocities, these are represented as a statistical distribution in addition with other features. These are included as: a) *Density* which is measured as number of people per unit area. This is used to model levels of service as described by Fruin [12] and the expected presence of people within target areas in a venue; and b) *Direction*: A symbolic information which described that a group is intentionally moving towards an explicitly described target (e.g. an exit) with a certain degree of certainty. This is used additionally to model the expected flow of people
3. *Macro-scale*: Average quantities such as crowd density, dominant motions (Translations), structure and internal energies are determined in this scale. They specifically include the following features: a) *Internal Energy*: Normalized between 0 and 1, it estimates the amount of oscillations of elements within a crowd; b) *Structure*: Normalized between 0 and 1, it estimates the strength of the connections within a crowd; and c) *Predominant Translation*: Used to measure the degree of mobility of the crowd.

4.3 Ontology Modules and Sensor Data Ingestion Architecture

As mentioned in Section 4.1, behaviour templates can be generalized and reused for different domains (venues) and sub-classing. The behaviour template in Section 4.1 concerning the "Stadium domain" is further detailed. As depicted in Fig. 2, the Event Behaviour Template captures the pre-event period (i.e. before the event takes place) with the expected effect as a Gathering Effect. This effect manifests itself at the Gates and Corridors, while the crowd moves towards the stands. The Crowd direction of motion is depicted with a target → Stadium Stands. As a result, the expected usual crowd(s) Gathering Behaviour at a Stadium (Football match event) states the crowd(s) move without running, while they maintain a high structure. This is expected from groups moving towards shared destinations and not scattering around the venue.

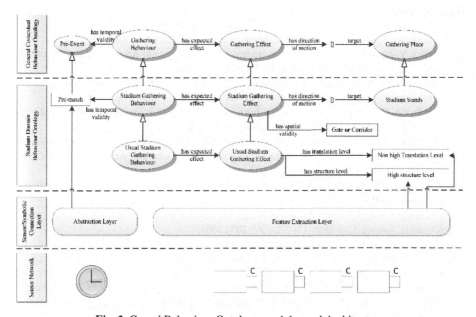

Fig. 2. Crowd Behaviour Ontology modules and Architecture

It is clear from Fig. 2 that the described concepts of Gathering Behaviour, Effect, and Gathering Place in a general ontology can be imported by various domain ontologies that will refine their definition for specific venue types. Equally, the mentioned sensory video feeds and further context relevant information, such as time and event occurrences, need to go through abstraction steps with symbolic representations in the terms of the domain ontology used (i.e. pre-match symbol instead of a date time).

5   Conclusions

This early research describes an approach for semantically enhancing the ingestion of sensor data which may describe the links to crowd behaviour, context and detectable sensor observations. The approach is inspired from script theory which suggests that humans follow scripts which are linked to past experience and observed situations. The paper presents an approach which models such scripts as causal chains in an OWL ontology language. The ontology can be reused to describe domain specific behaviour(s) at different venues. Moreover, a general schema is introduced on how sensor data is processed prior to behaviour classification using the ontology.

Acknowledgments. eVACUATE is co-funded by the European Commission under Grant FP7-EC-313161. One of the Authors (ZAS) would especially like to thank project partners for cooperation, including AIA S.A (Greece) for data sample acquisition; and Katholieke Universiteit Leuven (Belgium), for assisting in the use of workpackage11 recommendations on data Ethics, Legal and Regulatory Activities.

References

1. Schank, R.C., Abelson, R.P.: Scripts, plans, and knowledge. Yale University (1975)
2. Chang, Y.-H., Yang, H.-H.: Aviation occupant survival factors: An empirical study of the SQ006 accident. Accid. Anal. Prev. 42(2), 695–703 (2010)
3. Gonzàlez i Sabaté, J.: Human sequence evaluation: the key-frame approach. info:eurepo/semantics/doctoralThesis, Universitat Autonoma de Barcelona (2004)
4. Fernández, C., Gonzàlez, J.: Ontology for semantic integration in a cognitive surveillance system. In: Semantic Multimedia, pp. 260–263. Springer (2007)
5. Dey, A.K., Abowd, G.D.: The context toolkit: Aiding the development of context-aware applications. In: Workshop on Software Engineering for wearable and pervasive computing, pp. 431–441 (2000)
6. Remagnino, P., Hagras, H., Velastin, S., Monekosso, N.: Ambient intelligence: a gentle introduction (2005)
7. Chen, H., Finin, T., Joshi, A.: An ontology for context-aware pervasive computing environments. Knowl. Eng. Rev. 18(03), 197–207 (2003)
8. Gu, T., Pung, H.K., Zhang, D.Q.: A middleware for building context-aware mobile services. In: 2004 IEEE 59th Vehicular Technology Conference, VTC 2004-Spring, vol. 5, pp. 2656–2660 (2004)
9. ten Teije, A., van Harmelen, F.: An extended spectrum of logical definitions for diagnostic systems. In: Proceedings of DX-94 Fifth International Workshop on Principles of Diagnosis, pp. 334–342 (1994)
10. Cox, S.: Observations and Measurements. Open GIS Consortium Inc., 03-022r3 (2003)
11. Compton, M., Barnaghi, P., Bermudez, L., García-Castro, R., Corcho, O., Cox, S., Graybeal, J., Hauswirth, M., Henson, C., Herzog, A., Huang, V., Janowicz, K., Kelsey, W.D., Le Phuoc, D., Lefort, L., Leggieri, M., Neuhaus, H., Nikolov, A., Page, K., Passant, A., Sheth, A., Taylor, K.: The SSN ontology of the W3C semantic sensor network incubator group. Web Semant. Sci. Serv. Agents World Wide Web 17, 25–32 (2012)
12. Fruin, J.J.: Designing for Pedestrians: A Level-of-Service Concept. New York Metropolitan Association of Urban Designers and Environmental Planners. Highw. Res. Rec. (355) (1971)

Reconstructing the Carbon Dioxide Absorption Patterns of World Oceans Using a Feed-Forward Neural Network: Software Implementation and Employment Techniques

Jiye Zeng, Hideaki Nakajima, Yukihiro Nojiri, and Shin-ichiro Nakaoka

National Institute for Environmental Studies, Tsukuba, Japan
zeng@nies.go.jp

Abstract. Oceans play a major role in the global carbon budget, absorbing approximately 27% of anthropogenic carbon dioxide (CO2). As the degree to which an ocean can serve as a carbon sink is determined by the partial pressure of CO2 in the surface water, it is critical to obtain an accurate estimate of the spatial distributions of CO2 and its temporal variation on a global scale. However, this is extremely challenging due to insufficient measurements, large seasonal variability, and short spatial de-correlation scales. This paper presents an open source software package that implements a feed-forward neural network and a back-propagation training algorithm to solve a problem with one output variable and a large number of training patterns. We discuss the employment of the neural network for global ocean CO2 mapping.

Keywords: CO2, climate, neural network, ocean, software.

1   Introduction

Recent changes in the global climate are closely related to increasing atmospheric levels of anthropogenic greenhouse gases [1], particularly carbon dioxide (CO2). According to the global carbon budget 2013 report [2], the total global carbon emissions increased from 3.9 GtC/yr in 1959 to 10.7 GtC/yr in 2012, of which approximately 43% remained in the atmosphere, 30% was taken by terrestrial sinks, and 27% was absorbed by the oceans. The uncertainty of the magnitude of the ocean sink is largely due to the uncertainty in estimating the CO2 at the ocean's surface, given that the flux at the air–water interface is determined by the difference in the partial pressure of CO2 between the two mediums, the transfer coefficient, and the wind at the surface [3]. Although the latter two parameters encompass some uncertainty, the CO2 in the surface ocean determines whether the oceans are a carbon sink or source.

The most challenging obstacle in estimating the capacity of the oceans as a carbon sink is the insufficiency of measurement data. Using the 1×1 gridded dataset from the Surface Ocean CO2 Atlas[1] (SOCAT) version 2 [4], which is the most complete and quality-controlled dataset, we calculated that no more than 4% of the surface waters

---

[1] http://www.socat.info/

R. Denzer et al. (Eds.): ISESS 2015, IFIP AICT 448, pp. 417–425, 2015.

of the world's oceans had been sampled in any single month between 1990 and 2011. This motivated us to examine robust and reliable methods for interpolating the available CO2 data, both spatially and temporarily. However, most existing models use a basin scale (e.g., [5,6,7,8,9,10,11,12,13,14]) as the spatial de-correlation length scale of CO2 is on the order of 100 km, which is about 10 times smaller than the marine atmosphere CO2 [15], and the seasonal changes in the surface ocean CO2 can be 100 μatm or more [16]. The most used product to estimate the global ocean CO2 levels is the monthly climatology data of [17], which uses a 5×4 degree mesh.

This work presents open-source software that implements a feed-forward neural network (FNN) specifically developed for modeling environmental problems such as reconstructing the global ocean CO2. The software has been used by [18] to produce monthly maps of the climatology of CO2 with a spatial resolution of 1×1 degrees. We discuss possible techniques to extend the work of [18] to reconstruct the time variant distribution of the global ocean CO2 from 1990 to 2011.

2 Method

2.1 Software Package

Our software package[2] implements the FNN shown in Figure 1. The FNN comprises three layers: input, hidden, and output. A neuron in the input layer takes the value of an input variable and passes it to all neurons in the hidden layer. A neuron in the hidden or output layer adds a bias to the weighted sum of all of the outputs from its upstream neurons and transforms the sum to yield its output:

$$y = f(x) = \frac{1}{1+e^{-x}}$$ (1)

$$x = b + \sum_{i=1}^{M} w_i y_{i,upstream}$$

The sigmoid transform function was chosen because it increases monotonically from 0 to 1 for x from -∞ to +∞ and the derivative of y with respect to x yields a simple form that affiliates the so-called back-propagation [19] algorithm for training the FNN. In training, the algorithm changes the weight and bias parameters proportionally according to the negative gradient of the error cost function, i.e., the sum of squared error between the network output y and the target d:

$$F(\mathbf{w}) = \frac{1}{2}\sum_{l}^{P}(d^l - y^l)^2 = \frac{1}{2}\mathbf{e}^T\mathbf{e}$$ (2)

$$\mathbf{e}^T = [e^1 \quad e^2 \quad ... \quad e^P]$$

$$e^l = d^l - y^l$$

---

[2] http://db.cger.nies.go.jp/ged/Open-Data/JTECH-D-13-00137/ann-c++.zip

where P is the total number of training patterns (a pattern comprises a set of data of all input variables). In the simplest form, the algorithm uses the first-order derivative of the cost function as the gradient $\mathbf{g}$ to find the minima in the error space:

$$\mathbf{g} = \nabla F(\mathbf{w}) = \mathbf{J}^T \mathbf{e} \tag{3}$$

where the vector $\mathbf{w}$ includes both weight and bias parameters and $\mathbf{J}$ is the Jacobian matrix. Assuming $\mathbf{w}$ has N elements, $\mathbf{J}$ has the form of

$$\mathbf{J} = \begin{bmatrix} \dfrac{\partial e^1}{\partial w_1} & \dfrac{\partial e^1}{\partial w_2} & \cdots & \dfrac{\partial e^1}{\partial w_N} \\ \dfrac{\partial e^2}{\partial w_1} & \dfrac{\partial e^2}{\partial w_2} & \cdots & \dfrac{\partial e^2}{\partial w_N} \\ \cdots & \cdots & \cdots & \cdots \\ \dfrac{\partial e^P}{\partial w_1} & \dfrac{\partial e^P}{\partial w_2} & \cdots & \dfrac{\partial e^P}{\partial w_N} \end{bmatrix} \tag{4}$$

Regarding the output neuron and a training pattern, the partial differentiation by the weights and bias for the jth hidden neuron can be derived as

$$\frac{\partial e}{\partial w_{o,j}} = -\frac{\partial y_o}{\partial w_{o,j}} = -\frac{\partial y_o}{\partial x_o}\frac{\partial x_o}{\partial w_{o,j}} = -\delta_o y_j$$

$$\frac{\partial e}{\partial b_o} = -\frac{\partial y_o}{\partial b_o} = -\frac{\partial y_o}{\partial x_o}\frac{\partial x_o}{\partial b_o} = -\delta_o \tag{5}$$

$$\delta_o = \frac{\partial y_o}{\partial x_o} = (1 - y_o)y_o$$

and the partial differentiations by the weights and bias of the jth hidden neuron for the ith input neuron can be expressed as

$$\frac{\partial e}{\partial w_{j,i}} = -\frac{\partial y_o}{\partial w_{j,i}} = -\frac{\partial y_o}{\partial x_o}\frac{\partial x_o}{\partial y_j}\frac{\partial y_j}{\partial x_j}\frac{\partial x_j}{\partial w_{j,i}} = -\delta_j y_i$$

$$\frac{\partial e}{\partial b_j} = -\frac{\partial y_o}{\partial b_j} = -\frac{\partial y_o}{\partial x_o}\frac{\partial x_o}{\partial y_j}\frac{\partial y_j}{\partial x_j}\frac{\partial x_j}{\partial b_j} = -\delta_j \tag{6}$$

$$\delta_j = \frac{\partial y_o}{\partial x_o}\frac{\partial x_o}{\partial y_j}\frac{\partial y_j}{\partial x_j} = \delta_o w_j (1 - y_j)y_j$$

Updating neuron parameters for the tth training epoch (a complete loop through all training patterns) can be expressed as

$$\mathbf{w}(t) = \mathbf{w}(t-1) + \Delta\mathbf{w}(t) = \mathbf{w}(t-1) + \alpha\mathbf{g} \tag{7}$$

where α is the learning rate with a value between 0 and 1. The convergence of training the FNN by the gradient expressed in equation (3) is slow. The Levenberg–Marquardt algorithm (see [20,21]) improves the convergence speed by considering the second-order derivative of the cost function, resulting in a new estimation for the gradient as

$$\mathbf{g} = (\mathbf{J}^T \mathbf{J} + \mu\mathbf{I})^{-1} \mathbf{J}^T \mathbf{e} \tag{8}$$

where μ is the regularization constant and $\mathbf{I}$ is a unit matrix. In our implementation, we set μ proportional to the root mean square error:

$$\mu = \beta \sqrt{\frac{1}{P}\sum_{l}^{P}(d^l - y^l)^2}$$

(9)

We call β the regularization coefficient.

We implemented several methods in the software to achieve efficient computing and simple usage. First, the method of [21] was used to eliminate the necessity of storing a large Jacobian matrix in the memory. Second, the software scales all input variable data to have a zero mean and unit standard deviation and scales the target variable data to vary from 0.1 to 0.9. This method not only improves convergence speed but also makes it possible to use a default α and β for a variety of cases. Third, the software allows a user to use a text file and select any given number of columns in any order as input and output variables.

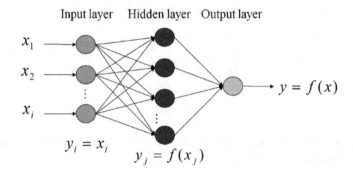

Fig. 1. Illustration of the feed forward neural network. Neurons in different layers are fully connected, but no connection exists among neurons of the same layer.

2.2   CO2 Model

Our basic model equation defines the fugacity of CO2 (fCO2) as a nonlinear function of month (MON), latitude (LAT), and longitude (LON):

$$fCO2 = F(MON, LAT, LON)$$

(10)

Because of insufficient measurements, we introduced sea surface temperature (SST), sea surface salinity (SSS), and chlorophyll-a concentration (CHL) as proxy variables in space and time. Therefore, the model equation becomes

$$fCO2 = F(MON, LAT, LON, SST, SSS, CHL)$$

(11)

In a global setting for long-term modeling, MON and LON must be transformed to account for their circular properties. As a result, the complete model equation becomes

$$fCO2 = F(CMON, SMON, LAT, CLON, SLON, SST, SSS, CHL) \qquad (12)$$

where

$$CMON = \cos(MON)$$
$$SMON = \sin(MON)$$
$$CLON = \cos(LON)$$
$$SLON = \sin(LON)$$

The model equation establishes the relationship between the eight input variables and the one output variable of the neural network.

2.3   Employment Issues

Two issues often cloud the proper use of an FNN: landing on a local minimum in training and choosing the "right" number of hidden neurons. The first issue can be detected using a different random number seeds to initialize the weight and bias parameters, or using different learning rates and regularization parameters. We have experimented with the Levenberg-Marquardt algorithm with these approaches and found that landing on a local minimum rarely occurred in our case.

The second issue is notorious. It is well known that an FNN can approximate any finite function given a sufficiently large number of hidden neurons [22,23]. That means that if the fCO2 values are unique in corresponding to unique values of MON, LAT, LON, SST, SSS, and CHL, equation (12) can be fitted accurately with a larger number of hidden neurons. An FNN configured as such remembers all training patterns and thus loses the capability to filter out erroneous information in measurement data. Unfortunately, there is no theoretically approved rule for choosing the right number of hidden neurons [24]. Our criterion for selecting the number is that the standard deviation of the difference between model outputs and observations (std1) is no larger than the standard deviations of repeated fCO2 measurements averaged over all months and grid boxes (std2) by 20%, i.e., |std1-std2|/std2<0.2.

An FNN configuration needs validation before it can be used to make predictions. Our approach uses 90% of the randomly selected data points for training and the remaining 10% for validation [18]. Once a configuration is validated, we used all data points to train the FNN to obtain a final product for prediction.

3   Results

We succeeded in using the FNN to model the mean global rate of increase in CO2 fugacity at the ocean's surface [18], yielding a value of 1.5 µatm/yr, which is in agreement with the commonly accepted value. Prior to this work, the rate was estimated from a collection of rates [17] that vary greatly. Using our rate, we were able to obtain the monthly climatology maps of CO_2 for the reference year of 2000 [18]. The results agree well with both measurements and the values reported by [17], which is the most used resource for calculating ocean sinks.

Extending the work of Zeng et al. [18], we reconstructed monthly CO_2 maps for 1990–2011 (see the examples in Fig. 2). Two new steps were taken to improve the mapping. First, we excluded the LAT and LON variables in equation (12) to obtain a first guess of CO_2 for areas where measurements were scarce, i.e., the Southern Pacific Ocean. As a large spatial gap may lead to overestimating the nonlinear interpolation of the FNN, we used the first guess for gap-filling every 10 degrees. Second, a version of the FNN without CHL was used to estimate CO_2 for areas where CHL data were not available. This step completes the coverage of the global oceans. The yielded product provides an alternative for estimating the time-variant ocean carbon sinks for 1990–2011.

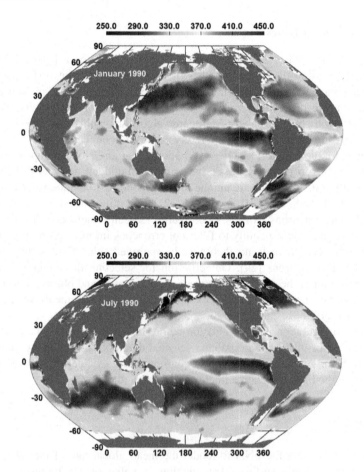

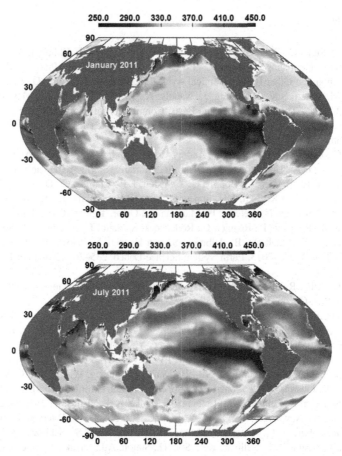

Fig. 2. Distributions of CO2 fugacity (µatm) in 1990 and 2011. The blank areas were either covered by ice or the depth is less than 500 m, which is our criterion for identifying open oceans.

4   Conclusions

Our results show that the FNN is an effective model for reconstructing global ocean CO2 sinks. As the model only establishes the dependence of the output variable on the input variables, and makes no assumption on the explicit expression of the model equation, it's straightforward to employ in practice. However, users must be aware of its nonlinear property and take appropriate steps to prevent over-fitting and over-shooting.

We made efforts to minimize the user interaction required, and the FNN converges quickly and steadily. In our experiments, the error of the cost function decreased steadily and changed very slightly after about 100 epochs for over 100,000 training patterns. The software only requires an ordinary PC to obtain results in 10 to 30 min for large datasets. We expect the software to be used for solving environmental problems similar to the carbon sink example discussed herein.

References

1. Ciais, P., Sabine, C., Bala, G., Bopp, L., Brovkin, V., Canadell, J., Chhabra, A., DeFries, R., Galloway, J., Heimann, M., Jones, C., Le Quéré, C., Myneni, R.B., Piao, S., Thornton, P.: 2013: Carbon and Other Biogeochemical Cycles. In: Stocker, T.F., Qin, D., Plattner, G.-K., Tignor, M., Allen, S.K., Boschung, J., Nauels, A., Xia, Y., Bex, V., Midgley, P.M. (eds.) Climate Change: The Physical Science Basis. Contribution of Working Group I to the Fifth Assessment Report of the Intergovernmental Panel on Climate Change, Cambridge University Press, Cambridge (2013)

2. Quéré, C., Le, G.P., Peters, R.J., Andres, R.M., Andrew, T.A., Boden, P., Ciais, P., Friedlingstein, R.A., Houghton, G., Marland, R., Moriarty, S., Sitch, P., Tans, A., Arneth, A., Arvanitis, D.C.E., Bakker, L., Bopp, J.G., Canadell, L.P., Chini, S.C., Doney, A., Harper, I., Harris, J.I., House, A.K., Jain, S.D., Jones, E., Kato, R.F., Keeling, K., Klein Goldewijk, A., Körtzinger, C., Koven, N., Lefèvre, F., Maignan, A., Omar, T., Ono, G.-H., Park, B., Pfeil, B., Poulter, M.R., Raupach, P., Regnier, C., Rödenbeck, S., Saito, J., Schwinger, J., Segschneider, B.D., Stocker, T., Takahashi, B., Tilbrook, S., van Heuven, N., Viovy, R., Wanninkhof, A.:: Global Carbon Budget 2013. Earth System Science Data 6, 235–263 (2014) doi:10.5194/essd-6-235-2014

3. Wanninkhof, R.: Relationship between Wind-Speed and Gas-Exchange over the Ocean. J. Geophys. Res.-Oceans 97, 7373–7382 (1992)

4. Bakker, D.C.E., Pfeil, B., Smith, K., Hankin, S., Olsen, A., Alin, S.R., Cosca, C., Harasawa, S., Kozyr, A., Nojiri, Y., O'Brien, K.M., Schuster, U., Telszewski, M., Tilbrook, B., Wada, C., Akl, J., Barbero, L., Bates, N.R., Boutin, J., Bozec, Y., Cai1, W.-J., Castle, R.D., Chavez, F.P., Chen, L., Chierici, M., Currie, K., de Baar, H.J.W., Evans, W., Feely, R.A., Fransson, A., Gao, Z., Hales, B., Hardman-Mountford, N.J., Hoppema, M., Huang, W.-J., Hunt, C.W., Huss, B., Ichikawa, T., Johannessen, T., Jones, E.M., Jones, S.D., Jutterström, S., Kitidis, V., Körtzinger, A., Landschützer, P., Lauvset, S.K., Lefèvre, N., Manke, A.B., Mathis, J.T., Merlivat, L., Metzl, N., Murata, A., Newberger, T., Omar, A.M., Ono, T., Park, G.-H., Paterson, K., Pierrot, D., Ríos, A.F., Sabine, C.L., Saito, S., Salisbury, J., Sarma, V.V.S.S., Schlitzer, R., Sieger, R., Skjelvan, I., Steinhoff, T., Sullivan, K.F., Sun, H., Sutton, A.J., Suzuki, T., Sweeney, C., Takahashi, T., Tjiputra, J., Tsurushima, N., van Heuven, S.M.A.C., Vandemark, D., Vlahos, P., Wallace, D.W.R., Wanninkhof, R., Watson, A.J.: An update to the Surface Ocean CO2 Atlas (SOCAT version 2). Earth System Science Data Discussions 6, 465–512 (2013), doi:10.5194/essdd-6-465-2013.

5. Zeng, J.Y., Nojiri, Y., Murphy, P.P., Wong, C.S., Fujinuma, Y.: A comparison of Delta pCO2 distributions in the northern North Pacific using results from a commercial vessel in 1995-1999. Deep-Sea Res. Part II-Top. Stud. Oceanogr 49, 5303–5315 (2002)

6. Lefevre, N., Watson, A.J., Watson, A.R.: A comparison of multiple regression and neural network techniques for mapping in situ pCO2 data. Tellus Ser. B-Chem. Phys. Meteorol. 57, 375–384 (2005)

7. Chierici, M., Fransson, A., Nojiri, Y.: Biogeochemical processes as drivers of surface fCO(2) in contrasting provinces in the subarctic North Pacific Ocean. Glob. Biogeochem. Cycle 20 (2006)

8. Sarma, V.V.S.S., Saino, T., Sasaoka, K., Nojiri, Y., Ono, T., Ishii, M., Inoue, H.Y., Matsumoto, K.: Basin-scale pCO2 distribution using satellite sea surface temperature, Chla, and climatological salinity in the North Pacific in spring and summer. Glob. Biogeochem. Cycle 20 (2006)

9. Jamet, C., Moulin, C., Lefevre, N.: Estimation of the oceanic pCO2 in the North Atlantic from VOS lines in-situ measurements: parameters needed to generate seasonally mean maps. Ann. Geophys. 25, 2247–2257 (2007)

10. Friedrich, T., Oschlies, A.: Neural network-based estimates of North Atlantic surface pCO(2) from satellite data: A methodological study. J. Geophys. Res.-Oceans 114 (2009)

11. Telszewski, M., et al.: Estimating the monthly pCO2 distribution in the North Atlantic using a self-organizing neural network. Biogeosciences 6, 1405–1421 (2009)

12. Takamura, T.R., Inoue, H.Y., Midorikawa, T., Ishii, M., Nojiri, Y.: Seasonal and Inter-Annual Variations in pCO2sea and Air-Sea CO2 Fluxes in Mid-Latitudes of the Western and Eastern North Pacific during 1999-2006: Recent Results Utilizing Voluntary Observation Ships. Journal of the Meteorological Society of Japan 88, 883–898 (2010)

13. Landschützer, P., Gruber, N., Bakker, D.C.E., Schuster, U., Nakaoka, S., Payne, M.R., Sasse, T., Zeng, J.: A Neural Network-based Estimate of the Seasonal to Inter-annual Variability of the Atlantic Ocean Carbon Sink. Biogeosciences Discuss 10, 8799–8849 (2013)

14. Nakaoka, S., Telszewski, M., Nojiri, Y., Yasunaka, S., Miyazaki, C., Mukai, H., Usui, N.: Estimating temporal and spatial variation of ocean surface pCO2 in the North Pacific using a Self Organizing Map neural network technique. Biogeosciences 10, 6093–6106 (2013)

15. Li, Z., Adamec, D., Takahashi, T., Sutherland, S.C.: Global aurocorrelation scales of the partial pressure of oceanic CO2. J Geophys. Res. 110, C08002 (2005), doi:10.1029/2004JC002723.

16. Wanninkhof, R., Park, G.H., Takahashi, T., Sweeney, C., Feely, R., Nojiri, Y., Gruber, N., Doney, S.C., McKinley, G.A., Lenton, A., Le Quéré, C., Heinze, C., Schwinger, J., Graven, H., Khatiwala, S.: Global ocean carbon uptake: magnitude, variability and trends. Biogeosciences 10, 1983–2000 (2013)

17. Takahashi, T., Sutherland, S.C., Wanninkhof, R., Sweeney, C., Feely, R.A., Chipman, D.W., Hales, B., Friederich, G., Chavez, F., Sabine, C., Watson, A., Bakker, D.C.E., Schuster, U., Metzl, N., Inoue, H.Y., Ishii, M., Midorikawa, T., Nojiri, Y., Körtzinger, A., Steinhoff, T., Hoppema, M., Olafsson, J., Arnarson, T.S., Tilbrook, B., Johannessen, T., Olsen, A., Bellerby, R., Wong, C.S., Delille, B., Bates, N.R., de Baar, H.J.W.: Climatological mean and decadal change in surface ocean pCO2, and net sea-air CO2 flux over the global oceans (vol 56, pg 554, 2009). Deep-Sea Res. Part I-Oceanogr. Res. Pap. 56, 2075–2076 (2009)

18. Zeng, J., Nojiri, Y., Landschützer, P., Telszewski, M., Nakaoka, S.: A Global Surface Ocean fCO2 Climatology Based on a Feed-Forward Neural Network. Journalof Atmospheric and Oceanic Technology 31, 1838–1849 (2014)

19. Rumelhart, D.E., Hinton, G.E., Williams, R.J.: Learning Representations by Back-Propagating Errors. Nature 323, 533–536 (1986)

20. LeCun, Y., Bottou, L., Orr, G.B., Muller, K.R.: Efficient backprop. Neural Networks: Tricks of the Trade 1524, 9–50 (1998)

21. Wilamowski, B.M., Yu, H.: Improved Computation for Levenberg-Marquardt Training. IEEE Transactions on Neural Networks 21, 930–937 (2010)

22. Blum, E.K., Li, L.K.: Approximation-Theory and Feedforward Networks. Neural Networks 4, 511–515 (1991)

23. Hornik, K.: Approximation Capabilities of Multilayer Feedforward Networks. Neural Networks 4, 251–257 (1991)

24. Svozil, D., Kvasnicka, V., Pospichal, J.: Introduction to multi-layer feed-forward neural networks. Chemometrics and Intelligent Laboratory Systems 39, 43–62 (1997)

Three Levels of R Language Involvement in Global Monitoring Plan Warehouse Architecture

Jiří Kalina[1,2], Richard Hůlek[1], Jana Borůvkova[2], Jiří Jarkovský[1],
Jana Klánová[2], and Ladislav Dušek[1]

[1] Institute of Biostatistics and Analyses, Kamenice 126/3,
625 00 Brno, Czech Republic
[2] Research Centre for Toxic Compounds in the Environment, Kamenice 753/5,
625 00 Brno, Czech Republic
kalina@mail.muni.cz, {hulek,jarkovsky,dusek}@iba.muni.cz,
{boruvkova,klanova}@recetox.muni.cz

Abstract. Three different options for involving R statistical software in the infrastructure of the data warehouse and visualization tool of the Global Monitoring Plan for persistent organic pollutants are presented, all differing in their demands with respect to data transfer rates, numbers of concurrently connected users, total amounts of data transferred, and the possibilities of repeating statistical calculations within a short period. After the development stage, two of these options were used at different levels of the system, demonstrating the specificity of their use and enabling the deployment of the powerful features of R statistical software by a system created using conventional programming languages.

Keywords: R, JSON, JSONIO, jsonlite, ODBC, statistical computing, web application, system architecture, POPs, GMP.

1 Introduction

The ongoing collection of data on environmental pollution within the second campaign of the Global Monitoring Plan (GMP) concerning persistent organic pollutants (POPs) is benefiting from the experience gained during the first collection period (2003–2008) [1], which allowed the design and development of a system for the collection, statistical evaluation and visualization of data in order to achieve maximal efficiency of statistical processing while maintaining the highest possible information value hidden in the data.

The Global Monitoring Plan was established to provide the comparable monitoring of POPs listed in annexes of the Stockholm Convention (SC), i.e. their presence in the environment as well as their regional and global environmental transport. GMP implements this in the form of a worldwide overview of compliance by the monitoring and evaluation of SC 22 POPs concentration levels and their trends.

The data reporting model suggested in the updated Guidance involves compiling and archiving primary GMP data within a "regional data repository" in each of the

R. Denzer et al. (Eds.): ISESS 2015, IFIP AICT 448, pp. 426–433, 2015.

five UN regional groups. In addition, regional data centers and a single GMP "data warehouse" should be established to compile and archive aggregated data, data products and results, including supplementary data that would be used in the Stockholm Convention effectiveness evaluation.

Based on the facts stated above, a multi-modular, on-line working data warehouse has been developed for data collection, processing and reporting within the second and future GMP collection campaigns. It is based on fully parametric data sheets for data input, supplemented by a possibility to utilize all data contained within the Global ENvironmental ASsessment Information System (GENASIS) repository [2]. It has been designed especially to improve the quality of the collected global data sets on POPs concentrations in order to determine their fate in the environment.

2   Architecture of R Involvement in the GMP Data Repository

The comparability of reported data is one of the elementary principles of GMP and also an essential condition enabling the use of a single set of methods for processing truly global data from all five United Nations Environmental Program (UNEP) regions, collected by dozens of individual (national) providers. The GMP principles of comparability became the elementary requirement for the development of the second generation of data collection and analysis tools. This comparability consists not only in the unification of all code lists used in reporting, but also in the standardization of physical units, the unification of the handling of missing values, the mutual conversion of the results of different methods of measurement and the fractions of substances measured, and the unification of the period for reporting, which was established during the previous decade with a one-year period.

The principal requirement imposed on the system for the collection and visualization of GMP data is the possibility of the simultaneous input of data either by transfer from existing databases (especially the GENASIS), or by the manual import of primary and (annually) aggregated data. Based on the data type and their input into the warehouse, the data undergo different-length sections of a sequence of mathematical and statistical operations, culminating in final outputs and visualizations with high added information value.

Since implementation of the statistical operations performed is very complicated and practically impossible using standard main and database programming languages (PHP and SQL in case of GMP), the series of analyses following logically in sequence demands the use of these languages only as an interface to the server version of the powerful statistical software R [4].

During development, three options for the involvement of the R language in the environmental pollution data assessment infrastructure of the GMP data warehouse system were tested (the transfer of data between the data warehouse and the specialized R server as a text file and procedure calls of R language using the HTTP protocol; data transfer between servers using JavaScript Object Notation (JSON) and direct access to the R procedures using Open Database Connectivity (ODBC)) [3]. The advantages and disadvantages of different approaches have been shown to be specific in relation to the purpose for which the R script is used and the amount of data that is transmitted. Thus, the result of the development was mainly the differentiation of methods of integrating scripts of the R language into the rest of the GMP data warehouse systems according to the level at which this involvement occurs.

On their way through the GMP data warehouse system from their input in the form of primary data to the resulting plots and summary statistics, the data go through three levels:

1. The lowest level (data input): input and transformation of primary data inside the Genasis repository. Primary data go through the following four sub-steps:
   (a) Conversion of values measured by passive air samplers to atmospheric concentrations of pollutants using the method developed in the framework of the Global Atmospheric Passive Sampling network (GAPS) and implemented as a separate recalculating R package (genasis) [5].
   (b) Calculation of the parameter sums, defined as the sum of a large number of different parameters, including the calculation of the detection/quantification limits (LoD/LoQ) (e.g. sum of indicator PCBs).
   (c) Calculation of toxic equivalents for selected groups of substances defined as the weighted sum of concentrations of substances measured at the same time in the same locality, and the treatment of censored values (LoD, LoQ).
   (d) Aggregation of separately measured fractions of identical analytes to the general fractions (e.g. gaseous phase and dust for air sampling), and the treatment of censored values (LoD, LoQ).
2. The testing of prerequisites for the aggregation of measured values over time to mutually comparable annual averages, the aggregation itself, and the treatment of censored values (LoD, LoQ).
3. Real time calculations of descriptive statistics and trends while browsing individual analyses on the website.

Primary data enters into this sequence at the lowest level (1), the aggregated data at level 2. The necessity to implement the R script language in order to execute the calculations exists over the entire sequence (i.e. in all three steps and the four sub-steps):

2.1 Data Input Level

A specialized R package "genasis-recalc" was invented for elementary operations on primary data on persistent pollution in the atmosphere, water, human blood, and milk. Specific demands at different levels of aggregation (over fractions of the environmental matrix, groups of similar compounds and/or sets of toxic equivalent compounds, according to different toxic equivalents and factors schemes (TEQs & TEFs) of the World Health Organization), the substitution of left-censored data (LoD, LoQ) [6], and temperature-dependent coefficients of recalculations of passive air sampling were adopted inside the package and are used at the moment when the data enter the repository.

In this level, data transfer was implemented using txt files. Because the backend consisting of an R-server for statistical computing is, for safety reasons and for reasons of achieving better performance, separated from the DWH server as well as from the primary data source server GENASIS, the task of data transmission has become a key problem in terms of speed and stability. The numbers of individual records in primary databases range from thousands to millions, while each record contains tens of numerical and text values describing, besides the measured concentrations, also the site and date of measurement, the method used for the determination and recalculation of the values, the parameters of the measuring devices, data ownership, and the id of the measured substance and its chemical specification etc.

Recalculations of primary data are triggered manually by a data manager in logically defined batches containing up to tens of thousands of records, which is the equivalent of up to one million transferred numerical and text values. For building service-oriented infrastructure, the only viable solution, one necessitated by the conditions, is to use the text HTTP protocol, which raises the need to wrap different data structures (single values, vectors or numerical matrices) on the one hand, and expand them somehow on the other.

As a suitable language for both processes, the JSON notation for writing data structures was adopted, which was already used in the system. It is also involved within the relatively large OpenCPU computational platform used for the development of DWH. The JSONIO package was used on the R-server side, which, however, proved to be extremely memory-consuming for the order of thousands of records – on a server with limited memory, this approach led to overflow even at about 200,000 integer values and the increase in memory consumption appeared to be exponential.

The limiting factor was, therefore, not the complexity of the recalculations of the records on the chemicals themselves, but the coding of data into JSON notation, requiring extreme memory infrastructure regardless of the form of the extracted data (for the stated number of tens of thousands of entries, overflow occurred even in the case of a single vector, which itself would be insufficient for the transmission of real data).

A solution to extreme memory consumption was found by not using the JSONIO package but sending plain txt files with numerical and text values separated by a simple separator (a comma). It was, however, necessary to resolve the coding of complex structures (such as nested lists, matrices, etc.). In any event, such an approach solved the problem of memory consumption by large volumes of data. On the R-server side, the data were loaded from the file issued on the main language side using the scan() function, which excludes the use of the memory-consuming JSONIO package. The problem which arises from this approach is the need for the complicated coding of a more complex data structure to a simple text notation, which leads to inefficiency, instability, and a high frequency of errors. Furthermore, the time required by this approach is also relatively high.

As the most appropriate solution, the option of giving the R language direct access to the database was adopted, enabled by the RODBC R language package version 1.3-9 [7], published in late 2013 and implementing ODBC database connectivity. All R scripts are strictly separated from the GMP warehouse main language layer (there are no direct data transfers between the main language and R scripts) and involved in the system using ODBC.

This form has proven to be the most effective in terms of memory consumption and acceptable in terms of time consumption. Because the four recalculations are performed on the primary data only once, and following steps work only with the results, the time consumption of the algorithm was not a crucial parameter.

The versatility of the ODBC connection also significantly increases the efficiency of the database solution from the perspective of experts from non-IT disciplines (especially environmental chemists and statisticians), who may develop computational algorithms in R completely separately and independently of IT developers and with only a limited knowledge of the language SQL.

The implementation of primary data recalculations was then performed in the form of a pair of buffers, represented by database tables (a properly constructed DB view and table) within the GMP DWH, between which the four resulting computations run according to the following cyclic procedure:

1. The data manager selects a batch (containing at most tens of thousands of records) for recalculation and, using a data management application, starts the filling of the input buffer (DB view), which is performed in the main programming language layer in DWH.
2. Directly from SQL, using the EXEC command, the appropriate procedure is called by R language on the R-server. Deploying the RODBC package function sqlQuery(), all necessary data is loaded into the R environment in the form of a data.frame structure.
3. If the loaded data.frame passes through a check of data completeness, it is recalculated and the results are stored, using RODBC again, in the output buffer (plain database table).
4. Still using the RODBC package and EXEC command, a follow-up procedure is called in the SQL database language. It is performed comprehensively in the main language layer of DWH, in addition to other necessary database operations, and finally the result is written back to the primary data structures.

Since the recalculations are performed in a predefined order, the data iteratively pass through all four steps when repeating this procedure for each recalculation (the calculation of passive measurement results of air pollution, the calculation of sums and toxic equivalents, and the calculation of fractions).

If the RODBC option of data transfer is used, the algorithms are less time-consuming, with a typical duration of units of minutes for the recalculation of each batch consisting of less than 1 million numerical or text values.

2.2   Aggregation Level

Once the data are recalculated and transformed to comparable scales, a selection of representative samples is carried out. In this step, the regularity of individual measurements over time (within one year) and the number of primary data are assessed and, taking into account local specific conditions of monitoring, the representativeness of the primary data is checked.

At least 3 samples within one year and a form of monitoring regularity in which the longest gap between subsequent measurements is no more than 3 times longer than the smallest one are required in order for data to pass automatically through the selection process; in other cases, a manual check of representativeness is required.

Appropriate selected datasets are subsequently transformed to annual aggregations, which will culminate in achieving the maximal comparability of data from different data sources.

Since there are several specific aggregation functions within the process of annual aggregation, the R with ODBC connection to the DWH database was again used to avoid the complicated and unreliable constructions of computing values by means of SQL.

As in the previous case, the RODBC package is used for inputting and outputting R script data included in another special package "genasis-aggr". In addition to the usual statistics such as arithmetic and geometric mean and standard deviation, also maximum and minimum concentration values in each year, number of primary records, and several advanced statistics are computed:

- 5th and 95th percentiles as concentration values taken at regular intervals from the inverse of the estimated cumulative distribution function of the values within each year, which serves as a description of data variability without extreme values,
- the smallest, typical and largest gap between the start of the year, dates of subsequent measurements, and the end of the year, used for determining the regularity of the measurements,
- the number of values below detection/quantification limits.

These statistics cannot be computed directly by SQL without creating complicated procedures involving the complicated maintenance of special cases such as incomplete data records, low numbers of records etc., resulting in the low reliability of such a solution.

The use of direct access to the DWH database and the utilization of SQL commands within the R environment enable the determination of the optimal distribution of aggregation tasks between elementary steps, conducted with higher effectiveness by means of standard SQL commands and more specific computations.

2.3 Visualization Level

Another principle of R script involvement is implemented at the highest level of data visualization. The short response times and large number of multi-user operations associated with the use of a web-based data browser require a more flexible solution compared to working with ODBC data inputs and outputs. Moreover, a typical selection of parameters and localities for visualization inside a browser is highly restrictive and limits the amount of data to smaller values of hundreds of records, which can be rapidly transferred by the HTTP protocol between the components for processing individual tasks.

Another R package called "datavis-platform-gmp-r" was invented for this level of the visualization tool. JSON notation turned out to be the best transfer option for relatively small numbers of records. Both the input and output data of the R scripts used for visualization are translated to JSON notation using appropriate libraries (the jsonlite package on the side of the R-server is used [8]) and sent by the POST method of the HTTP protocol.

There are two visualizations where the use of R scripts was necessary due to complicated computations which cannot be implemented in either the SQL or PHP languages:

1. horizontal box and whisker plots of the descriptive statistics of selected measurements with different measures of central tendency and data variance (similar statistics as in the aggregation step are computed here using standard R statistical commands),
2. time series plots including linear and exponential interlacing curves and their confidence intervals, using several parametric statistical techniques not present in main level programming languages.

A data structure of nested data lists is the most appropriate for both these visualizations. This structure is highly suitable for translation to JSON by the jsonlite package, with the exception of singleton lists, which are translated as simple elements. This unsystematic property necessitates the special measure of adding one zero element to each level of the nested list to obtain a minimum length of two elements for each list.

3   Conclusion

There are different demands with respect to data transfer rates, numbers of concurrently connected users, total amounts of transferred data, and the possibilities of repeating statistical computations within a short period at different levels of the GMP data warehouse and visualization system. During the development of second generation GMP data browsers, three different options for involving R statistical software were tested and assessed for final use.

The method of using JavaScript Object Notation (JSON) for coding data transferred between a database running on a data warehouse server and a separate R-server for statistical computations was shown to be fast but unsuitable for larger amounts of data (the order of millions of values) due to its extreme memory-consuming properties (using the RJSONIO package in the R environment).

A different method of data transfer in the form of specially devised coding within txt files, which should have solved the problem, exhibited problems with more complicated data structures such as matrices and nested lists; in addition, it was also more time-consuming.

As the best option for huge amounts of data, direct access from the R-server to the data warehouse database was implemented, using the Open Database Connectivity (ODBC) standard, made available by means of the RODBC package. This solution allows SQL and R functions to be combined within one script and provides a simple, effective and comfortable environment for the development of enviro-statistical structures separate from the rest of the IT infrastructure.

The main disadvantage of the ODBC approach, namely lower speeds of multiuser access to the database, was solved by using JSON whenever smaller numbers (in the order of hundreds) of values are transferred, such as in web-based visualizations.

References

1. Hůlek, R., Jarkovský, J., Borůvková, J., Kalina, J., Gregor, J., Šebková, K., Schwarz, D., Klánová, J., Dušek, L.: Global Monitoring Plan of the Stockholm Convention on Persistent Organic Pollutants: visualization and on-line analysis of data from the monitoring reports (2013)
2. Jarkovský, J., Dušek, L., Klánová, J., Hůlek, R., Šebková, K., Borůvková, J., Kalina, J., Gregor, J., Bednářová, Z., Novák, R., Šalko, M., Hřebíček, J., Holoubek, I.: Multi-matrix online data browser for environmental analysis and assessment. Masaryk University, Version 1.0 (2014), http://www.genasis.cz (Version 3.10. March 2014)
3. Hůlek, R., Kalina, J., Dušek, L., Jarkovský, J.: Integration of R Statistical Environment into ICT Infrastructure of GMP and GENASIS. In: Hřebíček, J., Schimak, G., Kubásek, M., Rizzoli, A.E. (eds.) ISESS 2013. IFIP Advances in Information and Communication Technology, vol. 413, pp. 240–252. Springer, Heidelberg (2013)
4. The R Project for Statistical Computing (2014), http://www.r-project.org/
5. Kalina, J., Klánová, J., Dušek, L., Harner, T., Borůvková, J., Jarkovský, J.: genasis: Global ENvironmental ASsessment Information System (GENASIS) computational tools. R packageversion 1.0 (2014), http://CRAN.R-project.org/package=genasis
6. Van den Berg, M., Birnbaum, L.S., Denison, M., De Vito, M., Farland, W., Feeley, M., Fiedler, H., Hakansson, H., Hanberg, A., Haws, L., Rose, M., Safe, S., Schrenk, D.: Tohyama, Ch., Tritscher, A., Tuomisto, J., Tysklind, M., Walker, N., Peterson, R.E.: The, World Health Organization Reevaluation of Human and Mammalian Toxic Equivalency Factors for Dioxins and Dioxin-Like Compounds. Toxicological Sciences 93(2),223-241 (2005), doi: 10.1093/toxsci/kfl055
7. Ripley, B., Lapsley, M.: RODBC: ODBC Database Access. R package version 1.3-9 (2013), http://CRAN.R-project.org/package=RODBC
8. Ooms, J., Duncan, T.L., Hilaiel, L.: jsonlite: A Robust, High Performance JSON Parser and Generator for R. R package version 0.9.13, http://cran.r-project.org/web/packages/jsonlite/index.html

Process Design Patterns in Emergency Management

Tomáš Ludík[1,2] and Tomáš Pitner[2]

[1] Department of Emergency Management: University of Defence, Brno, Czech Republic
[2] Faculty of Informatics: Masaryk University, Brno, Czech Republic
tomas.ludik@unob.cz, tomp@fi.muni.cz

Abstract. Emergency management is a discipline of dealing with and avoiding risks. In case of any emergency the immediate and fast intervention is necessary. It is possible only because of well-prepared contingency plans and adequate software support. Therefore, the aim of this paper is to focus on the common characteristics of process modelling within emergency management and to define the design patterns that are typical of this area. These Design Patterns enable faster and simpler generation of emergency processes and contingency plans as well as subsequent software support. They result from the current documentation and legislation. Each design pattern does not represent a final emergency process, but only a certain structure which is necessary to further customize according to current user requirements. Specifically, 16 design patterns have been identified and described on more management levels. The present form of design patterns is a result of the consolidation of many real processes of emergency management that arose and were verified within several research projects or set of directed interviews with emergency management experts.

Keywords: emergency management, process framework, process modelling, contingency plans, design patterns, directed interviews.

1   Introduction

Process management is an implemented and often used approach in business practice which enables a variety of organisations to achieve better results from a long-term point of view (Weske, 2012). On the other hand, the functional management approach often predominates in public administration (Smith, 1776). With regard to the poorer utilisation of an organisation's sources and assets, the functional management approach does not enable the achievement of these results. It achieves the set objectives more slowly and handles constantly ongoing changes only with great difficulty. These properties can be seen especially in the area of emergency management, where a fast and efficient intervention will enable not only the rescue of assets and the environment, but above all human life. There is an unambiguous necessity to gradually reduce using the functional management approach to emergency situations and to start coping with these situations in a process manner.

In case of process management, it is not only a change in the management approach, but also the entire information support of processes. This differs from the

R. Denzer et al. (Eds.): ISESS 2015, IFIP AICT 448, pp. 434–444, 2015.

classical rigorous development of information systems. Process-oriented systems must react to the dynamic environment in an organisation quickly and be capable of adapting themselves to current needs and priorities (Pekárková et al., 2013). For this purpose, a lot of new approaches, methods and instruments have appeared in reaction to this trend (Barta, 2013). Moreover, emergency management is specific because of the distrust of information technologies, because of necessary interoperability with other information systems and because of the emergency information system's complexity and the necessity to develop resistance to breakdowns and crashes (Hiltz et al., 2010; Haddow et al., 2013).

Based on the abovementioned description, there are two principal requirements for emergency management. First, there must be a change from the functional to the process management approach and, at the same time, support for the new method of coping with emergency situations with information through advanced information technologies. For this purpose, the Process Framework for Emergency Management has been defined. It provides well-arranged, unambiguous and complex instructions of how to achieve this complex change in the management method as well as in the information support in the area of emergency management.

2   Process Framework for Emergency Management

The Process Framework for Emergency Management consists of five main components which describe the problems of different areas. In specific terms, it is process methodology, reference architecture, factors for implementation, design patterns and quality assurance processes.

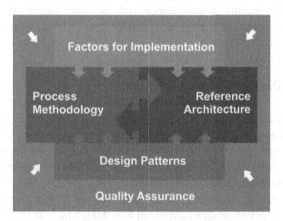

Fig. 1. Process framework for emergency management

Process methodology – the methodology contains the instructions of how to identify and describe the user roles and processes in the field of emergency management. For this, it recommends the appropriate recording forms of emergency management processes, which is the Business Process Modelling Notation combined with the Use Case diagram from the UML. If in need of automation, the methodology provides the instructions of how to further configure processes, how to add required data and services and subsequently how to interpret them through the workflow engine. For more information about process methodology, see (Ludík and Ráček, 2011a).

Reference architecture – this provides a view and recommendation concerning the particular software components which can be used in process automation and, at the same time, it reflects the requirements resulting from emergency management processes. The entire design is based on the Workflow reference model. Then this conceptual model is completed with specific tools and components which can be found in the sphere of information support of processes in organisations, whereas stress is laid on the independence of specific software from a particular provider. For more information about reference architecture, see (Ludík et al., 2011).

Factors for Implementation – the issue of emergency management processes is so comprehensive that the standard approaches used in the area of software engineering cannot be used. On this account, this part focuses on the description of factors and specific characteristics of emergency management. The identified factors can be divided into two groups, i.e. internal factors and external factors. For more information about factors for implementation, see (Ludík and Ráček, 2011a).

Design Patterns – these enable faster and simpler generation of emergency processes. They result from the current documentation and legislation and are defined based on many years' experience of emergency process modelling. No design pattern represents a final emergency process, but only a certain structure which it is necessary to further customise according to current user requirements. For more information about design patterns, see Section 4 of this paper.

Quality Assurance – this provides methods and tools to assure the quality of simulated processes that must be in compliance with not only legislation and current emergency plans, but especially in compliance with the requirements of bodies active in emergency management. For more information about quality assurance, see (Ludík and Ráček, 2011b).

3   Design Patterns State of the Art

In software engineering, a design pattern represents a general reusable solution to a commonly occurring problem within a given context in software design (Gamma et al., 1994). A design pattern is not a finished design that can be transformed directly into source or machine code. It is a description or template for how to solve a problem that can be used in many different situations.

In the same manner, it is possible to approach the design of process diagrams (workflow) and to define design patterns in this field. The Workflow Patterns Initiative is the greatest one in this field which is a joint effort of Eindhoven University of Technology and Queensland University of Technology and which started in 1999. The aim of this initiative is to provide a conceptual basis for process technology. In particular, the research provides a thorough examination of the various perspectives that need to be supported by a workflow language or a business process modelling language (Russell et al., 2006). There are a few similar efforts. As an example, a chapter in the book Designing Business Processes with Patterns (Glushko and McGrath, 2005) or a paper entitled Applying Patterns during Business Process Modelling (Gschwind et al., 2008) can be mentioned.

The design patterns can serve the purpose only in the event that they are comprehensible and described sufficiently. There is no single, standard format for documenting the design patterns. Rather, a variety of different formats has been used by different pattern authors. However, according to Martin Fowler, certain pattern forms have become more well-known than others, and consequently become common starting points for new pattern-writing efforts (Fowler, 2006). One example of a commonly used documentation format is the one used by Erich Gamma, Richard Helm, Ralph Johnson and John Vlissides in their book entitled Design Patterns (Gamma et al., 1994). It contains the following sections:

- *Pattern Name and Classification* – a descriptive and unique name that helps in identifying and referring to the pattern;
- *Intent* – a description of the goal behind the pattern and the reason for using it;
- *Also Known As* – other names for the pattern;
- *Motivation (Forces)* – a scenario consisting of a problem and a context in which this pattern can be used;
- *Applicability* – situations in which this pattern is usable; the context for the pattern;
- *Structure* – a graphical representation of the pattern. Class diagrams and Interaction diagrams may be used for this purpose;
- *Participants* – a listing of the classes and objects used in the pattern and their roles in the design;
- *Collaboration* – a description of how classes and objects used in the pattern interact with each other;
- *Consequences* – a description of the results, side effects, and trade-offs caused by using the pattern;
- *Implementation* – a description of an implementation of the pattern; the solution part of the pattern;
- *Sample Code* – an illustration of how the pattern can be used in a programming language;
- *Known Uses* – examples of real usages of the pattern; and
- *Related Patterns* – other patterns that have a relationship with the pattern; discussion of the differences between the pattern and similar patterns.

4   Design Patterns for Emergency Processes

The process approach is applicable in different domains whereas each of them has certain specific characteristics. The aim of this section is to focus on the common characteristics of process modelling within emergency management and to define the design patterns that are typical of this area. The design patterns described in this section are an essential part of the process framework for emergency management in the Czech Republic which was presented in Section 2.

Analogous to other parts of the process framework, it is possible to independently use the design patterns already created, without any links to the designed framework. Even in this example, the defined design patterns will enable a faster and better identification, analysis and emergency processes design at all levels of emergency management.The identified design patterns are divided into three groups according to the level of management at which emergency processes occur. These are strategic, operational and tactical levels.

4.1 Strategic Patterns

The strategic level represents the top-level management view of the solution of extraordinary events and emergency situations. Emergency-related legislation and other strategic documents defining general strategic procedures of coping with emergency situations on the territory of the Czech Republic are among the most fundamental documents influencing the design patterns. On the basis of these documents, it is possible to derive generally valid procedures used in coping with emergency situations, and to define them in a process way. Higher level processes develop in this manner and describe a general level of intervention management. This level is suitable for further decomposition.

Emergency Management Process, Solving an Extraordinary Event, Solving an Emergency and *Solving a Flood Situation* are included among the strategic design patterns of emergency management. Each design pattern is identifiable unambiguously through an *Identifier*. The *Title, Motivation, Description, Structure, User Roles, Known Uses, Related Patterns* and *Regulations* have been selected as further attributes for describing a design pattern.

SP-2: Solving an Extraordinary Event
Motivation – The aim of the design pattern is to show how to efficiently solve an extraordinary event in compliance with legislative requirements within the shortest possible time. An extraordinary event that occurs in a certain environment is usually solved by the Integrated Rescue System (IRS) components in a regular way.

Description – The solution of an extraordinary event proceeds in a few basic steps. First of all, the emergency operational centre receives a notification of the occurrence of an extraordinary event such as a fire, road traffic accident or leak of a hazardous substance. Based on the received information, the situation is analysed. According to its extent, the particular rescue components are activated. Their task is to come to the intervention site as fast as possible. After the arrival of particular components, the intervention commander who is responsible for coping with the emergency situation is appointed. First of all, he analyses the intervention site and assigns tasks to subordinate units. Afterwards, he monitors and evaluates the situation and responds to the development of the situation as a whole. The individual rescue components, such as firefighters, ambulance services and the police perform rescue and clean-up works. At the end of the intervention, the activities connected with finishing the intervention as well as evaluating the extraordinary situation that took place.

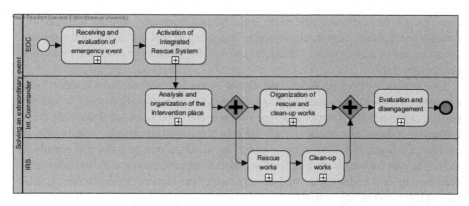

Fig. 2. Solving an extraordinary event (SP-2)

User Roles – Emergency Operational Centre, Intervention Commander, Integrated Rescue System.

Known Uses – Extraordinary events in the Czech Republic are solved every day. It may be e.g. a road traffic accident on the motorway, a hazardous substance leak, fire, explosion or other situations which need the assistance of the IRS. The entire process is initiated by an emergency call and subsequently it continues based on the type and characteristics of a given event.

Related Patterns – The described design pattern specifies the Response activity in the Emergency Management Process (SP-1) pattern in case of an extraordinary event.

Regulations – The defined process as such is primarily based on the Act on the Integrated Rescue System (Act No. 239/2000 Coll.).

4.2   Operational Patterns

The processes at the operational level are among the group of design patterns that have to be customised most, as they are markedly dependent on the site and characteristics of an extraordinary event or an emergency situation. The emergency plans of particular regions and municipalities have been developed with regard to local knowledge, e.g. the specific experience of emergency components or available resources in a given region. The IRS operational plans, which also are a basic starting point for creating the design patterns, describe the so-called ideal case of how to solve a given situation. However, it is necessary to take into account the fact that a real solution of a situation may be affected by other facts in practice. The operational design patterns serve primarily as a general starting point for process modelling at the operational management level. It is necessary to further adapt these processes according to specific user and territorial requirements. In the next part, one of seven specific operational design patterns within emergency management is presented.

OP-1: Reception of Information on an Extraordinary Event

Motivation – Each extraordinary event or emergency situation is dealt with as soon as it is reported to the IRS operational centre. Here, it is very important to recognise the character of the extraordinary event quickly and correctly, and to respond to it through intervening components. It is also necessary to find out which of the reported situations are of an emergency character and in which cases the emergency call number was abused.

Description – The emergency operational centre operator receives a report on an extraordinary event. He must find out the necessary information from a reporting person, especially the address and type of the event. In case of suspicion that the information is false, the operator calls back to the reporting person. Afterwards, the operator evaluates the extraordinary event; he selects a unit or units and sounds the alert. The unit for which the alert was sounded must confirm the alert and subsequent departure up to a certain time limit or may cancel the alert or departure for e.g. a defect on intervention equipment.

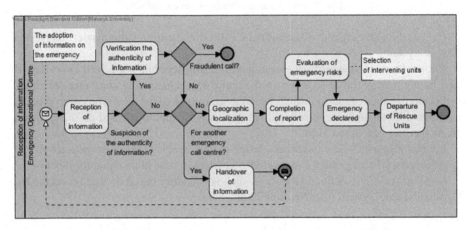

Fig. 3. Reception of information on an extraordinary event (OP-1)

User Roles – Operator of Emergency Operational Centre, Rescue Units.

Known Uses – The process is executed not only in the emergency operational centre of emergency calls 112, but also in other operational centres of the IRS components. The process is initiated by an incoming call, through which an extraordinary event is reported and completed by the departure of particular IRS components.

Related Patterns – The presented design pattern specifies the method of acquiring the information on an emergency situation which is a part of both the Solving an Extraordinary Event design pattern (SP-2) and Solving an Emergency design pattern (SP-3).

Regulations – Design pattern is based on the Combat Order of Fire Security Units. As another starting point to define the design pattern, the Act on the Integrated Rescue System and the Emergency Management Act were used.

4.3   Tactical Patterns

The design patterns at tactical level describe the activities of the intervention commander and other IRS components intervening in the scene of an extraordinary event.

The defined tactical design patterns are based on the general low-level standardised procedures which describe the activities of intervening components in the intervention site. It is necessary to state that these procedures are not formalised sufficiently in some of the basic components of the IRS. For this reason, the designed tactical patterns are primarily based on the Combat Order of Fire Security Units. This is a set of documents containing standardised procedures for the Fire Rescue Service units in the intervention site. The following tactical patterns have been defined: *Issue, Confirmation and Fulfilment of Order*, *Information Exchange*, *Management of Intervention*, *Establishment of Crisis Staff* and *Organisation of Intervention Site*.

TP-1: Issue, Confirmation and Fulfilment of Order

Motivation – The design pattern defines the general procedure of issuing, confirming and fulfilling the orders. Order, command, direction and instruction are control acts for conducting an intervention through which every commander discloses his decision to his subordinates to perform a definite task. To issue orders, commands, directions and instructions in the intervention site is not only an authorisation, but also a task of each management level.

Description – The superior issues an order to the addressee (subordinate). The order must be confirmed or, if need be, repeated by the addressee, which proves that the addressee understands the order. It is necessary to make sure that the order has really reached the addressee. If the addressee does not understand or does not confirm the order, the order is repeated again. When the order is issued, the subordinates follow it and the superior checks its fulfilment. After that, the subordinate reports the fulfilment of the order to the superior who issued the order and the design pattern is completed. In issuing an order, the principles apply as follows: an order must be performable and structured logically so that it is evident what its aim is. It is also important to stress the purpose of the order. It must be apparent that the commander is convinced of his decision. The content of the order must be clear, unambiguous and understandable. In case of an urgent situation, the order must be brief and must be issued rapidly.

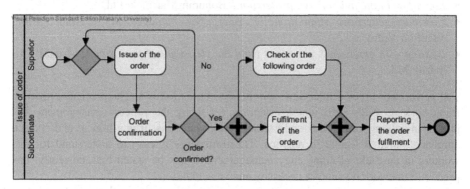

Fig. 4. Issue, confirmation and fulfilment of order (TP-1)

User Roles – Superior, Subordinate.

Known Uses – The design pattern is applied regularly within coping with every extraordinary event or emergency situation. Emergency management is based on the clear hierarchical structure of management. The particular intervening persons are obliged to fulfil orders and instructions of their unit commanders in the intervention site. The unambiguous responsibility for fulfilling all the activities is allocated in the intervention site.

Related Patterns – The design pattern supplements the operational design patterns which primarily describe rescue and clean-up works in the intervention site.

Regulations – The design pattern is defined based on the Code of Practice of Chapter Ř which is a part of the Combat Order of Fire Security Units.

5   Interviews with Experts

Set of directed interviews with emergency management experts, was used as method for verifying the process framework as well as design patterns applicability in practice (Pitner et al., 2014). The experts answered 8 questions. The addressed experts were chosen to cover the field of handling extraordinary events and emergency situations. For this reason, the key areas of emergency management, within which the application of the process framework is relevant, were identified. Out of these areas the experts were addressed and asked for assessing the defined framework. The experts are introduced in the alphabetical order as follows:

- *Emergency management and its impact on the environment* – Assoc. Prof. Vladimír Adamec;
- *Emergency management economic aspects* – Eduard Bakoš, PhD;
- *Dealing with emergency issues from the viewpoint of the municipality* – Aleš Kudlák, MSc;
- *Emergency management in power plant engineering* – Oldřich Mach, PhD;
- *Education in the field of civil protection* – Bohumír Martínek, PhD;
- *Computer-generated simulation in emergency management* – Assoc. Prof. Vladimír Vráb;
- *Dealing with emergency situations from the viewpoint of fire brigade* –Lukáš Vymazal, MSc.

The performed directed interviews can be sum up as follows. The presented process framework provides sufficient instructions for using the process management approach in solving emergency and extraordinary situations. It is a logical and correct approach which is usable in practice. The framework is easy to understand for the workers in the field of emergency management. It can be stated that, currently, the process framework becomes a necessity and an actual trend.

Individual parts of the framework are divided logically and their description provides information about their relevance. The description of individual parts is well-arranged, adequate and accurate. Some of the experts have recommended emphasising the strengths of the designed system, refining the terminology and describing the framework to be easy to understand for the lay public.

The identification of emergency processes, their subsequent optimisation and visualization can be considered as the main contributions of the process framework. The automation of processes and the information support to cope with emergency situations have been evaluated as the biggest contribution. The emergency processes defined clearly will enable a relative independence of the human factor. Further contributions can be seen in the savings of time, personnel and finance.

6   Conclusion

The process design patterns are defined based on the authors´ many years´ experience with modelling the emergency management processes. The present form of design patterns is a result of the consolidation of many real processes of emergency management that arose and were verified within several research projects, directed interviews with emergency management experts or within the development of bachelor´s and master theses. The aim of this paper is not only to create a basic set of design patterns for the area of emergency management, but also to show the method of how the design patterns can be defined in this area and, subsequently, to use them in modelling the emergency management processes.

References

1. Barta, J.: The Use of Simulations for the Need of Environment Protection. In: Hřebíček, J., Schimak, G., Kubásek, M., Rizzoli, A.E. (eds.) ISESS 2013. IFIP AICT, vol. 413, pp. 294–301. Springer, Heidelberg (2013)
2. Fowler, M.: Writing Software Patterns. Martin Fowler (2006), http://www.martinfowler.com/articles/writingPatterns.html (June 20, 2014)
3. Gamma, E., Helm, R., Johnson, R., et al.: Design Patterns: Elements of Reusable Object-Oriented Software. Addison-Wesley. 395 p. (1994), ISBN 0-201-63361-2
4. Glushko, R., McGrath, T.: Document Engineering: Analyzing and Designing Documents for Business Informatics and Web Services. MIT Press (2005)
5. Gschwind, T., Koehler, J., Wong, J.: Applying Patterns during Business Process Modeling. In: Dumas, M., Reichert, M., Shan, M.-C. (eds.) BPM 2008. LNCS, vol. 5240, pp. 4–19. Springer, Heidelberg (2008)
6. Haddow, G., Bullock, J., Coppola, D.: Introduction to Emergency Management. 5th edn. Butterworth-Heinemann (2013), ISBN 978-0124077843
7. Hiltz, S., Walle, B., Turoff, M.: The Domain of Emergency Management Information. In: Information Systems for Emergency Management. Advances in Management Information Systems, vol. 16, M.E. Sharpe, Armonk (2010) ISSN 1554-6152
8. Ludík, T., Ráček, J.: Process Methodology for Emergency Management. In: Hřebíček, J., Schimak, G., Denzer, R. (eds.) Environmental Software Systems. IFIP AICT, vol. 359, pp. 302–309. Springer, Heidelberg (2011a)

9. Ludík, T., Ráček, J.: Process Framework for Emergency Management. In: Proceedings of the 6th International Conference on Software and Database Technologies. SciTePress, Portugal (2011b) ISBN 978-989-8425-77-5

10. Ludík, T., Navrátil, J., Langerová, A.: Process Oriented Architecture for Emergency Scenarios in the Czech Republic. In: International Conference on Business Process Management. World Academy of Science, Engineering and Technology, Venice (2011) ISSN 2010-3778

11. Pekárková, L., Eibenová, P., Pitner, T.: A Framework for Monitoring and Evaluation of Learning Processes. In: Environmental Software Systems. Fostering Information Sharing, pp. 525–532. Springer, Heidelberg (2013) ISBN 978-3-642-41150-2

12. Pitner, T., Motschnig, R., Kozlíková, B., et al.: Constructive Communication in International Teams: An Experience-Based Guide, 1st edn., p. 248. Waxmann Verlag, Münster (2014) ISBN 978-3-8309-3025-9

13. Russell, N., Hofstede, A., Aalst, W., et al.: Workflow Control-Flow Patterns: A Revised View. BPM Center Report BPM-06-22 (2006) BPMcenter.org

14. Smith, A.: An Inquiry into the Nature and Causes of the Wealth of Nations. W. Strahan and T. Cadell, London (1776)

15. Weske, M.: Business Process Management, Concepts, Languages, Architectures. Springer, Haidelberg (2012) ISBN 978-3-642-28616-2

Advanced Data Analytics and Visualisation for the Management of Human Perception of Safety and Security in Urban Spaces

Panos Melas, Gianluca Correndo, Lee Middleton, and Zoheir A. Sabeur

University of Southampton IT Innovation Centre, Electronics and Computer Science,
Faculty of Physical Sciences and Engineering, Southampton, United Kingdom
{pm,gc,ljm,zas}@it-innovation.soton.ac.uk

Abstract. The genesis of this work began during the DESURBS[1] project. The scope of the project was to help build a collaborative decision-support system portal where spatial planning professionals could learn about designing much more secure and safer spaces in urban areas. The portal achieved this via integrating a number of tools under a common, simple to use, interface. However, the deficiencies in the project became apparent with subsequent development. Many of the open data employed changed format while applications were increasingly custom built for a single dataset. In order to overcome this a system called KnowDS was redesigned. The essence of the new design includes decoupling acquisition, analysis and overall presentation of data components. The acquisition component was designed to snap-shot the "data providing methods" and query data provenance in a similar way to a source code repository. The analysis component is built under a number of modular tools with a common interface which allows analysis to build in a plug&play approach. Finally, the data presentation component is where the custom logic goes. Under such design approach, the building of future applications becomes less challenging. As a consequence, two case studies using the new framework were considered. Firstly, a UK crime web-browser which allows data analytics performances at various granularities of crime types while correlating crimes across various UK cities has been achieved. Secondly, a mobile application which enables to generate reports on citizens' perception of safety in urban zones has also been developed. The two applications were efficiently built under the new design framework; and they clearly demonstrate the capacity of the new system while they actively generate new knowledge about safety in urban spaces.

Keywords: safety perception, urban security, data analytics, visualisation, open data.

1 Introduction

Large volumes of open observation and contextual data concerning urban spaces have become more accessible for processing in recent years. The open data can be

---

[1] DESURBS: Designing Safer Urban Spaces: http://www.desurbs.eu

R. Denzer et al. (Eds.): ISESS 2015, IFIP AICT 448, pp. 445–454, 2015.

potentially aggregated for better usage and improvement of existing decision-support systems, specializing in the dissemination of safety related issues in cities to the public [1]. The potentially useful data aggregation exercise starts with the use of the various open data sources which are provided as part of the open government movements globally [2]. Additionally, social network data, or so-called social sensing [3] data can be used [4, 5]. Furthermore, survey information from custom written mobile applications can be employed. The aggregation with private (closed) data such as local authority data or data from telecom providers can be employed [6]. The heterogeneous nature of the data can be improved via a data normalisation process. This converts all data to a common schema. However, the data is semi-structured and therefore concepts from NoSQL databases can be adopted [7]. Thus, all sources of data are analogous to a function which maps from space-time to a series of values. Data collection is performed using a periodic process which polls the data source for any changes. Because the data sources are potentially changing, it is important that the system not only stores the latest snapshot but also changes in data. For both operations, i.e. data collection and data normalisation, different filters/adapters are developed in order to fetch and normalise data. For example, the anonymisation of sensitive data might take place during normalisation. The system should be able to handle multiple adapters in order to fetch and normalise data accordingly.

An advanced Knowledge Discovery System (KnowDS) that can aggregate open data provided on the cloud has been developed in this study following the progress made in the DESURBS project [8]. The system partially structures the data in terms of a common schema and provides methodologies for updating and analysing urban data. Furthermore, the use of common external API allows applications to be built efficiently on top of the system. This paper is structured as follows. Firstly, a technical overview of KnowDS is presented with highlights on the encountered significant components and challenges. Secondly, a set of concrete examples of the framework in operation are described. Finally, conclusions are drawn along with future work and recommendations.

2   KnowDS   Design Overview

It is becoming increasingly common for data platforms to bring together open datasets and perform visualisations upon them. Such systems have three main components. Firstly, there is the acquisition system which downloads the data from an external API and stores in a custom database. Secondly, there is the processing system which takes the data form the database and converts it ready for display. Finally, there is a client application, typically web-based, which embeds the data and displays it. As they are designed for a specific purpose and each steps feeds to the next, it is difficult to re-purpose the data easily and efficiently. As an example a change in the external API may break the system completely. This issue was experienced in the early ongoing work phase of the DESURBS project.

Building upon such experience in DESURBS, the KnowDS framework was developed. The framework is divided into three components: Data collection and normalisation; Data processing and analysis; and applications. These are illustrated in Fig. 1

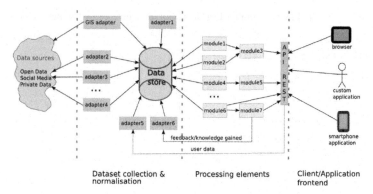

Fig. 1. Overall Design of KnowDS

above and delineated by the dashed lines. Each component is composed from individual modules, i.e. adapters and processing elements. Processing elements can provide a standardised API that frontend client applications and employ to interact with the system. Both adaptors and processing elements have clear interfaces while they perform a single specified task. Nevertheless, more complex tasks and analyses can be achieved by combining a set of processing elements. The overall system design is open and flexible to extend and accommodate new data sources as well as new data processing elements for performing knowledge discovery. The core implementation is primarily based on open source technologies and languages. The core technologies include Python, PostgreSQL, PostGIS, Django and Apache. The various components are discussed with more details in the next sub-sections.

2.1 Data Collection and Normalisation

The purpose of the *Data Collection and Normalisation* component is to gather and extract data of interest from various data sources. This has a similar purpose to conventional ETL (Extract-Transform-Load) [9, 10] systems which are common in data warehouses. In the extract process consumes web APIs (but more generally any data source). The transform serves to add structure to the original data which is often unstructured and heterogeneous. In contrast to ETL systems the reconstruction of the history of the data as well as current snapshot is enabled. For example, it is important to know that a specific API splits one field into two at specific date and provide snapshots of the data before and after the change. In order to achieve this, a method of tracking the changes to the data, similar to those employed by version control systems, has been purposely implemented. The KnowDS data store is composed of a combination of databases, directory structure and a storage archiving system. The current implementation of the data store employs a combination of databases and an auxiliary hierarchical directory structure to store binaries and data blobs. In order to realise the above vision, the nature of the datasets available (i.e. from data.gov.uk) to classify their nature was studied. In all cases the dataset was modelled as a functional mapping from a spatio-temporal attribute with a resource identifier to a multi-dimensional vector.

Table 1. Exemplar Datasets with the Common Attributes

Dataset	Spatial	Temporal	ID
Twitter	$\times^1/\checkmark$	$\checkmark$	$\checkmark$
Postcodes	$\checkmark$		$\checkmark$
UK Crime	$\checkmark$	$\checkmark$	
Weather	$\checkmark$	$\checkmark$	$\checkmark$
Pollution	$\checkmark$	$\checkmark$	$\checkmark$
Conservation Areas	$\checkmark$		$\checkmark$
Building information	$\checkmark$		$\checkmark$
House prices	$\checkmark$	$\checkmark$	
StreetView data	$\checkmark$		

This vision is fully documented for multiple datasets, as illustrated in Table 1 above. The fields often require conversions in order to put them under a common representation. For instance, geographical data for twitter are in WGS84 format, while the UK crime data are in Easting/Northing. Thus, the structuring process of data takes the arbitrary dataset and converts it into table format with several mandatory fields and a blob which contains the remainder of the data. It is for this reason that semi-structured data formats need to be described. The specific implementation of the component is made up of a number of autonomous modules (adapters) that are capable of accessing the source data, conversion, structuring, and storage. Specific adapters are lightweight and reusable since they are coded in a common pattern. Typical activities with the adapters include fetching the data from the source (one shot or periodic), data normalisation and anonymisation (of sensitive data). An example of data conversion processing can be illustrated through a relatively simple geographical dataset. Urban spaces can be simply defined as geospatial polygons. However, their representations differ among local authorities. Among the representations commonly used in the UK include:

- **Cities**: A boundary dataset containing polygons for each one of our cities. Defined at the level of government.
- **Neighbourhoods**: This is defined by the census Middle Layer Super Output Areas (MSOAs) are population-wise similar (~7400). Provided by Ordinance Survey.
- **Postcodes**: The highest level of resolution. Often down to the granularity of a few households. This is provided by the postal service.

These each are at a different zoom level and size. While some of the boundaries match (city and neighbourhood) together, others do not (postcodes). This means that a typical postcode can be contained in 1 or more neighbourhoods. Additionally, different schemes use different coordinate systems. WGS84[2] was used as a common coordinate scheme for our geographical coordinates. This means that on ingest the conversion to the WGS84 reference coordinates will be required. In order to cope with changes in data structure, many sorts of transformations that happen over the

---

[2] http://earth-info.nga.mil/GandG/wgs84/index.html

lifetime of datasets were addressed. The mapping relationship which was described earlier can be considered as data model. The model transformations are thus: *Creation, Modification and Deletion.* In order to handle such transformations, the history of the dataset which can be used for replay has been maintained. Hence, the restoration of previous states of the data even when the dataset has changed can be achieved. An example of the need for changes can be seen by studying the history of a particular API. For example the UK Police crime data API. In 2013, there were several breaking changes to it. Firstly, a refresh of the crime data meant that several crime types were re-classified. Secondly, the ability to obtain crimes in a specific Police neighbourhood (in Easting/Northing) was removed and replaced by street-level information (WGS84). As a result, several police administrative regions were merged. The re-classification of the crime types required the addition and removal of fields to the data model. The API change can be dealt with via the addition of a new model for the data. The merging of regions can be solved via modification of the data in the model.

2.2   Dataset Processing Modules

Whilst the purpose of the previous module was to collect and structure the data, the data processing module performs operations on the data for subsequent use by an application. The processing takes place in the central portion of Fig. 1. There are a number of specialised modules which perform processing of data which are contained within the dataset and provide output. Like the data collection adaptors, the modules are written under a common pattern. They specifically manage the access to the dataset and analyse it for a given specific task. Once analysed the output can be exposed via an API or passed to another module for subsequent processing. In this sense the modules can be classified in terms of whether the goal is to analyse data or aid in client applications.

The analysis takes place depending on the current client requirements and needs. In this model the back-end acts as a broker for data which is passed to an analytics engine. The analytics engine also stores data internally in a database. However, the data

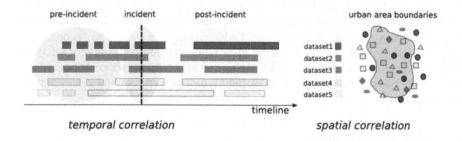

Fig. 2. Timeline, or location based analysis combining a heterogeneity of data sources revealing a pattern

is in processed form from the broker. There are a number of different data processing techniques that can be applied by the analytics engine. They are:

- *Simple analysis of data* (From a particular resource).
- *Combining data from different resources* (e.g. Timeline analysis on data from different sources, identification of patterns, behaviour.)
- *Incident timeline analysis* (Which includes combined data from available resources at a given time of an event.)

In particular, the analysis of data can split into pre-incident, during-incident, and post-incident analyses (see Fig. 2). Spatial analysis can also be applied on predefined urban spaces using multiple datasets as shown in Fig. 2. Higher level analysis, or custo-mised user defined analysis should be facilitated, i.e. in terms of describing an analy-sis as a workflow/process that can be loaded and run by the system. The analysis and study of identified patterns/behaviour, which are external to the system, might require input from knowledge domain experts.

2.3   The Application Front-End

At the frontend level, the business logic for the specific application should be con-tained. This is specific to the application and/or visualisation and does not enable the degree of code reuse as exhibited for the previous components. No analysis of data takes place at this level, however, data processing for visualisation or conversion to another format might be required. The connection between the clients and platform is via an established API such as HTTP/REST. Many applications will require some processing of the raw data, while this is triggered via the API. The results are cached within the data-store for subsequent use. This is illustrated in the right-most compo-nent of **Fig. 1**. Some examples of the sorts of modules that can be provided are: *Mash-up visualisations* (where data from different datasets are normalised on similar coordinates); *Custom data exporting*; and *Entering of user contributed data*.

3   Case Studies

Two case studies using the KnowDS framework are presented in this section. The first case study is an application which extracts data from the open UK crime API and visualises it using spatial analytics with Ordinance Survey data. The second case study is a mobile application that enables users report on their perception of safety at urban spaces which they frequent. The application shows how user contributed data can be used along with other sources of public data to generate and discover new knowledge.

3.1   UK Crime Application

This is an application that was developed for the system, while it takes into account existing work on crime analysis in the literature. The main dataset of this application

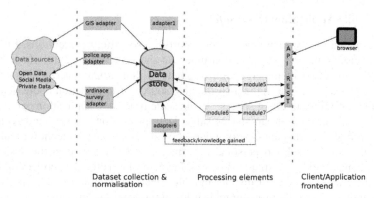

Fig. 3. UK Crime Application Design

is the UK Police Crime data which is available under a public API[3]. The Police crime application examines crime data in 13 major UK cities based in the South of England, the Midlands, the North of England and Greater London. The processing tools of this application allow comparison and visualisation of different crime types at various levels of spatial granularities and zoom levels. Additionally, analytics are performed on the data to allow quantified on-demand statistical comparisons of specific urban crimes and type of crimes across UK cities. An overview of the system as implemented in the KnowDS framework is illustrated in Fig. 3. The main function of the adaptors in this case is to fetch data from the UK police API and store it in the database. Additionally, as the crime location data is stored in Easting/Northing conversion to WGS84 is required. Finally, the adaptor periodically downloads and updates the data (on a monthly cycle) accordingly. In order to process the data and compare at differing zoom levels, access to Ordinance Survey definitions is also required. These are ingested into the data-store via an additional adaptor.

There are a number of distinct modules present in the system. Firstly, there is a tool that aggregates the normalised crime data for a specific crime-type and produces a "heat map" as a result. The output is archived within the data-store to reduce processing load. Secondly, there are raw crimes data which are exposed as a JSON object. This can be used to create maps on the client side. Thirdly, analytics are performed to cross-correlate various types of crime with each other. The results of the analysis are equally exposed via JSON. Finally, a simple aggregate of crimes at a given specific location (and level of zoom) is presented via a JSON object. The Police application front-end visualisation UI is a browser driven tool that can visualise various crime points and intelligent statistics on maps with cross-comparisons between different crime areas, e.g. city, neighbourhood, or postal code level. This is shown in Fig. 4. The data is generated dynamically from the framework and represents new investigative knowledge about urban and cross-urban crimes.

---

[3] http://data.police.uk/

3.2   Mobile Application (*YourSafe*)

This is a native android application for reporting user safety perceptions. End users are the dataset suppliers and also consumers at the same time. YourSafe is built to allow users to report their perception of safety within urban spaces. The aim is to show that end users can become a sustainable source of information about geospatial perception of safety in urban spaces. At the same time such application can implicitly lead to making local urban spaces safer. Data protection, privacy and security is considered highly in this application under the European Data protection regulations. Device ID's are hashed and personal information is NOT stored in the system. An overall schematic of the design is shown in Fig.5. As far as the data collection is concerned, there are a number of distinct modules which are implemented. Firstly, there is an adaptor which pulls in geographical locations from Ordinance Survey. Specifically, this is re-used from the police application. Additionally, UK crime data is re-used from the application as well. The final adaptor was built in the system in order to save reports into the data-store. Optionally, a binary object such as an image, can be sent as an attachment with the report. This adaptor converts the incoming report from the API to a space-time location and stores the report alongside the user. There is very little analysis that is performed for usage in the tool. The tool provides a simple visualisation of reports and crime data at a given location. Thus a pair of modules are written to perform a spatial query to return results via JSON. In addition there are tools related to user management. Specifically, creation and deletion of users lead to updates to the underlying data store. These are called via the rest API from an external client. The Android client is pictured in Fig. 6. The user can create a report either online or later on via the interface in Fig. 6(a). As well as the title and description, the user can add free tags to describe what is happening in terms of safety around their spaces and upload incident images. The visualisation interface (Fig. 6(b)) shows reports in the local neighbourhood but also Police crime reports (shown in blue). These are aggregated to an icon when there are several reports in close geographical proximities. Early participatory experimentations of Citizens has shown that the submitted

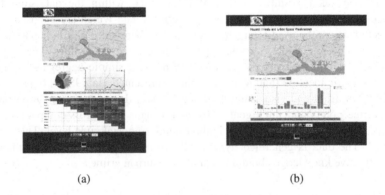

(a)   (b)

Fig. 4. (a) Illustration of the application showing crime data for a specific city (b) Comparison of two cities

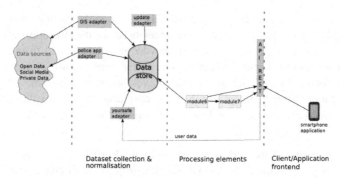

Fig. 5. The design of the YourSafe mobile application

reports are a valuable source of new knowledge. Although the number of participants in the early trial was limited, around 60% of the reports concerned safety perception narratives, 25% on alerted incidents; and 15% were on joint reporting of incidents and perception of safety in urban zones.

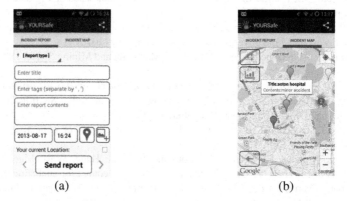

(a)   (b)

Fig. 6. Client application for YourSafe (a) report creation (b) visualisation

4   Conclusions

This paper provides an overview of the KnowDS framework for City crime data analytics. It illustrated its usefulness on two distinct applications: a UK crime web-application, and YourSafe mobile application. The essence of the design was to decouple the data gathering, data analysis, and data visualisation parts. The data gathering phase consists of a number of independent adapters which can ingest data into a data-store. Additionally, the history of the dataset is maintained and enabled to querying over historical data. This component of the framework is a data repository similar to a source code repository. The data analysis also consists of a number of modules which perform analyses on data. Processing is achieved by combining one or more of these modules. The last component is the specific application which varies depending on the application. The specific applications are very different in nature but share some common data (Police crime data). Using KnowDS allowed the mobile application to be built simply by concentrating on the differences between the two applications. Additionally, the framework demonstrated that knowledge can be mined from data content either via novel use of disparate datasets (UK Crime application); or user contributed data along existing data (YourSafe). Further development of the framework will continue in the future. More adaptors which allow more datasets to be explored will be put in place. Additionally, the range of data analytics tools will be deployed.

Acknowledgements . This work is co-funded by the European Commission under the 7th Framework programme under the DESURBS project: Grant Number 261652. Also the EVACUATE project: Grant Number FP7-EC-313161.

References

1. Vilajosana, I., Llosa, J., Martinez, B., Domingo-Prieto, M., Angles, A., Vilajosana, X.: Bootstrapping smart cities through a self-sustainable model based on big data flows. IEEE Communications Magazine 51, 6 (2013)
2. Chun, S., Shulman, S., Sandoval, R., Hovy, E.: Government 2.0: Making connections between citizens, data, and government. Informaiton Policy (2010)
3. Aggarwal, C., Abdelzaher, T.: Social Sensing. Managing and Mining Sensor Data, 237–297 (2013)
4. Prasetyo, P.K., Gao, M., Lim, E.-P., Scollon, C.N.: Social sensing for urban crisis management: The case of singapore haze. In: Jatowt, A., et al. (eds.) SocInfo 2013. LNCS, vol. 8238, pp. 478–491. Springer, Heidelberg (2013)
5. Lehmann, J., Goncalves, B., Cattuto, J.J.: Dynamical classes of collective attention in Twitter. In: WWW (2012)
6. Ceolin, D., Moreau, L., O'Hara, K., Fokkink, W., Van Hage, W.R., Maccatrozzo, V., Sackley, A., Schreiber, G.: Guus, N. Shadbolt.: Two procedures for analyzing the reliability of open government data. In: International Conference on Information Processing and Management of Uncertainty in Knowledge-Based Systems (IPMU) (2014)
7. Leavett, N.: Will NoSQL databases live up to their promise? IEEE Computer 43, 2 (2010)
8. Bonastos, A., Middleton, L., Melas, P., Sabeur, Z.: Crime Open data aggregation and management for the design of safer spaces in urban environments. In: Environmental Software Systems: Fostering Information Sharing, ISESS (2013)
9. Agrawal, H., Chafle, G., Goyal, S., Mittal, S., Mukherjea, S.: An Enhanced Extract-Transform-Load System for Migrating Data in Telecom Billing. In: IEEE International Conference on Data Engineering, ICDE (2008)
10. Henrard, J., Hick, J.-M., Thiran, P.: Strategies for data reengineering, Working Conference on Reverse Engineering, WCRE (2002)

Combined Aggregation and Column Generation for Land-Use Trade-Off Optimisation

Asef Nazari[1], Andreas Ernst[1], Simon Dunstall[1], Brett Bryan[2], Jeff Connor[2], Martin Nolan[2], and Florian Stock[3]

[1]CSIRO: Digital Productivity and Services, Melbourne, Australia
{asef.nazari,andreas.ernst,simon.dunstall}@csiro.au
[2]CSIRO: Land and Water, Adelaide, Australia
{brett.bryan,jeff.connor,martin.nolan}@csiro.au
[3]CSIRO: Digital Productivity and Services, Melbourne, Australia, and InnoZ – Innovation Centre for Mobility and Societal Change, Berlin, Germany
florian-stock@gmex.de

Abstract. In this paper we developed a combination of aggregation-disaggregation technique with the concept of column generation to solve a large scale LP problem originating from land use management in the Australian agricultural sector. The problem is to optimally allocate the most profitable land use activities including agriculture, carbon sequestration, environmental planting, bio-fuel, bio-energy, etc., and is constrained to satisfy some food demand considerations and expansion policies for each year from 2013 to 2050. In this research we produce a higher resolution solution by dividing Australia's agricultural areas into square kilometer cells, which leads to more than thirteen million cells to be assigned, totally or partially, to different activities. By accepting a scenario on agricultural products' return, carbon related activities, future energy prices, water availability, global climate change, etc. a linear programming problem is composed for each year. However, even by using a state of the art commercial LP solver it takes a long time to find an optimal solution for one year. Therefore, it is almost impossible to think about simultaneous scenarios to be incorporated, as the corresponding model will become even larger. Based on the properties of the problem, such as similar economical and geographical properties of nearby land parcels, the combination of clustering ideas with column generation to decompose the large problem into smaller sub-problems yields a computationally efficient algorithm for the large scale problem.

Keywords: aggregation-disaggregation, column generation, clustering, land use allocation.

1 Introduction

Predicting land use change in Australian agriculture in the context of increasing energy prices stimulating bio-fuels and bio-energy land uses, and a carbon policy with possibilities for increasing carbon price over time requires solving a large scale linear programming problem. The model covers the domain of southern and eastern Australian land currently in intensive agricultural use on a one square kilometer grid cell resolution over

R. Denzer et al. (Eds.): ISESS 2015, IFIP AICT 448, pp. 455–466, 2015.

813,000 square kilometers resulting in more than thirteen million square cells, including active and inactive cells, as shown in Fig. 1. Starting with the agricultural land present in 2013, the model finds the optimal land use each year forward in time until 2050 where optimality is defined as maximizing profit and social welfare (the sum of profit and consumers' surplus). In the highest resolution with land parcels of size one square kilometer, for each year the corresponding LP has 7,313,847 continuous variables and 814,811 constraints. The focus is on the change from current agricultural production to alternative land uses such as carbon plantings, environmental plantings, bio-energy or bio-fuels. Food prices are computed endogenously following a maximum welfare approach whereas costs and revenues for non-agricultural commodities depend on scenarios and exogenous modeling. The platform is built to model a range of scenarios involving alternate assumptions about global climate change, world carbon emissions trajectories, emissions limits and prices of carbon credits, price trajectories for energy, world food demand, supply and price trajectories, and agricultural productivity growth [11].

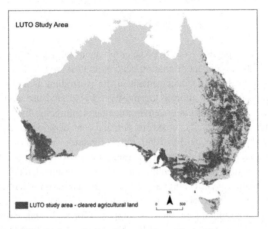

Fig. 1. Area for land use trade optimisation

Efficiently solving a large scale LP problem is the main difficulty that we address in this paper. At the present setting, finding an optimal solution for each year takes a long time even using commercial software packages. Also, considering that the model is build based on one set of fixed scenarios, the further expansion of the project to consider simultaneous scenarios for the sake of stochastic optimisation is almost impossible at this stage. Therefore, our first aim is to develop an algorithm which can solve the large LP pertaining to a particular year in a shorter amount of time.

One important fact in terms of agricultural land allocation for different products is that nearby land parcels have similar economical and geographical properties. They indeed have similar proximity to water resources, and main roads leading to similar transportation and production costs. In reality it is easy to detect that huge parcels of land are allocated to the same agricultural commodity while passing large farms in countryside. By drawing inspiration from this fact, instead of considering cells of size one square kilometer, the whole Australia is divided into big chunks of land (lower resolution) called clusters. The economical properties of each cluster are calculated based upon cells in each cluster. This type of aggregation technique in optimisation is a handy tool to create a set of smaller problems out of a large problem. However, the smaller problem size comes at the cost of lower accuracy. We remedy this by using an iterative disaggregation approach. The smaller problem is gradually made a better approximation of the original problem by breaking down big clusters into smaller clusters, and add new clusters as new column to the small problem.

There is an increasing level of attention to use optimisation techniques in agricultural and other land use management planning context. As an example, in [7] a hierarchical approach is presented for large-scale forest planning. The algorithm is based on solving an aggregate problem, which is of moderate size. Another example, in [8] authors argue the usage of optimisation techniques in combination with scenario analysis can provide efficient land use management options for sustainable land use from global to sub-global scales. In terms of water resource management, in [9] a spatial optimisation techniques implemented among four diffuse source pathways in a mixed-use watershed to maximize total reduction of phosphorus loading to streams while minimizing associated costs. An interesting utilization of a multi-objective optimisation technique is reported for identifying optimum land management adaptations to climate change [10].

The rest of the paper is arranged as follows. In the next sections, we describe the model in more details. Then a short description of column generation and aggregation techniques is provided. The new algorithm is introduced at the next section, and numerical results and the conclusion will conclude the paper.

2   The Model

In order to insert demand-production equilibrium, a segmentation of the domain is necessary to approximate the nonlinear relationship between the demand and production using piecewise linear functions. Also, an appropriate model needs to consider satisfaction of the Australian agricultural food demand by imposing supply-production and supply-demand constraints. As we should allocate every cell, partially or totally, to the activities, a set of land-use constraints are introduced. Furthermore, in case there are some particular expansion plans for particular activities, some new expansion constraints are introduced to fulfill existing capacity for each activity. The complete model of the land-use trade-off optimization (LUTO) project is represented by equation (1).   Some necessary and technical information of the model is represented in Table 1.

With resolution set to one, which is the highest resolution with land parcels of size one km^2, there are $|R|=812,383$ regional active cells. Also, there exist $|S|=100$ price and demand segmentation, $|J|=9$ activities and $|F|=24$ food commodities. The linear model has $|R|*|J|+|S|*|F| \approx 7,313,847$ continuous variables and $|N|+|R|+|F|+|S|*|F| \approx 814,811$ constraints. The number of variables is almost nine times more than the number of constraints.

$$\left\{ \begin{array}{l} \max \sum_{j \in F} \sum_{s \in S} P_{sj} y_{sj} - \sum_{j \in F} \sum_{r \in R} C_{r,ag_j} Q_{r,ag_j} x_{r,ag} + \sum_{j \in N} \sum_{r \in R} \delta_{rj} Q_{rj} x_{rj} \\[2em]

s.t. \quad \sum_{r \in R} Q_{rj} x_{rj} \leq Lim_j \quad j \in \{carbon, biofule, bioenergy\} \subset N \quad \text{Expansion} \\[2em]

\qquad \sum_{r \in R} Q_{r,epB} x_{r,epB} \leq Lim_{epB} \qquad\qquad\qquad\qquad \text{Biodiversity} \\[2em]

\qquad \sum_{j \in J} x_{rj} \leq 1 \qquad \forall r \in R \qquad\qquad\qquad\quad \text{Land-Use} \\[2em]

\qquad \sum_{s \in S} y_{sj} \leq \sum_{r \in R} Q_{r,ag_j} x_{r,ag} \quad \forall j \in F \qquad\quad \text{Supply} - \text{Production} \\[2em]

\qquad y_{sj} \leq D_{sj} \qquad \forall s \in S, \quad j \in F \qquad\qquad \text{Supply} - \text{demand} \\[1em]

\qquad x_{rj}, y_{sj} \geq 0 \qquad\qquad\qquad\qquad \forall s \in S, r \in R, i \in F, j \in J \end{array} \right. \tag{1}$$

Table 1. Components of the model

Sets	
J	Set of 9 activities including agriculture, carbon sequestration, environmental planting, biodiversity, tree-based bioenergy, wheat-based bioenergy, wheat-based biofuel, tree-based biofuel and wheat-based biofuel and food represented as $\{Ag, Cp, Ep, EpB, BeWP, BeS, \text{BfGS}, \text{BfWP}, \text{BfFS}\}$.
F	Set of 24 food commodities, ag_j's.
N	Non-food activities including Carbon, bioenergy, biofuel and environmental planting activities; In other words activities in J other than Ag.
R	Set of regions.
S	Set of segments in discrete food demand function.
Variables	
x_{rj}	Ratio allocated to activity $j \in J$ at cell $r \in R$ ($0 \leq x_{rj} \leq 1$),
y_{sj}	Amount of commodity $j \in F$ should be produced at the segment $s \in S$ at price P_{sj} .
Constants	
Q_{sj}	Quantity of activity j that can be produced at cell r.
δ_{rj}	Annualized economic return of activity j at r.
D_{sj}	Demand for commodity j at segment s, $\sum_s D_{sj} = D_j$.
C_{rj}	Production cost of commodity j at region r.
P_{sj}	Price of commodity j in segment s at demand level y_{sj}.

3   Column Generation

Column generation is a widely used technique to solve large scale linear and integer programming problems starting from pioneering publications [1] and [2]. The technique is frequently utilized when the number of variables is much larger that the number of constraints. In such large scale problems, the vast majority of the variables are zero at optimality, hence the fundamental concept underlying column generation is to solve a smaller problem instead of the original LP by considering a subset of columns (variables). The smaller problem is referred as restricted master problem (RMP), and new columns are added as required. The generation of new columns is accomplished by solving another problem called pricing sub-problem following each optimisation of the RMP. In the pricing stage of each iteration, the column(s) with minimum (maximum, depending on the objective) reduced cost(s) are added to the RMP. The optimality is achieved if it is impossible to add a new column to the RMP. For comprehensive surveys on column generation interested readers can consult [3] and [4].

For a formal explanation of the column generation algorithm consider the linear programming (1) where the p_j is the jth column of the coefficient matrix, and the number of variables is extremely greater than the number of constraints. Assume that an initial basic feasible solution, x_B, is available, with associated basis matrix B, and cost coefficient c_B. The simplex multipliers associated with this basis could be calculated as $\pi = c_B B^{-1}$ and are always available at each iteration of the simplex algorithm. To improve the basic feasible solution we "price out" all columns corresponding to non-basic variables by forming their corresponding reduced cost $\bar{c}_j = c_j - \pi p_j$. If $\max \bar{c}_j = \bar{c}_s > 0$, then considering non-degeneracy, the current solution may be improved by introducing x_s into the basis via a pivot transformation.

4   Aggregation Techniques

An important issue in obtaining an optimal solution of large scale optimisation problems is the trade-off between the level of details and the ease of solving the model in an acceptable amount of time. Aggregation-disaggregation techniques provide some methodologies for handling large optimisation problems by combining data, or using aggregated problems which are reduced in size. One main approach to construct an aggregated problem for a large scale LP is by partitioning the variables and forming corresponding columns by weighted average of columns in each partition. A feasible solution of the original problem is then achieved by applying a special transformation, called disaggregation, to an optimal solution of the aggregated problem. The aggregation error calculated as the difference between the original optimal objective value and the optimal value for the disaggregated solution guides the algorithm towards the optimality in an iterative scheme. In this section, a concise description of aggregation inspired from [5] is provided.

Consider the original linear programming problem in the form of

$$(LP) \begin{cases} z^* = \max cx \\ s.t. \ Ax \le b \\ x \ge 0 \end{cases} \tag{2}$$

A column aggregation is explained here, which means only variables in (2) are aggregated. Let σ be a partition of the column indices $\{1, \dots, n\}$ into a set of ters $S_k, k = 1, \dots, K$, such that $S_k \cap S_p = \emptyset$, $\bigcup_{k=1}^{K} S_k = \{1, \dots, n\}$. For the kth cluster, let its size as $|S_k| = n_k$, so that $\sum_k n_k = n$. The matrix A^k is defined to be the submatrix of A consisting of those columns whose indices are in S_k. Also, the sub-vectors c^k and x^k are defined in the same way. Consider a nonnegative n_k-vector $g^k = (g_j^k)$, satisfying the following normalizing condition

$$g \in G = \{g | \sum_{j \in S_k} g_j^k = 1, \ g_j^k \ge 0, \ k = 1, \dots, K, j \in S_k\}$$

and form

$$\overline{A^k} = A^k g^k, \qquad \overline{c^k} = c^k g^k, \qquad k = 1, \dots, K$$

such that $\overline{A^k}$ is a column m-vector equal to the linear combination of the columns $a_j, j \in S_k$ with the coefficients g_j^k, and $\overline{c^k}$ is a scalar defined similarly. The vectors g^k are called weighting vectors or the weights of aggregation.

Define the matrix $\bar{A} = [\overline{A^1}, \dots, \overline{A^K}] = [\overline{a_{ik}}]$, and the vector $\bar{c} = (\overline{c^1}, \dots, \overline{c^k})$. Then the problem

$$(ALP) \begin{cases} \bar{z} = \max \bar{c}X \\ s.t. \ \bar{A}X \le b \\ X \ge 0 \end{cases} \tag{3}$$

defines the (column or variable) aggregated problem corresponding to (2). In (3), X is a K-vector of aggregated variables. For a given original problem, then, an aggregated problem is determined by the pair (σ, g). It is assumed that (σ, g) has been chosen so that (3) is feasible. The optimal primal and dual solutions of the aggregated problem are denoted as (X^*, π^*). Interested readers could consult [6] for a general framework for aggregation and disaggregation technique and a survey on previous works.

5   The New Approach

Solving LP (1) takes a long time even using state of the art LP solver CPLEX as depicted in Fig. 2. For a particular instance of LP (1) used to sketch the chart, finding an optimal solution of the LP takes maximum time of 1:08:34, minimum amount of 0:21:34, and in average it takes 36 minutes per year for a complete run for a period of 38 years. Considering that the model should be solved for several consecutive years, at least for 38 years in this project, obtaining the optimal land allocation policy for a long planning horizon becomes quite time consuming. In addition, all the economic data, demand and supply figures along with energy price paths are acquired based on only one scenario out of thousands of scenarios. As a consequence, considering more than one scenario simultaneously for the sake of a stochastic model will result in an even larger problem and will require longer computational time. Therefore, for more comprehensive investigations on optimal land allocations an efficient solution methodology is necessary to solve the large LP problem in a reasonably shorter amount of CPU time.

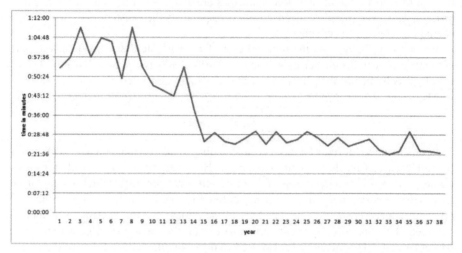

Fig. 2. CPU time for solving the LP for each year from 2013 to 2050

There are some interesting properties associated with agricultural land allocation that are utilized in our aggregation process. For example, it is quite plausible that nearby land parcels would be allocated to similar activities. The reason for this assumption is that geographically close areas have similar economical and soil properties, and the most profitable land allocation should be almost the same considering accessibility, water resources and costs. Therefore, instead of considering land parcels (cells) of size one square kilometer, we aggregate them into larger chunks of land which are called clusters. Each cluster will act as a decision making unit in the optimisation model, and its economic data are obtained by summing over the data related to all   active cells in that cluster.

We start by a lower resolution, say R_0, and divide Australia into a number of large parcels of land. Consider the set of clusters $C = \{C_k\}$, where $C_{k_i} \cap C_{k_j} = \emptyset$ for $k_i \neq k_j$, and $\bigcup_k C_k = R$. Each C_k is a nonempty subset of R. For each cluster, all the economic data including profits and costs of all nine activities and all 24 food products, in addition to other related quantities and capacities are calculated based on related data of active cells in that cluster. Note that in the aggregated LP model the number of land-use constraints is less than in the original problem. The reason is that in the original model there is one land-use constraint for each cell. However, in the aggregated model we are dealing with clusters of cells, and there is one land-use constraint for each cluster. The number of other constraints remains the same as the original problem. An aggregated LP is constructed as explained in section 4 with far fewer variables and constraints, and the optimal primal and dual solutions are obtained by solving the problem using CPLEX.

The plan is to improve the aggregated models consecutively to become as close as possible to the original LP with highest resolution but without solving a large scale problem. Towards this aim, one possible way is to subdivide large clusters and construct smaller ones, and introduce new clusters into the model as new columns. We incorporated reduced costs to separate cells with positive amount inside a cluster from the rest of cells in that cluster. Reduced costs are available at the end of optimisation process. However, these reduced costs correspond to the clusters, and we need to extend this concept to cells inside each cluster.

If, for example, $r_{k,ag}$ is the reduced cost of the variable that corresponds to agricultural activity in the cluster k, we need to distribute it between the agricultural activity of all cells inside the cluster k so that the total sum is equal to $r_{k,ag}$. In other words,

$$\sum_{c \in C_k} r_{k_c,ag} = r_{k,ag}.$$

In this manner, all reduced costs corresponding to all variables related to all activities for each cell in cluster k are calculated. However, before the calculation of reduced costs, we introduce a new concept of semi-reduced costs which is part of the final reduced costs and will be formally defined in the next paragraph. For each cell all semi-reduced costs are calculated for all activities, and the maximum of them is recorded. This quantity represents, to some extent, the most profitable activity for a particular cell. This quantity is also used to distribute the reduced cost of the cluster between all cells proportional to the size of its most profitable activity. The reduced costs are calculated based on semi-reduced costs, and by means of the sign of final reduced costs we can partition each cluster into two sub-clusters containing cells with positive and non-positive reduced costs. The economical quantities for newly constructed clusters are calculated using the information of cells belonging to it, and related information for shrunk clusters are modified considering cells remaining in those clusters. The changes in the old cluster transferred into the LP, and a new column is introduced for each new cluster.

Mathematically, in iteration t, after solving LP_t, we obtain optimal primal solution x_t^* and optimal dual solution π_t^*. At this stage, it is easy to calculate the reduced cost of each activity j of each cluster k using $r_{k_j} = c_{k_j} - \pi_t^* p_{k_j}$. To calculate reduced costs of each cell, perhaps the easiest way is to distribute r_{k_j} uniformly between all cells included in cluster k. However, this approach treats all the cells with equity, and there is not a distinction based on profitability. Another, smarter approach is to distribute r_{k_j} in a way that supports cells with higher profit potentials. In order to calculate reduced cost of each cell in each cluster, first we calculate semi-reduced costs, $\widehat{r_{c_j}}$, for the problem in this paper. The semi-reduced cost is the reduced cost without the portion related to the optimal dual value of the corresponding land-use constraint. In other words, for cell c in cluster k, $r_{c_j} = \widehat{r_{c_j}} - \alpha_c \pi_k^l$. For a cell c in cluster k, if $\max_j\{\widehat{r_{c_j}}\}$ is positive for activity j, the quantity α_c is defined as

$$\alpha_c = \max_j\{0, \frac{\max_j\{\widehat{r_{c_j}}\}}{\sum_c \max_j\{\widehat{r_{c_j}}\}}\}$$

After calculation of reduced costs of each cell in each cluster, the cluster is divided into two sub-clusters. One sub-cluster contains all the cells with positive reduced costs, and the other one contains all the cells with non-positive reduced costs. The economic data of each cluster is updated and new clusters are added into the previous aggregated model as new columns. The model is solved again, and the process of dividing clusters is continued until further bifurcation is impossible.

Algorithm 1. Aggregation and Column Generation
___

1: Make clusters with a low resolution R_0, and calculate economic attributes of each cluster.

2: Build the aggregated LP, and get optimal primal and dual solutions.

3: Calculate reduced costs of each activity for each cell in each cluster, and subdivide each cluster into two clusters based on the sign of reduced costs of containing cells.

4: If no new clusters created (no cells with negative reduced cost) then the solution is optimal. Stop.

5: Calculate economic attributes of new clusters, and update corresponding data in old clusters.

6: Improve the aggregated LP and include new columns for each recently created cluster, and get the optimal primal and dual solutions.

7: If a stopping criterion is not met, go to Step 3.

---

6   Computational Results

In this section we present some of the numerical results we obtained through working on application of our algorithm to solve the large scale linear programming problem originated from land use allocation. As seen in Fig. 2 solving a LP problem for each year takes a long amount of time averaging 36 minutes. For a fare comparison, all the numerical experiments are carried out on the same computer. It is worthwhile to mention that the optimisation technique discussed in this paper and all linear programming problems were coded in Python 2.7 language and executed on a computer running a dual core 64-bit Intel(R) Xeon(R) processor at 2.79 GHz with 64 GB RAM. The linear programming problems were solved using IBM CPLEX 12.5 solver.

Table 2 summarizes the output of solving the large scale optimisation problem starting with different resolutions. For our algorithm the stopping criterion is met if we are unable to subdivide the existing clusters further into new, smaller clusters. Resolution 1 is the finest resolution and creates the largest problem. Also, the resolution level of 7569 divides Australia into 417 clusters at the beginning of the computation, and creates the smallest possible LP problem in our experiments.

We recorded starting number of clusters, n_{start}, final number of clusters, n_{end}, the number of iterations to obtain the final optimal value, and the percentage difference between our optimal value with the optimal value of the original problem for each resolution. The original problem in its finest resolution of 1 has 812,383 clusters, due to considering each cell as a cluster. The algorithm could find the optimal solution in one iteration, as it is impossible to break down clusters. We also record the amount of time taken for CPLEX to find the optimal solution for each resolution in minutes. This column provides us a good measure to compare time performance of our approach. We did not consider the time necessary for the extraction and calculation of parameters in this column, and in the execution time provided in section 5.

Table 2. Results on running the algorithm of different resolutions

resolution	iterations	n_{start}	n_{end}	Difference (%)	t (min)
1	1	812383	812383	0.0	53.598
9	4	138329	138368	0.16	25.930
81	5	20402	20482	0.27	0.694
784	5	2784	2899	0.27	0.020
1600	7	1608	1742	0.26	0.016
7569	7	417	484	0.49	0.009

The data in the table demonstrates some interesting facts about our approach and its capability to deal with large scale linear programming problems. Instead of solving the largest possible problem, the algorithm tries to solve an aggregated problem which is a considerably smaller problem. After each iteration, it tries to subdivide clusters based on their reduced costs. As an example, starting with resolution 7,569 which divides Australia into 417 clusters at the beginning, only in seven iterations and with addition of 67 clusters, the algorithm could reach to the optimal objective function with only 0.49 percent deviation in a small portion of a minute. Comparing this outcome with solving the original problem which needs 53 minutes shows how fast the new algorithm could find the optimal solution. Furthermore, Fig. 3 represents the convergence rate to the optimal solution considering each resolution factor.

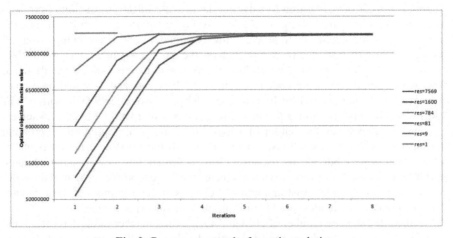

Fig. 3. Convergence results for each resolution

It is interesting to notice that choosing a lower resolution of 1,600 causes to start with a worse bound than 7,569. However, as shown in the Fig 3 it gets better quick, meaning that less clusters do not necessarily mean worse bounds, and also the smaller clusters are not necessarily all subsets of the larger clusters.

Combining the information presented in Table 2 and Fig 3 it is apparent that there is a smarter approach of solving the large scale LP in a noticeably shorter amount of time by choosing a lower resolution at the beginning and gradually refining the resolution of clusters in the sequel iterations. With this approach, it is meaningful to build a stochastic optimisation model of the land allocation planning problem, and obtain sensible outcomes in reasonable amount of time and effort.

7   Conclusion

In this paper we presented a new efficient algorithm to solve large scale linear programming problem originated from optimal land allocation planning. The algorithm combines techniques of column generation, aggregation and disaggregation particularly suitable for this problem. We approximated the large problem with a small LP problem by considering huge parcels of land as a cluster, and then tried to improve the approximation iteratively by subdividing clusters when it is possible. The use of our custom aggregation and disaggregation method allows us to easily solve land use models at a much higher resolution than would otherwise be possible, thus improving the fidelity of the models. In addition, the huge reduction in computational time lays the ground for more complex models. For example an extension to stochastic optimisation incorporating multiple scenarios in a single model is being considered.

References

1. Dantzig, G., Wolfe, P.: Decomposition principle for linear programs. Oper. Res. 8(1), 101–111 (1960)
2. Gilmore, P.C., Gomory, R.E.: A linear programming approach to the cutting-stock problem. Oper. Res. 9(6), 849–859 (1961)
3. Desaulniers, G., Desrosiers, J., Solomon, M.: Column Generation. Springer, New York (2005)
4. Lübbecke, M.E., Desrosiers, J.: Selected topics in column generation. Oper. Res. 53(6), 1007–1023 (2005)
5. Litvinchev, I., Tsurkov, V.: Aggregation in Large-Scale Optimization. Springer (2003)
6. Rogers, D.F., Plante, R.D., Wong, R.T., Evans, J.R.: Aggregation and Disaggregation Tech-niques and Methodology in Optimization. Operations Research 39(4), 553–582 (1991)
7. Weintraub, A., Cholaky, A.: A Hierarchical Approach to Forest Planning. Forest Science 37(2), 439–460 (1991)
8. Seppelt, R., Lautenbach, S., Volk, M.: Identifying trade-offs between ecosystem services, land use, and biodiversity: a plea for combining scenario analysis and optimization on different spatial scales. Current Opinion in Environmental Sustainability 5(5), 458–463 (2013)

9. Gaddis, E.J.B., Voinov, A., Seppelt, R., Rizzo, D.M.: Spatial Optimization of Best Management Practices to Attain Water Quality Targets. Water Resources Management 28(6), 1485–1499 (2014)
10. Klein, T., Holzkämper, A., Calanca, P., Seppelt, R., Fuhrer, J.: Adapting agricultural land management to climate change: a regional multi-objective optimization approach. Landscape Ecology 28(10), 2029–2047 (2013)
11. Bryan, B.A., Nolan, M., Harwood, T.D., Connor, J.D., Navarro-Garcia, J., King, D., Summers, D.M., Newth, D., Cai, Y., Grigg, N., Harman, I., Crossman, N.D., Grundy, M.J., Fin-Niganj, J., Ferrier, S., Williams, K.J., Wilson, K.A., Law, E.A., Hatfield-Dodds, S.: Supply of carbon sequestration and biodiversity services from Australia's agricultural land under global change. Global Environmental Change 28, 166–181 (2014)

A Software Package for Automated Partitioning of Catchments

Ralf Denzer, Tobias Kalmes, and Udo Gauer

Environmental Informatics Group (EIG), Saarbrücken, Germany
`ralf.denzer@enviromatics.org`

Abstract. This paper reports about a software package which has been developed to automatically partition hydrological networks (catchments) into clusters of similar size. Such clustering is useful for parallel simulation of catchments on distributed computing systems and is typically based on heuristic graph algorithms.

There have been a few approaches to automatically partition catchments, but literature research indicates that there seems to be no systematic investigation of the usefulness of different graph algorithms for catchment partitioning over a reasonable number of real world data sets. Our study aims at making a step in this direction.

The paper describes the software package, which has been implemented in Java, its pluggable architecture, and initial experiments using the European catchment dataset ECRINS. The paper presents work in progress.

Keywords: parallel simulation, hydrological network, graph clustering.

1 Introduction

Some computational problems of river catchment simulations require large amounts of computing time. It is therefore just natural to aim at parallelizing such computations. At the core of any parallelization, the first question is whether an algorithm can be parallelized and how. As catchment simulations are dynamic flow problems, both spatial and temporal subdivision is an option.

A look at the literature suggests that while there have been several proposed solution, a systematic study is lacking. The aim of the work presented in this paper is a long term one: to start with a systematic approach coping with the parallelization of the problem (which means the partitioning of the catchments here) and to end in computational infrastructures for easy deployment of parallelized models.

In order to approach the catchment partitioning problem systematically, we chose to apply a divide and conquer strategy, starting with the most simple problem setup. The experiments reported in this paper are based on the following preconditions:

1. Precondition 1: the catchment is represented by a binary graph.
2. Precondition 2: the algorithm to be parallelized is the same in every node.

R. Denzer et al. (Eds.): ISESS 2015, IFIP AICT 448, pp. 467–474, 2015.

It is clear that in reality other cases may occur: the graph may contain cycles and the algorithms may be different for different parts of the catchment, but many applications in the literature satisfy the above requirements anyway and binary graphs are common representations for catchments.

For the purpose of this study we have also completely ignored the question when the parallelization of a problem will start to pay off, depending of the compute time per time step per node compared to the amount and latency of data transfer between computing nodes. We were only interested in the first step, the automatic partitioning.

A *binary graph* is a special form of a directed acyclic graph (DAG). Each graph node has a maximum of two predecessor upstream nodes, and a maximum of one downstream node. The problem of our study is defined as follows:

For a binary graph **G**, find a clustering

$$C = \{ S_i, i = 1,n \} \tag{1}$$

into **n** clusters, where S_i are binary graphs and

$$\cup \, S_{i,\, i=1,n} = G \tag{2}$$

which means that the clusters taken together represent the graph **G**. Let |G| be the graph norm (number of nodes) in a binary graph. An optimal clustering C_{opt} is one which satisfies the following equation:

$$|S_i| = |S_j|, \text{ for all } i,j \tag{3}$$

Equation (3) means that for the purpose of parallel computing, it is desired that all clusters have equal size. This reflects precondition 2.

2   Space and Time Parallelization

A dynamic flow problem can be parallelized in space and time, as long as the flow is represented by a DAG in which downstream nodes only receive input from upstream nodes. There are two principle possibilities to use a distributed computing infrastructure for parallelization: a) a large catchment is split spatially into several catchments, which are computed in parallel, and b) for different time steps or time periods there is a different processor per node. Theoretically one could assign |G| * T (T being the number of time steps) processors to the computing problem, which would however result in unrealistically large hardware needs. In reality it makes sense to allocate one computing node for a clustering of nodes, to compute a time period of reasonable size and then to communicate a partial time series between the clusterings through connecting nodes, in order to balance the trade-off between using multiple processors (positive influence) and communication delays and latencies (negative influence).

The long term interest of this study is to get a better understanding of the different trade-offs, based on a large number of real world datasets, and not based on very few (or only one) dataset or very small (or even toy) datasets. For this purpose it is necessary

1. to spatially cluster many different datasets, including large datasets with many nodes, in order to gain experience how good the spatial partitioning is in reality – for this step a concrete model is not needed,
2. to actually run many model runs based on these clusterings in a distributed environment and measure their performance (which will be quite an effort and will require a lot of automation), or
3. to try to build a theoretical model of the distributed computing system based on execution per time step, average latencies and communication overhead, or
4. to experiment with a dummy model on a real distributed computing system

To this end we have started with the first step, and have implemented a software suite for spatial partitioning (or clustering). Along with the core software package, three published algorithms and one new algorithm have been implemented which we have used for the first batch of partitioning experiments.

It is our intention to carry on with the first step with as many datasets as we can get hold of and to implement more algorithms in the future. We also intend to conduct experiments according to step 4. We are also investigating how to move the clustering into a cloud infrastructure in order to provide a dynamic and scalable clustering service.

It should be noted though that this study is carried out with groups of Masters students only, without any external funding sources and support.

3   Related Work

The literature base on partitioning of catchments is not large but very diverse, approaching the problem from different angles. A 2001 article by M. Grübsch and O. David [1] gives a good introduction into the problem, its computational complexity and graph properties which may be taken into account when developing partitioning algorithms. They also propose a heuristic algorithm as a solution. In [2], a generalised computational architecture is proposed which allocates computing nodes over a master-slave pattern using load balancing, which is a standard approach in distributed computing. In [3], a SWAT model is parallelized but it remains unclear how the subcatchments have been partitioned. In [4] the authors state that a more generalized approach based on well understood software patterns would help practitioners develop parallel simulation solutions. One commonality of published papers is that whatever is proposed, the examples included in published studies have been small sets of case studies. Our study intends to start a systematic investigation over large sets of cases, starting with the partitioning problem.

4   The Software Package

The software implementation uses a pluggable architecture. At the core is a class called `ClusteringSuite` which dynamically manages a clustering run (see fig. 1). It loads clustering algorithms and test criteria (algorithms computing some quality measure of the generated clusters).

A new clustering algorithm or a new test criterion respectively only has to implement a simple interface and will be dynamically loaded based on entries in a property file denoting the algorithms and test criteria to be used. The suite dynamically loads algorithms via a method called addAlgorithm() add test criteria via a method called addTestCriterion().

```
class ClusteringSuite {
    ...
    addAlgorithm() { load and add an algorithm }
    addTestCriterion() { load and add a test criterion }
    ...
    List<ExperimentBundle<String>> doCluster {
    for all samples
        for all algorithms
            call clustering algorithm for sample
                for all test criteria
                    calculate criterion
                save clustering result in json file
}
```

Fig. 1. Parts of the clustering suite interface

The current implementation provides the following test criteria as built-in elements:

- AverageSize — gives the average size of the clusters
- AboveAverageSize — counts how many clusters are above average
- BelowAverageSize — counts how many clusters are below average
- MedianSize — gives the median size of the clusters
- AverageWeight — gives the average weight of the clusters
- MedianWeight — gives the median weight of the clusters
- DeltaMedianAverageSize — gives the delta of average size and median size
- Correctness — determines whether the algorithm is correct at all

The package contains two different executable programs, one called `Clusterer` and one called `ExperimentController`. While the clusterer will cluster one set of samples given by the user (respectively passed to the program), the experiment controller will generate samples which cluster the same catchment into many different sizes. This is for automation of the clustering experiments.

5   The Experiment

5.1   The Catchment Dataset

For the first study we have used the ECRINS[1] dataset, which can be downloaded from the web site of the European Environment Agency[2]. The dataset contains amongst others

---

[1] http://www.eea.europa.eu/data-and-maps/data/
european-catchments-and-rivers-network
[2] http://www.eea.europa.eu/

a European-wide hydrological network with approximately 1.2 million river segments. The download section of the EEA site contains several datasets. In order to access the hydrological network data, the "EcrRiv" dataset is needed. The dataset is well documented in [5]. For the experiments we have chosen a variation of catchment size from 1500 nodes to nearly 1460000 nodes (see table 1). The *river id* is the column *river_id* in table *c_tr* of ECRINS and the *end node* is the draining node (column *nodid* in table *c_node* of ECRINS). This data was run against several algorithms.

Table 1. Catchments used in initial experiments

River	River id	End node	Nodes
Volga	Z_C0000603	Y000601274	146585
Danube	Z_C0000897	Y000828008	114318
Kama	Z_C0000605	Y000312116	64024
Dnieper	Z_C0000089	Y000728340	42962
Don	Z_C0000631	Y000640649	32398
Rhine	Z_C0000823	Y000617080	25270
Po	Z_C0000025	Y000962481	23074
Ural	Z_C0000588	Y000537580	21391
Ebro	Z_C0000053	Y001234399	15648
Douro	Z_C0000049	Y001129129	12459
Drave	Z_C0000933	Y000912526	11966
Loire	Z_C0000067	Y000774881	9815
Adige	Z_C0000088	Y000952540	7608
Isere	Z_C0000750	Y000956258	6954
Adda	Z_C0000020	Y000955093	3385
Moselle	Z_C0000899	Y000660011	3054
Neckar	Z_C0000896	Y000693135	1578

5.2 Clustering Algorithms Used

After literature research, 3 algorithms were chosen for the implementation of the first experiments. The choice of algorithms was not easy, as many proposed graph clustering algorithms cope with more general graphs, and the documentation is not always clear and detailed enough to use it as a blueprint for implementation. As a start, we decided to implement three algorithms: *K-Means* [6], *RNSC* [7] and *Spectral Clustering* [8]. During the course of the investigation, an idea lead to the implementation of a new algorithm called *Neighbourhood Clustering*. This algorithm was also used in the tests and may be published at a later stage after more experimentation.

5.3 Aims

If you want to distribute a catchment simulation over a distributed homogeneous computing infrastructure, it is desirable that all clusters have the same size. Then different computing nodes would not have to wait for each other when they are passing messages between clusters between time steps (or time periods) simulated. In reality this is never achievable with cluster size greater than 1 (one computing node per graph node), because the binary graphs representing real world catchments are highly unbalanced. Real results have clusterings in which clusters are not of equal size.

It was our goal to achieve clusterings where the maximum cluster size and the minimum cluster size do differ only *by a factor of 2 to 2.5*. The rationale behind this aim is that due to the asynchronous nature of operating systems, network communication, latencies and so forth the overall runtime behaviour of a distributed simulation is not predictable anyway, and this aim seemed reasonable, achievable and still practical for distributed simulation. In order to make the results more visible we define the *maximum spread* as that factor (*maximum spread := maxsize / minsize*), and the *spread curve* (figure 2) as a curve which shows the spread for all generated clusters, where the clusters are ordered by size from left to right.

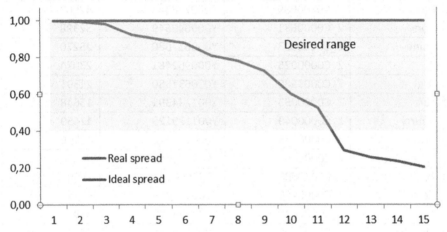

Fig. 2. Real vs. ideal spread curve (Neckar, 1500+ nodes, NH algorithm, 15 clusters)

5.4   Experiment Setup

In our initial experiments we ran all catchments against several algorithms where it was practical. Spectral clustering, for instance, was not used in all cases as it has considerable runtime requirements. Also clustering the largest catchments is a problem of run-time om standard machines. For each catchment in the experiment, the *desired cluster count* was chosen, starting with approximately 1/100 of the catchment size and iterating to approximately 1/10 of the catchment size with different step sizes, depending on the size of the catchment (for instance for river Neckar with 1578 nodes, an iteration was performed from desired cluster size 15 to 150, for each integer in between. These initial experiments were aimed at getting a first idea what might be achievable with the algorithms chosen.

6   Discussion

Our initial findings are that not all results are in the order of magnitude which we had hoped. Some clusterings have a very large variation in number of nodes. The best spreads are in the order of magnitude of 2.5, but particularly the very large catchments seem to be difficult to cluster evenly.

Some algorithms produce stray nodes, clusters of very small size – in some cases many of them. It is not clear yet whether those can be easily re-connected to other clusters (or to each other) in post-processing without unbalancing the quality of the solution again.

We have also not quality-checked the implemented algorithms over a large number of experiments, and a real problem is that there are no datasets in the literature to which we could compare our results to.

Also the choice of starting points influences the clustering, and some algorithms do have parameters which influence their behaviour. We have not yet done any variation over the automatically chosen starting points and over these parameters.

The computation time for the clusterings is another problem. It is just not practical to run many clustering runs over reasonable size clusters on standard machines, as some algorithms (particularly Spectral Clustering) just need too long to compute one clustering. Therefore particularly the large catchment have not been run over all variations of algorithms and cluster sizes which we had initially planned.

Therefore, in another project course in 2014/2015, we plan to extend our solution to a cloud infrastructure, in which we aim at running many more variations of experiments in order to find better solutions.

Acknowledgements. This experiment was carried out as part of a Master level project course in 2013/2014, with a group of 6 students, of which 2 agreed to co-author this paper. The resulting software was cleaned and refactored by the main author after the course had produced the first results. It is our intention to continue these investigations and we welcome collaboration with external partners.

References

1. Grübsch, M., David, O.: How to Divide a Catchment to Conquer Its Parallel Processing, an Efficient Algorithm for the Partitioning of Water Catchments. Mathematical and Computer Modelling 33, 723–731 (2001)
2. Wang, H., et al.: A common parallel computing framework for modeling hydrological processes of river basins. Parallel Computing 37, 302–315 (2011)
3. Yalew, S., et al.: Distributed computation of large scale SWAT models on the Grid. Environmental Modelling & Software 41, 223–230 (2013)
4. Denzer, R., Fitch, P., Athanasiadis, I.N., Ames, D.P.: Parallel simulation of environmental phenomena. International Congress on Environmental Modelling and Software 2014 (2014), http://www.iemss.org/sites/iemss2014/proceedings.php ISBN: 978-88-9035-744-2
5. EEA, EEA Catchments and Rivers Network System, ECRINSv1.1, EEA Technical report No 7/2012, European Environment Agency (2012) ISSN 1725-2237

6. Kanungo, T., Mount, D.M., Netanyahu, N.S., Piatko, C.D., Silverman, R., Wu, A.Y.: An efficient k-means clustering algorithm: Analysis and implementation. IEEE Trans. Pattern Analysis and MachineIntelligence 24, S. 881–S. 892 (2002), doi:10.1109/TPAMI.2002.1017616 (Abgerufen am April 24, 2009)
7. King, A.D.: Graph Clustering with Restricted Neighbourhood Search, Thesis (2004), http://citeseerx.ist.psu.edu/viewdoc/download?doi=10.1.1.129.2497&rep=rep1&type=pdf
8. Ng, A.Y., Jordan, M.I., Weiss, Y.: On spectral clustering: analysis and an algorithm, http://snap.stanford.edu/class/cs224w-readings/ng01spectralcluster.pdf

Understanding Connectivity between Groundwater Chemistry Data and Geological Stratigraphy via 3D Sub-surface Visualization and Analysis

Jane Hunter, Andre Gebers, Lucy Reading, and Sue Vink

The University of Queensland, Brisbane, Australia
{j.hunter,a.gebers,l.reading,s.vink}@uq.edu.au

Abstract. This paper describes the 3D Water Chemistry Atlas[1] - an open source, Web-based system that enables the three-dimensional (3D) sub-surface visualization of ground water monitoring data, overlaid on the local geological model. Following a review of existing technologies, the system adopts Cesium (an open source Web-based 3D mapping and visualization interface) together with a PostGreSQL/PostGIS database, for the technical architecture. In addition a range of the search, filtering, browse and analysis tools were developed that enable users to interactively explore the groundwater monitoring data and interpret it spatially and temporally relative to the local geological formations and aquifers via the Cesium interface. The result is an integrated 3D visualization system that enables environmental managers and regulators to assess groundwater conditions, identify inconsistencies in the data, manage impacts and risks and make more informed decisions about activities such as coal seam gas extraction, waste water extraction and re-use.

Keywords: 3D, sub-surface visualization, groundwater, chemistry, geological model.

1   Introduction

The Coal Seam Gas (CSG) industry is rapidly expanding within Australia but it faces concerns from governments and communities, worried about the environmental impact of coal seam gas exploration and production [1]. Consequently, extensive regulatory frameworks have been established by both the Commonwealth and the States to minimise risks and mitigate any adverse impacts of from CSG exploration and extraction [2,3,4]. For example, in Queensland, companies are required to undertake baseline assessments for water bores in areas where petroleum and gas production or testing is planned or underway. The Office of Groundwater Impact Assessment (OGIA), stores the baseline assessment information (which includes bore registration, aquifer, casing, stratigraphy, and water analysis records) in the Bore Baseline Assessment Database (BBAD) and uses it to produce groundwater impact report.

---

[1] http://3dwa.metadata.net/

R. Denzer et al. (Eds.): ISESS 2015, IFIP AICT 448, pp. 475–483, 2015.

In addition to OGIA's BBAD database, a number of other sources of groundwater and geological information provide complementary data for assessing the impact of CSG extraction on groundwater (e.g., the Groundwater Database (GWDB) maintained by the State Government and the Surat Super geological model developed by the University of Queensland [5,6]).

Stakeholders (including government, industry and research organizations) all agree that the rapid expansion of the Coal Seam Gas (CSG) industry in Queensland has led to growing demands for enhancements to groundwater data management services. These include the need for: improved data collation and integration across multiple organizations and monitoring programs; more rigorous and streamlined QA/QC procedures; and accessible easy-to-use tools for evaluating changes in groundwater chemistry due to analytical, environmental, human or geological factors.

2   Objectives

The 3D Water Chemistry Atlas project was established in 2013, through a collaboration between the University of Queensland's Centre for Coal Seam Gas (CCSG), Centre for Water In the Minerals Industry (CWIMI), School of Earth Sciences and the School of Information Technology and Electrical Engineering (ITEE). The aims of the 3D Water Atlas project are to tackle some of the gaps in groundwater data management in Queensland, as identified by stakeholders, by developing:

- A Web Portal to a unified, quality controlled database of groundwater chemistry data that is integrated with a reliable and consistent geological model, together with other freely available and relevant geospatial layers (e.g. satellite imagery, rad networks, property boundaries and mining lease boundaries).
- Streamlined QA/QC processes that automatically detect and filter erroneous data and help to guide future ground water monitoring practices.
- New visualization and analysis tools which take advantage of spatio-temporal overlay of water chemistry data and 3D geological data to enable regional interpretations of spatial and temporal water chemistry trends, by displaying outputs from multivariate statistical analyses and geochemical modelling.
- Interfaces that increase public access to water chemistry data whilst protecting commercially sensitive data.

3   Technical Architecture

One of the critical requirements for the system was that it should support 3D sub-surface visualization of geological and ground water data. Hence one of the first tasks was to assess existing platforms and to choose the optimum for this application. Although there are a plethora of "virtual globe" software systems available, they mostly support spatial information layers displayed above the earth's surface (street maps, digital elevation models, satellite imagery, etc.) i.e., they do not support 3-D subsurface data or strata visualisation. Five visualisation systems were identified that could potentially provide the visualisation capabilities required for the 3-D Water Chemistry Atlas:

- NASA World Wind [7] including Geoscience Australia's World Wind Suite [8] and EarthSci [9];
- Google Earth [10];
- ParaViewGeo [11];
- QUT's Groundwater Visualisation System (GVS) [12];
- Cesium [13];

To evaluate each of these systems, three sets of data were acquired (OGIA's Baseline Assessment data, the GWDB and GOCAD geological layers/models) and the relative ease and precision with which these datasets were ingested, searched, browsed and visualized was assessed. The criteria used for evaluating each system included: speed/efficiency; open source, free software; easy to install; cross-platform (Windows, Mac, Linux); intuitive user interface; support for common formats; visualisation richness; customisability; cross browser support (Chrome, Firefox, Internet Explorer).

Following an evaluation of the five visualization platforms above, the decision was made to use Cesium[2], "a JavaScript library for creating 3D globes and 2D maps in a web browser without a plugin". Because Cesium uses WebGL, it is cross-platform, cross-browser, and supports dynamic-data visualization enled by hardware-accelerated graphics. In addition, NICTA's "ground-push" plugin[3] was adopted to enable sub-surface excavation and visualization. Figure 1 provides a high-level view of the system's components:

- A PostGreSQL database with PostGIS indexing for storing the Groundwater and Baseline Assessment datasets and the CSG companies' borehole datasets;
- Cesium – the visualization platform that enables 3D sub-surface visualization of groundwater chemistry data and geological strata using "ground push" and runs on WebGL compatible browsers, including Chrome or Firefox.
- Geological Models, Map data and Digital Terrain models (acquired from the UQ School of Earth Sciences) that are loaded into Cesium on-the-fly.

4   QA/QC Process

It is critical to apply a rigorous QA/QC procedure to the geochemical data before producing geochemical plots and interpreting geochemical trends as this ensures that the data presented is of a consistent quality [14]. Incorrect data may be introduced due to errors in groundwater sampling methodologies and/or laboratory analysis methods. The QA/QC process applied to the data in the 3D Water Atlas, was based on a review of previous studies [15,16,17].

Some examples of specific QA/QC criteria that were applied to the geochemical data include: 1) removal of geochemical results that were produced through chemical analysis prior to 1950; 2) removal of geochemical results where the major ion "charge

---

[2] http://cesiumjs.org/
[3] https://github.com/NICTA/cesium-groundpush-plugin

balance error" is outside of the range of ± 5%. These criteria account for errors introduced by laboratory analyses. The first criteria relates to changes in analysis methods
over time [15], the second criteria relates to incomplete analyses and errors in analyses [16,17].

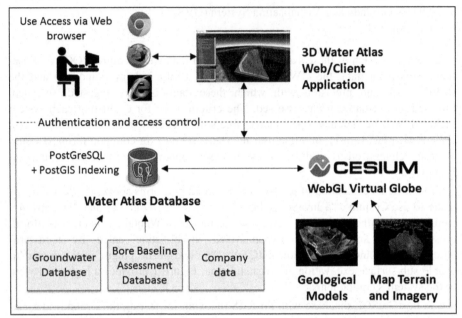

Fig. 1. High Level Architectural View of the 3D Water Chemistry Atlas

Automating the QA/QC steps saves time and hence reduces the time lag between
analysis of water quality samples and release of the geochemical data to regulators
(and ultimately to the general public). Automation also enables flexible implementation of QA/QC steps (e.g. user defined QC criteria) – allowing raw data to be displayed if it is of interest to specific users or enabling easy modification of QA/QC
criteria if thresholds change over time or location.

5   Search, Filtering, Analytical Services

Access to the 3D CSG Water Atlas Portal is via a secure login interface on the
project's Web site[4]. The user interface currently supports the following capabilities:

- Ability to overlay and visualize wells/bores and their water chemistry data overlaid on the 3D Geological (Gocad) Model and geological strata (Figure 2);
- Ability to search/filter and retrieve datasets based on specific spatial regions,
  well/bore numbers, time periods or company/organization bore data (Figure 3);
- A range of analytical services including:

---

[4] http://3dwa.metadata.net/?page=Portal

- o Groundwater analysis charts (e.g. Piper diagrams, Stiff diagrams, line charts and pie charts) (Figure 4);
- o Geological model cross-sections (Figure 5);
- o Comparison of formation assignments from different sources

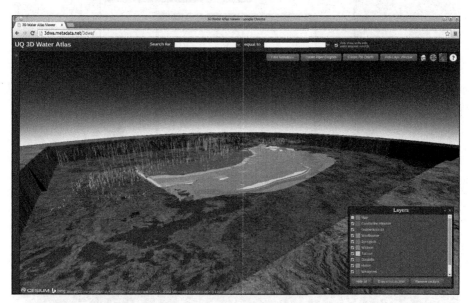

Fig. 2. Groundwater Monitoring Wells overlaid on the Surat Basin Supermodel

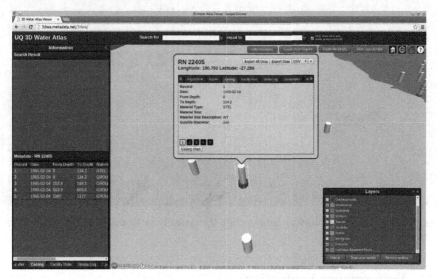

Fig. 3. Metadata and Data displayed for a single selected Well

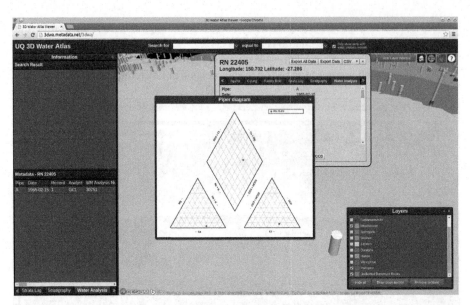

Fig. 4. Example of a Stiff Diagram generated for a particular well

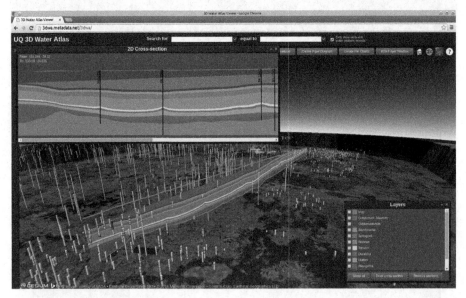

Fig. 5. Example of a geological cross-section dynamically generated from two user-defined endpoints

6   Performance Evaluation

To evaluate the system performance as the size of the geological model is scaled up, multiple copies of the Surat Basin geological model were rendered simultaneously within different locations/offsets in the 3D scene. The sizes of the compressed and uncompressed models are listed in Table 1 below.

Table 1. Sizes of the compressed and uncompressed geological models

Name	Compressed Size	Uncompressed Size	No. of Layers
Surat_gocad	18 Mb	48 Mb	11
Surat_gocad x 2	35 Mb	87 Mb	22
Surat_gocad x 3	53 Mb	131 Mb	33
Surat_gocad x 4	71 Mb	174 Mb	44

Caching of the model was disabled so that the model is reloaded each time and the benefits of caching won't impact on download and rendering speeds. For performance testing, the Google Chrome browser version 38 (which comes with simulated network throttling) was used. Tests conducted were with no throttling (on campus), 30mbps (wifi), 2mbps (dsl, residential broadband), and 750kbps (3G, mobile broadband).

Table 2. Time to download the model to the client (secs)

Connection Speed	SuraGocad	Gocadx2	Gocadx3	Gocadx4
AarNet	9	19	33	48
30 Mbps	9	20	33	48
2Mbps	72	144	216	282
750 Kbps	198	384	582	774

Table 3. Time for the 3D Water Atlas to become responsive to user input (secs)

Connection speed	No model (wells only)	SuratGocad	Gocadx2	Gocadx3	Gocadx4
AarNet	5	20	30	51	60
30 Mbps	6	22	42	64	70
2 Mbps	20	77	151	227	305
750 Kbps	60	208	410	604	792

Table 4. Comparison of Cesium's performance (frames per sec) on different clients

System	No model (wells only)	SuratGocad	Gocadx2	Gocadx3	Gocadx4
Dell Latitude E7740 Windows 64 bit	20-25 fps	8-10	5-6	4	2
Dell Optiplex 980 ubuntu 64 bit	11-12 fps	6	3-4	3	2

The evaluation results indicate that the 3D Water Atlas performance depends primarily on model size and network speed. If the model becomes 4 times larger than the current model, it would take about 1 minute on a high speed network before the 3D Water Atlas becomes responsive. On the Cesium performance side, the frame rate drops quite a bit on a 4 times larger model. On the largest model the frame rate dropped to 2 fps on both systems but the Water Atlas was still usable. The test hardware used were not the latest models and performance would improve on faster systems with better graphic cards. This is not a problem specific to Cesium but would be present with any 3D visualization systems. Further research is required to optimize performance as the model scales up to cover a larger region beyond just the Surat basin.

7   Feedback and Conclusions

Stakeholder feedback from both government agencies and CSG companies has provided valuable direction for future development, including: requests for: the ability to upload, overlay and compare different geological models; interactive selection of regions, time periods and formations to display geochemistry using standard tools (e.g. piper diagrams, stiff diagrams; pie charts, scatter plots); incorporation of new datasets including: property boundaries, mining lease boundaries, road networks; more sophisticated authentication and access control mechanisms to support restricted access to certain datasets, models, services; predictive models that enable users to choose different scenarios and to visualize modelled outcomes.

By combining the open source Cesium virtual globe platform with a common data model and PostgreSQL database, we have been able to quickly develop a rich 3D subsurface visualisation interface to an integrated knowledge-base that provides an effective communication tool for CSG stakeholders (industry, government and community groups), project partners and the general public. The availability of a common Web-based portal to multiple integrated datasets that have undergone rigorous QA/QC, will facilitate greater sharing and re-use of data and knowledge, encourage engagement between stakeholders and streamline interpretations of the monitoring data, ultimately improving our ability to assess the impact of human activities (CSG extraction, agriculture, coal mining) on ground water chemistry.

Acknowledgments. We would like to acknowledge funding from the Centre for Coal Seam Gas (CCSG), as well as the valuable contributions to the project from the other team members: Charles Brooking and Chih-hao Yu (School of ITEE), Joan Esterle (School of Earth Sciences), Alex Wolhuter and Jiajia Zheng (CWIMI) and Jim Underschultz (Sustainable Minerals Institute (SMI)).

References

1. NSW Government Chief Scientist and Engineer, Independent Review of Coal Seam Gas Activities in NSW. Managing environmental and human health risks from CSG activities (September 2014)
2. Australian Government, The Environmental Protection and Biodiversity Conservation Act 1999 (Cth) (EPBC) (1999)
3. Thompson, S., Loeliger, J.: Australia: Coal seam gas (CSG) – national regulatory update, Holding Redlich (2013), http://www.mondaq.com/australia/x/274750/

4. SCER. 2013. The National Harmonised Regulatory Framework for Natural Gas from Coal Seams 2013, Standing Council on Energy and Resources, Canberra (May 2013), http://scer.govspace.gov.au/files/2013/06/National-Harmonised-Regulatory-Framework-for-Natural-Gas-from-Coal-Seams.pdf

5. Tyson, S., Esterle, J., Shields, D., Reilly, M., McKillop, M., Roslin, A.: Geological modelling approach for the Eastern Surat Basin (Priority model area). Report to OGIA (2014)

6. Sliwa, R., Esterle, J.: Notes on lithostratgraphic correlation of the Eastern Surat basin model (Priority Area Model). Report to OGIA (2014)

7. NASA (2014), NASA World Wind Java SDK, http://worldwind.arc.nasa.gov/java/

8. Geoscience Australia, World Wind Suite (2014a), https://github.com/ga-m3dv/ga-worldwind-suite

9. Geoscience Australia. EarthSci (2014b), https://github.com/GeoscienceAustralia/earthsci

10. Google, Google Earth (2014), http://www.google.com/earth/

11. ParaViewGeo, Open Source Viusalization for Geoscience (2014), http://paraviewgeo.objectivity.ca/

12. Cox, M.E., James, A., Hawke, A., Raiber, M.: Groundwater Visualisation System (GVS): a software framework for integrated display and interrogation of conceptual hydrogeological models, data and time-series animation. Journal of Hydrology 491, 56–72 (2013)

13. Analytical Graphics, Inc. Cesium – WebGL Virtual Globe and Map Engine (2013), http://cesiumjs.org

14. Thyne, G., Guler, C., Poeter, E.: Sequential Analysis of Hydrochemical Data for Watershed Characterization. Ground Water 42, 711–723 (2004)

15. Grigorescu, M.: Jurassic groundwater hydrochemical types, Surat Basin, Queensland — a carbon geostorage perspective. Queensland Geological Record (2011)

16. Hodgkinson, J., Grigorescu, M.: Background research for selection of potential geostorage targets-case studies from the Surat Basin, Queensland. Australian Journal of Earth Sciences 60(1), 71–89 (2013)

17. Hitchon, B., Brulotte, M.: Culling criteria for "standard" formation water analyses. Applied Geochemistry 9, 637–645 (1994)

Distributed Minimum Temperature Prediction Using Mixtures of Gaussian Processes

Sergio Hernández[1] and Philip Sallis[2]

[1] Laboratorio de Procesamiento de Información Geoespacial,
Universidad Católica del Maule, Talca, Chile
[2] Geoinformatics Research Centre,
Auckland University of Technology, Auckland, New Zealand

Abstract. Minimum temperature predictions are required for agricultural producers in order to assess the magnitude of potential frost events. Several regression models can be used for the estimation problem at a single location but one common problem is the amount of required data for training, testing and validation. Nowadays, sensor networks can be used to gather environmental data from multiple locations. In order to alleviate the amount of data needed to model a single site, we can combine information from the different sources and then estimate the performance of the estimator using hold-out test sites. A mixture of Gaussian Processes (MGP) model is proposed for the distributed estimation problem and an efficient Hybrid Monte Carlo approach is also proposed for the estimation of the model parameters.

1 Introduction

Crop damages due to frost events is an important issue in many agricultural areas. There are several empirical models that attempt to predict or anticipate the occurrence of the minimum temperature at a given time and location. These methods deliver descriptive results, however calibration is required for the model parameters in order to account for the time of the year and the local conditions [13]. Artificial neural networks (ANN) models have been previously proposed as an alternative to the empirical methods for the estimation task [5]. For instance, ANN models were used to predict air temperature at hourly intervals from one to 12 hours ahead [12] using meteorological data such as temperature, relative humidity, solar radiation, wind speed and direction, as well as seasonal variables to account for the day of the year.

More recently, an ensemble of twelve ANN models was used to achieve temperature predictions throughout an entire year [11]. The ANN models were able to achieve low prediction error when using a large dataset for training consisting of 1.5 million records. To alleviate the issues related to the high dimensionality estimation problem, a support vector regression model was proposed for the prediction task using a reduced training set ($300,000$ records) [3].

In this paper we present a Bayesian framework for minimum temperature prediction using multiple sources of environmental data. A Mixture of Gaussian

R. Denzer et al. (Eds.): ISESS 2015, IFIP AICT 448, pp. 484–491, 2015.

Process (MGP) model is then proposed as an alternative to the ANN model for dealing with a reduced amount of data. The idea behind the MGP approach is to use local Gaussian Process regression models on different subsets of the input data and a gating network that is responsible of assigning input data points to one of the local experts [14].

The parameters of the MGP model includes a set of hyper-parameters for each Gaussian process model and the gating network. A Bayesian approach for estimating the model hyper-parameters from data is also presented [10]. Nevertheless, even for the reduced amount of data, the running time of the algorithm can be prohibitively slow. Therefore, we propose an efficient Hybrid Monte Carlo implementation in a shared memory machine that may overcome some of the estimation issues in high dimensional problems.

As a result, our framework is able to deal with deal with a large number of instances and deliver several predictions at test locations.

2   Gaussian Processes Regression

Regression problems deal with datasets in the form $\mathcal{D} = \{\mathbf{x}, y\}_{i=1}^{n}$, where $\mathbf{x}_i$ is an input vector and y_i is a continuous variable representing output data. In our case, the input data contains several environmental variables such as temperature, humidity and solar radiation measured at different times of the day (e.g. 18pm and 15pm) and the output data is the minimum temperature measured at any time of the following next day.

A Gaussian process regression model consists of a non-linear mapping between the input and the output data, such that:

$$y_i = f(\mathbf{x}_i) + \epsilon_i \tag{1}$$

where $\epsilon_i \sim \mathcal{N}(0, \sigma^2)$ represents a zero-mean noise term. More formally, a Gaussian process defines a prior over the function $f(\mathbf{x}) \sim GP(0, \kappa(\mathbf{x}, \mathbf{x}'))$ and $\mathbf{K}$ is a positive-definite kernel or covariance matrix with elements $[K_{ij}] = \kappa(\mathbf{x}_i, \mathbf{x}_j)$. Now, we can write the marginal distribution $p(y|\mathbf{x})$ as:

$$p(y|\mathbf{x}) = \int p(y|f, \mathbf{x})p(f|\mathbf{x})df \tag{2}$$

Integrating f in Equation 2 also leaves a normal distribution with covariance $\mathbf{K}_x = \mathbf{K} + \sigma^2\mathbf{I}$. If we now observe new data $\mathbf{x}_*$, we can write the predictive distribution as follows:

$$p(f_*|\mathbf{x}_*, \mathcal{D}) = \mathcal{N}(\mathbf{k}_*^T \mathbf{K}_x^{-1} y, k_{**} - \mathbf{k}_*^T \mathbf{K}_x^{-1} \mathbf{k}_*) \tag{3}$$

where $\mathbf{k}_*$ denotes the vector of covariances between the test point and the training data. Similarly, $\mathbf{k}_{**} = \kappa(\mathbf{x}_*, \mathbf{x}_*)$ is the covariance function of the test data.

2.1   Mixtures of Gaussian Processes

Wireless sensor networks make use of sensor nodes to collect environmental data from multiple locations [15,9]. Instead of having one single dataset, our interest is to gather data from different farming sites and perform centralized learning using a horizontally partitioned dataset $\mathcal{D} = \mathcal{D}_1 \cup \mathcal{D}_2 \ldots \cup \mathcal{D}_n$. Figure 1 depicts the data collection mechanism.

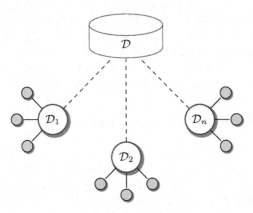

Fig. 1. Distributed environmental data from wireless sensor networks. Data is collected from multiples sites, each one having multiple sensor nodes. Every node reports the same information collected at different spots.

Compared to the cost of analyzing single datasets, the computational complexity of learning from a central dataset is increased [8]. This is specially problematic in Gaussian processes calculations that uses inversion of matrices and linear solvers that require approximation methods for large datasets [6]. One of such approaches is the Mixture of Gaussian Processes (MGP), that builds several regression or classification models on different subsets of the data. In this case, the complexity of performing large-scale training is reduced since each model can be trained independently and because of the centralized nature of the data collection mechanism, there is no requirement on the number of models to be trained.

In this case, we consider a set of models which are responsible of different groups of measurements $\mathcal{S} = \{S_1, \ldots, S_M\}$ [10]. A gating network parametrized by a discrete latent variable $\mathbf{z}$ is used to assign data points to any of the M local experts with prior probability π_m, such that $p(z_i = m) = \pi_m$. The MGP prior can be now written as follows:

$$f(\mathbf{x}) \sim \sum_i^M \pi_i \, GP(0, \kappa_i(\mathbf{x}, \mathbf{x}')) \tag{4}$$

3   Fast Inference for Mixtures of Gaussian Processes

The parameters of the MGP model include a set of hyper-parameters for each model $\Theta = (\theta_1, \ldots, \theta_M)$ and the gating network $\pi = (\pi_1, \ldots, \pi_M)$. In this paper we consider kernels based on the squared exponential function:

$$\kappa(\mathbf{x}_i, \mathbf{x}_j) = \sigma_f^2 \exp(-\frac{1}{2} \sum_d \nu_d^2 (x_{id} - x_{jd})^2) + \sigma_y^2 \delta_{ij} \tag{5}$$

where $\theta = (\sigma_f, \sigma_y, \nu_1, \ldots, \nu_D)$ and D being the dimensionality of the input vector $\mathbf{x}$. The posterior distribution of the model and the gating network parameters takes the form:

$$p(\Theta, \pi | \mathcal{D}) \propto p(\Theta, \pi) p(\mathcal{D} | \Theta, \pi) \tag{6}$$

Unlike Equation 3, in the MGP model we cannot compute the marginal posterior analytically. Instead, we could use the E-M algorithm to iteratively maximize the complete data log-likelihood $\log p(\mathcal{D} | \Theta, \pi)$ [16]. Instead, we sample from the marginal posterior distribution (see Equation 6) using a Hybrid Monte Carlo approach. The iterative procedure is given as follows:

1. Given the current kernel hyper-parameters Θ, sample the gating network parameters from the posterior distribution $p(z_i = m | \Theta, \mathcal{D})$
2. Sample π from a Dirichlet distribution $p(\pi_1, \ldots, \pi_M) \sim \mathrm{Dir}(\delta + c_1, \ldots, \delta + c_M)$, where δ is a concentration parameter and c_m is the number of times $z_i = m$ for all i.
3. Update Θ using hybrid Monte Carlo sampling.

Distributed Gibbs sampling for latent variable models were discussed in [1]. In this case, we can partition the dataset according to the expert assignments, such that a different processor performs computations on different data subsets S_m. GP computations require several linear algebra operations, however authors have noticed that good performance on multi-core machines can be achieved by using threaded BLAS libraries [7,2].

4   Experimental Results

4.1   Dataset

In this section we provide experimental results for the distributed minimum temperature prediction using the MGP approach. The data consists of agro-meteorological variables collected using Wireless Sensor Networks from 5 different locations in the region of Maule in south central Chile[1]. The data was sampled every 10 minutes but only the mean temperature, mean humidity and

---

[1] http://www.agrosense.cl

488 S. Hernández and P. Sallis

Table 1. Variables used for minimum temperature prediction and sensor nodes locations

x_1	Temp15	Mean Temperature at 15hrs
x_2	Hum15	Mean Humidity at 15hrs
x_3	Rad15	Mean Solar Radiation at 15hrs
x_4	Temp18	Mean Temperature 18hrs
x_5	Hum18	Mean Humidity 18hrs
x_6	Rad18	Mean Solar Radiation at 18hrs
y	*MinNext*	Next day minimum temperature

Lat	Lon	Site ID
-35.463882	-71.612818	donoso_1
-35.466391	-71.617502	donoso_2
-35.588004	-71.910842	gillmore_2
-35.857414	-71.602135	niceblue_1
-35.858761	-71.601540	niceblue_2
-35.858845	-71.601852	niceblue_3
-35.013470	-71.432918	canepa_1

mean solar radiation values at 15pm and 18pm were used to predict the minimum temperature for next the day. Table 1 describes the variables used in the predictive model. In order to create the training and test patterns, each node is used independently. Therefore, in the training data set we incorporate sensor nodes from different locations. Table 1 also shows the locations of the sensor nodes used in the training and test datasets.

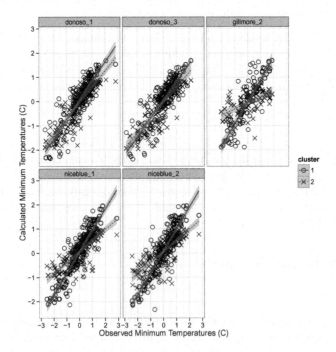

Fig. 2. Comparison between observed and calculated next day minimum temperatures at training locations

4.2   Model

The priors used for the gating network and the kernel hyper-parameters follow the settings suggested in [6,10]. In order to get the initial values of Θ, we partition the data using k-means and ran 100 iterations of Hybrid Monte Carlo with 10 leapfrog steps. The Hybrid Monte Carlo sampler was done in C + + and the data partitioning and parallel execution was performed in R. In order to ensure that valid random numbers were generated in parallel, the TNRG random number generator was used. This approach combines the flexibility of the R environment for data processing with the fast execution of C + + shared libraries [4].

A number of 1000 iterations and 3 leapfrog sets were used to train the MGP model. Figure 2 compares the predicted and observed minimum temperatures at the training sites.

As shown in Figure 2, each model produces different predictions. Figure 3 shows the predicted minimum temperatures at the test site. Figure 3 shows the predicted minimum temperatures at a single test site.

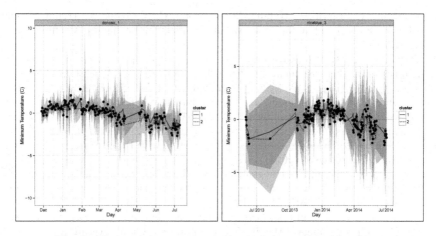

Fig. 3. Minimum temperatures at a training and test locations

Table 2 summarizes results using the Root Mean Square (RMS) error for the 3 test sites. It is important to notice that the ensemble RMS error is lower for all test locations.

Table 2. RMS values for the MGP model at test locations

Site ID	RMS Cluster 1	RMS Cluster 2	RMS Ensemble Mean
niceblue_3	0.4314506	0.4521971	0.3712023
canepa_1	0.5649653	0.6597936	0.5737617
canepa_2	0.7197888	0.6106701	0.5600180
canepa_3	0.5906937	0.6441202	0.5677543

5   Conclusions

In this paper we combine data from multiple and distributed sources and we are able to predict at previously unseen test locations. A mixture of Gaussian process model is introduced as a method to handle the distributed learning problem. The model has the appealing property of being able to handle multimodal regression or classification tasks. This is a new approach for distributed learning, since most methods used in the literature use locally trained models and then combine the output. In our case, we overcome the problem of having the same number of models and training locations by imposing the number of mixture components. However, this is also one of the limitations of this approach since we need to choose beforehand the number of components. Future work will involve automatic methods for model selection and model averaging procedures for the MGP model.

References

1. Asuncion, A., Smyth, P., Welling, M., Newman, D., Porteous, I., Triglia, S.: Distributed Gibbs sampling for latent variable models. In: Scaling up Machine Learning (2012)
2. Chandola, V., Vatsavai, R.R.: Implementing a gaussian process learning algorithm in mixed parallel environment. In: Proceedings of the Second Workshop on Scalable Algorithms for Large-Scale Systems, pp. 3–6. ACM, New York (2011)
3. Chevalier, R.F., Hoogenboom, G., McClendon, R.W., Paz, J.A.: Support vector regression with reduced training sets for air temperature prediction: a comparison with artificial neural networks. Neural Comput. Appl. 20(1), 151–159 (2011)
4. Eddelbuettel, D.: Seamless R and C++ Integration with Rcpp. Springer Publishing Company, Incorporated (2013)
5. Jain, A., McClendon, R., Hoogenboom, G., Ramyaa, R.: Prediction of frost for fruit protection using artificial neural networks. American Society of Agricultural Engineers, St. Joseph, MI, ASAE Paper pp. 03–3075 (2003)
6. Neal, R.: Regression and classification using Gaussian process priors. In: Bayesian Statistics 6: Proceedings of the Sixth Valencia International Meeting, vol. 6, p. 475 (1998)
7. Nguyen, T., Bonilla, E.: Fast allocation of gaussian process experts. In: Proceedings of The 31st International Conference on Machine Learning, pp. 145–153 (2014)
8. Peteiro-Barral, D., Guijarro-Berdiñas, B.: A survey of methods for distributed machine learning. Progress in Artificial Intelligence 2(1), 1–11 (2013)
9. Ruiz-Garcia, L., Lunadei, L., Barreiro, P., Robla, I.: A review of wireless sensor technologies and applications in agriculture and food industry: State of the art and current trends. Sensors 9(6), 4728–4750 (2009)
10. Shi, J.Q., Murray-Smith, R., Titterington, D.: Hierarchical gaussian process mixtures for regression. Statistics and Computing 15(1), 31–41 (2005)
11. Smith, B.A., Hoogenboom, G., McClendon, R.W.: Artificial neural networks for automated year-round temperature prediction. Computers and Electronics in Agriculture 68(1), 52–61 (2009)
12. Smith, B.A., McClendon, R.W., Hoogenboom, G.: Improving air temperature prediction with artificial neural networks. International Journal of Computational Intelligence 3(3), 179–186 (2006)

13. Snyder, R.L., de Melo-Abreu, J.: Frost forecasting and monitoring. Frost Protection: Fundamentals, Practice, and Economics 1, 91–112 (2005)
14. Tresp, V.: Mixtures of Gaussian processes. In: Advances in Neural Information Processing Systems, pp. 654–660 (2001)
15. Wang, N., Zhang, N., Wang, M.: Wireless sensors in agriculture and food industry–recent development and future perspective. Computers and Electronics in Agriculture 50(1), 1–14 (2006)
16. Yang, Y., Ma, J.: An efficient EM approach to parameter learning of the mixture of gaussian processes. In: Advances in Neural Networks–ISNN 2011, pp. 165–174. Springer (2011)

A Framework for Optimal Assessment of Planning Investments in Urban Water Systems

Rodolfo García-Flores[1], Magnus Moglia[2], and David Marlow[3]

[1]CSIRO Digital Productivity and Services Flagship, Clayton South, Australia
Rodolfo.Garcia-Flores@csiro.au
[2]CSIRO Land and Water Flagship, Highett, Australia
Magnus.Moglia@csiro.au
[3]Wiser Analysis, Keysborough, Australia
David.Marlow@wiseranalysis.com

Abstract. The functionality expected by governments and citizens from urban water management systems (UWMS) has evolved in time from delivering basic services to enabling complex issues such as healthy ecosystems, environmental sustainability, and economic growth. Alongside these changing expectations, the pressure on policy makers to fulfill disparate performance metrics with diminishing resources is increasing. In this paper, we introduce the Water Assets and Infrastructure Network Decision Support (WAND) framework for modelling and planning urban water systems with the aim of assisting medium to long-term investment decisions. The framework combines economic performance measures with liveabililty and sustainability, and uses optimisation as a crucial component. To demonstrate its feasibility, we present a prototype environmental software system built upon the principles of legibility, adherence to engineering conventions, and extensive unit testing. We use the prototype system to analyse a model of a hypothetical urban water system formed by two coupled water networks, one for freshwater and one for stormwater collection, and which handles six different commodities. Our results suggest to planners the optimal combination of planning investments while considering capacities, service levels and network operating conditions.

Keywords: urban water planning, infrastructure planning, decision making for water networks.

1   Introduction

The Water Services Association of Australia (WSAA, 2013) estimate that the urban water sector delivers services to over 20 million Australians in more than 9 million connected properties. It manages over AUD $120 billion in assets and between 2006-07 and 2011-12 capital expenditure was estimated at over $33 billion. Operational expenditure in 2011-12 was estimated at $7.2 billion. The urban water sector is a significant part of the Australian economy. More than that, urban water infrastructure represents a significant capital stock and future generations will inherit the cumulative impact of our ongoing investment decisions (Nolan, 2007; Marlow et al., 2010).

R. Denzer et al. (Eds.): ISESS 2015, IFIP AICT 448, pp. 492–502, 2015.
© IFIP International Federation for Information Processing 2015

The core urban water services involve the management of three water streams: water supply, sewage (and used water), and stormwater. Traditionally, each of these streams has been managed separately, but pressures on these systems have, however, grown over time and there is an increasing clash between the demand for and limits of water resources. This clash results in ecological, economic and cultural 'strains' (Vlachos and Braga, 2001), which have led various authors to suggest that the current model of water service provision is not sustainable, especially when considered in light of future uncertainties such as climate change and population growth (Ashley et al. 2003; Milly et al. 2008; Wong and Brown 2008).

From a practical perspective, innovations are being introduced into systems dominated by traditional centralised solutions to produce hybrid systems that combine decentralized green infrastructure systems, such as storm water harvesting, and traditional capital-intensive infrastructure. Balancing the costs, benefits and risks of both approaches requires enhanced capacity to predict the future and consider multiple tradeoffs. This to a large extent becomes an optimisation problem, which involves effective management of infrastructure assets. Further discussion of such management strategies is provided by Maheepala et al. (2010) or Marlow et al. (2013).

Regarding optimal design of water networks, Daganzo (2012) considered public infrastructure systems where the policy-making body chooses prices and system design by maximising society's welfare. This combined problem was decomposed into subproblems, and optimal operation was induced by structuring payments adequately. Bieupoude et al. (2012) used a geometric optimisation method known as "constructal" design to optimize water distribution network architectures subject to operational water quality constraints. Marinoni et al. (2011) developed a method based on mathematical programming to determine the impact of development on a waterway that receives treated water based on water quality criteria, and applied it to Greater Sydney Metropolitan Area.

There exist environmental software systems that inform investment in UWMS, including a small number of commercial products which inform optimal investments in urban water systems. However, none of these consider all the metrics simultaneously. Among the most widely used are PIONEER[1] (Lumbers et al., 2010), and WilCO[2] (Burns et al., 2012), which are suites of models built as environments for planning water infrastructure. Both WiLCO and PIONEER have been developed in the UK institutional and regulatory context in mind, though their parent companies claim that they can be extended to the requirements of other sectors. The modelling undertaken within WILCO and PIONEER focuses on water and wastewater assets, which are considered in isolation from each other, and trade-offs are thus analysed within each service area, but not across service areas. Furthermore, neither WiLCO nor PIONEER were designed to represent the urban water system as a whole, so they do not consider wastewater, drinking water and stormwater in an integrated manner.

In this paper, we introduce the Water Assets and Infrastructure Network Decision Support (WAND) framework, which has the aim of assisting medium- to long-term investment decisions, and relies on optimisation as a crucial component. The proof-of-concept solves a mathematical model of a hypothetical UWMS. Our results suggest to

---

[1] http://www.tynemarch.co.uk/products/pioneer/index.shtml,   accessed on February 28, 2014.

[2] http://www.seamsltd.com, accessed on February 28, 2014.

planners the optimal combination of investments, while considering capacities, service levels and operating conditions for sets of equipment and facilities.

2   The WAND Framework

The WAND framework (Figure 1) is based on the fact that baseline performance as reflected in the system of representative metrics (related to liveability, sustainability and productivity) will vary over time due to natural changes, including the impact of asset deterioration and other *natural* factors such as of climate change. Performance will also be influenced by *anthropogenic* factors such as changes in customer requirements/expectations, regulatory requirements, population growth or macro-economic development. The impact of these changes on system performance can only be countered by making investments in capital and non-capital interventions; informing these is the purpose of the *core engine* of WAND, which relies on optimisation to reduce the gap between actual and target performance. To feed the optimiser, information is required on the policies and strategies to implement and the effectiveness of the associated intervention options. The optimal investment decisions, selected from a *feasible option space*, alter the system as part of a feedback loop that operates at strategic, tactic and operational time scales. This helps form a self-similar model, in the sense that it is as representative to consider specific service areas as it is to consider the complete urban water system. In fact, in theory the framework could be expanded to include all urban systems at the three key decision scales and provide systemic insights into the impact of investments across a whole range of service provision areas.

The WAND prototype software system introduced in this paper implements the tasks of the core engine, and its purpose is to assess the tradeoffs on livability, sustainability and productivity associated with different portfolios of investment within a single framework. The prototype handles investments by distinguishing between asset operation, replacement, maintenance and construction.

To illustrate the purpose of the WAND environmental software system, we address on the problem of *urban water runoffs*. As cities grow the landscape changes and there is an increase in the area of land that is covered by impervious surfaces. This means that, when rain falls on the city, much of the water that would otherwise have penetrated into the soil now gathers as urban runoff. This changes the flow patterns in rivers and creeks, with further impacts on ecosystems and erosion of river banks, as well as increasing the risk of urban flooding with consequent societal costs. Furthermore, the runoff in cities goes directly to receiving waters without treatment (Burns et al., 2012), becoming a significant source of pollution. WAND addresses runoffs by assisting investment decisions in:

- Capture and use of stormwater; i.e. stormwater or rainwater harvesting (Sharma et al., 2009). This includes the treatment of urban runoff as per local regulations.
- Water Sensitive Urban Design features (Wong, 2006), which are helpful in order to achieve a more natural water cycle and provide additional treatment of urban runoff, such as stormwater bioretention systems and constructed wetlands. These are also known as *green infrastructure*.

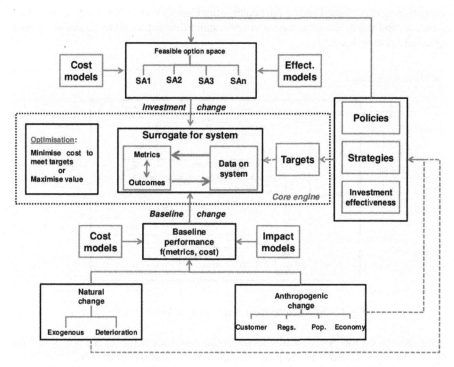

Fig. 1. The Water Assets and Infrastructure Network Decision Support (WAND) framework

3   Computational System

The optimiser in the WAND framework was implemented in Clojure[3] 1.5 and CPLEX[4] 12.4 with an Excel interface, as the UML 2 component diagram (Jacobson et al., 1999) in Figure 2 shows. Clojure is a compiled dynamic programming language of the LISP family built for the Java Virtual Machine (JVM) that has features that make it an attractive alternative to code the solution of problems that depend crucially on a correct mathematical representation. First, it has all the flexibility and power of LISP, but without the burden of backward compatibility with historical versions (Halloway, 2009). Second, it connects seamlessly to the mainstream infrastructure provided by Java by embracing the JVM. It does not attempt to build wrappers around Java, but tries to access it idiomatically, enabling the programmer to leverage on his past programming experience and on the huge amount of legacy code available for Java. Additional advantages include good concurrency support, a small core, laziness and conditions for error handling. Our WAND implementation makes extensive use of the symbolic features of LISP, for example for indexing of variables, making the order of the indexes irrelevant. This is extremely useful because the client's expert

---

[3] http://clojure.org/, accessed on the 8 of April of 2013.

4 http://www-01.ibm.com/software/integration/optimization/cplex-optimizer/, accessed on the 8 of April 2013.

knowledge is often based in the particular situations of individual water management resources, and using names is easier to understand than referring to elements by looking up tables of indexes.

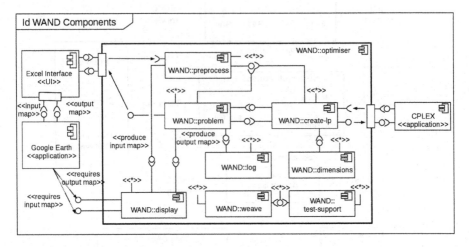

Fig. 2. UML 2 component diagram of the WAND optimiser

We developed the system with *clarity* as the core requirement. We aimed at keeping the problem as close to its mathematical representation as possible. To achieve this goal, we incorporated the following development principles:

1. *Literate approach.* When coded in literate style, a program should explain a problem and its solution to a human reader because its concepts have been introduced in an order that is best for human understanding (Knuth, 1984). This implies that software writing has more to do with the craft of writing, including its gradual process of improvement and refinement of ideas, than with merely laying down instructions for a machine to perform. The project was designed with namespace WAND::weave to process the documentation by *weaving* as introduced by Knuth (1984). All documentation in Clojure is stored as metadata, which in our system is retrieved by the functions in this namespace and "woven" (i.e., formatted) into L^AT_EX source. The documentation in the woven document is divided in sections, each of which corresponds to a namespace in the optimiser. Each section includes a description of the namespace's functions and variables. L^AT_EX enables the inclusion of formulas or typesetting commands as part of the documentation.

2. *Unit test design.* Unit testing takes advantage of the structure that Clojure gives to metadata. The :test field of the metadata enables the storage of a test function as part of a variable. By retrieving the names of all functions (i.e., data members that have argument lists) in a namespace, it is possible to generate lists of functions to be tested automatically, greatly facilitating unit testing. An extensive and automated unit testing namespace was implemented in WAND::test-support.

3. *Dimensional analysis.* In our experience, the lack of support for dimensional analysis has been the source of multiple problems in the past. We decided to take advantage of existing code from the JScience[5] library. Re-using Java code is encouraged in languages developed for the Java Virtual Machine, and is a particularly simple task in Clojure. Because dimensional analysis is one of the most basic engineering tools, the selected framework should be easy to reuse (namespace WAND::dimensions).

Namespace WAND::preprocess translates Excel input data into a data structure that can be handled by the optimiser. This is used by WAND::problem to produce the mathematical formulation, using the support functions stored in WAND::create-lp. Namespaces WAND::log and WAND::display keep a log of calculation progress and format the input and output data as KML maps, respectively. For the external components, the Excel interface captures input data regarding existing and proposed infrastructure, demand, intake levels and capacities, and retrieves the results in spreadsheet format. It also has the capacity to display input and solutions as maps in KML format, by invoking Google Earth[6]. CPLEX is a commercial solver for mixed integer linear programming problems.

Although there is great variety of tools available for development of environmental software systems (Argent and Houghton, 2001), we tried to keep the number of tools to a minimum to enhance clarity. The structure of the WAND optimiser in Figure 1 is the product of assimilating previous and successful experiences in coding similar optimisation problems (Higgins et al.; 2013, García-Flores et al., 2014) using the above-mentioned coding principles. The main advantages we perceive from the approach to software development adopted for WAND include shorter length of source code, legibility, reliability and facility to produce documentation. Most importantly, because the code is close to the notation of the mathematical formulation, we also expect WAND's optimisation module to be refined further and reused in future projects.

4   Example – Melbourne Urban Water System

This example illustrates the implementation of the framework to the Melbourne water system (Figure 3), which consists of two coupled water distribution networks.

- The *fresh water network*, which also incorporates wastewater streams, is shown in solid arrows and transports fresh water (that is, water for indoor and outdoor use) from reservoirs (sources marked with s_f in Figure 3) to the clients in Melbourne's suburbs (marked r). After use, the waste water collected is sent to treatment plants, marked u_f, and part of it is used again, (this is shown as double arrows to indicate separate pipelines) and part is disposed of in Port Philip Bay (shown as a gray block arrow). The "return" direction of the double arrows represents what is known as "purple pipes", which is a separate network of limited reach. Most areas do not have purple pipes going to them.

---

[5] http://jscience.org/, accessed on the 30 of October 2014.
[6] https://www.google.com/earth/, accessed on the 30 of October 2014.

- The *stormwater collection network*, shown in dashed arrows, collects rain water in catchments s_m in different points in the city. After some treatment in sites marked as u_m (wetlands, for example), part of it is used, depending on the setup, as indoor or outdoor water (or indoor only or outdoor only), and part of it ends in Port Philip Bay.

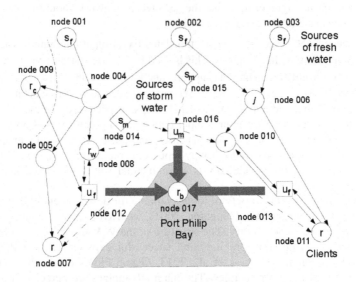

Fig. 3. The Greater Melbourne Water System

One of the objectives of the treatment facilites u_f and u_m is to reduce the amount of nutrients thrown into the bay. Irrigation areas can be considered sinks, and green infrastructure is modelled as a subset of treatment facilities u_m, which comprise wetlands, vegetated swales and biofiltration. The success of these facilities depends on their ability to store, retain or detain spill-overs, which means that they should also be modelled as reservoirs. Green infrastructure has a positive impact on stormwater flows in different areas. In the model, sewer overflows need to be penalised, whereas stormwater overflows need to be managed.

The WAND model considers six commodities and their transformations:

- *Indoor water* is mostly potable water, but some of the indoor water use may be covered by non-potable sources, i.e., not treated to class A standard.
- *Outdoor water* is mostly irrigation water. It travels from treatment facilities u_m to clients r, and from treatment plants u_f back to clients r, in both cases to be used as outdoor water. In the path from u_f to r, outdoor water is really treated waste water. The final destination of outdoor water is the client nodes.
- *Fresh water* is an aggregate of indoor and outdoor water. It travels from sources of fresh water s_f to households r. At the households, the water becomes indoor or outdoor, depending on its use.
- *Stormwater* is sent from stormwater catchments s_m to treatment facilities u_m. Stormwater can only be used for outdoor purposes.

- *Waste water* is sent from clients r to water treatment plants u_f.
- *Discharge water* is the water returned to the environment into the bay r_b.

The problem is formulated as a multi-period mixed-integer linear program whose aim is finding the optimal topology and capacities of pipelines connecting the nodes of the water network. This is done by minimising the total costs (i.e., the *objective function*), expressed as the sum of operation costs (including spillage costs and the costs of exceeding the control limits of sites that act as reservoir), replacement, maintenance and construction costs of all infrastructure assets.

Along the time horizon, the solution of the problem provides information about facility and pipeline segment replacement, upgrade and new construction. The constraints of the problem describe the conservation of flow at facilities and the conversion between water commodities. Some of the facilities are modeled as reservoirs, such as the waste water treatment facilities and green infrastructure (e.g., wetlands). These facilities need constraints with an upper capacity limit, which, if violated, (that is, if the facility overflows) are penalized in the objective function. Sources and stormwater catchments are facilities that provide an influx of fresh and stormwater, respectively, into the system, based on experts' forecasts and which also act as reservoirs, but are not penalised for spillage.

5   Results and Discussion

The planning horizon considered was from 2014 to 2019, in annual periods, and the tested scenarios were:

1. The creation of a new suburb in 2017 in node 009 with the consequent increase in fresh water demand, together with a linear increase in demand of node 011 from 481 ML of indoor use water per year in 2014 to 1000 ML in 2019 in node 011. All pipeline segments start with a diameter of 150 mm, except for the segments connecting the network to node 009, which do not exist at the beginning of the time horizon.
2. A "business as usual" scenario where no new suburb is projected and no increase in demand for node 011 is foreseen.

The demands of the clients to test in the scenario are shown in Table 1; the assumed available technologies and their capacities, which represent the investment options, are listed in Table 2. The calculation parameters are listed in Table 3.

Table 1. Demands of clients in the Greater Melbourne case study in ML/year

Node (clients)	Indoor water demand	Outdoor water demand
Node 007	1326.151	241.092
Node 008	648.180	90.411
Node 009	165.758 (after 2017)	23.121 (after 2017)
Node 010	117.47	16.385
Node 011	481.356 (increasing to 1000 by 2019)	67.142

Table 2. Available technologies to install in nodes and pipeline segments

Infrastructure type	Available technologies
Nodes	Site 200 ML, Site 500 ML, Site 1000 ML, Site 1500 ML.
Pipeline segments	Pipe 150 mm, Pipe 250 mm, Pipe 350 mm

Table 3. Penalisation parameters to enforce supply and operational levels in reservoirs

Penalty for failing to deliver indoor water	Penalty for failing to deliver outdoor water	Penalty for violating control limit in storm-water collection point	Penalty for overflow-ing stormwater collec-tion point
$10.0M /ML	$10.0M /ML	AUD $1000 /ML	AUD $0.1M /ML

We obtained all the following results in a 64-bit Intel Xeon CPU with 2 processors of eight cores (2.27 GHz) each and 48 GB of RAM. The linear program problem has 22,542 real variables, of which 14,880 are binary and 7,762 are real, and 50,421 constraints. A typical run takes around two hours and forty minutes to complete. Tables 4 and 5 show the suggested investments under scenario 1. These are, first, the construction of a fresh water pipeline and on-site infrastructure for node 009 to fulfill the new demand, as expected. Second, the increase in capacity of the pipelines connected to the waste water treatment plant in node 012. These also occur under scenario 2, as the initial pipe diameter assumed for the flows to node 012 is insufficient. Third, we can see the increase in capacity of the pipelines that connect node 011 to node 013, due to the increase in demand in node 011. Finally, we note in Table 5 that the optimiser suggests a "downgrade" of the fresh water source in node 002. This is probably not an action that a policy maker would take, but in this case we obtain this result because the cost of downgrading is not high enough. The decision maker can easily change the value of this parameter. Finally, scenario 2 turns out to be 11.3% more costly than "business as usual".

Table 4. Results for the upgrade and construction of new pipeline infrastructure

Origin node	Destination node	Commodity	Year	Old infrastruc-ture (mm)	New infra-structure (mm)
012	007	Fresh water	2015	150	350
012	008	Fresh water	2015	150	350
013	011	Fresh water	2015	150	350
007	012	Waste water	2015	150	350
008	012	Waste water	2015	150	350
011	013	Waste water	2015	150	350
004	009	Fresh water	2017	None	350

Table 5. Results for the upgrade and construction of new node infrastructure

Node	Node type	Commodity	Year	Old infrastructure (ML)	New infrastruc-ture (ML)
002	Source	Fresh water	2016	1500	500
002	Source	Fresh water	2017	500	200
004	Junction	Fresh water	2017	None	200
009	Client	Fresh water	2016	None	200

6   Summary, Conclusions and Future Applications

The expectations from urban water management systems have grown to include not only the provision of basic services, but also enabling healthy ecosystems, environmental sustainability, and economic growth. To achieve these goals, we have introduced the Water Assets and Infrastructure Network Decision Support framework. WAND uses optimisation and is built using the principles of legibility, adherence to engineering conventions, and extensive unit testing. To demonstrate its feasibility, we applied a prototype software system to a model of an urban water network that handles six different water commodities. The results suggest to planners the optimal combination of planning investments, while considering capacities, service levels and network operating conditions.

The main advantages we perceive from using standard engineering conventions (such as dimensional analysis) and the coding principles of literate programming and unit test design are, first, a shorter length of source code when compared to similar C++ developments; second, it is easier to produce documentation; and third, increased legibility and reliability. The main strength of the WAND optimiser is that it attempts to keep source code as close to the mathematical representation of the problem as possible by taking advantage of LISP's flexibility. This facilitates debugging and enables new members of the development team to "hit the ground running". On the downside, the disadvantages of our approach are the slow execution times when compared to C++ code and the unavoidable learning curve if the analyst is not familiar with LISP syntax. Nevertheless, we expect WAND's optimisation module to continue being refined and reused in future projects, although concepts such as deterioration are yet to be incorporated.

References

1. Argent, R.M., Houghton, B.: Land and water resources model integra-tion: software engineering and beyond. Advances in Environmental Research 5, 359–359 (2001)
2. Ashley, R.M., Blackwood, D.J., Butler, D., Davies, J.A., Jowitt, P., Smith, H.: Sustainable decision making for the UK water industry. Engineering Sustainability 156(ES1), 41–49 (2003)
3. Bieupoude, P., Azoumah, Y., Neveu, P.: Optimization of drinking water distribution networks: Computer-based methods and constructal design. Computers, Environment and Urban Systems 36(5), 434–444 (2012)
4. Burns, M.J., Fletcher, T.D., Walsh, C.J., Ladson, A.R., Hatt, B.E.: Hydrologic shortcomings of conventional urban stormwater management and opportunities for reform. Landscape and Urban Planning 105(3), 230–240 (2012)
5. Daganzo, C.: On the design of public infrastructure systems with elastic demand. Transportation Research Part B: Methodological 46(9), 1288–1293 (2012)
6. García-Flores, R., Higgins, A., Prestwidge, D., McFallan, S.: Optimal location of spelling yards for the northern Australian beef supply chain. Computers and Electronics in Agriculture 102, 134–145 (2014)
7. Halloway, S.: Programming Clojure. The Pragmatic Programmers (2009)

 8. Higgins, A., Watson, I., Chilcott, I., Zhou, M., García-Flores, R., Eady, S., McFallan, S., Prestwidge, D., Laredo, L.: A framework for optimizing capital investment and operations in livestock logistics. Rangeland Journal 35, 181–191 (2013)
 9. Rumbaugh, J., Jacobsen, I., Booch, G.: The Unified Software Development Process. Addison Wesley (1999)
10. Knuth, D.E.: Literate programming. The Computer Journal 27(2), 97–111 (1984)
11. Lumbers, J., Conway, T., Fynn, T., Heywood, G.: Optimal asset management planning: advances in water mains and sewers analysis within a new modelling environment. Water Asset Management International 6, 10–13 (2010)
12. Maheepala, S., Blackmore, J., Diaper, C., Moglia, M., Sharma, A., Kenway, S.: Integrated Urban Water Management Planning Manual. Denver, CO, Water Research Foundation (2010)
13. Marinoni, O., Higgins, A., Coad, P., Navarro, J., McPherson, R.: Directing urban development to the right places: Assessing the impact of urban development in an estuarine environment. In: Chan, F., Marinova, D., Anderssen, R. (eds.) MODSIM2011 19th International Congress on Modelling and Simulation, pp. 1902–1908. Modelling and Simulation Society of Australia and New Zealand (2011)
14. Marlow, D.R., Beale, D.J., Burn, S.: A pathway to a more sustainable water sector: sustainability-based asset management. Water Science & Technology 61(5), 1245–1255 (2010)
15. Marlow, D.R., Moglia, M., Cook, S., Beale, D.J.: Towards sustainable urban water management: A critical reassessment. Water Research 47(20), 7150–7161 (2013)
16. Milly, P.C.D., Betancourt, J., Falkenmark, M., Hirsch, R.M., Kundzewicz, Z.W., Lettenmaier, D.P., Stouffer, R.J.: Climate change: Stationarity is dead: Whither water management? Science 319, 573–574 (2008)
17. Mitchell, V.G.: Applying Integrated Urban Water Management Concepts: A Review of Australian Experience. Journal of Environmental Management 37(5), 589–605 (2006)
18. Nolan, B.: Funding Water and Wastewater Projects: Growing Communities Seek Strategic Alternatives. American Water Works Association Journal 99(5), 42–42 (2007)
19. Sharma, A.K., Grant, A.L., Grant, T., Pamminger, F., Opray, L.: Environmental and Economic Assessment of Urban Water Services for a Greenfield Development. Environmental Engineering Science 26(5), 921–934 (2009)
20. Maksimovic, C., Tejada-Guibert, J.A.: Frontiers in urban water management, deadlock or hope. In: Vlachos, P.E., Braga, P.B. (eds.) Chapter 1: The challenge of urban water management, pp. 1–34. IWA Publishing, London (2001)
21. Walsh, C.J., Fletcher, T.D., Ladson, A.R.: Stream Restoration in Urban Catchments through Redesigning Stormwater Systems: Looking to the Catchment to Save the Stream. Journal of the North American Benthological Society 24(3), 690–705 (2005)
22. Wong, T., Brown, R.: Transitioning to Water Sensitive Cities: Ensuring Resilience through a new Hydro-Social Contract. In: 11th International Conference on Urban Drainage, Edinburgh, Scotland, UK, vol. 10 (2008)
23. Wong, T.H.F.: An Overview of Water Sensitive Urban Design Practices in Australia. Water Practice & Technology 1(1) (2006)
24. WSAA, The future of the urban water industry. Submission to the National Water Commission's Triennial Assessment (2013)

Measuring and Benchmarking Corporate Environmental Performance

Marie Pavláková Dočekalová, Alena Kocmanová, and Jana Hornungová

University of Technology, Faculty of Business and Management, Brno, Czech Republic
{docekalova,kocmanova,hornungova}@fbm.vutbr.cz

Abstract. Corporate environmental performance is discussed in this paper. The aim of the paper is to propose a framework for an environmental performance benchmarking model. Corporate environmental performance is measured by key performance indicators (KPIs): Emissions of Greenhouse Gases, Water Consumption, Waste Production and Gross Value Added. Performance is benchmarked against the production frontier estimated by Data Envelopment Analysis. The environmental performance benchmarking model was created and tested on real corporate data. The model determines relative corporate environmental performance, identifies weaknesses in performance and quantifies performance gaps.

Keywords: corporate environmental performance, benchmarking, data envelopment analysis.

1 Introduction

Reporting corporate environmental performance is now commonplace among large enterprises. Twenty years ago, it was performed by just a few pioneers, and in the Czech Republic, for example, it can be said with little exaggeration that no companies informed their stakeholders about their environmental performance. In April 2014, the European Parliament adopted a directive that introduces the obligation that companies with more than 500 employees report on their social responsibility and, therefore, the impact of their business activities on the environment. Corporate environmental performance directly affects many corporate stakeholders – employees, consumers, the community, government bodies, etc. These stakeholders create a demand for clear and relevant information to support their decision-making. Traditional performance evaluation systems do not reflect the requirements of corporate stakeholders. The aim of this paper is to integrate the measuring of corporate environmental performance into performance measurement systems by proposing a framework for an environmental performance benchmarking model.

2 A Theoretical Approach to Environmental Performance

Corporate environmental performance is defined as the impact of the company on the environment. A company's influence on the environment is assessed in terms of

R. Denzer et al. (Eds.): ISESS 2015, IFIP AICT 448, pp. 503–511, 2015.

harmful activities affecting the environment [1]. ISO 14031 defines environmental performance evaluation as a "process to facilitate management decisions regarding an organization's environmental performance by selecting indicators, collecting and analyzing data, assessing information about environmental performance, reporting and communicating, and periodically reviewing and improving this process" [2].

There has been a great debate about the relationship between corporate environmental performance and economic performance. Both positive and negative statements can be found in scientific publications. The authors in [3] concluded that environmental and economic corporate performance are positively linked and that industry growth moderates the relationship, with the returns in environmental performance being higher in high-growth industries. The authors in [4, 5, 6] state that economic benefits are attained by the use of brands and advertisements providing information about the sustainability of products, thereby supporting product differentiation. On the other hand, a meta-analysis focusing on 37 empirical studies examining the relationship between environmental and economic performance shows that the results remain ambiguous despite three decades of theoretical and empirical research [7].

2.1   Environmental Benchmarking

Benchmarking represents a way of finding quality and achieving success on the basis of organic growth. The approach taken by companies to environmental benchmarking is influenced by the regulatory context, company strategy, product type, corporate and national culture, resource costs and stakeholder demands [8]. According to [8], environmental benchmarking can be split into four categories: regulatory, gross emissions, efficiency and life cycle.

The principle of benchmarking is included in the ISO 14000 standards relating to environmental management. The process of implementing environmental benchmarking based on the ISO 14001 EMS standard is described in, for example, [9]. Corporate environmental performance is benchmarked against:

- the organization's environmental policy,
- environmental objectives,
- environmental targets, or
- other environmental performance requirements [10].

The Best Available Techniques (BAT) can also be used as a benchmark for environmental benchmarking [11]. At the EU level, BAT for selected industrial and agricultural activities are defined and quantified in Best Available Techniques Reference Documents (BREF).

The use of the following factors is an extremely common approach in setting benchmarks:

- the average value in an industry,
- the best-performing company in an industry,
- the value of the previous period.

Performance can also be measured against the production frontier. Data Envelopment Analysis (DEA) and Stochastic Frontier Analysis (SFA) are methods that can be used for the purposes of estimating the production frontier. SFA has been defined by the authors [12, 13]. SFA is based on the estimation of a stochastic frontier production function by econometric methods. DEA has been defined by the authors [14] and is based on the estimation of a production function by techniques of linear programming. The DEA method was used for performance evaluation and benchmarking by, for example, [15, 16].

3 Methodology

An environmental performance benchmarking model was created and tested on real corporate data. The given data was taken from large Czech manufacturing companies for the year 2012. This industry was chosen because manufacturing companies exert a significant impact on the environment. The sample is described in Table 1.

Table 1. Research sample(N – number of companies, % - percentage in the sample)

Criterion	N	%
Number of employees		
250-500	10	55.5
501-1000	3	16.7
1001-2000	2	11.1
above 2000	3	16.7
Sector (as consistent with CZ-NACE)		
20. Manufacture of chemicals and chemical products	3	16.7
24. Manufacture of basic metals	3	16.7
25. Manufacture of fabricated metal products	7	38.9
27. Manufacture of electrical equipment	2	11.1
28. Manufacture of machinery and equipment n.e.c.	3	16.7
Legal form		
Joint-stock company	11	61.1
Limited company	7	38.9

The first step in creating a corporate performance measurement system is identifying relevant key performance indicators (KPIs). Environmental KPIs are often non-financial metrics. Mathematical and statistical methods were used to determine the environmental performance indicators. For a detailed description of the construction of environmental KPIs see [17, 18, 19].

Originally, the set of environmental KPIs consisted of seven variables: *Environmental Non-investment Costs, Air Emissions, Emissions of Greenhouse Gases, Energy Consumption, Water Consumption, Waste Production* and *Hazardous Waste Production*.

The first step in data processing was a quality check carried out in order to find out whether there were any erroneous or missing data. The following statistic measures were computed in order to obtain a basic knowledge of performance indicators: mean, range, standard deviation and variance. A correlation analysis was performed in order to understand the relationship between the variables. High values of pair correlation coefficients, i.e. |r| > 0.8, suggest multicollinearity. The variance inflation factor (VIF) was also used to detect multicollinearity. The VIF can be detected from an inversion matrix of the correlation matrix. Redundant KPIs were removed from the model. The reduced set of environmental KPIs then contained: *Emissions of Greenhouse Gases, Water Consumption* and *Waste Production*.

In this paper corporate performance is benchmarked against the production frontier – efficient frontier, which is constructed by efficient companies. The production frontier is estimated by Data Envelopment Analysis (DEA). The DEA method potential consists of identifying the best practice in the industry. The DEA model is based on assessing the quantity of consumed inputs by the produced outputs and estimation of the production possibility frontier. Three environmental KPIs (*Emissions of Greenhouse Gases, Water Consumption* and *Waste Production*) are considered as inputs. The goal of every business is to minimize values of these KPIs. *Gross Value Added* (GVA) is considered an output. GVA is the difference between the total production of goods and services and consumption (the value of goods and services consumed in production) – this approach is taken from the Eco Management and Audit Scheme (EMAS III). An input-oriented model with constant returns to scale (CCR model) is computed. The mathematical background of the model is described in [14].

The mathematical model of the primary input-oriented CCR model:

$$\max z = \sum_i^r u_i y_{iq},$$ (1)

on conditions: $\sum_i^r u_i y_{iq} \leq \sum_j^m v_j x_{jk}, \ \sum_j^m v_j x_{jq} = 1, \ u_i \geq \varepsilon, \ v_j \geq \varepsilon.$ (2)

Where z is the coefficient of the technical efficiency of a company C_q. u_i and v_j are individual weights assigned so as to maximize efficiency and ε is an infinitesimal constant that ensures that all weights of inputs and outputs are positive.

The professional optimization program Frontier Analyst from the company Banxia Software, which is very user friendly, was used for the model. The simplest method from the viewpoint of demands on software is the computation of DEA models with the use of MS Excel or using programmed applications such as DEA-Excel by Professor Jablonský and DEA Excel Solver by Professor Zhu. The specialized optimization software Lingo developed by the company Lindo Systems uses a special modelling language for notation. The model can also be imported into the program in MPS format. MPL for Windows from the company Maximal Software is an open optimization system.

4   Results and Discussion

Figure 1 shows an environmental performance measurement system based on a benchmarking model. An environmental performance measurement system must be part of a corporate performance measurement system. In order to provide the whole picture about corporate performance, the corporate performance measurement system must also consider the social dimension in addition to the environmental and eco-nomic dimension. A balance between these three factors of corporate performance creates a triple-bottom-line and brings sustainability to organizations [20, 21, 22].

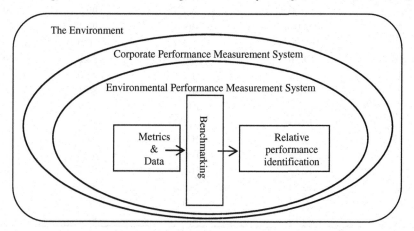

Fig. 1. Environmental performance measurement system

Metrics (environmental KPIs) and their values (data) are entered into the environ-mental performance benchmarking model. The outputs of the model are identification of:

- relative corporate performance and benchmarks,
- the best practice in the group of analyzed companies.

Table 2 presents the relative performance of all companies in the group given by the coefficient of technical efficiency derived from the DEA model. Performance is relative because it expresses the efficiency of the company within the studied group of companies. If it is equal to 100 %, this means that there is no company in the group that has a better performance. If the value is less than 100 %, there is at least one other company which is more effective. Both absolute and relative potential im-provements are part of the output of the DEA model calculations. Table 2 gives rela-tive potential improvements. The best-performing companies are "A", "G" and "Q". These efficient companies are referred to as "peer companies" and determine the efficiency frontier, i.e. they use the minimum quantity of inputs to produce the same quantity of outputs.

Table 2. Corporate Performance – results of the environmental performance benchmarking model

Company	Relative per-formance (%)	Potential improvement (%)		
		Emissions of Greenhouse Gases	Water Con-sumption	Waste Pro-duction
A	100.00	0.0	0.0	0.0
B	27.16	-99.9	-72.8	-83.0
C	3.9	-96.9	-99.7	-96.9
D	1.41	-98.6	-100.0	-98.6
E	1.00	-99.0	-99.7	-99.0
F	2.00	-98.0	-99.1	-99.5
G	100.00	0.0	0.0	0.0
H	**69.36**	**-30.6**	**-54.5**	**-30.6**
I	30.71	-69.3	-85.0	-69.3
J	11.88	-89.0	-88.1	-88.1
K	10.56	-100.0	-89.4	-97.3
L	90.43	-9.6	-67.2	-9.6
M	4.78	-100.0	-95.2	-98.7
N	7.28	-100.0	-92.7	-96.7
O	7.53	-100.0	-92.5	-92.5
P	50.54	-49.5	-87.4	-49.5
Q	100.00	0.0	0.0	0.0
R	30.12	-69.9	-97.7	-69.9

Let us analyze the performance of company "H" further. This company is not effective from the viewpoint of environmental KPIs per Gross Value Added. Table 3 gives the benchmarks for the environmental KPIs that will make sure that the company "H" becomes effective at the current level of Gross Value Added which is 378,433 thousand CZK.

Table 3. Environmental performance of company "H"

KPIs	Emissions of Greenhouse Gases (t)	Water Con-sumption (m³)	Waste Pro-duction (t)
Actual performance	0.01	4116.00	308.57
Benchmark	0.01	1873.07	214.04

Individual environmental KPIs together with their benchmarks can be visually integrated in an AMOEBA graph. In Figure 2, the benchmark is considered 100 % and the actual performance of company "H" is relative to the benchmark. Users can see at a glance that Water Consumption significantly exceeds its benchmark and is therefore the weakest point in the environmental performance of this particular company.

The graphic presentation of environmental KPIs in the context of their benchmarks makes the model outputs clear and easy to understand because it is obvious at a glance which KPIs effect environmental performance positively and negatively.

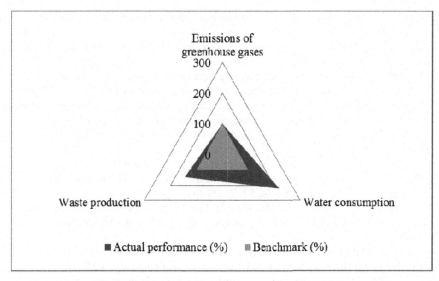

Fig. 2. Environmental performance of company "H"

The model outputs allow users to identify weaknesses in performance and to quantify performance gaps, for which reason the environmental performance benchmarking model can serve its users as a basis for decision-making and performance management. Information about environmental performance should be an integral part of corporate reporting [23, 24].

5   Conclusions

A framework for an environmental performance benchmarking model was proposed in this paper. Data Envelopment Analysis is the benchmarking method used in the model. This approach has the following advantages: the performance of the company is expressed in one number given by the coefficient of technical efficiency, the model quantifies necessary improvements – performance gaps and also identifies the "best practice" in the particular industry. Information then becomes an important source material for quality decisions by the management. The weakness of the model is that performance is relative, and adding another company to the analyzed group will change the environmental performance.

Acknowledgements. This paper is supported by grant no. 14-23079S Measuring Corporate Sustainability in Selected Sectors from the Czech Science Foundation.

References

1. Lankoski, L.: Environmental and Economic Performance. The Basic Links. In: Schaltegger, S., Wagner, M. (eds.) Managing Business Case for Sustainability, pp. 82–106. Greenleaf Publishing, Sheffield (2006)

2. ISO 14031:2013 Environmental management — Environmental performance evaluation — Guidelines

3. Russo, M.V., Fouts, P.A.: A resource-based perspective on corporate environmental performance and profitability. Academy of management Journal 40, 534–559 (1997)

4. Kirchhoff, S.: Green business and blue angels: a model of voluntary overcompliance with asymmetric information. Environmental and Resource Economics 15, 403–420 (2000)

5. Feddersen, T.J., Gilligan, T.W.: Saints and markets: activists and the supply of credence goods. Journal of Economics and Management Strategy 10, 149–171 (2001)

6. Fisman, R., Heal, G., Nair, V.B.: A Model of Corporate Philanthropy. New York, Columbia University (2008),
   http://d1c25a6gwz7q5e.cloudfront.net/papers/1331.pdf

7. Horváthová, E.: Does environmental performance affect financial performance? A meta-analysis. Ecological Economics 70, 52–59 (2010)

8. Rothenberg, S., Schenck, B., Maxwell, J.: Lessons from benchmarking environmental performance at automobile assembly plants. Benchmarking: An International Journal 12, 5–15 (2005)

9. Matthews, D.H.: Environmental management systems for internal corporate environmental benchmarking. Benchmarking: An International Journal 10, 95–106 (2003)

10. ISO 14001:2004 Environmental management systems — Requirements with guidance for use

11. Tokos, H., Pintarič, Z.N., Krajnc, D.: An integrated sustainability performance assessment and benchmarking of breweries. Clean Technologies and Environmental Policy 14, 173–193 (2012)

12. Aigner, D., Lovell, C.A.K., Schmidt, P.: Formulation and estimation of stochastic frontier production function models. Journal of Econometrics 6, 21–37 (1977)

13. Meeusen, W., van den Broeck, J.: Efficiency estimation from Cobb-Douglas production functions with composed error. International Economic Review 8, 435–444 (1997)

14. Charnes, A., Cooper, W., Rhodes, E.: Measuring the efficiency of decision-making units. European Journal of Operational Research 2, 429–444 (1978)

15. Zhu, J.: Quantitative Models for Performance Evaluation and Benchmarking: DEA with Spreadsheets. Springer, Boston (2009)

16. Post, T., Spronk, J.: Performance benchmarking using interactive data envelopment analysis. European Journal of Operational Research 115, 472–487 (1999)

17. Kocmanová, A., Klímková, M., Karpíšek, Z.: The Construction of Environmental Indicators for Determination of Performance of ESG Indicators to Support Decision-Making of investors. Business: Theory and Practice 13, 333–342 (2012)

18. Kocmanová, A., Němeček, P., Dočekalová, M.: Environmental, Social and Governance (ESG) Key Performance Indicators for Sustainable Reporting. In: 7th International Scientific Conference, pp. 655–663. Gediminas Technical University, Vilnius (2012)

19. Hřebíček, J., Piliar, F., Soukopová, J., Štencl, M., Trenz, O.: Corporate Key Performance Indicators for Environmental Management and Reporting. Acta Universitatis Agriculturaeet Silviculturae Mendelianae Brunensis 59, 99–108 (2011)

20. Elkington, J.: Cannibals with Forks: The Triple Bottom Line of the 21st Century. New Society Publishers, Stoney Creek (1998)

21. Kocmanová, A., Dočekalová, M.: Construction of the economic indicators of performance in relation to environmental, social and corporate governance (ESG) factors. Acta Universitatis Agriculturaeet Silviculturae Mendelianae Brunensis 60, 141–149 (2012)

22. Chvátalová, Z., Kocmanová, A., Dočekalová, M.: Corporate Sustainability Reporting and Measuring Corporate Performance. In: 9th IFIP WG 5.11 International Symposium on Environmental Software Systems, pp. 245–254. ISESS, Brno (2011)
23. Hřebíček, J.: Voluntary Reporting in the Czech Republic and Indicators of Sustainable Development. Linde, Praha, pp. 257–264 (2009)
24. Hřebíček, J., Soukopová, J.: Voluntary Company Assessment Report on the Linkages between Environment, Economy and Society. Ministry of Environment of the Czech Republic, Praha (2011) (in Czech)

GeneralBlock: A C++ Program for Identifying and Analyzing Rock Blocks Formed by Finite-Sized Fractures

Lu Xia[1], Qingchun Yu[1,*], Youhua Chen[2], Maohua Li[2], Guofu Xue[2], and Deji Chen[2]

[1]School of Water Resources and Environment Science, China University of Geosciences, Beijing 100083, China
yuqch@cugb.edu.cn
[2]Changjiang Conservancy Commission, Yichang 443003, China

Abstract. GeneralBlock is a software tool for identifying and analyzing rock blocks formed by finite-sized fractures. It was developed in C++ with a friendly user interface, and can analyze the blocks of a complex-shaped modeling domain, such as slopes, tunnels, underground caverns, or their combinations. The heterogeneity of materials was taken fully into account. Both the rocks and the fractures can be heterogeneous. The program can either accept deterministic fractures obtained from a field survey, or generate random fractures by stochastic modeling. The program identifies all of the blocks formed by the excavations and the fractures, classifies the blocks, and outputs a result table that shows the type, volume, factor of safety, sliding fractures, sliding force, friction force, cohesion force, and so on for each block. It also displays three-dimensional (3D) graphics of the blocks. With GeneralBlock, rock anchors and anchor cables can be designed with the visual assistance of 3D graphics of blocks and the excavation. The anchor, cables, and blocks are shown within the same window of 3D graphics. The spatial relationship between the blocks and the anchors and cables is thus very clear.

Keywords: GeneralBlock, finite-sized fracture, rock block identification and analysis.

1 Introduction

A computer program for identifying and analyzing rock blocks formed by finite-sized fractures is a useful tool in many problems involving fractured rocks. If a rock is slightly fractured, the blocks are infrequent in the rock mass. In this case the number, dimensions and locations of the blocks are a major concern. The rock blocks, which are commonly buried in the rock mass under natural conditions, may be exposed by artificial excavations and may fall into the openings formed by the excavation. Many authors have discussed the possibilities of the occurrence of unstable blocks caused by the intersection between fractures and excavations [1-4]. On the other hand, if a

---

* Corresponding author.

R. Denzer et al. (Eds.): ISESS 2015, IFIP AICT 448, pp. 512–519, 2015.

rock is heavily fractured, the rock may be visualized as an assemblage of isolated rock blocks. In this case, the mechanical behavior of the rock is often simulated as the behavior of a system of rock blocks [5-7].

Because the geometry of the blocks exerts a strong influence on the mechanical properties of the rocks, and the geometry of the blocks is determined by the geometry of the fractures, many authors have studied the relationship between the geometries of fractures and rock blocks. Basically, their approaches may be divided into two types. The major difference between the two methods is whether or not the shape of the fractures has a definition prior to block identification. In the first method, the shapes of the fractures are defined before block identification; this approach was used by many authors [8-12], and is adopted in GeneralBlock. In this method, the fractures can cross each other and terminate in intact rock; an individual fracture can be contributive, noncontributive, or partly contributive. The second method uses a block generation language [13-14], whereby the fractures always form fully connected networks and all of the fractures are completely contributive.

GeneralBlock is written in Visual C++ 6.0 using the OpenGL library. In the program, the modeling domain or the excavation may be of arbitrarily complex shape. The rock and fractures may be heterogeneous. The fractures may be either deterministic fractures obtained from a field survey or random fractures generated by stochastic modeling. The program identifies all blocks formed by the excavations and the fractures, classifies the blocks, and outputs a result table that shows the type, volume, factor of safety, sliding fractures, sliding force, friction force, cohesion force, and so on for each block. It also outputs three-dimensional (3D) graphics of each block. With GeneralBlock, anchors and cables may be added, and are shown with the blocks within the same window of 3D graphics, making the spatial relationship between the blocks, anchors, and cables very clear. The user can therefore edit rock anchors and anchor cables with the visual assistance of 3D graphics of blocks and excavation faces.

2   Algorithm

Some authors have discussed the issues in block identification. In initial studies, the fractures were assumed to be infinitely large, and hence, the blocks were limited to convex shapes. Lin et al. [8] and Ikegawa and Hudson [9] presented their block identification approaches for finite extended fractures based on topological concepts. In these approaches, the intersections of the fractures are calculated first to define the sets of vertices, edges, and faces. Then, the sets were regularized to discard any isolated and dangling vertices, edges, and faces. Finally, the blocks were identified through boundary-chain operations of the closed surfaces and the Euler–Poincare formula for a polyhedron. Similar methods have also been discussed in detail [10][12][15].

GeneralBlock was developed based on the procedure presented by Yu et al. [16]. It decomposes a complex block into a finite number of convex element blocks during the identification process. The adoption of the concept of an element block makes it possible to represent a complex block using an assemblage of simple convex blocks, and thus, to transform the difficult calculations involved in identifying the blocks around complex excavations into simple calculations using convex geometry. In the procedure, the complexity of the modeling domains and the heterogeneity of a material are taken fully into account.

In the procedure, a complex modeling domain is initially divided into convex subdomains, and each subdomain is further decomposed into convex blocks with infinite fractures. Then, the fractures are restored to finite dimensions, and the domain is reassembled by combining the subdomains into a full domain. Thus, the procedure is comprised of the following major steps:

1. Subdividing the modeling domain into a finite number of convex subdomains;
2. Removing the non-contributive fractures;
3. Decomposing the subdomains into element blocks with the fractures, which are temporarily taken as infinitely large at this stage;
4. Restoring the infinite fractures to finite;
5. Assembling the modeling domain.

3   User Interface

The solution of a block identification and analysis problem with GeneralBlock usually includes the following major steps.

1. Open a new project. This creates a new directory in which to store the data for the problem. All ensuing data for this problem will be stored in this directory.
2. Define the modeling domain.
3. Input deterministic fractures and/or generate stochastic fractures.
4. Calculate and observe the traces of the fractures.
5. Filter fractures.
6. Identify blocks and analyze their stability.
7. Display analysis results.
8. Design rock anchors and anchor cables.

3.1   Defining the Model Domain

The first step in block identification and analysis is defining the model domain. A major process in the definition is to decompose the problem domain into a number of convex subdomains. The subdivision of a problem domain is similar to the subdivision of a model domain into elements in the FEM, and the geometry and the associated data structure of a subdomain are also similar to those of an element in the FEM technique. The subdomains, surface polygons, and vertices must be numbered uniquely, and no overlap among the subdomains or surface polygons is allowed.

Manually decomposing a problem domain into subdomains is not difficult, even for a problem domain with a very complex shape. However, it is not simple to code a computer program to automatically decompose different-shaped rock masses. Thus, GeneralBlock provides graphical user interfaces for the subdivision of some common rock structures, including slopes, tunnels, and underground caverns. For these common structures, the user only enters a few data values through a graphical window to define the rock masses. The subdivision of the domain is performed automatically by GeneralBlock, and the user is not required to be aware of it.

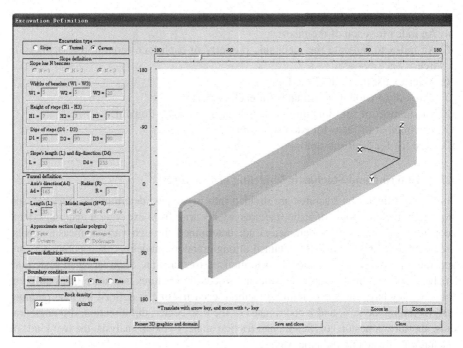

Fig. 1. The window defining the model domain (the example of the underground powerhouse cavern in the Three Gorges Project defined by GeneralBlock)

3.1.1 The Window Defining the Model Domain.
GeneralBlock provides graphical interfaces for three kinds of structures: slope, tunnel, and underground cavern. Accurately speaking, a tunnel is a kind of underground cavern. As an example, figure 1 shows the actual underground powerhouse cavern 311.3 m long and 71 m high in the Three Gorges Project. In the lower part of the powerhouse, the distance between the two vertical sidewalls is 31 m, and in the upper part the span of the crown is 32.6 m.

3.1.2 The Format of "model_domain.dat"
The data defining the model domain and sub-domains are all stored in an ASCII file named "model_domain.dat". This file can be edited by a text editor. The user can prepare it and have GeneralBlock read it to perform block analyses.

The rock masses and the excavations of study domains may have various shapes, e.g., slopes, tunnels, and their combinations. However, all of the data arising from domain definitions and subdivisions are stored in this file, and all of them always have the same format. This file includes the following data.

1. Direction of x-axis (in deg), excavation type (slope = 0; tunnel = 1; cavern = 3; complex = 4);
2. Number of the nodes to define the domain, number of the faces to define the domain;

3. Number of the nodes to define each of the faces;
4. An index for each of the faces;
5. An index to indicate the mechanic property of each face (common = 0; fix = 1; free = 2);
6. A vertex list for each of the face;
7. Three-dimensional coordinates for each vertex;
8. The number of sub-domains, rock density of each sub-domain;
9. The number of faces for each sub-domain;
10. Face list for each sub-domain.

3.2   Entering and Stochastic Modeling of Fractures

For GeneralBlock, the fractures are divided into two types: deterministic fractures and stochastic fractures. Deterministic fractures usually arise from excavation mappings; their geometric and mechanical parameters are determined through various measurements. Stochastic fractures are usually obtained through random modeling; their parameters are generated from a stochastic model. Deterministic fractures are often larger in scale than stochastic ones. Although deterministic and stochastic fractures may arise from different sources, they have the same defining method: each fracture is defined by nine parameters, including the x, y, and z coordinates of the disc center, dip direction, dip angle, radius, aperture, cohesion coefficient, and friction angle. In block analysis, the two kinds of fractures are treated in the same way.

After inputting deterministic fractures or simulating stochastic fractures, filtering fractures is necessary. The objective of fracture filtering is to find and eliminate the fractures that are evidently non-contributive to block formation. And fractures below the size specified by user may be neglected in block identification. For most practical engineering, the blocks close to the excavations are usually of more concern than more distant ones. Thus, it is often the case that only the fractures near the excavations are taken into account. In GeneralBlock, the distance of a fracture from an excavation is an integer. If the fracture intersects directly with the excavation, the distance is zero; if the fracture does not intersect directly with the excavation but is connected indirectly to the excavation through one fracture, the distance is one; the rest may be deduced by analogy.

The remaining fractures after fracture filtering are stored in the file "contributive_fracture_xyzabr.dat". GeneralBlock reads all fractures in this file when performing block identification.

Calculating and showing the traces of fractures should be done next. A trace is an intersection line between a fracture and a rock surface, e.g., an excavation or a natural exposure. Calculating the traces of fractures on specified excavations and displaying them through 3D graphics is a useful function of GeneralBlock. In practical rock engineering, when a fault is encountered by a borehole or an exploration tunnel, the engineering geologist is often confronted with the problem of predicting where the fault would be reencountered by other excavations.

Figure 2 shows the example traces shown in this figure are the traces of main faults in vaults on excavation of underground powerhouse in the Three Gorges Project.

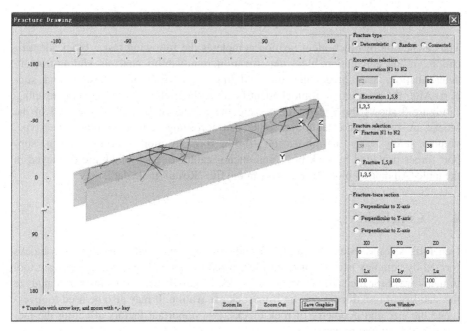

Fig. 2. The window for calculating and displaying the trace of fractures (traces of main faults in vaults on excavation of underground powerhouse in the Three Gorges Project)

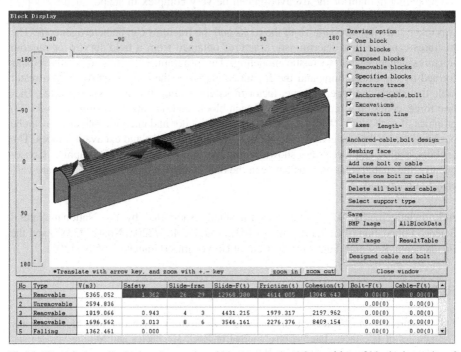

Fig. 3. The window displaying the results of block analysis (3D graphics of blocks in vaults of underground powerhouse in the Three Gorges Project using GeneralBlock)

3.3   Identifying Blocks and Displaying Results

The calculation of block identification completes the following tasks: block identification, volume calculation, block classification, removability analysis, sliding fracture determination, and force calculation (sliding force, friction, cohesion, and support).After the completion of block identification, the user can investigate the results.

Figure 3 shows the window displaying the results of block analysis. All of the blocks are listed in the table and sequenced according to their volumes. The type, volume, safety factor, sliding fracture, sliding force, friction, cohesion, and the support forces provided by rock bolts and anchor cables of each block are displayed in the table. All data of block results save in the file "Result_table.dat".

4   Conclusion

GeneralBlock has been developed for identifying and analyzing the rock blocks formed by complex excavations and finite-sized fractures. It is a useful software tool in many ways for the study of fractured rocks. It may be used to identify and analyze the stability of rock blocks arising from rock excavation. It may also be used to investigate the size and geometry of rock blocks, two important factors affecting the mechanics of fractured rocks.

GeneralBlock was developed in C++ with a friendly user interface. In the program, the modeling domain or the excavation can be very complex in shape, such as slopes, tunnels, underground caverns, or their combinations. The heterogeneity of the materials was taken fully into account. Both the rocks and the fractures can be heterogeneous. The fractures can be either deterministic fractures obtained from a field survey, or random fractures generated by stochastic modeling. The program: identifies all of the blocks formed by the excavations and the fractures; classifies the blocks and outputs a result table that shows the type, volume, factor of safety, sliding fractures, sliding force, friction force, cohesion force, and so on, of each block; and outputs three-dimensional (3D) graphics of each block. With GeneralBlock, rock anchor and anchor cable design can be performed with the visual assistance of 3D graphics of blocks and excavation faces. The anchors, cables, and blocks are shown within the same window of 3D graphics. Consequently, the spatial relationships between the blocks and the anchors and cables are very easy to understand.

Acknowledgements. This study was financially supported by the National Natural Science Foundation of China (Grant No.40372134, No.40772208, No.41272387) and the Fundamental Research Funds for the Central Universities (Grant No.2652011305).

References

1. Warburton, P.M.: Vector stability analysis of an arbitrary polyhedral rock block with any number of free faces. International Journal of Rock Mechanics and Mining Science and Geomech. Abstracts 18, 415–427 (1981)

2. Goodman, R.E., Shi, G.: Block theory and its application to rock engineering. Prentice-Hall, Englewood Cliffs (1985)
3. Lin, D., Fairhurst, C.: Static analysis of the stability of three-dimensional blocky systems around excavation in rock. International Journal of Rock Mechanics and Mining Science and Geomech. Abstracts 25, 139–147 (1988)
4. Hoek, E., Kaiser, P.K., Bawden, W.F.: Support of underground excavation in hard rock. Balkema, Rotterdam (1995)
5. Cundall, P.A.: Formulation of a three-dimensional distinct element model—part 1: A scheme to detect and represent contacts in a system composed of many polyhedral blocks. International Journal of Rock Mechanics and Mining Science and Geomech. Abstracts 25, 107–116 (1988)
6. Shi, G.: Discontinuous deformation analysis: A new numerical model for the statics and dynamics of block systems, PhD thesis, University of California, Berkeley, USA (1989)
7. Wu, J.H., Ohnishi, Y., Nishiyama, S.: A development of the discontinuous deformation analysis for rock fall analysis. International Journal of Numerical and Analytical Methods in Geomechanics 29, 971–988 (2005)
8. Lin, D., Fairhurst, C., Starfield, A.M.: Geometrical identification of three-dimensional rock block system using topological techniques. International Journal of Rock Mechanics and Mining Science and Geomech. Abstracts 24, 331–338 (1987)
9. Ikegawa, Y., Hudson, J.A.: A novel automatic identification system for three-dimensional multi-block systems. Engineering Computing 9, 169–179 (1992)
10. Jing, L.: Block construction for three-dimensional discrete element models of fractured rocks. International Journal of Rock Mechanics and Mining Science and Geomech. Abstracts 37, 645–659 (2000)
11. Ohnishi, Y., Yu, Q.: 3D block analyses for fractured rock. In: Desai, et al. (eds.) Computer methods and advances in geomechanics, pp. 577–580. Balkema, Rotterdam (2001)
12. Lu, J.: Systematic identification of polyhedral blocks with arbitrary joints and faults. Comput Geotech 29, 49–72 (2002)
13. Heliot, D.: Generating a blocky rock mass. International Journal of Rock Mechanics and Mining Science and Geomech. Abstracts 25, 127–138 (1988)
14. Empereur-Mot, L., Villemin, T.: OBSIFRAC: database-supported software for 3D modeling of rock mass fragmentation. Computers & Geosciences 29, 173–181 (2003)
15. Yu, Q.: Analyses for fluid flow and solute transport in discrete fracture network, PhD thesis, Kyoto University, Kyoto, Japan (2000)
16. Yu, Q., Ohnishi, Y., Xue, G., Chen, D.: A generalized procedure to identify three-dimensional rock blocks around complex excavations. International Journal of Numerical and Analytical Methods in Geomechanics 33, 355–375 (2009)

On the Volume of Geo-referenced Tweets
and Their Relationship to Events Relevant
for Migration Tracking

Georg Neubauer[1], Hermann Huber[1], Armin Vogl[2], Bettina Jager[1],
Alexander Preinerstorfer[1], Stefan Schirnhofer[1], Gerald Schimak[1], and Denis Havlik[1]

[1] AIT Austrian Institute of Technology GmbH, Vienna, Austria
{Georg.Neubauer,Hermann.Huber,Bettina.Jager,
Alexander.Preinerstorfer,Stefan.Schirnhofer,
Gerald.Schimak,Denis.Havlik}@ait.ac.at
[2] Federal Ministry of Interior, Republic of Austria, Vienna, Austria
Armin.vogl@bmi.gv.at

Abstract. Migration is a major challenge for the European Union, resulting in early preparedness being an imperative for target states and their stakeholders such as border police forces. This preparedness is necessary for multiple reasons, including the provision of adequate search and rescue measures. To support preparedness, there is a need for early indicators for detection of developing migratory push-factors related to imminent migration flows. To address this need, we have investigated the daily number of geo-referenced Tweets in three regions of Ukraine and the whole of Japan from August 2014 until October 2014. This analysis was done by using the data handling tool Ubicity. Additionally, we have identified days when relevant natural, civil or political events took place in order to identify possible event triggered changes of the daily number of Tweets. In all the examined Ukrainian regions a considerable increase in the number of daily Tweets was observed for the election day of a new parliament. Furthermore, we identified a significant decrease in the number of daily Tweets for the Crimea for the whole examined period which could be related to the political changes that took place. The natural disasters identified in Japan do not show a clear relationship with the changes in the degree of use of the social media tool Twitter. The results are a good basis to use communication patterns as future key indicator for migration analysis.

Keywords: migration, tweets, geolocation, early indicator, push factor.

1   Introduction

In recent years the importance of migration has increased considerably in EU member states, and is seen as one of the major challenges by the European Union. A number of events have led to issues of migration becoming more important in Europe, including the "Arab spring" crisis situations in North-Africa, natural disasters such as draughts or large scale flooding, and wars and warlike situations in the Middle-East, Sub-Sahara and South Asia. These events have caused an overwhelming migration

R. Denzer et al. (Eds.): ISESS 2015, IFIP AICT 448, pp. 520–530, 2015.

wave with a steadily growing number of refugees who are trying to reach European countries. European societies are struggling with the socioeconomic impact of these crises. Consequently, these societies are searching for political solutions which can cope with the humanitarian responsibilities, as well as the protection of their demographic and economic structures.

It is important for possible destination countries to be well-prepared for such large influxes of refugees so they can grant migrants a liveable and worthy reception. As an example, the southern border of Italy is facing a soaring migratory wave, as more than 100.000 illegal migrants had to be rescued in open-sea during 2014 and brought to the Italian coast. This mass immigration caused a socioeconomic crisis in this region. Human disasters, such as the drowning of hundreds of human beings, could be avoided if better information is available to alert search and rescue teams in timely manner. Currently, European authorities seem ill-prepared to cope with this overwhelming situation and therefore new information sources have to be found in order to better observe possible migration-causing incidents. Early and reliable indicators on migration movements are therefore imperative for multiple stakeholders such as border police forces or first responders in the field. So far, data on volume and flow of migration is mainly inconsistent, outdated or does not exist at all. This paper investigates the suitability of using the volume of geo-referenced Tweets versus time as potential early indicators of migration movements, whilst taking into account both long term impacting situations and specific high-profile events.

1.1   Related Work

In recent years, extensive research was done in identifying events by studying human communication behavior on social media. In this context the micro-blogging platform Twitter has been the focus of much research. The benefit of gathering information about events from social media services, such as Twitter, relates to the fact that people turn to these platforms in the face of exceptional circumstances [1]. This study stresses that irrespective of whether these events are emergencies, natural disasters or political protests, a significant factor for changes in communication patterns is a disruption to normal routines. Besides a certain content of Twitter messages, [2] pointed out, that volunteered information with geographic footprints is displaying people's current position, which can facilitate a wide range of possibilities to support situational awareness. The tracking of recent trends in migration patterns by using geo-located data gathered from Twitter has been discussed in [3] as a specific type of application.

Based on the monitoring of real-time migration flows, statements can be made on migration trends, i.e. increasing or decreasing mobility from a certain country to OECD countries. Political and civil events are frequently chosen as research use cases. An analysis of Twitter data in the reference period of five months exposed a relation between communications behaviour and the occurrence of exceptional events during the troubled time. As a main result of [4], highly publicised events in Egypt have been reflected in the amount of communication via Twitter in a certain spatial area. Furthermore, the paper states that the amount of communication in different Egyptian cities is comparable.

Another study focusing on the Middle East was made by [5] and showed the potential for the detection of trending topics on the basis of content-based geo-location of Arabic and English language Tweets. An extensive range of applications has been presented by [6], who have employed techniques for the SNOW Data Challenge 2014. By combining aggressive filtering of Tweets with hierarchical clustering of Tweets, events around the US presidential elections in 2012 and the recent events in Ukraine, etc. have been detected.

1.2   Developments in the Aftermath of the Ukrainian Conflict

In the course of the escalating conflict between Russia and Ukraine in the early 2014, a Ukrainian crisis emerged. Accompanied by demonstrations at the Independence Square in Kiev a strong commitment to Europe had been expressed by Ukrainian protesters, which has acquired visibility during the Euromaidan protest wave. Although the situation in the Crimea has seemed to calm down since the Crimean status referendum in March 2014, [7] pointed out, that the annexation of the Crimea has caused radical changes, especially for ethnic Ukrainians, Crimean Tatars and representatives of minority groups generally.

An increasing number of incidents have been recorded in the east and Crimea, which have been identified as an important factor for emigration from the Crimea. A research of the conflict events in the archive of Center for Strategic and International Studies (CSIS)[1] delivers therefore a huge number of hits. Table 1 illustrates the most relevant events for each category summarized on a monthly basis. The categories "civil events" and "political events" comprise the majority of results. In particular the combats in the eastern Ukraine have been highly publicized. The majority of events can be clearly attributed to one of the pre-defined categories. Solely, the category "natural events" remains vacant, which can be explained by the overwhelming media response to human induced events or the fact, that there were no natural induced disasters in the period from August 2014 to October 2014.

Table 1. Events in Ukraine in the second reference period (August 2014 – October 2014)

Month	No. of Events	Exemplary Event
August 2014	32	Over 300 Ukrainian soldiers flee across border to Russia European leaders threaten Russia with further sanctions Suspicion surrounds Russian convoy carrying aid to Ukraine
September 2014	28	Ceasefire strained as fighting near Donetsk kills nine Party of regions plans election boycott as fighting continues Drop in Russian gas supplies to Europe
October 2014	27	Separatists are violating ceasefire Ukraine elects new parliament Russia and Ukraine remain at impasse over gas

[1] http://csis.org/ukraine/index.htm#130

1.3   Environmental Events in Japan

Japan is one of the countries most affected by natural disasters. Due to its geographic location in the pacific in the geologic fracture zone of four tectonic plates, earthquakes happen frequently in the Japanese archipelago. Since Japan has over 100 active volcanoes eruptions are also occurring occasionally in Japan. Other relevant disasters caused by natural events in Japan are extreme temperatures, floods, storms (e.g. tropical cyclones) and mass movements [8]. Japan leads in the list of economic damage due to earthquakes in the world from 1900 up to the present day with the huge number of 360 billion US $ [9]. In the actual World Risk Report [10] Japan is in the top five countries with the highest urban risk. Urban risk is defined as the product of urban vulnerability and urban hazards. Several natural events occurred in Japan during the observation period from August 2014 up to October 2014, which can be seen in Table 2. These natural events were extracted using the search engine GLIDEnumber [11].

Table 2. Natural events in Japan in the period (August 2014 – October 2014) extracted from GLIDEnumber V2.0 [11]

Date	Type of Event	Event
08/08/2014	Tropical Cyclone	Typhoon Halong killed one person in Japan and injured 33, as authorities ordered 1.6 million people out of the path of the storm that battered the west of the country
20/08/2014	Landslide	At least 36 people were killed in Japan on 20 August 2014, when landslides triggered by torrential rain
27/09/2014	Volcanic Eruption	Mt. Ontake, a central Japan volcano popular with tourists particularly in the fall, erupted without warning just before noon 27 September 2014
06/10/2014	Tropical Cyclone	At least one person was dead and six were missing on 6 October as a strong typhoon whipped through the Tokyo metropolitan area after making landfall further south
12/10/2014	Tropical Cyclone	Typhoon Vongfong, the strongest storm to hit Japan this year, has made landfall on the country's main islands

2   Method

2.1   Data Acquisition

In contrast to many other platforms, Twitters data access policy is quite liberal. The programming interface provides access to 1% of the twitter traffic on a just-in-time basis. Users are free to downstream either a random sample or provide data filters in order to decrease data volume and ensure that Tweets match various criteria like the presence of certain hashtags. However, if the data volume after the application of filters still exceeds the 1% threshold, twitter randomly truncates the subset to meet the data limitation policy. In order to examine spatiotemporal frequencies, we applied a geo-location filter to only download Tweets that feature geographic positioning attributes in terms of latitude and longitude. In this way, Twitter provides roughly 7 million geo-referenced Tweets a day, originating from mobile devices equipped with GPS sensors.

During the three month evaluation period we downloaded 698 million Tweets (261GB). AIT has developed a data analysis tool called Ubicity in order to extract, aggregate and analyse social media data. It routes the data between all kinds of data stores and analysis components like search engines, graph databases or mobile phones. We used its geo-polygon query capability to extract the tweets emitted in certain areas of the Ukraine and Japan.

2.2   Data Analysis

We approximated the national borders of the Ukraine and Japan and retrieved all of the collected messages tweeted within the geo-polygons. In the case of Ukraine, we subdivided the territory into three subareas with respect to the distribution of the Russian language according to a national census in 2001 [12]. Polygon (a) in Fig. 1 depicts the area in which less than 10% of the population identified Russian as their native language. Polygons (b) and (c) depict areas with a rate higher than 50%. Area (b) encompasses the administrative districts Donetsk and Luhansk; (c) encompasses the Crimea peninsula. We selected the three Ukrainian areas because of their geopolitical importance in the conflict between the Ukrainian government and the Pro-Russian separatists.

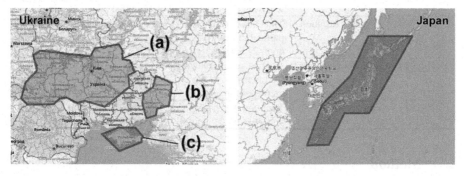

Fig. 1. The Geo-Polygons approximate the national borders of parts of the Ukraine and Japan. We analyzed all Tweets provided by the Twitter public streaming interface submitted within these areas – (a) West Ukraine, (b) East Ukraine and (c) Crimea.

In the period of investigation, we leached from a total number of 698 million Tweets (261GB), 1.1 million Tweets in Ukrainian areas and 25.9 million in the Japanese polygon. The geo-polygon query consists of multiple latitude/longitude pairs to approximate the borders of the respective country. As our twitter stream was partly interrupted due to maintenance work, we identified those interruptions of at least one hour and excluded affected days from our investigation. Our analysis is based on the spatiotemporal dimension only. The main advantage of this approach is that it is language and text understanding independent. Advanced analysis might also take term frequency and co-occurrence as well as hashtags and network relations into account. Depending on the use case we identified tight filters as a promising solution. Keeping the data rates low (below 1% of the overall traffic) avoids spurious frequency changes in the first place.

3   Results

Statistical tests highlight, that the communication behavior differs significantly between Japan, the Crimea and the regions in the Ukraine (Table 3). In comparison to the Japanese Tweets, the number of Tweets is lower by a factor of rounded 30 in the region of the West of Ukraine (see the mean values). However these numbers do not take the difference in the number of inhabitants between the regions from Ukraine and Japan into account.

Table 3. Statistical parameters for Tweets gathered in Japan, the Crimea and the East and the West of Ukraine

Statistical Parameter	Japan	Crimea	East Ukraine	West Ukraine
Mean	375316.8	1314.8	1416.3	13868.8
Median	375090.0	1105.0	1407.0	13774.0
Maximum	498847.0	2882.0	1855.0	17383.0
Minimum	212669.0	306.0	1094.0	10791.0
1st Quartile	328671.0	706.5	1309.0	13251.0
2nd Quartile	375090.0	1105.0	1407.0	13774.0
3rd Quartile	419217.0	1954.3	1498.0	14516.5

3.1   Results Obtained for the Crimea, the East and the West of Ukraine

As illustrated in Fig. 1 (left picture), the analysis of Tweets in the Crimea, the East and the West of Ukraine considers the three regions separately. Fig. 2 displays that the course of the curve shows a permanently downward trend from the beginning of the reference period to the end. Apart from the peaks in the second half of August, no comparable extent of Tweets could be reached in later stages.

The flat curve shape of the number of Tweets (not shown here) indicates a moderate increase over the period of three months in the East of Ukraine. Determined by daily peaks, the events around the foray of Ukrainian forces into Lugansk and Donetsk are reflected in the communication identified in the eastern region of the Ukraine. Aside from the middle section of the curve in Fig. 3, a permanent decrease of the number of Tweets per day in the West Ukraine can be recognized. The line is slightly curved and the most disruptive events are not clearly reflected therein. Mirrored by monthly top rates a marked increase of communication can be noticed at the beginning of September 2014. In this time frame, NATO became more visible in Ukrainian conflict and in general, the largest number of political events had been observed regarding, foreign sanctions and economic degradation.

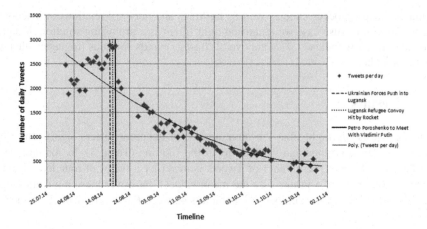

Fig. 2. Number of Tweets from August 2014 to October 2014 in Crimea

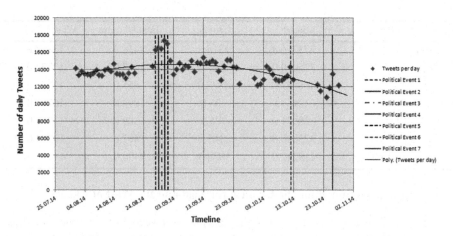

Fig. 3. Number of Tweets from August 2014 to October 2014 in West Ukraine

3.2   Results Obtained for Japan

The timeline of the daily number of geo-located Tweets in Japan describes a linear decrease over the whole period (Figure not shown). An interesting result is that the communication behavior around all the tropical cyclones is located over the trend line, but after the landslide no such trend is recognizable. This might be explained by the missing data from our dataset, which was caused by system maintenance. In this time period no political events with an increase of Twitter communication were found. On a culture-bounded basis, Japan naturally exhibits a higher number of Tweets when compared to the other observed areas – the Crimea, East and West Ukraine.

4   Discussion

4.1   Discussion of Communication Patterns Related to Natural Events

Analysis of the Tweets from Japan showed no clear patterns. Five major natural disasters and three political events were identified in the period of investigation. Looking at the two cyclones on August 8th and October 12th 2014, an increase of about 10% in number of Tweets was observed the day after the event. However, a decrease of about 16% was observed for the cyclone occurring on October 6th. The observed changes lay within typical variations of the daily number of Tweets. A landslide took place on August 20th causing 36 casualties. This event did not lead to an increase of messages on the day of the event nor in the days afterwards. This is in contrast to the results from [4], in which a snowstorm in Egypt was associated with the highest number of Tweets in the observed period. The reason for this difference might be the uniqueness of the Egyptian snowstorm, whereas cyclones are rather common events in Japan. The identified political events did not occur with an obvious increased number of Tweets.

4.2   Discussion of Communication Patterns Related to Man – Made Events

We examined three regions in Ukraine in order to identify possible differences in communication patterns between these regions that were caused by different human induced factors. We identified for almost every day a political or civil event, however no natural disaster was documented. It is interesting to note that in all examined regions, the number of Tweets augmented on October 26th, the day the election of a new parliament took place.

The Crimea shows a remarkable decrease in the daily number of Tweets during the three investigated months. The median of daily Tweets in August is 2,279, whereas the median in the month of October went down to 647, corresponding to 28 % of the Tweets of August. Apart from the peaks in the second half of August, no comparable extent of Tweets was identified afterwards. There are a number of possible reasons for this decrease. For instance, new types of social media might have been introduced by the new potentates. Another possibility would be the restriction of communication services in general or a new taxing policy making use of social media not affordable to a considerable part of the population. Finally, it is possible that a large proportion of former Twitter users just left the region.

On August 17th the highest number of geo-referenced daily Tweets was observed, this day a push of Ukrainian forces into Lugansk and Donetsk was reported. In the eastern region of Ukraine, the highest number of daily Tweets can be seen for September 20th, the day a large explosion took place in Donetsk. Compared to the median of all daily Tweets this corresponds to an increase of about 32% in the total number of Tweets.

In contrast to the investigations on Egypt performed by [4], in which the number of Tweets across the whole Egypt and the cities of Cairo and Alexandria correlated highly, correlations were low for the regions of Ukraine, e.g., 0.16 in case of the West of Ukraine and Crimea. Communication patterns using Twitter seem to differ considerably between the examined regions in Ukraine.

Looking at the methodology applied to extract Tweets several aspects need to be discussed in detail. The authors of [13] indicate that the 1% streaming limitation is not constant over time. Hence, long-term frequency analysis that is based on the public twitter programming interface requires advanced data normalization approaches to avoid misinterpretation. Our approach to focus on the amount of Tweets in a pre-defined area builds on the concept, which is based on the assumption that monitoring of the dimension of the crowd at a certain hotspot is more meaningful than the content of the communication. Without pursuing a thematic priority the approach of extracting geo-references from Tweets facilitate novel insights in human behavior and opens multiple application, as mentioned in [6], [14] [15] and [16]. Especially, the study of [16] have provided an outlook on how Social Media technology can be used as a support module for real time alerting systems for any type of event.

5   Conclusion

It is the purpose of our ongoing investigations to develop a method for the identification of early indicators of migration movements. The method has to optimize required man power of the stakeholders (e.g. border police forces) as well as their time investment, it has to serve to respond to developing or already ongoing migration movements in very early stages in order to mitigate the effects of such developments. The method consists of several steps:

1. Identification of typical communication patterns such as elevated number of daily Tweets associated with natural as well as man-made events having the potential to become push factors for migration based on analysis of historical data

2. Continuously observation of the quantity of social media communication for unstable regions without analyzing the content and comparison the developing patterns of communication with archival patterns being typical for migration triggering events. Identification of developing situations affecting the well-being of migration endangered populations leading to the imminent readiness for emigration by observing the individual base relevance of the region

3. In case of identifying communication patterns indicative for migration developments such as exceptional frequency of Tweets or non-typical increases or decreases of daily number of Tweets more detailed investigations such as text mining can be performed to obtain a more precise operational picture. Moreover, profound knowledge on the ongoing developments in specific critical regions is required to interpret changes in communication patterns correctly

So far, we examine the relation between communication patterns and historical data and restrict our work to item 1 of the above described approach. We intend to find specific types of events such as riots or natural disasters, that are associated with typical "communication curves". In some cases several developments in communication intensity may become potential indicators of migration movements. For instance, the very large decrease in transmitted Tweets in Crimea is likely to be a sign for one or several civil and political changes occurring in a period of several months.

References

1. Starbird, K.: Crowdwork, Crisis and Convergence: How the Connected Crowd Organizes Information during Mass Disruption Events. Colorado (2012)
2. Stefanidis, A., Crooks, A., Radzikowski, J.: Harvesting ambient geospatial information from social media feeds. GeoJournal 78(2), 319–338 (2011)
3. Zagheni, E.G.V., Weber, I.: Inferring international and internal migration patterns from Twitter data. In: Proceedings of the Companion Publication of the 23rd International Conference on World Wide Web Companion, Geneva, Switzerland (2014)
4. Neubauer, G., Huber, H., Jager, B., Vogl, A.: Detecting Events in Egypt Based on Geo-Referenced Tweets. In: 22nd Proceedings of IDIMT-2014. Networking Societies – Cooperation and Conflict, Czech Republic, Poděbrady (2014)
5. Khanwalkar, S., Seldin, M., Srivastava, A., Kumar, A., Colbath, S.: Content-Based Geo-Location Detection for Placing Tweets Pertaining To Trending News on Map. In: The Fourth International Workshop on Mining Ubiquitous and Social Environments (MUSE 2013), Prague, Czech Republic (2013)
6. Ifrim, G., Shi, B., Brigadir, I.: Event Detection in Twitter using Aggressive Filtering and Hierarchical Tweet Clustering. In: Proceedings of the SNOW 2014 Data Challenge, Seoul, Korea (2014)
7. Office of the United Nations High Commissioner for Human Rights, Report on the human rights situation in Ukraine (2014)
8. PreventionWeb,
   `http://www.preventionweb.net/english/countries/statistics/?c`
   `id=87` (accessed November 5, 2014)
9. Statista,
   `http://de.statista.com/statistik/daten/studie/163492/umfrage`
   `/oekonomischer-schaden-durch-erdbeben-nach-laendern/` (accessed November 5, 2014)
10. United Nations University-Institute for Environment and Human Security, World Risk Report 2014, Bonn, Germany (2014)
11. Glidenumber,
    `http://glidenumber.net/glide/public/search/search.jsp` (accessed November 5, 2014)
12. Washington Post, The main advantage is the independence in terms of language understanding. Advanced analysis might also take term frequency and co-occurrence as well as hashtags and network relations into account. We discovered the stability of the public twitter data de (accessed November 5, 2014)
13. Morstatter, F., Pfeffer, J., Liu, H., Carley, K.M.: Is the Sample Good Enough? Comparing Data from Twitter's Streaming API and Twitter's Firehose. In: Proceedings of ICWSM (2013)
14. Abdelhaq, H., Sengstock, C., Gertz, M.: EvenTweet: Online Localized Event Detection from Twitter. In: Proceedings of the VLDB Endowment, Riva del Garda, Trento, Italy (2013)

15. Kraft, T., Wang, D., Delawder, J., Dou, W., Li, Y., Ribarsky, W.: Less After-the-Fact: Investigative visual analysis of events from streaming twitter. In: IEEE Symposium on Large-Scale Data Analysis and Visualization, LDAV (2013)
16. Schaust, S., Walther, M., Kaisser, M.: Avalanche: Prepare, Manage, and Understand Crisis Situations Using Social Media Analytics. In: Proceedings of the 10th International ISCRAM Conference, Baden-Baden (2013)

Benchmarking Systems and Methods for Environmental Performance Models

Zuzana Chvátalová[1], Jiří Hřebíček[2], and Oldřich Trenz[2]

[1] Brno University of Technology, Faculty of Business and Management,
Kolejní 4, 612 00 Brno, Czech Republic
chvatalova@fbm.vutbr.cz
[2] Mendel University, Faculty of Business and Economics,
Zemědělská 1, 613 00 Brno, Czech Republic
{jiri.hrebicek,oldrich.trenz}@mendelu.cz

Abstract. Many business activities and procedures influence the environment. This environmental impact has to be assessed. We consider companies where the procedure of measuring environmental performance is applied through an environmental management system. The benchmark methodology has been developed precisely for these companies. This benchmark methodology can be used in the initial assessment as a screening method in sectors of different economic activities. The paper surveys the methodology that is designated for the environmental performance assessment of companies in the food-processing sector and introduces the architecture of the Web environmental benchmarking and reporting system that has been also developed.

Keywords: benchmark methodology, criteria, environmental performance, information system, environmental indicators, environmental performance evaluation, environmental reporting.

1   Introduction

Benchmarking is the process of improving performance by identifying, understanding, adapting and implementing best practices and processes that are found inside and outside a company. It involves the creation of partnerships to exchange information on processes and measurements, resulting in the setting of realistic improvement goals. Effective benchmarking is a process of continuous improvement [1].

Benchmarking is a framework within which performance indicators and the best practices are examined in order to determine areas where the company performance can be improved. Although most benchmarking initiatives concern financial and management issues, environmental benchmarking is becoming a major element in the environmental management of companies.

Environmental benchmarking is an environmental management tool that can provide a substantial contribution to the improvement of environmental performances by facilitating the identification of the gap between company performance and an optimal performance [3]. It helps the company's management to find out how to

R. Denzer et al. (Eds.): ISESS 2015, IFIP AICT 448, pp. 531–541, 2015.

continuously and exactly monitor the development of the company's environmental impacts in the chosen sector (economic activities connected with NACE - Statistical classification of economic activities [6]) and to find relationships between the environment, the economy and society and to transform them into Key Performance Indicators (KPIs) [5], [7], [8] for the measurement of environmental performance.

What is benchmarked in environmental benchmarking? The scope of environmental benchmarking should include all areas of the given company's activities, and not be restricted solely to those activities that have an obvious environmental impact. Therefore, it may include an assessment of Environmental Management Systems (EMS), management performance, Environmental Management Accounting (EMA), resource and waste management, product environmental quality, environmental education and training, customer relations and emergency response [2].

Let us consider the environmental performance and the KPIs for the food processing sectors with NACE codes: C10 - Manufacture of food products and C11 - Manufacture of beverages in the section 2 of the paper. Here we have taken into account the Global Reporting Initiative (GRI), its G4 Guidelines [9] and the Food processing guideline of G4 Sector Disclosures [10] and our past research [12] to specify the KPIs. We have also analyzed the Sustainability Assessment of Food and Agriculture systems (SAFA) [11] of the Food and Agriculture Organization of United Nations (FAO), its holistic global framework for the assessment of sustainability along the food and agriculture value chains, and this in order to optimize the environmental performance and the KPIs [14]. Furthermore, we consider benchmarking as an ongoing process of actions, steps, functions and activities that aims to identify and adopt best practices for improving environmental performance specified by a given company's KPIs. A number of different methods for benchmarking have been developed [15], [16]. We have considered the process based on EEA methodology [2] in the section 3 of the paper and we have applied this to chosen companies' food processing sector in the section 4 where we mention the architecture of the Web information system that has been developed as a part of our project [13].

2   Key Performance Indicators of the Food Processing Sector

The ISO 14031:2013 international standard [17] sets out *Environmental Performance* (EP) as measurable results of a company's management of its environmental aspects. The *Environmental Performance Evaluation* (EPE) is defined in ISO 14031:2013 as follows: A process to facilitate management decisions regarding a company's EP by selecting indicators, collecting and analysing data, assessing information about EP, reporting and communicating, and periodically reviewing and improving this process. Therefore, the EPE is a process which enables companies to measure, evaluate and communicate their EP using KPIs, based on reliable and verifiable information.

The ISO 14031:2013 standard describes two general categories of indicators for EPE: Environmental Performance Indicators (EPIs); and Environmental Condition Indicators (ECIs). There are two types of EPIs:

1. Management performance indicators (MPIs) provide information about management efforts to influence the environmental performance of the company's operations.
2. Operational performance indicators (OPIs) provide information about the environmental performance of the company's operations.

The EPE process defined in ISO 14031:2013 and likewise in ISO 14031:1999 is too general including methods how to determine KPIs and choose appropriate EPIs and ECIs indicators. In addition, there are many international standards for implementing and certifying the sustainability pillars of environmental indicators, like for instance ISO 9000, ISO 14000, ISO 18000 [18]; ISO 26000 [19]; GRI [9], [10]; SAFA [11]; the Eco-Management and Audit Scheme [20] and the Organization for Economic Cooperation and Development (OECD) Guidelines for Multinational Enterprises [21].

We have been developing specified KPIs for the food processing sector [4], [5], [8], [12] since 2007. We introduce the results of our research of KPIs' determinants in the food processing sector C10 and C11 in Table 1, where we follow the trends which brought the frameworks of the GRI and SAFA principles with our conclusions [4], [12], [14], [22] and [23].

Table 1. List of KPI Indicators [23]

Area	Indicator	Title	Unit
Investment	EN1	Investments into environmental protection	Czech crown
	EN2	The cost of investment into environmental protection	Czech crown
Emission	EN3	Total air-emissions (at least SO_2, NO_x, CO, VOC, NH_3 and $PM_{20,.50,.10}$)	Ton
	EN4	Total greenhouse gas emissions (CO_2, CH_4, N_2O, HFCs, PFCs and SF_6)	kg of CO_2-eq
Resource consumption	EN5	Total annual energy consumption	MWh
	EN6	Total consumption of renewable energy	%
	EN7	Material use (except water and energy)	Ton
	EN8	Recyclable input material use	%
	EN9	Total annual water consumption	m^3
Waste	EN10	Total annual waste production	Ton
	EN11	Total annual production of hazardous waste	Ton

3   Benchmarking Systems Methodology

The benchmarking process is a series of actions, steps, functions, or activities that bring about an end or a result: *the identification and importance of best practices for the improvement of EP*. There are dozens of sources which describe the benchmarking process. It is called by some "the nine-step benchmarking process", or by others "the

534   Z. Chvátalová, J. Hřebíček, and O. Trenz

four steps of benchmarking". The following description of phases is based on Andersen and Pettersen [1], who call the process "the benchmarking wheel", in order to indicate that benchmarking is an ongoing process [23]:

1. *Plan*: During the planning phase, the scope and type of environmental benchmarking are determined. The focus here lies in process benchmarking, because, through the analysis of best practices, it provides a basis for substantial improvements. The planning stage involves: selecting what is to be benchmarked; analysing the organization processes; establishing performance measures for the process; selecting benchmarking partners that will participate in the benchmarking process; and determining the data collection methods that will be employed.

2. *Search*: A primary task is to search for and identify suitable benchmarking partners in the investigated sector. This includes the following activities: to design a list of criteria which an ideal benchmarking partner should satisfy (e.g., geographical location, size, structure, products, technology, economic activity, and organisational climate); to search for potential benchmarking partners (i.e., companies that are better than oneself at the process in question); to compare the candidates and select the best-suited benchmarking partner(s) (it is recommended to select more than one possible benchmarking partner); to establish contact with the selected partner(s) and gain their acceptance for participation in the benchmarking study. The companies of the food processing sector (NACE codes C10, C11) were selected on the basis of the database of the Czech Environmental Information Agency of the Ministry of the Environment of the Czech Republic, which have enabled and certified their EMS with the ISO 14001 or EMAS standards in 2007 [23].

3. *Observe and Collect Data*: The steps of the observation phase are as follows: to assess the information needs (data and information should be collected on EP levels, which indicate how good the partner is compared to oneself; practices or methods which make it possible to achieve these EP levels, and enablers who make it possible to perform the process according to these practices or methods); select the method and tool for collecting the information and data; observe and debrief (it is important that after the visit a debriefing is conducted as soon as possible in order not to lose any details of the observation). We have combined the collection of data through the abovementioned Web Information System and also through personal visits of the investigated company's responsible environmentalists [16]. The selected companies were further explored (we have used their annual reports, website, etc.) and submitted for evaluation according to additional criteria that were relevant to the selection of companies for our research [23].

4. *Analyse*: The descriptive statistics were made on the grounds that certain specifics of variables have an influence on the result of the methods and timing, and this can be seen in the descriptive statistics of the individual indicators. The average, standard deviation, variance and coefficient of variation were calculated. To determine the dominant factors which affect the company the method of the main components was used; the appropriateness of the data was tested using Bartlett's Test of Sphericity and the Kaiser-Meyer-Olkin Measure of Sampling Adequacy [23]. The main purpose of this phase is to determine: the EP gaps between benchmarking partners; the causes of the gaps, such as the methods and practices

that make it possible for partners to achieve higher performance levels; the factors that facilitate or hinder the adoption of best practices and methods.

5. *Adapt*: The main findings of the analysis phase are communicated and discussed with the benchmarking partners. The best practices identified during the benchmarking were adapted and improved by the companies and recommendations were developed for their implementation [23].

6. *Continuous Improvement*: Benchmarking should not be a one-time event but an interactive, continuous and dynamic process for improving a company's EP. This involves monitoring the process, introducing continuous learning and providing input for the company's continuous improvement. It could be done by means of the Web information system that has been developed.

3.1   Environmental Benchmarking Information Tools

Some information and communication technology (ICT) tools are available for the purposes of environmental benchmarking. There exist both generic and specific ICT tools for environmental benchmarking [16]. We mention several of them here:

- e-Bench [24] is a Web-enabled audit and simulation/modelling tool that is used to record systematically whatever energy or utilities an organization is consuming and to relate these to the core business activity. The system then benchmarks these input factors to identify how efficiently they are used with other users in the database. e-Bench has been successfully used in the USA, Australia and New Zealand.
- The Global Environmental Management Initiative (GEMI) [25] is a coalition of large businesses aimed at providing strategies for businesses to achieve Environmental, Health and Safety (EHS) excellence, economic success, and corporate citizenship. The group introduced their primer for environmental benchmarking in 1994. The primer is not industry or sector-specific, and is accessible to everyone free of charge on the Internet. This ICT tool can be used as a framework for any kind of benchmarking, whether focusing on roles, strategic issues, processes or performance.
- The Safety, Health and Environment Intra Industry Benchmarking Association (SHEIIBA) [26] was formed in 1996 in response to the recognition that many leading companies were eager to learn how others in different sectors managed EHS and to compare their accident performance. Corporate Benchmarking Ltd. (in SHEIIBA) has built and runs bespoke safety benchmarking programmes for industry sectors. Participating companies enter accident and ill-health data into an online form each month. The data is divided by cause and type and can by split into different employee groups. Data can be viewed in graphic or tabular format as fixed periods, rolling years or time spans (up to 12 quarters or years.) The system is currently in use in 14 United Kingdom water utilities.
- Environmental Management Assessment and Benchmarking (EMAB) [27] is a Web application (portal) designed for the maturity assessment and benchmarking of corporate environmental management efforts [28]. The portal enables the measuring of corporate environmental management efforts via a survey that is based on criteria pursuant to the ISO 14000 family [17] and the EMAS III [20] standards.

In addition to the assessment, there is a benchmarking function that allows the comparison with other participating companies. Its development started in 2009 at the Ostnabrück University as part of the project IT-for-Green [29] and has been going since spring 2014. The portal is in both German and English and is open especially for German companies.

Our analysis of known environmental benchmarking ICT tools together with the evaluation [16] show: an efficient ICT tool has to be based on reliable and purely scientific information of the main environmental impacts and aspects of companies of the given sector. Based on this the information environmental KPIs are worked out, and these are the foundations of a well-structured management benchmarking system. This system then has potential to be eco-efficient and easy to use [23].

4   Web Information System

We have applied the abovementioned ideas of section 3.1 to companies in the food processing sector of the Czech Republic, where we have identified the environmental performance model based on the specific conditions of the EMS implementation [16], [23] and we have furthermore developed a Web Information System for the environmental benchmarking of companies in this sector, where we have also used our experiences with the development of the Web Information System for the corporate performance and reporting [4], [14], [23], [30].

4.1   System Requirements and Objectives

In our vision, we foresee two main objectives of the developed Web Environmental Benchmarking and Reporting Information System (WEBRIS) [30]. A company may use such a system to create various reports and share its data with both its stakeholders and, in the future, with the state administrations concerned with regulatory demands and mandatory corporate reporting [23, p. 165-177].

The second objective of WEBRIS is the EPE performed by evaluating input KPIs (Tab. 1). This way, the company can share its EP with the public or check its EP development progress. EPE can be done through various reports as stated above or through custom dashboards [23, p. 223-228].

We define the following three main generic actors:

- *Reporter* – a person responsible for ensuring company mandatory environmental reporting (especially a company environmentalist) or reporting for stakeholders [23, p. 166]; this would typically be a member of the management team or a contractor..
- *Evaluator* – a person responsible for the EPE of a company [23, p. 212]; this role can be represented by a wide range of people starting from managers, auditors and various internal interested parties. The evaluator may also enter data into the information system, but it is not his/her primary task; typically, this would be the additional data required for the report generation, but not required as a part of mandatory reporting (e.g., company strategy, goals a targets, vision, etc.)

- *Administrator* – the administrator of the information system responsible for defining the report templates and business rules used to generate reports [23, p. 212].

Basic high-level requirements for the Web information system are [23, 211-217], [30]:

- to store source company data; to evaluate KPIs according to the selected sector and methodology;
- to generate environmental benchmarking reports in the selected format for offline storage, printing and archiving;
- to import source company data from its company information system in the prescribed format;
- to provide selected information in the form of reports accessible online to the general public or only to selected persons;
- to provide selected information in the standardized XBRL (eXtensible Business Reporting Language) format for interchange with other systems [32];
- to provide the possibility to evaluate the company EP anonymously;
- to provide the possibility to define report data and business logic;
- to dynamically generate the XBRL taxonomies for a given report [32];
- to provide the possibility to customize standardized reports and to generate fully customized reports;
- to provide the possibility to compare reports among the companies of the given sector.

4.2   WEBRIS Structure

The Fig. 1 shows an overview of WEBRIS architecture based on an XBRL database. The main idea of this approach is a possibility of direct storing of XBRL data into an XML database that allows relational access to these data. The logical relational data model and the XBRL contents simplify the Business Intelligence integration [30, 31, 32]. The architecture of WEBRIS is divided into application, processing and data layers.

The application layer accepts report submissions and provides the results of report queries. It is composed of various interfaces such as a web application user interface or some defined APIs. The application layer communicates with the storage layer via SQL queries or via the XQuery language. It defines the access tools and internet protocols used for the following purposes: SOAP, REST, JDBC or file access via WebDAV.

The data layer is composed of both the RDB system and the XBRL database. The data layer exposes both the relational and the XML interface so that the data can be queried by both SQL and XQuery languages. The application layer provides a wide range of APIs to connect the database to various sources. This offers a high interoperability of the WEBRIS system. Alongside the application layer is the Business Intelligence engine [32], which can benefit from direct access to the data layer. This will be possible if the data layer is self-containing, i.e., if it can provide an XBRL document with all the necessary taxonomies and templates.

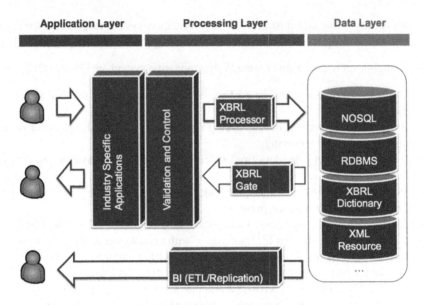

Fig. 1. WEBRIS architecture [30]

4.3 WEBRIS Environmental Benchmarking Validation

The pilot implementation of WEBRIS has been performed in the set of twenty four SME breweries in the Czech Republic which belong to C11 - Manufacture of beverages NACE section and which have determined their KPIs according to Tab. 1. The benchmark values were calculated firstly as the mean of the KPIs of the registered companies and after further analysis as the optimum value" consulted with environmental experts. The choice was made vis á vis the availability of comprehensive data from the given market segment and the willingness of companies to   develop further. Another direction of the software implementation will be connected with improving the user-friendliness (in accord with feedback) and the integration of complementary methods for measuring company performance, together with an extension into other market segments.

Every user of WEBRIS, after completing the registration of his company, can input their KPIs (see Tab. 1) and thereupon the output benchmark will be determined. Based on the input KPIs, the benchmark will be shown. This means that the company EPE is performed based on the assessment of the KPIs that have been entered. The individual criteria are displayed in a ray chart (Fig. 2). The closer the partial value to the outer edge, the closer it is to the maximum evaluation level of the given segment (company benchmark). Emphasis in assessment is placed on sustainability. One part of benchmarking are recommendations useable for the further development of the company.

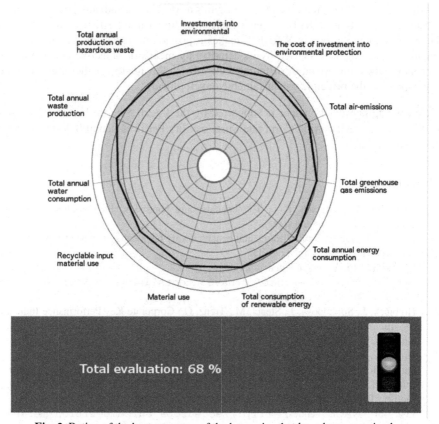

Fig. 2. Rating of the best company of the breweries that have been examined

5   Conclusion

Our research [4, 5], [8], [13, 14], [23], [30, 32] has focused the possibility of the utilization of ICT and XBRL taxonomy for environmental benchmarking and reporting of food processing organizations. We have suggested the formalization of this system on the basis of the universal XML markup language by means of the use of the XBRL [30, 32] and we have developed WEBRIS based on KPIs. We have assumed that it will minimize the main barriers that prevent the tested organizations (C10 and C11 NACE codes) from supporting environmental reporting. Some of their objections have been for example:

- Collecting and managing environmental data is expensive, technical issues with data collection are also a problem.
- Determining a set of appropriate KPIs to monitor and measure EP is difficult.
- Disclosure can create business risks which competitors and regulators may seize upon.
- Environmental reporting is seen as a superfluous and burdening activity.

The core of these barriers is the time-demanding nature of creating the breweries' data-processing reports, and the absence of positive feedback of their managers.

By using WEBRIS, the given brewery gains a whole set of advantages. The administration and editing of KPIs is much easier and much more effective for EPE. The benchmark methodology in WEBRIS makes it possible to assess the given brewery's environmental impacts (caused by its activity) by means of objective considerations; to conduct the comparison of different breweries and evaluate whether their activities correspond to the principles of sustainable development.

Acknowledgments. The paper is supported by the Czech Science Foundation. Name of the Projects: "Measuring Corporate Sustainability Performance in Selected Sectors" Reg. No. 14-23079S.

References

1. Andersen, B., Pettersen, P.G.: The benchmaking handbook. Step-by-step instructions. Chapman & Hall, London (1996)
2. Bolli, A., Emtairah, T.: Environmental benchmarking for local authorities:From concept to practice. EEA, Copenhagen (2001)
3. ECOSMES. Environmental benchmarking, http://www.ecosmes.net/cm/navContents?l=EN&navID=envBenchmar king&subNavID=1&pagID=1
4. Hřebíček, J., Soukopová, J., Štencl, M., Trenz, O.: Corporate Key Performance Indicators for Environmental Management and Reporting. Actauniv. Agric. etsilvic. Mendel. Brun. 59, 99–108 (2011)
5. Hřebíček, J., Pekárková, L.: Key Performance Indicators for Sustainable Reporting According toNACE. In: Möller, A., Schreiber, M. (eds.) 22nd International Conference on Informatics fo Environmental Protection, Enviroinfo 2008. Environmental Informatics and Industry Ecology, pp. 45–53. Shaker Verlag, Aachen (2008)
6. List of NACE codes, http://ec.europa.eu/competition/mergers/ cases/index/nace_all.html
7. Hermann, B.G., Kroeze, C., Jawjit, W.: Assessing environmental performance by combining life cycle assessment, multi-criteria analysis and environmental performance indicators. Journal of Cleaner Production 15, 1787–1796 (2007)
8. Hřebíček, J., Mísařová, P., Hyršlová, J.: Environmental Key Performance Indicators and Corporate Reporting. In: International Conference EA-SDI 2007. Environmental Accounting and Sustainable Development Indicators, pp. 147–155. University Jana Evangelisty-Purkyně, Ústí (2007)
9. G4 Sustainability Reporting Guidelines, https://www.globalreporting.org/reporting/g4/
10. G4 Sector Disclosures. Food processing, https://www.globalreporting.org/resourcelibrary/ GRI-G4-Food-Processing-Sector-Disclosures.pdf
11. SAFA, Sustainability Assessment of Food and Agriculture systems (SAFA) (2013), http://www.fao.org/nr/sustainability/ sustainability-assessments-safa/en/
12. Hřebíček, J., Valtinyová, S., Křen, J., Hodinka, M., Trenz, O., Marada, P.: Sustainability Indicators: Development and Application for the Agriculture Sector. In: Erechtchoukova, M.G., Khaiter, P.A., Golinska, P. (eds.) Sustainability Appraisal: Quantitative Methods and Mathematical Techniques for Environmental Performance Evaluation, pp. 63–102. Springer, Heidelberg (2013)

13. Measuring Corporate Sustainability in Selected Sectors. Project GACR GA14/23079S, http://gacr.pefka.mendelu.cz/en/index.php
14. Hřebíček, J., Soukopová, J., Trenz, O.: Current Trends of Economic Modelling of Sustainable Corporate Performance and Reporting – Review and Research Agenda. In: Nerudová, D. (ed.) Procedia Economics and Finance, vol. 12, pp. 234–242 (2014)
15. Hee-jeong, Y., Kun-mo, L.: Environmental Benchmarking Methodology for Identification of Key Environmental Aspects of Product. In: IEEE International Symposium onElectronics & the Environment, pp. 21–26. IEEE Press, New York (2002)
16. Jónsdóttir, H., Sparf, A.M., Hanssen, O.J.: Enviromental Benchmarking a Tool for Continuous Environmental Improvements in the SME Sector. Nordic Innovation Centre, Oslo (2005)
17. EN ISO 14031: 2013. Environmental Management – Environmental Performance Evaluation – Guidelines (2013)
18. Integrated Management System Documentation / Manuals for Integrated Certification, http://www.isohelpline.com/ims_iso_9000_iso_14000_ohsas_1800 0_docu-ment_manual.htm
19. ISO 26000:2010. Social responsibility, http://www.iso.org/iso/iso26000
20. EMAS, http://ec.europa.eu/environment/emas/index_en.htm
21. OECD Guidelines for Multinational Enterprises, http://www.oecd.org/document/28/ 0,3746,en_2649_34889_2397532_1_1_1_1,00.html
22. Hřebíček, J., Trenz, O., Vernerová, E.: Optimal set of agri-environmental indicators for the agricultural sector of Czech Republic. Agric. etsilvic. Mendel. Brun. 61, 2171–2181 (2013)
23. Kocmanová, A., Hřebíček, J., Dočekalová, M., Hodinka, M., Hor-Nungová, J., Chvátalová, Z., Kubálek, T., Popelka, O., Šimberová, I., Topolová, I., Trenz, O.: Corporate performance measurement, Littera, Brno (2013) (in Czech)
24. e-Bench, http://www.e-bench.com/eBench/index.jsp
25. GEMI – Global Environmental Management Initiative, http://www.gemi.org/GEMIHome.aspx
26. SHEIIBA - Safety, Health and Environmental Intra Industry Benchmarking Service, http://www.sheiiba.com/
27. EMAB - Environmental Management Assessment and Benchmarking, http://www.emab.ertemis.eu/contao/homepage.html
28. Frehe, V., Stiel, F., Teuteberg, F.: A Maturity Model and Web Application forEnvironmental Management Benchmarking. AMCIS 2014, 1–14 (2014), http://aisel.aisnet.org/amcis2014/GreenIS/ GeneralPresentations/1/
29. IT-for-Green -, http://it-for-green.eu/
30. Hodinka, M., Štencl, M., Hřebíček, J., Trenz, O.: Business Intelligence in Environmental Reporting Powered by XBRL. Acta Univ. Agric. Silvic. MendelianaeBrun. 62, 355–362 (2014)
31. XBRL, https://www.xbrl.org/
32. Hodinka, M.: Formalization of Business Rules and Methodology of their Implementation to the Information System. Ph.D. thesis. Mendel University, Brno (2013)
33. Popelka, O., Hodinka, M., Hřebíček, J., Trenz, O.: Information System for Corporate Performance Assessment and Reporting. In: Long, C.A., Mastorakis, N.E., Mladenov, V. (eds.) 2013 International Conference on Systems, Control, Signal Processing and Informatics (SCSI 2013), pp. 247–253. EUROPMENT Press, New York (2013)

Scalability of Global 0.25° Ocean Simulations Using MOM

Marshall Ward[1] and Yuanyuan Zhang[2]

[1] National Computational Infrastructure, Canberra, Australia
marshall.ward@anu.edu.au
[2] Fujitsu Australia Limited, Canberra, Australia
yuanyuan.zhang@au.fujitsu.com

Abstract. We investigate the scalability of global 0.25° resolution ocean-sea ice simulations using the Modular Ocean Model (MOM). We focus on two major platforms, hosted at the National Computational Infrastructure (NCI) National Facility: an x86-based PRIMERGY cluster with InfiniBand interconnects, and a SPARC-based FX10 system using the Tofu interconnect. We show that such models produce efficient, scalable results on both platforms up to 960 CPUs. Speeds are notably faster on Raijin when either hyperthreading or fewer cores per node are used. We also show that the ocean submodel scales up to 1920 CPUs with negligible loss of efficiency, but the sea ice and coupler components quickly become inefficient and represent substantial bottlenecks in future scalability. Our results show that both platforms offer sufficient performance for future scientific research, and highlight to the challenges for future scalability and optimization.

Keywords: ocean modeling, performance profiling, high performance computing, parallel computing.

1 Introduction

Current global climate simulations typically rely on coarse ocean models of approximately 1° resolution, but there is growing demand for a greater resolution of the ocean eddy fields, with corresponding resolutions on the order of 0.25° or 0.1° [1]. The very strong stratification of the ocean causes its most turbulent currents to emerge at these smaller resolutions [2], which are absent from coarse-resolution climate models. Such turbulent processes are expected to have a major role in the maintenance of the ocean's strongest currents, and in the vertical mixing and stratification of the ocean [3].

Along with the many scientific challenges of high-resolution climate modelling, an additional impediment in the adoption of greater resolutions in the ocean is the significant computational cost. A typical climate simulation requires decades, if not centuries, of simulation time to achieve a scientifically valuable result, and can require hundreds of such runs to perfect the tuning of their numerous parameters [1]. In such an environment, one needs the capacity to simulate many years per day. To achieve such results will require proven scalability into hundreds, if not thousands, of CPUs.

R. Denzer et al. (Eds.): ISESS 2015, IFIP AICT 448, pp. 542–551, 2015.

In this paper, we assess the ability to run high-resolution simulations on computing platforms of Australia's National Computational Infrastructure (NCI). We focus on scalability up to 1920 CPUs on the Raijin and Fujin computing platforms. We consider a selection of configurations on each platform and assess their efficiencies for use in future scientific research.

2   Methods

2.1   Numerical Model

The experiment used in this study is the global ocean-sea ice model of [4], which was based on the Geophysical Fluid Dynamics Laboratory (GFDL) CM2.5 model [5]. The numerical submodels are the Modular Ocean Model (MOM) and the Sea Ice Simulator (SIS), built from the Flexible Modeling System (FMS) framework, which also includes the ocean-ice coupler [6]. The simulations presented here use the MOM 5.1 source code release, which includes the SIS and FMS components.

The numerical grid of the ocean and sea ice models is a curvilinear grid with a nominal resolution of 0.25° and contains 1440 × 1080 horizontal grid points. The ocean and sea ice models use 50 and 6 vertical levels, respectively.

Parallelisation is achieved by decomposing the horizontal grid into tiles of equal size, with additional halo grid points surrounding each tile. For each timestep, the halos of adjacent and diagonally adjacent tiles are updated, requiring 8 messages per field.

Standard experiments are run for 31 days, using 1488 timesteps of 1800 second resolution. Each ocean timestep requires 72 additional sea ice timesteps. A longer simulation time was chosen to represent a typical integration time for scientific analysis, and to reduce any statistical variability of the observed walltimes. Simulations using 960 CPUs were run three times to confirm the reproducibility of the results, and the median walltimes was used to select the run in this study. For all other runs, a single simulation was used for each configuration.

Diagnostic output consists of 4 three-dimensional fields, which are saved to disk after every 5 days. This output rate was chosen to reflect a comparable rate of scientific value while also not overshadowing the model calculations.

2.2   Raijin

Raijin is the principal supercomputer of the NCI National Facility. It is a Fujitsu PRIMERGY cluster comprised of 3592 computing nodes, with each containing two 2.6 GHz 8-core Intel Xeon Sandy Bridge (E5-2670) CPUs, with a total core count of 57472. Turbo boost is enabled for these runs, increasing the maximum clock speed of 16 cores to 3.0 GHz. Operational nodes have approximately 32 GiB of memory, with more memory available on selected nodes.

The cluster network uses InfiniBand (IB) FDR-14 interconnects, which provide peak (4x aggregate) transfer speeds up to 56 Gb/s between nodes. There are 18 nodes connected to each top-of-rack (ToR) IB switch. The 72 nodes in each rack use 4 ToR switches. Each ToR switch connects to a top-level director switch, with 3 connections per ToR to each director. Because of the high usage rate of Raijin, it is prohibitive to arrange jobs within the network, and we assume that all experiments in this study depend on the director switches.

The operating system platform is CentOS 6.5, which uses the Linux 2.6.32 kernel. Jobs are managed using the PBSPro scheduler, and files are kept under a Lustre 2.5 filesystem.

We use the Intel Compiler Suite 14.3.172 for model compilation. MPI communication uses Open MPI 1.8.2 and data IO uses NetCDF 4.3.0, which was built using HDF5 1.8.10. The model is built with the -O2 and -xhost optimisation flags.

We consider three experiment configurations on Raijin: a standard configuration using 16 model processes per node (herein "default"), a similar configuration using hyperthreaded cores, and a third configuration running 12 model processes per node (herein "12 PPN"). For the 12 PPN configuration, turbo-boosted clock speeds are increased to 3.1 GHz.

2.3   Fujin

Fujin is NCI's Fujitsu FX10 cluster consisting of 96 compute nodes, each containing a 1.848 GHz 16-core SPARC64 IXfx CPU. For our investigation, numerical experiments were limited to a maximum of 84 nodes, or 1344 cores.

The interconnect is a streamlined version of the K-Computer's Tofu interconnect system, and consists of 8 serially connected Tofu units. Each unit contains 12 compute nodes arranged as a 3D torus of shape $2 \times 3 \times 2$. Nodes are connected by 10 bidirectional links with 5 Gb/s transfer rates, yielding a peak transfer rate of 100 Gb/s between nodes. Tofu interconnects also include the Tofu barrier hardware module for optimised MPI reductions and broadcasts, but we do not use it in this study.

When compared to Raijin, the lower clock speed of Fujin's CPUs will necessarily result in lower optimal performance for computationally-bound software. However, the fixed Tofu interconnect offers the potential for optimized node layout and efficient scalability for higher CPU counts.

The FX10 operating system is Fujitsu XTC OS 1.3.6, with a Linux 2.6.25 kernel. Jobs are managed by the scheduler of the Parallelnavi suite. The filesystem is the Fujitsu Exabyte File System (FEFS) 1.3.1, which is based on the Lustre 1.8.5 filesystem.

The model is compiled using the Fujitsu compiler suite 1.2.1 and includes Fujitsu's MPI library, which is based on Open MPI 1.4.3. Data IO uses NetCDF 4.3.2, built with HDF5 1.8.12 and NetCDF-Fortran 4.2. The model is compiled using the -Kfast, -Kocl, and -O2 optimization flags.

We consider two configurations on Fujin, denoted here as snake and ladder layouts. Node placement for a single Tofu unit for each layout is illustrated in Figure 1. The snake layout guarantees that all communications is exclusively between neighbour nodes, but also requires that each node span an entire latitude line. The ladder layout divides each latitude line across two nodes, allowing for smaller tile widths, but it also requires diagonally adjacent tiles to send data through non-neighbour nodes.

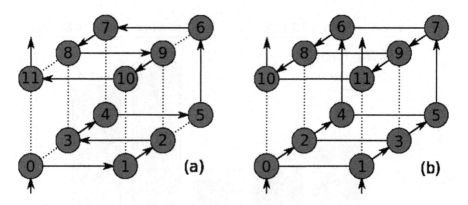

Fig. 1. Node layouts for each Tofu unit. Each node number corresponds to 16 domain tiles. Figure (a) shows the snake layout and figure (b) shows the ladder layout.

2.4   Timing

On Raijin, we use the IPM 2.0.2 profiler to construct basic runtime statistics. Model runtime and MPI usage times are based on IPM output logs. On Fujin, runtime and MPI usage times are from the `fipp` profiler output logs.

Submodel runtimes are provided by the internal timers of the MOM ocean model, which are based on the `system_clock` subroutine of the Intel Fortran compiler and the system clock of the Linux kernel.

3   Results

3.1   Platform Configuration

Figure 2a shows the total runtime for a 480-CPU experiment across different hardware platforms and configurations. The configuration choice on Raijin had a major impact on performance, with observed speedups of 28% and 60% for hyperthreaded and 12 PPN experiments, respectively. Process layout on Fujin had an observable but less notable impact, with the snake layout achieving a 15% speedup in comparison to the ladder layout.

Experiment runtimes on Raijin are faster than on Fujin, with the fastest runs on Raijin outperforming the Fujin jobs by more than a factor of two. Much of this difference in performance can be attributed to the clock speeds of the two platforms. However, the clock speed ratio of the Raijin and Fujin CPUs is only 1.62, and cannot alone account for the differences in performance.

Figure 2b attempts to clarify this performance difference across the platforms by estimating the mean number of cycles per CPU with the following formula:

$$N_c = f(1 - p)\tau_o$$

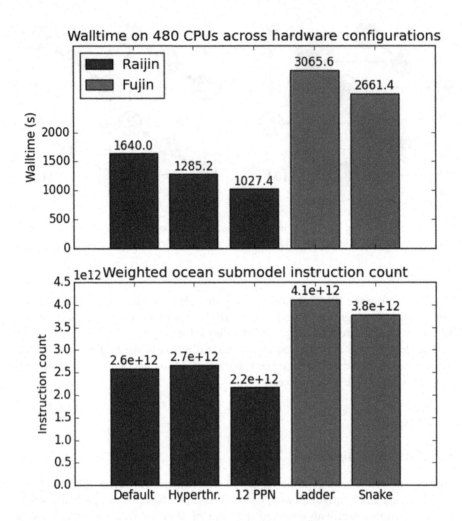

Fig. 2. Model performance across platforms and configurations. Figure (a) compares walltimes in seconds, and figure (b) compares cycle counts in the ocean submodel.

where f is the CPU clock speed, p is the mean fraction of MPI instructions across all ranks, and τ_o is the ocean submodel runtime. We focus on the ocean submodel because it is strongly dominated by floating point arithmetic, and is shown in the next section to demonstrate high scalability up to 1920 CPUs.

N_c is an imperfect estimate of cycle count, since total communication time may not accurately represent communication time in the ocean model. There may also be additional communication costs outside of the MPI library. But it can provide an approximation of the number of computational cycles, as well as the relative efficiency of vector arithmetic on each platform.

After correcting for clock speed and focusing on the ocean model, our estimate indicates that the performance of the two platforms is comparable, with SPARC operations requiring only 15% more cycles than the x86 operations for its simulation.

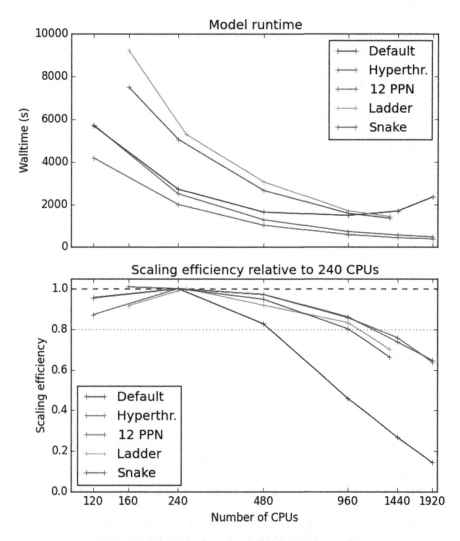

Fig. 3. Model walltime (a) and scaling efficiency (b)

3.2   Scaling

The general performance and scalability of each experiment across different CPUs is shown in Figure 3. The general trends shown in the previous section are also observed in Figure 3a, with simulations on Raijin generally outperforming those on Fujin. Hyperthreaded and 12 PPN jobs continue to outperform the default runs on Raijin, and snake layouts outperform ladder layouts on Fujin.

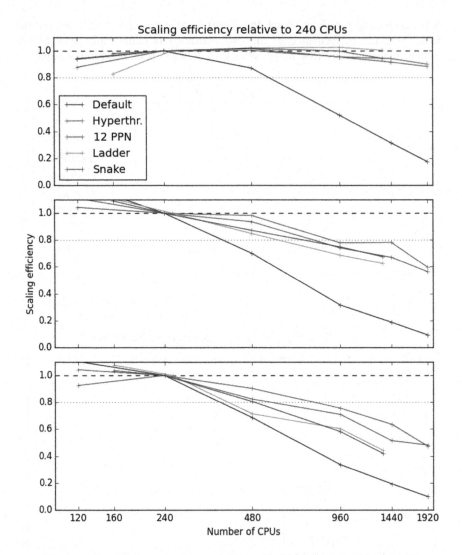

Fig. 4. Scaling efficiency for the ocean (a), sea ice (b), and coupler (c) submodels

The most notable observation is the dramatic loss of performance of the default experiments on Raijin, where scalability begins to diminish at 480 CPUs and wall-times begin to increase after 960 CPUs. Scalability is restored by either introducing hyperthreading or by using fewer cores, indicating the presence of a computational bottleneck related to the number of processes per node.

The relative efficiency of each configuration is shown in Figure 3b, which is computed as

$$\varepsilon = \frac{r\tau_r}{n\tau_n}$$

where n is the number of CPUs, τ_n is the runtime using n CPUs, and r is the reference experiment, which is 240 CPUs for all configurations except the ladder Fujin runs, which use 255 CPUs.

Figure 3b shows that, with the exception of the default Raijin setup, all runs demonstrate scalable performance up to 960 CPUs and maintain an efficiency greater than 80%. Experiments on Raijin scale slightly better than on Fujin, although the results are comparable over all platforms and configurations. Beyond 960 CPUs, all experiments begin to drop substantially and no longer provide a reasonable level of performance.

Model performance can be further clarified by investigating the scalability of the respective submodels, as shown in Figure 4. Figure 4a shows that, despite a reduction of general scalability around 960 CPUs, the ocean submodel continues to scale efficiently to 1920 CPUs. However, the sea ice and coupling model subcomponents, shown in Figures 4b and 4c, grow progressively worse in performance as the number of CPUs increase, indicating major bottlenecks in the sea ice model and submodel flux exchange components.

There is some evidence of improved efficiency in the ocean model, indicating that the communication bottlenecks in the sea ice and coupler models may also be freeing additional resources for the ocean model. Scaling efficiency on Fujin appears to be better than Raijin for the ocean model, although it is notably lower in the other model components.

4   Discussion

4.1   Configuration

Scalability on Raijin beyond 480 CPUs was only possible after either reducing the number of processes per node, or enabling hyperthreading on the core. In both situations, we reduced the number of processes per computational core. While the underlying cause is not known, one point of consideration is use of subthreads within Open MPI. Since each model instance create four MPI subthreads, there is a competition for resources between these processes on each core. By allowing the kernel to shift some of these jobs to other computational cores, we may be relieving any bottlenecks related to shared memory management or context switching. But further investigations are required to confirm this explanation, and to determine if it is a consequence of x86 architecture, kernel scheduling, or Open MPI implementation.

Scalability on Fujin was not affected by processor layout, although the performance of the snake layout was measurably faster than the ladder layout. From this, we conclude that even a modest dependence on non-neighbor communication, such as in our ladder layouts, can have a detrimental effect on performance, and that snake layouts should be used when possible.

4.2   Platform Comparison

An additional observation in this study is the significant discrepancy in performance between the Raijin and Fujin platforms. Our estimate of cycle count indicates that most of this difference can be attributed to CPU clock speed. However, the x86 CPUs still demonstrate somewhat better performance per cycle. This can be attributed to various factors, such as differences in CPU cache architecture or compilers, but a more thorough investigation would be required to confirm the level of efficiency and underlying cause.

An unexplored opportunity for improved hardware performance on Fujin is the Tofu barrier acceleration of the MPI reductions and broadcasts. Such operations are a dominant part of most diagnostic calculations, and the Tofu barrier could have an major impact on future simulations with high levels of diagnostic output.

Another point of consideration is the increasing trend of greater numbers of cores on each node, including MIC architectures such as Xeon Phi accelerators. Although Raijin outperformed Fujin in runtime, scalability was not possible without the introduction of redundant computational cores. No such additional resources were required to achieve scalable results on Fujin.

4.3   Submodel Performance

The difference in ocean scalability versus the ice and coupler submodel also indicates a potential target for optimization. Running the ocean and sea ice serially on each process is a potential bottleneck that could be addressed by moving the sea ice calculations onto separate core. In such a configuration, load balancing would become a greater concern, and a separation of ocean and ice would put a greater burden on the coupler. But given the inability of SIS to scale beyond 480 CPUs, and the very large number of sea ice timesteps required per ocean timestep, this may become a requirement in the future.

The poor scalability of the coupling subroutines indicate that a parallelisation of of ocean and sea ice timesteps will not be sufficient to achieve future scalability. Efficient field exchange between models must also be a target of future optimisation efforts.

5   Conclusion

We have shown that the global 0.25° resolution ocean-sea ice configurations of the MOM ocean model can run efficiently on both x86 PRIMERGY and SPARC FX10 platforms. On the x86-based Raijin system, we were able to simulate over 10 model years per day at a sufficiently high level of efficiency. On the FX10 Fujin platform, we can simulate over 4 model years per day at a similar level of efficiency.

In order to achieve a high level of performance on the Raijin platform, we were required to either reduce the number of model processes per node to 12, leaving four cores to run idle during the simulation, or to enable hyperthreading on our CPUs, allowing two computational threads per core. Although reducing the number of cores yields a greater level of performance, hyperthreaded runs yield comparable results without any idle cores, thereby achieving much greater efficiency. When all 16 cores on each node were used without hyperthreading, the runtimes increased by a factor of three and were unable to scale beyond 480 CPUs.

Comparison of the submodels within the ice-ocean configuration shows that the ocean model scales up to 1920 cores with only a negligible loss of efficiency, while the sea ice and coupling components cease to scale after 480 CPUs. Future efforts to improve the scalability of MOM should target these subcomponents.

Both platforms have proven capable of running global high-resolution simulations of the ocean, and enable scientists to investigate the impacts of turbulent-scale processes on global climate. Development towards resolutions of 0.1° and beyond will require further investigations of the underlying codes and their resource requirements, and ongoing collaborations between industry and the academic research community.

Acknowledgements. This work was conducted as part of the ACCESS Optimisation Project, a collaboration between NCI, Fujitsu, and the Australian Bureau of Meteorology. Research was undertaken with the assistance of resources from NCI, which is supported by the Australian Government. We are grateful to Mark Cheeseman of NCI, Symon Swann of Fujitsu Australia, and Motohiro Yamada of Fujitsu Japan for constructive reviews on an earlier draft of this paper.

References

1. Taylor, K.E., Stouffer, R.J., Meehl, G.A.: An Overview of CMIP5 and the Experiment Design. Bull. Amer. Meteor. Soc. 93, 485–498 (2012)
2. Chelton, D.B., de Szoeke, R.A., Schlax, M.G., El Naggar, K., Siwertz, N.: Geographical variability of the first baroclinicRossby radius of deformation. J. Phys. Oceanogr. 28, 433–459 (1998)
3. Farneti, R., Delworth, T.L., Rosati, A.J., Griffies, S.M., Zeng, F.: The Role of Mesoscale Eddies in the Rectification of the Southern Ocean Response to Climate Change. J. Phys. Oceanogr. 40, 1539–1557 (2010)
4. Spence, P., Griffies, S.M., England, M.H., Hogg, A., Mc, C., Saenko, O.A., Jourdain, N.C.: Rapid subsurface warming and circulation changes of Antarctic coastal waters by poleward shifting winds. Geophys. Res. Lett. 41, 4601–4610 (2014)
5. Delworth, T.L., Rosati, A., Anderson, W.G., Adcroft, A., Balaji, V., Benson, R., Dixon, K.W., Griffies, S.M., Lee, H.C., Pacanowski, R.C., Vecchi, G.A., Wittenberg, A.T., Zeng, F., Zhang, R.: Simulated climate and climate change in the GFDL CM2.5 high-resolution coupled climate model. Journal of Climate 25(8) (2012)
6. Griffies, S.M.: Elements of the Modular Ocean Model (MOM), GFDL Ocean Group Technical Report No. 7. NOAA/Geophysical Fluid Dynamics Laboratory. 618 + xiii pages (2012 release)

A Performance Assessment of the Unified Model

Dale Roberts and Mark Cheeseman

National Computational Infrastructure, Canberra, Australia
{ds.roberts,mark.cheeseman}@anu.edu.au

Abstract. The Unified Model (UM) is a model produced by the UK MetOffice for Numerical Weather Prediction (NWP) and climate simulation. It is used extensively by various university, government and other research organizations on the large supercomputer hosted at the National Computing Infrastructure (NCI). A 3-year collaboration between NCI, the Australian Bureau of Meteorology and Fujitsu is underway to address performance and scalability issues in the UM on NCI's supercomputer, Raijin.

IO performance in the UM is the most dominant factor in its overall performance. The IO server approach employed is sophisticated and requires proper calibration to achieve acceptable performance. Global synchronization and file lock contention is a problem that can be remedied with simple MPI global collective calls. Complimentary IO strategies, such as MPI-IO and directed IO, are being investigated for implementation.

The OpenMP implementation employed in the UM is investigated, and is found to have inefficiencies that are detrimental to the load balance of the model. Only loop-wise parallelism is employed. Due to the inherently imbalanced nature of the model, a task-wise approach could yield improved threading efficiency.

Keywords: unified model, numerical weather prediction, performance analysis, high performance computing.

1   Introduction

The Unified Model, produced by the UK MetOffice, is a model used for atmospheric simulation over time scales ranging from a few hours for numerical weather prediction (NWP) to decades for climate modeling. An overview of its development can be found in [1]. It is used in the Australian Bureau of Meteorology's (BoM) operational NWP forecasts at both a global and regional resolution. It also serves as the atmosphere component of the Australian Community Climate and Earth System Simulator (ACCESS) coupled climate model. Its complexity and scale demand the use of supercomputers. For this paper, we focus on a global configuration of the UM on the National Computational Infrastructure's supercomputer, Raijin. Raijin is a Fujitsu Primergy cluster consisting of 3592 nodes. Each node possesses two Intel Xeon E5-2670 8 core CPUs giving Raijin a total of 57,472 CPU cores and a theoretical peak performance of 1.2 Petaflops. The nodes are connected by a fast Infiniband network, capable of 56GBit/s between any two nodes. Raijin also provides a fast lustre-based

R. Denzer et al. (Eds.): ISESS 2015, IFIP AICT 448, pp. 552–560, 2015.

[2] file system with approximately 10PB of storage capacity and a peak write performance in excess of 150GB/s. For this paper Intel FORTRAN and C compilers are used along with OpenMPI [3] for MPI (Message Passing Interface) support.

The UM configuration of interest for the presented performance assessment and optimization work is the global N512L70 configuration. It possesses an approximately 25km horizontal resolution (making for a horizontal grid of dimensions 1024 by 769) at mid latitudes and contains 70 model vertical levels. Optimization of configuration is important to BoM's future operational weather forecasting suite, as it will lead to greater accuracy in both weather and climate prediction. BoM has mandated a strict performance target of 10 model days per wallclock hour if this global configuration is to be included in its operational forecast suite. We suspect that performance issues observed at N512L70 (such as I/O and efficient OpenMP use) may be more severe at higher resolutions, such as N768L85, the global resolution of the next BoM operational forecast suite. Thus any solutions implemented at the N512L70 configuration should be applicable and valuable for them as well.

2   Initial Scaling Tests

Using version 8.4 of the Unified Model [4] a strong scaling analysis of the global N512L70 configuration is performed. Each run lasts 24 model hours with a time step of 10 minutes. The UM is capable of using a multi-threaded model, in that each MPI task is able to spawn multiple OpenMP threads. When this multi-threaded mode is enabled, the IO can be performed using the IO Server asynchronous dump feature. In this feature a number of MPI tasks are set aside to perform the expensive process of writing model output to disk as the remaining MPI tasks perform the normal computational work in the atmosphere model run. If this feature is not activated, all output is passed to and written by a single MPI task while all other MPI tasks sit idle – thereby interrupting the normal model calculations.

Figure (1) shows observed strong scaling of the model with the IO Server feature disabled and with all output switched off. It's clear that the single task writing approach severely limits scalability. There is no observed benefit in using more than 512 CPU cores with output enabled in this case. With an averaged runtime of 984 seconds at 2048 CPU cores (over 5 runs), it will not be possible to meet BoM's operational performance requirement with this configuration.

With the IO Server feature enabled, observed strong scaling improves substantially as illustrated in Figure (2). The UM must be run in multithreaded mode here. (I.e. at least 2 OpenMP threads need to be spawned and available to each MPI task). This requirement comes from the IO Server design that uses two threads per IO Server MPI task. Thus, the use of IO servers will be an integral part in meeting operational performance requirement.

The two sets of points at 512 cores in Fig. (2) denote two different runs performed on Raijin, one with 2 OpenMP threads per MPI task, and one with 4 OpenMP threads per MPI task. It is clear that the best utilization of 512 cores is to have 256 MPI tasks each with 2 OpenMP threads. This type of observation leads us to believe that improved performance in the UM could be achieved through additional OpenMP optimization. In spite of the IO now residing on separate MPI tasks, Figure (2) shows that the performance with IO disabled altogether is still better than when IO is enabled on the IO servers.

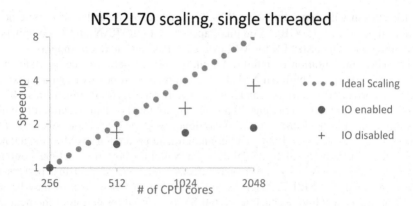

Fig. 1. Observed strong scaling of the global N512L70 configuration using the single MPI task I/O approach. We define 'Speedup' as the ratio of the runtime at 256 cores compared to that at larger stated core counts. Ideal scaling would see a job run on twice as many cores take half the time, a speedup factor of 2.

It is possible for an IO server to possess more than 1 MPI task. For the 'IO enabled' runs shown in Figure (2), we used IO servers containing 8 MPI tasks each. Write performance can be enhanced by fine-tuning the layout and structure of the IO servers used –including the number of MPI tasks allocated to each. As an example, in Figure (2), we display the difference in observed strong scaling at 4096 cores using 8 and 16 MPI tasks per IO Server (e.g. the green cross). While IO Server tuning does improve observed runtimes, it is not enough to significantly change the overall scalability of the global configuration.

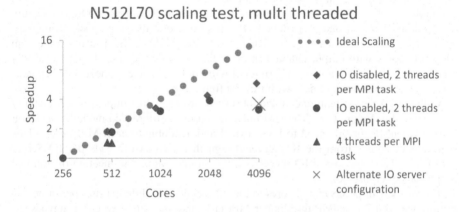

Fig. 2. Observed strong scaling of global N512L70 configuration with IO Servers enabled

3   Threading Performance

Investigations showed that, while the UM can be run with up to 16 OpenMP threads per MPI task on Raijin, performance decreases significantly when more than two threads per MPI task are employed. A detailed analysis of the OpenMP performance was completed using the Score-P [5] profiling and tracing tool, in conjunction with the Vampir trace viewer [6]. For this particular analysis, the UM N512L70 configuration was run in a 16×30 decomposition, with 4 IO servers, each comprising 8 tasks; giving a total of 512 MPI tasks, each with 2 OpenMP threads. Score-P adds approximately 20% to the model run time for a full performance trace. Vampir categorizes all function calls, and displays each category in with different colors according to the legend in Figure (3).

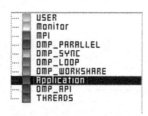

Fig. 3. The function group legend used by Vampir. An ideal trace will spend the majority of its time in the 'Application', 'OMP_LOOP' or 'OMP_WORKSHARE' states. These categories denote function calls in which useful computational work is occurring. Time spent in 'OMP_SYNC' and 'MPI' denotes points where one OpenMP thread is waiting for another to compete a task, or waiting for data to be received from another process, and no useful computation is occurring.

Fig. (4) shows a selection of atmosphere tasks in the 'Master Timeline' view from Vampir version 8.3.0. The view has been zoomed in on a single atmosphere time step, without radiation calculations, that is performed every 6 time steps.

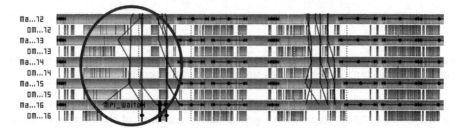

Fig. 4. The 'Master Timeline' view of 5 MPI processes performing a single UM atmosphere step. Function groups are colored as per Fig. (3). Note the significant load imbalance in the circled region.

The vast majority of time between the start of the atmosphere step and the first 'MPI_WaitAll' call (the circled section of the trace) is spent in the 'OMP_SYNC' category of calls. This category denotes every time an OpenMP thread needs to wait for another thread to complete. In this case, the large scale precipitation calculation in the microphysics section of the atmosphere step contains an !$OMP PARALLEL declaration, which then proceeds to be executed in serial, whilst the newly created OpenMP thread waits for the completion of the main thread. This section of the code is potentially taking twice as long as necessary, thereby increasing the load imbalance among the tasks. Load imbalance comes about when each MPI task performs a different amount of work on the data it has. When this occurs, the tasks that complete that section first need to wait for the final tasks to complete that section. This can be seen in the circled region of Fig. (4). During this wait period, they will not be doing any useful work, and are considered wasted. One of key activities in improving the performance of this UM configuration will be eliminating this type of observed load imbalance. Fig. (5) illustrates a similar scenario. Here we display the work done by two OpenMP threads assigned to a single MPI task running an atmosphere step.

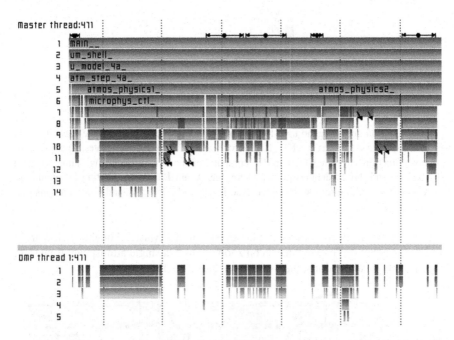

Fig. 5. Vampir's view of the call stack of 2 OpenMP threads allocated to an MPI task running a portion of one atmosphere step. Function groups are colored as per Fig (3).

For the entire atmosphere step, OMP thread 1 is active (i.e. the program is inside an !$OMP PARALLEL region) for approximately one third of the time and spends over a quarter of its time in in the OMP_SYNC category. Though we have selected an arbitrary task for this comparison, this behavior is observed in all non-IO MPI tasks.

Consequently, one OpenMP thread on each atmosphere MPI task spends approximately 30% of its time in MPI_WaitAll calls. This load imbalance is further exacerbated as the halo exchange immediately follows, resulting in more idle CPU time as neighbor tasks wait for threads to synchronize.

OpenMP use in the UM atmosphere code is overwhelmingly data-based parallelization, in which separate iterations of a 'DO' loop are executed on individual OpenMP threads. For a model as inherently load imbalanced as the UM, this may not be sufficient. An alternative approach could be to employing work-share OpenMP constructs where separate independent tasks are allocated to different OpenMP threads. A potential target for this approach would be the convection control subroutines. Every atmosphere tile may undergo one of deep, shallow or congestus convection, as well as mid-level convection. This routine is particularly load imbalanced, as the entire model area on a particular MPI task may only undergo mid-level convection, whereas other MPI tasks may spend a significant amount of time in one of the other convection routines as well as mid-level convection. One could separate the deep, shallow and congestus convection routines on to different OpenMP tasks, such that they are calculated simultaneously, and then revert to data-based parallelism for the mid-level convection calculation.

4   IO Performance

Jobs ran at the global N512L70 configuration run for 1 model day and generate approximately 151GB of output data to disk. If one ignores the UM code completely and just performs a single low-level sequential write to Raijin's high-speed filesystem, then it takes about 220 seconds to perform the write. BoM's current operational forecast suite requires the global UM configuration to run for 10 model days and generate an accordingly ten-fold increase in output. If one ignores the UM code and gain just performs a single low-level sequential write, the time required for generating the output jumps to approximately 36 minutes. BoM's operational forecast suite cannot last longer than one wallclock hour. Thus, one has (at best) 24 minutes to complete all computations in a N521L70 run which is not feasible currently. (Both I/O approaches, IO Server and single MPI task output, use sequential writes for data output.)

In the IO server implementation, model output can be written concurrently with normal atmospheric calculations. At each write, each MPI task performing atmosphere computations sends relevant output data to the nearest IO task (by MPI rank) of each IO server. The first IO server to receive all necessary output data commences the writing of the first output/dump file. The remaining IO servers will flush out all data pertaining to that output file and focus on the next output file.

The 1 model-day runs of the N512L70 configuration produces fifteen dump files in total. Testing showed that the optimal IO Server setting for this configuration varies depending on the number of MPI tasks assigned to the atmosphere model. Fig. (6) shows that for fewer than 1024 or fewer MPI tasks (2048 total cores), 8 MPI tasks per IO server and up to 4 IO servers. Moving to 4096 total cores, gives 8 IO servers in total, which is seen to harm performance. In the 8 IO server setup, several servers seem to remain idle as fewer than 8 files are being written to simultaneously for the majority of the time. Furthermore, the overhead associated with synchronizing all files across 8 IO servers will ultimately increase the time spent in IO, to the point where the IO will take longer than the model run when a large number of MPI tasks are utilized. Reducing the number of IO servers by increasing the number of tasks per server but retaining the total number of MPI tasks for IO is also seen to be detrimental

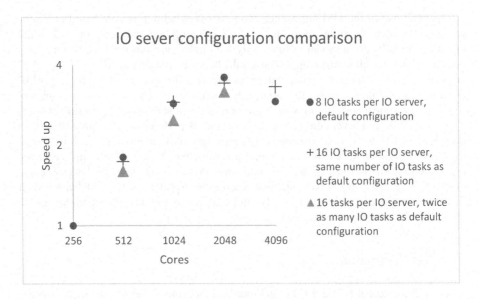

Fig. 6. Comparison of different IO server configurations with the same number of total MPI tasks

to performance for 1024 or fewer MPI tasks, as this limits the ability of the IO servers to write multiple files in parallel. Furthermore, increasing the number of IO tasks and retaining the same number of IO servers is also seen to reduce performance, as in this case, fewer MPI tasks are being allocated to the model itself.

Even when IO servers are employed, there is still a significant overhead due to IO. At 4096 cores, it takes approximately 185 seconds to complete the 24-model hour run without IO, and 305 seconds to complete it with IO enabled. Fig. (7) shows a time-sampled profile of the speed of UM output writes during a run with IO servers enabled.

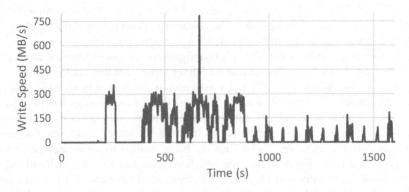

Fig. 7. Observed write speeds for a model day run of the N512L70 configuration. The model produces output at approximately 200, 400, 600 and 800 seconds.

Raijin's high-speed file system is capable of sequentially writing to a single file at around 700MB/s. The observed average write speed for a UM model dump is around 300MB/s. This is due to the overhead of the IO servers moving all data across to the main IO server MPI task in 4MB segments, and writing each segment as it is received. Fig. (8) shows the effect this has on atmosphere tasks.

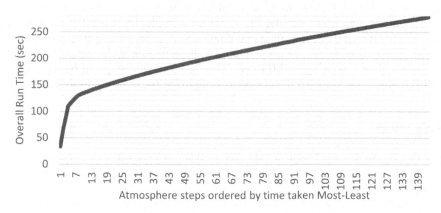

Fig. 8. Cumulative time spent in UM atmosphere steps, ordered by longest time step to shortest. This was performed with a 32×62 decomposition using 4 IO servers each with 16 MPI tasks, for a total of 4096 cores.

Over half of the total run time was spent in the twelve longest atmosphere steps. The long duration of these steps is caused by IO servers being unable to complete some given request. There are a variety of reasons for this, for instance, an insufficient amount of memory has been allocated to the IO servers, which, when full, will cause the model to stop whilst the data in memory on the IO servers is written to disk. Many of these issues could be alleviated with tuning of the IO server parameters. However, as one increase the model resolution, this type of fine-tuning will not prevent such stalling. The number of output files will not increase as resolution increase. Thus one will need to either a) increase the amount of memory to each IO server task so that it can hold more output data, or b) increase the number of MPI tasks dedicated to IO server activity (eg. Increase number of IO servers and/or increase number of MPI tasks belonging to each IO server). Each alternative will suffer from the same stalling behavior. Thus alternate I/O methods should be explored. One possible approach is MPI-IO [7] where multiple IO server tasks can write to files concurrently thereby achieving greater write speeds. The overhead of sending entire files across to a single MPI task would also be eliminated.

5   Conclusions and Future Work

We have investigated the overall performance of the UM MetOffice's Unified Model focusing on the OpenMP and IO server implementation. We found inefficiency in the threading, with the second OpenMP thread of each MPI task spending approximately 75% of the time idle. OpenMP parallelism has been predominantly loop/data-wise. A more task-wise OpenMP parallelism strategy could improve the treading efficiency significantly. In particular, the sections of code identified in Section 3, namely, the different convection subroutines, will be the first target for optimization.

IO is a significant factor in the run time of the UM, even with the IO server approach. Tuning of available IO server parameters can improve the performance at N512L70, but it is unlikely that parameter tuning will have sufficient performance for higher resolution configurations. One possible way to provide such speeds is to make use of Raijin's high-speed parallel file systems by employing a parallel IO standard, such as MPI-IO. In particular, the large dump and post-processing files produced, at several gigabytes each, rely on accumulating data from each IO server process before writing the data from a single MPI task. This accumulation step can be replaced by MPI-IO calls that allow each IO process to write to the file in lustre-aware manner.

References

1. Brown, A., Milton, S., Golding, B., Mitchell, J., Shelly, A.: Unified Modeling and Prediction of Weather and Climate A 25-Year Journey. American Meteorological Society, 1865-1877 (December 2012)
2. Braam, P.: The Lustre Storage Architecture (2004), ftp://ftp.uni-duisburg.de/pub/linux/filesys/Lustre/lustre.pdf
3. Gabriel, E., et al.: Open MPI: Goals, concept, and design of a next generation MPI implementation. In: Kranzlmüller, D., Kacsuk, P., Dongarra, J. (eds.) EuroPVM/MPI 2004. LNCS, vol. 3241, pp. 97–104. Springer, Heidelberg (2004)
4. Wood, N., Staniforth, A., White, A., Allen, T., Diamantakis, M., Gross, M., Melvin, T., Smith, C., Vosper, S., Zerroukat, M., Thuburn, J.: An inherently mass-conserving semi-implicit semi-Lagrangian discretization of the deep-atmosphere global non-hydrostatic equations. Q.J.R. Meteorol. Soc. 140, 1505–1520 (2014), doi:10.1002/qj.2235
5. Schlutter, M., Philippen, P., Morin, L., Geimer, M., Mohr, B.: Profiling Hybrid HMPP Applications with Score-P on Heterogeneous Hardware. In: Bader, M., Bode, A., Bungartz, H.-J., Gerndt, M., Joubert, G.R., Peters, F.J. (eds.) Parallel Computing: Accelerating Computational Science and Engineering (CSE), vol. 25, pp. 773–782. IOS Press (2014)
6. Knüpfer, H., Brunst, J., Doleschal, M., Jurenz, M., Lieber, H., Mickler, M., Müller, S., Nagel, W.E.: The Vampir Performance Analysis Tool-Set, pp. 139–155. Springer, Heidelberg (2008)
7. Thakur, R., Gropp, W., Lusk, E.: Data sieving and collective I/O in ROMIO. In: The Seventh Symposium on the Frontiers of Massively Parallel Computation, Frontiers 1999, pp. 182–189. IEEE (February 1999)

The Czech e-Infrastructure and the European Grid Infrastructure Perspective

Ludek Matyska

CERIT-SC, Masaryk University, Brno, Czech Republic and CESNET, Prague, Czech Republic
ludek@ics.muni.cz

Abstract. National e-Infrastructures are playing an increasingly important role in the support of complex computational and data requirements from all scientific disciplines, environmental informatics not excepting. Since 1996, such an e-Infrastructure is developed and operated in the Czech Republic, with its emphasis shifting from a shared uniform distributed infrastructure to a more user-tailored environment. Its development relates (and in some cases precedes) the evolution of European Grid Infrastructure (EGI), with its current vision of an Open Science Commons concept. While the current e-Infrastructure concept and its implementation is of a very generic nature, it can be tailored to specifically cover different needs of environmental applications. This paper gives an overview of the Czech national e-Infrastructure, its connection to EGI and a number of applications from environmental science domains.

Keywords: e-Infrastructures, high throughput computing, compute and storage resources, weather forecast and modelling.

1   Introduction

Nowadays, high quality research and education is practically impossible without an extensive information and communication technology support. As there is an ever increasing request for more resources, it is necessary to combine compute and storage resources from different sites leading to the development of a concept of an e-Infrastructure (known also as Cyberinfrastructure in the USA). The e-Infrastructure is a distributed system that could span an institution, country or even a continent, combining resources sufficient for even the most demanding needs.

2   The Czech e-Infrastructure

2.1   Brief History

The history of a modern complex e-Infrastructure in the Czech Republic dates back to 1996, when Masaryk University through its Supercomputing Centre Brno coordinated the first project to build a distributed shared computing infrastructure known as "MetaCentrum" [1]. In 1998, the MetaCentrum coordination was transferred to CESNET,

R. Denzer et al. (Eds.): ISESS 2015, IFIP AICT 448, pp. 561–568, 2015.

the Czech National Research and Educational Network provider (NREN). The Meta-Centrum evolved gradually into the Czech National Grid Initiative.

The primary goal of the MetaCentrum was to build a distributed computing environment that exposed a uniform interface to its users; the emphasis was on uniformity, hiding the complexity of the used technology, but in the same time forcing users to adapt to the environment which MetaCentrum provided. MetaCentrum created a true grid – a combination of resources provided by different resource providers (public universities and institutes of Academy of Science) that together created a uniform compute and storage infrastructure. Recently, CESNET complemented the computing resources (clusters) with a distributed infrastructure of large scale hierarchical storage systems to cover also needs for big data storage and processing (the dawn of big data analytics).

MetaCentrum connects some 10 000 cores at 6 major and several more minor locations. The largest is at CERIT-SC. All the cores use x86_64 architecture, some nodes are also equipped with NVidia graphics. The total storage capacity are near 30 PB at four major installations throughout the country.

The SCB at Masaryk University, while offloading the responsibility for the management of the large scale distributed e-infrastructure to CESNET, continued to develop new concepts for the e-Infrastructure. In 2011, it started a transformation into the center CERIT Scientific Cloud, a highly flexible computing and data center focusing on user-tailored e-Infrastructure development and operation. CERIT-SC provides some 4500 cores and additional 4 PB of storage capacity; among the resources is also a SGI Ultraviolet 2 system with 6 TB of RAM shared among its 284 cores (a slightly larger system is expected to be delivered in the mid of November 2014).

Approximately at the same time, Technical University of Ostrava started its "IT4Innovations" project, to build a full scale national supercomputing center. In October 2014, SGI won a tender on the national supercomputer with its ICE X system that will include almost 600 basic nodes with nearly 900 Xeon Phi multicore processors—this will be the largest Xeon Phi installation in Europe.

Currently, the national e-Infrastructure landscape of the Czech Republic is composed of these three centers: CESNET with its MetaCentrum and extensive storage capacities, IT4Innovations supercomputing center and CERIT-SC as the grid and cloud center for collaborative research. All these centers are connected through the high speed network backbone provided by CESNET. The network provides capacity of ten of gigabits per second (with the main trunks recently upgraded to 100 Gbps lines). The network connects all the university cities and has sufficient capacity to support even the most demanding data transfers within the country.

2.2   Technology and Access

The basic distributed e-Infrastructure provided currently by MetaCentrum and CERIT-SC is based on a lightweight model of shared resources offered through a scheduling system (i.e., targeting a job submission mechanism). The system, built around the Torque schedulers [2], offers several queues that differ in their priority, the maximum time each job is allowed to run, and the queue capacity (how many jobs an individual user can submit simultaneously). When submitting a job, users must select the appropriate queue and could annotate their job with additional information like number of cores needed, amount of needed disk space or extent of RAM needed for successful job completion. To support complex requirements, a specific web service is provided that can be used to check whether the used combination could be actually fulfilled by the e-Infrastructure, which combination of resources could serve the job with the given annotation (and how many such combinations exists). This service helps users to optimize their job descriptions to best meet their needs while taking into account the limits of the e-Infrastructure and its capacity.

Practically the whole computing infrastructure is virtualized, with part accessible through standard cloud interface as provided by OpenNebula [3]. This gives the system higher flexibility, as users are not restricted to the "standard" environment (operating system—in this case Debian—set of defined libraries plus an extensible set of applications), but they could submit whole virtual machines (either from a pre-defined pool or their own) with their own specific environment (including a completely different operating system like MS Windows).

With the virtualized nodes and the cloud interface, users are able to ask also for interactive access to the individual nodes or their sets. MetaCentrum provides even full virtual clusters [4,5], where a set of nodes could be connected through a virtualized private network and used as a whole. Use of network virtualization guarantees separation from other users, creating thus a secured (encapsulated) environment that is accessible through specified interfaces only (or not at all).

2.3   Scheduling and Fairshare

The whole e-Infrastructure is available free of charge to all bona-fide scientists and academicians in the Czech Republic (this includes also all university students). Users can just register with MetaCentrum and are immediately given access to the resources. With its near 900 users the demands of the e-Infrastructure exceed its capacity; therefore some scheduling is needed. The Czech national e-Infrastructure uses a specific fairshare mechanism [6] that dynamically adjust individual user's priorities with respect to the extent of past computations.

When a user joins MetaCentrum, he is given some basic priority. The priority is automatically decreased when he uses the e-Infrastructure above average use; and it is increased when the usage is low. This means all users get a "fair" access to the e-Infrastructure. To support excellent research, user's priority can be (permanently) increased if a result (usually a publication) is registered with MetaCentrum. This priority increase is immediately taken into account by the fairshare scheduler, giving such users better access to the resources. Users with high (and high quality) research output are thus visibly prioritized without any unnecessary bureaucracy (i.e. this system does not need to evaluate any a-priori user's proposals for the use of e-Infrastructure while guaranteeing to highly productive users that they will have access regardless of the number of average users).

2.4   Flexibility and CERIT-SC

The center CERIT-SC has a specific position in the national landscape. It is not only the largest individual resource provider in the Czech Republic, but the center focuses on collaborative research with other user communities and also on further development of the e-Infrastructure itself. The center promotes the wide adoption of cloud technologies to provide highly flexible and adaptable compute and storage environment. The center works closely with its partners from other research fields to analyze the problem and to find out the most efficient ways of the use of the e-infrastructure, At the same time, it supports extensive modifications and adaptation to the e-Infrastructure itself to support its most innovative use.

The basic mode of work is the establishment of joint research teams together with users. Computer Science experts contributed by the center complement domain scientists from the application area; such interdisciplinary teams are best prepared to maximize the potential offered by the e-Infrastructure. These teams usually involve also bachelor, master and especially PhD students (both from the Computer Science and the particular research discipline) that are thus given an opportunity to directly participate in high quality research. See [7] for examples of successful collaborations.

3   European Grid I

The Czech e-Infrastructure is a part of the European Grid Infrastructure (EGI) [8]. The current EGI infrastructure is a result of 15 years of development. It currently connects 347 data centers in 57 participating countries (not all of them in Europe, one is even in Australia) and it provides 487,600 CPU cores, 286 PB disk and 118 PB tape storage. Its measured reliability is above 99.6 % and it runs around 1.5 million jobs each day (this is equivalent of almost 5 million core-hours per day). Since 2011, more than 2000 publications with EGI acknowledgment have been produced in almost all scientific disciplines in more than 200 projects.

Since the initial EU activities in the DataGrid project in late nineties, CESNET has been a strong partner in all major activities related to the European grid infrastructure. CESNET was a coordinator of the EGI Design Study project that led to the proposal EGI and its first consolidated project, EGI InSPIRE.

More recently, CESNET together with CERIT-SC are major players in the Federated Cloud activity that allows multiple IaaS cloud providers to become visible to the user as a single system that scales to user needs, providers resilience, prevents provider/vendor lock-in and could be targeted towards the research community. The Federated Cloud infrastructure currently includes resources from 12 countries; the Czech partners provide not only necessary resources but also play a strong role in the development of individual software components—the major contribution lies in the development of the rOCCI implementation to guarantee standards compliance of the federated Cloud approaches [9].

CESNET and CERIT-SC are also working together in the area of AAI and Identity management, especially through a joint development of the Perun system. Perun serves as an extensive identity management and consolidation system supporting also authorization through VO and group concept, both at the national and also at international levels [10].

3.1   EGI Vision

As the primary grid (i.e., batch processing oriented) the EGI infrastructure is considered too static and inflexible by an increasing number of research communities: Therefore a new EGI vision has been developed and presented recently.

The vision states:

Researchers from all disciplines have easy and open access to the digital services, data, knowledge and expertise they need to collaborate and perform excellent research.

This vision found its expression through **Open Science Commons**, a concept based on three complementary pillars:

e-Infrastructure Commons: a flexible and dynamic ecosystem providing integrated services through interoperable infrastructures;

Open Data Commons: Observations, results, applications of scientific activities available for anyone to use and reuse;

Open Knowledge Commons: Easy access to knowledge and expertise to address challenges in education and research.

EGI positions itself to be the key provider of open access to compute, storage, data, knowledge and expertise complementing the community specific capabilities (the EGI Mission).

This mission is currently being implemented through a portfolio of platforms based on a middleware agnostic infrastructure. It covers and integrates all previous approaches like desktop grids, high throughput and high performance computing systems and is primary based on the cloud Infrastructure as a Service (IaaS) concept.

4   Environmental Applications

While the original grid-based e-Infrastructure provided a rather uniform environment that forced its users to adapt their applications to the environment, the recent trends are much more user-friendly. Using techniques of virtualization of all e-Infrastructure component, smart scheduling and cloud access policies, it is the e-Infrastructure that is adapted and tailored to best fit the applications, data manipulation, and workflows. Such user orientation is naturally beneficial for the environmental sciences, with their complex workflows, whose elements have extremely different requirements on the e-infrastructure.

An example is the SDI4Apps project (*Uptake of open geographic information through innovative services based on linked data*; http://sdi4apps.eu/, co-funded by the EU). Its main objectives are to integrate a new generation of spatial data infrastructure (SDI) based on user participation and social validation, support easy discovery and accessibility of spatial data for everybody, and link spatial and non-spatial data using the Linked Open Data principles. To actually implement these objectives, the SDI4Apps rely extensively on a scalable cloud infrastructure, whose architecture is developed and continuously updated with the input from six pilot applications. These applications focus on easy access to data, tourism, sensor network, land use mapping, education and ecosystem services evaluation. The projects is trying to bridge the 1) top-down managed word of INSPIRE, Copernicus and GEOSS initiatives with 2) the bottom-up mobile world of voluntary initiatives and thousands of micro SMEs and individuals developing ad ho applications based on geospatial information. CERIT-SC is responsible for the architecture, development, and operation of the cloud infrastructure for SDI4Apps, making it a natural part of the national e-Infrastructure landscape. The experience built through the development for Federated Cloud infrastructure is directly used by the SDI4Apps, while the know-how achieved through this project implementation is transferred to other areas and disciplines, esp. in the area of storage and processing of geospatial data in a federated cloud environment.

The *Platform for the provision of specialized meteo-predictions for power plants*, a project funded by the Technology Agency of the Czech Republic, targets the development and implementation of a modular software system for prediction of electricity production from solar and wind power plants. It combines numerical models of weather forecast, whose outputs are among other intensity fields of global microwave radiation, cloudiness, air humidity, wind and temperature. The individual models are cross-correlated and the forecast values are used to remove errors and improve precision of the inputs into the model of power prediction [11]. The reliability and universality of the power production prediction is increased through "real-time" verification, using both the real-time weather and power production data to modify the forecast. The resulting highly reliable, modular and at the same time flexible system can be used by wide range of power generating plants. The development of this system extensively relies on the national e-Infrastructure that supports fast combination of different models, collection of data from real-time sensors and on demand processing in a virtualized environment.

The national e-Infrastructure is used to support reconstruction of 3D models of forest covers from full-waveform LiDAR and multispectral scans. This ultimate goal of such a reconstruction is to increase prediction precision for ecological models that simulate processes in natural and also human controlled ecosystems, to analyze the photosynthetic activity in the large vegetation covers etc. The precise 3D models of studied ecosystems play essential role in the prediction. These 3D models could be created from a combination of data provided through different techniques of surface and air scans (full-waveform LiDAR, hyperspectral scans, thermal scans etc.), eventually combined with "in-situ" measurements. Again, the target is to combine all the available data and improve thus analysis of independent individual data sets. The collaboration between experts in both environmental prediction and computer science already lead to the development of highly optimized 3D reconstruction algorithms of individual trees that are two orders of magnitude faster than other currently available methods [12].

The Atmospheric processes and modelling group, part of the Research Center for Toxic Compounds in the Environment (Recetox), studies processes which influence concentration of persistent organic pollutants in the atmosphere and other parts of the environment. The group aims to understand the processes important for the geographical distribution of pollutant and study time trends of their concentration. The studies use complex atmospheric models, e.g. to study air quality in Europe between 2009 and 2010 with hourly temporal resolution, space resolution 12x12 km and 28 vertical layers. The study uses the chemical transport model CMAQ (Community Multiscale Air Quality Model), the weather is forecast using the WRF (Weather Research and Forecasting Model). The WRF produces meteorological input fields for the CMAQ model which then performs modelling of advection, diffusion and chemistry of gas phase, aerosols and clouds [7:2011-2012].

All these examples of successful collaboration between domain science (in this case environment sciences) and e-Infrastructure experts demonstrate the validity and strength of the most recent evolution in the e-Infrastructures, namely their increased ability to support large scale data collections combined with extensive simulations on a tailored e-Infrastructure.

5   Conclusion

e-Infrastructures are becoming an indispensable tool for environmental sciences. The previous phase of the e-Infrastructure development required massive adaptation of applications and workflows to fit the provided e-Infrastructure; this lead to rather disappointing experience that resulted in rather reluctant uptake of the large scale e-Infrastructures. Recently, with the shift to more user-tailored and user-friendly e-Infrastructures, using the most advanced techniques of virtualization and clouds to provide highly flexible and adaptable environments, the environmental sciences widely benefit from the existence of large scale e-Infrastructures. The Open Science Commons concept defines a novel way for the joint development of the e-Infrastructure and the ways it is used. At the Czech national level, CERIT-SC is the forerunner of such activities, through extensive collaboration with research communities and focusing on mutual co-development of both the e-infrastructure and the applications that are expected to run on it.

References

1. Matyska, L., Vocu, M., Krenek, A.: MetaCenter—Building a Virtual Supercomputer. ERCIM News, vol. 45 (2001)
2. Toth, S., Ruda, M.: Practical Experiences with Torque Meta-Scheduling in the Czech National Grid. In: Cracow Grid Workshop 2011, Cracow, Poland, pp. 33–45 (2012)
3. Sotomayor, B., Montero, R.S., Llorente, L.M., Foster, I.: Virtual Infrastructure management in private and hybrid clouds. IEEE Internet Computing 13(5), 14–22 (2009)
4. Antos, D., Sitera, J., Matyska, L., Holub, P.: Metacenter Virtual Networks. In: Cracow Grid Workshop 2008, Cracow, Poland, pp. 86–93 (2009)

5. Antos, D., Matyska, L., Holub, P., Sitera, J.: VirtCloud: Virtualizing Network for Grid Environments—First Experience. In: The 23rd IEEE International Conference on Advanced Information Networking and Applications (AINA) 2009, pp. 876–883. IEEE Comp. Soc., Bradford (2009)

6. Isard, M., Prabhakaran, V., Currey, J., Wieder, U., Talvar, K., Goldberg, A.: Quincy: Fair scheduling for distributed computing clusters. In: ACM SIGOPS 22nd Symposium on Operating Systems Principles, pp. 261–276 (2009)

7. The MetaCentrum Yearbooks,
   http://www.metacentrum.cz/en/about/results/yearbooks/

8. Kranzlmueller, D., Lucas de, J.M., Oster, P.: The European Grid Initiative (EGI). In: Remote Instrumentation and Virtual Laboratories, pp. 61–66. Springer (2010)

9. Rochwerger, B., et al.: The reservoir model and architecture for open federated cloud computing. IBM Journal of Research and Development 53(4), 1–11 (2009)

10. Prochazka, M., Licehammer, S., Matyska, L.: Perun—Modern Approach for user and Service Management. In: IST4Africa Conference Proceedings, Mauritius, 11p. (2014)

11. Stepanek, P., Zahradnicek, P., Farda, A.: Experiences with data quality control and homogenization of daily records of various meteorological elements in the Czech Republic in the period 1961–2010. Idöjárás. Quarterly journal of the Hungarian meteorological society 117(1), 123–141 (2013)

12. Sloup, P., Rebok, T.: Automatic reconstruction of Norway spruce tree models from LiDAR data. In: ISPRS2013-SSG (2013)

The NCI High Performance Computing and High Performance Data Platform to Support the Analysis of Petascale Environmental Data Collections

Ben Evans[1], Lesley Wyborn[1], Tim Pugh[2], Chris Allen[1], Joseph Antony[1], Kashif Gohar[1], David Porter[1], Jon Smillie[1], Claire Trenham[1], Jingbo Wang[1], Alex Ip[3], and Gavin Bell[4]

[1] National Computational Infrastructure (NCI), Australian National University, Canberra, Australia
[2] Bureau of Meteorology, Melbourne, Australia
[3] Geoscience Australia, Canberra, Australia
[4] The 6th Column Project, Berlin, Germany
{Ben.Evans,Lesley.Wyborn,Chris.Allen,Joseph.Antony,
Kashif Gohar,David.Porter,Jon.Smillie,
Claire.Trenham,Jingbo.Wang}@anu.edu.au,
T.Pugh@bom.gov.au,
Alex.Ip@ga.gov.au,
gavin@6thcolumn.org

Abstract. The National Computational Infrastructure (NCI) at the Australian National University (ANU) has co-located a priority set of over 10 PetaBytes (PBytes) of national data collections within a HPC research facility. The facility provides an integrated high-performance computational and storage platform, or a High Performance Data (HPD) platform, to serve and analyse the massive amounts of data across the spectrum of environmental collections – in particular from the climate, environmental and geoscientific domains. The data is managed in concert with the government agencies, major academic research communities and collaborating overseas organisations. By co-locating the vast data collections with high performance computing environments and harmonising these large valuable data assets, new opportunities have arisen for Data-Intensive interdisciplinary science at scales and resolutions not hitherto possible.

Keywords: high performance computing, high performance data, cloud Computing, data-intensive science, scalable data services, data cube, virtual laboratories.

1   Introduction

The National Computational Infrastructure (NCI) at the Australian National University (ANU) has organised a priority set of large volume national environmental data assets on a High Performance Data (HPD) Node within a High Performance

R. Denzer et al. (Eds.): ISESS 2015, IFIP AICT 448, pp. 569–577, 2015.
© IFIP International Federation for Information Processing 2015

Computing (HPC) facility, as a special node under the Australian Government's National Collaborative Research Infrastructure Strategy [1] Research Data Storage Infrastructure (RDSI) program [2]. The colocation of these large volume collections with a high performance and flexible computational infrastructure is part of an emergent area of the Data-Intensive Science, at times referred to as the Fourth Paradigm of Science [3].

NCI operates as a formal partnership between the ANU and the three major Australian National Scientific Agencies: the Commonwealth Scientific and Industrial Research Organisation (CSIRO), the Bureau of Meteorology (BoM) and Geoscience Australia (GA) who are also the custodians of many of the large volume national scientific data records. The data from these national agencies and collaborating overseas organisations are either replicated to or produced at NCI, and in many cases processed to higher-level data products. Model data from computational workflows at NCI are also captured and released as modelling products. NCI then manages both data services and computational environments, known as Virtual Laboratories, to use that data effectively and efficiently.

This paper examines the data collections, the underlying High Performance Data (HPD) infrastructure, the management of trusted environments, and opportunities and challenges that this new research platform at NCI offers.

2   Data Collections

There are 31 (and growing) data collections in the initial ingestion at NCI [4] requiring over 10 Petabytes (PBytes) in storage volume (Table 1). They are currently categorised into six major fields all related to the environmental sciences:

1) earth system sciences, climate and weather model data assets and products;
2) earth and marine observations and products;
3) geosciences;
4) terrestrial ecosystem;
5) water management and hydrology; and
6) astronomy, social science and biosciences.

These data collections are predicted to grow exponentially over time. For example, the datasets for the international Coupled Model Inter-comparison Project (CMIP5) [5] experiment completed in 2013 are well over 3 PBytes; the data for the next CMIP6 experiment will be an order of magnitude larger again by 2020 due to higher resolution spatial grids. Current satellite remote sensing data collections, along with their higher products derived from large time-series of Australian Landsat collection, Moderate Resolution Imaging Spectroradiometer (MODIS), Advanced Very High Resolution Radiometer (AVHRR) and Visible Infrared Imaging Radiometer Suite (VIIRS) are in the order of 2 PBytes. The next generation of satellites such as Japanese Himawari-8/9 mission [6] and the European Space Agency's Copernicus programme [7] are about to come online, with higher spatial resolution sensors and data volumes that in time will dwarf the earlier satellite data collections.

To facilitate effective and efficient use of large volume data collections and to support their use in high performance computing environments, attention must be placed

Table 1. Data Collections hosted at the NCI RDSI node as of 27 November, 2014. The fields are 1) earth system sciences, climate and weather model data assets and products, 2) earth and marine observations and products, 3) geosciences, 4) terrestrial ecosystem, 5) water management and hydrology, and 6) astronomy, social science and biosciences.

Field	Collection Name	TBytes
1	Ocean General Circulation Model for the Earth Simulator	27
1	Year Of Tropical Convection (YOTC) Re-analysis	17
1	Community Atmosphere Biosphere Land Exchange (CABLE) Datasets	23
1	Coordinated Regional Climate Downscaling Experiment (CORDEX)	52
1	Coupled Model Inter-Comparison Project (CMIP5)	3077
1	Atmospheric Reanalysis Products	104
1	Australian Community Climate and Earth-System Simulator (ACCESS)	2350
1	Seasonal Climate Prediction	546
2	Australian Bathymetry and Elevation reference data	105
2	Australian Marine Video and Imagery Collection	6
2	Global Navigation Satellite System (GNSS) (Geodesy)	5
2	Digitised Australian Aerial Survey Photography	72
2	Earth Observation (Satellite: Landsat, etc)	1587
2	Satellite Imagery (NOAA/AVHRR, MODIS, VIIRS, AusCover)	152
2	Satellite Soil Moisture Products	5
2	Synthetic Aperture Radar	27
2	Remote and In-Situ Observations Products for Earth System Modelling	341
2	Ocean-Marine Collections	399
3	Australian 3D Geological Models and supporting data	3
3	Australian Geophysical Data Collection	307
3	Australian Natural Hazards Archive	26
3	National CT-Lab Tomographic Collection	190
4	ecosystem Modelling And Scaling faciliTy (eMAST)	84
4	Phenology Monitoring (Near Surface Remote Sensing)	11
5	eMAST Data Assimilation	102
5	Key Water Assets	41
5	Models of Land and Water Dynamics from Space	20
6	Skymapper (Astronomy)	207
6	Australian Data Archive (Social Sciences)	4
6	BioPlatforms Australia (BPA) Melanoma Dataset (Biosciences)	120
6	Plant Phenomics (Biosciences)	102

on the whole data workflow from creation to publication, including data management plans, provenance capture, and unique identification of the data through Digital Object Identifiers (DOIs) and other forms of data discovery and access. As there is also a move towards enabling HPC analytics directly on the data content, increasingly attributes will need to be self-describing and conform to international standards for vocabularies and ontologies.

Because of the scale of the data collections at NCI, some aspects of data management are now active areas of ongoing research and development collaboration. One example is provenance systems, where specialized databases will be created to allow use-dependent provenance graphs to be generated on-the-fly.

3   High Performance Data (HPD)

With both the increased data volumes, and the increased computing power required to effectively process and analyse them, the coupled computational environments are increasingly too large or complicated to be architected separately: they must be co-designed at inception. This has given rise to High Performance Data (HPD), as a complementary approach to the traditional High Performance Computing (HPC).

We define High Performance Data (HPD) as data that is carefully prepared, standardised and structured so that it can be used in Data-Intensive Science on HPC.

To achieve this, the use of the data needs to be considered as part of the production and management of the data, rather than an after-thought for data curation.

Many of the data sets that have been assembled on the NCI are ones that were considered too large to process and access by conventional means; bandwidth limits the capacity to move them, data transfers are too slow; and latencies to access them are too high. Even if the data sets can be moved, few can afford to store them locally, the energy costs are substantial, and provenance and versioning of the large data collections at multiple sites are too complex to manage. We predict the increasing scale of data, its associated processing, and complexity of software environments will be too difficult or affordable to host beyond a few trusted international centres.

Properly structured, the HPD collections provide new opportunities to integrate and process large volumes of data at resolutions and at scales never before possible. Once created, HPD enables in-situ processing of the data and requires users changing their processing to use trusted online applications and services on the data in-situ.

4   High Performance Data Infrastructure

4.1   Design Considerations

The infrastructure at NCI has been designed to support Data-Intensive Science within HPC environments. The new infrastructure was designed to reduce the time taken to process the data and required a balance between the available processing power and the ability to access data.

More specifically the infrastructure to support HPD at NCI was designed and programmed, and is operated in a way that enables multiple users to rapidly invoke dynamic high performance computation on these large volume data collections from a variety of use-cases. Processing can take place in a variety of modes: batch-style deep processing; interactive environments for preparing model and analysis computation; web-time data processing including the Open Geospatial Consortium (OGC) Web Processing Service (WPS) [8], Virtual Desktop Interfaces (VDIs) for fully assembled software environments; and various server-side visualisation capabilities.

4.2   Computer Platforms for HPD

To ensure that HPD techniques can scale out for the demands of Data-Intensive Science, all parts of the data and services need to be considered for their ability to scale out and for high bandwidth and low latency access to data. This includes batch-mode HPC platforms, cloud infrastructure, and high performance filesystems.

NCI provides a 1.2 PetaFLOP supercomputer (Raijin) with over 57,000 processing cores and an approximately 10 PBytes Lustre filesystem. The system includes Fujitsu compute nodes consisting of Intel SandyBridge processors, a QDR InfiniBand network, and a Lustre filesystem for a cluster-wide namespace and a PBSPro batch system.

For its private cloud, (Tenjin), NCI selected OpenStack [9] as its underlying cloud technology on a HPC-class 3000 processor core system using the same generation of technology as the Raijin supercomputer, including Intel's SandyBridge processors and a Mellanox QDR InfiniBand interconnect. In addition, each node of Tenjin has local Solid State Drives (SSDs) to allow high IOPs workloads. When using virtual machines, the performance of the hypervisor is critical for the performance of both computational and IO systems. Over time, the performance of these hypervisors has improved. Future work on OpenStack will see bare-metal nodes used as part of the node structure where virtualisation is the limiting factor for operations.

Both the supercomputer and cloud can mount several facility wide Lustre [10] file systems, which maintain the data collections and other persistent reference data. The Lustre systems use a mixture of NetApp and DDN storage arrays, which are managed by Object Storage Servers (OSS) within scalable units. There are currently over 50 OSSes serving approximately 20 PBytes of filesystem space.

To provide operational robustness, each layer of the infrastructure has its own management domain. The connection to both the supercomputer and the cloud are managed with a scalable set of data serving bridging infrastructure using Lustre LNET and NFS that manages both the performance and security to each of the systems over the InfiniBand network fabric.

4.3   Software Stack Management

The variety of both environments and services for Data-Intensive HPD environmental science has required a deeper consideration of the software environment including management and deployment practices and the supporting software infrastructure.

This involves the two key concepts of the Development-to-Operations (DevOps) process which includes firstly testing and integration, and secondly re-usable trusted software stacks.

To manage the software systems, NCI has developed a system of Puppet Bundles based on Puppet [11] and Git [12]. The NCI Puppet Bundles are run in a masterless mode, where the coordination of nodes and deployment is achieved through standard Git management. All operational stacks are maintained to a high degree of traceability and reproducibility through this system.

All shareable services of the NCI environment have been written to make use of the underlying Puppet core framework. This provides easy integration, simplified sharing and re-use, and the ability to more easily scale-out the infrastructure. Other technologies (e.g., Docker [13]) can be deployed in a layered ecosystem of software deployments.

4.4   Scalable Data Access

Modern Data-Intensive environments require much more than just discovery and access to filesystems. To find data, a research problem requires the ability to pro-grammatically search for attributes and extract data using defined services like the Data Access Protocol (DAP), and other geospatial services such as those defined by the OGC including Web Map Service (WMS) [14], Web Coverage Service (WCS) [15] and Web Feature Service (WFS) [16].

NCI have developed a scalable catalogue framework using a combination of Geo-Network [17] and ElasticSearch [18] to record the metadata, and allows for rapid search across key attributes and respond with the relevant data service URI or filesys-tem location for access.

All data is registered in the catalogue framework including the services that are meaningful to the data, e.g., THREDDS [19], Hyrax [20], and GeoServer [21]. To find the data, programs have begun to standardize on JSON [22] objects for interact-ing with the search infrastructure.

4.5   Datacube Technologies

For analysis in high performance environments, those collections that comprise mul-tiple data sets and data series, even if they conform to agreed international standards, need to be aggregated into seamless data arrays. The datasets being assembled are often of different spatial and temporal resolution. To analyse these data as coherent units, the data will increasingly need to be stored, aligned and indexed using datacube methodologies.

A number of collaborations have now been established to address this issue. For example, GA, CSIRO and NCI are collaborating on a project called the Australian Geoscience Data Cube (AGDC) [23]. For this project, the data is prepared to allow rapid analysis of the data in several dimensions (e.g., spectral, spatial and temporal) by converting to consistent grids, each with a fixed and consistent geospatial foot-print, forming a space-time 'data cube'. In the development phase of the AGDC, some 636,000 Landsat product scenes were converted to 4 million spatially-regular, time-stamped, band-aggregated tiles. This consistent gridding minimised the geospatial processing necessary to locate individual pixels of data across multiple scenes (or files) of Earth observation data. Tile-based analyses could then be distributed across thousands of compute nodes for parallel computation underpinned by the high-performance Lustre filesystems of the NCI facility. As a result of this successful development phase, the AGDC project is now being expanded to incorporate other data Earth Observation imagery including MODIS data and elevation data.

5   Interdisciplinary and Collaborative Virtual Laboratories

Virtual Laboratories are a set of integrated software stacks that provides workflow software, specialised tools, web services, and visualisation services. The nature of the Virtual Laboratories is that they consist of a mixture of software stacks that are sourced from independent, trusted software and data repositories and are integrated as an interoperable stack.

Common software stack components may also be reused, and re-integrated by the individual Virtual Laboratory that requires them. This is a key way where software (and ultimately data) can be reused and/or repurposed for multiple Virtual Laboratories and will ultimately assist in achieving interdisciplinary outcomes.

The development of these trusted software stacks usually involves large-scale engineering efforts, often entailing global collaborations. Some well-known examples used at NCI include the Earth Systems Grid Federation (ESGF) [24] (of which NCI is a core member), and model management environments such as Cylc [25] and Rose [26] and visualisation software such as UV-CDAT [27] and the Oceans Data Interoperability Platform (ODIP) [28].

The release and integration of the software environments at NCI are managed using our Puppet Bundles approach, which ensures that software is both upgradable and maintainable. By carefully managing the software stack to track the upstream software repository, the trustworthiness of individual Virtual Laboratory stacks can be maintained.

6   Opportunities and Challenges

The new infrastructure developed at the NCI has enabled:

- A dramatic improvement in the scale, resolution and reach of Australian environmental research;
- High performance access to nationally significant research collections using new Data-Intensive capabilities to support cutting-edge research methods; and
- The realisation of synergies with related international research infrastructure programs.

Further, by co-locating major diverse environmental data collections with HPC infrastructures an interdisciplinary approach to solving key global Environmental Science issues such as impacts of climate change; sustainably exploiting scarce water, mineral and energy resources; and protecting our communities through better prediction of the behaviour of natural hazards is now feasible.

However, these opportunities cannot be easily realised unless some key remaining challenges are addressed, including common licensing framework, authentication and authorisation, semantic enablement of data using controlled vocabularies, and provenance tracking of workflows. There is also a growing recognition of the need for the development of new specialised skills, in particular in data science. There is also a need to deploy these skills in multi-faceted interdisciplinary teams.

7   Conclusions

We have reached the following conclusions about the future directions of computational and Data-Intensive methods in environmental and earth systems science through the course of this work:

1. The need to access the large and exponentially increasing data volumes in Environmental Science is now acute; traditional data access and HPC technologies no longer scale.
2. We define High Performance Data (HPD) as data that is carefully prepared, standardised and structured so that it can be used in Data-Intensive Science on HPC.
3. HPC can now be combined with HPD to support the more complex workflows of Data-Intensive Science.
4. The coupled HPC-HPD environments and the data are increasingly too large or complicated to be architected separately: they must be co-designed at inception.
5. HPC and HPD are now integral to Earth and Environmental Research. Combined they offer new opportunities to collaboratively address problems such as climate change; sustainable exploitation of our water, mineral and energy resources; and better prediction of natural hazards.

Acknowledgements. The authors wish to acknowledge funding from the Australian Government Department of Education, through the National Collaboration Research Infrastructure Strategy (NCRIS) and Education Investment Fund (EIF) Superscience fund through the NCI, RDSI and National eResearch Collaboration Tools and Resources (NeCTAR) projects.

References

1. Department of Education: National Collaboration Research Infrastructure Strategy, retrieved from https://education.gov.au/national-collaborative-research-infrastructure-strategy-ncrison (retrieve on November 27, 2014)
2. Department of Education: Information Sheet Research Data Storage Initiative (RDSI) Australian Government,
   http://docs.education.gov.au/documents/information-sheet-research-data-storage-initiative-rdsi (modified September 24, 2014)
3. Hey, T., Tansley, S., Tolle, K.: Jim Grey on eScience: a transformed scientific method. In: Hey, T., Tansley, S., Tolle, K. (eds.) The Fourth Paradigm: Data-Intensive Science Discovery, pp. xvii–xxxi. Microsoft Corporation, USA (2009)

4. National Computational Infrastructure: National Collections, retrieved from `http://nci.org.au/data-collections/data-collections/`, and the Geo-Network catalogue `http://nci.org.au/data-collections/data-collections/and` (November 27, 2014)

5. Taylor, K.E., Stouffer, R.J., Meehl, G.A.: An Overview of CMIP5 and the experiment design. Bull. Amer. Meteor. Soc. 93, 485–498 (2012), doi:10.1175/BAMS-D-11-00094.1

6. Japan Meteorological Agency: Himarwari-8/9 of the Meteorological Satellite Center (MSC) of the JMA, retrieved from `http://www.data.jma.go.jp/mscweb/en/himawari89/index.html` (November 27, 2014)

7. European Space Agency: The Copernicus programme, retrieved from `http://www.esa.int/Our_Activities/Observing_the_Earth/Copernicus/Overview4` (November 27, 2014)

8. Open Geospatial Consortium Web Processing Service, OGC, retrieved from `http://www.opengeospatial.org/standards/wps` (November 27, 2014)

9. OpenStack, retrieved from `http://www.openstack.org/on` (November 27, 2014)

10. Lustre file system, retrieved from `http://wiki.lustre.org/index.php/Main_Page` (November 27, 2014)

11. PuppetLabs Inc., retrieved from `http://puppetlabs.com/` (November 27, 2014)

12. Git, retrieved from `http://git-scm.com/` (November 27, 2014)

13. Docker, retrieved from `https://www.docker.com/` (November 27, 2014)

14. Open Geospatial Consortium: Web Map Service, retrieved from `http://www.opengeospatial.org/standards/wms` (November 27, 2014)

15. Open Geospatial Consortium: Web Coverage Service, OGC, retrieved from `http://www.opengeospatial.org/standards/wcs` (November 27, 2014)

16. Open Geospatial Consortium: Web Feature Service, OGC, retrieved from `http://www.opengeospatial.org/standards/wfs` (November 27, 2014)

17. Open Source Geospatial Foundation:GeoNetwork, retrieved from `http://geonetwork-opensource.org/` (modified January 31, 2014)

18. ElasticSearch, retrieved from `http://www.elasticsearch.org/` (November 27, 2014)

19. THREDDS, retrieved from `http://www.unidata.ucar.edu/software/thredds/current/tds/` (November 27, 2014)

20. OpenDAPInc: Hyrax, retrieved from `http://docs.opendap.org/index.php/Hyrax` (November 27, 2014)

21. Open Source Geospatial Foundation: GeoServer, retrieved from `http://geoserver.org/` (November 27, 2014)

22. JSON, retrieved from `http://www.json.org/` (November 27, 2014)

23. Australian Geoscience Data Cube (AGDC), retrieved from `https://github.com/GeoscienceAustralia/agdc/wikion` (November 27, 2014)

24. Earth Systems Grid Federation: About the Earth System Grid, retrieved, from `https://www.earthsystemgrid.org/about/overview.htm` (November 27, 2014)

25. Oliver, H.: The Cylc Suite Engine, retrieved from `http://cylc.github.io/cylc/html/single/cug-html.html` (November 27, 2014)

26. UK Met Office: Rose, retrieved from `https://github.com/metomi/rose/` and `http://www.metoffice.gov.uk/research/collaboration/rose` (November 27, 2014)

27. Williams, D.N., et al.: UV-CDAT (2014), doi:10.5281/zenodo.12251, `http://uvcdat.llnl.gov/`

28. Oceans Data Interoperability Platform (ODIP), retrieved from `http://www.odip.org/` (November 27, 2014)

Big Data Architecture for Environmental Analytics

Ritaban Dutta[1], Cecil Li[1], Daniel Smith[1], Aruneema Das[2], and Jagannath Aryal[2]

[1] CSIRO Digital Productivity Flagship, CSIRO Hobart, TAS 7001, Australia
[2] University of Tasmania, CSIRO Hobart, TAS 7001, Australia
ritaban.dutta@csiro.au

Abstract. This paper aims to develop big data based knowledge recommendation framework architecture for sustainable precision agricultural decision support system using Computational Intelligence (Machine Learning Analytics) and Semantic Web Technology (Ontological Knowledge Representation). Capturing domain knowledge about agricultural processes, understanding about soil, climatic condition based harvesting optimization and undocumented farmers' valuable experiences are essential requirements to develop a suitable system. Architecture to integrate data and knowledge from various heterogeneous data sources, combined with domain knowledge captured from the agricultural industry has been proposed. The proposed architecture suitability for heterogeneous big data integration has been examined for various environmental analytics based decision support case studies.

Keywords: big data, architecture, machine learning, semantics.

1 Introduction

The ultimate challenge in agricultural decision support systems is to overcome the data unavailability and uncertainty to improve the natural resource management efficiency and achieve better business objectives. Uncertainty factors in the agricultural and environmental monitoring processes are more evident than before due to current technological transparency achieved by most recent advanced communication technologies. Poor data quality and uncertainties make most agricultural decision support systems unreliable and inefficient. This inefficiency leads to failure of agricultural and environmental resource management [1-3].

It is evident that there is a serious need to capture and integrate environmental and agricultural knowledge from various heterogeneous data sources including sensor networks, individual sensory systems, large scale simulated models, patched historical weather data, satellite imagery, domain knowledge and contextual user experience for better decision support with high reliability and confidence. This approach would be able to provide a much wider framework for complementary knowledge validation and meaningful utilization of the acquired knowledge. In agricultural domain knowledge is very volatile in nature, which can only be passed from generation to generation, can vary on a daily basis based on requirements. The farmers can understand and only tell the story of the field, just by looking at the colour of the soil

R. Denzer et al. (Eds.): ISESS 2015, IFIP AICT 448, pp. 578–588, 2015.
© IFIP International Federation for Information Processing 2015

or by looking at the sky. One of the key motivations of this research was to develop an architecture, which can incorporate unstructured, undocumented, ad-hoc knowledge into a structure rule base to be used directly in the big data analytics for better decision support system. Recent development of heterogeneous big data analytics and architectural development for big data integration for agricultural solution was the main motivation behind this work.

2   Big Data Centric Architecture

In the intelligent environmental knowledgebase (i-EKBase) project we aimed to integrate multi scale heterogeneous data from 'Australian Water Availability Project (AWAP)', 'Australian National Cosmic Ray Soil Moisture Monitoring Facility (CosmOz)', 'SILO Data', 'ASRIS Soil data', '250m resolution \ NASA MODIS data', '30m resolution NASA LANDSAT data', 'Australian Digital Elevation Data', and finally 'Domain knowledge is available (i.e. farmer's long experience of daily decision making based on generation wise climate adaptation knowledge). Then on top of this large data integration, our novelty was to apply data driven spatio-temporal artificial intelligence (machine learning) analytics to learn and establish new environmental correlations to make the decision support system more sustainable and scientifically justified to improve business profitability and productivity [4-6].

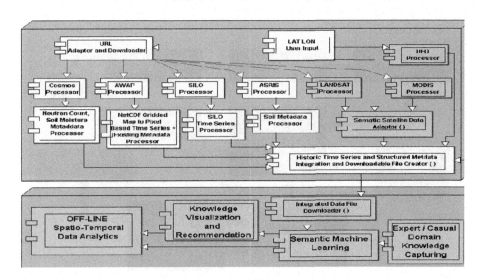

Fig. 1. UML diagram of the proposed architecture

Fig.1 shows the UML diagram of the system architecture that has been proposed and implemented in this study. In the proposed mechanism we process the available metadata separately from the data observations. Feature extraction process was applied to the metadata to create a unique feature base from the individual data source. This processing was done using data mining and text mining techniques. It also involved unsupervised machine learning techniques (i.e. unsupervised clustering techniques). Main application area of machine learning technique was in the processing of actual observations from various sensors and systems. Various supervised machine-learning techniques (i.e. neural networks) were used to extract feature base from the observation database. Uniqueness of the architecture in this context was in the selection of machine learning methodology to extract targeted feature base from the observations. The targeted feature base was determined on the basis of the actual application and also based on the available domain expert knowledge usually undocumented and belonging to individuals (i.e. farmers) as long-term field experience. We used the domain knowledge to provide guidance to the machine learning processes to extract the desired feature space. This was done to make the feature extraction process more meaningful and unique. This approach was able to make the machine learning process (so called black box approach) more usable in terms of biophysically explanations for the domain people. Domain guided extraction using machine learning was named as semantic extraction hence it produced semantic feature base. Meta-feature base and semantic feature base were integrated to form an enriched feature space, which was a most significant representation of the heterogeneous big data. The dimension reduction is important step in any big data related architecture, especially when extremely large number of highly correlated observations is present. In this architecture we show that dimension reduction could be done in a domain specific meaningful way to increase the efficiency of the system, and also to increase the accuracy of the system by enriching the data semantically [1-5].

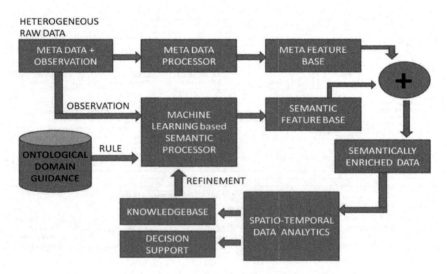

Fig. 2. Concept diagram of the proposed architectural overview to integrate big heterogeneous knowledge

In the second phase of the architecture, various supervised and unsupervised algorithms were used to analyze the extracted and enriched spatio-temporal feature space. Temporality of the feature space was determined based on the required decision support frequency of the targeted domain and the application. Fig. 2 shows the concept diagram of the proposed architecture for agricultural decision support system based on true heterogeneous data integration.

3   Architecture for Domain Knowledge Capturing

In this part of the work we investigated how domain knowledge can be efficiently represented in Linked Open Data (LOD) and how this representation can be incorporated for use with machine learning models. Further, we will investigate how to perform learning, inference and prediction tasks with LOD. The work package aims to demonstrate the value of combining semantic and machine learning representations for environmental modeling. Primary objective of this part of the architecture was to establish a standard protocol for capturing essential domain knowledge in a way that could directly be used in automated reasoning and machine learning based processes. Agricultural domain experts and farmers could potentially define the complete feature space required to optimize the harvesting. Often that could be in a casual format or unstructured know-ledge that makes it inaccessible from the system point of view. It is also true that domain knowledge often get lost in translation from generation to generation due to lack of standard mechanism to capture. In all kind of agricultural decision support system there are some essential environ-mental attributes and prior defined thresholds for those variables. The farmers based on their best experience and business profitability in the past usually predefine these thresholds. They also have some special features (i.e. soil colour to determine soil moisture) that they use in the daily decision making process. Decision making process is always a classification problem with two or more possible solutions. It is also possible to find some historical ground truth data (scattered over long time frame) from the farming companies that could be used for cross validations. Fig. 3 shows this part of the architecture.

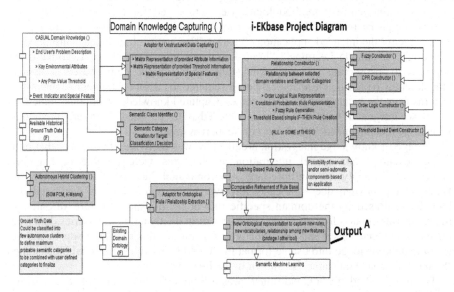

Fig. 3. UML diagram of the domain knowledge capturing architecture

In this architecture we have applied data driven autonomous hybrid unsupervised clustering techniques (combining Principal Component Analysis (PCA), Self Organizing Map (SOM) and Fuzzy C Means (FCM) to automatically create and match class labels for possible decisions those are defined and stored in farmers mind. Advantage of this autonomous clustering was that this architecture was able to establish few more class definitions. We have defined this part as semantic class identifier. Any of these class labels defining a kind of decision should be related to a set of essential attributes defined by the farmers. We have defined these labels as semantic categories of the decision-making system. Attributes, thresholds and associated decision class could be modeled as a complete association set that was captured as rule in our architecture. This was captured within the relationship constructor module. Four different rule constructors were used to formulate these relationship, namely, fuzzy rule constructor (using fuzzy rule base creation), conditional probabilistic rule constructor (using conditional probability rule generation), order logic constructor (using order logic to formulate rules) and threshold based significant event rule constructor (where threshold of few environmental variables, directly defined by the farmers in conjunction with an event which led to make an unusual decision). In this architecture we proposed to use all or some of these rule constructors based on requirements and availability of ground truth data.

4   Analytics Driven Big Data Architecture

The i-EKbase" knowledgebase architecture represents semantically enriched spatio-temporal features from the environment in a unified manner. The purpose of this work was to learn spatio-temporal patterns acquired from different knowledge sources, translating the learned knowledge into a more efficient decision support system. In this part we describe the detailed architecture behind the semantic analysis. Data driven machine-learning methodologies were employed for this purpose. Machine learning could be used for autonomous knowledge discovery and online inference of knowledge for the intended application scenarios. This approach included "Unsupervised Learning", "Ensemble Learning", "Deep Learning", and "State Based Learning". The aim was to incorporate various learning algorithms on the cloud based computing infrastructure to provide the analytical power required to capture and integrate interesting patterns from the heterogeneous data sources. Captured knowledge from this framework was also integrated with the domain knowledge to be used in future prediction, knowledge recommendation, and decision support systems.

Design of knowledge integration architecture was motivated by the fact that none of the existing data model integration architectures were capable of handling, processing and analyzing multiple large environmental data sources simultaneously. Database on its own does not carry any weightage unless data is converted into knowledge. Based on the domain specific rule or relationship structure an ontology translator was created for automatic reasoning from the dynamic time series data from the environmental sensor and sensor networks. A task of this translator was to convert the domain knowledge into usable format that could be used in functional block called 'Semantic Signal Translator' (as shown in the Fig. 4).

The block called 'Data Conditioner' was a time series integrator for the semantic signal selector function. Pre-processed time series data were batch processed and represented as daily averaged data for this study. Data from the different sources measuring the same environmental attribute were harmonized. Again different measured attributes from the same node were also harmonized according to the daily average. Simultaneously a generic time window selector function was developed to define the required temporal frequency defined by the domain ontology.

Combination of this kind formed a pool of similar variables, which should be able to validate or complement each other in case of missing values in the time series. Complementary method identified the missing value segments of a time series and replaced those segments with an average segment based on other available time series in the same pool. Next a 'cross-correlation technique' was used to measure the similarities between two complemented time series signals representing similar scenarios (in terms of location and time period).

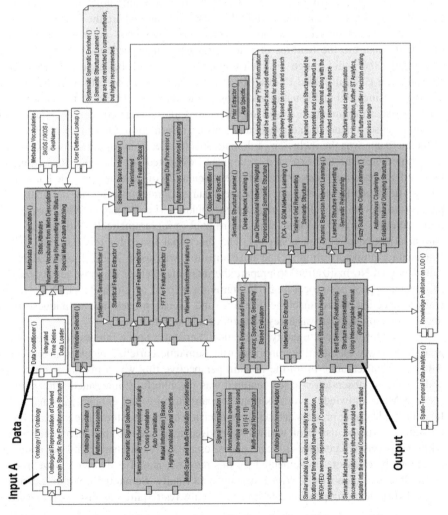

Fig. 4. UML diagram of the semantic machine learning based big data architecture

Other purpose of this step was to cross validate similar time series data in the same pool to find a representative time series regarding that particular pool. If the two signals being compared were completely identical then the cross-correlation coefficient should be equal to 1 and if there are no similarities between the signals it should be equal to 0. A scoring protocol was designed on cross correlation results. The time series with highest score were selected from each sub group as best representative of the associated environmental variable for that time period. Semantics representations are usually intended as a medium for conveying meaning about some world or environment. One of the significant novelties of this architecture was to implement a generic mechanism to parameterize all possible available metadata into static attributes (i.e. Boolean flag for each of the metadata or a numeric representation with a library of definition). Metadata is "data about the data" and it can provide the description of the what, where, who and how about data. For example, a sensor node metadata could describe when and where the sensor node was deployed, who deployed that node, which environmental attributes are being measured, what are the features or characteristics of that particular sensory system, and finally the valid range of measurement that could be expected. However, metadata are generally used to describe the principal aspect of data with the aim of sharing, reusing, and understanding heterogeneous data sets. In fact, different types of sensor or sensor-simulation model metadata may be considered, namely, static and dynamic sensor metadata and associated sensing information. Other important aspect of the metadata was the inclusion of domain specific decision support class categories and experience based expected outcomes, extracted in the previous domain knowledge extraction block. Parametric representation of metadata provided us with a unique functionality to reason with metadata programmatically in an analytical process. In this process already existing vocabularies (i.e. Geoname, XKOS etc.) and user defined lookup tables were consulted programmatically to refine the parameterization of the metadata [1]. The functional block for this part was called 'Metadata Parameterization'. Data normalization was used in the functional block called 'Signal Normalization' to prepare the integrated sensor response matrix for the subsequent signal pre-processing paradigms on a local or global level. Wide range feature selection using machine learning and signal processing techniques, in a domain specific manner was a key element of this architecture.

The next level of functionality was called 'Semantic Space integrator' where integration of newly extracted features from the semantic enriched block was combined with the Meta features. From the domain perspective this was a pivotal point where wide range of observation-based features was meaningfully integrated with domain specific Meta knowledge. At this point the architecture had enough information to formulate a learning process and design a decision support system. The primary focus moved towards the usage of various supervised machine-learning techniques along with unsupervised techniques to learn about semantically enriched data. Four essential functional blocks were implemented for this purpose, namely, 'Training Data processor', 'Objective Identifier', 'Prior Extractor' and finally 'Semantic Structure Learner'. In the hybrid learning process a training set is always required against a ground truth data set as training target. The 'Semantic Structural Learner' functional block was the core body for learning and spatio-temporal analytics. Four different learners were used which were based on 'Deep Network Learning (for low dimensional network weights representing semantic structure)', 'Principal Component Analysis (PCA) – Guided Self Organizing Map (G-SOM) network learning (to train a grid structure to represent the semantic structure)', 'Dynamic Bayesian Network Learning (for learning the structure behind the semantic relationship)' and 'Fuzzy Subtractive Cluster Learner (for learning the natural grouping among the feature space using autonomous clustering)'. The parallelization was implemented to establish a wide range of cross-validation and complementary learning. An autonomous unsupervised learner algorithm was implemented to select randomized training sets for the learning phase. The 'Training Data Processor' was responsible for this step. The other two functional blocks, the Objective Identifier' and the 'Prior Extractor' were responsible to generate the ground truth based training target for the training phase and also for the testing phase which is called 'Objective Evaluation and Fusion'. Testing of the learning phase was based on evaluation parameters i.e. accuracy, specificity and sensitivity. To process the evaluation and accuracy estimates from the testing of the trained structure learner models a functional block called 'Network Rule Extractor' was implemented. These rules could be structured representation of some existing rules or they could also be new associations derived as part of the learning. The functionality of this block was to identify new rules those are being generated during semantic structure learning processes. The new rules were represented as new knowledge into the original domain ontology marked as 'Input A'. This was done as part of the implemented enrichment block called 'Ontology Enrichment Adaptor'.

The functional block called 'Optimum Structure Exchanger' was implemented to perform this stage of the architecture. This block was constructed based on Resource description framework (RDF), uniform resource identifier (URI) and triple store technologies. Extracted rules were converted into RDF format to be represented on the LOD. This i-EKbase architecture was implemented on the CSIRO's Bowen research cloud infrastructure. In order to establish the effectiveness of this newly proposed heterogeneous big data analytical framework, this paper presents few real life case studies and associated performance factors to highlight the principal achievements of this architecture [1-8].

5   Big Data Architecture Based Environmental Case Studies

This case study has three main achievements. Firstly a multi-source environmental knowledge framework (i-EKbase) was developed to provide large-scale availability of relevant sensor-model databases for any environmental application. We have developed lightweight ontologies based on extracted metadata from heterogeneous data sources. Next historic surface water balance for one location in Tasmania, Australia was estimated using unsupervised machine learning knowledge recommendation [8].

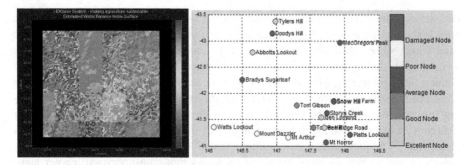

Fig. 5. (a). Area wise water balance estimation using multi source heterogeneous data architecture; **(b)** Dynamic Annotation and Recommendation about the sensor network's node based data quality

The traditional water balance model based method does not include several other environmental parameters (i.e. solar radiation, temperature and humidity), which might have significant influence on the water balance. This issue has been addressed by using multi dimensional and heterogeneous data in i-EKbase system. The machine learning based data driven approach behind i-EKbase system was demonstrated as an effective method to estimate water balance with potentially higher accuracy. Supervised machine learning paradigms were experimented to explore generalization capability and prediction accuracy of this proposed water resource management solution based on multi sensor – model integration [7].

The Radial Basis Function Network based 91.3% accuracy performance proved that newly proposed predictive water resource estimation method based on large multi scale knowledge integration could potentially make the irrigation decision support systems more robust and efficient. Fig. 5(a) shows the area wise water balance estimated using newly developed big data analytical architecture [1, 7-8].

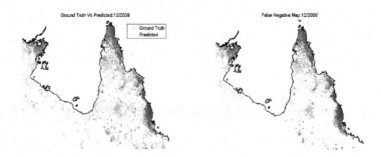

Fig. 6. Bush-fire hot-spot estimation and prediction based on the proposed analytical architecture

In a different case study we focused on automatic sensor data annotation and visualisation of dynamic weather data acquired from a large sensor network using this newly proposed big data analytics platform. Aim was to develop a data visualisation method for CSIRO's South Esk hydrological sensor web to evaluate the overall network performance and visual data quality assessment. This visual data quality technique developed from this study could be used for quality assurance of any sensor network (See Fig 5(b)). In another case study, Main aspect of this study was to establish a methodology to predict wild fire prone locations as spots on the Australian map based on publicly available gridded maps of Australian weather variables and hydrological variables. Integrated data sets were created from the gridded maps available from Australian Water Availability Project (AWAP) and Bureau of Meteorology (BOM). On the other hand, NASA-MODIS historical active fire image archives for Australia were used as ground truth. 70% of the data (2008-2009) were used to train all the neural networks where as the monthly image data from 2010 (30% of the data set) were used to test the networks. Independent training and testing were critical for this study to prove the generalization capability of the hybrid architecture based on the neural networks. 94% overall prediction accuracy was achieved from this approach, with 93% sensitivity and 95.3% specificity. Maximum false positive rate was 0.7% whereas overall precision was 96% (Fig. 6) [6].

6   Conclusions

Our understanding of the environment is greatly associated with the interlinked knowledge of the phenomena surrounding to us. Such knowledge is a result of data and extracted information. With the availability of very high and even ultra-high resolution sensor data there is a greater need of managing data, information and essentially the knowledge. With the advent of technological novelties and their wider applications the generated data is surpassing our capacities to store it. There is an urgent need for improved methods and advancement in data-intensive science to retrieve, filter, integrate, and share data.

Data and meaningful information are key for the actors in every walk of life, however, how to conceive, perceive, recognize and interpret such data in space and time is a big question and a big challenge. Taking this challenge into the perspective, we have presented an opportunity of recommending environmental big data using machine learning approaches. We have a firm belief that our simple approach will contribute to the body of knowledge in big data study and big knowledge management in this era of data intensive science.

References

1. Dutta, R., et al.: Recommending Environmental Big Data Using Semantic Machine Learning. In: CRC Book on Future Trend on Big Data Analytics, pp. 463–494. CRC Press, Taylor & Francis Group (2014)
2. Plaisant, C., et al.: Interface and data architecture for query preview in networked information systems. ACM Transactions on Information Systems (TOIS) 17(3), 320–341 (1999)
3. Marchal, S., et al.: A Big Data Architecture for Large Scale Security Monitoring. In: 2014 IEEE International Congress on Big Data (BigData Congress). IEEE (2014)
4. Zhong, T., et al.: On mixing high-speed updates and in-memory queries: big-data architecture for real-time analytics. In: 2013 IEEE International Conference on Big Data. IEEE (2013)

5. Luo, Y., et al.: A Component-based Software Development Method Combined with Enterprise Architecture. In: 2013 International Conference on Advanced Computer Science and Electronics Information (ICACSEI 2013). Atlantis Press (2013)
6. Dutta, R., et al.: Deep cognitive imaging systems enable estimation of continental-scale fire incidence from climate data. Nature Scientific Reports 3, 3188 (10.1038/srep03188), 1-4 (2013)
7. Dutta, R., et al.: Performance Evaluation of South Esk Hydrological Sensor Web: Using Machine Learning and Semantic Linked Data Approach. IEEE Sensors Journal 13(10), 3806-3815 (2013)
8. Ce, L., et al.: Area Wise High Resolution Water Availability Estimation Using Heterogeneous Remote Sensing and Ensemble Machine Learning. Accepted in 13th IEEE Sensors 2014, Valencia, Spain (2014)

A Performance Study of Applications in the Australian Community Climate and Earth System Simulator

Mark Cheeseman, Ben Evans, Dale Roberts, and Marshall Ward

National Computational Infrastructure, Canberra, Australia
{mark.cheeseman,ben.evans,ds.roberts,marshall.ward}@anu.edu.au

Abstract. A 3-year investigation is underway into the performance of applications used in the Australian Community Climate and Earth System Simulator on the petascale supercomputer Raijin hosted at the National Computational Infrastructure. Several applications have been identified as candidates for this investigation including the UK MetOffice's Unified Model (UM) atmospheric model and Princeton University's Modular Ocean Model (MOM). In this paper we present initial results of the investigation of the performance and scalability of UM and MOM on Raijin. We also present initial results of a performance study on the data assimilation package (VAR) developed by the UK MetOffice and used by the Australian Bureau of Meteorology in its operational weather forecasting suite. Further investigation and optimization is envisioned for each application investigated and will be discussed.

Keywords: climate simulation, Unified Model, performance evaluation.

1 Introduction

1.1 Australian Community Climate and Earth System Simulator Optimization Project

The Australian Community Climate and Earth System Simulator, or ACCESS (Keenan, et al., 2014), is an integrated software system for coupled climate and earth system simulations. It is a joint initiative of the Australian Bureau of Meteorology (Bureau) and the Commonwealth Scientific and Industrial Research Organization (CSIRO) in cooperation with the university community in Australia. It is used extensively by the Australian academic community through the Australian Research Council Centre of Excellence for Climate System Science (ARCCSS) (ARC Centre of Excellence for Climate System Science, 2011). The simulation work performed within ACCESS is so computationally intensive that supercomputers are needed to complete this work at a reasonable rate. One such supercomputer heavily used for ACCESS-related work is Raijin –a petascale supercomputer installed at the National Computational Infrastructure (NCI) in Canberra, Australia. With ACCESS-related research being a core activity, knowing (and improving) the performance of ACCESS-related simulations on Raijin is of great interest. Improved performance will translate into additional and/or larger simulations that achieve greater scientific output.

R. Denzer et al. (Eds.): ISESS 2015, IFIP AICT 448, pp. 589–598, 2015.

To date, no coordinated effort has been done to gauge the current performance of the ACCESS framework at NCI and what could be done to increase it. The ACCESS Optimization project (referred to as ACCESS-Opt henceforth) was created to address the issue. This three-year collaboration between NCI, Bureau and Fujitsu has clear performance-driven goals: 1) determine strategically important ACCESS simulations being run on Raijin (or to be run in the very near future), 2) assess the performance of these configurations on Raijin, and 3) implement upgrades for identified performance issues in these simulations.

ACCESS-Opt provides an opportunity for high performance computing experts to engage with Australian weather/climate researchers. It is hoped that this collaboration will further their scientific deliverables and aspirations with ACCESS.

1.2   Raijin Supercomputer

ACCESS simulations performed at NCI use Raijin -an x86 based cluster comprised of 3592 nodes connected by Infiniband FDR interconnect. Each node contains two 8-core Intel Sandybridge CPUs running at 2.6 MHz clock speed. At least 32 GB of physical memory is available and shared between the two CPUs on a node. A high-speed Lustre-based filesystem containing approximately ten petabytes of space is available for high-speed storage. Intel FORTRAN and C compilers are used for source code compilation. OpenMPI (Gabriel, et al., 2004) is used for message-passing support in the parallel applications.

2   Project Methodology

2.1   Organizational Collaboration

Cooperation and collaboration between the member organizations is key to ACCESS-Opt's success and methodology. NCI specialists first interact with climate and NWP researchers at Bureau, CSIRO and ARCCSS with the goal of determining which ACCESS applications (and corresponding configurations) should be investigated. The same specialists, with input and assistance from staff at the before-mentioned organizations, then conduct performance assessments and possible optimizations on the selected configurations. The results are then relayed back to the same researchers for dissemination. Wider distribution of the results is made through publications and presentations.

2.2   Software Benchmarking

Figure 1 outlines the methodology followed when assessing an application's performance. The first step is to perform what is known as a strong scaling analysis. Here, a particular configuration of an ACCESS simulation is run multiple times. All runs are identical except for the number of CPU cores being used –which is increased at a constant factor (usually two). Ideally, as the number of cores is doubled, the simulation's runtime should be halved. So, if one were to plot the ratio of the observed runtimes at increasing numbers of cores to the observed runtime at the smallest number of cores used, one would get a straight line if the vertical axis is logarithmic with a base of 2. There are multiple examples of such strong scaling plots in the paper stating with Figure 3.

Fig. 1. Performance assessment methodology

Strong scaling plots generally will indicate the point where adding additional CPUs to a given simulation is no longer prudent. At this point, one needs to take a more detailed look at the application's performance by creating a performance profile. A performance profile summarizes where an application's runtime is being spent. The profile's specificity is up to the investigator –one can record the time spent in general types of activity observed (I/O, communication, computational, etc) or in individual subroutines and functions. Figure 2 shows a basic profile for a data assimilation code ran on Raijin using 384 CPU cores –with each core running a single MPI task. One sees that communication-related activity clearly dominates the application's runtime. Profiling was performed with the open-sourced tool, Score-P (Schlutter, Philippen, Morin, Geimer, & Mohr, 2014).

The final step is to generate traces for selected configurations on ACCESS-related jobs. In a trace, snapshots of activity within a running job are gathered at a specified frequency for the duration of the entire job. While a performance profile can indicate which parts of an application take up significant portions of its runtime, a trace can show how and when these "hot-spots" accumulate during a run. Visualization of trace logs is performed using the Vampir software (Overview: Vampir 8.3, 2014).

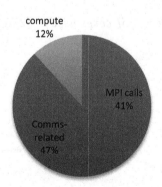

Fig. 2. Profile of the data assimilation application at 384 CPU cores

3   Preliminary Results

3.1   Unified Model

The Unified Model (UM) is a general atmospheric circulation model developed by the United Kingdom MetOffice (UKMO). An overview of its development can be found in (Brown, Milton, Golding, Mitchell, & Shelly, 2012). UM is used operationally for numerical weather prediction in Australia, New Zealand and other countries. Under ACCESS, it is used for atmosphere-alone simulations and serves as the atmospheric component in coupled climate model configurations.

Initial UM optimization work uses version 8.4 of the UM and has focused on a global N512L70 configuration (eg. ~25km horizontal resolution with 70 model vertical levels) -which we will refer to as UM-N512L70 from this point onwards. This configuration due for use by the Bureau for operational weather forecasting duties and is also well known by a number of supercomputer vendors (including Fujitsu). It uses distributed memory parallelism almost exclusively with the addition of OpenMP threading in certain subroutines and areas such as I/O.

I/O is typically a dominant factor in the performance of any earth-system application. UM has adopted an asynchronous IO server approach to improve its I/O performance –particularly in the output of large datasets. In this approach, a subset of MPI tasks being used for the UM job are dedicated to IO activity only -thereby freeing the remaining MPI tasks to concentrate on "normal" computational work. This approach has been successfully adopted in other codes (Edwards & Roy, 2010) but requires proper configuration of the IO servers for optimal performance. This fine-tuning involves manipulating a number of parameters such as the number of active IO servers, number of MPI tasks dedicated to each IO server, frequency at which data is passed to IO servers and so forth. A strong scaling analysis was performed on UM-N512L70 with and without the use of IO servers as shown in Figure 3. All runs lasted one model day. We define strong scaling factor as the logarithmic base 2 of the ratio of the recorded run time at each number of CPU cores to the lowest number of CPU cores used (256 in this case).

$$\log_2\left(\frac{runtime_i}{runtime_{256\,CPUs}}\right), i = \#\,of\,cores\,used \in \{256, 512, 1024, 2048, 4096\}$$

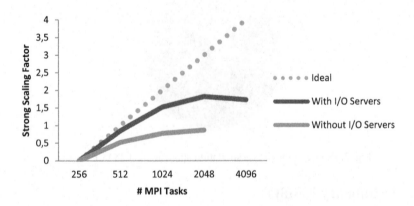

Fig. 3. Strong scaling for the N512L70 global UM configuration

The use of IO servers reduces observed runtimes while also improving scalability as shown in Figure 4.

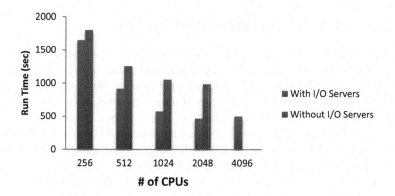

Fig. 4. Observed run times for the N512L70 global UM configuration

Strong scaling significantly improves up to 2048 cores with IO servers. At 4096 cores, observed runtime increases again due to the design of the IO server implementation in UM. Output data is replicated and passed between MPI tasks acting as IO servers in order to balance the workload among them. The "least-busy" IO server will output the next datafield to be written while the remaining IO server MPI tasks will flush data belonging to that field from their memory buffer and concentrate on other output datafields. However, this data replication/sharing can become excessive and can stall the overall writing process. A potential remedy would be incorporating MPI-IO into the IO server design. Instead of passing data between the individual IO servers, all the MPI tasks holding out the parts of the output datafield(s) could concurrently write to the same file.

The existing OpenMP implementation in UM is inefficient in a number of areas in the code –particularly in the convection routines. In such areas, 1 or more OpenMP threads are idle for long periods of time. Most existing OpenMP was added for loop and small-scale data parallelism only. Task-wise parallelism would be a more beneficial use of OpenMP and future work will focus on this. Also, some existing OpenMP use is architecture dependent (for the IBM Power architecture). Removing this dependence should yield significant performance benefits for Raijin.

The CPUs used in Raijin are capable of running more than one thread per physical core by using hyper-threading (Intel Corporation, 2014). In certain circumstances, enabling hyper-threading can increase application performance however this was not the case with the UM. Because of the low utilization of present OpenMP threads, hyper-threading is not necessary to effectively deal with extra processes spun up by OpenMPI and other system software.

Additional UM configurations to be assessed include the N768L85 global configuration that is scheduled to be part of the Bureau's next generation operational forecast suite in 2016/17. Performance issues flagged in UM-N512L70 (I/O, OpenMP) are expected to be more severe at this higher resolution.

3.2   UK MetOffice Data Assimilation Package (VAR)

In 2006, the UK MetOffice developed a 4D variational data assimilation (known simply as VAR) scheme for use in its operational weather forecasting suites (Rawlins, et al., 2007). This scheme has since been adopted by other organizations worldwide including the Bureau. In VAR, time series of observational data for certain parameters (such as temperature and pressure) are fitted to data from a Unified Model weather forecast. Fitting the observations involves repeated running of a simplified low resolution of the UM to assess the impact small changes to the model states has on the fit to the observations and to determine new perturbations to improve this fit. These simplified versions of the model are currently run at the horizontal resolutions of N108 and N216 (approximately 120km and 60km respectively) with the same number of vertical levels (70). Performance tests are conducted on version 30.0 of VAR.

Observed strong scaling is persistently good up to 384 MPI tasks as seen in Figure 5. After this point, performance depended on the number of MPI tasks assigned to each multicore CPU on Raijin. Observed strong scaling and associated runtimes continued favorably up to 1536 MPI tasks (the limit for domain decomposition) when only 4 MPI tasks were assigned to each 8-corPU (while still reserving the entire CPU). However, when the CPUs are fully populated with 8 MPI tasks, observed runtimes increased significantly at all MPI task counts as seen in Figure 6. At lower counts (eg, 192 and less), memory bandwidth contention is the main culprit for the increased runtimes. With large computational sub-domains and the use of three and four-dimensional data arrays, cache stalling is prevalent. At larger MPI task counts (over 384), OS jitter becomes apparent. The main control daemon for PBS (the job scheduling software used on Raijin) frequently interrupts the execution on a single CPU core on each node as it checks resource usage. It was observed that OpenMPI would spawn 4 hardware threads per MPI task it created. These threads are used to enable OpenMPI's asynchronous non-blocking communication calls as explained in (Wittmann, Hager, Zeiser, & Wellein, 2013). While they do overload physical CPU cores, we do not believe these additional OpenMPI threads contribute significantly to the observed OS jitter. Enabling hyper-threading (Intel Corporation, 2014) on the Intel CPUs alleviated the OS jitter issue by efficiently scheduling the non-compute processes onto logical threads. Observed runtimes dropped dramatically -at 1536 MPI tasks, there is now only a 12% difference in runtime between using full and half populated CPUs. Table 1 shows the observed run times for VAR as the number of MPI tasks is increased. It also highlights the OS jitter effect apparent when fully-allocated CPUs are utilized on the Raijin supercomputer (and how hyperthreading and under-allocating CPUs are effective workarounds).

Future VAR work includes the assessment of a higher resolution configuration using N320L70 of the outermost loop. No OpenMP was used in the current assessment. Addressing its effective use in VAR will be the target of upcoming work.

Table 1. Measured run times for the N216/108L70 configuration of VAR

# of MPI Tasks	Run Time (seconds)		
	4 MPI tasks / CPU (no hyperthreading)	8 MPI tasks / CPU (no hyperthreading)	8 MPI tasks / CPU (hyperthreading)
24	8751	15033	15315
48	4342	8057	7629
96	2180	4002	3828
192	1158	2000	1821
384	705	1425	1013
768	491	1586	941
1536	471	2440	539

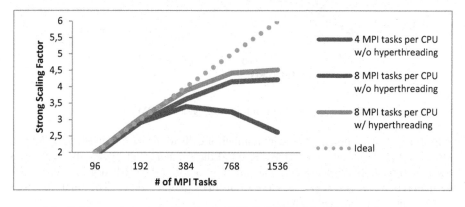

Fig. 5. Observed strong scaling for the N216/108L70 global VAR configuration

3.3 Modular Ocean Model

The Modular Ocean Model (MOM) (Griffies, Harrison, Pacanowski, & Rosati, 2004)
is a general ocean circulation model developed at the Geophysical Fluids Dynamics
Laboratory (GFDL) at Princeton University. It is a finite difference application written in FORTRAN90/95 using MPI distributed parallelization. Domain decomposition is performed along the horizontal dimensions only (eg. longitude and latitude).
MOM is one of the main earth science models used by the ACCESS user community.
It is employed for standalone ocean simulations and serves as the ocean component
for coupled climate model configurations. Performance assessment work has targeted version 5.1 of MOM using a global configuration with a 0.25° horizontal resolution and 50 model levels. Sea-ice representation is done by GFDL's Sea Ice Simulator
model (Winton, 2001) that is coupled to MOM. Observed strong scaling of the 0.25°
global configuration is shown in Figure 6. The issue of an observed difference in

performance between using fully and partially populated CPUs on Raijin is present just like with VAR. The cause of the inflated runtimes (see Figure 6) when using 8 MPI tasks per CPU is the same as with VAR. The observed differences in performance at lower core counts is smaller than that observed with VAR. We believe that this is due to less memory bandwidth contention in MOM. At 1920 CPU cores, OS jitter becomes a serious impediment to performance. The same interrupting behavior from the PBS scheduler is still present. Enabling hyper-threading on the CPUs alleviated the problem just like with VAR.

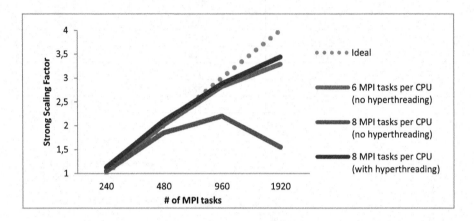

Fig. 6. Strong scaling results for the 0.25° global MOM configuration

Profiling showed that a significant number of calls to the MPI_Allreduce collective operation. Code modifications have reduced the frequency of these calls leading to lower runtimes. Introducing land masking (eg. ignoring land-filled grid cells during the integration steps) dropped observed run times another 20%. The final observed run times are given in Table 2 below.

Table 2. Observed run times for the 0.25o global MOM configuration

# of MPI Tasks	Run Time (seconds)		
	6 MPI tasks / CPU (no hyperthreading)	8 MPI tasks / CPU (no hyperthreading)	8 MPI tasks / CPU (hyperthreading)
120	4112	5298	5220
240	1970	2558	2393
480	1013	1469	1221
960	583	1152	707
1920	419	1810	480

Additional profiling on Raijin revealed that approximately 50% of all observed runtime is concentrated in three areas of the model: a) tracer advection, b) horizontal viscosity determination, and c) vertical mixing. These areas will be the focus of renewed optimization efforts in the upcoming year.

4   Future Work

Optimization work will continue on the applications and configurations previously discussed. NCI, Bureau, ARCCSS and Fujitsu staff frequently meet to discuss the project's status and to explore new goals. Higher resolution configurations are to be assessed for UM (N768L85), MOM (0.1° horizontal resolution) and VAR (N320L70).

Emphasis will be placed on the performance assessment and optimization of version 1.4 of the coupled climate model ACCESS-CM (Bi, et al., 2013). This model couples UM 9.1, MOM 5.1 the sea ice mode, CICE 5.0 (Los Alamos National Laboratory, 2013) and the land surface model, CABLE 2.0 (Kowalczyk, Wang, Law, Davies, McGregor, & Abramowitz, 2006) via the OASIS3-MCT library (Valcke, Craig, & Coquart, 2013).

Acknowledgements. We wish to thank all the Bureau and CSIRO staff who have assisted us –in particular, Dr. Ilia Bermous, Dr Justin Freeman, Dr Martin Dix, Dr. Simon Marsland, Dr. Vicki Steinle and Dr Peter Steinle. We would also like to acknowledge several individuals from ARCCSS: Dr. Scott Wales, Prof. Andy Hogg and Dr. Nic Hannah.

Finally we extend a special thanks to ACCESS-Opt's steering committee for their continued guidance and support (Ben Evans and Mark Cheeseman of NCI, Robin Bowen and Tim Pugh of the Bureau, Ross Nobes and Tomohiro Yamada of Fujitsu).

References

Altair: PBS Works, `http://www.pbsworks.com` (retrieved October 23, 2014)

Home: ARC Centre of Excellence for Climate System Science, `http://www.climatescience.org.au` (retrieved October 23, 2014)

Bi, D., Dix, M., Marsland, S., O'Farrell, S., Rashid, H., Uotila, P., et al.: The ACCESS coupled model: description, control climate and evaluation. Australian Meteorological and Oceanographic Journal 63(1), 41–64 (2013)

Brown, A., Milton, S., Golding, B., Mitchell, J., Shelly, A.: Unified Modeling and Prediction of Weather and Climate A 25-Year Journey. American Meteorological Society, 1865–1877 (2012)

Cullen, M.J.: The unified forecast/climate model. Meteorological Magazine 122, 81-94

Edwards, T., Roy, K.: Using I/O Servers to Improve Application Performance on Cray XT Technology, Cray Users Group, pp. 1–4. Edinburgh (2010)

Gabriel, E., Fagg, G.E., Bosilca, G., Angskun, T., Dongarra, J.J., Squyres, J.M., et al.: Open MPI: Goals, Concept and Design of a Next Generation MPI Implementation. In: Proceedings 11th European PVM/MPI Users' Group Meeting, pp. 97–104. Budapest (2004)

Griffies, S.M., Harrison, M.J., Pacanowski, R.C., Rosati, A.: A Technical Guide to MOM4. Technical Report, Princeton University, Geophysical Fluids Dynamics Laboratory, Princeton (2004)

Intel Corporation, Intel Hyper-Threading Technology, from Intel Corporation website: `http://www.intel.com/content/www/us/en/architecture-and-technology/hyper-threading/hyper-threading-technology.html` (retrieved October 25, 2014)

Keenan, T., Puri, K., Pugh, T., Evans, B., Dix, M., Pitman, A., et al.: Next Generation Australian Community Climate and Earth-System Simulator (NGACCESS) - A Roadmap 2014-2019. Technical, Centre for Australian Weather and Climate Research, CAWCR (2014)

Kowalczyk, E., Wang, Y., Law, R., Davies, H., McGregor, J., Abramowitz, G.: The CSIRO Atmosphere Biosphere Land Exchange (CABLE) model for use in climate models and as an offline model. Technical, Commonwealth Scientific and Industrial Research Organisation (2006)

Los Alamos National Laboratory, The Los Alamos sea ice model (CICE) (2013), From COSIM: The Climate, Ocean and Sea Ice Modeling Group: http://oceans11.lanl.gov/drupal/CICE (retrieved November 7, 2014)

Rawlins, F., Ballard, S.P., Bovis, K.J., Clayton, A.M., Li, D., Inverarity, W., et al.: The Met Office global four-dimensional variational data assimilation scheme. Quarterly Journal of the Royal Meteorological Society 133, 347–362 (2007)

Schlutter, M., Philippen, P., Morin, L., Geimer, M., Mohr, B.: Profiling Hybrid HMPP Applications with Score-P on Heterogeneous Hardware. In: Bader, M., Bode, A., Bungartz, H.-J., Gerndt, M., Joubert, G.R., Peters, F.J. (eds.) Parallel Computing: Accelerating Computational Science and Engineering (CSE), vol. 25, pp. 773–782. IOS Press (2014)

Valcke, S., Craig, T., Coquart, L.: OASIS3-MCT User Guide. Technical Report, CERFACS, CNRS, Toulouse (2013)

Winton, M.: FMS Sea Ice Simulator. Princeton University, Geophysical Fluid Dynamics Laboratory, Princeton (2001)

Wittmann, M., Hager, G., Zeiser, T., Wellein, G.: Asynchronous MPI for the Masses. Cornell University, Department of Computer Science, Ithaca (2013)

A New Approach for Coupled Regional Climate Modeling Using More than 10,000 Cores

Marcus Thatcher, John McGregor, Martin Dix, and Jack Katzfey

CSIRO Ocean and Atmosphere Flagship, Melbourne, Australia
{Marcus.Thatcher,John.McGregor,
Martin.Dix,Jack.Katzfey}@csiro.au

Abstract. This paper describes an alternative method for coupling atmosphere-ocean regional climate models that communicates momentum, radiation, heat and moisture fluxes between the atmosphere and ocean every time-step, while scaling to more than 10,000 cores. The approach is based on the reversibly staggered grid, which possesses excellent dispersive properties for modeling the geophysical fluid dynamics of both the atmosphere and the ocean. Since a common reversibly staggered grid can be used for both atmosphere and ocean models, we can eliminate the coupling overhead associated with message passing and improve simulation timings. We have constructed a prototype of a reversibly staggered, atmosphere-ocean coupled regional climate model based on the Conformal Cubic Atmospheric Model, which employs a global variable resolution cube-based grid to model the regional climate without lateral boundary conditions. With some optimization, the single precision, semi-implicit, semi-Lagrangian prototype model achieved 5 simulation years per day at a global 13 km resolution using 13,824 cores. This result is competitive with state-of-the-art Global Climate Models than can use more than 100,000 cores for comparable timings, making CCAM well suited for regional modeling.

Keywords: geophysical fluid dynamics, MPI, regional climate modeling.

1 Introduction

Regional Climate Models (RCMs) are used to study how changes in global climate can affect meteorology at fine spatial scales. Such models are commonly used to dynamically downscale climate change projections from Global Climate Models (GCMs) to regional and local spatial scales appropriate for impact studies. There are four main components in the construction of an RCM:

- The dynamical core that simulates the atmosphere as a geophysical fluid.
- Parameterization of atmospheric physical processes, such as solar radiation, clouds, boundary layer turbulent mixing and aerosols.
- Parameterization of surface interactions at fine spatial scales, such as mountain ranges, forests, deserts, ice and oceans, which significantly influence the regional meteorology.

R. Denzer et al. (Eds.): ISESS 2015, IFIP AICT 448, pp. 599–607, 2015.

- An assimilation or nudging system to ingest large scale changes in atmospheric circulation and sea surface temperatures, as predicted by GCMs for different global warming scenarios.

The RCM integrates these four components to produce a consistent representation of the meteorology at regional spatial scales (i.e., 1 to 100 km). RCMs face a difficult computational challenge as they are required to simulate atmospheric processes that may last seconds to minutes, whilst integrating the simulations for time periods greater than one hundred years. Computational load-balancing issues arise as the various simulated atmospheric processes are not uniformly distributed over the simulation grid. Furthermore, assimilating climate data also requires the RCM to be reading and writing atmospheric datasets while running on hundreds to thousands of cores.

Traditionally the ocean is simply represented in an RCM by interpolating Sea Surface Temperatures (SSTs) from a GCM dataset. This approach neglects any feedback between the atmosphere and ocean and smoothes out variability arising from ocean surface eddies. Most attempts to construct an atmosphere-ocean coupled RCM are extensions of the GCM approach, where a 'coupler' is used to manage communication between atmosphere and ocean processors. Since the atmosphere and ocean usually use different grids, complex communication patterns can arise, resulting in considerable inter-node message passing that slows down the simulation. To minimize the impact of this communication bottleneck, couplers usually only exchange information between the atmosphere and ocean models every few simulation hours.

This paper proposes an alternative approach to developing an atmosphere-ocean coupled RCM that has good wave dispersion properties and allows frequent coupling without increasing simulation time. Our approach is based on a reversibly staggered grid [1], which was originally developed for the Conformal Cubic Atmospheric Model (CCAM) [2]. CCAM is a global atmospheric model based on a variable-resolution conformal-cubic grid so that it can simulate regional scales without lateral boundary conditions. The reversibly staggered grid handles horizontal velocity components and was introduced into CCAM to provide good gravity wave dispersion properties. However, the reversibly staggered grid has also been found to possess excellent dispersive properties when simulating the ocean [1], making it suitable as a universal grid for an atmosphere-ocean coupled model. Using a common grid for the atmosphere and ocean avoids the communication bottleneck associated with traditional coupling methods and improves the simulation timings. We have constructed such a reversibly staggered ocean model within CCAM to assess its potential for coupled regional climate modeling. After some optimization, the coupled model prototype was found to exhibit strong scaling beyond 10,000 cores while exchanging fluxes between the atmosphere and ocean models every time-step (e.g., 3 minutes).

CCAM and its variable-resolution conformal-cubic grid are described in Section 2. Section 3 outlines the CCAM software architecture and parallel programming issues. Section 4 explains how the regional ocean model was integrated into CCAM using the reversibly staggered grid. Section 5 describes the performance of the prototype atmosphere-ocean coupled regional model, including timings for different size grids and scaling issues. Conclusions and future work plans are presented in Section 6.

2   The Conformal Cubic Atmospheric Model

The Conformal Cubic Atmospheric Model (CCAM) is based on the conformal cubic projection [2] (see Fig. 1). CCAM was the first three-dimensional atmospheric model to use a cube-based grid, which provides significant computational advantages due to avoiding coordinate singularities while still locally resembling a Cartesian grid. The CCAM grid can be focused over a region of interest using the Schmidt transformation [3] and was part of the first generation of variable-resolution global atmospheric models [4]. By using a global, variable-resolution grid, CCAM avoids lateral boundary conditions and facilitates coupling between the global and regional spatial scales on the same grid. CCAM currently employs a non-hydrostatic, semi-implicit, semi-Lagrangian dynamical core that is efficient for regional climate modeling due to the relatively large time-step allowed by semi-Lagrangian methods. CCAM also has an extensive series of physical parameterizations to describe the behavior of the land-surface, aerosols, convection, cloud microphysics, radiation, gravity wave drag and boundary layer turbulence.

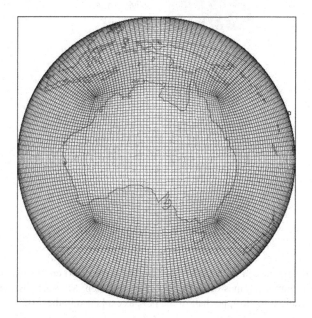

Fig. 1. Example of a stretched conformal cubic grid employed by CCAM, focused over Australia, using a Schmidt factor of 3 (i.e., the front panel of the cube has shrunk by a factor of 3)

For assimilation, CCAM employs a convolution-based scale-selective filter [6], that nudges the atmosphere at large length scales (e.g., greater than 3,000 km) towards a specified GCM projection of future climate. We base our filter on a convolution as it can be easily applied to CCAM's variable-resolution cubic grid and can accommodate irregular coastlines when assimilating ocean data in the atmosphere-ocean coupled RCM.

3   Software Design

The software components of CCAM are represented in Fig. 2, where initial conditions and configuration data are read by the initialize component at the start of the simulation. Prognostic variables are transported around the model by the dynamics component. Assimilation perturbs CCAM towards a global GCM dataset. Additional or unresolved processes that need to be parameterized are included under physics. Prognostic and diagnostic data are periodically written to a history file from the output routines. Lastly, the finalize component stores all prognostic variables at the end of each simulation month in a restart file. The restart file is read as initial conditions for the next simulation month when CCAM is restarted with new configuration data. Each component in Fig. 2 can be further divided into atmosphere, ocean and land-surface sub-components.

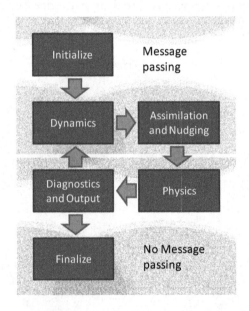

Fig. 2. Schematic diagram of the CCAM software components, where the dynamics, assimilation, physics and output routines cycle every model time-step. Message passing between processors is only required in the upper half of the plot, as explained in the text.

CCAM is written in Fortran and uses the Message Passing Interface (MPI) system to communicate between parallel processors [5]. The conformal cubic grid is decomposed over the available processors into equal rectangular parts, with no partitioning in the vertical direction. This is because the atmospheric physics, with its faster processes, depends on the entire vertical column during a time-step. Communication between parallel processors is only required for the initialize, dynamics and assimilation components (i.e., the upper half of Fig 2). There is no communication between processors in the lower half of Fig. 2, as physics routines independently update the prognostic variables for each vertical column of grid-points and the output and finalize routines write separate NetCDF files for each processor. CCAM output variables are selectively re-combined from the parallel output files using post-processing software, which also interpolates the simulation results to a latitude/longitude grid.

Fluxes are exchanged between the CCAM atmosphere and ocean models in the physics component, due to the use of a common reversibly staggered grid. This is because the fluxes between the atmosphere and ocean are independent for each grid-point on the common grid, in contrast to models where atmosphere and ocean grids are misaligned so that additional message passing is required to communicate fluxes. Atmosphere and ocean wave dispersion properties are not compromised when using a common reversibly staggered grid, as discussed in the Section 4.

To maximize the scaling properties of CCAM, most of the dynamics software routines use non-blocking, point-to-point communication between neighboring processors to exchange portions of atmosphere and ocean data at processor boundaries. However, CCAM's semi-implicit, semi-Lagrangian dynamical core relies on an implicit solution to the Helmholtz equation, with the model performance being largely determined by the numerical algorithm used. We found that a custom-designed geometric multi-grid solver for the Helmholtz equation demonstrated the best timings for more than 1,000 processors, although Conjugate-Gradient and Successive Over-Relaxation methods are also available.

The scale-selective filter, which is used to assimilate host GCM data into CCAM at large spatial scales, naively requires $O(N^2)$ computations where N is the number of horizontal grid points. However, the efficiency of the scale-selective filter was improved by approximating the two-dimensional convolution with two separate one-dimensional convolutions. Although this approach reduces the number of computations to $O(N^{3/2})$, processors still require data from all other processors whose grid-points lie along a common row or column on the CCAM cubic grid. We found that using MPI-2's Remote Memory Access (RMA) allowed us to efficiently pass the required information around the cubic grid, improving the filter timings by a factor of 5 compared to a naïve global 'gatherall' approach.

CCAM can be compiled for single precision as well as double precision computations, where the use of the single precision mode can significantly reduce communication bandwidth problems. Care is taken to avoid any degradation to model performance when using single precision, such as always using double precision for the radiation code and improving the precision for calculating global sums.

4   A Reversibly Staggered Ocean Model for CCAM

Our atmosphere-ocean coupled regional climate model exploits CCAM's reversibly staggered grid so that a common grid can be used for both the atmosphere and ocean. The atmosphere and ocean models can then be coupled together in the physics component, avoiding additional message passing overheads associated with exchanging momentum, radiation, temperature and moisture fluxes between models. The reversibly staggered grid determines the location of the velocity fields on the model grid as shown in Fig. 3. Most atmospheric models are based on the staggered Arakawa C-grid due to poor wave dispersion properties associated with the unstaggered A-grid. However, the A-grid is suitable for computing Coriolis terms that couple the U and V

velocity components, related to the rotation of the Earth. The A-grid is also conve-
nient for carrying out the physical parameterizations at coincident grid points.
CCAM's reversibly staggered grid switches between the Arakawa A-grid and the C-
grid, thereby exploiting the advantages of both grids. Importantly, the reversible
transformation can switch between the staggered grids without any loss of information. It has been shown that the reversibly staggered grid approach provides excellent
dispersive properties for both atmosphere and ocean geophysical fluid dynamics [1].

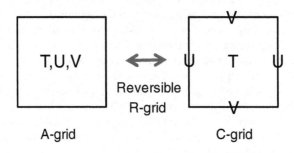

Fig. 3. Schematic representation of the reversibly staggered grid that switches between the
Arakawa A-grid (left) and the C-grid (right). T represents a scalar field (e.g., temperature) at
the center of the grid box, whereas the velocity components U and V can be reversibly staggered with respect to T to improve the dispersive properties of the simulation.

The CCAM ocean model has prognostic equations for the currents, potential temperature, salinity and the surface displacement height of the ocean. We also include a
cavitating fluid model of sea-ice, although we do not discuss sea-ice further in this
paper. Both the atmosphere and ocean models use a semi-implicit, semi-Lagngian
dynamical core, but with some differences such as different equations of state for
density. The ocean model adopts bathymetry-following sigma-z coordinates such
that that the vertical grid stretches and compresses as the ocean depth changes. Careful treatment of the pressure gradient terms was required to avoid spurious pressure
gradients arising from discretization errors.
The Vandermonde formula, used for constructing the reversibly staggered grid in
CCAM, is represented as a periodic tri-diagonal matrix that circles the globe. As
there is a portion of the tri-diagonal matrix on each processor, we iteratively solve the
tri-diagonal matrix to improve the scaling of CCAM, thereby avoiding global MPI
communications. Typically six iterations are sufficient for the problem to converge.
In the case of the ocean model, special treatment of the reversibly staggered grid is
required along coastlines to be consistent with the non-slip boundary condition for
currents. In practice, this problem is solved by reducing the order of the Vandermonde formula when approaching coastlines (i.e., reduced to a linear model) so that
no information is lost when switching between the Arakawa A and C-grids.
Our atmosphere-ocean coupling method is particularly suited to RCMs, since the
spatial resolution of the shared reversibly staggered grid is sufficient to resolve eddies
in both the atmosphere and ocean. RCMs can also capitalize on the frequent exchange
of information between the atmosphere and ocean models, which can be important for

simulating extreme weather events such as cyclones. Although different numbers of land and ocean points on different processors can result in load imbalance issues, this problem already existed with the simple interpolated SST approach used by most RCMs and is not exacerbated by our coupling method.

An example of how the reversibly staggered ocean model modifies the structure of SSTs can be seen in Fig. 4, where ocean surface eddies were spun up by the coupled model and can be seen in the small-scale structure of the simulated SSTs.

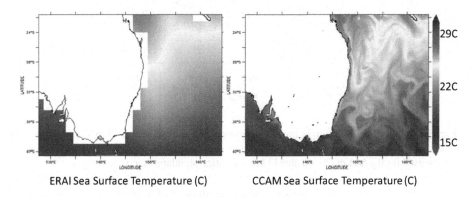

ERAI Sea Surface Temperature (C)   CCAM Sea Surface Temperature (C)

Fig. 4. Comparison between interpolated SSTs from ERA-Interim 'observations' (left) and spun-up SSTs by the reversibly staggered ocean model (right) at 10 km resolution over the target domain. SSTs are in units of degrees Celsius.

5   Performance of the Atmosphere-Ocean Coupled Model

Figure 5 shows the timings for (unstretched) global, atmosphere-ocean coupled CCAM simulations as a function of the number of processors for various grid resolutions. These simulations were performed on the Pawsey Centre's Magnus, which is a Cray XC40 system using Intel Xeon "Haswell" processors. The CCAM simulations employed 35 vertical levels over a 40 km height for the atmosphere and 30 levels over a 5 km depth for the ocean, including a minimum of 10 levels in the top 200 m of the ocean. We used CCAM in single precision mode, which reduced the required internode message passing bandwidth. Finally, we applied the scale-selective filter every six simulation hours to perturb the air temperature, winds, surface pressure and SSTs towards ERA-Interim reanalyses (i.e., an atmospheric dataset that is constrained by observations). For the case of a 13 km resolution simulation, the size of the raw output files is approximately 10 GB per month, although the output is split into separate parallel output files for each processor. The 13 km resolution single precision result of 5 simulation years per day with 13,824 cores is competitive with state-of-the-art models such as the double precision NCAR GCM that produced 2.6 simulation years per day for the same horizontal resolution, but required 200,000 cores [7]. Hence CCAM's design allows it to simulate the regional climate with considerably less computing resources than typically required for RCM experiments.

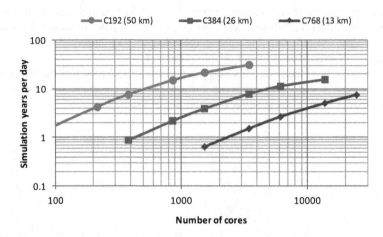

Fig. 5. Scaling results for single precision, atmosphere-ocean coupled CCAM simulations on IVEC's Magnus for three different global grid resolutions. Time-steps of 900 s, 360 s and 240 s were used for the 50 km, 26 km and 13 km resolution simulations, respectively.

We note that the CCAM timings are a consequence of a number of factors including the use of single precision, the semi-Lagrangian dynamical core, the geometric multi-grid algorithm, as well as the reversibly staggered coupling strategy. The multi-grid solver and the scale-selective filter were found to be the weakest components of CCAM with respect to scaling, as the atmosphere-ocean coupling has no communication overhead. The scale-selective filter was found to scale proportionally to the square root of the number of processors when using RMA, but is only called every six simulation hours. Therefore the relative cost of the filter remains the same portion of the total run time when the resolution is increased and the model time-step is decreased. We are then left with the geometric multi-grid solver as the primary limitation on model scaling. Although our custom-designed geometric multi-grid solver has competitive timings compared to other multi-grid solvers reported in the literature, it can be difficult to fully exploit the available parallel processing with multi-grid methods. For this reason, we are investigating explicit methods for the dynamical core as described in Section 6.

6   Conclusions

This paper describes an alternative approach to atmosphere-ocean coupled regional climate modeling that is based on a reversibly staggered grid. The excellent dispersive properties of this grid are suitable for simulating both atmosphere and ocean geophysical fluid dynamics, making it appropriate as a common grid for integrating the two models. The message passing overhead associated with exchanging fluxes between the atmosphere and ocean models can then be eliminated. The approach is valid when both atmosphere and ocean eddies are resolved on the common grid and the frequent exchange of fluxes between the models is important, making the method well suited for RCMs. We have constructed a prototype of the reversibly staggered, atmosphere-ocean coupled regional model using CCAM and show that the single precision version can produce timings of 5 simulation years per day using 13,824 cores. Factors contributing to this result include the use of single precision, the semi-Lagrangian dynamical core, the geometric multi-grid algorithm, as well as the reversibly staggered grid coupling strategy. The CCAM timings are comparable to a state-of-the-art GCM using 200,000 cores [7], although CCAM requires considerably fewer cores making it well suited to regional climate modeling.

Although entirely adequate for petascale computing resources currently available in Australia, CCAM scaling will eventually be limited by the implicit geometric multi-grid solver for the Helmholtz equation. This issue is being addressed with the development of a split-explicit, flux-conserving dynamical core that will use an equi-angular, gnomonic cubic grid. Nevertheless, the current semi-implicit, semi-Lagrangian prototype successfully demonstrates the viability of the reversible staggering approach for atmosphere-ocean coupled regional climate modeling. It may also be possible to use the reversibly staggered grid for other types of geophysical fluids, although the feasibility of our approach will depend on the dispersive properties of the reversibly staggered grid for the modeled system.

Acknowledgements. The authors wish to thank Pawsey Centre's Petascale Pioneer program for providing computing resources for the simulations described in this paper. Thanks to Aaron McDonough and Paul Ryan for their technical advice. We also acknowledge the constructive feedback on the manuscript from Peter Dobrohotoff and the two anonymous reviewers.

References

1. McGregor, J.L.: Geostrophic adjustment for reversibly staggered grids. Mon.Wea. Rev. 133, 1119–1128 (2005)
2. McGregor, J.L.: C-CAM: Geometric aspects and dynamical formulation. CSIRO Marine and Atmospheric Research Technical Report 70 (2005),
   http://www.cmar.csiro.au/e-print/open/mcgregor_2005a.pdf
3. Schmidt, F.: Variable fine mesh in spectral global models. Beitr. Phys. Atmos. 50, 211–217 (1977)
4. Fox-Rabinovitz, M., Cote, J., Dugas, B., Deque, M., McGregor, J.L.: Variable resolution general circulation models: Stretchedgrid model intercomparison project (SGMIP). J. Geophys. Res. 111, D16104 (2006)
5. McGregor, J.L., Dix, M.: An updated description of the conformal-cubic atmospheric model. In: Hamilton, K., Ohfuchi, W. (eds.) High Resolution Simulation of the Atmosphere and Ocean, pp. 51–76. Springer (2008)
6. Thatcher, M., McGregor, J.L.: Using a scale-selective filter for dynamical downscaling with the conformal cubic atmospheric model. Mon. Wea. Rev. 137, 1742–1752 (2009)
7. Worley, P., Craig, A., Dennis, J.: Performance ofthe community earth system model. In: 2011 International Conference High Performance Computing, Networking, Storage and Analysis (SC), Seattle, WA, pp. 1–11 (2011)

Author Index

Printed in the United States
by Bookmasters

Printed in the United States
By Bookmasters